PASSPORT TO PEKING

Frontispiece: Paul Hogarth, *Man and Cart*, China, 1954, conté.

Passport to Peking

A VERY BRITISH MISSION
TO MAO'S CHINA

PATRICK WRIGHT

OXFORD
UNIVERSITY PRESS

OXFORD

UNIVERSITY PRESS

Great Clarendon Street, Oxford ox2 6DP

Oxford University Press is a department of the University of Oxford.
It furthers the University's objective of excellence in research, scholarship,
and education by publishing worldwide in

Oxford New York

Auckland Cape Town Dar es Salaam Hong Kong Karachi
Kuala Lumpur Madrid Melbourne Mexico City Nairobi
New Delhi Shanghai Taipei Toronto

With offices in

Argentina Austria Brazil Chile Czech Republic France Greece
Guatemala Hungary Italy Japan Poland Portugal Singapore
South Korea Switzerland Thailand Turkey Ukraine Vietnam

Oxford is a registered trade mark of Oxford University Press
in the UK and in certain other countries

Published in the United States
by Oxford University Press Inc., New York

British Library Cataloguing in Publication Data

Data available

Library of Congress Cataloging in Publication Data
Library of Congress Control Number: 2010933105

Typeset by SPI Publisher Services, Pondicherry, India
Printed in Great Britain
on acid-free paper by
Clays Ltd, St Ives plc

ISBN 978-0-19-954193-5

1 3 5 7 9 10 8 6 4 2

My empire is made of the stuff of crystals, its molecules arranged in a perfect pattern. Amid the surge of the elements, a splendid hard diamond takes shape, an immense, faceted, transparent mountain. Why do your travel impressions stop at disappointing appearances, never catching this implacable process? Why do you linger over inessential melancholies? Why do you hide from the emperor the grandeur of his destiny?'

Kublai Khan to Marco Polo, Italo Calvino,
Invisible Cities (1972)

In comparing an alien culture with one's own, one is forced to ask oneself questions more fundamental than any that usually arise in regard to home affairs. One is forced to ask: What are the things that I ultimately value? What would make me judge one sort of society more desirable than another sort? What sort of ends should I most wish to see realized in the world?

Bertrand Russell, *The Problem of China* (1922)

What was the good of going to Peking when it was just like Shrewsbury? Why return to Shrewsbury when it would all be like Peking? Men seldom moved their bodies; all unrest was concentrated in the soul.

E. M. Forster, 'The Machine Stops' (1909)

If you've ever been part of an official delegation, you learn less about a country than sitting in the British Museum and reading about it.

Joe Slovo, *New York Times*, 4 December 1994

Say! When's this guy going to get to China?

Stanley Spencer, speaking to
the Bourne End Parents Association, 1957

To Claire

Preface and Acknowledgements

Stanley Spencer was a peculiarly home-loving artist. So closely did he cleave to the Berkshire village of Cookham that he once feared he might have damaged his vision irreparably just by walking a few miles along the Thames to fulfil a commission in neighbouring Bourne End. What, then, was he doing drawing and painting in the People's Republic of China?

I first pondered this question in 2001, when working as a curator of Tate Britain's exhibition of Spencer's paintings and drawings.[1] Looking further into the matter, I found that Spencer had travelled in September 1954 as an invited guest of the Communist-led government in Peking. Far from being alone in his unexpected journey to the Orient, he went along with several planeloads of Britons gathered in from various sometimes very loosely defined positions on the left of the political spectrum. A group from the Labour Party leadership flew first, including the former Prime Minister Clement Attlee and his Minister of Health, Aneurin Bevan. A party of dissenting 'Bevanite' Labour MPs departed later, packed together, not always happily, with a clutch of their more right-wing and pro-American colleagues. The flight over Eastern Europe, Soviet Russia, and Mongolia was also undertaken by a strangely mixed company of scientists and artists, architects and writers. Various trade unionists and local councillors embarked, and so too did the national secretary of the Women's Co-operative Guilds of Great Britain. There were liberal-minded sceptics aboard the planes, as well as partisan admirers of the new regime and some allegedly quite ignorant freeloaders too. And all this took place nearly eighteen years before February 1972, when President Richard Nixon and his wife Pat stepped down onto the tarmac at Beijing to commence the visit that is now often assumed to mark the opening of relations between the People's Republic of China and the West.

The occasion for these east-bound flights was provided by the fifth anniversary celebrations of the Communist 'Liberation', proclaimed by Mao on 1 October 1949. The invitations, which were not approved by the elderly Winston Churchill's Conservative government, followed years of acute international tension. The Iron Curtain, which was first brought down around Communist Russia in 1919/20, had been lowered again very shortly after the Second World War, this time dividing Europe from the Baltic to the Adriatic, as Winston Churchill declared in his famous Fulton oration of 5 March 1946. An Asian extension, a 'cordon sanitaire' that was quickly dubbed the 'Bamboo Curtain', was placed around Communist China a few years later. These largely impenetrable barriers were never just closed frontiers. They were shored up by opposed and contrary propagandas as well as by censorship, trade embargos, blockading warships, and governments that were learning how to play the game of 'brinkmanship' with the threat of nuclear catastrophe.

If the post-war decade was a time of 'containment' and bloc-building, in which there was much talk about monolithic centres of power and their closely controlled 'satellites',[2] it also saw new kinds of conflict. First named by George Orwell in 1945, the 'Cold War' had become a prevailing reality in Europe. In Asia, the wars had been altogether hotter, and not just in Korea. As a colonial power, Britain had also been faced with nationalist and Communist insurgencies in India, Indonesia, Malaya, Burma, and elsewhere.

By the summer of 1954, further tensions were being provoked by more recent initiatives, two of which especially had combined to divide the British Labour Party into feuding factions. One was the proposed rearmament of West Germany. The other was the formation of the South-East Asia Treaty Organization, promoted as an Eastern consort to NATO by President Eisenhower's fiercely anti-Communist Secretary of State John Foster Dulles, and brought into existence when its charter was signed on 8 September 1954. These initiatives were supported by the leadership of the Labour Party, and opposed vigorously by the left of the party, gathered as its *Tribune* reading members were around the charismatic figure of Aneurin Bevan. The defeat of the Bevanites on both counts was confirmed at the Labour Party's annual conference, held in Scarborough at the end of September.

At the time of the flights to Peking, Britain's political life was being pressed into the 'Natopolitan' mould that would be denounced at the end of the decade by the no longer Communist

4

historian E. P. Thompson.[3] In his view, this forceful manoeuvre had been successfully completed by the General Election of 26 May 1955, which was won by the Conservatives under Anthony Eden after a campaign that was 'conducted entirely within the political and strategic premises of NATO'.[4] Thompson attributed the British people's compliance with this redefinition of their possibilities to various causes: apathy, the persistence of attitudes derived from 'exhausted imperialism', and the allure of capitalism's promise of yet to be delivered 'affluence'. Disenchantment with the idea of radical political transformation was also widespread, thanks not least to the increasingly unmistakable horrors of Stalinism, which, as Thompson suggested, had also worked to discredit more native radical traditions, which actually had nothing to do with Soviet Communism.

Through much of 1954, however, there were many Britons who resisted the drift into 'Natopolitan' conformity. The year had opened with encouraging signs of a thaw in the Cold War. Stalin had died in March 1953, and a somewhat more conciliatory attitude seemed to be emerging in Moscow. At the end of July an armistice had brought the Korean War to the state of suspension in which it still hangs to this day, and the year had opened with new signs of a possible settlement in Indo-China, where French forces were fighting a losing war against Ho Chi Minh's Viet Minh. Early in 1954, it emerged that the Chinese Premier Chou En-lai would be leading a Chinese delegation to Geneva, where he would take part in an international conference which, though shunned by America, would consider ways of settling France's continuing war in Indo-China.

The Geneva Conference of 1954 may not feature as much more than a footnote in the Cold War histories of our time. Yet to those who looked on eagerly as the participants struggled their way through various impasses, its final resolution seemed a marvellous return to sanity. Britain's Conservative Foreign Secretary Anthony Eden was widely praised for his diplomacy. For many, however, the real hero was Chou En-lai, who had proved himself quite unlike the manipulated Soviet puppet of anti-Communist expectation. A mantle of Western admiration and hope settled over the shoulders of this handsome Chinese leader, and the invitations to visit China followed before the smiles had time to fade.

Having previously written about the Western visitors who travelled to Stalin's Soviet Union and came back either cursing what they had found or praising the regime to the skies,[5] I decided to look more closely at the experience of the Britons who flew to 'New China' in the wake of the Geneva Conference. Were they really as their often American critics described them: culpable adherents or credulous 'pilgrims' who had really only toured their own naive illusions? To what extent were they duped by the Chinese authorities, who had surely learned much about the arts of 'friendship' and hospitality, and of constructing show projects and other such 'Potemkin villages', from their far more experienced allies in the USSR?

There are, to be sure, a number of unwavering adherents in this story and some holy fools too, including the notorious 'Red Dean of Canterbury', Hewlett Johnson. False perceptions abounded, and yet a considerable number of the visitors also confronted the limitations of their own thinking as they sought a renewal not just of foreign trade but of exchange in the fields of science, archaeology, culture, and the visual arts. In none of these arenas were they as naively 'pro-Communist' as their accusers—and in a few cases they themselves—would go on to suggest. I was impressed by the vehemence with which the familiar charges of 'useful idiocy' were dismissed by two of the surviving travellers—Barbara Castle and the Sinologist John Chinnery. As far as they were concerned, retrospective accusations of the kind that can so easily be launched from the pulpit of hindsight quite fail to grasp that 1954 was a time of real potential—and one, as Castle added, that demanded courageous political decisions. The future really had seemed to stand open, and if anyone had been irresponsible it was surely those in positions of power who refused to rise to the challenges of the moment.

James Cameron, a correspondent who made the journey to China for the *News Chronicle*, would later warn that nothing could be less worthy of recounting than 'the inexpressively tedious details of a long trunk flight'.[6] I have taken a different view, using the admittedly sometimes desperate comedy of those exhausting and much broken flights as the departure point for a wider investigation. I have surveyed the backgrounds of selected travellers, probing the sources of their interest in China in the first place. I have also used the story of their journey to explore the historical relations between Britain and China, and, in particular, to review some of the ways in which China has figured as a land of contrast and otherness within the British imagination: not as another 'post-Bronze Age society' that has actually long existed in 'alternation'[7] with Europe, as has recently been suggested is really the case, but as a contrastingly static and unaccomplished land of silk and tinkling teacups, which had long since been left behind by the dynamic West, and where 'revolution' was now presented as the answer to centuries of misery, oppression, and foreign exploitation.

As this implies, the book is far more about post-war Britain and its inherited perspectives than it is about the reality of China, either now or then. It is partly for this reason that I have, with a few exceptions, retained the old system of romanized spellings as opposed to the more recently introduced *pinyin*, and partly in order to acknowledge that, whatever lens it may be viewed through, the walled city that was 'Peking' in 1954 really is not the same city as the 'Beijing' of the early twenty-first century. Britain, meanwhile, was a financially straitened place, with currency restrictions that made extended overseas travel very difficult. Its distinctive character may, perhaps, be suggested by three stories that were running around the edges of the press coverage devoted to the international events of the Cold War: the spread of the recently imported myxomatosis virus among the nation's rabbit population; the 'inscrutable demon'[8] of metal fatigue, which had been causing Comet airliners to break up in mid-air at such speed that bodies recovered from the Mediterranean Sea showed no sign of contact with the aircraft; the approaching launch of commercial television in the form of ITV—a development which might, it was briefly anticipated, require viewers to fit a second aerial to their homes.

I incurred my first debts at Tate Britain, where Richard Humphreys, Sheena Wagstaff, and Stephen Deuchar encouraged me to think more seriously about the work of Stanley Spencer. Timothy Hyman was tolerant of my initial ignorance, and Chris Stephens, Adrian Glew, Martin Myrone, Joanna Banham, and Robert Upstone also helped me get focused. My early enquiries about Spencer's visit to China led to several meetings with John and Ying Chinnery, who were generous with recollections, advice, and contacts. They put me in touch with the Chinese expatriate artist Chang Chien-ying ('Mrs. Fei' as she was known to many in Britain), and also Nong Priestley who, together with her husband David, has greatly assisted my attempt to understand Chang and Fei Cheng-wu's experience as Chinese artists in mid-twentieth-century Britain. Not long afterwards I met the late Dr Elizabeth James, who talked most informatively about her husband Dr Derrick James's slightly later journey to China. I would like to thank Diana Hogarth, who welcomed me when I visited her husband Paul in Cirencester, and who has toler- ated many subsequent enquiries with impressive equanimity. Margaret Mathews generously shared her recollections and also loaned me a considerable collection of photographs and notes made in China by her husband Denis Mathews. I am grateful to Professor Edwin G. Pulleyblank, emeritus professor of the Depart- ment of Asian Studies, University of British Columbia, who will, I hope, not object too strongly to finding himself in such oddly mixed company all over again. Michael Foot remembered a lot about the Bevanite MPs of 1954, including several who joined that year's flights to Peking. He also urged me not to hang around if I wanted to talk with Barbara Castle, who kindly agreed to share her memories of China and the Geneva Conference, and who provided me with a typed transcript of her diary. I also learned from various people who were in China before 1954. Sybille Van der Sprenkel remembered staying in the British legation compound during the Peking siege of 1949. Michael and Julian Morgan provided additional information about the same beleaguered bastion in later years—as did the late Derek Bryan, who also informed me about the early years of the Britain–China Friendship Association. My cousin James Buxton lent me the letters written in Peking by his father, Martin Buxton, and I am also grateful to his sister Eleanor Kovacs for sharing her memo- ries of growing up in the British embassy compound.

Stephen E. Tabachnik kindly sent me proofs of his then still forthcoming study of the life and works of Rex Warner, *Fiercer than Tigers*. He also put me in touch with Mrs Frances Warner, who gave me permission to quote from her husband Rex Warner's diary of the China trip. I must thank the internet for my correspondence with Grant Heyter-Menzies of British Columbia, with whom it has been a pleasure to share information about the empress dowager, the American ambassador's wife, and the difficulty of telling connoisseurship from looting in early twentieth-century Peking.

Heather Glen alerted me to the Chinese dimensions of the Festival of Britain—without her prompting there would be no Chinese junk sailing through the pages that follow. Neal Ascherson gave me helpful information about Alan Winnington and his eventual return to Britain. Anthony Day trusted me with his Paul Hogarth drawing. Simon Hilton helped me find others, and Peter Mennim of Cambridge obligingly photographed several of the works reproduced here.

My research into Cedric Dover has been greatly assisted by his widow, Maureen Alexander-Sinclair, by his daughter, Valerie Robertson, sadly now deceased, and by his granddaughter Vicki Mitchell. I am also indebted to Michael Banton, who knew Dover in the 1950s and has made available to me his very useful collection of papers and manuscripts. I benefited too from the recollections of the late Tania Alexander, who worked as Dover's publisher before the Second World War, and also those of Anthony C. Hall, a bookseller in Staines, who found me a number of Dover's scattered books and publications.

I am obliged to both Ann Danks and Dr Jeremy Harvey, who have generously helped me trace Stanley Spencer's correspondence about China, and also to Katy Talati, who shared her memories of Spencer and also China before the Liberation. The late John Smethurst provided me with a useful and sympathetic description of Ellis Smith and his position and reputation in Salford and the north-west, and the late Peter Vansittart talked most helpfully about his friendship with A. J. Ayer in the 1950s. Dinah Casson and Carola Zogolovich have been generous in providing me access to their memories as well as to the diaries and drawings of their father, Sir Hugh Casson. Many thanks also to James Lindsay, who kindly gave me permission to reprint two photographs from his father, Michael Lindsay's book *The Unknown War*; to Tim James who has allowed me to use his father, Derrick James's diary as the spine of several chapters; to David Cope, of Left on the Shelf, who helped me trace various leaflets, pamphlets, and other publications concerned with various British campaigns about China and also the early years of New China; and to Andrzej Krauze for information about some of the Polish artists encountered by Paul Hogarth during his travels behind the Iron Curtain. My thanks are also due to the Syndics of Cambridge University Library for permission to quote from the papers of J. D. Bernal.

Jamie Muir and Chris Mitchell have read and helpfully commented on various chapters. I also gained from the attention and occasional raised eyebrow of Simon Coates, who produced a series of radio 'essays' drawn from my researches, and transmitted under the name 'English Takeaway' on BBC Radio Three in 2008. I'm grateful to Dr. Judith Green and other participants in the 'Exhibiting East Asia' symposium at King's College, Cambridge (June 2004). Thanks also to Marina Warner, Robert MacFarlane, Leo Mellor, and others involved with 'Passionate Natures' (2007) and 'Memory Maps' (2008), conferences organized through the University of Cambridge's Centre for Research in the Arts, Social Sciences, and Humanities at which I presented my account of Stanley Spencer's encounter with the Ming Tombs. I have also benefited from seminars held as part of the 'Great British Art Debate', a continuing collaboration involving Tate Britain and public galleries in Norwich, Newcastle, and Sheffield—the latter being one of the places where Chang Chien-ying and Fei Cheng-wu demonstrated the art of Chinese paintings during their first years in Britain.

I have been assisted in a more diffuse but no less real way by my colleagues in various institutions: Barry Curtis, Steve Connor, and others at the London Consortium; Patrick Keiller, Doreen Massey, and Mathew Flintham, with whom I have shared a parallel project funded by the Arts and Humanities Research Council at the Royal College of Art; John Tomlinson, Patrick Williams, and everyone else at the Institute of Cultural Analysis at Nottingham Trent University.

I would also like to acknowledge the generosity of the Paul Mellon Centre for British Art. My initial enquiries were assisted by a Mellon fellowship held at Tate Britain, and this book also benefits greatly from a subsequent award that has made it possible for Oxford University Press to include illustrations throughout. Finally, I am grateful to everyone at OUP. Thanks especially to my editors Luciana O'Flaherty and Matt Cotton, to Celia Dearing, whose picture research has taken her into some unlikely and very hidden crypts, and also to Mary Worthington, who suggested a number of highly desirable improvements in the course of preparing the text for the press.

Patrick Wright

www.patrickwright.net

Contents

Part V. The Artist's Reckoning (*China*)

List of Plates

List of Figures

PART I

In the Spirit of Geneva
(London to Minsk)

1

Embarkation

Shortly before eight o'clock in the morning of Tuesday, 14 September 1954, a flight clerk at Heathrow Airport looked up to see a party of six men approaching his desk. 'Are you the cultural delegation?' he asked, adding dryly: 'Mind you, I am only guessing.'[1]

'It was a safe bet', as one of the party scribbled in his notebook, 'for if ever a crew was motley this was it.' The scribe, Sir Hugh Casson, also records that the man at the head of this unlikely cohort resembled a 'totem pole topped with a scarlet face' that would sporadically splinter into sudden laughter. Tall and thin, with blue eyes and a reserved manner, Leonard Hawkes was Professor of Geology at Bedford College (a women's college within the University of London), President of the Mineralogical Society, and a Fellow of the Royal Society too. Sixty-three years of age and clad in grey flannels and a ginger tweed jacket, he was respected within his profession for his work on volcanoes, the fluctuation of sea levels, and the ongoing movement of the earth's crust. Newspapers had brought him wider notoriety as a boffin: the 'recognised authority' who had revealed that England was not just losing its empire or declining metaphorically into abject reliance on American loans, but actually sinking, as the fatal floods of 1953 may have suggested, south-east first into the North Sea.[2] The professor who had provoked the headline 'Fish will one day swim over London',[3] is himself said to have resembled a pike and to have kept a cigarette permanently trembling on his jutting lower jaw.

Next came a fellow in suede shoes with unusually smart luggage. Lofty like Hawkes but of thicker build, Rex Warner had the shoulders and haunches of a rugger player and, as Casson also noticed, carried his head thrown back as though permanently surprised by whatever the world placed in front of him. A classicist and translator, most recently of Thucydides' *The Peloponnesian War*,[4] Warner had been a friend of C. Day Lewis and W. H. Auden in Oxford in the 1930s. A sports-loving head boy who had gone on to become a schoolmaster, he had also been known both as a left-wing poet[5]— an ornithological Marxist who hymned dippers and long-tailed tits as well as hammers and sickles—and as the author of 'allegorical' novels in which sundry twentieth-century ideologies were tested.[6]

Warner had travelled through Germany immediately after the Second World War, visiting Belsen shortly after its liberation and scripting a film about displaced persons before going on to work for the British Council, first in Greece, where he spent two years as Director of the British Institute in Athens, and later in Berlin. In 1946, he had published *The Cult of Power*, a collection of essays in which he reflected on the truth of the poet W. B. Yeats's warning that 'the centre cannot hold', issued in 'The Second Coming' shortly after the First World War. It was Yeats, he declared, rather than the optimistic prophets of the League of Nations, who had foreseen the 'rough beast' that can emerge when there are 'no agreed standards or values which go deeper than the trivialities of common sense'.[7] Looking back over the Nazi catastrophe at the moment of its final defeat, Warner had pronounced his own warning that 'the new world cannot be built with the old bricks of legality and monetary arrangements', nor only with 'science and efficiency' nor, for that matter, with 'planning' which, whilst a necessary responsibility of the emerging welfare state, might also leave people 'without aim or responsibility or enthusiasm'.

By the time he turned up at Heathrow, however, Warner was no longer so worried about the God-shaped hole at the centre of modern culture. Divorced and remarried to the wealthy Barbara Rothschild, he was living a grand life in Woodstock, Oxfordshire— his biographer mentions a 'magnificent study' along with white-gloved Italian servants[8]—and writing decidedly un-Marxist books about 'eternal Greece', bird-watching, and cricket.[9] His most recent novel, *Escapade* (1953), was a light-hearted romp in which Stalin and Hitler are imagined to have taken up residence, disguised as a vicar and a retired Colonel respectively, in a little English village named Average. Seeing no gain in Warner's earlier reputation as a political writer, the publishers had even used the jacket to emphasize that *Escapade* had been written for 'enjoyment and entertainment' alone: 'no lesson is expected to be drawn from it'.[10] Warner, who had brought along the letters of Cicero to read over the arduous days ahead, was also an alcoholic who would be remembered for stepping off the aeroplane at the many stops that punctuated the delegation's journey and asking, even in the most unlikely places, 'Where's the bar?'[11]

The third man was as short as the first two were tall. Standing only a fraction over five feet high and wearing a white panama hat, the 63-year-old Stanley Spencer 'peered out, like a friendly tortoise, from the shell of an ulster coat that enveloped him from chin to toe'. A notoriously unkempt figure who may well, as one friend admits, have had blackheads in the nape of his neck,[12] Spencer carried an unfurled umbrella and a 'shapeless shopping bag' from which protruded a sketchbook and also, so Casson would allege, the trailing end of a pyjama cord. Known as an artist and visionary, he was famous for his love of Cookham, the village by the Thames in Berkshire that he had made the measure, at once erotic (or 'pornographic', as had also been alleged of his paintings) and divine, of all human life. A Christian Socialist of his own highly idiosyncratic kind, Spencer owed nothing to the upper-class trajectory—public school, Cambridge or Oxford—of his fellow delegates. He had attended the Slade School of Art in London in the early years of the twentieth century. Yet as the son of an upper-working-class family much devoted to music as well as to building (the trade of his grandfather), he had received his earlier education in Cookham: partly at home, where the prophetic language of the King James Bible mixed with the guild socialist vision of John Ruskin (greatly admired by Spencer's father), and partly at the dame school run by his two elder sisters in 'a corrugated iron hut in the next-door garden'.[13] Though peculiarly self-absorbed, Spencer would turn out to have a larger conception of village life than Warner had revealed in *Escapade*.

Only one member of this curious delegation could ever be described as 'a dapper figure in a dark suit'. A. J. Ayer was a small man: thin and curly-haired, says Casson, with sharp-brown eyes and restless movements. A philosopher who aspired to the style of Fred Astaire,[14] he was Grote Professor of Mind and Logic at University College, London, where he had built a considerable department of philosophy. Though he had published his *Philosophical Essays* the previous year, Ayer was still best known as the author of *Language, Truth and Logic* (1937), a work of logical positivism that was said, and surely not only by Ayer himself, to have brought about the end of philosophy as the world had previously known it.

Ayer, who would describe himself as 'half rodent—half fire-fly', was on easy terms with the man who recorded that utterance in his notebook—a duffle-coated fellow with a sharp nose and straggly hair, who was, in the words of a biographer, as 'small and nimble as a monkey'.[15] The architect and writer Sir Hugh Casson had made a great splash as Director of Architecture for the Festival of Britain in 1951 and a smaller one, shortly afterwards, when he redesigned the interior of the royal yacht, *Britannia*. Knighted in 1952 and recently appointed Professor of Interior Design at the Royal College of Art, Casson was a Modernist of the house-trained English variety, and an enthusiastic brightener of Britain's drab post-war public realm. More austere architects may already have looked down on him as a superficial manipulator of appearances who thought one could lift a city merely by painting its lamp-posts pale blue, as Casson had stipulated in his Coronation decorations for the City of Westminster in 1953. Others, who deplored the dinginess of post-war London but were less keen to call in the bulldozers, may have reckoned that brightening up the lamp-posts was not such a terrible way to begin.

Given Professor Hawkes's reported contempt for the burdens of administration,[16] John Chinnery may perhaps have been the man with the tickets. He was by far the youngest member of the party. A lecturer in Chinese from London University's School of Oriental Studies, he had joined the delegation as interpreter, secretary, and guide. According to Sir Hugh, he approached the departure desk with 'the diffident demeanor of a man who had yet to size up the dimensions of the task in front of him'.

Having been picked up from a London hotel at seven o'clock that morning, these six hastily mustered representatives of the British arts and sciences were embarking on the first leg of a journey to Peking, where they would take part, as invited guests of the Chinese government, in the celebrations marking the fifth anniversary of Mao Tse-tung's Proclamation of the People's Republic of China on 1 October 1949. The trip promised to be quite an adventure and yet Casson recalls that the group looked sombre and damp-spirited as they approached their plane.

Stalin's death, on 5 March 1953, had combined with the more recent ceasefire and armistice in Korea to initiate a thaw in the Cold War, yet this had been insufficiently convincing to prevent the travellers from encountering raised eyebrows, pursed lips, and facetious witticisms when they told friends, colleagues, and also their bank managers where they were going. When Stanley Spencer went to collect his passport, the lady who served him remarked, 'You're rather sticking your neck out aren't you?'[17] After the storms of outrage that had broken over various returning 'fellow-travellers' in recent years, the delegates had good reason to feel apprehensive about the adventure. They may also have glanced at one another with some concern as to how they would get on together in the tightly fuselaged days ahead. As Casson noted, a guest 'is always a prisoner', and 'beyond the Iron Curtain there are no bystanders—only players'. Their journey, which would actually stretch out far beyond the five days estimated by its organizers, also promised to be 'paved with memorials to compromises and tolerations of each other's peculiarities'.

Stanley Spencer can hardly have known the upper-class boarder's feeling of 'off-to-school depression' remembered by Casson, but he too had good reason to glance nervously at the KLM plane that would convey them to Amsterdam on the first leg of their flight. Three years later, he would recall feeling oddly reassured by the fact that the car which carried them to Heathrow from the London hotel in which the delegation had assembled the evening before had actually been heading in the direction of his home in Cookham. It was, nevertheless, an anxious embarkation: 'I saw the fins shining in the early morning sun & felt very trembly.'[18]

Recognition: A Hand-Shake and a Scowl

These apprehensive emissaries were by no means the first Britons to embark for Communist China that year. They were flying in the wake of the leader of the Labour Party and erstwhile Prime Minister, Clement Attlee, who had made the same journey earlier in the summer, together with Aneurin Bevan, his former Minister of Health, and also Dr Edith Summerskill, who had been Minister of National Insurance in the same epoch-making post-war government.

There is one land, nevertheless, where Professor Hawkes's scratched-up band of English peacemakers may still seem to have climbed into their plane many years too early. In American perceptions, after all, the story of the West's rapprochement with the People's Republic of China tends to be focused around the events of February 1972, when President Richard Nixon, a seasoned Red-baiter who had now embarked on a 'journey for peace',[19] flew to Peking and stepped down onto the tarmac with his arm held out towards the smiling Chinese Premier, Chou En-lai.

As the opening act of a performance that Nixon himself dubbed 'the Week that Changed the World',[20] that handshake would indeed be a momentous gesture. It would herald the end of America's increasingly surreal insistence that Chiang Kai-shek's nationalist regime, installed on the violently cleansed island of Taiwan (Formosa) since being driven out of the mainland by the victorious People's Liberation Army in early 1949, was the legitimate government of all China.

In reality, things were nothing like so simple. Indeed, if Nixon's future handshake would be deliberately held for the cameras, this was because it had a great deal of symbolic work to do. The aides responsible for scripting this theatrical coup knew very well that the government of the People's Republic of China had long nursed the memory of a snub alleged to have taken place in Geneva in 1954.[21]

On 24 April that year, Chou En-lai had arrived in Europe at the head of the Chinese delegation to a Five Power conference called to seek ways of settling the Indo-Chinese War, in which France was struggling, unsuccessfully, against the advancing forces of Ho Chi Minh's Communist League for the Independence of Vietnam (Viet Minh). Over the following three months, Chou was pictured shaking hands with many leaders, including, as a matter of course, the Soviet Foreign Minister, Vyacheslav Molotov. Yet America's Secretary of State, John Foster Dulles, had brusquely rejected his offer to meet on civil terms. Indeed, members of the American delegation, who were present in Geneva but not formally participating in the conference, are reputed to have engaged in special manoeuvres to avoid even having to acknowledge the Chinese in the buffet between sessions. On one occasion the Under-Secretary of State for Far Eastern Affairs, Walter Robertson, was artfully cornered by the secretary-general of the Chinese delegation, Wang Bingnan. Such was the power of anti-Communism in America, where Senator Joseph McCarthy's influence was still pervasive, that he is said to have 'nearly fainted' when the British cabinet minister Walter Monckton jokingly brandished a miniature camera and wondered aloud how much *Life* magazine would pay for the picture he had just taken of the two men in apparently friendly conversation.[22]

Unyielding as he was in his hatred of Communism, it is most unlikely that Dulles ever actually stood in front of Chou En-lai stubbornly refusing to shake his proffered hand. Indeed, over the course of the Geneva Conference, the coordinator of the American delegation had actually held four meetings with his Chinese

Fig 1. Clement Attlee and Mao Tse-tung, 31 August 1954.

counterpart to discuss the fate of detained citizens on both sides, and hands were shaken too.[23] Yet this was the persistent image of friendliness spurned that Nixon's rigorous clasp at that airfield outside Peking would be intended to melt nearly eighteen years later.

The USA would hold out until the year after the People's Republic of China had been admitted to the United Nations on 25 October 1971, insisting that Peking was really Peiping, as Chiang Kai-shek's defeated nationalists had called the northern capital, and that China belonged to Taiwan rather than the other way around. Britain, however, had disconcerted official American opinion by recognizing 'New China' in January 1950. The decision had been the responsibility of Ernest Bevin, Foreign Secretary in the post-war Labour government, who announced it only three months after Mao's proclamation of the People's Republic on 1 October 1949.

And why not, as many Britons wondered. After two years of bloody civil war in which the brutality, incompetence, and corruption of Chiang Kai-shek's regime had become apparent to all but its most zealous supporters in the West, there were surely grounds for at least some optimism about the intentions of the victorious Communists, who had been considered 'agrarian reformers'[24] rather than strict advocates of the Soviet model by wartime observers of their isolated regime in the remote north-western province of Yenan. During the negotiations of 1944, the Chinese Communists had shown themselves prepared to collaborate with Chiang Kai-shek's Kuomintang against the common Japanese enemy, as long as the nationalist government granted legal status to their party and abolished one-party rule. Despite his recent vitriolic denunciations of Chiang Kai-shek as the 'running dog' of American imperialism, Mao and other Communist leaders had continued to talk of leading a coalition government—a People's Democratic United Front—and proceeding towards the socialist future in comparatively decorous stages. There could be no doubt that, in foreign policy, Mao advocated 'leaning to one side' (i.e. towards the USSR) and fiercely dismissed the idea of neutrality as 'merely a camouflage; a third road does not exist'.[25] Yet there were other indications that the proclaimed 'New Democratic Revolution' need not necessarily culminate in a Stalinist dictatorship—especially if it wasn't isolated behind the 'Bamboo Curtain' already being lowered by America.

The Sino-Soviet Treaty of Friendship, Alliance and Mutual Assistance, agreed with Stalin in Moscow in February 1950, brought Soviet military aid to China as well as cultural and economic exchange. Yet the 'Common Programme' drawn up by the Communist Party and adopted by the wider Political Consultative Conference at the end of September 1949 had not consisted only of warlike expostulations against 'imperialist aggression'. It also promised to establish legal rights, to break the medieval bondage in which Chinese women were held, and to grant equal rights to all nationalities in the People's Republic. In Britain, it was by no means only a handful of partisan Communists who looked back over China's many dreadful decades of imperialist intervention and invasion, of civil war, flood, and famine, and considered these to be admirable ambitions. A wide range of more or less left-wing opinion also subscribed to the view, expressed by Richard Crossman, Iain Mikardo, Michael Foot, and twelve other Labour MPs in a pamphlet published in May 1947, that, whilst Britain still had a role to play both in Europe and on the wider international stage, it should definitely not just be that of an indebted 'outpost of America'[26] locked into Churchill's rearguard policy of seeking to preserve at least some of the British empire as a Washington-backed 'bulwark against Bolshevism' in a world divided into hostile blocs.

There had been no fullscale McCarthyist terror in Britain: not even, really, the systematic 'cleansing' of the 'public services' demanded by Lord Vansittart, who claimed, while speaking in the House of Lords on 29 March 1950, to have identified Communists in the BBC, the universities, the offices of the approaching Festival of Britain and the civil service (he claimed sixteen card-carrying suspects in the Department of Inland Revenue alone).[27] And yet, as defensive officials would explain, Britain's recognition of the People's Republic of China had been a reluctant and partly self-interested concession. *The Times* had described it as a merely 'pragmatic' measure, while at the same time lamenting the prospect of Britain and the United States 'recognizing opposite sides in a squalid and useless struggle in the China seas'.[28] It was carried out against strong objection at home as well as in the USA, which continued, again in the estimate of *The Times'* leader writer, to regard the Pacific Ocean as the British had long viewed both North Sea and English Channel: that is, as 'the last ditch between it and a hostile world'. Further infuriated by the new Chinese government's announcement that they would be requisitioning the 'former military barracks'[29] of the American, British, French, and Dutch embassies in Peking, the Americans, who are said to have lost both their radio mast and their Consul General's office in this provocative adjustment, had withdrawn from the People's Republic, with Dean Acheson insisting that Red China was already in cahoots with Soviet Russia, and doing so in a belligerent manner that, so his critics argued, only made that outcome much more likely. So inflamed was the political climate in America by the end of 1950 that the recalled Consul General, Oliver Edmund Clubb, would be accused of being a fellow-traveller and distanced from the Foreign Service as a 'security risk'.[30] Such accusations had been in the air over America since November 1945, when the US ambassador to China, Brigadier General Patrick Hurley, had resigned, accusing the China experts in the State Department of supporting Communism. The charge that had been intensified during the 'tawdry reign of terror'[31] imposed by Senator Joe McCarthy when witch-hunting not-so-cold warriors set out, assisted by Chiang Kai-shek's loyal 'China lobby' in the US, to make a crypto-Communist even of the late General 'Vinegar Joe' Stilwell. He had been Commanding General of American forces in China, Burma, and India during the Second World War, when both Communists and nationalists in China had suspended their civil war to fight the Japanese with the Western Allies, and he knew very well the folly of associating Chiang Kai-shek, whom he habitually derided as 'Peanut',[32] with the cause of democracy.

Curtains, Flies, and Dope

Based on the pragmatic realization that the Communists were now irreversibly in control of the Chinese mainland, British recognition was announced partly in the hope of safeguarding the country's extensive commercial interests in China and Hong Kong, and also of avoiding tensions within the fracturing empire (both India and Pakistan had recognized the People's Republic of China shortly beforehand). In the event, it would lead to little in the way of mutual understanding. Yet Chou En-lai did accept the appointment of an 'ad interim' chargé d'affaires to prepare the way for the establishment of formally agreed diplomatic relations in the future.

On 13 February 1950 this new official, John Hutchinson, had arrived in Peking, together with most of the staff from the British embassy, which had been moved first to Nanking after Chiang Kai-shek declared it his capital in 1927, and later to Chungking after Nanking fell to the Japanese in December 1937. From the perspective of the People's Republic, at least, the aim was to negotiate 'preliminary and procedural questions' relevant to the eventual establishment of diplomatic relations between the two countries.[33] These questions turned out to be large and, indeed, largely beyond resolution. The revolutionary authorities resented the British government's maintenance of relations with its defeated nationalist ally in Taiwan (the old name, 'Formosa' was already considered an imperialist provocation). They were infuriated by Britain's abstention from voting over the proposed expulsion of the Kuomintang delegates occupying China's place in the United Nations, and they found further provocation in British collusion with the nationalists' disposal of Chinese state property: including seventy aeroplanes, which had been flown to Hong Kong by the nationalist airline and sold to a conveniently established American company from there.[34]

Faltering attempts to overcome these objections were obliterated on 25 June 1950, when Kim Il Sung's Soviet-backed North Korean army advanced across the 38th Parallel (the opening of hostilities was described very differently by the People's Republic of China: 'At daybreak, South Korean troops suddenly attacked North Korea along the entire length of the 38th Parallel'[35]). The Korean War was joined by America together with Britain and other Western allies, whose intervention on the side of South Korea was sanctioned by a resolution of the United Nations Security Council. The People's Republic of China entered the conflict on Kim Il Sung's side at the end of October.

The outbreak of the Korean War greatly stiffened the 'Bamboo Curtain' between Communist China and the West. Thanks to this new extension of the 'Iron Curtain', which Churchill had so famously condemned Stalin for bringing down across Europe in his Fulton oration of March 1946, the quest for diplomatic understanding was displaced by an atrocity show in which nothing could be communicated except in the service of duelling ideological narratives. One of the most dramatic controversies to be played out in this smoke-filled theatre of accusations was initiated by Alan Winnington, a British Communist who had been sent to China in 1948 and who travelled with North Korean forces as reporter for the London-based *Daily Worker*. In a notorious pamphlet named *I Saw the Truth in Korea* (1950), speedily denounced as a contemptible act of treachery by Britain's Labour government, he reported from a recently captured valley at Rangwul where he described being shown a mass grave filled with the corpses of some 7,000 political prisoners.[36] He also claimed to have seen the tell-tale Lucky Strike cigarette packets discarded by American observers presumed to have attended, and perhaps also overseen, their murder by South Korean forces. Comparable claims were made not long afterwards by Monica Felton, who would be removed from the Chairmanship of the Stevenage New Town Development Corporation for visiting North Korea with a women's delegation and publishing a pamphlet, *What I Saw in Korea*,[37] in which she likened the prisoner-of-war camps sanctioned by UN forces to Nazi concentration camps.

In another of the most sensational charges of the ongoing propaganda war, the Chinese authorities cited 'irrefutable facts'[38] proving that, since January 1952, the American military had been using 'large-scale bacteriological warfare'[39] against China and North Korea: dropping infected voles, anthrax-contaminated chicken feathers, and even plague-bearing tarantulas along with flies, mosquitoes, and midges from their planes, exploiting techniques developed by Japan's infamous Unit 731 in Manchuria and employed against China with monstrous, and no doubt also vividly remembered, consequences between 1932 and 1945.

The Americans denied all such charges, firing off counter-accusations alleging Chinese abuse of prisoners of war. The claims of biological warfare were, however, accepted by the British biochemist Joseph Needham and the other members of an 'International Scientific Commission' convened by the Moscow-led World Peace Council, at the request of the President of the

Chinese People's Committee for World Peace, Dr Kuo Mo-jo, who insisted that the International Red Cross Committee was too biased to carry out an impartial investigation.[40] It was during the closely chaperoned visit of this commission of largely Western European scientists, in the summer of 1952, that the acting British Consul in Peking, Martin Buxton, wrote to his father (a professor at the London School of Hygiene and Tropical Medicine), asking 'Do you know Professor Needham? Peking diplomats are split on the germ warfare question. Since neither side can admit the possibility that its own government is a liar, and somebody must be telling lies somewhere.'[41]

The confusion was indeed considerable and it would prove long-lasting too. Embarrassed by captured US airmen who admitted the Chinese charges of germ warfare, the Western authorities were further horrified, in January 1954, that is, after the ceasefire, when a handful of US and British soldiers held by the Chinese in North Korea volunteered to move to Peking rather than returning to the West in an agreed exchange of prisoners.

Having already published claimed confessions of British and American soldiers admitting to 'torture, rape, arson, looting and cold-blooded murder of defenceless civilians and prisoners of war in Korea',[42] the PRC now proceeded to display these 'turncoats' as brave 'thinking soldiers',[43] who were prepared to condemn their own governments, to denounce the racism and class exploitation of the capitalist regimes that had tried to use them as murderous 'robots', and to sing the praises of Maoist internationalism too. American analysts countered with the assertion that these renegades were undereducated, dysfunctional, and mentally challenged types, many of them products of broken homes, who had been brutalized by the Chinese: blasted with incessant propaganda and then tempted into making recorded confessions in return for 'liquor and marijuana'.[44]

The accusations flew in both directions, with China and her Western supporters claiming that murderous nationalists in South Korean prison camps were terrorizing Communist prisoners into volunteering to transfer their allegiances. As one of the journalists who made these claims, Alan Winnington never wavered in his insistence that American and British prisoners in North Korea had been kept under tolerable conditions. Lacking solidarity and doomed by their own traditions of 'free enterprise and devil-take-the-hindmost', the American prisoners had, so he gleefully proclaimed, proved liable to demoralization—some, he alleged, had just given up and died.[45] The 978 British prisoners, being mostly 'depression children'[46] from working-class homes, were said to have fared a lot better. Kept in open settlements on the south bank of the Yalu River, they organized themselves according to their own cooperative and radical traditions. Provided with good medical treatment and quite able to withstand attempts at political re-education, they enjoyed skating and other recreations. As for marijuana, it was in this company that Winnington claimed to have first smoked the stuff, which the British prisoners—far from having been more or less forcibly doped—had found growing wild in the nearby hills and gladly planted 'around their cottages'.[47]

Infuriated by Winnington, his accomplice the Australian reporter Wilfred Burchett (*Daily Express* and *Ce Soir*), and other renegades who would continue to 'dislocate the propaganda machine'[48] for some time to come, the American government greeted this new development as further proof that Red China had been engaging in insidious, if not uniquely Oriental, techniques of mind control. In 1950 the hugely influential term 'brain-washing' had been launched into circulation by an American journalist and CIA propagandist named Edward Hunter. Having 'peeped through the bamboo curtain'[49] as a correspondent based in Hong Kong, he used the term to describe the coercive techniques the Chinese Communists had started to promote as 'thought reform'. That condemnation of 'brain-washing' may have impressed many Westerners, including, perhaps, a few who had already read *Nineteen Eighty-Four*, published the previous year (1949), and could therefore recognize its 'Orwellian' resonances from the start. Yet the emerging term was strongly resisted by other Western witnesses who were predisposed to offer a more appreciative definition of the process. The French observer Claude Roy, who visited China in 1952/3, thought that Communist 'brain-washing' was actually a process of 'heart searching', associated with the innumerable little 'brain-storms' with which the Peoples Liberation Army was said to have won over those degraded converts who had once been loyal to Chiang Kai-shek.[50]

For Peter Townsend, a Briton who went to China with the Friends Ambulance Unit in 1941 and stayed through the first years of the People's Republic, the alleged 'brain-washing' was just such a form of remoralization, also known as 'Opening One's Thoughts' and 'Changing One's Thinking': a benign, if at times also painful, therapeutic process through which the new collective taught its members that an intellectual who was really intent on 'serving the people' had to do more to overcome his unrevolutionary past than merely 'picking up a few Marxist phrases'.[51] William G. Sewell, a British Quaker and biologist who was then teaching at the West China Union University in the south-western city of Chengdu, also looked back quite positively on the searching group discussions introduced following the liberation of the last city on the Chinese mainland to be taken by the Communists: 'It was the foundation of life in the new China that everyone should know what it was all about, that he should become politically conscious, and realize fully his own responsibilities.'[52]

The Korean War was suspended by 1954 but, even with the thaw produced earlier in the year by the Geneva conference on Indo-China, it was still a challenging time for Westerners invited to go behind the 'Bamboo Curtain'. On 11 August Chou En-lai had announced that the People's Republic intended to liberate Taiwan from Chiang Kai-shek. Indeed, on 3 September, less than two weeks before the members of the British cultural delegation embarked at Heathrow, the People's Liberation Army had shelled Kuomintang positions on the islands of Quemoy in the Taiwan Strait. No wonder A. J. Ayer had hesitated at the thought of joining a 'group of fellow-travellers', only accepting the Chinese government's invitation after phoning Hugh Casson, whom he knew to be a man of Conservative political opinions, and establishing that he too would be willing to go.[53] No wonder, either, that the members of the cultural delegation had chosen the geologist Professor Leonard Hawkes as their Chairman: a safe as well as senior pair of hands, he could scarcely be branded an ideological renegade by suspicious onlookers.

Advance of the Death-Watch Beetles

A dry dock, built to accommodate the old tea clipper *Cutty Sark*, had nearly been completed at Greenwich. The World Meteorological Organization was hoping to involve both American and Russian scientists in probing the extent to which atomic tests might be affecting the world's weather... 'Trembly' or not, the now airborne members of the British cultural delegation may briefly have felt comforted by the stories in that September morning's edition of *The Times*. Not long after taking off from Heathrow, however, they would set aside their papers and start watching as the cities of divided Europe slid by.

Amsterdam

STANLEY SPENCER: '...very nice airport. I thought of my self-portrait in the Museum of Modern Art there.'[54]

REX WARNER: 'About 1 hour and 2 Bols in excellent airport.'[55]

HUGH CASSON: 'Amsterdam finds us still depressed. The eyes prick with nostalgia as loud-speakers announce the flight leaving for London. I have not experienced this dull, trapped-dog feeling since going back to school. Our fellow passengers on the K.L.M. plane to Prague include a British football team. Lunch is served over the Rhine. Below us stretches a huge American airfield. Are the American wives, thumbing over the comics in those little villas below, as homesick as we are? At 1 p.m. we penetrate the Iron Curtain...low, rolling, sun-dappled hills, a deserted autobahn, a bomb-shattered airfield. Over Czechoslovakia the sky is grey, sad and autumnal. I read and reread the unreadable areas of *The Times*..."E.D.C."... "Sugar Project in Barbadoes"'.[56]

Prague

SPENCER: 'We came down at Prague where we stayed 2 days & walked about on the bridges & saw the Cathedral up on the Hill. We went to it by an endless taxi drive. It seemed a bit deserted.'

AYER: 'Five or six years had passed since the death of Jan Masaryk and the purge of Slansky and his followers but an air of listlessness, of hopeless depression, greeted the visitor like a clammy southern wind. Presumably some people were thriving under the current regime and others bravely engaging in clandestine opposition but there was no mistaking the general sense of defeat and despair. Even the beauty of the city had been marred by the erection in white marble, of a gigantic monument to Stalin and the Red Army, which was so placed on the heights of the city that it seemed to meet the eye at every turn.' '... pictures of the leading Czech Communists greeted us everywhere, in conjunction with those of Malenkov whom the Czechs had wrongly forecast as Stalin's successor.'[57]

CASSON: 'The knife of homesickness is given a further twist by the poignancy of a tiny homely label, "Thrupp & Maberly" on the sill of the taxi door.'

'Despite a friendly hotel, spirits drop to zero in this grey despairing city, visually ruined by the vast and vulgar memorial to the Red Army which now dominates the heights above the river. I have forgotten shaving soap, the Philosopher his razor. There is nothing gay in the shops—still less on the face of the shoppers. The Painter says we are deathwatch beetles condemned only to go forward.'

WARNER: 'Reached Prague at 1.35 & were met by Chinamen. After some delay got to the Palace Hotel. Went round cathedral & walked back via Charles Bridge. City curiously silent. Most people have to share rooms. Ayer and I were lucky in the drawing of lots. Think they really wanted us to go on to Moscow today...Good drink in "Film Club". Spencer is reminded of Purgatory. Early bed.'

[September 15]

CASSON: 'Next morning we complete our Chinese visa forms—fifty questions, the final one of which states "Please now write your autobiography"—and embark upon our first Russian aeroplane, twin-engined, tricycle-undercarriage, sturdy, Turkey-carpeted and well kept. No reading lamps or safety straps. The stewardess, pale, and dressed in a blue-serge coat and skirt, welcomes us gravely aboard and hands round tea in glasses. Her hands are shapely, the nails pinkly varnished.'

Minsk

SPENCER: 'an unexpected landing at Minsk 'because of a "storm over Moscow" that sounded very dramatic to me'.

CASSON: 'Brand new airport. Meet our first example of the contemporary Russian interior—fringed velvet curtains, serge table-cloths, draped portieres, cut-glass vases, huge oil paintings in heavy gilded frames, a Victorian preface to a Victorian country.'

WARNER: 'Down at Minsk at 7.00 (9.00 local time). Drinkless meal, then told that our plane will not leave till tomorrow morning. We are shown into a huge dormitory, brightly lighted, & surrounded by continuous whistling of trains. 9 beds.'[58]

JOHN CHINNERY: 'It reminded me of the dormitory of an English boarding school, with iron beds lined up in rows and kitsch paintings on the wall—snow scenes or landscapes with birch trees. I remember Spencer coming up to me and asking: "Do you think it's time for me to go to byes?"'[59]

AYER: 'I cannot explain why the name "Minsk" still has a romantic sound for me. It draws no support from anything that we discovered in the city.'

2

Holding Out in the Legation Quarter

Smooth lawns flowed round clumps of spiky fir trees which half concealed the stout Victorian houses. A wing showed here, an arched verandah there...I went up to an open side gate in a wall. A rifle was leaning against a stool, but there seemed to be no sentry. On the other side of a wide, paved court, stood a pavilion roofed with treacle-yellow tiles. Weeds sprouted between the paving-stones and the tiles. A snake of crimson wall encircled everything. It was dreamlike and utterly still, like a *surréaliste* picture.

Denton Welch, *Maiden Voyage*[1]

Though spared the ferocious accusations made against State Department officials in America during the years of Senator Joe McCarthy's witch hunt, the handful of British diplomats in Peking had nevertheless found themselves under considerable pressure during the first years of Communist rule.

The government of the new People's Republic ignored them, except at moments of particular tension when it would confine them to their walled embassy compound and orchestrate anti-imperialist demonstrations outside the gate. However, these isolated representatives also knew the mistrust of the Foreign Office in London. Such were the suspicions of the time, to say nothing of the scrutiny from Washington, that trouble awaited a British diplomat who admitted any sympathy with Communist China's revolutionary reforms. Derek Bryan, a former First Secretary (Chinese Affairs) in Peking, did just that while on home leave in 1951. Offered a choice between a post as commercial attaché in Peru and early retirement, he opted for the latter.[2] Humphrey Trevelyan, who would eventually become Britain's first officially tolerated chargé d'affaires in the People's Republic of China, recalls arriving as head of mission in Peking to find a letter from a

Whitehall official berating consular staff for not employing inverted commas when using the word 'liberation' to describe the Communist victory of 1949, as if they too were dupes of the new regime's propaganda.[3] 'We were', as he wrote of the isolated diplomatic community he had joined, 'living at the end of the line.'

White Peking: the Allure of Maladjustment and Stagnation

Trevelyan had arrived in Peking shortly after the armistice that brought the Korean War to a close in July 1953.[4] Having made his way through the 'Bamboo Curtain' from Hong Kong, he sailed upriver through intensely cultivated farmland to Tientsin, an industrialized former Treaty Port, which impressed him as having 'attained an intensity of ugliness and desolation achieved by no other town in the world'.[5] From here, he took a train across the North China plain to find that Peking, at least, remained an ancient city wrapped in high crenellated walls some 40 kilometres long and accessed through sixteen multi-storeyed gate towers. Surrounded by a moat and many duck farms, Peking was still recognizable as the city of Kublai Khan: a 'Tartar encampment in stone',[6] in the words of one early twentieth-century guide. There were other walled cities in the world and yet, as a recently departed German photographer would insist, 'there has never been anything to compare with the walls of Peking'.[7]

Much had happened since 1 October 1949, when this repeatedly looted city of jade and silk was hauled out of the no man's land it had occupied during the recent civil war and proclaimed the capital of 'New China'. Lakes had been drained and sewers cleaned, reputedly for the first time since the Manchu defeat of the Ming dynasty in 1644.[8] Streets that had long seemed 'a never-ending pageant'[9] teeming with hawkers, beggars, jugglers, barbers, clowns, fortune-tellers, and bird-sellers, now also featured busy 'New China' bookshops selling political pamphlets and novels. The air had long confronted arriving Western visitors with a panic-inducing 'excess of sound':[10] a cacophony in which the noise of clappers, gongs, and trumpets was mixed with the 'plaintive singing cries' of peddlers, the grinding of cart wheels turning on ungreased wooden axles, and the eerie fluting of pigeons swooping about with bamboo whistles attached to the base of their tails.[11]

It was now also filled with propaganda slogans, revolutionary songs, and public confessions too.

The imperial eunuchs had gone but Peking remained an 'archetypal' city laid out according to the principles of 'marvellous symmetry'[12] noted by the visiting Arnold Toynbee in 1929, with palaces, peony beds,[13] lotus-filled lakes, pagodas, dragon walls, carved lions embodying the antithetical yet also complimentary principles of yin and yang, and boulevards on which coal-bearing camels were scarcely yet challenged by limousines full of party officials. Arrayed around the palaces and gardens of the Forbidden City, and well viewed from the wooded and temple-clad artificial mound known as Coal Hill, the Tartar City remained, as a more recent British visitor had noted, an 'anonymous muddle'[14] of narrow walled alleys ('hutongs') with gates leading to residential compounds containing internal courtyards joined by 'moon gates' and south-facing single-storey houses with pitched roofs, paper-covered windows, and ancient wooden lattices. 'Remoulding' and 'Thought reform' may recently have become the order of the day for the residents, including the beggars and tramps, who had been swept up for retraining in the industrious ways of the new order. Yet the approaching foreigner was more likely to notice that Peking still resembled the imperial capital of the ancient Middle Kingdom: an impression that was still scenically confirmed, as it had been for Toynbee, by the distant Western Hills, which 'magically advance or retreat or disappear in accordance with changes in the atmosphere'.[15]

Trevelyan found the British consular mission still clinging to its 'princely town palace' in the Legation Quarter.[16] Extending westward from the wall of the Tartar City and bordering the Mongolian Market and the Imperial Carriage Sheds, the British embassy compound at 1 Hsing Kuo Lu was itself a monument to the troubled history of contact between China and the British empire. To begin with, the Chinese emperors had refused the thought of a Western presence in their lands. For many years, indeed, the imperial authorities are said to have considered Western diplomats as of no higher status than messengers from Korea, Mongolia, Tibet, and other 'tributary states', insisting that they too must prostrate themselves as they approached the emperor, and trying to confine their access to the distant southern city of Canton and

Portuguese Macau.[17] Perhaps the most famous example of this lofty indifference was provided by Emperor Ch'en Lung in a letter written in 1793 in response to Lord Macartney's mission, sent to China by William Pitt with the aim of creating an embassy in Peking: 'I have perused your Memorial. The earnest terms in which it is couched reveal a respectful humility on your part which is highly praiseworthy ... As to your entreaty to send one of your nationals to be accredited to my Celestial Court and to be in control of your country's trade with China, this request is contrary to all usages of my dynasty and cannot possibly be entertained.'[18]

The matter was eventually resolved by force. The Treaty of Nanking, an 'unequal treaty' imposed after the First Opium War of 1839–42, established British rule in Hong Kong and opened a system of five Treaty Ports, including Canton and Shanghai. Ten more were established, together with further rights of navigation, trade, and settlement, after the Second Opium War of 1856–60. As Karl Marx wrote in the *New York Daily Tribune* in June 1853, 'the superstitious faith in the eternity of the Celestial Empire' collapsed as British forces ended the isolation that had secured the old China of the Manchu dynasty: 'That isolation having come to a violent end by the medium of England, dissolution must follow as surely as that of any mummy carefully preserved in a hermetically sealed coffin, whenever it is brought into contact with the open air.'[19]

After the Second Opium War, in which Peking was violently subjugated by Lord Elgin in 1860 and the old Summer Palace to the north-west of the city was burned and looted by vengeful British troops, the British Legation had been installed in a decayed Manchu palace compound, formerly owned by the dukes of Liang and equipped with stone lions, red-pillared pavilions, and ornamental kiosks in the garden. To begin with, this walled and now 'extraterritorial' enclave is said to have been leased from the Imperial Foreign Office for £500 per year,[20] while further palaces and buildings were taken over by other foreign powers to form what would eventually become the international Legation Quarter. The legations of Japan, Russia, and many other Western nations were to be found here, as were various banks, hotels, churches, schools, an art gallery, and the Peking Club too.

Fig 2. Entrance gateway to British Legation, Peking, 1919.

Possessing a larger acreage than any other foreign compound in the city, and being enclosed, on one side at least, by the massive wall of the ancient Tartar City, the British embassy had been barricaded and defended as the refuge for all Westerners in the Legation Quarter during the Boxer Rebellion of 1900, when the European powers in China came under attack from the 'Society of Righteous and Harmonious Fists', originally a peasant movement determined to rid China of Christians and foreigners. Many missionaries and their converts were murdered in outbreaks across north China. And the uprising spread to Peking, where it was encouraged by Prince Tuan and tolerated, if not exactly 'mothered',[21] by T'zu-Hsi (Cixi), the empress dowager, a famously reactionary figure who had kept Peking largely unchanged and, in English usage, 'mummified' in the years that saw the coastal cities of Shanghai and Canton transformed by overseas trade, and who seemed to her enemies to exhale 'the last gasp of a corpse-like civilisation'.[22] In the words of one outraged missionary observer, the Boxers plunged Peking into 'a pandemonium, a

Fig 3. The dining room of the British Legation, c.1900.

rehearsal of hell.... the condition of the capital became like that of Paris under the wildest orgies of the Commune'.[23]

The siege of the Legation Quarter, and of the British embassy compound in particular, lasted fifty-five days. For a time no news of the fate of the various legations escaped, except for exaggerated rumours alleging that all had been overthrown and their occupants massacred. There was uproar in France, where it was believed that the French minister in Peking, Stephen Jean-Marie Pichon, had been murdered by 'slavering Chinese fiends',[24] and also in Germany, whose hard man in the city, Baron von Ketteler, really was shot dead in the street. Premature obituaries were published in Britain too, including that of *The Times* correspondent, Dr George Morrison, who is said to have secured a pay rise and, indeed, a job for life on account of the extravagant valedictory praise lavished on him by his own mistaken paper.[25]

Eyewitness accounts of events in the barricaded compound tell of a cemetery quickly dug in the Councillor's garden, 'unnecessary walls and brick walks' torn up for barricades,[26] and the verandahs of the much shelled main house being defended against rifle fire and cannon balls by a multicoloured array of sandbags improvised from 'silks and satins, curtains, carpets and embroideries', all 'ruthlessly cut up' to meet the requirements of the moment.[27] Responsible for this and other defensive measures, the women in the compound were described by one proud witness as 'marvels of pluck'.[28] The surviving marines were highly praised too.

The siege of the Legations and also of the North Cathedral, where over three thousand had been protected by a force of forty-three French and Italian marines, was lifted by the combined forces of the Eight-Nation Alliance (Japan, USA, Britain, Russia, Italy, Germany, France, and Austro-Hungary), which assembled in Tientsin and then marched for five days over deep sand with the temperature nearing 100 degrees. The Japanese were said to have survived these arduous conditions best, but it was the British or, more specifically, General Gasalee's company of Sikhs who, on 14 August, entered the city through the sewage canal, emerging to be greeted on the British Legation's tennis court and, indeed, patted on the back by those they had relieved. It was reported that the defenders' 'mainstay' during the siege had been an ancient cannon, recovered from a junkshop by a loyal Chinese coolie and put into action as 'The International Gun'.[29] Mounted on a Russian carriage and loaded with Italian ammunition (in some accounts the carriage was Italian and the ammunition Russian), this relic was put to work by an American gunner. It can safely be said to have done less damage than the looting that, once again, followed the Allied occupation of the burned and much devastated city.

Abandoned by the empress dowager, her imperial court, and much of its rebellious population, Peking was systematically 'sacked'. One pseudonymous 'eyewitness', an English resident who would later be ostracized by the white community for the honesty of his account, told of rape and pillage, of captured 'coolies' being dispatched with a shotgun, of vast amounts of treasure being ransacked from deserted palaces, and much priceless porcelain being smashed by marauding soldiers with eyes only for precious metal. 'Everyone has piles of it', wrote Bertram Simpson, of the silver amassed during this period of 'quiet looting', in which 'all our armies are becoming armies of traders'.[30] It was said that even the wife of the British Minister in Peking, Sir Claude MacDonald, had 'devoted herself most earnestly to looting'.[31]

The wife of the American Minister, Sarah Pike Conger, appears to have felt very differently about the siege and its consequences. Admitting the 'fiendish cruelty' and 'most lamentable'[32] methods of the Boxers, she nevertheless understood the Chinese desire to repel foreign influences. Writing to a niece on 30 September 1900, she declared 'Poor China! Why cannot foreigners let her alone with her own? China has been wronged, and in her desperation she has striven as best she could to stop the inroads, and to blot out those already made. My sympathy is with China. A very unpopular thing to say, but it is an honest conviction, honestly uttered.'[33] Be that as it may, when she was later reduced to auctioning off her collection of Chinese treasures in New York, a year or so after the death of her husband in 1907, Mrs Conger was forced to admit that some of her own valuable items had been looted too.[34]

With the Peace Treaty signed a year or so after the defeat of the Boxer Rebellion, the Legation Quarter in Peking was brought under Western control. The Chinese houses scattered through and around it were cleared, partly to create defensible open space, and the entire area was walled (Chinese observers would remember that the wall 'actually had hundreds of gunholes facing the city')[35] and turned into a small extraterritorial city with its own Administrative Commission, paved streets, electric lighting, and police force. The curious anthropology of expatriate life was renewed too. Visiting the city some three years later, Denton Welch would find that the Western residents had long since returned to their customary ways, which included impressing visitors with their well-stocked homes: preferably not just one of those 'stout'

Victorian villas in the British compound but a fabulous mandarin's palace in the Tartar City with carp pools in the courtyard, doors and windows shaped like leaves, carpets of gold thread, and huge jade carvings proudly said to have been looted from the burning Summer Palace in 1860.[36]

The defeat of the Boxer Uprising may have marked the effective end of the Manchu court as an 'independent Chinese ancien régime',[37] but the social life of Peking's doubly jaded expatriate circle had continued to revolve around dinner parties like the one described in Somerset Maugham's book *On a Chinese Screen* (1922). Here, the impeccably tailored First Secretary of the British legation stands tall among his international guests. These include a Swiss businessman whose wife, a former *cocotte*, displayed 'her opulent charms so generously that it made you a little nervous', and a Guatemalan Minister, whose frilled shirt and dazzlingly displayed orders serve only to embarrass the underdressed chargé d'affaires from Montenegro. The French military attaché is also present: his exotically scented and latecoming spouse proves more than a match for the ageing and therefore no longer quite so melodramatic Russian princess, who wears black silk from ankle to neck and has no tolerance for English writings about her lost homeland. As for the conversation, these more or less animate period pieces

> talked of this Minister who had just written from Bucharest or Lima, and that Counsellor's wife who found it so dull in Christiania or so expensive in Washington. On the whole it made little difference to them in what capital they found themselves, for they did precisely the same things in Constantinople, Berne, Stockholm and Peking. Entrenched within their diplomatic privileges and supported by a lively sense of their social consequence, they dwelt in a world in which Copernicus had never existed, for to them sun and stars circled obsequiously round this earth of ours, and they were its centre.[38]

Even outside the British legation compound, the international lifestyle seems scarcely to have been interrupted by the struggles of the warlords who spent much of the 1920s tearing an already shattered China into smaller pieces. Together with her artist husband, Cyrus LeRoy Baldridge, the American writer and cosmopolitan Caroline Singer arrived in Peking just in time for the coup of October 1924, in which Feng Yü-hsiang, the 'Christian General' who is famously said to have used a fire hose to baptize his troops, deposed President Cao, and placed the Chinese under martial law. The two Americans saw the heads of executed looters mounted on the city walls, watched Feng's 'hymn-singing' soldiers carry machine guns into Buddhist temples, and heard that the secretary of the outgoing regime had been shot dead in the street before he could disclose 'the uses to which public funds were put'.[39] Some of the overthrown regime's officials took refuge on foreign soil represented by the Legation Quarter, which Baldridge described as resembling 'a European suburb inhabited by rich of ultra-conservative tastes' even though its hotels were suddenly 'jammed from cellar to attic with Chinese'.[40] Others quit the city altogether, having tried to save their houses from government confiscation by lending them to foreigners, and Americans best of all.

Thanks to the awkward situation in which the 'ashen-faced' General of the gendarmerie suddenly found himself, Singer and Baldridge were themselves invited to take up residence in his house near the Drum Tower in the northern reaches of the Tartar City. It was a fabulous place of blue silk and pearl-inlaid teakwood, with lotus pools, temples, paved courtyards, a dramatic 'rock garden', and various smaller houses all spread out over three acres. Agreed with the hastily departing owner, their 'lease', which Baldridge wrote himself, demanded no rent. The only plea made by their landlord before he set off on his urgent 'business trip' was that they should do what they could to protect the property against the police and other claimants, even though Baldridge warned that he and his wife, who were of markedly liberal and internationalist outlook, would never be prepared to 'claim immunity' from the Chinese government by 'hoisting the American flag or yelping for marines'.[41]

The armies poured in and out of Peking during these chaotic years, but the convulsions do not appear to have had much effect on the systematic 'maladjustment'[42] of the 'white colony' in the Legation Quarter. Singer, who shared her anti-imperialism with her artist husband, remarks dryly that 'Ladies endlessly gyrating in the cycle of at-homes form a droll international pageant'.[43] The other activities of these 'white imperialists'—a phrase Baldridge adopted from the 'characteristically unsparing' analysis of Bertrand Russell, who had taught in Peking in 1921—included gun-running, gambling, much of it centred on the efforts of Mongolian ponies at the nearby racecourse, and clipping hunks out of their cats' fur in order to discourage the Chinese from converting these pets into lining for winter jackets.[44] Many foreign residents, including some of the missionaries and educationalists, had come to terms with Peking as a city of bribery, rake-offs, and 'squeeze', not the least of it connected to the thriving trade in antiquities cast into circulation by the various crises that had engulfed the imperial city since the opium wars.

Some who took the opportunity of such moments when treasures were shaken or, indeed, violently pulled free of their customary imperial settings, went on to become respected scholars and collectors—few, after all, were as extravagant in their peculiarities as Sir Edmund Backhouse, the notorious 'hermit of Peking', who turned out also to have been a swindler and forger, as well as a fantasist who claimed to have been the empress dowager's lover.[45] Sir Percival David, a Briton who assembled one of the most valuable and influential collections in the West, managed to acquire a number of rare ceramic works from the imperial collection in 1927/8. The pieces in question had been given to a bank by the empress dowager, who used them as collateral when raising funds to cover the cost of her final removal from the Forbidden City in 1901. Previous prospective purchasers had been frightened off by the death threats awaiting anyone who proposed to remove these precious items from Peking, but Percival managed to spirit them out with the help of a Japanese art-dealer friend.[46] They became central exhibits in his collection, and were displayed alongside works lent by the Chinese government and other Western collectors at the International Exhibition of Chinese Art, a vast and influential show directed by David and opened at the Royal Academy of Arts in London on 28 November 1935.

Having surveyed the lower reaches of this expatriate world in which connoisseurship coexisted so fruitfully with looting, Cyrus Baldridge records that 'tourists in Peking were always being shown treasures with which Old China Hands would then reluctantly agree to part. In several homes one only with difficulty could get through dinner without buying the amber beads from around the hostess's neck. And it was sheer rudeness, when dining with a retired English major, not to avail ourselves of the opportunity of depriving him of his choice Chinese jewellery.'[47] Such was the scale of this informal trade that 'drawing rooms sometimes underwent startling refurnishing between cocktail parties'.

Together with the silk-robed and square-hatted servants on which its participants depended, the expatriate way of life was still intact in 1934, when a young American named Haldore Hanson arrived in Peiping (Peking) from Northfield, Minnesota, and took up residence as secretary to a Chinese official. This future foreign correspondent joined a settlement of about 4,000 Americans and Europeans. It impressed him as resembling a small farming community back home in Minnesota, where gossip passed like wildfire and people were at once on first name terms and 'sharply divided on moral issues':

> a dominant colony of missionaries invoked the wrath of the Lord upon a small but vocal group of homosexuals and nymphomaniacs who entertained lavishly, drank freely, and discussed without a twitch their respective modes of life. The battle lines were not always distinct; more than one pervert went to church and at least two missionaries of my acquaintance became little 'hellers'. Others in the community, not partisans of either side, mingled tolerantly with both.[48]

China was still a land of exotic special effects in 1935, when Peter Fleming, a dashing British adventurer and correspondent for *The Times*, journeyed overland from Peking to India—a testing and at times dangerous undertaking he would throw off as 'this escapade in Tartary'.[49] Leaving from Peking station at midnight on 15 February, Fleming and his route companion, the Swiss athlete and writer Ella Maillart, were seen off by a gaggle of expatriate friends who had come directly from a fancy dress party still decked out in fur coats and burnt cork. Smiling into the faces of these 'pierrettes and apaches', he thought that Peking was just like Oxford in its tendency to be 'characteristic'[50] and realized, nervously, that 'it was really a very long way to India'.[51]

Maillart described Peking as 'the decaying capital'[52] but its condition had worsened again in 1937, when the outbreak of the

second Sino–Japanese War prompted the closure of many legations and put startlingly new pressure on the 'infinitely bored'[53]
Westerners accustomed to floating through this city of 'peculiar
ruined magnificence'.[54] Sir Harold Acton, the Oxford aesthete
who lived in Peking from 1932 until the outbreak of the Second
World War in 1939, provided one of the pre-war British community's last testimonials in *Peonies and Ponies*, published in 1941.
Here was another anthology of lapsed missionaries and frayed
fantasists, who spend their time searching out the Tao or 'Way' of
ancient China, setting up night clubs, 'adopting' Chinese sons
and daughters, and leafing their way through much-thumbed
copies of the *Illustrated London News* as they tried to relieve the
torpor of expatriate life in a city that had actually been a place of
'sheer stagnation',[55] since 1927, when Chiang Kai-shek established
his new capital in Nanking. In the judgement of Derk Bodde, an
American researcher who returned to Peking on a Fulbright
fellowship at the end of August 1948, the fate of the non-American
foreigners in Peking seemed by then 'even more pathetic' than
that of the Chinese, who could at least work to stay alive. The
game, finally, was up. Whether they were Russian, French, British
or German, the Europeans who stayed now did so 'simply because
there is nowhere else to go. Many have lived here for decades.
Now they have almost nothing, and before them lies the prospect
of even less.'[56]

'Liberation' and a Diplomatic Christening

The British embassy compound had suffered during the Second
World War: looted under the Japanese occupation, it had also
been used to house infirm British internees. Yet it was still operating when Trevelyan turned up in 1953, albeit only barely
furnished and already reduced, through acquisitions made by the
new authorities, to an area of some 18 acres. With its tennis, squash,
and fives courts, its library, chapel, social club and other remaining
amenities, the compound impressed Britain's arriving chargé
d'affaires as a peculiar relic. Trevelyan likened it to 'a superior
mental home provided with every comfort',[57] but weirdly disconnected from the world beyond its walls—except for the sound of
revolutionary propaganda, songs, and music pouring in from the

loudspeakers outside. It was only in the late 1950s, when the British embassy was finally moved and its compound in the Legation Quarter taken over by the Ministry of Public Security, that the stable block, chapel, and other buildings would be cleared of the vast accumulation of documents, gilt communion chalices and ewers gathered in from various churches across north China, and personal possessions stored there by departing British subjects, including *The Times* correspondent and also Sir Harold Acton, who had hurriedly left in 1939, when the ongoing hostilities between China and its Japanese invader were quickly swept up into the Second World War.[58]

According to Trevelyan, the small consular staff living in the British compound had endured three and a half years in 'an anomalous and humiliating' limbo. Spurned by the government of 'New China', they had spent much of their time playing bridge as well as tennis, while attending as best they could to the interests of the few remaining American as well as British, Australian, and other foreign residents, be they arbitrarily imprisoned missionaries or trapped businessmen whose companies were being systematically squeezed into the ground (assailed with wild tax demands and prevented from either working or laying off their employees, Western businesses in China were effectively held hostage under impossible conditions). The embassy compound felt like 'an internment camp'[59] in the early 1950s, and it would continue to serve as a refuge, not just for Peking's remaining Westerners, but for other threatened creatures too. Its collection of mongrels would become all the more unique as the dogs in the city outside were killed off by Maoist decree. Even the sparrows roosting in the compound's tall trees would come to be seen as a threat, and not just during the campaign against the 'Four Evils' unleashed in 1957. According to Douglas Hurd, who took up his post in the Peking embassy compound as a young member of the Foreign Office in the summer of 1954, these 'enemies of the people' were already in the sights of the Young Pioneers who wanted to come in and slaughter them as grain-stealing pests.[60]

An impression of the first years under the new Communist-led government in Peking can be gathered from letters written by Trevelyan's predecessor at the British legation. On 7 October 1952, Martin Buxton, who was then acting as Britain's officially unrecognized consul in Peking, wrote to inform his mother in England of the recent christening of his second daughter. Since there was no longer a resident minister in the compound, the service had been conducted by the Reverend Canon Farnham E. Maynard of St Peters in Melbourne, who had conveniently 'turned up' some two weeks earlier as an Australian delegate to the ongoing Asian-Pacific Peace Conference.

It had proved difficult to assemble that particular delegation. Convinced that China would only exploit 'Peace' as a propaganda weapon, the Australian government had, so Buxton explained, taken draconian measures to prevent its citizens leaving for Peking, and the delegates had to be found among Australians who were already out of the country. Among them was Nancy Lapwood, a missionary teacher and friend of the Buxtons, who had worked at Yenching University, an establishment a few miles outside the walls of old Peking. Besides giving a 'grand, simple and moving speech'[61] at this gathering of representatives from thirty-seven countries, this daughter of a medical missionary had introduced Buxton and his wife to the Canon, who turned out to be 'an elderly man who is more interested in meeting people and wandering around than in sitting on commissions and framing resolutions'.

The christening service was well attended, given the circumstances and the small number of Britons remaining in Peking at that time. As Buxton wrote, 'social duty and friendliness' raised the congregation at the British embassy chapel from its customary fifteen to about sixty. After the ceremony, the Buxtons gave a party on their lawn in the embassy compound. The consul informed his mother that the garden had looked 'magnificent' with its scarlet salvias, michaelmas daisies, and yellow chrysanthemums. 'All the British community' came to the service, including the Buxtons' oldest friends in Peking, and about ten children with their parents. The elderly Canon Maynard was there, as was Nancy Lapwood and her British husband and fellow teacher, Ralph,[62] and the atmosphere was 'very friendly, which, considering how much some of the Embassy staff mistrust and dislike Peace Conferences of this sort, was very gratifying'.

It was, nonetheless, a dwindling community. John Haffenden records that only thirty-six people had participated when the entire

British community was invited to Christmas Dinner at the embassy in 1951, and the shrinkage had continued since then. The poet and English teacher William Empson had already left in August, together with his Communist wife, Hetta, and their two children. He had stayed on as long as possible at the National Peking University, presenting unaltered lectures—'because they were never reactionary',[63] as he would explain in a letter to his Chinese Professor, then committed to the forceful new policy of 'thought reform'. Eventually, however, the increasingly defeated British Council had terminated his contract.[64] Others followed. A fortnight or so after their christening party, on 24 October 1952, Buxton wrote to his father remarking: 'Our friends the Lapwoods have gone back to England, practically the last of the non-diplomatic community and about our only link with Chinese life.'

That sense of growing isolation pervades Buxton's letters home. He and his wife write mostly of family matters, but they also tell of steps taken to relieve tedium within the embassy compound. There were bridge parties, tombola, and dances. The circulation of disintegrating copies of English women's magazines is said to have done much to reduce the barrier dividing ordinary members of the embassy staff from the superior beings they were inclined to resent as 'dips'. Buxton's letters also include vivid descriptions of excursions on days when the embassy compound's inmates were allowed out. As he explained to his father, 'Although we live in the lap of material luxury, everyone feels the lack of freedom to move around and go places. The whole western diplomatic community was childishly happy last Sunday on a trip to the Great Wall, partly because the weather was nice, but chiefly because we were really "out" for once, and without even a protocol official to stop us going too far.'[65]

Martin Buxton had been posted to China while still in his twenties, and not long out of Trinity College Cambridge. In 1948, he was sent as a vice-consul to Mukden (Shenyang) in Manchuria. As the Communist armies proved increasingly victorious in their civil war against the Kuomintang, he was quickly moved on to Peking, where he would remain consul until 1953 (he later returned for a further four years in 1955). According to William Empson, who had made his own return to the city in the summer of 1947, Peking was then at least still blessed by its lack of a 'sense of sin'. Empson associated the city with 'a diffused homosexual feeling, that is, you will seldom go through a street without seeing at least one agreeable young man, and you feel affectionately towards him because he seems so content with himself and there is no need for anything to be done. I do not think this is a peculiarity of mine; considering the high proportion of buggers among the foreigners who genuinely "love China" it seems to be the chief thing the country has to offer.'[66] The Legation Quarter no longer looked like a thriving city of its own and the Peking Club was, as *The Times* correspondent regretted in 1949, 'a mere shadow of itself', just as the days of horse racing and polo were only 'memories of the joyous past'.[67] As Britain's only representative in the city, Buxton was described as the 'solitary vice-consul' who had been in charge of the British embassy compound through the last days of the civil war. He was there to witness the hyper-inflation and also the six-week siege that preceded the arrival of the victorious People's Liberation Army (PLA) on 23 January 1949. The siege was ended by a ceasefire negotiated with the nationalist commander General Fu Tso-yi, who had withdrawn behind the city walls, the stoutness of which may have reassured him—if not the remaining American Fulbright fellow who feared these ancient fortifications might actually turn the city into 'a gigantic potential deathtrap'.[68] While that deliberation went on, the nationalist regime prepared to hold out. Chinese residents were forced to work on fortifications. Pill boxes and wire barricades appeared in the streets, and thousands of houses were cleared from the area outside the city wall. Airfields were rushed into existence, one occupying the Tung-tan glacis, an area of open ground around the Legation Quarter which had been cleared of Chinese houses after the siege of 1900, and since drafted into service as a polo field for the foreigners. Another demanded the hasty destruction of 400 ancient cypress trees in the sacred enclosure of the Temple of Heaven.[69] Having made various alarming noises about defending the city 'at all costs',[70] General Fu (who appears to have been in secret communication with the Communists) changed his mind as the enemy closed in, announcing that he had no intention of 'fighting to the last man'.[71]

Communist victory was heralded by an encouraging 'great illumination', in which the city's interrupted electricity supply was restored by the advancing forces who had already 'liberated' the nearby power plant.[72] Then, on Monday, 31 January, the long anticipated 'red tide'[73] finally poured in through Peking's West Gate in the form of the Eighth Route Army: cavalrymen mounted on Mongolian ponies, well-formed infantry, and then 'miles of captured American vehicles and weapons'. According to Alan Winnington, the British Communist journalist who was pleased to observe proceedings from an armoured car near the head of this triumphant force, the 'liberation' was something of an anticlimax. 'Not an egg was thrown',[74] he recalled, having apparently expected some signs of loyalty to the nationalists who had previously plastered the walls of the city with slogans proclaiming that 'The liquidation of the bandits is the only way to preserve the city'.[75]

Derk Bodde, the American Fulbright scholar who also watched these events unfold in Peking, notes that Western press agencies took a deliberately dim view of the 'Liberation', suggesting that the people of Peking greeted the People's Army cautiously with the kind of 'wait-and-see' attitude with which they had received so many 'conquerors' over the centuries, and making far too much of a story in which a band of revolutionary students were said to have come across a rich fur-clad Chinese lady, and commanded her to crawl on the street like a fox.[76] Condemning this Western coverage as 'not only injudicious but unfair', Bodde was in no doubt that the Communists actually arrived to find 'the bulk of the people on their side'.[77] Sybille van der Sprenkel, a British Council worker who watched events from the British embassy compound, remembers the Communists looking 'pretty scruffy' as they entered the old capital, but adds that the liberation turned out to be 'all very civilized and orderly'.[78] Some of the city's foreign residents stepped out to join the applauding crowd as the 'red-cheeked' and healthy-looking PLA soldiers followed their blaring propaganda truck through the streets.[79] 'Extremely thrilling', enthused Hetta Empson, after watching the military parade with which the People's Republic was inaugurated on 1 October.[80] Her husband, William, remarked: 'It seems natural in England by this time to give a pretty gloomy jeer at the term "liberation"... but [the students] honestly did think they were liberated from serious danger when the Communist troops finally walked in'.[81]

At the time, there was a lot to be said in justification of this enthusiasm, and Derk Bodde, the American Fulbright scholar, was not afraid to commit some of it to his diary. Recoiling from the biased reports of the Western press agencies, he noted that the Communists had been sustained through years of hardship and self-sacrifice by 'a genuine idealism' that should be acknowledged by 'even the severest critic of their cause'.[82] He also reckoned that the United States, by supporting the corrupt and reactionary Kuomintang, had 'done as much as anyone else to discredit, in the eyes of thinking Chinese', the proclaimed democratic principles that John Dewey and others had tried to apply to China some fifteen years earlier.[83]

According to the Lapwoods, who watched the victorious Red Army pass nearby Yenching University on their approach to Peking, 'the Communists...took neither food nor fuel from the villagers, and would not accept any presents or services. They paid with their "Great Wall" currency, for all they needed. Whatever furniture they borrowed, they carefully returned, replacing anything damaged or broken. They carried water and swept the courtyards for their hosts. They chatted cheerfully with everyone, and the air was full of stories of their astonishing behaviour. Peking had known many armies through the past fifty years, but never one like this.'[84] It was the same in Shanghai, where Alun Falconer registered the liberating troops as tired but noble— prepared to accept an enthusiastically proffered glass of water, but insistent on paying for the cigarettes forced on them.[85]

Events in Tientsin were described by Otto B. van der Sprenkel, a lecturer in Chinese History at London's School of Oriental and African Studies, who was then a visiting Professor at Nankai University. Glad to see the collapse of the degenerate Kuomintang government, he too welcomed the liberation ('Chieh-fang') and the 'gigantic effort of organization'[86] with which the PLA went on to prove that its soldiers were not the 'Red devils' of nationalist propaganda. They had entered Tientsin on 15 January 1949, well armed and equipped with scraps of paper bearing the addresses at which they were to be billeted. Their first contact with the people often consisted of a polite bow, followed by an enquiry about the whereabouts of the street or house in question. 'These must have been some of the first occasions in

Tientsin's history of uniformed soldiers using all the forms of Chinese courtesy to ordinary civilians. On the civilians, at first astounded, and in the end mightily pleased, the effect was enormous.'[87] The exception that proved the superiority of the new rule was provided by a single peasant from the north-east. Said to have been unable to resist the temptation to steal a teaspoon from the Astor House Hotel, he was promptly brought back and made to apologize for his transgression. In a land that had seen so many bloodbaths, what, as van der Sprenkel's readers may well have wondered, could be seriously wrong with an army that behaved like that?

Though not to be compared with the events of 1900, the siege of Peking had nevertheless been a fairly nerve-racking experience for the Westerners inside the city. As one of the Britons who had been gathered into the embassy compound for their safety, Sybille van der Sprenkel remembers Martin Buxton giving a 'very good lead' during that crisis, despite his youth, his lack of 'side', and his disregard for 'the niceties of diplomatic etiquette'.[88] There was, as she adds, 'not much to be formal about' at that time of scarcity and apprehension, and it was Buxton's 'calm imperturbability and fairmindedness' rather than any reliance on protocol that came into its own in the rationing of food supplies, or in distributing kerosene, left in the legation compound by the Shell oil company, to Western families who would then sell it on for dollars with which to buy food.[89]

Perhaps exaggerated family lore tells of a time towards the end of the siege when there was nothing left to eat in the British embassy compound, except for half a bag of millet and a single remaining pat of butter, which passed back and forth between cupboard and table, gathering its own layer of Peking's famously pervasive yellow dust because nobody was prepared to be the one who finished it off. In that respect, at least, things had eased considerably by the time of the Buxtons' christening party in 1952, when guests were provided with coffee, a cup of South African wine mixed with soda water and pineapple juice, asparagus rolls, and slices of a large sponge christening cake.

The situation was still improving in the summer of 1954, when the young Douglas Hurd arrived from the Foreign Office to begin his first diplomatic posting in China. He came with 'large quantities of wine, toothpaste and razor-blades', acquired in London as requested. Indeed, while passing through Hong Kong, he appears to have stocked up further with 'quantities of sherry and Indian tea'.[90] Dismayed to find nothing to study but 'Marxism or porcelain', Hurd would follow Trevelyan in likening the Peking embassy to 'the end of the world'.[91] Installed in this barely staffed fortress (and yet to be granted permission even to visit Britain's empty consular buildings in Kunming, Chungking, and Hankow), he joined the grindingly familiar circuit of 'endless amiable diplomatic buffet dinners, night after night balancing lukewarm curry on one's knees, dancing to the same records with the same nice women, drinking a little too much, staying a little late, rising limp and fragile the next day'.[92] The sense of routine may only have been modestly relieved by the regular screening of Ealing comedies in the club room but, by Hurd's time, at least, there was also an increasing supply of unofficial British visitors for the diplomats to entertain and deplore as idyll-hunting freeloaders—including the 'real left-wingers', who, as Hurd would later charge, treated the rising Communist dictatorship 'as if it was a gate to Paradise' but still found their way to the embassy compound for 'whisky, home news, and the sound of an English voice'.[93] No doubt some of these extramural visitors really did enjoy lecturing the sequestered diplomats about what was really going on in China—a land they themselves were still only intermittently allowed to see.

3

Paul Hogarth's Marxist Shudder

Paul Hogarth was 84 years old by the time I met up with him. It was the beginning of November 2001, and he was still settling into a house in Cirencester, having reluctantly just moved from Hidcote Manor in the North Cotswolds, where his long-standing tenancy with the National Trust had been inconveniently terminated a few weeks earlier.

He was a man of considerable stature: a senior fellow of the Royal Academy of Arts, an Officer of the Order of the British Empire, a well-respected teacher, and a prolific graphic artist whose illustrations had been much in demand over five decades. In his time, Hogarth had collaborated with Brendan Behan, Doris Lessing, Malcolm Muggeridge, Robert Graves, and John Betjeman among many others. His drawings had adorned editions of Shakespeare, diverse books on wine, and the covers of many Penguins including, perhaps most famously, the novels of Graham Greene. He had recently illustrated a special edition of *A Year in Provence*, Peter Mayles's best-seller about being English in the south of France, and he was a regular contributor to Richard Ingrams's anti-lifestyle magazine, the *Oldie*.

I, however, had come to enquire after the young Paul Hogarth, remembered by his friend Ronald Searle as 'the original angry young man'[1] and 'all aggressiveness and pure crusader-earnestness'.[2] Surviving photographs show this ardent 'artist reporter' going about his business in China in 1954. Thanks to these, I had seen him clad in windcheater and beret and sketching in Canton, smiling out from between two nameless Chinese attendants, or locked in earnest conversation with Jack Chen, a procommunist artist and journalist of mixed Chinese and Caribbean extraction. None, however, show him sipping whisky with Douglas Hurd in the Peking embassy compound, and it seems most unlikely that this fiercely partisan artist would have allowed himself to do any such thing...

'They were just handing out visas',[3] Hogarth recalled of his departure to China in September that year, and he had certainly

Fig 4. Paul Hogarth, drawing in Canton.

been among the most obvious British candidates for an invitation. An apparently still resolute member of the Communist Party of Great Britain, Hogarth had been lionized by John Berger, then known primarily as a socialist art critic with the *New Statesman*, who hailed him as a 'talented artist and a rare man: rare because he is utterly without compromise'.[4]

Born in Kendal, Westmoreland, in 1917, Hogarth had grown up in Manchester and trained at Manchester School of Art. Radical-ized as a student in the 1930s, he had joined Joan Littlewood's Theatre Union, a group that went on to become famous as 'Theatre Workshop', and also the emerging Manchester branch of the Artists International Association, in which company he learned 'the agitprop skills of graphic design' and producing posters, banners, and murals for the left-wing causes of the time.[5] He joined the International Brigades and, in 1937, went to Spain to fight for the republican cause (he was among the volunteers who were repatriated as too young shortly after arriving). During the Second World War, he served briefly with the British army and then worked in industrial camouflage as a brush-hand and carpenter before going on to produce war propaganda for the Ministry of Information.[6] After 1945, he found employment in Shell's publicity department thanks to James Boswell, the art director who was also chairman of the Artists' International Alliance.

Hogarth made many drawings in Britain during the first post-war years: his chosen scenes included slums, sweatshops, political rallies, and, in one noteworthy example, a great mass of industrial workers pouring out of the factories and workshops at Trafford Park. Yet he had also embarked on various working excursions behind the recently descended Iron Curtain, going *East of Stettin-Trieste*, to quote the title of a partisan travel book by Stanley Evans, a Communist-symphathizing Church of England canon who revealed himself to be an enthusiastic observer of the most vile Stalinist show trials in this mercifully forgotten volume: published as an anti-Churchillian 'book without Iron Curtains' and illustrated, somewhat sparingly, with drawings made by Hogarth in the course of his own travels in Eastern Europe.[7]

Art of the Potemkin Village?

Such were the initiatives Hogarth had in mind when, nearly half a century later, he repudiated the drawings he had made during his travels behind the Iron and Bamboo curtains. Writing in 1998, he would also suggest that, no matter how resolute his outward demeanour may have appeared, doubts were already growing in his mind by the time he embarked for China. On that occasion he took his cue from a story told him by Jerzy Zaruba, an 'irrepressible caricaturist' (and one who also let his pen serve the Stalinist cause), whom he had befriended in Poland in 1953:

> There once lived an old king whose last wish was to have his portrait painted. So the most distinguished painter in the land was commissioned and the portrait duly painted. But the old king was not an easy subject to paint. He was blind in one eye, had a withered arm and was lame in one leg. The portrait revealed these physical defects all too clearly. The artist was shot at dawn. A second artist was summoned and he painted much of what he saw before him,

rendering the old king's physical defects in a more romantic manner. But he, too, was shot. A third artist, an American, was given the commission and his picture received royal acclaim. For he had depicted the king shooting a deer, kneeling on one knee in profile, thus concealing his lame leg. His blind eye, closed up as if to sight his rifle, also concealed his withered arm. This, said everyone, was pure Socialist Realism.[8]

Having repeated that tale, in which the failings of official Stalinist aesthetics were strategically displaced into an allegorical past, Hogarth confessed that 'I too, like the American mentioned in the story, was now turning out drawings which concealed what was really going on in Poland, the GDR, Czechoslovakia and other Eastern Bloc countries. Minders dutifully produced statuesque heroes of socialist labour for me to draw in industrial enterprises from Anshan to Bucharest, from Kladno to Cracow. If I occasionally depicted a historic old town without any apparent political significance, they would be most upset.' Hogarth spared none of his drawings from this time, insisting that 'Such graphic art, was by its very nature, essentially ephemeral and downright misleading'.

In this repudiation Hogarth finds no mitigation in the fact that his early drawings, the best of which are searching and compassionate portrayals of the people and realities they seek to record, were actually produced in strongly argued opposition to socialist realism of the officially approved Stalinist variety. Instead, he abandons his early work to an accusation that had been made many times, from the left as well as the anti-Communist right of the political spectrum, since the first Western visitors started reporting on Soviet Russia from the time of the Bolshevik coup of October 1917. It was charged, repeatedly and not always with good reason, that those who travelled behind the Iron Curtain were either adherents, who only saw what they wanted to see, or equally culpable dupes who allowed themselves to be taken in by the 'techniques of hospitality'[9] used to flatter and seduce them, and who mistook their impressions for reality as they were wafted through a series of show projects and stage-managed Potemkin villages.[10]

Hogarth had every right to repudiate his early drawings as he looked back through the ruins of the Cold War, the Great Leap Forward, and the Cultural Revolution. Yet it was hardly thanks to craven obedience to the party line that he also emerged from his

Communist travels as one of the most promising draughtsmen of his generation. He had already learned the necessity of resisting prescriptive orthodoxy when working as an art editor on various left-wing journals in London during the years immediately following the Second World War. Appointed art editor of *Our Time* in January 1949, he was soon fending off the ideological drones who kept coming in from Communist Party headquarters in King Street, brandishing what he later recalled as 'lugubriously Marxist articles'[11] guaranteed to sent the circulation into a dive. Hogarth was no chaotic Bohemian like his mentor Randall Swingler, the writer, editor, and virtuoso drinker who had given him that particular job, but he knew from the start that a good drawing was not the same as a visualized slogan, and that to be 'independently minded' meant being viewed with suspicion by the Communist Party bosses.

Hogarth was 30 years old when he embarked on the first of the many journeys he would devote to recording the reconstruction of Europe as its nations emerged from the Second World War. In 1947, he had organized a party of four artists, including Ronald Searle, Laurence Scarfe, and Percy Horton, and gone with them to Yugoslavia where they would record the construction of a 'youth railway' being built in East Bosnia by international student volunteers including the future historians Edward and Dorothy Thompson.[12] In 1948, he and Searle visited Prague and then went on to Poland where they saw various wrecked cities and attended the Congress of Intellectuals for Peace at Wroclaw. In 1949, he was in Spain, revisiting places he had first encountered during the Spanish Civil War, and there would also be visits to France and also Italy, where he came across the work of Gabriele Mucchi, Renato Guttuso, and other younger artists aligned with the Communist Party. He later described his own party card as 'the equivalent of the certificate that the medieval pilgrim carried',[13] remembering how it allowed him to stay free of charge at the many Houses of Culture that were then under Communist control.

Hogarth's drawings of his travels—produced over a few snatched minutes in the street, factory, conference hall, or courtroom—had quickly become a fixture of the European left. Like Picasso's ubiquitous peace doves, they adorned many more or less Communist-affiliated journals in various countries on both sides of the division. They also filled special supplements issued to coincide with Moscow-backed international congresses of the kind that caused such dismay to the British Labour government, including the Congress of the Peoples for Peace, held in the Konzerthaus in Vienna over a week in December 1952.[14] As for his journeys behind the Iron Curtain, these increased, both in frequency and in profile, after Hogarth carried out a mission to Greece in August 1952. He had gone at the request of a Welsh woman named Betty Ambaticlos, who approached Hogarth after seeing his drawings of Spain in the left-wing press.[15] Her husband was Tony Ambatielos, the Communist leader of the since suppressed Confederation of Greek Seamen's Union (OENO), which he had helped to establish while living in Britain during the Second World War, and through which he had gone on to aid Communist rebels fighting the military and Royalist regime of Marshall Papagos.

Fig 5. Paul Hogarth, Tony Ambetielos on trial in Athens, 1952, conté (from Hogarth's *Defiant People: Drawings of Greece Today* (London: Lawrence & Wishart, 1953).

Ambatielos was now imprisoned in Athens, having been sentenced to death as a traitor, together with nine other trade unionists, in October 1948. In August 1952, he and his comrades were brought before a military tribunal, which confirmed the internationally deplored death sentences—although these were automatically commuted to life imprisonment in accordance with Greece's recently enacted 'Pacification' law.

While in Athens to watch, seethe, and draw as Ambatielos and his comrades turned the tribunal into 'an indictment of Fascism',[16] Hogarth lodged in 'cheap hotels and safe houses'[17] in working-class districts. He drew the famous view of the city from the steps of the Parthenon, but only in order to challenge received views with many other drawings showing 'the Athens the tourists do not see'.[18] He sketched fishermen and melon-sellers, blacksmiths and boatbuilders, as well as unemployed workers and women queuing to visit their incarcerated husbands outside the notorious Averoff prison. His drawings were fully aligned with the cause of the jailed Communists (Ambatielos would not be released until 1964), and further fired by a sense of shame at the fact that the Papagos regime had been backed by Britain's Labour government as well as by America. In a furious introduction to Hogarth's drawings of these heroically 'defiant people', the Australian-born reporter James Aldridge, who had covered the Greek campaign during the Second World War for *Time* magazine, pointed out not just that Greek Communists like Ambatielos had played a leading role in the fight against Nazism, but that they had since been on the receiving end of the first napalm ever used in warfare—said to have been dropped by British and American planes in an attempt to drive Communist partisans out of their strongholds in the mountains.[19] Greece, concluded Aldridge, had emerged from its battle with Nazism only to become 'the first victim of the cold war'.

In December 1952, Hogarth's 'Drawings of Greece Today' went on show at the Galerie Apollinaire in London, and new invitations arrived as the artist followed them to later exhibitions in Warsaw, Prague, Bucharest, and Sofia. At the opening at the Book and Press Club in Warsaw, Hogarth was approached by officials of the Ministry of Culture, who invited him to draw the ongoing reconstruction of Poland. Having previously visited the country in 1948, he could, as he later recalled, hardly escape seeing the many signs of the ongoing 'Sovietization'—epitomized by the vast and hideously 'ornate' Palace of Culture and Science dominating the centre of Warsaw. At the time, however, his 'Drawings of Poland' were given a very different presentation. In an introductory text that would accompany them as they toured Britain, the Australian-born Communist novelist Jack Lindsay reads the drawings into conformity with the party line. Lindsay had been in Poland with Hogarth in 1948. Remembering the barely conceivable extent of the ruin they had encountered there, he was now delighted to see 'the familiar machinery of building' given 'an heroic character' in Hogarth's more recent drawings.[20] As for the fact that Hogarth had apparently not pursued any explicit political message in his sketches of various historical towns and landscapes, from 'the wild Tatras' to the 'pleasant wooden shapes of peasant Poland', Lindsay quickly recuperated this apparent failure of judgement: it 'helps us to feel the closeness to the earth in the other men who have left the land and are carrying on the titanic works of construction'.

Hogarth had indeed been determined to record 'the epic sense of collective endeavour' involved in post-war 'Reconstruction'[21] as he saw it in various socialist countries in Eastern Europe. He also provided various publications on the far side of the Iron Curtain with ideologically packaged selections of drawings of life in capitalist Britain: both in Poland and in East Germany, readers would be invited to learn from his drawings of the grimy north of England, the Welsh mining districts, or the hard streets of East London. There was, to be sure, a Communist zealot in the young Paul Hogarth. Yet even in these early days, his pencil saved him from becoming the merely ideological zombie suggested by his later recantation and assumed by some recent critical commentary.[22] Hogarth drew portraits of Communist heroes, young and old, and approving sketches of official Soviet largesse too—the newly rebuilt old town in Warsaw, or of Stalin's Palace of Arts and Culture soaring upwards out of the ruins of the same horribly savaged city. Even so, however, relatively few of his drawings are merely visual equivalents of the slogans displayed in the window of an apron-clad London housewife he showed quarrelling with a dismayed Conservative canvasser on her doorstep ('a vote for the

Communist candidate is a vote for peace').[23] Just as Cervantes's madly idealistic Don Quixote was challenged by the paunchy realism of Sancho Panza,[24] so Hogarth's stance could be complicated by his own pencil. The partisan in Hogarth may have wanted to nail his drawings down to a position of one-sided allegiance, but his crayon was inclined to walk off with the nail as it engaged with the ambiguities and contrasts, the folds and subtle gradations, of the reality before it. It was in that tension, between one-sided and battle-hardened commitment and a more open and exploratory artistic practice, that Hogarth pursued his search for a new kind of realism—sourced, as he would repeatedly explain, not in the nineteenth-century naturalist conventions adopted by Stalinist 'socialist realism', but in the new forms of figuration pioneered by Picasso, Renato Guttuso, and others.

Writing long after he had discarded the leaden overcoat of his Communist past, Hogarth would emphasize different aspects of the four weeks he had spent drawing in Poland. He would recall the previously unadmitted fact that the country had been 'gripped by a xenophobia reminiscent of Nazi Germany', expressed in 'orchestrated mass demonstrations, marching songs and strength-through-joy youth camps'.[25] He would also suggest that his drawings of historical buildings and unmodernized landscapes—and perhaps also those of individual people, many of them portrayed in their traditional occupations—had actually been a compensatory strategy, and by no means an attempt to suggest that the Sovietization of 'New Poland' had gone to the very roots of national experience. It was, he would now plead, actually in reaction against the ongoing Sovietization that he had felt 'more at home depicting the architecture of the past'—the restored Warsaw Old Town, the monasteries, churches, and palaces of Cracow, the City Hall in Gdansk. He would also claim to have had some quite searching conversations with Polish graphic artists, including officially approved cartoonists such as Ignacy Witz, who would introduce a very handsomely produced and officially published portfolio of twenty-four of Hogarth's drawings of Poland,[26] and Jerzy Zaruba, the latter being an 'Anglophile' who had lived in Britain during the Second World War and who is said to have been responsible for the 'most vitriolic'[27] portrayals of the anti-Communist Polish settlement in London.

Zaruba and his friends eased the way for ideologically framed selections of Hogarth's drawings of Britain to be published in Polish magazines and art journals under such headings as 'American Occupation of Great Britain'[28] and 'Poor District of London' (in the latter, Hogarth added a commentary claiming that the East End was proof—which it may indeed have been—of how capitalism had 'taken the urban poor' and 'squashed' them into 'overcrowded dwellings').[29] Zaruba also invited the English artist to spend a week with him at his retreat at Szlembark in the Tatra Mountains. Here Hogarth was moved, as he would later write of the drawings he made here, by the sight of a local community that remained untouched by the 'tidal wave of authoritarianism and industrialization that had all but engulfed Poland'. It was here also that he met Tadeusz Kulisciewicz, a famous print-maker who would resist serving Stalinism more bravely and consistently than Zaruba. Both artists, so Hogarth later claimed, had been 'incredulous that I, an Englishman, a Westerner, could possibly believe in the edicts Socialism imposed on artists and writers to portray a perfect world'.[30]

By the time Hogarth moved on to Czechoslovakia, later in 1953, the tensions between Communism and his developing artistry had become considerably more pronounced. At the opening of his Greek drawings at the Union of Czechoslovak Artists' gallery in Prague, he had been asked to return to Czechoslovakia to produce drawings of 'socialism under construction'. Travelling in the early summer of 1953, he took Randall Swingler as his writer—they were paid £200 each by the Czechoslovak embassy in London—but things went from bad to worse once they had arrived. Swingler, who was by no means prospering as a well-known Communist writer in Cold War Britain, turned up wearing a beer-stained tweed jacket, Oxford bags, and an ancient rucksack preserved from his student days. His appearance horrified the Czech officials, whose disgust was far from alleviated when Hogarth managed to have his Bohemian friend's garments cleaned and pressed while he was sleeping off a hangover in their smart Prague hotel.[31] The pair had been lumbered with an interpreter named Olga Klusakova, already possessed of a formidable track record. In 1949, she had driven a visiting Dylan Thomas to such despair that he is said to have 'embraced a Baroque statue on the Charles bridge' and threatened to throw himself into the river below unless she was 'banished from his sight'.[32]

Swingler may have pleased Olga when, in the course of denouncing the 'baleful' impact of American imperialism on English literature in a lecture delivered at Charles University, he suggested that Graham Greene, who was actually fiercely anti-American, wrote his books with the aim of appealing to the Hollywood producers who might make him rich. Far more often, however, this dissolute visitor alarmed and disgusted her. An infuriatingly persistent 'pain in the neck', Olga proved reluctant to let her charges out of her sight as they toured the country in a black Tatra limousine, but Swingler still managed to indulge his weakness for the bottle and also to seek out various left-wing writers, including some soon-to-be-persecuted figures who were not part of the official tour.

Hogarth remembered spending time with Vítězslav Nezval (1900–58), an avant-garde writer who had been among the founders of the surrealist movement in Czechoslovakia, and was now 'critical of the party establishment'. They also met up with Paul Eisler, who had become a friend of Swingler's whilst working at the Czechoslovak embassy in London. He had since been an economics adviser for the recently overthrown and executed Communist leader Rudolf Slansky but was now working a lathe in a factory, and extremely critical of the regime and its continuing show trials. As for the commissioned book of their unsuccessfully chaperoned travels, Hogarth's sixty or so planned drawings were made and Swingler's long-delayed text was also finished in the end. An extract was printed in *The Countryman*, illustrated with a handful of pleasantly pastoral and apparently wholly unpolitical drawings by Hogarth. In the text, Swingler babbles on about 'a country in which industry has learnt to beautify and not befoul the landscape, to enrich and not impoverish the land'.[33] Far from mentioning the critical judgements of his fallen friend, Paul Eisler, he recites the regime-friendly story of an unnamed 'philosopher', said to have felt so enthusiastic about the socialist reconstruction that he had voluntarily abandoned his university post to work as a crane operator in the building of the Orava dam.

Swingler's biographer, Andy Croft, has described the text of 'the Czechoslovakia book' as 'a triumph of finely judged criticism, studied omission and disingenuous special pleading'.[34] It was never published. In an interview with Croft, conducted on 19 November 1993, Hogarth seems to suggest that this was largely because the Czechoslovak publishing house Orbis wanted 'a more upbeat' text than Swingler was prepared, in the end, to produce. Croft indicates that the problem may actually have been related to the fact that Stalin had died in March 1953, and the Czechoslovak Communist Party was slowly coming round to the realization that it might be appropriate to adopt a less abjectly enthusiastic stance towards his deeds and works.[35] Whatever the exact circumstance, the proposed British edition never appeared either.

The visit to Czechoslovakia was definitely not Randall Swingler's finest hour, but Hogarth would later claim to have been following his pencil, which had, once again, proved reluctant to turn reality into 'poetic substance'[36] of the doctrinaire 'socialist realist' variety favoured by Olga. Asked, in November 1993, whether he and Swingler had been used by the Czechoslovaks, he told Croft, 'I always felt I was using them! I was learning a lot, partly bored and partly stimulated. I knew it was propaganda, but I had to learn to be an artist and that was what interested me. But I also had a sense, going through the war, that something worthwhile might be happening.'[37]

To Hell with Francis Bacon

As they were expressed in print, meanwhile, the young Hogarth's views of the role of art remained furiously dogmatic. Indeed, his writings reveal Hogarth to have been a fierce hater of 'bourgeois decadence'. In an article written for *Marxist Quarterly* in 1954, he declared himself on the side of 'Humanism versus Despair in British Art Today'.[38] He was vitriolic about the mainstream art world, in which art was 'merely the pastime of wealthy collectors', and he condemned the public galleries supported by the recently founded Arts Council for failing to establish an alternative idea of value. During the war, the art establishment, together with its 'reactionary doctrine of art for art's sake', had been displaced by necessity. The Council for the Encouragement of Music and Arts (CEMA) had broken with the polite confinement of art to conventional museums and galleries, and started

promoting exhibitions in factory canteens and other such places
where they might help to stiffen working class resolve. In CEMA's
programmes, art had become, once again, 'a natural means of
communication; asserting its true social function in the life of
the nation'. The need to rally the entire nation to the war against
fascism had also encouraged realist art of the kind Hogarth
considered 'a true social expression' rather than 'a mere trifle
reflecting no other content or purpose than that of decoration
in the worst sense of the word'.

By the mid-1950s, so Hogarth asserted, this moment had been
betrayed. Though elected on a landslide of popular enthusiasm,
the Labour government of 1945 had quickly turned into 'a grave-
yard for these hopes', with the new Arts Council leading the
retreat back to the gallery and museum and to an associated bourgeois aesthetic divided between the two evils of 'academic naturalism and abstract art'. Meanwhile, the commercialization of
book publishing had reduced the opportunities for artists in
literary illustration: a problem that was compounded by the
economic effects of 'rearmament and cold-war thinking', which
prompted the death or degeneration of a number of the 'more
intelligent' magazines in which a socially engaged kind of illustration had once flourished.

Add the bank-rolling power of American art foundations to this
mix, and the result was a new abstract 'formalism' that was influen-
tially advocated by British followers such as Herbert Read, who had
spoken against realism, prompting Hogarth to take a passing swipe
at this American-funded 'lotus-eater'. In Hogarth's view, the British
abstract artists riding this new wave were quite lacking the 'humanism'
of Leger, Chagall, Juan Gris, and other members of 'the older generation of formalists'. They produced 'meaningless structures of metal
and plaster' or, in the uniquely awful case of Francis Bacon, 'revolting'
portrayals of 'headless and limbless figures'. In embracing such
work, so Hogarth wrote, 'bourgeois society has embraced the true
pictorial expression of its decay'. Its institutions, exemplified by the
recently founded Institute of Contemporary Art in London, were
guilty of turning younger artists away from 'the cultural heritage
and the tangible problems of reality'.[39]

As a self-declared 'artist-reporter' as well as a social realist,
Hogarth placed himself in a contrary line of descent that both

John Berger and he would describe at some length. It included the work of Kathe Kollwitz in Germany, and of Winslow Homer and Thomas Eakins in the USA. Its British representatives included James Boswell and Paul Nash among the twentieth-century war artists, and also nineteenth-century forerunners such as Arthur Boyd-Houghton and Luke Fildes, who had worked for *The Graphic* and other illustrated papers in the Victorian age. Gustave Doré's depictions of the London poor were also enlisted to the cause.

Such, then, was the young British Communist artist who, in 1954, had been invited to make a series of drawings in China. Hogarth's invitation came from the World Peace Organization, a Moscow-funded front, as he told me with a loud guffaw, which commissioned him to spend several months depicting the life and landscape of 'New China'. News of his invitation had been too much for some. Hogarth remembers how frantically the painter Felix Topolski tried but failed to secure a similar invitation. And there was also trouble at the Central School of Arts and Crafts in London, where Hogarth had been working since 1951. Informed that his junior tutor was once again setting off on a new series of exotic travels, the eminent Scottish artist, William Johnstone, who was principal of the school, summoned Hogarth into his office and faced him with an ultimatum. '"Either," he said in a not unfriendly manner, "ye arrange for me to be invited to China, or indeed to any of those damned countries, or I'll have to ask ye to resign".'[40] Hogarth tried but failed, and Johnstone proved true to his word.

The invitation was a solo commission, and yet Hogarth's political links in London were such that he could hardly avoid making the journey in company. As a seasoned traveller behind the Iron Curtain, he was asked to serve as the chaperone of what he remembered as 'a very unpleasant, rather third-rate Labour delegation'. As he recalled, the Chinese authorities had only invited this particular delegation at the last minute, by which time the more resourceful members of the British labour movement were either already busy or away on their summer holidays. So he ended up flying with a scratched-up party of previously untravelled shop stewards, local councillors, and rank opportunists who had 'no desire to get to know the Chinese people better', but were happy to 'get pissed every night at the Chinese government's expense'.

Ginger beer had been the preferred drink in young British Communist circles in the 1930s, and even Randall Swingler had not been able really to corrupt Paul Hogarth, who described himself as pretty much a teetotaller at the time of his trip. Yet as a puritanical Marxist—'boring, doctrinaire' as he sneered at his younger self—he had additional reasons to recoil from those he was obliged to chaperone on their journey to Peking. Though undeniably proletarian, his delegates would prove far from progressive in their working-class consciousness. Hogarth would be dismayed by their ignorance and prejudice, by their bad jokes, their fearful rejection of otherness, their inert stupidity, which he could do nothing to shift. In his sharply polarized mind, this delegation would come to represent the corpse of the Labour Party's landslide general election victory of 1945: a historic opportunity that had been squandered and then lost to the elderly Winston Churchill's Conservative Party, which regained power in October 1951. Hogarth was flying with the defeated aspirations of British socialism slouched in the seats all around him. Nearly fifty years later, the memory of those delegates, who had surely represented the very 'dregs of the labour movement', still sent an involuntary shudder through this distinguished graphic artist's long since reformed shoulders.

4

The Battle of British 'Friendship'

For Humphrey Trevelyan, arriving in Peking at the end of the Korean War in 1953, the handful of non-diplomatic Westerners remaining in the city were 'the twilight brigade'.[1] He remembers a couple of stranded German antique dealers, who struggled on for a few difficult years before being parted from their collections and forced to leave. As for the political stragglers, 'they were the Communists, mostly old journalists, employed by the Chinese on minor literary tasks. They were pathetic.'

Perhaps he was thinking of Alan Winnington, the *Daily Worker* correspondent who had backed the Chinese and North Korean Communists in their propaganda claims during the recent war. Trevelyan had not long been in Peking before Winnington turned up at the British embassy compound hoping to renew his expired passport so that he might attend the approaching Geneva Conference. His request was rejected on the order of the British Foreign Secretary. Like Clement Attlee's Labour cabinet before him, Anthony Eden viewed Winnington as a traitor who had 'interrogated British prisoners of war on behalf of the Chinese in Korea'[2]—a charge Winnington would mock, attributing the British authorities' decision to pressure from the American government: still fuming, as he assumed, at the success with which he and Wilfred Burchett had undermined US propaganda statements during the Korean War.

Trevelyan's 'twilight brigade' may also have included Rewi Alley, a New Zealander who had moved to Shanghai in 1927, motivated partly, as has recently been suggested, by the city's tolerance of homosexual activity.[3] Having arrived at the time of Chiang Kai-shek's murderous assault on Communists and trade unionists in the city, he had been radicalized by his experiences as a factory inspector for the Fire Department, joining the circle of Western Communist sympathizers in the city and going on to play a leading role in the industrial cooperative movement (also known by its slogan 'Gung Ho', or 'Work Together'), which he had helped to launch in 1938, using funds from overseas to help equip the combined Communist and Nationalist forces of 'Free China' against invading Japan.[4] At the time of the Liberation, this seasoned ally of the new People's Republic was still running the Bailie School he had founded in 1944 at Shandan in the far north-west. As pressure mounted against this foreign-run institution (rumours were circulated alleging that the teachers were US spies, nationalist agents were unmasked among the teachers, and a coup attempt was mounted by a group of 'super revolutionary' students),[5] he moved to Peking. Taking up residence as one of the regime's most loyal foreign 'friends', he was soon penning brutally simplified poems praising 'this new and lovely Peking'[6] and refusing to regret that the 'escapist' dreams of China's ancient poets were being replaced by 'a new poetry in action', manifest in 'the determined lift' that new China's industrious garbage collector gave to his shovel: 'First they'll live poetry, | then they'll write it, and the language of tomorrow | will be tied to factual living; total man | triumphant over nature.'[7]

'Pathetic' or not, these fellow-travelling expatriates were not entirely unrelieved in their isolation. Indeed, they were already accustomed to welcoming the international visitors who kept turning up to marvel at the 'new China'. Marian Ramelson had been among the first to pass through. A trade unionist from Leeds, she went to China in 1949 as British representative at the Women's International Democratic Federation's Asian Women's Conference. She was ablaze with hope for a post-war 'peace' in which 'the black night of war' would be 'abolished from the history of mankind'.[8]

Together with women from the USA, France, Cuba, the Ivory Coast, and elsewhere, Ramelson spent eight days and nights talking as the group rode to China from Moscow on the Trans-Siberian Express: 'We knew that we were on a voyage of discovery. We were going to meet women who a few short years ago were not considered to have any intelligence at all, who for centuries had been condemned to hard toil and black illiteracy, but who today are playing a leading part in helping to build up a new life in their own countries.'

The First Indian Goodwill Mission sailed through on a wave of fiercely anti-imperialist optimism in September/October 1951. 'Thus dream becomes reality, life confirms the conceptions of wishful thinking and Utopia is woven into the fabric of this wonderful new world,' wrote its deputy leader, the journalist R. K. Karanjia, as he recalled the vision that came to him during a post-prandial snooze beside a high section of the Great Wall, where Mao was said once to have stood and longed to 'bind up the monster' on the southern side.[9]

A year later, in October 1952, the delegates to the Asian and Pacific Peace Conference had assembled to give 'the people's answer to germ warfare and atom bombs'.[10] Rewi Alley, who was drafted into this event, himself as a member of the New Zealand delegation, remembered it as 'an astounding meeting':

> Latin America met China and India; Australasia looked up and learned from Mother Asia. A peasant leader from Colombia pushed back the felt hat from his head and looked across at the Vietnam and Lao delegates. Pakistani and Indian representatives walked arm-in-arm. A Black American led the American delegation, which included his Japanese-American wife and a Japanese-American publisher. Among other Americans present was Joan Hinton, now a worker in a Chinese animal-breeding station, once a young scientist who had worked on the bomb dropped at Nagasaki. Her speech was a masterpiece of direct simplicity.

The Foreign Office may have encouraged its diplomats to view the Britons among these wide-eyed 'Friends' of New China as gullible fools, yet there was a lot more to be said about their optimism than that. They were among the inheritors of an older perspective that was indeed quite unlike the views customarily associated with the foreign inhabitants of the Legation Quarter, or the Bund in Shanghai. The political left in Britain had long had an eye on China and its people's struggle to emerge from misery. Contrary voices had been raised since Britain first smashed its way into China in the interests of commercial extraction. In the nineteenth century, and as later campaigners remembered, the cause of Chinese freedom had been embraced by the Chartists, who commended the imperial Chinese court's resistance to the British imposition of opium on the Chinese people, and who strongly opposed British intervention during the First Opium War of 1839–42.[11] While imperialist opinion considered China a pitifully backward land that could only be improved by trade with the West, the Chartists deplored those who 'prated about National Honour' in their defence of British policy, and condemned the onslaught as another application of the same violence that was being used to suppress Chartism at home.[12]

By the early twentieth century, there was a definite movement within China working for the creation of a new and independent national republic, and this too had attracted considerable unofficial sympathy in the West. The pacifist Bertrand Russell, who spent a year teaching philosophy in Peking in 1921, yoked together the three foreign 'evils' of Imperialism, Bolshevism, and the YMCA, condemning these Western imports for failing to engage with 'the Chinese outlook' and attempting instead to 'force other people to realize our conception of the world'.[13] Having looked into the faces of his students, Russell believed that the collapse of the Manchu Qing dynasty had released 'a renaissance spirit' that made it possible, if only foreign powers could be prevented from wreaking the usual havoc, for Young China 'to develop a new civilization better than any that the world has yet known'.[14]

The 'Young China' in which Russell and other liberal-minded Western observers placed their hopes had been created after decades of rising hostility to both the decadent Manchu court and to the foreign powers which continued to open China with gunboats, railways, additional treaty ports, and strategically placed advisers appointed to the imperial government. The revolt, which was also a modernizing impulse, developed in the coastal south while the north of China was still dominated by the traditional values maintained by the empress dowager. It was directly descended from the events of 1894 when a 'Revive China Society' had been formed by Sun Yat-sen, a Western-educated 28-year-old physician from Canton, who had lived both in British Hong Kong and in Hawaii, and who himself drew inspiration from the earlier example of the Taiping Rebellion, bloodily suppressed with the help of French and British forces in the 1860s.

Not content with inspiring students to cut off their pigtails to demonstrate their rejection of Manchu custom, Sun plotted against the imperial authorities. After the failure of an attempted uprising in 1895, he spent eleven years in exile in Europe, North

America, and Japan. The breakthrough came with the Xinhai Revolution of October 1911, when revolutionaries took the Viceroy's headquarters in Wuhan, triggering a series of uprisings that saw the Qing dynasty, already weakened by the failure of the Boxer Rebellion of 1900, finally disintegrate in chaos. Foreign powers manoeuvred for advantage as provinces started to fall into the hands of corrupt governors and warlords, and powerful interests in remoter reaches of the collapsed Chinese empire—Tibet, Sinkiang, Mongolia—were increasingly tempted by the thought of independence. The 'dissolution' that, in 1853, Karl Marx, had predicted for the Manchu emperors and their allegedly mummified version of China, had finally arrived.

On 1 January 1912, Sun Yat-sen, who had recently returned from political exile abroad, was elected the first President of the new Republic of China. Sun established a revolutionary government based in the southern city of Canton, but he failed in his first attempts to reunify the collapsing former empire around the 'Three People's Principles' of nationalism, democracy, and the social consideration often translated as 'the people's livelihood'. According to the American philosopher John Dewey, who was teaching in Peking in 1919, 'the so-called republic is a joke; all it has meant so far is that instead of the Emperor having a steady job, the job of ruling and looting is passed around to the clique that grabs power.'[15]

Yet the nationalist movement was actually greatly strengthened after the First World War, when the Paris Conference ceded German concessions in Shantung to Japan, prompting justified outrage in China and the protests of the student-led May Fourth movement. Dewey, who was in China to lecture on what democracy might actually come to mean in that Asian context, saw this 'Peking tempest'[16] as an explosion of hope, in which women had evidently found a considerable role, but which had yet to develop the pragmatic programme necessary if it were to produce more than just 'a flash in the pan'.[17]

Frustrated in his attempts to win Western support for his struggling republic as it was relaunched in 1919, Sun turned towards Soviet Moscow, which that year disowned Russia's Chinese treaties and the concessions and extraterritorial rights of the tsarist period. The Bolsheviks were prepared to assist Sun's new 'People's

Party', the Kuomintang, as well as the Chinese Communist Party, forged out of various geographically scattered Communist groups under Comintern guidance in 1921. From 1923, therefore, and in line with a 'united front' policy imposed on the two parties, the Kuomintang was guided by a Soviet Mission to China. Directed by the 'special envoy' Mikhail Borodin, the Soviet advisers established the Whampoa Military Academy for training Kuomintang forces, helped to organize propaganda, and also reformed the Party along Leninist lines to create the centralized machine that would eventually serve Chiang Kai-shek most effectively, although hardly as those Soviet advisers had anticipated.

Accompanied by a policy of inflaming the Chinese masses against British and other foreign imperialism, much of Borodin's work was concentrated in the coastal cities, including Canton to the south and Shanghai, where the Central Committee of the Chinese Communist Party was based. However the Soviet influence also reached into the old imperial capital. The American artist Cyrus Baldridge was in Peking to see the Russian legation, which had been deserted since the revolution of 1917, reopened in the winter of 1924. The high wall surrounding the legation garden was painted bright red, the hammer and sickle was raised over the gates, and Ambassador Lev Karakhan moved in, while other residents of the Legation Quarter looked on in horrified fascination.[18] Three years later, in the spring of 1927, Peking's foreign residents, by this time inflamed by widely reported outrages perpetrated against Europeans when the nationalists took Hankow and other cities, would watch again as soldiers from the 'Country Tranquillizing Army' of the Manchurian warlord Chang Tso-lin, who had taken Peking that April, entered the Legation Quarter while the ambassadors and ministers of the treaty powers turned a blind eye to this flagrant breach of diplomatic immunity, and proceeded to raid a building connected to the Russian embassy. Here they discovered arms, propaganda materials, and a sizeable cohort of forty Chinese Communists, who were 'dragged shrieking down Legation street' to be imprisoned, tortured, and, in the case of twenty, including Li Ta-chao, a founder of the Chinese Communist Party, executed by slow strangulation while Chang Tso-lin sipped tea nearby, so *Time* magazine reported, in the company of a visiting Senator Hiram Bingham of Connecticut.[19]

After Sun Yat-sen's death in 1925, his party, the Kuomintang, had been taken over by one its generals, Chiang Kai-shek, who launched the Northern Expedition (1926–8) from Canton, proclaiming the new nationalism and successfully breaking the warlords south of the Yangtze River. Not long afterwards Chiang Kai-shek turned on the Communists, who had reluctantly followed Stalin's line and remained in membership of his party (Stalin had spoken of going along with Chiang Kai-shek until he was 'squeezed out like a lemon and then flung away').[20] Increasingly alarmed by the rise of the left, Chiang seized control of the party in the coup of 20 March 1926. Eleven months later, and with the support of Western companies, his troops entered working-class districts of Shanghai and, together with their gangster accomplices, launched a ruthless campaign of slaughter and suppression against the leaders of the workers' uprising without which he could not have taken the city in the first place. In a famous statement, published on I July 1927, Madame Sun Yat-sen condemned Chiang for abandoning her late husband's policy of 'leading and strengthening the people' and turning the Kuomintang into 'a machine, the agent of repression, a parasite fattening on the present enslaving system'.[21] While Chiang Kai-shek established his own government in Nanking, a left-wing government had emerged at Hankow, the largest of the three cities of Wuhan, at the beginning of 1927. However, the White Terror was quickly extended to Canton, Wuhan, and elsewhere, leaving hundreds of thousands dead, and the leadership of the Communist Party overthrown and in hiding. The Northern Expedition was completed in 1928, when Chiang's army, which now travelled in alliance with the forces of two warlords, took Peking.

There were many in Britain who supported the new Republic, formed under Sun Yat-sen in 1911, and who recognized that China had been cheated by the Treaty of Versailles. After the slaughter of 1927, however, dissenting Western opinion about China would be shaped by successive campaigns associated with the increasingly Moscow-ruled Communist International. A 'Hands Off China' campaign was launched in Britain that same year— carrying over both its methods and much of its membership from the 'Hands Off Russia' committee that had earlier opposed the British government's hostility towards the Bolshevik revolution.

The founders called for committees to be formed in every town, warning that British banks were funding Chiang Kai-shek's forces in their torture and murder of true Chinese nationalists, and that the British government was 'deliberately trying to create' bloody incidents at Hankow and Shanghai, the latter being 'the greatest stronghold of imperialism in China'.[22]

The charge would be adjusted after the Japanese seized Manchuria in 1931. Once again, there was considerable outrage in Britain, which the left quickly set out to promote and articulate. This time it was the Comintern-formed 'League against Imperialism', the British section of which had been established by Fenner Brockway, George Lansbury, and others in April 1927,[23] that published China's Appeal to British Workers, and accused the Western powers of being 'prepared to see Japan march forward to crush the successful Chinese Soviets'.[24]

The most consequential of these 'Aid China' campaigns, the China Campaign Committee, was launched in response to Japan's invasion of China in the early autumn of 1937. By this time Japan was backed by Nazi Germany and fascist Italy, and engaged in a full-scale assault against China that would later be recognized as the opening engagement of the Second World War in Asia. As has been described by Arthur Clegg, a British Communist who had joined the League against Imperialism while still a student at the London School of Economics, the inaugural meeting was held at the National Trade Union Club in High Holborn, London, and chaired by Victor Gollancz, publisher of the newly formed Left Book Club.[25] The senior trade unionist and Communist Ben Tillett was there, as were representatives of the International Peace Campaign, the Women's International League, the Union of Democratic Control, the National Peace Council, and the Friends of the Chinese People, the latter being an organization that had given 'some safe political scope' to Chinese in London who could not, thanks to the watchful eye of the Kuomintang secret police, afford to appear explicitly left wing. 'Aid China' committees were formed up and down the country, and a central office was established in the Union of Democratic Control's office in Victoria Street, London—staffed by Dorothy Woodman, also secretary of the Union of Democratic Control, Arthur Clegg, who became National Organizer, and eventually also George Hardy who, in the late 1920s, had lived in Shanghai as a Comintern operative working with the Pan-Pacific Trade Union Secretariat.[26] In the office, so Clegg would later write, 'we were all Communists', although the voluntary assistants extended to a wider circle of elderly suffragettes, vicar's wives, and Special Branch snoops. In accordance with the 'popular front' tactics of the time, the organizers went on to galvanize a much wider constituency of support in trade unions, churches, and business circles too.

Though opposed to the stories emerging from the nationalist 'China Information Office' in London, the China Campaign Committee was not averse to exploiting public taste for old-fashioned *chinoiserie*. It printed photographs of the Great Wall, the Ming Tombs and famous pagodas, and articles extolling traditional Chinese literature and technique. Yet if China could be praised as 'The Fountain-head of Oriental Culture and Beauty',[27] it was to be defended as a new inspiration born out of the revolutionary initiative of the late Sun Yat-sen. The campaign's literature set the bobbed hair of the republic's emancipated girls against the bound feet of women who had grown up in old China. It exhibited the 'cultural achievements' of Japan (bombed universities and closed schools, lacerated children, widespread and deliberately fomented opium addiction, massacre in Nanking, etc.), and opposed this gallery of evils with a celebration of the 'free China' in which Chiang Kai-shek, thanks to the united front policy, was accepted as overall leader. It approved of the League of Nations, which, though impotent in military terms, had at least passed a resolution condemning the Japanese bombing of undefended towns in China.

Not content with issuing leaflets—picturesque, furious, and informative—the China Campaign Committee (CCC) became widely known through its practical demonstrations. There were China rallies in London (favourite venues included Trafalgar Square, Friends House, the People's Palace in Mile End Road, and Conway Hall in Red Lion Square) and events across the country too, some of them organized to coincide with Gollancz's publication, in 1938, of the American reporter Edgar Snow's *Red Star Over China*, a hugely influential account of the Long March, which also included the first interviews with Mao Tse-tung, Chou En-lai and other Communist leaders who had welcomed Snow in their remote and blockaded areas in north-west China. The campaign demanded and organized many marches for a boycott of Japanese goods, issuing a detailed inventory of items ranging from silk to 'hard hewn oak'. Individual acts of refusal were called for but the boycott was also enacted by a number of organizations, including various Co-ops, the Black and White Milk Bar chain, which cancelled its order for a million Japanese straws, and the dockers' union, which refused to unload Japanese goods.[28]

In its fund-raising, the CCC and its local committees specialized in 'China Weeks', sometimes featuring 'bowl of rice' or 'bread and cheese' dinners:[29] symbolic forms of self-denial of a kind that would later be used by other charities including Oxfam and War on Want. It fielded a panel of speakers who went out to address Peace Councils, trade union meetings, and church groups. Working in conjunction with the Artists International Association, it toured an exhibition of Contemporary Chinese Woodcuts, Drawings, and Cartoons, which had been assesmbled in Shanghai by the political artist and writer Jack Chen and, earlier in 1937, exhibited in Moscow by the International Society for Aid to the Victims of Fascism. It sponsored performances by a Chinese orchestra and also by Paul Robeson, who sang for the Committee at the Queen's Hall, performing 'A New Song of Freedom' and a Chinese Army march: 'The enemy will be silent. China will rise again.'[30] A number of its most effective speakers and presenters were themselves Chinese. Wang Si-Li had been a member of the Fukien government, set up in defiance of Chiang Kai-shek by the Chinese Nineteenth Route Army in 1934 and defeated shortly afterwards.[31] Sent to 'study' in London, he became known as Shelley Wang, a poet whose work was published in journals and collections associated with the British left.[32] Jack Chen, who was actually of mixed Chinese and Caribbean Creole ancestry (he was the son of Eugene Chen, who had assisted Sun Yat-sen in the Revolution of 1911), would later remember following his exhibition from Moscow to London: no sooner had he arrived than he found himself immediately thrust onto a CCC platform in Trafalgar Square and asked to address the vast audience alongside Dean Hewlett Johnson, Paul Robeson, and Victor Gollancz, who advised him to speak from the heart but keep his sentences short.[33] He went on to introduce a printed selection of the Chinese woodcuts for the campaign, and would also produce a strip-like series of drawings telling the story of the industrial cooperatives of Rewi Alley for American readers.[34]

At some of its meetings, the campaign also had the help of a visiting General Yang Hu-chung, who was among those who had taken Chiang Kai-shek prisoner at Sian in December 1937, the famous kidnapping incident in which Chiang was forcibly confronted by Chou En-lai and others and driven to suspend his ten-year-long civil war against the Communists and to enter a new united front against the common Japanese enemy.[35] The writers who spoke from its platform included Jack Lindsay, who wrote his 'Agony of China' for the cause, and the poet W. H. Auden, who briefly became involved after visiting China with Christopher Isherwood: before the couple 'fled'[36] to America, he gave a lantern lecture on China for the Left Book Club, and spoke at a 'self denial dinner' in Birmingham Town Hall.[37] J. B. Priestley announced that China was 'The only country that offers hope for the future of mankind'.[38] Eric Gill stepped up, as did the anthropologist Bronislaw Malinowski, and an array of more or less predictable left-wing figures: Sylvia Townsend Warner, Rebecca West, Sylvia Pankhurst, J. D. Bernal, Margaret Gardiner, Ellen Wilkinson, the Marxist biologist J. B. S. Haldane, Harold Laski, and the Christian Socialist economist and historian R. H. Tawney. The sinologist Arthur Waley gave his name to the campaign, as did Laurence Binyon, formerly in charge of Oriental departments at the British Museum. Urged on by a legion of local vicars, Britain's archbishops signed up too.

When it came to spending its fund, the China Campaign Committee did not share the priorities of the Lord Mayor's Fund, launched in October 1937 by the British Red Cross Society, the Association of British Missionary Societies, and an association of British firms with interests in China.[39] Unlike its establishment rival, which dispensed its money through the British ambassador in China and the Governor of Hong Kong, it was determined to ensure that medical assistance reached the Red Army, which Chiang Kai-shek's national government was by no means keen on supplying with Western aid despite the united front. The funds raised were used to sustain 'International Peace Hospitals' in the Communist-held areas, including the one where the Canadian

Dr Norman Bethune had worked at Wutaishan. The campaign also gave funds to the Anglo-Chinese Development Society, which existed to assist Rewi Alley's 'Gung Ho' Industrial Cooperatives.

Friend against Friend: The Making of Mr Attlee's Guide

These 'Aid China' campaigns were susceptible to internal tensions as liberals, Christians, democratic socialists, and Communists eyed one another in mutual suspicion. Pressure from the Labour Party camp ensured that the British section of the League Against Imperialism parted with Fenner Brockway as its Chairman, although his triumphant ejecters are unlikely to have felt reassured when he was replaced by the Reverend Conrad Noel, the famously 'red' vicar of Thaxted. In October 1937, the London Labour Party had teamed up with the London Trades Council to organize its own Trafalgar Square Rally for China, only a week after the CCC's similar event, with Clement Attlee as main speaker.[40] These political differences became insurmountable as the Second World War gave way to the Cold War. Indeed, it was not just over its policy towards Communist China that critics had been questioning the Labour government's apparent submission to America in a world increasingly divided into two hostile blocs. Clement Attlee's policies were fiercely disliked by many on the left, and his anti-Communist Foreign Secretary Ernest Bevin was seen as a particularly disreputable turncoat. The Labour government responded to these challenges by setting up a Cabinet Committee on Subversive Activities,[41] and by proscribing 'Communist' bodies from its own membership.

These animosities also exploded in the China Campaign Committee, aggravated by the outbreak of guerrilla war in Malaya, which Britain's Labour government blamed on Chinese Communist intervention, and also by the events of April 1949, when the British frigate HMS *Amethyst* ran aground in the Yangtze River after being fired on by Communist forces. By this time, the China Campaign Committee was chaired by the man who, in the summer of 1954, would accompany and guide Attlee, Bevan, and the rest of the Labour leadership's delegation around China. A graduate of Balliol College, Oxford, Michael Lindsay had first gone to China in 1937, sailing from Vancouver on a ship that also carried

Norman Bethune, to teach economics and introduce an Oxford-style tutorial system at Yenching, the American university near Peking. Lindsay would later claim to have first encountered the Chinese Communists by travelling behind the Japanese lines during his vacations: first in 1938, when he met up again with Bethune, by then working with the Communist army in Wutaishan; and again, this time in the company of the British mathematics lecturer, Ralph Lapwood, in 1939. He had found the Communists both reasonable and practically concerned to help the ordinary peasants in areas under their control. Indeed, they impressed him as a species apart from the 'extremely doctrinaire' British Communists he had earlier encountered while carrying out an industrial survey in England and South Wales: zealots who had actually opposed attempts to help unemployed miners on the grounds that such measures would sap their revolutionary will.[42] Though never a Communist himself, Lindsay admired the Chinese Communists' stand against the Japanese and started secretly supplying them with medical supplies and radio components.

As an American institution, Yenching University had been an extraterritorial island of immunity in occupied China, but all such security was lost when war was declared after the Japanese attack on Pearl Harbor on 7 December 1941. That same day Lindsay and his wife, former student Hsiao Li, had driven out of the university, leaving a few minutes before the Japanese secret police came in to arrest them.[43] After reaching the Western Hills, they abandoned the car in which they had made their escape and went on, assisted by local villagers, to cross the Japanese lines and join the Communist guerrillas in the remote north-west. They stayed for nearly four years, travelling with the Communist forces in the front-line areas and later settling at Yenan. Appointed a 'technical adviser', Lindsay used his knowledge as an amateur enthusiast to create radios for the Communist forces. While in Yenan, he and Hsiao Li, whose children were both born in these arduous years, were in regular contact with the leading Communists.

During 1944, Lindsay, perhaps assisted by his earlier experience as a press attaché with the British embassy in Chungking, produced an influential series of articles for Western publications, which would be hailed as the first 'detailed and impartial' reports by a Western observer of the guerrilla areas in North China'[44] since Edgar Snow's reports had appeared in 1939. Some of Lindsay's reports, quickly reprinted as a pamphlet by the China Campaign Committee, first appeared in the American journal *Amerasia*, while others appeared as the work of an unnamed 'special correspondent' for the London *Times*. In these dispatches, Lindsay set out to cut through Western ignorance and illusion to explain the standpoint of the Communists on both Japan and the nationalist government in Chungking. He described the remarkable success of the Communists' methods of mass mobilization, detailing their achievements in education, landownership, marriage reform, the formation of cooperatives, currency, and taxation. He also reviewed the techniques with which the underequipped guerrilla warriors, assisted by an extensive network of local 'self-defence corps', had so successfully withstood a far more powerful Japanese enemy. He concluded that, if properly armed and supplied by the Allies, the Communists could 'produce a marked influence on the course of the war against Japan'.[45] He was pleased by the fact that non-Communist, and even some Kuomintang, staff held influential positions, and also that the Communists had restrained any impulse to introduce collective farming, a measure that would have been strongly opposed by the peasantry. He backed the Communists not in their ideological zeal, but for their understanding of the need for compromise and cooperation. There was, he reckoned, nothing in the 'new democracy' outlined by Mao Tse-tung that might not be fitted into a genuinely 'democratic China after the war'. Far from being the omen of an inevitably totalitarian regime to come, 'the elaborate political organization which has aroused a great deal of suspicion is really a necessary condition for carrying on guerrilla warfare against a superior enemy'.[46]

It was not just for Western readers that Lindsay wrote as a critical and far from doctrinaire supporter of the Communist regime in North China. A week or so before leaving Yenan to return to England, he had circulated a report entitled *What is Wrong with Yenan?*,[47] in which he outlined the organizational inefficiencies that came with Communist Party control. He pointed out that the Communist Party failed to communicate openly, its cadres often failing to back their political accusations with even the slightest evidence. He indicated the organizational weaknesses that came about because no one, perhaps especially at lower levels, dared to question Party decisions. Things were, as he pointed out, run much more effectively in the front-line areas where non-Communists held many responsible positions.

Lindsay would later declare that the Chinese Communist Party's fierce anti-Americanism was rooted in the disappointments of this time. The Americans and the Chinese Communists had a common enemy in the Japanese, and Lindsay, who had been in close contact with them, knew that the Communist leaders had wanted to improve relations with America as distinct from the imperialist European powers. Yet they became convinced that the Americans were using the war as a second front in the dispute between Chiang Kai-shek's nationalists and Communism. A key moment in their disillusionment came in November 1944, when America's ambassador general, Major General Patrick Hurley, whom Lindsay judged to be a bull-headed man with no understanding of what was really going on in the Communist areas, visited Yenan to work out the terms of a proposed settlement between the Communists and the Kuomintang. After the discussion, Hurley had drafted, and even personally signed, a settlement that would have granted the Communists a coalition government and military command, recognition of all the armies fighting the Japanese, and a fair distribution of American supplies. When these terms were later rejected by the Nationalists, Hurley repudiated his promises and, to the dismay of Chou En-lai and the other Communist leaders, tried instead to press the Communists into submission.[48] According to Lindsay, this was only one example of the 'bad faith' shown by the American authorities as they manoeuvred between their anti-Communism and their commitment to resourcing 'Free China's' war against Japan.

After a special farewell dinner at the international guest house at Yenan, given by Mao and his wife, the Lindsays returned to Britain at the end of November 1945. Like their hosts in Yenan, they hoped to continue their attempt to inform Western policy towards China. Their difficult journey was made possible by Chou En-lai, who gave them the considerable sum of US $3,000 for travel expenses. A photograph shows Lindsay, his wife, and their

Fig 6. Michael Lindsay, Hsiao Li Lindsay, and family at the Master's Building, Balliol, Oxford, 1945.

two rebel-born infants immediately after their arrival in Oxford. Still dressed in guerrilla clothes, they look splendidly out of place in the lodge at Balliol College, Oxford, where Lindsay's father, the Scottish academic and recently ennobled Labour peer Lord A. D. Lindsay of Birker, was Master.

Back in Britain, Lindsay made little headway in his attempts to persuade the authorities to take steps to prevent a resumption of civil war between the Communists and Nationalists in China. Indeed, he found himself viewed with suspicion from both sides of the increasingly exacerbated division between left and right. The new Labour government seemed all too content to leave

China in 'the American sphere of influence',[49] and his pleas for an independent British policy were ignored by the Foreign Office, which, as he found out later, had been notified that he was an anti-American Communist by the (still Nationalist) Chinese ambassador in London.[50] Shortly after his election as Chairman of the China Campaign Committee, Lindsay went to America, where he worked as a visiting lecturer at Harvard during the academic year of 1946/7. Returning to Britain, he took up a post teaching economics at Hull University in 1948. By the spring of 1949, with the People's Liberation Army (PLA) established in Peking and set to extend its victory to Nanking, Shanghai, Tsingtao, and other cities, his furious and no doubt also 'doctrinaire' Communist critics on the left of the China Campaign Committee were determined to displace him.

Together with his 'excellent series of articles'[51] published in *The Times* in 1944, Lindsay's personal contact with the Communist leaders in China had once bestowed considerable authority on his views. He himself would continue to believe that for the first three years after its election victory of 1945, the British Labour government was 'thoroughly discreditable and cowardly'[52] for treating China as 'an American sphere of influence' and failing to establish its own policy. He would remain convinced that, 'in the period from 1938 to 1945, the existence of defects did not alter the fact that the overall record of the Chinese Communist Party was such as to justify approval and support from people who were doing their best to make an objective judgement'.[53] However, he had also seen a 'progressive deterioration' in China's Communist regime since 1946, and was becoming increasingly convinced that the Chinese leaders, who were nursing 'infantile'[54] grudges about Britain's exploitative past in China and showing no interest in establishing normal diplomatic relations with Britain, were also now leaning so heavily towards Soviet Russia that they were becoming a copybook regime adept at turning a blind eye to ongoing Soviet imperialism in Eastern Europe. In short, he was well on the way to concluding that the leaders he had once known and respected in Yenan were now operating in a 'psychopathic state of emotional and intellectual confusion'.[55] By the spring of 1949, he was preparing to visit Peking with a statement that seemed, so his furious critics alleged, to assume Chinese responsibility for the war in Malaya and also to abandon the China Campaign Committee's long-standing commitment to returning Hong Kong to China.

As Arthur Clegg and other hard-boiled Communists in the CCC saw it, this backsliding revisionism was to turn the campaign into a defender of the very imperialism it had been launched to oppose.[56] Borrowing a term from Mao Tse-tung, Clegg condemned it as a victory for the despised '"third roaders" who, pretending to be both anti-capitalist and anti-Communist, in fact spend all their efforts on making impossible a united progressive stand against the building of Wall Street's empire'.[57] A breakaway meeting was held in April 1949, with the Marxist lawyer and recently expelled Labour MP, John Platts Mills, the novelist Jack Lindsay, the British Communist Party's Jack Woddis, and also the young John Chinnery, who had learned some Chinese while serving as a Lieutenant in the war and was then a student at the School of Oriental Studies in London. A statement of aims was drafted by Arthur Clegg and the Britain–China Friendship Association was established shortly afterwards.

Joseph Needham attended the inaugural meeting, as did the former British representative in China, Derek Bryan, and the veteran American journalist and former Comintern agent, Agnes Smedley, whom the China Campaign Committee had recently helped move to Britain from America, where she was being harried by McCarthyite anti-Communists on account of her pre-war reports from China.[58] Needham became the new association's President, and its first sponsors included the sinologist and translator Arthur Waley, Lord Boyd Orr (an advocate of world government and former Director General of the United Nations Food and Agriculture Organization), and the barrister and independent Labour MP D. N. Pritt, an anti-fascist who was also one of Britain's most notorious Soviet apologists—a 'paid liar' as George Orwell called him.[59]

Michael Lindsay went on calling down a plague on the extremists of both sides, like the 'third roader' his 'doctrinaire' critics judged him to be. He condemned totalitarianism and its 'suppression of freedom' in Soviet Russia as well as Franco's Spain.[60] When it came to China he rejected the views of 'extreme anti-Communists, who have no objection to the Nazi techniques of government'[61] so long as they are used by an anti-Communist regime such as that of Chiang Kai-shek. He also urged Britain's Labour government to moderate its policy of 'blind anti-Communism',[62] which merely chained it to 'the doctrinaire thesis of two irreconcilable factions in the world'.[63] If British recognition of New China had done nothing to improve Sino-British relations, this was partly because the two countries were divided between 'the empirical and theoretical ways of thinking',[64] and nothing was likely to improve 'until British representatives are prepared to take the trouble to state their case in terms that could be understood by the Communists', who were both 'ignorant of the normal conventions of diplomatic intercourse and deeply suspicious of the West'.[65]

At the same time, Lindsay had identified various causes for alarm when he did revisit China in the summer of 1949. He reported on the dismal state of the Chinese press, which tended to spout the party line on all subjects and also printed shockingly distorted coverage of the West. He warned, once again, of the 'doctrinaire' tendencies of the new regime, worrying that if these triumphed over the 'scientific' and experimental approach, the Chinese Communist Party could easily 'degenerate into a dominant minority exploiting the masses'.[66] He pointed out the menace of slogans such as the one he saw displayed in a Communist book-shop in Tientsin: 'All facts that are not in accordance with revolutionary theory are not real facts.'[67] In a discussion of 'Educational Problems in Communist China', written for the Institute of Pacific Relations in 1950, he noted that, even before the Liberation of 1949, the Chinese Communists had been alarmingly ambivalent about 'the unresolved contradiction between education and indoctrination',[68] between open discussion and the subordination of individual and group to the party line. He also suggested that the more 'doctrinaire cadres' within the party were 'cases for psychiatry rather than education'.[69] It was a claim that he would later elaborate with reference to both Chinese and Western Communists, associating their refusal to face reality with George Orwell's condemnation of 'doublethink', and observing that 'mental illness can take the form of emotional attachment to some unsatisfactory theory which substitutes a simplified mental world for the real world whose complications the mentally ill are unable to face'.[70] And yet, for a time at least, Lindsay continued to believe that 'New China' had different potentialities and didn't necessarily have to submit to this disorder. If the propaganda war were lifted and Western leaders such as the American Secretary of State Dean Acheson stopped forcing China into a conveniently hideous Stalinist mould, it might proceed by experiment and reason to develop 'a new form of Communism which would really serve the people and could become fully democratic'.[71] It was, perhaps, an unconscious reprise of the superior 'new civilization'[72] that, in 1921, Bertrand Russell had imagined might emerge from the wreckage of the Manchu dynasty.

5

The Charms of Anti-Americanism

As Chairman of the defunct China Campaign Committee, Michael Lindsay may have worried about the difference between 'doctrinaire' and democratic interpretations of socialism, but the Britain–China Friendship Association admitted no such hesitations as it dug in on its chosen side of the Cold War division. The new campaign was firmly pro 'New China' at its core, as would repeatedly be claimed by those who reviled it as a Communist front. Some controlling members, including Arthur Clegg, were indeed dogmatic Stalinists, but the B–CFA also appealed to a wider public dismayed by America's pursuit of the 'Truman doctrine', perceived by many Britons to be bellicose and culpably determined to divide the entire world into hostile blocs. However alarming the conduct of the USSR and its new Chinese ally, many in Britain, as elsewhere in West Europe, had become strongly critical of the USA since the start of the Cold War in 1948. Indeed, recent years had seen successive moments of conflict in which British liberals combined with socialists and the usual handful of orthodox Communists, to oppose American conduct in the name of liberty and independence.

In May 1949, diverse Britons had rallied to the defence of Gerhardt Eisler, brother of the composer Hanns Eisler and a seasoned agent of the Communist International under Stalin (he was denounced before the House Un-American Activities Committee by his own sister, Ruth Fischer, who would condemn him for having served as one of Stalin's loyal henchman in China during the interwar years).[1] Eisler had jumped bail in America and escaped by boarding the Polish liner *Batory*, when it was about to sail for Europe from New York City. He is said to have walked up the gangplank carrying a large bunch of flowers to give the impression that he was merely a visitor bidding farewell to a departing friend. He then sat down in a deck chair and waited until the ship was safely in the Atlantic before revealing himself and asking to buy a first-class ticket.[2] When the *Batory* docked in

Southampton, Eisler made an appealing drama of being forcibly removed by British police and jailed in advance of an extradition hearing. There was strong public outcry against this action, which had been carried out in the presence of two men from the American embassy. Successfully defended by the Stalinist lawyer D. N. Pritt, Eisler was freed by a Bow Street magistrate, who accepted that the outstanding perjury charge against him in America would never stand up in a British court. Having bought himself a new suit of clothes, he departed for East Germany, where he would soon enough join the leadership as 'one of the most rabid apologists'[3] for Walter Ulbricht's Communist regime. As the editor of the *New Statesman*, Kingsley Martin, MP, explained in a wireless talk written for the BBC's USSR section, Eisler's cause was taken up in Britain not just by predictable pro-Soviet figures such as Pritt and Willie Gallacher (the Communist MP for West Fife, who had condemned Eisler's arrest in the House of Commons), but by many others of more liberal persuasion who were intent on 'maintaining the right of asylum, and showing that the British intended to maintain their liberties and what we call "the rule of law", even though it was America which demanded Eisler's extraction'.[4]

It was with similarly liberal arguments that, two years later, Joseph Needham, Douglas Goldring, and other civil libertarians of the left objected to the rough and illegal manner in which bayonet-wielding American troops in West Germany and Austria had arrested British youth trying to reach the 'World Festival of Youth and Students for Peace', sponsored by the Communist 'World Federation of Democratic Youth', in East Berlin in August 1951.[5] Another characteristic explosion of British outrage had occurred in the summer of 1954. This time the victim was a young American medical researcher, Dr Joseph H. Cort. Together with his wife Ruth, also a doctor, the 26-year old physiologist had been working in Cambridge and Birmingham for a few years. On 12 June, however, it emerged that Cort was being squeezed out of the country by the British government, which had refused to extend his visa under pressure from the American embassy. Anti-Communist McCarthyites had named Cort as having belonged to a 'secret Communist cell' while at Yale, and he was now wanted as a draft evader. A considerable campaign was mounted in defence of Cort and the principle of British independence now threatened by what one trade unionist condemned as 'the long arm of McCarthyism'.[6] As a young Labour MP, Tony Benn led the attack in the House of Commons, and the cause was joined by Clement Attlee and Michael Foot, as well as by many academics and scientists, diverse trade unions, the National for Civil Liberties, and the *New Statesman and Nation.* Despite weeks of clamour, however, the Conservative Home Secretary, Sir David Maxwell Fyfe had refused to yield and, at the end of July, the two American doctors boarded a Polish freighter in the London docks, having thanked the British people for the strenuous efforts made on their behalf and revealed that they would be heading east for Czechoslovakia, where they intended to take up an offer of work and 'political asylum'.

These and other protests against American power reflected a rising belief in liberal as well as more decided left-wing circles that Britain, despite being abjectly dependent on American loans and aid through the Marshall Plan, still had an independent role to play in the world, and should under no circumstances be reduced to behaving like a bloc-minded stooge of its American paymasters. For many Britons, opposition to American power was sustained less by any pro-Soviet sympathies than by a strong sense of affronted patriotism. The Communist-sympathizing Anglican Canon Stanley Evans was a singular figure, to be sure. However, this 'back street pastor' (in 1955, Evans would become vicar of Holy Trinity Church in Dalston, East London), had surely not been alone in feeling that the rise of American power in the West gave new currency to the great English lament of John of Gaunt in Shakespeare's Richard II:

> This land of such dear souls, this dear, dear land,
> Dear for her reputation through the world,
> Is now leas'd out—I die pronouncing it—
> Like to a tenement, or pelting farm:
> England—is now bound in with shame.[7]

The Red Dean's Moment

Appealing to that same quite widely diffused anti-Americanism, the Britain–China Friendship Association created a fierce storm by defending China against America throughout the Korean War.

It published frankly partisan books and pamphlets, including those in which Burchett and Winnington challenged Anglo-American propaganda statements over Korea. Thanks to its Communist connections, it also became the principal conduit of exchange visits between Britain and New China, organizing partisan tours in which cavilling doubts of the sort sneeringly attributed to Michael Lindsay were not encouraged.

At the end of 1950, only a few weeks after Chinese forces crossed the Yalu River to enter the Korean War as the 'Chinese People's Volunteers', the Britain–China Friendship Association had brought a delegation of five Chinese visitors to Britain. Led by Liu Ning-yi of China's All-Union Federation of Labour, this was the first delegation to visit Britain from Communist China and the reports of its visit were shaped by the fierce ideological arguments that had attended the B–CFA's break with the China Campaign Committee.

Michael Lindsay wrote a frankly unimpressed report of the delegation's progress through Britain for the *Manchester Guardian*. There had, he remarked, been widespread interest in the party of Chinese visitors, which included three professors as well as its trade unionist leader. Invitations had been issued by Labour Cabinet Ministers, but though the 'Communist-controlled management of the Britain–China Friendship Association' had ostensibly welcomed non-Communist help (possibly including Lindsay's own) in arranging contacts in China, the delegation's tour of Britain had been carefully confined: 'The charges that a definite iron curtain was maintained round the delegates are exaggerated. But there was, during much of their visit, a smoke-screen of suspicion, misrepresentation, and conspiratorial methods. Though not impenetrable this was effective in shielding the delegates from non-Communist opinion.'[8]

As Lindsay would assert in a later account of this episode, 'the B–C.F.A management' encouraged the Chinese delegates' misunderstanding of various situations in which they found themselves and also made it difficult for the public to make contact with the delegation. 'When in London', indeed, 'they were housed at an obscure public house in Paddington in rooms which could be reached only through the bar counter.'[9] Non-Communist invitations were rejected with 'gross discourtesy'. The Lord Mayor of

Manchester was among those snubbed by the Chinese delegates and their British minders. Mistakenly expecting a formal reception of the sort that other cities had provided, they walked out when they were asked, as a courtesy, to sign the visitors' book prior to a merely private meeting (organized as such by the B–CFA) in the Lord Mayor's parlour. They refused to attend the Labour Party Conference at Margate (allegedly because they might hear 'opinions about Korea contrary to those of the Chinese government'). They were not prepared to accept hospitality from Labour MPs at the House of Commons, and they withdrew at very short notice from their scheduled meeting with the Parliamentary Labour Party's Foreign Affairs Group. They did consent to have lunch with the party's National Executive Committee at Transport House, but the occasion was a disaster. No sooner was the meal over than Liu Ning-yi, who, a year or so previously, had robustly commended Arthur Clegg as a tireless friend of the Chinese people who understood that 'Wall Street…can, and will, be defeated everywhere',[10] stood up and produced 'a tattered copy of a speech which he had used up and down the country at Anglo-Chinese friendship meetings'. According to Lindsay, he then denounced the Labour government as an 'international disgrace', guilty of placing Britain 'completely under the thumb of America'. Some of his minders in the Britain–China Friendship Association will have enjoyed this assault but observers in the Labour Party did not. As *Tribune* concluded: 'Surely this must be the rudest delegation that has ever left China, a country once renowned for the politeness of its inhabitants.'[11]

In April 1951, the Britain–China Friendship Association responded to a return invitation, issued by that same Liu Ning-yi, by sending its own delegation to China. Announced as 'the first British Delegation to Visit New China', the party was chaired by a Communist coal miner from Yorkshire, Jock Kane, and had eleven members including a doctor, Michael Rapoport, and the trade unionist Betty England, who recalled that 'Everywhere we went we were met with music and flowers, whether field flowers in the countryside or arum lilies and carnations in Shanghai'.[12] Arthur Clegg was among the adherents who joined this delegation, as was George Hardy, a widely travelled British-born Communist, who had first been dispatched to China as a Comintern agent in

1927. Having arrived in Hankow at the height of Chiang Kai-shek's murderous assault on Chinese Communists, he had spent three years working undercover with the Chinese Communist Party and the All-China Federation of Labour Unions.[13] Now 67 years old, this seasoned Stalinist smiled benignly throughout the trip, expressing 'supreme happiness' at the sight of a liberation that seemed to have wrought a magical transformation in the 'demeanour of the people' even though still only seventeen months old.[14] At a meeting organized by the Shanghai Labour Council, Hardy was greeted with tumultuous applause when he looked back on the struggles he had shared with Chou En-lai and others, and warned the 2,000 assembled Chinese citizens that 'the price of liberty is eternal vigilance. "The enemies," I said, "have not given up. They still exist in Shanghai and must be rooted out."' This advice 'brought the audience to their feet, shouting slogans and raising their right hands'.[15]

Michael Lindsay might have opposed 'the doctrinaire thesis of two irreconcilable factions in the world',[16] but these delegates betrayed no such worries. In Peking, they joined a meeting at which 5,000 people heard from witnesses who had survived the 'merciless bombing of Antung' by American planes from South Korea.[17] In Nanking, they visited 'the Home of Love', a children's home founded by Chiang Kai-shek where many babies were reported to have died and then been wrapped in newspaper and buried in mass graves by Catholic nuns who, so one employee told the delegation, had justified their neglect by asking 'What if they lived and became Communists?' As this heavily propagandized story was recited, Hardy glanced at Clegg, whose look asked 'Can this be possible?' Yet Hardy admitted no doubt: 'it was true enough. There is a madness abroad and it infects many otherwise goodhearted people. It broke loose once on the world and ended in Belsen, Buchenwald, Auschwitz. Now Churchill tells the living millions they are better dead than living under a different social order.'[18]

The delegation watched admiringly as 800,000 people took part in the great May Day demonstration in Peking ('children with flowers, but never a gun or a tank to be seen'). Yet for Hardy, the visit found its personal climax when Liu Shao-chi, the Communist leader and author of *How to Be a Good Communist* whom he had known in the 1920s, hailed him as 'an inspiration' to the Chinese people. 'I felt that my life had been rightly spent, as you would have felt, too, when Liu said these words: "Comrade Hardy, too, came to us in 1927, and helped us very much. He lived secretly. But if he had been caught they would have murdered him. Now he comes to China under different conditions."'[19] Hardy returned to Britain convinced that 'The dream has already come true in part'.[20]

A further delegation of thirty-one visited New China under the auspices of the Britain–China Friendship Association in September and October 1952. The membership this time included trade unionists, 'leading persons from the fields of arts and science',[21] and four left-wing Labour MPs including Geoffrey Bing, a radical barrister who was also a veteran of the International Brigades. On his return, Bing produced a B–CFA pamphlet insisting that Britain, as 'the greatest trading nation of the world', could not afford to remain 'divided from the biggest foreign market in the world' and must realize that, while 'the age of the "comprador" is over', trade should be re-established on new terms—especially since the alternative was to cede the market to Soviet Russia.[22] He derided the long-standing Western idea of 'the unchanging East' with its picturesque archetypes, dismissing such visions as really a foil for gangsterism, landlordism, prostitution, and opium addiction. In the course of praising New China's reform of the marriage laws, he claimed the continuation of child marriages in Muslim Pakistan (citing a recent example involving an 8-year-old girl) as proof that 'mere political independence' had not changed backward social conditions in Pakistan. As for the new regime's executions, 'it would appear' that the majority involved gangsters of the most deserving kind. No such statement would be issued by Desmond Donnelly, the Labour MP for Pembrokeshire. Though he had admired the 'simple, ragged people—all participating in the fabulous adventure of national resurgence',[23] Donnelly hated being guided around New China's show sites in a party of enraptured and gloating British Communists who denounced him as a 'Lackey of Wall Street', a 'Spy of the Foreign Office', and, indeed, 'a filthy swine' when he refused to sign their carefully prepared closing joint statement of support for the regime. It was, he later wrote of the trip, like 'being boiled alive in a form of political pressure cooker, with the lid bolted down tight'.[24]

By that time, however, the Britain–China Friendship Association had made a bigger splash by sponsoring a visit by the notorious 'Red Dean' of Canterbury. Hewlett Johnson had previously gone to China in 1932, when he had reeled in horror as 'China groaned under the blows of enemies external and internal'.[25] Returning in the summer of 1952, a year or so after being awarded the 'Stalin Peace Prize' in Moscow and having just been barred from visiting South Africa by the Malan government, who rightly recognized him as an enemy of apartheid, Johnson was delighted to discover that 'the new creative China had risen from the ground, had scattered her enemies, had smashed her fetters and was standing on her feet and, unbound, ready to assume her rightful place—in what Professor Arnold Toynbee felt would be the new centre of power in the coming centuries—in the East'.[26]

In the course of this visit Johnson met up with Peking's resident New Zealander, Rewi Alley, who gave him the party line on land reform, helping to ensure that he came away with a positive appreciation of the 'Accusation meetings' and the 'people's tribunals', which decided over 'the confiscation and redistribution of the landlord's holdings. This is a less lengthy process than might be supposed, and generally needs no preliminary surveys or measurements. The local people, fully familiar with land ownership, already know the details.'[27] As a clergyman, Johnson appreciated New China's cinema too: 'Films in the Eastern world are clean and serious, and film advertisements are clean and reflect a serious and cleanly life—a standard not yet reached in the West.'

The Red Dean's most provocative opinions were formed at a Peking exhibition devoted to 'phenomena of a very unusual character'.[28] Here he learned of voles that had fallen out of the sky, along with clouds of midges, flies, fleas, beetles, spiders, and even chicken feathers. Some of these objects were said to have descended 'like the falling of snow' while others crawled out of cardboard containers that had glided down on little silk parachutes.[29] The 'Exhibition on Bacteriological War Crimes Committed by the Government of the United States of America', opened in Peking during the summer of 1952. It was mounted with the aim of proving the Chinese accusation, launched by Chou En-lai on 24 February, that the Americans had been practising biological warfare on North Korea and parts of China too.[30]

Fig 7. Hewlett Johnson, Dean of Canterbury, inspecting the evidence at the Chinese 'Exhibition on Bacteriological War Crimes Committed by the United States of America'. Published by the Chinese People's Committee for World Peace in Peking, 1952.

There was actually much dispute about this claim, propagated as it was at a time when the Chinese people had been raised to a frenzy of exterminatory concern about flies and other naturally disease-bearing insects.[31] The cardboard containers were said to be flares, and the 'four-compartment bacteria bombs' to be nothing more insidious than leaflet bombs, just as it was claimed that the confessions of US airmen such as John Quinn or Lieutenant Kenneth L. Koch were the consequence of 'brainwashing' or other forms of duress. It was also vehemently asserted that the evidence for this outrage had been rigged with the help of scientists from the USSR.

The 'Red Dean of Canterbury' was among the international visitors who were convinced by the 'irrefutable ironclad evidence'[32] displayed at the exhibition. Indeed, a photograph of Johnson bending over to inspect a display of 'four-compartment bacteria bombs' features prominently on the opening page of the large English-language publication produced to carry news of the show around the world.[33] Though shared with other International 'friends', including Wilfrid Burchett and Rewi Alley, who was directing similar claims at Australia and New Zealand,[34] Johnson's support for China's allegations would be condemned as 'shameful'

by Revd Harold Rigden, an American missionary and the former
Rector of Fu Jen Catholic University in Peking, who was then
enduring severe ordeals in the Peking jail where he had been
incarcerated as an alleged American spy. Having watched the
Communist papers fill with cartoons showing the Americans using
various techniques to introduce disease-carrying rats into Korea,
Father Rigden had deduced that the germ warfare accusations
had been cooked up by the Chinese government in order to
'cover up' the severe losses their troops were suffering from
epidemics.[35] Rigden had developed a particular interest in the
allegations, having found himself being additionally persecuted
by the other prisoners, who reviled the incarcerated American as
the source of all the lice and fleas in their cell.

Advance reports of Johnson's conclusions ensured that, when
he and his wife landed in England, they found an 'angry storm'
raging around their muddled Christian heads. At a press conference organized by the Britain–China Friendship Association,
Johnson faced scores of reporters, who mocked his claims, and
ridiculed his suggestion that Chinese peasants had picked up
contaminated insects with chopsticks. Insisting on 'the exhaustive
and scientific assemblage of the evidence' the dean repeated that
'the facts about germ warfare are conclusive and irrefutable'.[36]
A group of Conservative MPs promptly tabled a motion demanding
that he be dismissed from his office as Dean of Canterbury. In the
House of Lords, the government was urged to consider taking
legal action against Johnson, who had insulted British troops and
brought the Church of England into 'contempt and disrepute'.
The suggestion met with considerable sympathy from the Archbishop of Canterbury, who nevertheless felt obliged to acknowledge that, 'public nuisance' as he may well be, Johnson was a
citizen as well as a dean and could hardly be prevented from
speaking his mind.[37]

The outcry was aggravated by Johnson's pamphlet *I Appeal*,[38]
published by the Britain–China Friendship Association in time to
be presented to all members of the House of Lords on the morning
of their debate on the subject. This reprinted the 'confessions' of
two captured US airmen, and also the texts of various appeals
from the regime-led Christian churches in China, all of which
accused the Americans of engaging in 'large-scale bacteriological

warfare' and condemned 'the warmongers that tie up their fate with rats and fleas'. Johnson appealed to 'the decency, the honesty and the courage of the whole British people to insist that they will have no part or lot in this crime of genocide, this crime of germ warfare'. In the event, so Johnson would later claim, the debate was truncated by Winston Churchill, who had seen Johnson's pamphlet and reckoned it advisable to let the matter drop rather than have the argument extended into the House of Lords. Having made his accusation, the Red Dean went back to Canterbury, sincerely dismayed that the Chinese churchmen's appeal had been so rudely dismissed by the Archbishop of Canterbury, but satisfied to think that his intervention might at least lead to 'happier relations between the Chinese Church and the Chinese State'.[39]

This was unconvincing stuff, which confirmed Johnson as a national laughing-stock. From the Britain–China Friendship Association's partisan point of view, however, an impressive explosion had been detonated. It would be repeated when Joseph Needham, who was also President of the B–CFA, returned to London in September 1952. By then it was widely known that the International Scientific Commission, with which he had spent several months reviewing China's allegations (but not repeating any of the tests on which those claims were said to rest), had reported that 'the peoples of Korea and China have indeed been the objective of bacteriological weapons... employed by units of the U.S.A. armed force'.[40] Needham's assent to this conclusion, which one historian has characterized as a reluctant 'leap of faith',[41] was made partly out of horror of American culture and what it had become under McCarthyism, and partly in defiance of a Western tendency to treat Asians as 'experimental animals', which Needham considered to have been confirmed by the atomic bombs dropped on Hiroshima and Nagasaki in 1945. It also represented Needham's defence of China's scientists: not just the sixty, including twenty-three with American Ph.D.s, selected to carry out investigations for the committee,[42] but others he had got to know personally while running the British Council's Science Cooperation Office during the Second World War.[43]

In Britain, Needham's ordeal began with a press conference, held on 26 September at the Hotel Russell in Bloomsbury.[44] Here he made statements of certainty that quite defied his own earlier reservations about joining the Commission in the first place, and claimed that the captured American airmen who had confessed to these hideous crimes were 'absolutely normal people' who had not been manipulated or tortured. He admitted that he had not spoken to these prisoners alone since he did not want to hurt the feelings of their captors, whom he appears later to have congratulated for awakening the American pilots to 'an appreciation of true spiritual values'.[45] The argument followed Needham as he worked his unapologetic way through a noisy lecture tour, and then continued to rage for years to come. Though Needham faced objection from sources that were politically quite close to home—including the editor of the *New Statesman*, the National Peace Council,[46] and also the United Nations Association,[47] of which he himself was an active member—the counter charge was largely orchestrated by the Information Research Department of the Foreign Office, which recognized that, unlike the Very Reverend Hewlett Johnson, this respected Fellow of the Royal Society could not so easily be written off as 'our national joke'.[48] The dispute escalated, not so much as a 'rational debate', so one historian has argued, but as an example of the new propaganda-led 'politics of absurdity' that would shape communication between the Cold War's polarized camps.[49] It was soon enough exported to the USA, where Needham was blacklisted, and his sympathizers censured or, in the case of the Columbia University anthropologist Gene Weltfish, fired from their jobs.[50]

Icebreakers and the Trade Embargo

While these arguments about germ warfare raged, the Communist-promoted idea of 'friendship' was unfolding on other fronts too. The Britons who visited China as the 'Icebreakers' in 1953 were businessmen, not scientists or culpably idealistic clergymen, and the barrier they were seeking to penetrate dated back to 31 March 1949, when Harold Wilson, President of the Board of Trade in the Labour government, had introduced a 'sweeping'[51] set of prohibitions against trade with the Soviet bloc.

An embargo list that had earlier been concentrated on objects of military value now included numerous items of general industrial use, including minerals, non-ferrous metals, metal-working machines, chemicals. A further tightening was introduced by America the following year, extending the list to 1,100 items and barring US ships and planes from carrying 'strategic items' destined for Hong Kong, Macao, or East Europe as well as Communist China—a decision that threatened Britain's crown colony in Hong Kong. Coordinated by a committee of the NATO countries based in Paris, the regulations were tightened against East European countries, and then extended to China. After 18 May 1951, when China was declared an 'aggressor' in the Korean War by the UN Security Council, it was decreed that member countries should impose a draconian ban on exports to China.

The blockade was further enforced by a US measure known as the Battle Act, or the Mutual Defence Assistance Control Act, enacted in October 1951, which introduced penalties against any country receiving US aid, which was found shipping embargoed goods to China or the Soviet bloc. That ban was meant to be applied to goods of 'strategic' significance but it soon became apparent to objectors that just about anything could be counted 'strategic' and that the ban was, in the words of its opponents, 'a bid to retard the industrial development of a third of the world'.[52]

These measures, which amounted to a full-scale embargo, caused objection among British companies and Hong Kong interests, and also among politicians concerned that trade restrictions of this sort would merely force China into closer alliance with the USSR. The tensions increased as Senator Joe McCarthy used his subcommittee to persuade US federal agencies to stop employing foreign shipping companies (including the British Blue Funnel Line) who were also trading with Communist Countries. McCarthy, who was apparently pressing for an absolute blockade of China, declared this practice of 'dual trading' to be 'the most inexcusable thing I have ever heard of'.[53] The official British response to this policy may have had much in common with *The Times*' editorial which regretted that McCarthy was exceeding even the American government in his advocacy of a measure that 'would mean, on the trade front, a general state of war'.[54] It would not, however, be the Labour government that steered British businesses into a first breach of the embargo.

The 'Icebreakers' were coaxed into existence by a businessman named Jack Perry, whose 'Dress Products Company' was based in

Hackney, East London.[55] He was among the economists and businessmen from both sides of the Iron Curtain who met in Copen-
hagen in October 1951 with the aim of coordinating opposition
to the trade restrictions which divided the hostile blocs. In April
1952, the deliberations were resumed at an international
economic conference in Moscow, involving 471 participants from
forty-nine countries. The twenty-nine-strong British delegation
was chaired by Lord Boyd-Orr, FRS, the first Director of the UN
Food and Agriculture Organization, and, of course, also the
Chairman of the Britain–China Friendship Society, while Jack
Perry went as its Secretary. Its members included manufacturers
and exporters, trade unionists, five MPs, and various academics
including the Keynesian economist Joan Robinson, her
Cambridge colleague, the Marxist economist Maurice Dobb, and
also Charles Madge, the founder of Mass Observation, who joined
as a member of the Faculty of Social Sciences at Birmingham
University. While in Moscow, the British participants held
informal discussions with the Chinese delegation. They agreed
to create lists of goods that might be exchanged despite the
American ban, and they went on to initiate Anglo-Chinese trade
in wool-tops, a non-embargoed item widely used in the production of worsted cloth.

It was Perry who forged this exchange, exploiting his contacts
in the Bradford textile trade, then suffering from a depressed
market at home, while at the same time ignoring the hostility of
both the Bradford press and the British banks which refused to
respect Chinese letters of credit.[56] On 4 May 1952, the British
delegates, who included MPs, economists, and trade unionists as
well as representatives of interested firms, went on to form the
British Council for the Promotion of International Trade
(BCPIT)—an unofficial body, which impressed some as nothing
more than a Communist front, and was chaired, once again, by
Lord Boyd Orr, FRS, who believed 'it is better to have wagons
crossing frontiers with goods people need than columns of
armoured vehicles carrying out manoeuvres'.[57]

With Joan Robinson as vice-chairman of its executive committee
and the former UN official Roland Berger as Director of the
Council, the BCPIT used its contacts both to unleash a 'barrage'[58]
of questions in the House of Commons, and to prepare the way

for a mission to China. The latter proposal was fiercely attacked in Westminster and also in the press. But the mission went ahead in June 1953, six or so weeks before the signing of the armistice that brought the Korean War to an end, with sixteen men representing companies such as Austin Motors, Enfield Cables, Brush Electrical Engineering, and Rubery Owen and Co. Ltd (the director of the latter engineering company having allegedly been summoned to the Foreign Office by Sir Anthony Eden and strongly advised to understand that the organizers were 'Commies', and that 'you can't touch pitch without being defiled').[59]

Encouraged by the success of a delegation of French businessmen, who had travelled to Peking a few weeks earlier and returned with a trade agreement for the exchange of £10m worth of goods,[60] the 'Icebreakers' entered China on 12 June and went on to agree £30 million worth of mutual trade between the two countries involving goods that might not fall foul of the widely drawn embargo. Irritated by this 'First Business Arrangement', signed in Peking on 6 July 1953, Sir Anthony Eden continued to advise British companies to spurn the BCIT as a 'communist front'.[61] He had no regard for a 'fellow-traveller' initiative taking place at a time when legitimate British businesses in China were still being persecuted by the Chinese government.

The 'Icebreakers', however, were not to be turned. Joan Robinson, the Cambridge economist and B–CFA member who accompanied the delegation on its three-week visit, noted that New China was 'bubbling over with babies'[62] and had only been improved by the 'hurricane' of land reform that had swept away the oppressive landlords ('You must not think of dukes, nor yet of village squires').[63] In letters home, she declared the old palaces of Peking to be 'like an enormous permanent Festival of Britain, with glories from the past instead of fancies for the future'.[64] As for Europe's official representatives in China, Robinson returned the contempt in which they were inclined to hold visiting delegates such as herself: 'the western diplomats live in isolation in the Legation Quarter chewing over their grievances and feeling superior about being white.'[65]

Such was the first 'Icebreaker' mission to China. The sequel came in April 1954, when representatives of forty-eight British companies met a Chinese trade mission at the offices of the China

National Import and Export Corporation in East Berlin (a location chosen because visas would not be available to enable the Chinese to visit Britain), agreeing £3.6 million worth of contracts. By this time, however, a new sense of conciliation was emerging. By 1954, indeed, the British government was also opposing the embargo lists and, indeed, actively seeking trade with China. Having made contact with the Chinese trade representative Lei Jen-min during the course of the Geneva conference, it would establish the Sino-British Trade Committee with a view to developing trade with China and organizing officially sanctioned exchange visits.[66] Thanks to the optimism that eventually triumphed at Geneva, there would be fewer allegations of Communist sympathy to trouble the British businessmen who visited China in 1955.

6

Barbara Castle's Bevanite Sigh

The sound was arresting, even mortifying. Provoked by an apparently uncontroversial question, it gathered up two words, slowly dismembered them and then hurled their remains far out into the row of amalgamated workers' cottages known as Hell Corner Farm that was Barbara Castle's home in Ibstone, Buckinghamshire. 'Oh' was a gasp of furious disappointment, pressurized, and then suddenly released.[1] 'America' was a drawn-out battle between furiously sharpened consonants and murdered vowels. This apparently involuntary exhalation, which might have accompanied a fit or a cardiac arrest, seemed an impressive memorial to the frustration of the many Britons who had remained convinced, in that post-war decade, that the world really didn't have to be divided in the way American policy dictated.

If the failure of the Labour Party was a rude if not actually belching fact on Paul Hogarth's plane, Barbara Castle, the left-wing Labour MP for Blackburn, travelled with America on her mind. Arranged by the Britain–China Friendship Association, on behalf of the Chinese People's Institute of Foreign Affairs, her delegation, which was led by Mr Ellis Smith, the Labour MP for Stoke-on-Trent South, did not depart until early October, 1954. The initial invitation had assumed this group would travel as an official delegation of the British Labour Party and attend the anniversary celebrations on 1 October. However, the appointed politicians were not prepared to miss the annual Labour Party conference in late September, at which a fierce internal dispute about party policy would come to a head. Attlee and his party managers were determined to bind the membership to supporting the proposed rearmament of West Germany and also the new South-East Asia Treaty Organization. In the event, they succeeded on both counts, despite strong opposition from Aneurin Bevan and the left-wing 'Bevanites' arrayed around him. It looked for a time as if the trip to China would be cancelled in the wake of this decision, but the Chinese authorities had eventually agreed—'reluctantly' as its attendant Sinologist,

Professor Edwin Pulleyblank, remembers—to go ahead on condition that it was reorganized and, as the politicians felt, downgraded into a 'cultural delegation'.[2]

The Second Labour Delegation consisted of ten Labour MPs, including Barbara Castle and a number of other leading Bevanites; seven senior trade unionists; Mrs Mabel Ridealgh, a former Labour MP who had been granted a month's unpaid leave from her present position as National Secretary of the Women's Cooperative Guild; and four hastily added 'cultural delegates'. Of the latter, Cedric Dover, the Calcutta-born Eurasian author of *Half-Caste* and other books concerned with race and imperialism, was enlisted as 'the anthropologist of the party'.[3] His three fellow 'professionals' were Dr Derrick James, a lecturer in anatomy at University College, London; the artist and critic Denis Mathews, who was also secretary of the Contemporary Art Society, based at the Tate Gallery; and Edwin G. Pulleyblank, a young Canadian who had recently been appointed Professor of Chinese at Cambridge University and who, like John Chinnery, was taking advantage of the opportunity to make his first visit to China.

When they arrived in Prague, the members of this late-travelling delegation were greeted by Chinese representatives, who informed them that, due to acute pressure on eastern-going planes, two of the party of twenty would have to stay overnight, and join the rest a day later in Moscow. All four of the delegation's cultural 'professionals' were intrigued by the offer, which was received with no enthusiasm at all by the MPs and trade unionists. According to Derrick James, who kept a detailed diary of the journey, the MPs were 'keen to get on, with the rather forlorn hope that they might reach Moscow for Moscow Dynamos v. the Arsenal'. As Mathews also records, 'the Trades Union boys were searching for cups of tea while they waited for the plane'.[4] The quest led them to the airport café, where they sat down by a table on which an 'enchanting' one-year-old baby lay sleeping. After 'lots of broad backchat about a "nice cup of char", "not enough to put strength into a man", and so on, they got back onto their aircraft and departed for Moscow'.

Having waved them off, the two who had volunteered to stay, Mathews and Derrick James, were taken through customs by Mr Chou ('thin and wiry, below our idea of average height, with a

Mongolian cast to his face') from the People's Republic of China's Czechoslovak embassy. Having endured a 'great palaver' about their money and cameras (Mathews travelled with no less than three, as suspicious customs officials duly noted), they were escorted to a Humber limousine with CD plates the size of 'soup tureens' and a 'most charmingly sinister chauffeur in a huge mackintosh and a Hollywood style felt hat'. Driven slowly through the suburbs, they noticed the tram system and new flats, which were not wholly successful in disguising the fact that Prague had 'a slightly dilapidated air, like so many towns in England'. The Czechs did not seem to go in for huge portraits of their leaders everywhere, and 'there is a happy absence of advertisements'.

Deposited in the Palace Hotel, they were invited to exploit its resources as guests of the Chinese embassy. James found the hotel to be 'much like any other, not in the luxury class but, for example, like the "Star"...in Maidstone'. Their double room was full of 'heavy Victorian furniture' and the bath was 'quite splendid': approached up a step, it was the size of a 'small lake' but quick to fill thanks to a torrential supply of hot water far superior to the spluttering dribble produced by the average British geyser.

Outside the hotel, however, cash remained a problem and not only on account of Britain's fierce currency restrictions. 'Unlike the Rumanians,' so James noted, 'the Chinese do not apparently hand out wads of dough to visitors.' Venturing out for a late afternoon walk, he and Mathews were horrified by the official exchange rate, which hiked prices by a factor of three. James maintained an optimistic view of the shops ('as much variety, I should say, as there is in Ashford'), while admitting that 'the window displays are not as clever as some of the London ones'. They walked along the river as the actress Constance Cummings had advised Mathews to do, and crossed the bridges of this 'lovely town', which they found to be dominated by 'a rather monstrous colossus of Stalin'. In the evening, they took a No. 1 tram up to the Castle and entered the Cathedral of St Vita to find 'a lovely Gothic interior in which the bishop was holding benediction'. The congregation, which 'probably numbered nearly a hundred', did not seem to Mathews quite so moribund as it had appeared to Stanley Spencer a few weeks earlier ('as always most women but quite a number of young men and some children too'). The light was fading as they returned to the lower town, following a long flight of steps 'flanked by pictur-esque houses' and, as Mathews' noted, 'not good enough to photo-graph the children playing on stilts in this pleasant setting'.

Dr James noted that there were 'lots and lots of soldiers and officers about Prague'—so many, indeed, that it was 'almost like London in wartime'. He also phoned Dr Joseph H. Cort, the young American doctor and medical scientist who had recently taken up 'political asylum' in Czechoslovakia. The members of the cultural delegation had merely glimpsed Dr Cort in the Palace Hotel, but James called him up on the phone and then conversed with him for several hours, drinking coffee and brandy, and comparing the Soviet and Western approaches to science. Cort informed him that his colleagues at the Czech Academy of Sciences, some of whom had been trained in Britain, regarded the Russians as 'a bit nuts' about Pavlov. And what, James asked, of the claims of Olga B. Lepeshinskaya, the elderly Bolshevik investigator whom Stalin had fêted for allegedly proving Engels's fantasy that living cells might be generated from non-cellular matter? In a recently published pamphlet, Lepeshinskaya had boasted that her experiments, said to be finding great interest in China as well as the USSR, had also been 'successfully repeated'[5] in various laboratories in Czechoslo-vakia. Cort, however, reported that the scientists with whom he was now working in Prague regarded the Stalin Prize winner's demoli-tion of 'bourgeois' cell theory as 'a great joke'. Cort described English science as 'meticulously quantitative', which James accepted as true. In his desire to go beyond that, however, he left James puzzled: 'Philosophical integration of science and society is OK, but just how you make science different, and still science, I don't know.' It was a good question, and one that James would take with him to China.

The rest of the delegates, meanwhile, were flying on towards Moscow. Like Hugh Casson's account of the earlier 'cultural dele-gation', Barbara Castle's diary describes a journey into an oddly familiar nineteenth-century past: 'the very plane is draped in Victorian idiom: the Russians cover their plane seats in loose covers that sweep the ground: just as the Victorians draped their table legs.' She also recalls that the protocol of flying was 'very irregular' in those early days. Seat belts were disregarded, if they existed at all, and the stewardesses would be walking about even during landings[6] (Castle later remembered one who was 'still upright when the plane hit the ground'). Passengers were able to wander around inside the plane throughout the journey and it was thanks to the resulting melée that Castle came across two American Congressmen who had joined the flight in Prague, and who may even have been the more important travellers for whom Mathews and James had surrendered their seats. One was Congressman Fisher of Texas, but Castle was altogether more interested in Laurie C. Battle, a Democrat from Alabama. Having established that he was indeed the member of the US Committee on Foreign Affairs who had given his name to the notorious Battle Act, also known as the Mutual Defence Assistance Control Act of October 1951, she told him, frankly, that he ought to be ashamed of himself.

Remembering this encounter in the midst of George W. Bush's 'War against Terror', Castle would heave another terrific sigh, before declaring emphatically that 'the Americans are heart-breaking'. At the time, however, she noted in her diary that Battle was 'a charming, good-looking American in his late 30s who argued pleasantly in the plane with us all the way to Minsk, assuring us that his Act was a very liberal alternative to the Kem amendment'.[7] It was a friendly dispute, involving a considerable number of the British delegates as well as Barbara Castle, who found herself sitting 'on the floor of the plane to join in'.

There was certainly a lot to argue about. For behind this chance encounter lay a thoroughly hated outcome of America's determination to wage 'economic warfare' against the Soviet bloc. The origins of this policy are customarily traced to the so-called 'long telegram' sent in 1946 to the Secretary of State by George Kennan, the US chargé d'affaires in Moscow. In this, Kennan had suggested that the USSR was implacably opposed to America, and should be economically isolated since it was most unlikely to be influenced by political or economic inducements. A trade embargo had been imposed not long afterwards, and in March 1951, Congressman Battle had convened hearings of a subcommittee of the House Foreign Affairs Committee, during which he openly accused the Allied countries of 'permitting exports while US soldiers lay dying on Korean battlefields'.[8] The Mutual Security Bill, enacted as a

result of those hearings on 10 May 1951, demanded the cancella-
tion of aid payments to Allied countries that did not enforce the
US embargo. That same summer, Battle had spent six weeks in
Europe investigating the Allies' compliance with the US embargo,
reporting, once again, that 'I am not satisfied with what I have
found'. Nevertheless, he was at least partly justified in claiming to
have become a counsel of moderation.

As the *Economist* had conceded in a generally hostile leading
article, the Battle Act was indeed in some respects more flexible
than the earlier Kem amendment, introduced as a rider to an
appropriation bill in May 1951.[9] Unlike the latter, it was informed
by the reluctant understanding that, not least for the sake of West
Berlin, some exports to the East would remain necessary. Introduced on 26 October, the Battle Act allowed for the appointment
of a Mutual Defence Assistance Officer, who would determine
what items should be embargoed as usable for purposes of war,
atomic energy, or strategic transport. Battle might also have
pointed out that concessions had indeed been made in the wake
of his Act, and that it was no simple matter for America to withdraw aid from an uncompliant and more or less bankrupt ally at
the very time when it was also trying to solidify its own bloc under
NATO.

By the time of these China-bound flights in 1954, Britain and
other European nations were deliberately flouting America's
embargo. British officials were proposing a 50 per cent reduction
in the lists of embargoed goods, particularly with regard to exports
to China and other Asian markets. The Churchill government
also objected to the so-called 'China differential', which ensured
that any liberalization of the lists applied to the Soviet Union
would not be extended to China. These decisions were the cause
of much international tension. Indeed, in the summer of 1954,
the Eisenhower Administration had recommended that Congress
cut off military aid to Great Britain and France for their lack of
compliance. In the event, however, and as Battle may perhaps
have reminded Castle and the other members of the Second
Labour Delegation, no threatened withdrawal of American aid
had ever actually taken place.

It is likely that familiar British arguments against those trade
embargoes were reprised in Castle's airborne conversation. Even

if they were not uniformly inclined to condemn American policy as an act of coercion against a former ally, some of the British MPs and trade unionists might reasonably have pointed out that America had never relied on trade with the Soviet Union, unlike Britain, which had previously had significant ties involving the import of essential foods and raw materials. They may have argued that the embargoes were by no means accurately or exclusively targeted against military expansionism, and that they recoiled harshly on West European economies: depriving their industries of markets; forcing them to buy food and raw materials from the USA at a time when the exchange rate against the dollar was highly disadvantageous; and, as Soviet critics of the system were also in the habit of asserting, creating unemployment too.

Congressmen Fisher and Battle may well have emerged from the argument confirmed in the suspicion that America's European allies were an unreliable bunch and far too soft on Communism. Yet politeness held. For a brief period, indeed, the two Americans even became reliant on an informal kind of British aid. At Minsk, the travellers were delayed for half an hour while Soviet officials checked their passports, and interrogated the Americans with particularly intense suspicion. Seeing that they had no language in common, Barbara Castle came to their assistance, relaying their answers in French via a bilingual Russian stewardess. The officials wanted to know who had invited the Americans to Russia and were puzzled by their insistence that no one had. Motivated 'more by a desire to test the Russians than anything else, they had applied for visas at the Russian Embassy in Washington and 10 days later had received them: just like that!' As Castle noted, 'we teased them while the officials cross-examined them at Minsk and they were deeply grateful when I got them in the clear'. Once that difficulty was resolved, Castle and the other delegates returned to their travels: 'we had a strange meal in the airport at Minsk: a Victorian-style dining room with red velvet curtains draped over the arched doorway and damask table cloths flowing to the ground.'

7

Chou En-Lai's Winning Smile

'Come and see'—these were not empty words.

Robert Guillain[1]

The political thaw that prompted the various China-bound flights of 1954 had set in a year or so earlier. American policy remained governed by a hard-line anti-Communism that had little interest in searching the utterances of Soviet or Chinese leaders for modest concessions such as had been offered by Chou En-lai early in 1946, when he told General George C. Marshall that, while the Chinese Communists would certainly 'lean to one side' as Mao had promised, the exact angle of their inclination towards Soviet Russia depended on the attitude taken by the Americans.[2] However, the Korean War had been brought to a close by the armistice of 27 July 1953, and there was growing interest in finding a settlement of France's protracted and failing war in Indo-China. Since Stalin's death in March 1953, a settlement had also become more imaginable in Soviet Russia, where the old Comintern policy of 'peaceful coexistence' was being redeveloped under the brief leadership of Malenkov, a colourless character judged by two British observers to be 'largely the representative of Stalinist bureaucracy'.[3] The same grey light was dawning over Red China, despite the suspicions of Michael Lindsay and other Western critics, who would continue to condemn the Chinese for abusing that pastoral term.[4] During the course of the Geneva Conference, however, the 'Five Principles of Peaceful Coexistence' would be accepted as fundamental to now pacified Sino-Indian relations by both Chou En-lai and Jawaharlal Nehru.[5] It was also apparent that Mao's first five-year plan, announced in 1953 to be commenced the following year, would be greatly assisted by the opening of trade relations with Western Europe.

The French authorities, meanwhile, had been increasingly keen on finding a settlement of the Indo-China War that might grant independence within the French Union to non-Communist regimes in the three 'Associated States' of Cambodia, Laos, and Vietnam.[6] For a time there was talk of 'negotiating from strength'. By the end of 1953, however, France was facing military humiliation at the hands of Hô Chi Minh's forces in Vietnam. The reinforcements demanded by the 'Navarre Plan' were not forthcoming and public opinion, in France as in Britain and elsewhere, was against sacrificing more men and resources for the sake of going along with American theories of containment. As the *Economist* concluded on 7 November 1953, 'the game no longer seems worth the candle'.[7]

So the international climate was already softening when news came that Hô Chi Minh was ready to consider French proposals for a negotiated settlement if the French suspended hostilities. A 'feeler' to this effect was communicated via the Stockholm paper *Expressen* on 29 November 1953,[8] and followed up in January 1954, when the Soviet Foreign Minister, Molotov, joined his counterparts from Britain, France, and the USA in Berlin for a Four Power meeting to discuss the future of Europe. The assembled ministers had found it quite impossible to reconcile Soviet and Western schemes for the reunification of Germany. However, it was here that Molotov proposed inviting China to a Five Power Conference in which South-East Asia might be discussed. Responding in a radio broadcast from Peking on 9 January, Chou En-lai gave immediate support to the suggestion.[9] As Eisenhower's fervently anti-Communist Secretary of State, John Foster Dulles was reluctant to go along with this. Yet he did consent to discussing 'particular' questions, including Korea and Indo-China, as long as others were present and it was understood that America's participation in such a meeting did not imply any wider recognition of the People's Republic of China.[10]

Between the Berlin and Geneva conferences, the latter scheduled to begin on 26 April 1954, Dulles tried to convince America's allies into taking 'united action' against Communism in South-East Asia. Promoted as the 'New Look', Dulles's policy imagined the 'free community', which included Britain, France, Australia, New Zealand, Thailand, and the Philippines, as well as the three Associated States of Indo-China, combining to threaten Red China with an internationalized policy of 'massive retaliation'.

This approach was justified by the 'domino theory', introduced by President Eisenhower during a press conference on 7 April 1954, in which Asian nations were imagined falling one after another before the advancing Communist Juggernaut. It was met with some alarm in Western Europe. Dulles, who impressed at least one British diplomat as suffering from 'linguistic incontinence',[11] huffed and harangued. And his fellow interventionist, Vice President Richard Nixon, contributed to the sense of anxiety when, on 16 April, he announced that it might be necessary to send American troops 'to save this embattled land'.[12] Yet this apparent attempt to escalate hostilities—Dulles was known for his belief in 'brinkmanship'—failed to convince the senior politician who was Foreign Minister in the elderly Winston Churchill's British government.

Anthony Eden temporized, declaring himself reluctant to preempt the approaching Geneva Conference. Nevertheless the joint communiqué he issued with Dulles admitted the possibility of organizing a 'collective defence', thereby infuriating many on the British left, including Aneurin Bevan, who had seen it as 'a surrender to American pressure' and resigned from the Shadow Cabinet when Clement Attlee failed to repudiate Eden's compliance with American policy.[13] Dulles, meanwhile, returned to Washington and announced that he would be contacting ambassadors of his intended axis to establish 'an informal working group'. This provoked Eden into action. In a response that has been likened to 'the petulant reaction of a cornered rabbit', he ordered Britain's ambassador in Washington not to attend any such meeting, and condemned Dulles's actions in a series of angry telegrams ('Americans may think the time past when they need consider the feelings or difficulties of their allies').[14]

Greatly concerned about the increasingly desperate plight of France's encircled garrison at Dien Bien Phu, the French Foreign Minister, Georges Bidault, was certainly tempted by the thought of an immediate American air attack. He was also under great stress and, indeed, inclined to appear drunk in the Chamber (in one debate, he is said to have collapsed, embarrassingly, onto the Communist benches). The American threat was restrained, however, thanks not least to Anthony Eden who, having woken a little slowly to the gravity of the situation and talked with the ailing

Prime Minister Winston Churchill, proposed that the British cabinet should adopt an eight-point directive that refused to commit Britain to such a policy ahead of the Geneva Conference. Dulles was left firing tirades against the 'increasing weakness' of the British attitude.

So the day had come when a delegation of nearly 200 officials from the People's Republic of China flew through, or perhaps over, the Iron Curtain from Moscow, and landed at Geneva for an international conference on Indo-China that, though not formally convened by the United Nations, would be held in the UN's Palais des Nations. They arrived at Cointrin airport alongside the Soviet delegation on the afternoon of Saturday, 24 April 1954. To begin with the photographers struggled to distinguish Mao Tse-tung's right-hand man from the other alighting Chinese delegates. When his name was called, however, Chou En-lai turned to the cameras and transfixed the West with a smile.

Describing the moment some five years later, two French authors would write: 'His were the instinctive reactions of the great actor and public figure. On the smooth ivory face, deeply lined, with its high forehead, huge mouth, and enormous pointed black eyebrows setting off the large and beautiful black eyes, there flashed a smile. It was a great, meaningful, ironic smile, showing dazzling teeth. It was a smile that would animate the pages of American magazines and be worth months of negotiations.'[15] Though considerably less disarmed by Chou's smile, the correspondent for the London *Times* conceded that Geneva, while 'always international in its aspect and atmosphere', was now 'brighter than ever because of the colourful dresses of visitors from the east'.[16] As for Grand Mont-Fleur, the considerable house where Chou would reside and hold court during the extended visit that formed his 'European debut',[17] *The Times* only noted in passing that 'some of the barbed wire with which it had been proposed to ring the country houses which Mr. Molotov and Mr. Chou En-lai are to occupy has been removed'.

No doubt this sudden splash of 'Eastern colour' was a welcome addition to Geneva's famously peaceful lakeside scene, but the Chinese Communist visitors surprised the Swiss by refusing to lodge in the same hotel as their Soviet Russian allies. They would also

Fig 8. Chou En-lai, Geneva, 1954.

offer observers a picture of forbidding otherness: not least in their use of bullet-proof limousines and their habit of marching about in ranks that seemed to confirm the Western image of Mao's China as a grimly regimented land of 'yellow hordes' and 'blue ants'.

It was not long, however, before the Chinese delegation started to make an altogether different impression. Just as, in May 1920, Britain had failed to discover a blood-soaked monster when Leonid Krassin arrived in London as the head of Bolshevik Russia's first trade delegation,[18] Western observers in 1954 soon realized that the 56-year-old Chou En-lai, who led the Chinese delegation in his combined role as Prime Minister and Foreign Minister of the People's Republic, was by no means identical with the monstrous creature of anti-Communist legend.

Chou had himself looked forward to Geneva as 'our first real show in the international arena', and he proved an able performer.[19] This, as he well knew, was the first time since the liberation that Western observers had been in any position to study Chou and to measure the man against the lurid images provided by hostile demonology. The American government remained intransigent, but many citizens of the West were considerably more impressed. Convinced that American policy was culpably bellicose, and beyond the influence of their largely consenting West European governments, they were predisposed to place their hopes in China and its representative. Indeed, the sight of Chou in Geneva may have seemed to confirm the extravagantly redemptive images offered by fellow-travelling pilgrims who had earlier encountered him in China, including the credulous 'Red Dean' of Canterbury who had fallen in rapture at the feet of the red saviour when visiting China in 1952:

> Mr Chou's face once seen is never forgotten. An alert and kindly face, youthful, almost boyish, set in a frame of dark hair, with dark eyes, shining beneath dark brows. A Chinese face, of course, but with unusually deep-set eyes for China. A very warmly kind face too, and with eyes that look straight at you. I cannot imagine a less aggressive face, or a gentler one,[20]

Anti-Communists and also more liberal sceptics had stood back from such reports as further proof of the nauseating deference with which 'useful idiots' gazed into the eye of totalitarian power. Yet the impression made by Chou as he stepped out in Geneva—not a rough-necked 'agrarian reformer' dressed in padded cotton but an urbane, cultured, and articulate man in a tailored suit and silk tie—was by no means confined to the perceptions of a few self-deluding zealots. According to the British journalist James Cameron, Chou was 'the man who on his brief appearance at Geneva produced the simultaneous double-effect of a nervous construction in the diplomatic hearts and a violent sexual impulse in the persons of almost every European woman who clapped eyes on him. This is both unusual and immaterial, politically, but might as well be noted.'[21] It was not an effect that anyone would claim for America's John Foster Dulles.

For Humphrey Trevelyan, who had made the journey from Peking to assist Anthony Eden, Geneva was a tedious business: 'An international conference is a painful affair for all except the principals. It consists largely in waiting around.'[22] That and listening to pre-cooked 'platitudes declaimed in the full glare of publicity'.[23] His new junior colleague in the British embassy compound in Peking would surely have agreed. Douglas Hurd would later recall the many hours he spent sitting under an ineffective fan in the embassy's sweltering high-security room, drinking Tsingtao beer and laboriously deciphering numerical telegrams in which every turn of the conference proceedings seemed to be reported in dreary detail.[24] He would not find his own use for the mistrusted jargon of 'peaceful coexistence' until nearly half a century later, when he looked back through his subsequent career as Britain's Home Secretary and then Foreign Secretary, and applied the phrase to the harmonious collection of ancient buildings in the spacious Great Court of Trinity College, Cambridge, where he had taken a first in History.[25]

Having opened against a chorus of pre-emptive American denigration, the Geneva Conference extended over three months, its programme of plenary sessions being interspersed with restricted sessions, backstage lobbying, and more or less conspiratorial dinners. There was plenty of ideological grandstanding of the kind that would become so familiar during the Cold War, with leaders addressing their voters at home, or the other members of their own bloc, and then withdrawing into more pragmatic compromises behind the scenes. It was an agonizing struggle in which every detail was argued: the agenda, the seating plan, even the languages to be declared official at the conference. Convened on 26 April, the first phase was intended to agree terms for the reunification of Korea. It ground to a halt a week or so later. The second phase, concerned with the Indo-China War, opened a day after the catastrophic fall of the French garrison at the long-beleaguered fortress at Dien Bien Phu on 7 May. It too went through moments of deadlock, thanks partly to a general election that brought down the French government. Indications were poor as the deadline approached, but then came the concessions, which made possible the declaration issued on 27 April 1954. Ceasefires were announced in three separate agreements concerned with Laos, Cambodia, and Vietnam.[26] The latter was to be divided at the 17th parallel, and troops withdrawn to positions on both sides. The territorial sovereignty and independence of Indochina was affirmed, providing independence from France and terminating foreign involvement in the region.

Ho Chi Minh's Viet Minh, which had been placed under great pressure by its ally in China, issued a formal protest against the agreement, reserving the right to press on with the war as it saw fit. The United States declared that it had 'taken note' of the ceasefire agreements but would not be formally associated with the agreements that came to be known as the Geneva Accords. There was talk of 'appeasement' and President Eisenhower, who declared himself unwilling to criticize the settlement, left no doubt it was 'not what we would have liked to have had'.[27] He would later describe Geneva as a 'terrible' settlement that had 'put great numbers of people under Communist domination'.[28] The general response in the USA may have been 'largely one of indifference'.[29] In Western Europe, however, the outcome was greeted with a profound sense of relief. Geneva marked a break in the apparently relentless march towards global nuclear conflict in which the world had been engaged since 1948/9, and which had reached a new level of alarm with the successful development of the Soviet hydrogen bomb, tested on 12 August 1953.

The London *Times* admitted to a feeling of 'deep thankfulness'[30] and Anthony Eden, who looked on the Accords as 'the best France could have obtained under the circumstances',[31] came home with a considerably enhanced reputation. Eden won the respect of his political opponents at home: he was commended in *Tribune* and even hailed by the *New Statesman* as 'the darling of the Labour Left'.[32] There were, of course, some on the British left who would have rejected this suggestion, and not just those who knew that, while the Churchill government presented itself as uninvolved in the Indo-China war, Britain had in fact been selling artillery and planes to the French forces.[33] Yet the wider view, expressed by a French historian, was that Britain had distinguished herself, maintaining an independent outlook that was more principled and elevated than anything available to politicians in beleaguered France, overwhelmed as they were by military defeat in Vietnam.[34] Geneva would come to be regarded as one of the last occasions, only two years before the Suez crisis, on which Britain exerted a decisive influence on international politics.

For many observers, however, the credit really belonged to Chou En-lai, who returned to China describing Geneva as a huge victory while the Chinese press continued to blast the American delegation for trying to obstruct the outcome. If Chou acquired an unearthly glow in the eyes of many British onlookers, this was partly thanks to the fact, relayed back to Washington by the *New York Times*, that 'many British regarded the [US] administration's China policy as the main impediment to peace in Asia'.[35] The Chinese delegation, meanwhile, had not emerged from behind the Iron Curtain spouting messianic dogma of the kind that might, only a few years earlier, have insisted that the way of struggle in all colonial settings was the 'way of Mao Tse-Tung'.[36] For all his ferocious diatribes against America, Chou had proved himself prepared to make concessions at key moments in the discussion. He had yielded ground on the composition of the international committee proposed to supervise the transformations in Indo-China. He had announced that the Viet Minh would undertake a ceasefire and join the Chinese in recognizing the non-Communist governments of Associated States such as Laos and Cambodia that might become independent members of the French Union.[37] He had agreed to separate consideration of Laos and Cambodia from discussion of the war in Vietnam.[38]

Chou had also engaged in a remarkable round of 'peripatetic diplomacy'[39] during a period when the conference was suspended towards the end of June. On the 24th, he flew off to India to discuss 'the Five Principles of peaceful coexistence' and, no doubt, other matters, with President Rajendra Prasad and Prime Minister Nehru, who had presented his own peace plan for Indo-China to India's House of the People a month previously.[40] He then flew on to Burma where he talked with Prime Minister U Nu, and smilingly presided over the issue of another friendly joint communiqué in which the rights of national self-determination were stressed and it was stated, in reassuringly plain terms, that 'Revolution is not for export'.[41] He had then returned briefly to China, landing at Canton and proceeding to the border with Vietnam where he would extract terms from Ho Chi Minh, who was actually highly reluctant to accept the division of Vietnam proposed in the Geneva Accords. While John Foster Dulles fumed, threatened, and set about countering the conciliatory developments at Geneva by drawing Asian nations into the defence pact that, in early September 1954, would establish the South-East Asia Treaty Organization, Chou had behaved as a world leader, not just engineering loyalty within his bloc, but performing exactly the kind of conciliatory peacemaking role that was claimed for the United

Nations, from which America insisted that the People's Republic of China should be barred. Having completed his tour Chou returned to Geneva via Moscow. Nine British sailors imprisoned by China were released with a carefully timed flourish just as he arrived. The smiling Chinese leader even found time for an audience and a toast of mao-tai with Charlie Chaplin.

As a British Conservative as well as a young diplomat in Peking, Douglas Hurd was predisposed to give the credit to Anthony Eden.[42] Yet Geneva was an altogether more emphatic triumph for the People's Republic of China. Without compromising in their hostility to America, which would remain at a peak for the rest of the year, the Chinese Communists had achieved an outcome that gave the USA no direct involvement in Indo-China.[43] They had sacrificed the Viet Minh yet they had also demonstrated that they were not mere stooges of the Soviet Union. In conduct that was no doubt coordinated with Molotov, they appeared instead as the regional power for South-East Asia, and one that was evidently capable of independent decision. They had opened a gap between West Europe and America, thereby preparing the way for trade relations to be established. The latter achievement was especially valuable given the importance that the Chinese government attached to the successful delivery of their first five-year plan, launched in 1954.[44]

It was with that aim in mind that Chou and his officials had started handing out invitations to interested British and European observers. 'Come and See' went the beaming message, which Chou En-lai would also relay to good effect when denying the existence of the so-called 'Bamboo Curtain' at the first Afro-Asian Conference at Bandung in April 1955, and delegations of more or less 'friendly' visitors were soon converging on airports around the world to travel to China—'all expenses paid',[45] as the salaried Douglas Hurd notes with remembered Foreign Office disgust.

Chou En-lai's performance at Geneva had been a sensation for many in Western Europe, one that filled them with a thrill of optimism about the chances of breaking out of the nuclear deadlock between the two blocs. In Britain, the optimistic 'spirit of Geneva' was embraced with particular enthusiasm by the Bevanite left. When I talked with Barbara Castle shortly before she died, she was still emphatic about the marvellous thing the Geneva breakthrough had been. It was, she remembered, 'absolutely thrilling': a chance to break the mould of conflict, and a moment of communication in which difficulties could actually be talked about. For politicians of the left, especially, it represented a challenge of the most testing variety. Nobody could know whether the thaw would last, but the chances of it so doing depended on Western politicians rising to the occasion in a way that would inevitably expose them to sharp criticism as fellow-travellers and dupes. As Castle insisted, the moment demanded righteous courage of the kind Aneurin Bevan had shown when he faced down Britain's almost unanimously hostile doctors to establish the National Health Service.

The British left appears to have been all but swept away by the optimistic contagion that was 'the spirit of Geneva'. Within the Labour Party the attempt at rapprochement may be dated back to a resolution passed, a few months after the end of the Korean War, at the annual Labour Party Conference at Margate in 1953. This had demanded that 'a mission of goodwill be sent to the Soviet Union and the People's Republic of China, by the Labour Party as a step forward to more friendly relations between East and West'. The resolution had been accepted by the National Executive Committee, but no reply was received when an approach was made to China's nearest representative in Geneva. The initiative had been renewed in 1954. Indeed, the secretary of the Labour Party, Morgan Phillips, travelled to Geneva to make arrangements for a delegation to visit China. He met Feng Hsuan on the afternoon of 2 June and went back to meet Chou En-lai in Geneva on 19 July, four days before the Chinese leader's return to China. The invitation was issued soon afterwards.

So, on 9 August 1954, eight delegates from the Labour Party's National Executive Committee set off on a 'Journey for Peace', claimed, with a sideways scowl at the Britain–China Friendship Association's earlier missions, to be the first 'independent Western Party delegation' to set foot in New China since 1949.[46] Clement Attlee, Aneurin Bevan, Edith Summerskill, and Wilfrid Burke were all prominent MPs. The party secretary Morgan Phillips also went, as did three powerful and far from radical trade union bosses: Harry Earnshaw of the United Textile Factory Workers Association, Henry Franklin of the National Union of Railwaymen, and Sam Watson of the Durham National Union of Mineworkers.

Fig 9. Departure: Edith Summerskill, Clement Attlee, and Aneurin Bevan at Heathrow, 9 August 1954.

With the Labour leadership embarked and seen off by a storm of adverse comment in the British as well as American press, further delegations were invited to follow them in time to attend the Liberation's fifth anniversary celebrations on 1 October. The 'very unpleasant rather third-rate Labour delegation' that Paul Hogarth was asked to chaperone had to be scraped up in a last-minute rush by the Britain–China Friendship Association. Though its members were appointed by the same organization, the late-travelling Second Labour Delegation was also a decidedly mixed group, and not just after it had been restructured as a 'cultural delegation'. Michael Foot remembered its Chairman, Ellis Smith, as 'a kind of middle of the roader in the Labour Party', while also describing the Gaitskellite George Lindgren of Wellingborough and Charles Royle, the MP for Salford West (whom Herbert Morrison had once described as 'the innocent butcher'—a trade that Royle had indeed pursued) as 'more central' than some of the others. As for Arthur Lewis, the member for West Ham North, he was an 'old-fashioned right winger', like some of the trade unionists.[47] Yet the delegation also included a clutch of left-wing Bevanite MPs—people, as Foot explains, who 'started on the left' and tended to stay there too. Captain John Baird, of Wolverhampton North-East, was Foot's dentist: 'I'm not sure he was a very good dentist but he was a damn good socialist, and a very strong supporter of Bevan and the NHS.' Will Griffiths of Manchester Exchange was 'a very nice chap indeed': an optician by practice, he was 'very courageous' and served as Parliamentary Private Secretary to Nye Bevan. The former schoolmaster Ben Parkin of Paddington North was 'a real left-winger too'. Among the four 'cultural' delegates added at the last minute, both Denis Mathews and Cedric Dover had Communist affiliations, as did John Horner, the General Secretary of the Fire Brigades Union: he was 'quite a formidable chap', as Foot recalled, who had got to know Rewi Alley in Shanghai before the Second World War.

As for the cultural delegation formed by Leonard Hawkes, Hugh Casson, John Chinnery, Stanley Spencer, Rex Warner, and A. J. Ayer, this really does appear to have been an improvisation. If asked why they were travelling to China, its members would have repeated, with varying degrees of amusement and disbelief, that they were going as representatives of the British arts and sciences. In their luggage, they carried a 'goodwill message'. Formally headed a 'Message from British Artists and Scientists to Chinese Colleagues', this document bore the signatures of 672 'well-known characters in British cultural life'. The list included just under a hundred architects, including Sir Patrick Abercrombie, Clough Williams Ellis, and Berthold Lubetkin. The artists included Ivon Hitchens, Augustus John, Peter Lanyon, Julian Trevelyan, Mary Fedden, Henry Moore, Ben Nicholson, Ceri Richards, and Roland Penrose. Among the many writers were E. M. Forster, Doris Lessing, Jack Lindsay, Kingsley Martin, Kathleen Raine, J. W. Robertson Scott (founder of the *Countryman*), Alex Comfort, Sylvia Townsend Warner, Naomi Mitchison, J. B. Priestley, Hugh MacDiarmid, Bertrand Russell, and Siegfried Sassoon. Benjamin Britain, Malcolm Arnold, and Sir Arthur Bliss were among the composers, and the signatories from the worlds of theatre and film included Paul Rotha, Basil Wright, Miles Malleson, Joyce Grenfell, and Dame Sybil Thorndike. There were many scientists and doctors, including Richard Doll and J. D. Bernal, while those listed under 'Universities' included G. D. H. Cole, E. R. Dodds, William Empson, who had himself recently returned from China, Bonamy Dobree, Lancelot Hogben, Arnold Kettle, C. Day Lewis, J. B. S. Haldane, Christopher Hill, J. H. Newth, Maurice Dobb, and Arthur Waley. The six 'cultural delegates' had been invited to travel to Peking in order present their 'Message from British Artists and Scientists to Chinese Colleagues' at a special ceremony held as part of the fifth anniversary celebrations. The text reads as follows:

'We, the undersigned men and women, who are concerned with the arts and sciences, send you our greetings.

We have a profound respect and admiration for the past achievements of Chinese civilization, from which we in the West have still much to learn. In particular we need more information about cultural and scientific activities in present-day China. We believe that the exchange of ideas and information between Britain and China can be fruitful for the future development of art and science in both countries, as such exchanges have been in the past. We believe that close cultural relations can do much to foster mutual understanding and friendship between our two peoples. It is our earnest wish to see an end to all the dissensions which at present threaten to separate us. With these aims in view we are determined to work for the fullest scientific and cultural exchange between our two countries. We feel sure that we can look forward to your cooperation.'

It may seem remarkable that anyone considered this bland statement worth lugging across the world. Though 'presumably drafted by Communists' as A. J. Ayer had quickly concluded, it was indeed 'extremely innocuous' in its contents—'effectively saying nothing more than that the signatories respected the ancient culture of China and hoped that any political differences that might arise between our respective governments could be settled by peaceful means'.[48] If it was indeed vague to the point of non-existence, this reflects its drafters' desire to open a passage through the polarized ideological sensitivities of the time, to skirt around the factionalism for which the left and its China campaigns were well known, and to avoid bringing down anti-Communist wrath on potential signatories who, only two years previously, had seen Joseph Needham being savaged and the Dean of Canterbury turned into a laughing stock. The statement sent 'greetings' without binding its signatories to any explicit ideological solidarity with the Communist 'Liberation'. It looked forward to 'future development' without expressing any idea of how, and under whom, it might be brought about. It regretted the division between East and West, but avoided openly taking sides in the ongoing war between Capitalism and Communism. It spoke of both science and the arts without engaging the polemics that had accompanied both as they had been taken in contrary directions on either side the Iron Curtain. Indeed, science and culture were projected as the neutral stuff of a benign new International in which common interests could be recognized across all frontiers and curtains too.

Three years later, it would be remarked as a matter of fact that these visitors had travelled 'at the invitation of the Chinese government through the Britain–China Friendship Association'.[49] This was true enough, despite the diplomatic note on the declaration insisting that their mission was not the work of any 'organization', whether newly established or already existing, but had been prepared by a number of 'friends of China in professional circles including some who visited China in 1952'. The sheets were circulated for signatures 'when it became clear that a message of this kind would receive the support of some of the men and women who have made distinguished contributions to the arts and sciences in our country'.

There had been no public campaign, announcement, or advertisement; and the 672 people who signed the statement of goodwill were raised by an 'informal committee' of three people: Andrew Boyd, an architect with the London County Council, Donald M. Ross, a Canadian biologist then working at University College Hospital, London (who had indeed visited China with the B–CFA delegation of 1952), and Denis Mathews, an artist and critic (not least on BBC Television's Panorama programme, launched in 1953), who was then running the Contemporary Art Society, and who would himself fly to China as a member of the Second Labour Delegation.

Such was the level of happenstance involved in the drafting of the statement of friendship, that Mathews almost missed the vital meeting. His widow Margaret remembers him describing how he happened to be driving past the Baker Street mansion block where it was held, when he looked down to see the invitation, which he had so far neglected, lying on the dashboard and realized that he happened to have arrived just in time. However loose the arrangements, the statement, together with the ramshackle cultural delegation formed in response to the Chinese government's invitation to take it to China, was indeed a product of the new 'Friendship' association. A. J. Ayer recognized it as a fellow-travelling if not openly Communist proposal when he got the call informing him that the Chinese government had invited him to go. And what of Stanley Spencer, who admitted to feeling 'trembly' as he surveyed the first plane at Heathrow Airport that September morning? Years later, it would be rumoured that this home-loving son of Cookham had only embarked for China because the authorities there had confused his name with that of the left-wing poet, Stephen Spender, and invited the wrong man.[50] This story may at moments have been tolerated by Spencer himself (perhaps it spared him raised eyebrows and accusations of fellow-travelling naiveté). Yet it is also wholly untrue, as both Paul Hogarth and John Chinnery would insist—'absolute nonsense' was Chinnery's emphatic retort.[51] The delegates had been selected in England and Spencer's letter of invitation, which was accurately addressed, had come from Dr Donald M. Ross. Writing on 19 August 1954, the Canadian zoologist reminded Spencer of the statement of friendship he had earlier signed and explained that the Chinese authorities 'would now like five of the signatories of the declaration to take it to them in person', and to spend a month in China as guests of the 'Chinese People's Society for Cultural Relations with Foreign Countries'.[52] By way of encouragement, Ross added that Sir Hugh Casson had 'accepted an invitation to represent the architects'.

That Spencer hesitated over the decision is indicated by the fact that he twice made his way to University College London to discuss the invitation with Dr Ross and, it would seem, to try to wriggle out of the trip. When he announced his reluctance to travel by air, giving the implausible grounds that 'I would like to have seen the country', Dr Ross insisted there would be plenty of opportunities since the journey, which he expected to take about five days, would consist of three-hour flights, with numerous stops along the way. Spencer also suggested his old friend and former brother-in-law Richard Carline as a far more appropriate representative of Britain's artists: 'I asked if he could not go as he was so good at immediately reacting to what he sees & doing on the spot the most original paintings.'[53]

Spencer described his quandary to members of his family. He would 'have hated to turn this chance down', as he explained to his niece and sister-in-law, yet his acceptance of Ross's invitation had been 'subject to getting such official information as will satisfy me'.[54] Though aware of widespread and by no means only official disapproval of such exercises in 'friendship', he more or less admitted the truth of his brother Gilbert's verdict: 'You only went because you were afraid not to.'[55]

Spencer's invitation had hardly come out of the blue. Even if not wholly conquered by the 'spirit of Geneva', he had his own ways of approving the 'friendliness' that might flower between the distant and ideologically divided peoples of China and Britain, and this was not the first time he had opposed the nuclear-enhanced hostilities of the early Cold War. In 1952 he had shown work in a group exhibition of realist work organized by 'Artists for Peace', an initiative formed by John Berger and others, including various members of the Artists International Alliance, after a proposed Sheffield Peace Conference had been abandoned thanks to government refusal to grant visas to all but Pablo Picasso and a handful of other international participants.[56] If Richard Carline came to mind in Spencer's discussions with Ross, this may be because Carline had helped to winkle Spencer out of Cookham and launch him on his way to Peking in the first place. Carline was, as his late wife once told me, a 'fellow-traveller'[57] but never a Communist Party member (Paul Hogarth would remember Carline as 'mildly radical').[58] Having been chairman of the Artist's

International Association and also campaigned for refugees from Nazism in the late 1930s, Carline had later joined the Britain–China Friendship Association, convening meetings of the 'artists' committee' at his house in Hampstead. Whether or not Carline had initially recommended Spencer as a possible signatory or delegate, he felt sufficiently involved to ask Paul Hogarth to keep an eye out for him should their paths cross in China.[59]

PART II

One Good Elk and Dinner with the Politburo
(Moscow)

'I'm not kidding… We've been in five countries since Prague. We've been round Everest and I don't know how Tensing climbed it. We've been to Moscow twice but we couldn't get across the river. And we were in the salt mines! They gave us swords. You slice the salt this way and that into blocks, then you pick a block up and hold it above your head and stagger up a big ladder.'

Tommy Lawton,
Arsenal player, Moscow, October 1954[1]

8

Flowers for Edith Summerskill

The first things to catch Paul Hogarth's eye were 'giant porcelain fruit bowls' placed on 'intensely blue chenille tablecloths'.[1] The waiting rooms resembled old-fashioned 'parlours' with their aspidistras, their 'out-sized' portraits of Stalin and Molotov, and the thickly piled carpet on which the travellers and their suitcases eventually came to rest. Hogarth's delegation had arrived in Moscow, and they would hardly stay long enough to measure how far the Soviet authorities' notoriously manipulative 'techniques of hospitality'[2] extended beyond strategically placed fruit bowls, potted plants, and sumptuous banquets of the kind that had been laid on for Western visitors ever since the early days of the Bolshevik revolution.

As they were driven along the 'broad Yaroslav highway', Hogarth and his band of previously untravelled shop stewards watched something resembling 'suburbia' give way to the 'vast planned area' of the new Moscow State University and glimpsed the city's other vigorously ornamented skyscrapers in the distance. Sometimes known as the 'seven sisters', these towers were Stalin's gift to Moscow: grandiose buildings of state intended, so the Secretary of the Labour Party, Morgan Phillips, had reckoned as he swept through with Attlee, Bevan, Summerskill, and other members of the National Executive Committee, to establish a 'great western metropolis' where previously there had been a 'haphazard' series of towns and villages clustered around the Kremlin.[3] Arriving to take up his post as British ambassador in October 1953, Sir William Hayter had seen these novel presences gleaming against an inky sky and momentarily imagined that the towers of the Kremlin must have been newly whitened as they had been in the eighteenth century.[4] By 1956, so Hayter would also recall, a British Minister of Housing, Duncan Sandys, only had to mention these skyscrapers to provoke Khrushchev into a tirade against Stalin's 'wasteful extravagance'. In Hogarth's eye, however, they were less provocative. They resembled nothing so much as 'insurance buildings of the 1920's' and their 'fretted silhouettes against the setting sun' gave 'the wide flat landscape a dream-like grandeur'.[5]

Like the members of Professor Hawkes's cultural delegation, Hogarth was put up at the Savoy Hotel, where he found not a shining new world but an unflushed labyrinth of reactionary fixtures: 'numerous chambers and passages...stuffed with a remarkable variety of elaborate furniture, paintings and bric-à-brac'. In pre-revolutionary days, this had been one of the *grands hôtels* of Europe, and it seemed to Hogarth that 'nothing except the clientele' had changed. A *belle époque* ceiling by Leon Bakst 'menaced' him as he unpacked his bags. He recorded 'brassy lifts, piloted by Tolstoyan porters' and 'platoons of elderly women servants' marching about beneath vast chandeliers. On the approach to the hotel's subterranean restaurant, 'a giant stuffed bear rampant was unexpectedly encountered in the chiaroscuro of an endless passage. I almost expected to meet Repin at dinner.'[6]

Hogarth spent a morning drawing the Kremlin churches from across the Moscow River, watched by curious children and a

Fig 10. Hugh Casson, hotel landing, Moscow, ink drawing, 1954.

group of building workers who treated his emerging sketch as the occasion for an argument about realist aesthetics. Though unable to speak Russian, he imagined that one of his proletarian critics was making the case for a dogmatic naturalism, insisting that 'everything must be put down', while his comrade, a more sophisticated realist like Hogarth himself, used vigorous thumb gestures to insist that 'liberties could be taken to express mood and atmosphere'. Another of these curious workers turned out to be a former gunner who spoke a little German and wanted to commission a drawing of his children. Hogarth was leaving for China the next evening, so he made a sketch of the man instead and then went off with the *Daily Worker's* Moscow correspondent, Ralph Parker (who would later translate Alexander Solzhenit-syn's *One Day in the Life of Ivan Denisovich*), to visit the vast monas-tery of Zagorsk where 'wrinkled-faced babushkas' chanted among marvellous icons and a group of youths departed for their national service, waved off by friends with flowers and folk songs performed to a nostalgic accordion accompaniment.

Hogarth and his party of more or less lumpen shop stewards would soon leave Moscow as scheduled. Not so the six members of Leonard Hawkes's cultural delegation. They passed through the same airport lounge as Hogarth (Casson registered 'fringed

Fig 11. Hugh Casson, Moscow skyline, ink drawing.

portières' as well as the electrical wires and tractors filling the background of the portrait of Stalin), and also found themselves sharing rooms in the Savoy Hotel, where Casson recorded the 'usual Edwardian sale room interior'. They were then stuck in the city for a period that threatened to stretch out indefinitely as Stanley Spencer babbled away with 'endless tales of Cookham & Macedonia & Belfast'. The cultural luminaries ate and drank, and became increasingly 'angst-ridden' about the delays to their flight, and mistrustful, too, of the 'promises' made by the Chinese embassy in response to the pleas of Rex Warner and John Chinnery, the latter being 'kept at it as dogsbody' (Casson). There was, as Chinnery himself recalls, intense pressure on China-bound flights and, regardless of their impotent warnings that they would soon have to turn round and go home, priority was given to more serious Communist delegations from Eastern Europe.[7]

With all expenses paid but no 'official' status to invoke, the cultural delegation experienced Moscow as five days in limbo. Interpreters made reassuring noises as they led the little party from one diverting attraction to the next, and the Britons may have felt additionally humiliated by the increasingly evident fact that the Soviet authorities did not even judge them worthy of the 'close surveillance' they had been warned to expect. By 20 September, which they did not yet know to be their last day in the city, they were reduced to mooching around Moscow Zoo. Three weeks later, Hewlett Johnson, the blindingly optimistic 'Red Dean of Canterbury', would find proof here that animals as well as people stood to be reconditioned in the Soviet New Jerusalem. He would be shown a lion and a dog kept together in the same cage, and assured that the peacefully coexisting lion had refused to eat when the dog was removed. Likewise, 'prairie dogs and wolves' were also being 'brought up together', and they too 'did not fight' provided that there was no anxiety about food.[8]

The cultural delegation drew no such improving lessons. 'Rather bad, though one good elk', as Rex Warner scribbled in his diary. 'Shabby and wistful', noted Casson, who apparently found nothing here to inspire the Elephant and Rhinoceros Pavilion his practice would soon be designing for London Zoo. Stanley Spencer admitted that the place was 'dilapidated' and not kept up and yet it was also 'just what I liked', with 'the usual concrete erections & trees' and 'the late afternoon sun on the people' and 'Russian peasant types appearing here & there among the shrubbery'.[9]

No such uncertainty awaited the Second Labour Delegation, which passed through Moscow after the main rush to be in China for the National Day celebrations of 1 October, and embarked on an officially scheduled programme of receptions and visits extended over four days. They arrived at 2 a.m. on 6 October, which happened to be Barbara Castle's birthday, an event that the All-Union Society for Cultural Relations with Foreign Countries (VOKS) representative who met them at the airport, Comrade Constantine (remembered by James as 'a small round faced chap, with scar under chin'), immediately had them toasting with vodka. They were then driven to the National Hotel. 'Very Comfortable', noted Dr Derrick James, when he and Denis Mathews caught up with the party after their night in Prague, and found themselves sharing a 'perhaps slightly Victorian' room: 'just off the Red Square', as James scribbled; 'very warm and stuffy' and 'with a view of Lenin's tomb in the distance from the window. Slept like a log'.

'Today, once behind the Iron Curtain, every building, however well-known, every monument—even such prosaic objects as trolley-buses or chocolate cake—are invested with a new mystery, an atmosphere of the other side of the looking glass which gives a keener edge to everything observed.' Hugh Casson's point would be confirmed as the various delegates woke up in their grand hotels and stepped out into a world where nothing was quite as familiar as it seemed.

They looked at the cars. Despite the National Hotel's double windows, Derrick James was roused early on his first morning by a 'terrible row of motor horns' blaring outside. Peering out, he noted the 'immensely wide street, and the cars hooting at 'uncontrolled pedestrians' who poured across the junctions in 'huge hordes'. He also saw why the taxi that had brought them from the airport the previous night seemed constantly to be getting lost. It was, he observed, forbidden to filter left at traffic lights, and drivers therefore had no choice but to drive over the crossroad, swing round at the end of the control strip and then come back to make their turn from the opposite direction.

Fig 12. Hugh Casson, Moscow street scene, ink drawing.

After an enormous breakfast of salmon, yoghurt, potato salads, and eggs that seemed only to come in multiples of three, James and his colleagues were picked up by the little fleet of Intourist cars that would haul them around Moscow. Sensitive about the status of their party ever since it had been downgraded to a merely 'cultural delegation', some of the more status-conscious trade union bosses may have noticed that they had not been provided with the best car made in the Soviet Union, namely the 'ZIS', which was built like an American Buick. Though unmistakably 'the grade II car of Russia', the ZIM, was, in James's assessment, 'comfortable, quiet and quite lively'. A seven-seater with cloth upholstery and instruments 'styled in a contemporary fashion', it had a dashboard of metal grained to make it look like wood, and a chrome grille containing a push button radio that allowed for six channels, even though, as James surmised, only two were actually available.

They looked at the buildings. Striding along 'wide sweeping streets', Paul Hogarth found Moscow an 'exciting tumultuous spectacle where a bizarre imagery of the past jostled with a metropolitan present'. He was struck by the vivid contrast between the 'numerous construction sites, with their prefabricated assembling

A Timber House - Moscow -

Fig 13. Hugh Casson, A timber house, Moscow.

techniques' and the 'flamboyantly Victorian department stores and gold-domed cathedrals'.[10] A. J. Ayer too was impressed by the extraordinary speed with which new buildings were shooting upwards among ubiquitous tower cranes. He noticed that 'the unskilled labour force seemed to consist mainly of women, who worked like the sturdy peasants they appeared to be. There was a gang of them whom we could watch from the windows of our hotel as they tossed bricks around from dawn till dusk.'[11] Eric Hobsbawm, who visited Moscow later that year, together with Christopher Hill and two other British Communist historians, saw a little further into the condition of those toiling middle-aged women, deducing, in passing, that they were probably war widows.[12]

They looked at the clothes if not into the lives of the people. Casson judged the Muscovites 'cheerful' if 'unglamorously dressed', and the atmosphere 'curiously inspiring. Everybody looks as if he had a niche in life & wasn't ashamed of it.'. Late on 16 September, Rex Warner could be found reclining, glass in hand, in the Savoy Hotel's 'perfect' restaurant. It was the end of the cultural delegation's first day in Moscow, and they had not sat down for dinner until 11.45 p.m., having just come from a 'terrific' production of Verdi's *Aida* at the Bolshoi Theatre. There were 'some western tunes' in the repertoire of the Hotel's 'modified jazz band', and Warner was sufficiently recovered from his delegation's 'drinkless' and sleepless ordeal in Minsk to be able to report 'a general feeling of things going well'. The restaurant was plainly an exclusive haunt of 'the governing class', yet the clientele impressed him as quite diverse. He saw 'a character like Vronsky, ordering two bottles of champagne', and he noted: 'Women's dress various, but no fashion.'

A. J. Ayer would confidently extend that observation to the crowds on the streets too: 'One thing that particularly struck us was the drabness of people's clothes, the absence of any attempt on the part of either sex to cut any sort of dash.'[13] Passing through in early October, Barbara Castle also registered the 'scruffy drab, even unkempt appearance of the crowds...It is not merely that they are drably clothed; they look every inch proletarians, sons of toil, manual labourers, peasants, who have no pretensions to taste in clothing, furniture or personal belongings.'

Clement Attlee had resisted any such line of thought. Recalling how 'drab' the Muscovites had looked on his only previous visit, he was pleased to see women in 'light summer frocks' and 'good shoes'. Despite a persistent lack of variety in the shops, he would inform readers of the *New York Times* that 'there undoubtedly had been a great advance in the standard of dress'.[14] Casting an adamantly pro-Communist eye over the Moscow crowd, Paul Hogarth noted 'a few distinguished-looking usually bearded characters and haughty women with the carriage of a Sarah Bernhardt'.[15] These dubious relics aside, however, he was pleased to record 'a strong sense of being in a plebeian society'. Where A. J. Ayer registered a miserable absence of sartorial flair, Hogarth saw proletarian virtue and a healthy refusal of bourgeois narcissism in the demeanour of 'ordinary working people' who looked as if they had 'faced their responsibilities heavily and carried them out in the knowledge that it was right to do so'. His Muscovites were not the oppressed creatures of a totalitarian state, but 'people walking upright', to use the terminology that the Marxist philosopher Ernst Bloch was then elaborating in East Germany.[16] Their clothes might lack style yet, in Hogarth's eye, these heroic strivers were true and active subjects of history and far superior to the grotesquely rigged creatures to be found mincing about on fashionable streets in the capitalist West.

The delegates looked at one another too. As Denis Mathews noted in a letter to his mother, he was travelling with 'a hearty bunch of English left-wing politicians and trade unionists' who were 'falling over backwards to find everything wonderful here'. He added that 'so much of it is that there is no necessity to strain the point'.[17]

Of the various British delegations that passed through Moscow on the way to China that year, the one that most concerned the British ambassador, Sir William Hayter, was the first and most official group consisting of Clement Attlee, Aneurin Bevan, Dr Edith Summerskill, and five other members of the Labour Party's National Executive Committee. Initially, as was reported by a suspicious British press, the party had intended to pause here for only a few hours. However, three days before they departed from London on 9 August, it was announced that the Moscow municipal authorities had invited them to extend their visit.[18] In the event they stayed for two days, providing Hayter with a unique opportunity to inspect the Soviet leadership from close up—something that had previously been impossible thanks to 'the puerile etiquette of the Cold War'.[19]

During Stalin's last years, as Hayter would later recall, the members of the Soviet Presidium had been unknown to Westerners, only glimpsed as 'distantly visible, squat, flat-capped figures, on Lenin's tomb during ceremonial parades'.[20] Perhaps because Stalin had disliked men taller than himself, 'they were all approximately the same size and shape, short, powerful men whom no one could really tell apart'. Some of these shadowy figures had appeared alongside Stalin at banquets held during the years of alliance in the Second World War, but they had receded during the subsequent Cold War and 'could hardly be distinguished except by the presence or absence of moustaches or spectacles'. After Stalin's death, in March 1953, those members of the Presidium had begun to step out of this isolation, encouraging Hayter, who had arrived in Moscow as British ambassador in October of that year, to hope that this new policy of 'accessibility' might lead to 'frank, confidential discussions' in which East–West problems were sorted out by reasonable human beings.

Experience would soon enough convince Hayter to draw a different conclusion: 'Each of the Soviet leaders carried his own private Iron Curtain around with him. Responses were predictable;

conversations were like *Pravda* articles on one side and *The Times* leading articles on the other; well-grooved long playing records went round and round.'[21] Such had been his growing sense of frustration at this ideological freeze that the British ambassador had started wondering whether his government might not be well advised to close its hugely expensive embassy in Moscow. Yet the optimism prompted by the death of Stalin had continued to flare, however fitfully, through the dinners and receptions of the following year.

The first occasion, so Hayter recalls, on which foreign ambassadors were invited to sit with Molotov and other members of the Council of Ministers had been the reception following the anniversary celebrations of the Russian revolution on 7 November 1953. The event was not without its difficulties. The Soviet Minister of Defence, Nikolai Bulganin, got so drunk that he had to be led away from the table—an awkward moment even though he was replaced by Marshal Zhukov, the great Red Army commander who had vanquished Hitler during the Second World War but had hardly been seen since falling from Stalin's favour and being demoted in 1946. The American ambassador, meanwhile, had been seated next to the East German leader Walter Ulbricht, a loyal, indeed craven, Stalinist with whom not the slightest thread of conversation was deemed permissible. It quickly became apparent that some of the toasts at these events were going to be awkward too. Even when not intended as hostile acts of Cold War, they served to test the limits of the 'peaceful coexistence' that was raising such hopes and fears in the wake of the Geneva Conference.[22]

Western ambassadors in Moscow had experienced an earlier encounter with the Soviet leadership in July 1954, when they were invited to participate in a dinner for the Chinese Prime Minister, Chou En-Lai, stopping over on his way back to Peking from Geneva. Soviet and Chinese leaders had not been seen together before, and the ambassadors studied their glances and gestures for any sign of stresses in the supposedly 'indissoluble relationship' between the two Communist regimes—a relationship that was perfectly flawness in official statements, and would remain so in the report Chou En-lai would give to the Chinese government on his return from Geneva, which betrayed no dissatisfaction with

China's place among 'the brother countries headed by the Soviet Union'.[23]

The Attlee delegation, which passed through a month later, was given a much closer view of the Soviet leadership than the British embassy had at first expected: perhaps, so Hayter suggests, because the Russians, whom he had seen being 'teased' by Chou En-lai on account of their refusal to learn foreign languages or to allow their wives to join them at receptions,[24] were apprehensive that the British mission might be a bloc-breaking exercise, intended, as they eventually suggested to the British visitors, to 'drive a wedge between Communist China and the Soviet Union'.[25] As protocol demanded, Hayter had approached Andrey Vyshinsky (formerly Stalin's infamous state prosecutor but now demoted to Deputy Minister of Foreign Affairs), to invite Khrushchev, then Secretary of the Communist Party, to join Attlee and the other Labour politicians for dinner at the embassy. The reply came that Khrushchev would indeed attend, and that he would be joined by the Premier and Chairman of the Council of Ministers, Georgy Malenkov, the Trade Minister Anastas Mikoyan, the Foreign Minister Vyacheslav Molotov, the Vice-Minister of Foreign Affairs Vyshinsky, the former Head of State and Chairman of the All Union Council of Trade Unions, Nikolay Shvernik, and by the Mayor of Moscow, Mr Mikhail Alekseyevich Yasnov. Moreover it was announced that the entire Labour delegation would be dining with the Soviet leadership the day before.[26]

That initial dinner with the Presidium had taken the unexpected form of a 'country house party', held in the former home of Maxim Gorky, a classical house set among silver birches and pines at Uspenskoye, some 25 miles from Moscow. In Hayter's account of the evening, Molotov features as 'the genial, fatherly host' and Mikoyan as 'the court jester'. Khrushchev, who did most of the talking, impressed the ambassador as 'repulsive and blundering, and startlingly ignorant of foreign affairs. I reported afterwards that he seemed to be practical and cunning, rather than intelligent, like a little bull who if aimed the right way would charge along and be certain to arrive with a crash at his objective, knocking down anything that was in his way.'[27] As for Georgy Malenkov, who would be ousted within a matter of months and replaced first by Nikolay Bulganin and then by Khrushchev himself, Hayter recalled him as 'mostly silent, smiling and playing with a flower'.

The Times report of this unexpected encounter was a bit more detailed, thanks to information gleaned from Morgan Phillips, who had attended the occasion as General Secretary of the Labour Party. He revealed that Malenkov, not content with expressing a desire for closer relations with Britain, had walked out into the gardens of that country mansion, which 'might easily have been the setting for a Turgenev play',[28] and gathered a bouquet of red, white, and blue phlox, which he then graciously presented to Dr Edith Summerskill.

Aneurin Bevan, who mistook Gorky's villa for Malenkov's 'private house', remembered the toasts as 'innumerable and tedious. Nothing seemed too trivial or banal to serve as an excuse for a toast'.[29] Though more impressed by Malenkov, whom he judged the 'ablest' of the Soviet leaders, Bevan also records that Khrushchev, who would explain that he was able to be more 'forthright' because his office lay outside the government, made 'a very blunt speech', explaining, with his glance shifting between Attlee and Bevan, that he 'realized there were differences in the Labour Party and even in the delegation'. He commended the newly published *Tribune* pamphlet, *It Need Not Happen*, in which Bevan, Barbara Castle, Harold Wilson, and three other 'Bevanite' MPs, had argued against the rearming of West Germany as part of the European Defence Community. He also declared himself unable to 'reconcile the delegation's good wishes for the Soviet Union with the Labour Party's support for the European Defence Community'. Aware that this line of conversation would quickly place him 'at loggerheads' with the other members of the delegation, including the trades union barons who remained in control of the NEC, Bevan manoeuvred the conversation into an only slightly less awkward discussion of China's place on the UN security council.

The Soviet Presidium had never dined at a foreign embassy before, but they came to the British embassy the next night, and sat in a dining room distinguished by its painted ceiling and red silk walls hung with portraits—including one of George V, which Russian guests routinely mistook for a picture of Nicholas II, George's first cousin and the last tsar of Russia. The delegation's report to the Labour Party National Executive Committee declared that the atmosphere was 'cordial' at both these dinners, 'and we have full opportunity of expressing out views'.[30] According to *The Times*, 'the occasion was informal and the talk was gay and punctuated with laughter as the champagne flowed'.[31] After the dinner, the party split into small groups in the embassy's 'White Room' to discuss 'peaceful coexistence', 'east–west trade', and other subsidiary issues of the moment.

As the host, Sir William Hayter remembered the five-hour meeting as a somewhat less harmonious affair.[32] No one 'wanted to be bothered with Khrushchev', except Mr Sam Watson, General Secretary of the Durham Miners' Association, who tried and failed to convince the future Soviet leader of the fallacies of Communism. Attlee tried and failed to come to terms with Mr Mikoyan on the subject of freedom and democracy. Battered in return with fiercely wielded references to economics and dialectical materialism, he confirmed for his American readers that 'there is this great mental gulf between the hard-shell Communist and the West'.[33] Indeed, 'I was reminded of the man in Wells's story, "The Country of the Blind" who tried to explain what sight was, but when he told of the sky he assured the reader that overhead was a smooth dome.' Sam Watson found Khrushchev just as 'tight' on the question of Formosa/Taiwan, which he plainly considered a supreme example of 'the aggressive and anti-Chinese machinations of the "American Imperialists"'.[34] His ignorance of the West and its people seemed 'almost immeasurable', and he wasn't forthcoming about what 'peaceful coexistence' might actually amount to, except increased trade and 'no compromise over ideology and propaganda'. It was enough to drive Watson to some plain speaking:

> After a couple of hours of this I said to him: 'Now look here, Comrade Khrushchev. You are a miner, and I am a miner, and miners in all countries can talk to one another openly and with respect for one another's intelligence. Are you ever going to call off your propaganda war against social democratic parties, Britain's included? In short, do you want co-existence in the field of commerce and chloroform in the field of politics?'

Bevan, meanwhile, sat with Malenkov, waving away the embassy staff who offered to assist in their conversation. Bevan's own notes reveal that they were discussing the rearming of West Germany, a step that Malenkov strongly opposed, not least because it might assist the re-emergence of 'those elements that proved so difficult before', and that he was less worried by the embassy staff than by Edith Summerskill, who 'kept barging in' on their conversation.[35] Despite her interruptions, Bevan detected 'a definite shift of emphasis from the ascendancy of one dominant individual to group rule', and concluded that Khrushchev 'certainly is not another Stalin'.[36]

The 72-year-old Clement Attlee, meanwhile, had grown tired and withdrawn to a corner with Morgan Phillips. When asked which of the Russians he would like to join in conversation, he replied that he wished to talk with 'none of them'. When the Minister of Trade, Mr Mikoyan stepped in anyway, Attlee 'attacked him violently about Marxism, astonishing Mikoyan by what seemed to him the perversity of his views'. In his record of this outbreak, Hayter paired it with another 'slightly alarming' conversation he had with Mr Attlee, who was staying at the embassy: 'He suddenly said to me at breakfast: "Have you read Marx?" This struck me as rather a loaded question, coming from the head of the British Socialist Party to the British Ambassador in a Marxist country. I said nervously that I hadn't read it all but that I'd read the potted version supplied to us by the Foreign Office. "Haven't read any of it myself," said Mr Attlee.'[37]

The Labour delegation's version of this encounter was somewhat more forthcoming about the content of the discussion. In his 'Private & Confidential' report to the Labour Party's National Executive Committee, Morgan Phillips notes that the Russians were strongly anti-American, and opposed to the rearmament of Western Germany. They had argued that Western European countries should be able to formulate their own security pact, without involving the United States. Yet they were not on the warpath, and accepted the desirability of 'peaceful coexistence'. Indeed, Phillips anticipated that they would probably be prepared to form a pact between East and West Europe even with the USA still involved. In articles written for various British papers, Morgan Phillips suggested that the Soviet Union needed a 'long peace' in order to carry out their ambitious plans for the development of their country.

Having previously visited the Soviet Union with a Labour delegation in 1946, Phillips was impressed to see the extent of reconstruction already carried out since the war. The first indication of this transformation was provided by the eight- or ten-storey blocks of flats glimpsed from the plane as they landed in Moscow, but he and the rest of the NEC delegation would see the same story in various spheres of Soviet life: boosted industrial output, massive housing programmes, expansion of social services and cultural facilities, the fact that shops were now better stocked and the people better fed too.

Phillips also reported 'big changes in the attitude of the Soviet leaders'. In 1946, Stalin had informed his British visitors that Soviet Communism and the British Labour Party's social democracy represented different approaches to the same goal. Interested in the Labour government's nationalization of basic industries, the dictator had warned them, 'in complete seriousness', to anticipate trouble from Britain's 'clever and experienced bourgeoisie'—including the dispossessed coal-owners who may well 'rise up and organize a counter-revolution'.[38]

Six years later, Phillips acknowledged 'big changes in the attitude of the soviet leaders' now that Stalin was gone, including 'a greater readiness to admit criticism and errors'. There had not 'for a long time been a better opportunity for British initiative to dispel fear and suspicion' and 'this new group of Soviet leaders must not be allowed to drift into permanent isolation'. The 'road to peace' would be long and difficult, but the intense international interest aroused by the Labour delegation's trip proved that the world was 'awaiting British initiative to set us on that road'.[39]

Phillips made his own attempt to capture the new Soviet leadership in words—something he had to do if he was to sell as many articles as possible to newspapers back home. In his drafts and finished articles, Malenkov, who was then little known to readers in the West, is variously described as 'short and stubby, 'cheerful and chubby',[40] 'cheerful and short', and even 'cheerfully chubby'. Phillips also insisted that the Labour delegation's conversation with the Soviet leaders had repeatedly come back to 'the problem of achieving the basis of peaceful coexistence'. Both sides had been the victim of 'international tension', and both were burdened with growing expenditure on armaments. Despite this, Phillips felt 'grounds for a renewal of optimism. The dread of a new war and the threat of the hydrogen bomb and worse is common to all people everywhere—to Russians as well as ourselves.' His point, made over Moscow Radio and then repeated in an article drafted for the *Daily Telegraph* (which had already cancelled Phillips's contract for articles on the delegation's progress, citing as its excuse his frequent contributions to the co-operative weekly *Reynolds News*): 'Men and women the world over have similar basic needs and interests and are victims of the same hopes and fears.'[41]

Phillips's reports were surely bland enough, but the Labour delegation's activities in Moscow still caused frenzy in some areas of the British press. The *Observer* thought the whole trip ill-advised, and the *Daily Sketch* went into paroxysms of Cold War outrage when it was reported, in the *Manchester Guardian*, that the Labour leaders had joined their Russian hosts in drinking a toast to their next meeting 'in London'.[42] Taking this provocative concession as proof that the Russians, who would obviously prefer to visit Downing Street rather than the Labour Party's HQ at Transport House, were counting on the Labour Party to win the next election, it asked 'How do you fancy having your government picked for you by Moscow?'

It was apparent that 'peaceful coexistence' was not going to be easy. The idea had been commended by Stalin in the years before his death. It had since been reasserted by Malenkov and also by Chou En-lai, who proclaimed the same belief on returning to China from Geneva. The cause had been commended by Churchill and also by his Foreign Secretary Anthony Eden, whose reports from Geneva had welcomed the prospect of 'improved relations with China' as 'a real contribution to peaceful coexistence, which is still our aim and object with every country'.[43] Yet if a Communist writer could hope that, after Geneva, 'peaceful coexistence' was 'the new mood'[44] in Europe, it was also fiercely resisted by others. In London, the *Economist* condemned both the elderly Winston Churchill and the United Nations Assembly for their deluded 'wishful thinking'[45] insisting that the Soviets, who were aggressively convinced of the superiority of their system, were actually trying to break the Western European countries away from their powerful ally across the Atlantic. For them, so the *Economist* declared on 7 August 1954, 'peaceful coexistence' meant 'one camp without America'.[46] That view was shared by officials at the American embassy in Moscow. Their views were conveyed to the *Manchester Guardian's* 'special correspondent', who reported, on 15 August 1954, that 'American opinion in Moscow' took a dim view of the Labour leadership's encounters with the Soviet government, condemning the Soviet hospitality as an attempt 'to create a breach between the Labour and Conservative Parties' and to 'soft-soap British opinion at the expense of Anglo-American relations'. The Labour leadership would come home convinced that while 'peaceful coexistence' should definitely not be understood to involve 'acceptance of all that the Government of another country stands for', it did at least imply 'something more than the mistrustful non-belligerence which passes for peace to-day'.[47] To those Americans in Moscow, however, it was plain that in this matter as in so much else, the NEC delegation had been 'fooled'.

9

Just Like Manchester a Hundred Years Ago

A few weeks later, the members of the cultural delegation would find themselves traipsing around the Soviet capital with Cold War stereotypes falling apart in their minds. Hugh Casson noted the disintegration as he entered Red Square: 'I find as usual that it doesn't tally either with my imagination or with recorded accounts I have read.' The Kremlin was an even greater surprise. In A. J. Ayer's phrase, they had expected 'a grim, sinister fortress',[1] a vast bunker from which atom bombs and the many tentacles of global Communist conspiracy protruded. Yet this legendary bastion dissolved before their eyes, turning into what Casson described as 'a collection of cracker hats peeping over a red brick wall and about as sinister-looking as a plate of biscuits'. Venturing inside, he found the place to be 'a magical architectural museum…as mad and highly coloured as a toyshop. Never again shall I read without smiling the familiar journalistic cliché "lights burn late in the dreaded Kremlin to-night".' In the main courtyard ('nearly as big as the Horse Guards Parade'), Casson was surprised to see 'a manhole suddenly opens in the ground and two soldiers emerge'. Yet the sudden appearance of these men, 'who replaced the lid and walk purposefully away', did not prevent him from telling Rex Warner that the reality in front of their eyes quite dispelled any idea of 'wicked men in the Kremlin'. The journalist Michael Davie, who was in Moscow to cover Arsenal's friendly match against Moscow Dynamo (the sluggish British team was politely thrashed 5:0 on 5 October), also found the Kremlin to be something other than the 'windowless monolith' of Western expectation: 'Its brick walls have the lovely maturity of Knole,' he wrote, 'and the enclosed fairy-tale city is primrose yellow, white and gold.'[2] The players, who spent three hours touring the Kremlin's cathedrals and museums, may not have been so seduced: 'They seem to queue to go to bed here', said one adding: 'They don't get much of a chance…'.

The cultural delegation spent its first full morning examining relics in this unexpectedly 'ridiculous and charming' place. They went around the Cathedral of the Annunciation and the Cathedral of the Assumption, which Spencer found 'so moving that I felt tears behind my eyelids',[3] and joined the parties of workers and peasants—'pilgrims',[4] as Ayer called them—shuffling reverentially through the salons of the old palace. Warner records that Stalin's room was only 'seen in the distance' but there were closer exhibits that seemed as unlikely as their own presence in Moscow—a pair of boots made by Peter the Great, a platinum model of the Trans-Siberian express, a working pocket watch in which every part, including the spring, was made of wood. 'Rather like the Victoria and Albert Museum',[5] as Denis Mathews would inform his mother, having scrutinized rooms full of trophies preserved from the age of the tsars, and heard about the difficulties the Soviets had encountered in developing adequate cleaning techniques for the medieval icons in the Kremlin's three small churches.

Fig 14. Hugh Casson, Inside the Kremlin.

Visiting the Kremlin with the Second Labour Delegation, Derrick James also surveyed the assembled 'products of our Russian Craftsmen' and found some of the gifts made to the tsars—ivories, armour, and coaches, including one presented by Elizabeth I—to be 'rather blatantly ornate'. When one such 'horror' was described by the guide, Ina the interpreter displayed her independence by turning to the delegates and shrugging, '*She* says its beautiful!' Among the various examples of the Russian founder's art was a huge cannon, claimed as the biggest in the world, and a 200-ton bell, cast in the age of wood smelting, which, as Mathews noted, 'aroused enormous interest in the chap from the Union of foundry workers'.

Hemmed in by their lack of Russian as well as by VOKS representatives and interpreters, the delegations experienced Moscow as an itinerary of guided visits, receptions, and dinners, with magnificent performances at the Bolshoi Theatre thrown in for good measure. The British ambassador, Sir William Hayter, considered the Ballet then to be in ossified if still splendid condition: spectacular but without any trace of the great innovations of Diaghilev, Fokine, and Massine, it had a limited repertoire dominated by *Swan Lake*.[6] Yet this conservatism did not trouble many of the China-bound British delegates. Thrilled to find himself in the theatre where Tolstoy's Vronsky and Anna Karenina had met, Stanley Spencer adored Prokofiev's ballet *Cinderella*—'very lovely music with great sweeping themes'.[7] The lead part was danced by Olga Lepeshinskaya, who, according to Ayer, 'then ranked third or fourth in the hierarchy of Russian ballerinas'.[8] Ayer confessed to being 'no connoisseur of the art of ballet, but for what my opinion is worth I thought she danced as well as anyone that I had ever seen. I had once seen Pavlova perform in London but only at a time when she was past her best.' Rex Warner was more simply enchanted. 'Absolutely wonderful. Pure joy', as he wrote of *Cinderella*. He had been just as impressed by Verdi's *Aida* the night before: 'Wonderful theatre. High gold. Packed house of all sorts. Hundreds on stage. V. clever Rider Haggard sets.'

Hugh Casson judged the intervals and the scenes in the crowded foyers to be just as engaging as the ballet—surveying the apparently quite 'classless' audience, he singled out a 'Tolstoyan farmer' and a group of 'East European peasants' among the teeming exhibition of boots, beards, and open necks. Derrick James, who attended a performance of *Carmen* with the Second Labour Delegation, also remembered the Russians promenading in the entrance hall, 'walking round and round with their guests on their arms, going anticlockwise'. Wandering upstairs, he found himself in a gilded hall, with side rooms full of paintings and sculptures ('mostly not to my taste') and also, rather enigmatically, a large model of a trolley bus. On the delegation's second visit, they watched the great ballerina Galina Ulanova in Prokofiev's *Romeo and Juliet*: 'She dances exquisitely, but I don't know enough to tell whether she's better than Fonteyn.' Remembering his ordinary life at home, where a lecturer in anatomy had to live without limousines, grand hotels, and official solicitation, he concluded his theatrical comparisons by writing: 'Must have boxes at Covent Garden in future! They're so much better than the gods.'

The more industrially minded members of the Second Labour delegation experienced their moments of envy during daytime meetings of an altogether less rarified kind. During their afternoon visit to the All Soviet Council of Trade Unions, they sat and listened, while their Soviet counterparts described a trade union system that dwarfed anything that could be claimed by even the largest of these British barons. The Soviet comrades boasted 40 million members, and an extensive network of factory, area, and city committees organized under thirty-nine Central Industrial Unions in various branches of industry. They also claimed a vast collection of housing, holiday camps, rest facilities, and even 'preventoriums' devoted to the avoidance of disease.

The British visitors were informed that the Soviet trade unions enjoyed a more expansive role than their equivalents in Britain, where the class war had yet to be properly won. The mission included 'Development of national economy of USSR' and 'bettering the economic and cultural relations and conditions of the workers'. Here, as they noted in their report, 'workers activity' was not 'restricted to WAGES but also helps to increase productivity and to increase the output of capital and consumer goods'. The workers competed with the output targets set by the State, trying collectively to surpass and improve on them. In their workplaces they would attend mass meetings, agreeing targets with the Plant Director, and they also 'can and do criticize the management'. The British visitors, who had their own experience of a kind of 'joint consultation' in which decision-making power rested entirely with managers, noted the existence of Grievance Committees, and also that Soviet workers did not have to contribute to the cost of their social insurance. All this was counted as highly impressive, better than had been achieved in Britain, even in the notorious 'workplace Kremlins' that emerged in some large engineering works during the Second World War.

This positive perception was further embedded by a visit to the Stalin Auto Plant, where the delegation got out their notebooks and dutifully practised the art of dictation. The factory, they were told, was thirty years old, and the first car and truck factory to be erected in the Soviet Union since the revolution. It produced fridges and bicycles as well as lorries specially equipped to deal with terrible road conditions, and a large 8-cylinder limousine which had 'the outward appearance of a large, modern, American motor car'. There were 35,000 workers, 40 per cent of them women, and they followed methods of 'sub-assembly and final assembly' similar to those used in Britain. As Barbara Castle recalls, George Doughty, who was General Secretary of the Association of Engineering and Shipbuilding Draughtsmen, declared the plant 'to be up to Ford's standard in layout and equipment, though he criticized individual points like lighting and safety devices'. Castle noted that 'Workers received from 700 to 2,500 roubles a month, but 'all share equally in social benefits and additional benefits provided by factory e.g., rest home, Palace of Culture'. The latter offered many 'cultural and social amenities for all employees and their families including a number of crèches and kindergartens'. The delegation was pleased to find that 'control of the Palace of Culture is very largely with the Trade Unions', and that the factory also had holiday camps at various resorts, and nutrition clinics for those employed on heavy jobs or with 'weaker constitutions'.

The Moscow subway elicited further gasps of admiration, and not just from Barbara Castle, who records 'Very beautiful stations and brightly painted trains, all spotlessly clean'. James and Mathews had planned to duck out of their delegation's visit to a metro station, but found it difficult to refuse to go, and were soon glad to have failed. Half the party got lost on the way to the station—'helpless bastards' as James notes of his trade unionist colleagues. But the two cultural delegates had been amazed when they got there, finding a spaciousness that contrasted dramatically with the 'cramped feeling of the tube', and commending the air-conditioning system that distributed fresh and sweet-smelling air throughout the system. Built like 'vast underground halls', the stations were, as James wrote, 'filled with paintings, mosaics and sculptures, and richly decorated in various styles'. This décor had reminded Ayer of 'Lyons Corner Houses', and James too had his misgivings. Confronted by what he now recognized as 'the same old architectural problem', he noted that 'I can't get used to the gilded and ornamented appearance of things like tube stations, but I must admit that I infinitely prefer the [Moscow] Metro to the Tube'. He was especially impressed by a station built in 1935. He couldn't recall the name, but it was an austere and 'exquisitely proportioned' study in blue and stainless steel, and James could hardly believe it was the work of the same architect as the 'horror of illuminated stained glass' that was next down the line.

Completed the previous year, Moscow State University's new science building provided further evidence of the freakish scale of Stalin's monumental projects. It may have been 'wonderfully equipped', as Rex Warner noted, right down to its 'velocity lift', yet Barbara Castle found the largest of Stalin's seven neo-classical skyscrapers 'hideous in its brash grandeur'. Indeed, she likened it to 'a battleship riding the night with red lights swung from mast to poop'. A similar judgement can be inferred from the faces of Attlee, Bevan, and Summerskill, photographed a month earlier by Morgan Phillips as they gazed out over Moscow from a balcony high up on the tallest building anywhere outside New York City. The Labour leaders stand there looking uncomfortable, even stunned—and not just by the sight of a formidable industrial hammer carried by a heroic worker in the vast sculpture behind them.

Hugh Casson thought the 'handling of space reasonably good' but the finish 'shoddy' and the exterior 'clumsily detailed'. He had more reason than most to be curious. By 1954, he was already thinking about the new Arts Faculty building his practice would design for the University of Cambridge. Commissioned in 1952 (and subsequently overwhelmed by a disputatious collection of 'signature' faculty buildings by more individualistic architects), Casson's plan for the Cambridge site has been hailed as 'Britain's first large post-war university plan' and his preliminary watercolours of the scheme show a sequence of low polytechnic-like buildings with courts and open spaces with bicycles leant against autumnal trees. As a work of 'gentlemanly modernism',[9] Casson's scheme required neither heroic proletarian sculptures nor a massive assembly hall such as Castle found in Moscow State University, with rows of white columns and a 'grim' backcloth showing 'Soviet youth marching through hammers and sickles to their glorious destiny'. Described by Pevsner as 'an Eden of picturesque beauty', it was certainly not to be measured by the criteria employed by the guide at Moscow State University who informed Casson, like every other delegate, that 'If a baby was born here and spent one day of its life in every room it would be 25 years old when it left'.

Having surveyed the official 'sights' of Moscow, Barbara Castle concluded that 'the most interesting thing about the new Russia is its failure to produce a modern idiom in architecture, painting or furnishing'. Casson would almost certainly have agreed—as did Denis Mathews, who declared more robustly that 'the paintings are hideous and the new buildings just imitation American skyscrapers'. The judgement was not so easily accepted by the more 'stolid' Labour politicians and trade unionists in Castle's delegation. While accepting that the grand 'sights' of Stalin's Moscow contrasted sharply with the 'drabness' and evident poverty of the people, it was apparent, as Castle herself felt obliged to admit, that at least some of these hard-pressed citizens felt a compensatory pride in the monumental constructions of the Stalinist state. This would surely have been understood by other delegates, including Chairman Ellis Smith and the MP for Salford West, Charles Royle, both of whom shared Barbara Castle's background in north-west England. The Labour movement in which they had grown up certainly took pride in its institutions, modest as they were by comparison: not immense new universities like Moscow's, but the labour colleges and Peabody libraries (a fine example still stands among the most prominent public buildings in Smith's home town Eccles); not ostentatious palaces of culture or trades union-owned resorts on the Black Sea, but the Labour club and perhaps the bank holiday charabanc trip too; not the massive Moscow 'Gastronome', which Barbara Castle found to be 'a very crude drab store' with a 'gaunt and white' director who discoursed on food distribution under the command economy, but the Co-op with its popular dividends, its modesty, and its friendly smiles. Ellis Smith's respect for the ongoing reconstruction underlies his later insistence that he and his fellow delegates had found the Soviet people living 'in dread'[10] of another war: worried about rearmament in West Germany, and most reluctant to see their 'new towns' and heroically reconstructed cities destroyed all over again. Soviet officials had attempted to reassure Attlee on the same point, claiming that Stalin's gargantuan projects were a 'source of pride to the people'. Unlike Smith, however, the Labour leader continued to feel oppressed by these spectacular new developments, which must have 'absorbed an amount of labour and material that might have been used for more social purposes'.[11]

As they travelled through Moscow the members of the various delegations tried to pin down the shifting sights with the help of English comparisons, both inane and surreal. Some of these Anglicizing tropes were little more than momentary flourishes, which actually worked to emphasize rather than overcome the distance between these British visitors and the Soviet world in which they found themselves. Just as Prague had stimulated thoughts of Maidstone and Ashford in Derrick James's diary, so Ayer likened the decor of Moscow's metro stations to that of Lyons Corner Houses and Casson compared the old wooden houses that survived among Moscow's many building sites to ornate college barges half-sunk in the mud of the Thames at Oxford.

As these travellers no doubt realized, such stretched comparisons often failed to make convincing sense of Russia. They also tended to reduce England to a pile of implausible debris toppling forward from the back of a disorientated mind. Among the more consistently employed of these airborne analogies was the idea that the planes that hauled them to Moscow had actually carried them back into another version of Victorian England. This conceit was shared by the members of the cultural delegation. In his memoir, *Red Lacquer Days*, Hugh Casson explained the basis for this comparison: 'More and more does Moscow in 1954 look like Manchester a century ago. The same bustling development, the excitement of the new railways and factories, the pinafored school-girls, the over-decorated buildings, the tyrannical working hours, the belief in progress, the confidence in self.' Ayer would summarize the perception a little differently: 'Our overall impression of Russia at that time was that on the surface it was very like Victorian England. There was the same expanding economy, the harsh conditions of labour, a comparable jingoism, a similar sanctimoniousness and moral earnestness, the same predilection for social realism, contemporary Soviet painting being very like English academic painting of the mid-nineteenth century.'[12]

The 'Victorian' analogy impressed members of other delegations too. For Derrick James, the 'Victorian' quality of mid-twentieth century Moscow extended to its partiality for kitsch porcelain ornaments extending from china doves, ballerinas, and performing dogs, to more contemporary examples in which the various races of the world stand united and radiant in Communist harmony. As artists, both Paul Hogarth and Denis Mathews saw the same 'Victorian' influence in the nineteenth-century academic painting that still seemed to govern Soviet ideas of socialist realism: 'pretty terrible stuff', Mathews told his mother, comparing the works he had seen at the Tretyakov Gallery of Russian Art to the 'more banal' Victorian subject paintings rightly left to moulder in 'the Tate basement'. He added, 'I have said this in most positive terms to all the Russians I meet. When I see so much that is excellent about this country I can see no harm in frank speaking.' The same dim retrospective tendency was also revealed in the gilded rooms or 'parlours' with their ornate furniture and décor: many delegates noticed the anti-macassars covering the Soviet Union's sofas and armchairs, but it took Barbara Castle to name the fabrics, be it the 'yellow and gold damask', which she saw 'looped back in Victorian style' over the windows of the new state university assembly hall, or the 'red chenille' draped over so much of Soviet reality: the legs of the seats in aeroplanes, the doors of airport waiting rooms, tables in hotels and conference rooms, even wireless sets.

If there was a single moment when Rex Warner discovered that homely recollections could be dragged to mind by a chaotic sense of discrepancy rather than likeness, it occurred on the evening of 19 September, when he found himself in the northern outskirts of Moscow, gazing over a collection of rams with 'delightful people looking after them'. Watching these bucolic folk as they wove gladioli into the wool of their charges, he found himself thinking that 'they looked just like English chaps at any agricultural show'. Perhaps, as he stood there with Stanley Spencer and Hugh Casson, he was reminded of the agricultural show he had invoked thirteen years previously in his novel *The Aerodrome*.[13] Held every year on meadows by the river just outside a little English village, this was an unashamedly local event with roundabouts, beer that flowed free of the constraints normally imposed by the licensing laws, and prize vegetables displayed in the big marquee. Its paths were planks laid down on the marshy ground, and it also featured a shooting gallery, a prize bull named 'Slazenger', and little booths from which traders sold dogs and rabbits, wicker baskets, and walking sticks of ash.

In Warner's little English show the technological future had been represented by an alarming display of stunt flying laid on by the neighbouring aerodrome—deafening fighter planes that roar and dive overhead, upsetting the ladies and prompting the Rector to denounce the airmen as 'Crazy Monkeys' who would 'come to some harm' one of these days. Moscow's All-Union Agricultural Exhibition was of a wholly different order, and not just because technological modernization was of its essence. This huge site had been reopened earlier in 1954, after its pavilions were closed and its land put back into agricultural production during the emergency of the Second World War. Progressive agriculturalists and scientists from around the world would be invited to this forceful showcase to exchange experience—including some who played a leading role in the post-war transformation of British agriculture[14]—and passing political delegations were guided round the vast installation as a matter of course. The Secretary of the Labour Party, Morgan Phillips, spent a couple of hours here in August, together with Attlee, Bevan, and the other members of the NEC delegation, some of whom were photographed admiring furs and coats displayed in front of a didactic mural of sheep-shearing scenes. Phillips noted that over 2,000 exhibitions were under way, and also that 'the right to exhibit' was confined to people who had 'attained certain targets in the field of production'. Clement Attlee thought the place 'finely laid out' and the 'exhibits of good quality'; there was, he added, 'no regimentation, and we mingled with the crowd'.[15] Used primarily as an instrument in the education of Soviet citizens, the Agricultural Exhibition was said to be receiving up to 50,000 visitors a day, about a third of whom came from rural communities. These visitors received five-day tickets, which included the cost of travel to Moscow and accommodation in hostels, more of which were then being built to accommodate them. In an article drafted for *Reynolds News*, Philips remarked that 'This effort of education by emulation is characteristic of the Soviet regime'.[16]

The entrance to this vast showground was no modest turnstile attended by boy scouts or volunteers from the Women's Institute. Instead it was a vast monumental *propylaea* rising out of

Fig 15. Moscow All–Union Agricultural Exhibition: entrance (contemporary postcard).

formal flowerbeds: a totalitarian confection of pilasters, pedestals, and cornices, adorned with reliefs of heroic peasants, flanked by high poles bearing red flags and capped with a 27-ton sculpture by Vera Mukhina in which a rampant industrial worker brandished his hammer alongside the sickle of an equally rampant female collective farm worker. Inside, the delegates found a vast open agora, in which visitors might feel squashed by the sky and further reduced by the scale of the 'pavilions' scattered through the site. The All-Union Agricultural Exhibition was a massive propaganda machine dedicated to the agricultural capabilities of Stalin's Soviet Union, and its 'pavilions' bore not the slightest resemblance to hired canvas marquees. Dating, in many cases, from the 1930s, they were vast works of wedding-cake architecture designed to assert the diverse styles associated with the Soviet Union's various provinces and to harness them as engines of state propaganda. There was a major pavilion for each of the USSR's sixteen republics, and some sixty others devoted to selected aspects of agricultural industry as it was being transformed by proletarian science. A small plantation of improved wheat or barley could be inspected by the Michurin Gate, but it was in the Ukrainian Pavilion that Rex Warner found his rams: enormous creatures that were exhibited alongside an unfamiliar variety of sheep equipped with prodigiously 'extended bottoms'. He also noticed a 'Pavilion of the Potato', and, had time allowed, he might have visited others dedicated to techniques of garden cultivation, duck and goose husbandry, and the Soviet creed of Mechanization too.

Stanley Spencer, who accompanied Rex Warner on this unanticipated excursion, was also familiar with agricultural shows of the traditional English kind, even though, in his Thames-side village of Cookham, the modern interruption was more likely to be provided by a passing steam launch full of raucous bean-feasters than by a diving stunt plane. It is said that Spencer would sometimes donate a painting to be given away as a tombola prize at Cookham's summer fair; and he had long been working on a series of paintings in which Christ materializes in the midst of the annual Regatta, suddenly converting that languid festival into a final Day of Judgement. Seated in a wicker chair in the horse-ferry barge on a Thames crowed with punts, he leans forward sharply

Fig 16. Moscow All-Union Agricultural Exhibition: people in rain (photo: Derrick James).

to condemn the smart-shoed hotel-keeper and his venal wife for making a financial killing rather than a resurrection out of Cookham's annual festival. There was no indication of divine intervention at Moscow's Agricultural Exhibition, yet Spencer found things to admire nonetheless. He delighted in the 'magical' lights playing across the fleeces of massed Ukrainian sheep, and he enjoyed walking out of doors among the 'gorgeous' fountains, including, no doubt, the new 'Friendship of Nations' exhibit in which water rained down on sixteen sculpted maidens representing the Soviet republics. In all, Spencer estimated, there were more than a thousand jets, and their spray cast a soft haze into 'the evening's goldenness'.[17]

Like Warner, Spencer was amazed by the 'gigantic' scale of the Soviet exhibition. An English village show might include three or four rams, confined on the local recreation ground with the help of string and a few bales of straw. But there were a good five hundred specimens in the Moscow exhibition, and each one was utterly enormous. John Chinnery remembers Spencer contemplating the testicles of one of these Soviet rams, and musing that, had he himself been so prodigiously equipped, he might have been better able to cope with Patricia Preece—a financially embarrassed and apparently also fortune-seeking Lesbian whom he had married after abandoning his first wife Hilda Carline. The other cultural delegates may not have known Spencer's cruelly rendered nudes of Preece (in one of the most famous she is placed against a raw and undressed leg of mutton), but they had heard more than enough by now about the scheming Patricia and the way she had got the better of a tiresome homunculus named Stanley.

The Second Labour Delegation passed through the Agricultural Exhibition on 8 October, by which time the nights were closing in and the whole site was glistening with rain. Derrick James recorded that the thing was done on a 'quite enormous

Fig 17. Moscow All-Union Agricultural Exhibition: large man with melon (photo: Derrick James).

Fig 18. Moscow All-Union Agricultural Exhibition: collective farmer from Uzbekistan (photo: Derrick James).

scale', all very lavish, and we saw only a fraction of it. He recalls meeting a 'wonderful old man from Uzbekistan', who was the officer in charge of the Uzbekistan pavilion. He was 74 years of age and had 'a grip like a mincing machine'. Having contrived a new way of growing grapes, he was 'a Stalin prizewinner, and a very important old boy'. A mural in the pavilion showed his innovative method, which seemed to involve nothing more progressively

Fig 19. Moscow All-Union Agricultural Exhibition. collective farmer from Georgia (photo: Derrick James).

scientific than training vines first up vertical supports, and then drawing them across on poles at a slight angle to the horizontal. The aim was to provide sufficient space between the ground and the fruiting vine for one of Stalin's red tractors to pass, thus enabling the introduction of 'mechanical cultivation'. Whatever they made of this new 'method', Dr James and his colleagues sampled the grapes and found them 'splendid, large and juicy'. The celebrated agriculturalist from Uzbekistan also sliced up an enormous melon for his visitors. James ate his piece to show willing ('I don't go for melon much') and deferred to the 'authorities present', including a hefty stooge, who declared this particular fruit of Soviet engineering to be 'splendid' too.

The grandiose scale and style of the Agricultural Exhibition precipitated another argument within the Second Labour Delegation on the subject of Soviet architecture. 'The Party boys' insisted that 'these pavilions are expressive of local cultures' but

Fig 20. Moscow All-Union Agricultural Exhibition: the Michurin Garden. 1954.

James himself found it 'difficult to believe that any local cultures are quite so flashy'. 'Perhaps,' as he noted, 'we shall never agree on this problem'. The pavilions at the Agricultural Exhibition impressed Barbara Castle as 'lavishly ornamental and flamboyant in design. The general effect is of splendour and some of the displays are well arranged (e.g. the grape hall in the Uzbekistan pavilion) but it is all very conventional: there are no creative flights of inspiration as in the Festival of Britain.' Centred around the Royal Festival Hall on the south bank of the Thames, that event may well have offered a more telling British comparison than the regatta or village agricultural show. Yet the comparison had apparently not detained the former architectural director of the Festival of Britain. After touring Moscow's crowded spectacle with Warner and Spencer, Sir Hugh Casson admitted only to 'a nightmare trek round the Agricultural Exhibition where, owing to some error of translation, we are taken for a party of experts on sheep and, falsely attired in white coats, spend two hours plunging incurious hands into thick fleeces'. That done, he and his tired colleagues made their way back to their hotel, unaware that, while some aspects of the mechanized and genetically improved future they had just inspected might indeed be realized over the decades to come, the All Union Agricultural Exhibition would only survive into the twenty-first century as a rather tacky and in part privately owned shopping mall.

10

The Tragic Thoughts of Chairman Smith

Prepared for another display of florid Victoriana, Derrick James was relieved to find the interior of the Palace of Moscow Soviets 'modern in a remarkably restrained way for the Russians'. Having arrived after lunch on Thursday, 7 October, he and the other delegates were ushered into a large room where they sat around a long felt-covered table laden with bottles and packets of cigarettes and cigars. A year or two previously, so James was informed, the bottles would have contained vodka. Now, however, a drive against drunkenness was under way, and the refreshments consisted of some 'remarkably nice aerated fruit drinks, of orange, blackcurrant, pear, grape etc. flavours. They are quite unlike anything I have had elsewhere, and after a time one gets to like them rather.'

The reception at which the Second Labour Delegation was officially welcomed to Moscow was altogether more modest than that extended to Attlee, Bevan, and the other members of the NEC some two months earlier. They were received by Mikhail Yasnov, the powerful Mayor of Moscow, his Deputy, and half a dozen representatives of the City Council. Yasnov spoke proudly of the vast building programme in which his city was engaged. He counted up new hospitals by the dozen, and chased the tally of recently built schools up into the hundreds. Remembering how the British Labour government of 1945 had struggled to get their public housing programme off the ground at all in the slumped post-war economy, the Labour delegates may have been disconcerted to hear not just that Russia's central government plan demanded that Moscow City Council produce 10 million square metres of housing by 1960, but also that 2 million of those had been delivered in the previous two years, while 564,000 were presently under construction.

After the Mayor's welcome it was the turn of the delegation's leader, Mr Ellis Smith, to respond. Smith was a great admirer of state planning—indeed, in the 1940s he had repeatedly argued for the British adoption of a 'Five Year Plan for Peace, Joy and Plenty'.[1] Yet this was not the theme on which the MP for Stoke-on-Trent South chose to elaborate during the course of his 'rather rambling' reply. Instead, as James noted in his diary, he talked about 'how he had been in Moscow in 1927 and the streets were cobbled & the people poor, and look at them now. He went on in this strain for some time, and said he had seen Trotsky pursued across the Red Square.'

Smith's speech was to become 'painfully familiar' (James) to his fellow delegates over the days and nights to come. They had to sit through it again two days later, on Saturday night of 9 October, at a big dinner organized by their host, the All-Union Society for Cultural Relations with Foreign Countries (VOKS). This, as Denis Mathews wrote, was 'a tremendous banquet that went on for hours—speeches of unbelievable platitudes and caviar, smoked salmon, meat, chicken, meat, fish, soup in endless relays with vodka all the way'.[2] The Chinese ambassador was there along with the USSR's Deputy Foreign Minister and the First Secretary of the British embassy, remembered by Barbara Castle as a congenial fellow named Dobbs, whose Australian wife entered fully into the spirit of the occasion, even replying in Russian to one of the toasts. As for Ellis Smith, Castle's diary records that he 'made our blood run cold with long incoherent speeches about his previous visits to Russia and his working class roots. His leadership keeps causing trouble but apart from that we are a reasonably happy delegation.'

Chairman Smith may have been a man of 'stupendous simplicity' but Derrick James came to view him quite sympathetically when discussing his own newborn son, delivered while the Second Labour Delegation was en route between London and Moscow:

Ellis is a short grey haired man in his fifties, of an almost painful sincerity. He is one of those people of whose integrity one is convinced within a few moments of meeting him. He speaks slowly, in a broad North Country accent, and is the senior Parliamentarian of the party. He is readily emotional. After I arranged to phone home from Moscow, I heard that he was about to become a grandfather for the first time, and suggested that he should phone to ask after his daughter. He swallowed, gripped my arm, and his eyes were moist when he said "You see, I nearly lost her", and turned away with something like a sob. I gathered from another MP that his daughter was nearly killed in a car crash some years ago. He is a dear old man, I think, but seems utterly unsophisticated. Of course he is probably damned smart in fact, but this is not the way everyone seems to regard him.

Sincerity, Integrity, Simplicity...Smith was much loved in the north-west of England: a caring and highly principled man who formed an inspiring role model for the young, he was even referred to as 'Saint Ellis' in his constituency in Stoke-on-Trent. And yet the words so frequently used to praise him were double-edged to say the least. On 14 November 1941, just after he had been elected to the Executive of the Parliamentary Labour Party and also elevated to the Opposition Front Bench, the *Manchester Guardian* had described Smith as 'one of the most sincere and selfless men who ever worked for the trade union and Labour movement', adding that 'these qualities richly compensate a rather strict orthodoxy of outlook' and made Smith liked 'by members of all Parties in the House of Commons'.[3] Clement Attlee, who had recently addressed a meeting with Smith in Stoke Town Hall, was said to have been 'astonished' at the warmth with which constituents had greeted their representative. There were others, however, who failed to register Smith's compensating qualities. After all, a man could be 'Sincere' and also plain wrong. He could be luminous in his 'Simplicity' or just plain thick. His 'integrity' might imply loyalty to delusions as well as 'orthodox' beliefs. That was how some of the more polished figures in the Labour Party saw their proletarian colleague. Writing in his diary in 1944, Hugh Dalton (Eton, Kings College, Cambridge) had placed Smith in 'a little group of second raters' who sat in a bunch and disapproved of everything'. In the following year he dismissed him as 'silly little Ellis Smith'.[4] Hugh Gaitskell (Winchester, New College, Oxford) briefed Smith in August 1945, when the resolute Lancastrian was appointed Parliamentary Secretary to the Board of Trade, and noted 'very nice...but I am afraid he will find some of the work rather beyond him'.[5] Smith had gone on to resign in January 1946: the first of the Attlee government resignations, but not, in his own mind at least, because he wasn't up to the job.

Born in 1896 and considerably older than the 'Bevanites' who heard his speeches with such dismay, Ellis Smith was also a strongly principled socialist of a decidedly 'old-fashioned' variety. An ardent believer in 'the great movement which we represent', Smith had answered the sneers of his well-born and more powerful colleagues in 1949, just after the municipal elections suggested that, while Labour had won 'a big vote', it may not have been big enough to overcome the fact that the Tories were now 'riding high'.[6] The following weekend, on 15 May 1949, he had picked up his copy of the socialist Sunday paper *Reynolds News* and been pleased to read an editorial ('What we think'), declaring that the time had come to 'toughen the moral and physical sinews of the Labour Movement in the next 12 months—or we risk defeat'. The article had called for the creation of 100,000 People's Commandos, and a 'People's Council of Action' in every constituency to improve the political education of the voters, and help the Movement 'purge itself of the smugness that has affected it

Fig 21. Ellis Smith and Derrick James at Hangchow.

for too long'. The imagined People's Commandos would set about bracing the people in the knowledge that 'We are a fighting movement of social change—or we are nothing'.

Already widened by this editorial plea, Smith's eye was drawn to another inspiring article entitled 'Why a singer must fight' and printed on the very same page. The latter was written by the great African-American singer Paul Robeson, who had recently completed the British leg of a four-month European tour organized after a series of eighty-five concerts in the USA had been cancelled due to savage anti-Communist pressure. Smith may well have been impressed by Robeson's account of his battle to keep ticket prices down, so that his concerts could be attended by workers who should neither be expected to fork out £1 a seat, nor be relegated to the balcony, an area that, in America's southern states, was the 'complete badge of inferiority of the Negro'.[7] Yet the British MP who is sometimes still remembered as 'the Champion of the North'[8] also rose to Robeson's larger point.

Fiercely condemning the American McCarthyites, who 'hate English socialism as much as the Communism they rave about in Goebbels-like terms', Robeson had called on the British left to widen its commitment to embrace the interests of millions in the colonies: 'No nation to-day can build in isolation. The continued progress of the British people is linked with the struggle for freedom all over the world. Above all it is linked with the fight for peace.' The persecuted singer then revealed his belief that 'advancing the human family' also meant taking a position on the primary division of the Cold War: 'Here, in Britain, I saw that there are very many people who think in terms of peace and peaceful reconstruction in the same way as they do in the Soviet Union and the Eastern democracies.'

Inspired by these arguments, Smith had set to work immediately. The next edition of *Reynolds News* carried his description of the 'New Ginger Group' he was launching within the Labour Party: 'We plan to fight for socialism in the spirit of the men who built up our Movement.'[9] The diagnosis was that the party had become too complacent: 'that burning enthusiasm all of us shared in 1945 has been replaced in many sections of our movement by apathy, or what is worse, cynical disillusionment.' An old socialist had told Smith, 'We are becoming too respectable', and Smith considered this to be 'a hundred times true'. 'It is not enough to recite statistics or exports, however inspiring they may be. Statistics alone do not foster the crusading spirit nor do they attract youth to our banners.' If the labour movement's 'great adventure' was not to fail, and the popular landslide of 1945 be wasted, its activists must 'provide an ideal, a cause worth fighting for and sacrificing for'.

Smith's Socialist Fellowship would set out to rekindle the flame that had once fired the Labour Party and revive the 'crusading spirit' of such men as George Lansbury, Bob Smillie, and Alfred Purcell. With its study groups, schools, and pamphlets, the Fellowship would make the case for Socialist Britain in the same spirit as the hard-hitting editorial of the previous week's *Reynolds News* and also the 'magnificent statements of faith' recently issued by Paul Robeson:

> We shall encourage comradeship and fellowship wherever we go. We will bring back the old ways that had such massive appeal to the common people in the early days of our Socialist, Co-operative and Trade Union Movement. Propaganda in the open air, at the street corners and market places will be revived throughout the country. We shall sing songs again and mean them—the great Socialist songs.

Declaring it 'Time for a Speed Up' all round, Smith had looked forward to rallying the 'active Socialists' who, unlike the Labour government's fiercely anti-Communist Foreign Secretary Ernest Bevin, were determined to see 'a Socialist inspiration in our conduct of foreign affairs'. The Socialist Fellowship was a good ship launched into a sea full of jagged rocks. Despite Smith's assurance that membership would be confined to 'people eligible for Labour Party Membership', the Trotskyists had also welcomed his initiative and, in accordance with the principle of 'entryism', duly clambered aboard and headed for the bridge. Smith had been inspired by the example of the old Independent Labour Party, which had persisted for many years within the national Labour Party it had helped to found in 1906. Yet no such long and fruitful voyage awaited the Socialist Fellowship. By July 1950, both Smith and Fenner Brockway had resigned, unable to accept the national council's policy of opposing British involvement in the Korean War. In April 1951, the Socialist Fellowship had been proscribed by the Labour Party's National Executive Committee. Ellis Smith's ship was sunk, and he would find no consolation in the fact that the associated magazine, *Socialist Outlook*, floated on for some time as a Trotskyist alternative to Michael Foot's *Tribune*.

Far from being the outcome of abstract intellectual decision, Ellis Smith's socialism was an organic expression of the working-class roots he insisted on digging up and waving before his hosts and fellow delegates as he talked his way through those Moscow receptions. Born the son of a carter in 1896, Smith had lived his entire life in Eccles, on the south bank of the Manchester ship canal. After attending council schools in Patricroft, he had been apprenticed in the pattern-making shop at British Westinghouse Company, an American-owned electrical engineering firm in Old Trafford that was taken into British ownership during the First World War and re-established as the Metropolitan Vickers Electrical Company in 1919. A member of the Independent Labour Party before he was out of his teens, Smith had developed his life-long interest in the trade union, the United Patternmakers Association, by listening to the conversation of the men around him during the First World War.

In the last months of that conflict, Smith had served as an engineer with the British Tank Corps at Erin in northern France. Trained as a gunner and driver, he helped salvage tanks along the Arras–Dullens Road, participated in a strike, and continued to read the *Daily Herald*, thanks to his wife, who was careful to use the banned socialist publication as wrapping in her weekly food parcels. Coming home to Eccles, he embraced the industrial militancy of the post-war years. As he himself put it in 'A Letter to an Engineer', written during the Second World War: 'Came home with great ideas, determined to play my part in preventing a repetition of the catastrophe of the kind that my generation had suffered. I was doing considerable reading now, and many of us were working and living for a new social order. It was at this time that the whole Labour Movement was alive, virile and at its best, and above all, we were united.'[10]

Back at Metropolitan Vickers, Smith had served on the Works Committee, helped to found the Eccles Branch of the United

Patternmakers Association in 1922, and become Secretary of the Eccles Trades and Labour Council in 1924. In his own time he read Dickens, the Webbs, and everything by Jack London he could lay hands on. He is also likely to have been a prominent participant in the lunchtime discussions of the Metropolitan Vickers debating society, founded in 1925 and used to 'ventilate social, political and other questions'.[11] Not content with studying history and Marxist dialectics, he attended a course on 'Method in Thinking', held at the Manchester office of the Assurance Agents Union.[12] He also achieved a First Class Certificate in Economics from the Cooperative College in Manchester and became a tutor in Economics for the National Council of Labour Colleges.

Smith worked as a pattern maker for Metropolitan Vickers until 1935, when he won Stoke-on-Trent for the Labour Party, having campaigned as 'a man of the people'. In north-west England, however, he had become known during the general strike of 1926. As secretary of the Eccles Trades Council, he had taken a leading role in his town's conduct of the strike, which he embraced as a wonderful demonstration of 'the power of Labour'. He attended the meetings, helped organize the action, and was there at the moment of greatest tension, when attempts were made to take a van loaded with food to the blacklegs who had managed to occupy Railway House in Patricroft. The threat of violence was increased by the fact that the van driver was accompanied in his attempt to break through the picket-line by a number of volunteer toffs. He was, as Smith noted later, 'assisted by some plus fours (complete with jazz pullovers etc), and looked ever so dirty'. The General Strike was defeated, but Smith remained proud of the solidarity demonstrated by his fellow workers and townspeople: 'It can be safely said that Eccles was as solid as any part of the country from beginning to end.'

Barbara Castle, who had grown up in Pontefract and Bradford, first came across Smith in 1932 when, just down from Oxford University, she worked as propaganda officer for the local Labour Party in Hyde, near Manchester. One of her jobs had been to find local politicians and trade unionists, who were prepared to come to Hyde on a Saturday night, step up onto her portable speaking platform in the market square, and rally the citizenry to the cause. The party was frankly demoralized following its huge defeat in the general election of 1931 but not Smith, who had gladly helped out on several occasions.[13] She had admired this 'dogged little trade unionist from Eccles' as 'one of the lesser-known stalwarts who built up the party again from the ashes' left by Ramsay McDonald.

By the time he entered the House of Commons Smith was, in the words of his own election press, 'a familiar and powerful figure on the Lancashire platform' and distinguished by his 'clear exposition of the contradictions of capitalism'. So what made Smith's speeches so alarming to his fellow delegates, and so very far from clear, thirty years later in Moscow? Smith was known to the *Daily Express* as 'the gravel-voiced MP for Stoke-on-Trent' (12 March 1954). Eight years later, the *Manchester Guardian* (8 June 1962) would claim that his slow 'Manchester quack' was scarcely modified even after a quarter of a century in Westminster. Yet it would take more than an accent to appall Barbara Castle, who herself knew what it was to take a northern voice south.

It might be suspected that some at least of Smith's speeches were thrown out of customary alignment by the influence of alcohol. Drunkenness was a characteristic hazard of Soviet hospitality—as Barbara Castle had known since at least 1946, when she and Charles Royle, the Salford MP who was also now with the Second Labour Delegation in Moscow, had visited the Soviet sector of Germany along with other members of an all-party delegation sent to visit the British Army on the Rhine. As Castle recalls, they were taken around by a Russian officer, whose 'idea of hospitality was to get everybody drunk except himself'.[14] Stopping at a guesthouse on the road to Leipzig, he set to work with the vodka. Royle had 'never drunk anything stronger than orange juice', but the Russian kept filling his glass with vodka, claiming it was water. The results were predictable, so Castle recalls. 'Having grown more and more loquacious during the meal Charlie suddenly sprung on to the table and tried to do a Russian dance. Then, with a final "Whoopee!" he had disappeared, only his feet visible over the table edge. He had to be carried out and was extremely ill.'

If drink played any part in Ellis Smith's difficulties in Moscow, this was certainly not because he was a habituated boozer of the kind that Paul Hogarth had found among his party of previously untravelled shop stewards. Like many who entered the labour movement through the Independent Labour Party in the early twentieth century, Ellis Smith came from a non-conformist background, where drinking was strongly disapproved. As a child he had attended the Patricroft Congregational Sunday school and, as a coming young socialist, he had considered alcohol an unmitigated evil to be avoided at all cost. His surviving papers record how, in 1934, he and a comrade visited Weymouth to attend the Trades Union Congress, held in Dorset that year to mark the Centenary of the transportation of the Tolpuddle Martyrs. They had found the town full and Smith recalls the horror with which he realized he may have no choice but to put up for the night in a room above a pub. Smith had softened his stance on drink by 1954. He was, as his friend and protégé Johny Smethurst recalls, quite prepared to take glass of sherry at receptions in Stoke or Eccles. He could still be highly 'volatile', however, on occasions when he suspected that funds might have been 'recycled' through the till of the Labour Club bar.[15]

The truth is that, even without vodka toasts, Smith was inclined to ramble about in the landscapes, both fallen and ideal, at the back of his mind. One of the other Labour MPs on the delegation informed Derrick James that their leader had once paused to hunt up an illustration while making a speech in the House of Commons: 'War is terrible', he was alleged to have said before slowly moving on to add, 'My wife's third cousin was killed in the war'. Whatever the accuracy of that observation, there can be no doubt that the House of Commons was familiar with Smith's memories of the First World War. On 20 May 1938, he had offered his fellow MPs, or the small number who remained in the Chamber to listen, an extended oration on the subject.[16] He started by telling of his recent visit to hospital, where he had met a despairing veteran whose difficulties stemmed, as the doctor confirmed, from the inadequate treatment he had received for a throat illness while he was serving in France. He moved on to the tribulations of a friend who had served in Gallipoli, and suffered predictable problems from having been obliged to stand waist-deep in water for long periods. After explaining at some length that he himself had not suffered anything like the worst of the experience he was about to describe, he detailed what it had been like to serve inside a tank, insisting that the horror of being cramped into that hellish little space, plagued by fumes and noise even without any engagement with the enemy, was amply sufficient to justify the call he was now making, more than twenty years later, for increased pensions for ex-servicemen.

Far from being an erratic consequence of drink, Smith's rambling, open-air style of address was a product of its own formation in the milieu of early twentieth-century English socialism. Examples did not necessarily come singly as he mixed analysis with personal testimony, sentiment with dogma, vehement denunciation with rousing invocations of the world as it might be if only the bosses were replaced by decent human beings. Smith's was a redemptive vision in which the pragmatics of everyday political management often came to seem like a betrayal of vision and principle. His speeches were powered by a sense of righteous purpose and a pronounced faith in doctrine—even if the Bible seems to have given way to the fervent dialectics of Marxist economics and class war. He would draw extensively on history as he spoke, and he saw the Russian Revolution through a thick lens of English precedents: the Peasants' Revolt, the Tolpuddle Martyrs, Milton, the Rochdale Co-operators, William Morris, Keir Hardie, and Bob Smillie of the old Independent Labour Party, Shelley's 'The Masque of Anarchy', and, of course, its heroes, the Manchester millworkers who were sabred and trampled to death by cavalry in the Peterloo Massacre of 1819.

On entering the House of Commons in 1935, Smith had indeed persisted with the 'tub-thumping style of speaking' he had developed in the northern Labour movement. He is said to have horrified some of his fellow Labour MPs by doing so.[17] Even Smith's friends concede that 'passages in some of his speeches were vacuous and self-opinionated', despite the 'sincere delivery' that only sometimes helped to disarm critics.[18]

That Smith was prepared to launch into a speech with only a rough sense of intended direction is proved by his surviving notes. Typically, these consist of truncated phrases typed in capitals and spaced out over the page, broadly sketched skeletons on which Smith plainly intended to improvise robustly. One speech that does survive in a fuller version was given in 1947 in Manchester, at a rally organized by the Lancashire & Cheshire Federation of Trades Councils, of which Smith was President for several decades, despite the sporadic attempts of the TUC to replace him with a more pliable brother. Entitled 'People of the World Unite for

Peace—Progress and World Brotherhood!', this prolix declamation was intended to introduce one of the few well-known American politicians who could be welcomed as a friend of the British left. Henry Wallace was a Democrat, and something of a socialist too. He had been Secretary for Agriculture during the New Deal and then served as Vice President to Roosevelt in the early 1940s—until 1946, when he was asked to resign after attacking the administration's hard-line policy against the Soviet Union.

Smith, who was on home ground as Westminster's emerging 'Champion of the North', opened by welcoming Wallace, who had come to speak out against the Anti-Communist witch hunts in the United States. He then launched into a tirade of his own—one that went on and on at a length that must have left the eminent American (who that same year became editor of *New Republic*) wondering whether his time would ever come. Eventually, after various crescendos marked in bold type, Smith issued a resounding call for 'the international brotherhood of Labour', and for the solidarity in which its members would set about 're-making the world'. In the words of 'The Internationale', the message was 'Workers of the World, unite'. But that was far too bald a statement for Smith's liking. He wanted to see those workers not just united but 'So united that they will overcome the birth pangs of the New World Order, subdue the past, dominate the present, exalt life, and render it peaceful, abundant and joyous to every man, woman and child. Forward to World Brotherhood.'

At this point, Wallace may well have started getting to his feet, but Smith launched himself into another swooping flight, quoting Roosevelt on the great programme of public works with which Wallace had transformed the Tennessee Valley under the New Deal, and insisting that comparable plans should have been prepared for Lancashire, North Staffs, South Wales, North Wales, Cumberland, and Scotland too. He quoted from Abraham Lincoln, President Woodrow Wilson, and Henry Wallace himself, before finally arriving at the internationalist slogan with which he eventually introduced the waiting American: 'The World is one Family with one future.'

For some of the British Labour MPs in his delegation, the main cause of embarrassment in Smith's Moscow speeches lay less in their vagrant prolixity, than in their reverence, at this time of cautious de-Stalinization, for the Soviet Union of the 1920s and 1930s. When it came to his experience of the great workers' state, Smith was not one to be 'cautiously statistical', as Barbara Castle declared that Attlee, Aneurin Bevan, and other members of the Labour leadership had been when they eventually reported to the National Executive Committee on their visit—all too aware of the suspicious, if not plain hostile British press that would be weighing up their words.[19] Instead, he went in for full-blooded hymns of praise to Stalin and the Bolshevik revolution, accompanied by swooping excursions into his own experiences as a long-term supporter of the USSR, and vigorous condemnation of the Western interests he now saw driving the Cold War.

Smith had only visited the Soviet Union once before 1954, so the 'previous visits to Russia' that Barbara Castle remembered him going on about are likely to have included a trip he made to Czechoslovakia, travelling with a delegation just after the war in 1946. That time he had taken with him a letter of introduction from Willie Gallacher, the Scottish President of the Communist Party of Great Britain, who enthusiastically commended him to Clement Gottwald, the Communist Prime Minister who, two years later, would become President and drive through the Staliniza-tion of his country. Gallacher had entered the House of Commons as Communist MP for West Fife in 1935, the same general elec-tion that had brought in Ellis Smith as the Labour member for Stoke-on-Trent, and his letter, dated 26 June 1946, described the English socialist as 'one of the best proletarian representatives in the House of Commons' and urged Gottwald to 'Give him the keys of the city. Treat him as a comrade of mine and make his visit something he will always remember. Signed Your old Comrade Wm Gallacher.'

Ellis Smith had visited the USSR a year after the General Strike, in 1927, when he travelled as a member of a forty-eight-strong British Workers' Delegation made up of militant trade unionists, activists and cooperators, all of them steeled by experience of the recent defeat. Smith, who had joined this rank-and-file delega-tion as a member the United Patternmakers' Association, would later recall that the trip was made at a time when 'conditions were very bad, and it was very cold'. His comrades in the pattern-making workshop at Metropolitan Vickers had 'collected to buy me a good new overcoat, which I wore for many years'.[20]

So it was that, on 7 November 1927, the young Ellis Smith had stood in a specially provided stand under the Kremlin wall, gazing out over a thronging Red Square, as the celebrations of the tenth anniversary of the Bolshevik revolution unfolded. He heard speeches by Voroshilov, Commissar for War, and also Kalinin, Chairman of the Communist Party, and, by repute, 'the most popular man in Russia'.[21] Then the massed bands broke into the Internationale, and guns fired inside the Kremlin, their smoke billowing out over the high wall. More speeches followed: Bukharin, and also the Glaswegian Communist Willie Gallacher, who had changed his ways since 1920, when Lenin judged him guilty of 'Left-Wing Communism; an Infantile Disorder', and who now spoke out in the name of the Communist International. Ellis Smith had watched with his heart in his mouth as a million Moscow workers filed passed the Lenin Mausoleum in 'a solid unbroken phalanx forty deep'. They came with banners, slogans, and ingenious moving effigies of the Revolution's enemies including Austen Chamberlain and Stanley Baldwin, the Tory leaders judged responsible for the British trade embargo against Communist Russia, and no doubt also for the British TUC's dissolution, a few weeks earlier on 7 September 1927, of the Anglo-Russian Trade Union Committee. As night fell, the whole scene was illuminated with four searchlights and Ellis Smith stood there, utterly transfixed, as the Red Cossack cavalry charged across the square at a terrific pace: their blue uniforms, shining lances, and magnificent black horses gleaming in the lights of triumphant Revolution.

Smith evoked that remembered scene in his speech at the VOKS banquet on 9 October 1954, including his glimpse of the protesting Trotsky being chased out of Red Square. The latter had indeed been among the more fateful occurrences of the day, marking as it did the successful tightening of Stalin's personal dictatorship over the Soviet party and state apparatus. Trotsky, Zinoviev, and others within the Communist Party had opposed Stalin, whose international policies had failed in Europe and also in China where, as was certainly understood by the Chinese ambassador who heard Ellis Smith's speech at the VOKS reception in Moscow

1954, the Communists had just suffered a catastrophic massacre at the hands of Chiang Kai-shek, with whose Kuomintang they had reluctantly stayed in alliance on Stalin's orders.[22] In Russia, as the German Communist Ruth Fischer put it, 'naked terror reigned', and the leading oppositionists were being closed down. 'When Trotsky appeared in the Moscow streets, he was pelted with rotten apples. Wherever he went, fights broke out and the demonstration was transformed into a riot. Surrounded by this "belt of incidents," he was never able to address the crowd.'[23] His protest at the tenth anniversary celebrations was among the last public acts of the opposition to Stalin, who responded to this latest act of defiance by expelling the transgressors from the Communist Party. Stalin had been dead for a year by the time Ellis Smith returned to Moscow in October 1954, but his reverence for Stalin was unshaken by the fact that the Russian functionaries gathered at that VOKS dinner were now beginning to take their distance from the late Great Leader. As for the sight of Trotsky being chased into exile across Red Square, Smith viewed that episode through the memory of his own more recent struggles against Trotskyism in the Socialist Fellowship, and considered it a case of good riddance.

As he addressed his hosts at the VOKS banquet, Chairman Smith may have described how his loyalty to Stalin's Soviet Union had been tested again, a few years after his visit to Moscow. In March 1933, six Metropolitan Vickers engineers working in the Soviet Union had been arrested, along with several Russians who worked with them. Charged with espionage and sabotage against Soviet hydro-electric plants, they were tried in Moscow under a rising prosecutor named A. Y. Vyshinsky. At Old Trafford the Metropolitan Vickers shop stewards were called together, and asked by the management to pass a resolution pledging their confidence in the integrity of the arrested engineers. Smith, who was then deputy chairman of the stewards, had been the only one to refuse, arguing that 'I could not pledge my confidence in men I did not know'. A difficult meeting with the Managing Director had followed, but Smith would yield no ground, advising his outraged boss to 'bear in mind that you might want to trade with Russia again'.

Unswervingly loyal to the Soviet Union, Smith would be pleased to record that Metropolitan Vickers had indeed resumed such trade not long afterwards. It was a good outcome for some in Moscow too. Having come to international notice in the 'Metro-Vickers' trial, State prosecutor Vyshinsky went on to do Stalin's bidding in the notorious show trials that commenced a few years later. Demoted since Stalin's death in 1953, Vyshinsky was now the Deputy Minister of Foreign Affairs, who had relayed Ambassador Hayter's invitation to Khrushchev to dine with Attlee and his colleagues at the London embassy earlier that summer. It was in the same role that he attended the VOKS reception at which he heard Chairman Smith give the verbose and wandering speech that made Barbara Castle's blood run cold.

Smith's loyalty to Stalin and the Soviet cause also made for difficulties at the British embassy in Moscow. Castle recalls the Second Labour Delegation's courtesy visit to the British ambassador. Sir William Hayter explained the congestion at food shops by suggesting that there were too few of them—all the embassy staff agreed unanimously that there was no shortage of food. Hayter also suggested that the Russians would actually favour a rapprochement with the US, since the two countries had so much in common: 'Russians', he explained with the hauteur of his class and station, 'like size and are a crude people.'

His comments certainly didn't impress Ellis Smith. Indeed, they soon added to the 'difficulties' that Castle associated with his leadership in her diaries. As Smith later remembered: 'In the British Embassy I overheard the conversations of the staff and saw their superior air. I said to the delegation's vice-chairman: will you move a vote of thanks to the British Embassy staff? He answered: no you should do that...I said—I cannot. If I could I wouldn't: I never heard such anti-Soviet talk.'[24]

For a while that undelivered vote of thanks passed back and forth between Smith and Vice Chairman George Lindgren, caught in a stand-off that reflected wider tensions within the Labour Party. Both men were sons of the working class, who had entered the House of Commons from a strong background in local activism. Lindgren, whose father was a carpenter in Islington, had worked as a railway clerk before winning the marginal seat of Wellingborough for Labour in the general election of 1945. A socialist of a more accommodating variety than Ellis Smith, he had supported Hugh Gaitskell, the Chancellor whose 1951 budget had split the Labour Party by introducing prescription charges into the NHS, and was still remembered with a burning sense of disappointment by Barbara Castle and other Bevanites. Indeed, it has been said that 'even his friends would have regarded George as being over-willing to trim Labour's policies when in Government in order to avert defeat at the polls in a subsequent election'.[25] Smith, meanwhile, had 'little sympathy with colleagues who trimmed their policies or disregarded the working-class base of their party'. It was Lindgren who eventually moved the vote of thanks.

11

Stanley Spencer's Pyjama Cord and the Socialist Tree

It was not just the political delegates who were falling out with one another by the time they got to Moscow. Hugh Casson leaves no doubt that the members of the cultural delegation had also been straining under the 'terrible fate' of being 'members of a party in the composition of which we have had no say'. Temperamental differences were aggravated by the long flights, the shared hotel rooms, and by the uncertainty as to when, if ever, they would get their next flight. Perhaps some also felt traces of the 'vague sense of self-disgust' once attributed to the 'decent, active, leisured'[1] cosmopolitans of nineteenth-century Europe, forced to think far too much about themselves by the habit of comparison thrust on them by continental travel.

The members of the cultural delegation had neither official functions nor a shared political ideology over which to bicker. Their progress was instead defined by the intense personal antagonism that developed between A. J. Ayer and Spencer. It is hard to imagine two less compatible Englishmen to be so closely thrust together. To meet Spencer was, as Paul Hogarth recalled, 'like meeting a plumber'. A. J. Ayer was an urbane old Etonian and a campaigner for secularism, who was more than at ease with his own celebrity as the man who had made logical positivism a subject of conversation among the British middle classes. Spencer was a home-taught religious painter, who found his oddly biblical messages among the charladies of his Berkshire village home. He was also a man of agonizing and disastrously incompetent relations with women. Ayer, on the contrary, was a contrastingly suave operator who, even by 1954, was rumoured to have bedded a hundred women ('All you have to do', he is said once to have remarked of his conquests, 'is to pay a woman the smallest attention. In this country, no one else does').[2]

In the second volume of his autobiography, *More of My Life*, Ayer recalls how he was 'repelled by the mixture of eroticism and religiosity' permeating Spencer's work, adding that he found the artist 'the most self-centred man that I have ever met. His gnome like appearance was not unappealing, and I could bear with his minor eccentricities, such as his taking pains to look disheveled and his wearing pyjamas as underclothes. It was his conversation that wore me down.'[3] He remembered Spencer maundering on about Cookham and Macedonia, or Mesopotamia, and talking about the various women in his apparently grubby life as if the whole world knew who Hilda, Patricia, and Daphne were. Peter Vansittart informs me that Ayer 'loathed Spencer'.[4] He quotes his friend as having described Spencer as 'a vile little man, boring on an unwholesomely lavish scale, intolerable…interested only in himself and women'.[5] As Vansittart adds, 'the last two objections sounded curious from Freddie, but the rest was unquestionable. Spencer would belabour at length what he called, too often, the vulgarity of law and morality, and found pleasure in inflicting and receiving pain, with women. For the artist, and his joyous creativity, all must be forgiven, all permitted.'

John Chinnery confirms that Spencer was a taxing travel companion. Unwell, and bad tempered, he 'bored us all to tears' with his 'highly illogical' conversation. Casson too would later look back on Spencer, carrying an unfurled umbrella and a shapeless shopping bag, as 'a most grotesque figure, in his long Ulster with a huge yellow woollen scarf wound round his head against the cold, his pyjama cord showing at the foot of his trouser, because he kept his pyjamas on under his clothes for virtually the whole trip as far as I remember'. That pyjama cord became a motif of the trip. Like a Chinese pigtail in one of Sax Rohmer's Fu Manchu stories, it keeps reappearing, getting longer and shorter as it trails out of different apertures of Spencer's clothing or luggage. The delegation's jokes were often at Spencer's expense. Speaking to a large audience at the Architectural Association on his return, Casson would pause theatrically after mounting the platform, gaze around the audience for several seconds and then declare, 'I think I can safely say I am the only person in this room who has slept with Stanley Spencer'.[6]

The four cultural members of the Second Labour Delegation had their problems too. While the trade unionists and politicians noted production figures, and admired the scale of the Soviet Union's economic and social achievements, they strained at the leash, impatient with Chairman Smith's attempt to include them in inspections of supermarkets and car factories. These difficulties appear to have come to a head at the Agricultural Exhibition. They had four interpreters for a party of twenty, but could not agree on what to go and see. The result was that James never got to the machinery section. 'This', he noted, 'was one of the failings of democracy, and in future we must split up into small groups, each if necessary with a different programme. I have lobbied Barbara to support this policy. She is a tough lass, and can probably handle it.' Denis Mathews was not prepared to wait for Chairman Smith and the delegation's trade unionist 'secretary' George Doughty to consent to the proposed adjustment, and made his own move against the enforced inanity of 'official tourism' while still at the Agricultural Exhibition. Wandering around that Stalinist fairyland, he came across 'a charming young interpreter' who had 'nothing to do with VOKS', their official host. He arranged to meet her the next day in Red Square, and was impressed when she turned up wearing an English camel hair coat. After taking a long walk around a poorer part of the city and visiting a museum, they agreed to meet again when Mathews made his way back from China: a trip to the Bolshoi was planned, where this interpreter's cousin was a dancer. She refused to take Mathews's money for the tickets, but he still posted all his Russian cash to her, so that he could join her for 'a gala evening' on his way home.

The easing of the itinerary allowed Derrick James to pursue his interest in Soviet science, greatly relieved not to be marching about in a column of twenty. Revisiting Moscow State University with Barbara Castle, who had missed the delegation's earlier visit, he noted that, however dismal the aesthetics of the building, the student quarters were 'amazingly luxurious' and the students' laboratory 'first class in its equipment: much better than ours'. James remained sceptical about the anti-cellular theories of Comrade Lepeshinskaya, but he continued his enquiries into

Soviet biology, attending a specially arranged meeting at VOKS together with Cedric Dover, whom he describes as 'the anthropologist of the party'. They went into 'a large room, again like a Victorian parlour blown up to an enormous size', and had a long conversation with Aleksander Ivanovich Oparin, an eminent and still powerful Soviet Academician who had presided over the elevation of Lysenko and his false 'proletarian science', and who remained widely known for his theory of the origin of life, which suggested that life first emerged in the 'primordial soup' of an ocean in a reducing atmosphere, and was similar to the hypothesis produced, also in the 1920s, by the British Marxist biologist J. B. S. Haldane.

Asking Oparin about Soviet methods of student selection, James was informed that applicants were selected by professorial interview, and that the few mistakes made were easily weeded out in the first year. After that, Oparin claimed, there were no rejects, except in cases of illness. James noted sceptically that 'This seemed quite amazing, but he was firm about it'. The two agreed to try to initiate an exchange of students between Britain and the Soviet Union—a theme that James pursued further when he met another Soviet biologist, A. N. Studitsky, to discuss his work on muscle grafting.

James was by no means entirely convinced by the claims he heard about Soviet medical research, the training of doctors, and the availability of medical services to the general public. He wrote them down, but he also noted contrary indications such as the pronounced scarcity of spectacles worn by people in the streets or, for that matter, by the delegation's interpreters, one of whom was extremely short-sighted and apparently without any optical aids at all.

Cedric Dover went along with this, even though he was not directly interested in questions of research funding and possible student exchanges. Dover had contributed dozens of articles to scientific journals around the world, but he had no university post and much of his writing also reflected his ongoing struggle to make a bare living. When blackouts were introduced during the first weeks of the Second World War, it had been he who stepped up to advise British readers of *Reynolds News* why they should increase their intake of Vitamin A if they wanted to improve their nocturnal vision.[7] He had also written the course on Biology for a popular compendium entitled *The Complete Self Educator*. Indeed, he had opened this introduction to 'the study of living things' with a flourish that claimed none of the 'objectivity' expected of academic publications: 'All material things are living (organic) or non-living (inorganic) things. A Rolls-Royce is easily recognized as a non-living thing; its owner, at least in the scientific sense, as a living thing.'[8]

Cedric Dover went along with James's scientific enquiries, but he also studied the trees of Moscow unusually closely. He did this as a member of 'The Men of the Trees', an ecological organization founded by Richard St Barbe Baker in 1924, which campaigned for afforestation in Africa and elsewhere. Dover was editor of this international association's journal, appropriately named *Trees*, and he was preparing an illustrated article about the specimens he encountered on the trip to China.[9] As the plane 'glided above whipped cream' on the way to Prague, he had gazed down on the rich 'farm and forest' agriculture of the Czechoslovak country-side: noting farms protected by lines of hardwoods and conifers, and patches of forest adjoining the fields. He had been pleased to find further evidence of 'tree-consciousness' in the city of Prague itself. It was, however, at the centre of Soviet power that he found the silvestral theme really coming into its own.

The Soviet Union was, he suggested, already known for its achievements in 'combining forestry with agriculture and land recreation', yet a new emphasis on 'amenity trees' in the cities suggested that Soviet Communism was a life-enhancing thing of soul and beauty and not just a noisy state-owned construction site devoted to badly designed prefabricated buildings that Mayor Yasnov and his boastful officials could count up in millions of square feet. Noting that 'Trees begin to delight the eye on the doorstep of the airport of Moscow', he suggested that 'new trees for new roads and new buildings seems to be, like electrification, a first principle of the Soviet economy'. To prove his point, he inserted Soviet-supplied photographs of the leafy delights of Sver-dlov Square, and of lime-washed trees squeezed into the tight space between the road and a new block of flats in Revolution Avenue, Podolsk, near Moscow.

Dover also noted that saplings alone could not fulfil the Soviet ambition for beauty: 'the Muscovite is proud of his trees and too impatient to watch new plantings grow—the forest, not the streets, is the place for them to grow, he thinks. Therefore, adult or nearly adult trees are planted for amenity or landscaping purposes.' Forty-year old trees had been planted along Gorky Street when it was widened and '50,000 near adults had been placed in the grounds of the recently completed Moscow State University, as well as 500,000 shrubs and 1,500,000 plants for flowers'. Yet the message that Dover found here was not only a matter of quantity, acceleration, and impatience for an improved future. Dover further orchestrated his theme by praising the harmonious diversity of the university's trees: 'they symbolise the national character of the University, for there are cork-oaks from the Amur River, red oaks from the Ukraine, blue spruce from the Caucasus, maples and lindens from Ryazan, and so on.' And who was to say that those trees, as they stood there in the late summer light, distinct in species and yet growing into a still emerging overall design, did not whisper a reassurance, at least in the more anthropologically inclined reaches of Dover's mind, that the Soviet Union was also delivering on its promises towards its various human nationalities? 'Today', as this 'Man of the Trees' had decreed in a since largely forgotten tract of 1939, 'the Soviet minorities are the only minorities without racialism and minority grievances. Stalin can claim with truth that the October Revolution dealt the legend of racial inequality a mortal blow.'[10] It was an optimistic, indeed frankly deluded, conclusion that would surely not have convinced Derrick James, who, that same year, had quit the Communist Party of Great Britain, horrified by news of the Nazi–Soviet pact, signed by Molotov and Ribbentrop in Moscow on 28 August that year.

Dover was not the only member of the Second Labour Delegation inclined to hear the spirit of socialism whispering in the trees of the USSR. He shared this perception with Chairman Ellis Smith, who would also praise the trees planted every few yards along the roadside to help make 'places of real beauty' of the USSR's rebuilt cities.[11] One might sense a tactical retreat here, as if the realities of life in the Soviet Union, with its drab lack of fashion, its slaving women labourers, its obvious lack of personal liberty, and the endless queues noticed by the visiting Arsenal players, had forced the precious idea of 'Socialism' to take to the woods in fright. Yet for Smith this was a long-standing preoccupation, and one that may have owed something to the leafy nineteenth century visions of John Ruskin and William Morris. Certainly, it had been in his mind by 1935, when he had arrived on the political scene as the new Labour MP for Stoke-on-Trent. His victory speech included predictable promises of class war and justice for the working man, but journalists reported that he also 'wants to see the City made beautiful': indeed, 'he pleaded for more open spaces, and for gardens, shrubs and trees on open land'.[12] During the First World War German prisoners had been employed to show what could be done in this direction, and Smith suggested that the people of Stoke should now prove the possibilities in peacetime too. He had revisited the idea in January 1949, when he had been involved in an argument over whether or not it was fair to call Stoke 'a beastly hole'.[13] A worker at the railway station had volunteered to beautify the derelict view from his window, and Smith urged other constituents to join in this project of planting shrubs and trees. 'Beautification' was the rallying cry by this time—'cleaning, brightening and greenification'—and for Smith it was connected to the view that 'Democracy is doing something yourself, not leaving it to the other fellow'. Like so much else in the country, the broken railings around the city's statue of 'Staffordshire's greatest son', Josiah Wedgewood, represented 'an attitude of mind' that 'must be fought'. It is anyone's guess what Mikhail Yasnov, the bulldozing Mayor of Moscow, would have made of that.

PART III

Anticipating China
(Moscow to Ulan Bator)

Do I really envy those who see the wonderful places of the earth before they have dreamed of them?

Vernon Lee,
'On Modern Travelling', 1897 [1]

The presence of the aeroplane does not so much alter the truth as assemble it before the mind in an overwhelming sweep.

Aneurin Bevan, 1954 [2]

12

Ghosts over Siberia

(Casson and Pulleyblank)

'One by one the stations are marked off…Sverdlovsk (Irish stew and vodka)…Omsk (hot tea and a wash)…Novosibirsk (sardines and brandy)…Krasnoyarsk (cocoa and salad)'.[1] Hugh Casson provides only a brief record of the flights that carried the cultural delegation from Moscow to China. They travelled in the company of two 'film types'—a Dutchman and a Frenchman who boarded the plane wearing a 'v chic black tie and Edwardian trousers'. The Marxist physicist J. D. Bernal, who made the same journey in a plane carrying the Bulgarian delegation, watched the Urals crawl by 'hardly more conspicuous than the South Downs'. For Casson, however, no idly scraped-up English analogy could undo the fact that it was an arduous transit in which airports and time zones dragged by in surreal procession: 'sunset and dawn, dinner and breakfast have been observed and eaten often, it seemed, in unfamiliar sequence.'

At one point in this bewildering journey, so Casson alleges, Stanley Spencer picked up his notebook and scribbled 'How wonderful to be really flying over Mongolia'—only to cross out the words when informed that he was actually 'ahead of fact'. At another, as his daughters recall, Casson walked into a hut-like airport dormitory to find a book abandoned by a previous traveller—who, he wondered, could ever have passed this way with a copy of one of Angela Brazil's boarding-school stories for upper-class English girls?[2]

The plane was a licensed Soviet version of the pre-war Douglas DC3, a twin-engined and deafeningly noisy 'rattletrap'[3] that vibrated constantly. Once again there were no seat belts, and those who wanted refreshment eventually learned to help themselves to tea from a flask in the front rack.[4] The delegates were reduced to a 'grey, dumb, brain-washed' condition by the time they tumbled out at Krasnoyarsk asking for coffee, which eventually arrived as cocoa. They were even worse off when they reached

Fig 22. Hugh Casson, Irkutsk, ink drawing.

Irkutsk, 'the last port of call in Russia'.[5] Grounded by fog, they found themselves in a 'fortified zone' and confined to the airport building for an indefinite period that dragged on for two nights. Ayer and Warner played picquet. Spencer, who may indeed have had a yellow scarf wrapped around his head against the cold, played 'sad music' on the parlour piano. Casson tried to draw in the airport garden, where the lights of planes manoeuvring on the runway gleamed suggestively in an aluminium bust of Molotov. He was disturbed by the French cameraman, who wanted to talk about Corbusier, and then by a suspicious policeman who insisted that 'Drawing is not necessary'. A delegation of khaki-clad figures stamped in, prompting Spencer to observe 'How terrible to see soldiers who have not come to protect you'.[6] He had them wrong too. Having quickly taken over the Englishmen's table in the restaurant, the 'soldiers' turned out to be a 'Parliamentary Delegation from Rumania—clearly more important than we are'.

Leafing through the airport visitors' book, the marooned Britons turned up a single unexpected entry in English: 'Have spent three useful days in lovely Irkutsk.' The words had been written by Hewlett Johnson, the notorious 'Red Dean of Canterbury', passing through a year or so previously. 'The "three days" strikes an ominous note, the "useful" a puzzling one,' wrote Casson. 'We wondered what a useless day in the Deanery could be like,'[7] remembered Ayer, before conceding that the Dean, unlike them, had probably been 'allowed to visit the town'. 'How?' asked Rex Warner, who had at first felt oddly at home in Irkutsk. 'Place looks v. like England,' he had

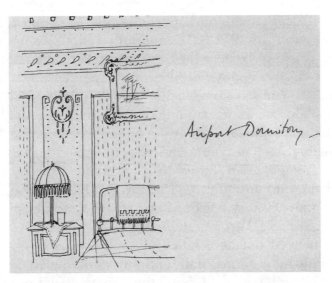

Fig 23. Hugh Casson, airport dormitory, ink drawing.

scribbled shortly after arrival, adding that he 'slept like a boy' after a lunch that was 'not bad' even though served at a crazy time. Since then, Irkutsk had melted into a grey limbo where the 'miseries of air travel' could no longer be alleviated: 'All our roubles & all our brandy now gone'. Casson's notebook confirms their 'penniless and hopeless' condition: 'Spent our last roubles on a bottle of Madeira. R. W. desperate for spirits.'

While Ayer withdrew into Gibbons's *Decline and Fall of the Roman Empire* and Spencer returned from the piano to start sketching his more amenable fellow delegates as they sat, Hugh Casson may have wondered whether the mirage-filled distance between Britain and China could really be closed by so laborious an act as flying to the far side of the world.

The problem can be introduced with the help of Joseph Needham. Speaking on 'Science & Society in Ancient China' in London's Conway Hall on May 1947, the Cambridge biochemist, who had recently spent four years in 'Free China' running the British Council's Sino-British Science Cooperation Office, commended Chinese civilization as having 'the over-powering beauty of the wholly other'.[8] He concluded his talk by declaring that 'only the wholly other can inspire the deepest love and the profoundest desire to learn'. The innocence of Needham's own 'desire to learn' had since been fiercely challenged after his corroboration, in 1952, of Communist China's claims alleging American use of bacteriological warfare. Yet it was not just on account of the splintered illusions generated by the newly descended 'bamboo curtain', that China's 'otherness' demanded a more elaborate understanding of distance than could be measured in miles alone. Europe had long been in the habit of recognizing itself in contrast with its imagined and thoroughly misrepresented Asian 'other'. Having pursued the roots of this habit back into antiquity, one researcher has gone so far as to suggest that 'History began when the West took cognizance of itself against a backdrop of the East'.[9]

Casson need not have relied only on the fabulous travels of Marco Polo for evidence of the antiquity of this persistent Western habit. He might have considered the dispatches of the Franciscan John De' Marignolli, who set out as an envoy of Pope Benedict XII in 1339, crossed the Black Sea, and then pressed on through the 'torrid zone' and the massive sand hills beyond which, until the Tartars ventured out from the far side, no habitable lands were thought to lie. He later sent back word that Paradise actually existed, and that four vast rivers flowed from the same fountain of Eden, and then fell to earth with such thunderous noise that the people living around them were born deaf.[10]

The British architect might also have considered the reports of the Italian Friar Odoric who, having reached the southern city of Canton a few years earlier, evoked a settlement 'as big as three Venices' and, beyond that, a land filled with other monstrously swollen presences: 'And as with the geese, so also with the ducks and fowls; they are so big that you would think them perfectly marvelous. Here there be serpents bigger than anywhere else in the world, many of which are taken and eaten with great relish.'[11] Odoric continued his inventory of enlarged amazements at the since vanished port of Zayton: 'And here be seen the biggest cocks in the world. And there be hens also that are white as snow, and have no feathers, but have wool upon them, like sheep.'[12] He wrote of 'a certain great mountain...And on the one side all the animals that dwell there are black, and the men and women have a very strange way of living. But on the other side all the animals are white, and the men and women have a quite different way of living with the others.' Vast melons were said to grow on the mountains of 'a certain great kingdom called Cadeil': 'And when these be ripe, they burst, and a little beast is found inside like a small lamb, that they have both melons and meat.'[13] In Peking, Odoric saw with his own eyes that all married women 'wear upon their heads the foot of a man as it were, a cubit and a half in length, and at the top of that foot there are certain cranes's feathers'.[14] He marvelled at Kublai Khan's palace, walled off within the Tartar city and attended by the 'Green Mount', 'a hill thrown up on which another palace is built, the most beautiful in the whole world. And this whole hill is planted over with trees...And at the side of this hill has been formed a lake and a most beautiful bridge built across it.'[15] It was on the same hill, which survived to impress twentieth-century tourists as the 'Coal Hill', that Marco Polo had described grown trees being planted with the soil still packed around their roots.

As an architect and former camoufleur, Casson would surely have taken particular pleasure in the testimony of the French Jesuit missionary and painter Jean Denis Attiret, who, in a letter written in 1743, described how he had first travelled to Peking under the command of the Emperor Kangxi. Carefully screened and forbidden even to glimpse the land during his journey, he stepped out of his conveyance to find Peking a world of breath-taking astonishments. As he wrote of the Summer Palace and its imperial gardens, 'I had never seen anything that bore any nature of resemblance to them'.[16] He marvelled at the flowering trees, pagodas, and valleys joined by bridges which 'generally wind about, and serpentize'.[17] He also noted how incredibly fast the city's single-storey buildings were erected: 'They look almost like those fabulous Palaces which are said to be raised by Inchantment all at once, in some beautiful Valley, or on the Brow of some Hill.'[18]

Struck by descriptive vertigo as all grounds for comparison failed him, Attiret also revealed that 'otherness' was a two-sided business. Having shown the emperor some pictures of European cities, he knew that the Chinese had their own way of looking back at the West in horrified amazement:

Their Eyes are so accustom'd to their own Architecture, that they have very little Taste for ours. May I tell you what they say when they speak of it, or when they are looking over the Prints of some of our most celebrated Buildings? The Height and Thickness of our Palaces amazes them. They look upon our Streets, as so many Ways hollowed into terrible Mountains; and upon our Houses, as Rocks pointing up in the Air, and full of Holes like Dens of Bears and other wild Beasts. Above all, our different Stories, piled up so high one above another, seem quite intolerable to them: and they cannot conceive, how we can bear to run the Risk of breaking our Necks, so commonly, in going up such a Number of Steps as is necessary to climb up to the Fourth and Fifth Floors. 'Undoubtedly, said the Emperor *Cang-hy* [Kangxi (r. 1662–1723)], whilst he was looking over some Plans of our *European* Houses, this *Europe* must be a very small and pitiful Country; since the Inhabitants cannot find Ground enough to spread out their Towns, but are obliged to live up this high in the Air.'[19]

On the other side of this doubled mirror, the Western cult of *chinoiserie* was born of European fancy and amazement.[20] Lacquer rooms appeared in seventeenth-century country houses, along with silk wallpapers and works of porcelain of the kind that inspired widespread European imitation. *Chinoiserie* entered the Baroque and the Rococo styles,[21] and 'Chinese' bedrooms became fashionable among the wealthy. A Chinese Summer House was created at Stowe in 1738. The queen of Sweden was presented with a Chinese Pavilion, complete with bells and dragons, at Drottningholm in 1753, and a few years later Frederick II of Prussia commissioned a Chinese Tea House in Potsdam. The European fantasy that was China went on to inspire diverse architects, furniture makers, and garden designers. The dragon-roofed Chinese Pagoda at Kew Gardens, designed by Sir William Chambers after the example of the Porcelain Pagoda in Nanking, was completed in 1762. Twenty or so years later Prince Franz of Anhalt-Dessau had the Oranien-baum palace and gardens at Dessau refashioned as 'most daintily and amusingly Chinese' in the sense later described by Vernon Lee: 'Chinese, because oranges are called "China-oranges," and also "mandarins." Make-believe eighteenth-century Chinese, of course, with pagodas and Chinamen on wall-papers and hangings, and slender, lacquered furniture: a little space all white and porce-lain-blue, and white and nasturtium colour, like the precious vases and teacups and saucers on the shelves.'[22] In Britain, Chinese galleries were added to many buildings, including Richard Brinsley Sheridan's Theatre Royal in London's Drury Lane (1809) and the Royal Pavilion at Brighton (1838). The cult of China moved poets—its literary manifestations include the stately pleasure dome of Xanadu in Coleridge's famously interrupted dream poem 'Kubla Khan'—and also political philosophers, who gazed into the shimmering Middle Kingdom to see their own predilections reflected back at them. Giambattista Vico's 'New Science' was influenced by Confucianism—not least in its conception of 'poetic cosmography'—and also by the account of China produced by Matteo Ripa, a Jesuit who had lived in China between 1711 and 1723, and then returned to found Europe's first School of Sinology in Naples in 1732. Leibniz also drew on a Confucian sense of organism, imagining a nature of subtle interrelatedness as opposed to Newtonian mechanism.

Such was the persistence of these imaginative appropriations that it was scarcely possible for a twentieth-century Westerner to go to China without already having more or less exotic versions of that Eastern land piled up at the back of his mind. Zealous fellow-travellers might have worked hard to redden up these lacquered scenes, but even those who professed themselves exclusively devoted to the cause of 'New China' still took with them something of legendary 'Cathay': 'a land of poetry and graciousness', as the best British historian of *chinoiserie* has described it: 'a spacious garden of azaleas, paeonies, and chrysanthemums, where the most serious business of life is to drink tea in a latticed pavilion, beside a silent lake, beneath a weeping willow; to listen to the music of piping and tinkling instruments; and to dance, to dance for ever, among the porcelain pagodas'.[23]

Junk History and the Museum of Embryos

Curiosity and fanciful admiration were certainly part of what the Western eye awarded China as its 'other'. Yet the operation also entailed denigration, mockery, and contempt such as was most forcefully expressed around the extravagant Victorian spectacle that, one hundred years later in 1951, would inspire the Festival of Britain at which Hugh Casson had made his mark as Director of Architecture.

The Great Exhibition of the Works of Industry of All Nations opened in Hyde Park, London, at the beginning of May 1851. The prodigious display was staged in Joseph Paxton's Crystal Palace, itself an astonishing structure of glass and cast iron, and the opening ceremony was enthusiastically reported in *Punch* magazine.

Noting the silence of the now overawed 'croakers and detractors' who had so loudly prejudged the Crystal Palace to be unsafe and, indeed, no better than a vast sparrow trap, 'Mr Punch' watched the arrival of Queen Victoria and Prince Albert, who had directed preparations for the exhibition, with a confidently patriotic smile.[24] He was gratified to see the royal party walking about informally among 25,000 people of all social ranks. Indeed, he hailed the sight as 'the result of our constitutional monarchy, and which all the despotism and republicanism of the world cannot obtain elsewhere'. It was, he thought, 'a magnificent lesson for foreigners—and especially for the Prussian princes, who cannot stir about without an armed escort—to see how securely and confidently a young female Sovereign and her family could walk in the closest possible contact, near enough to be touched by almost anyone'.

Yet this was not the only contrast with foreigners that came to mind. At the end of the opening ceremony, a Chinese man in full Mandarin regalia stepped out of the crowd—'carried away, or rather pushed forward', so Mr Punch reckoned, 'by his enthusiasm'. This unlikely fellow, whose performance was surely far less unprompted that it looked,[25] approached Queen Victoria and performed an 'elaborate salaam, consisting of a sudden act of prostration on his face'.

Here, in Hyde Park, was the kow-tow, a gesture that had already loomed large in Anglo-Chinese relations. The very first British mission to China, which took place in 1793, is said to have failed at least partly because George III's envoy, Lord Macartney, simply refused to prostrate himself before the Emperor Qianlong. Imperial Chinese protocol demanded that he touch the ground with his forehead no less than nine times in the manner expected of ambassadors from vassal states, but Macartney, who understood little of Qing guest ritual with its rules for 'Cherishing men from afar',[26] would have none of it. By the time of the Great Exhibition, the kow-tow was well known in Britain as 'the quintessential Chinese act', thanks not least to the interpretation of Protestant missionaries inclined to construe the Chinese as an effeminate and idolatrous people 'desperate for something to bow to'.[27] Certainly, Mr Punch enjoyed the sight of that Chinese man grovelling before Queen Victoria. He joked that this kow-towing must also be 'the cause of the general flatness of feature and particular squareness of nose of that flowery people, who, from their countenance, appear to have been sown broad-cast over a large tract of that country'.

This was by no means the first time that China had been viewed as a distant land of contrasts that was amusingly backward in its antiquity. Written for the *London Magazine* in the early 1820s, Charles Lamb's famous 'Dissertation on Roast Pig', ventured that the origin of roast pork lay in an accident suffered by a Chinese swineherd.[28] This simple fellow was said to have come home one day to find that his even more witless son had burned down the house, incinerating a sow and her newly farrowed litter in the process. It seemed an utter disaster, until he touched one of the scorched and sizzling piglets and then licked his finger to relieve the pain. Word of his discovery quickly spread, and China was soon filled with people burning down their houses in order that they too might sample the pleasures of roast suckling pig. A less comic version of this condescension was expressed in Alred Lord Tennyson's poem 'Locksley Hall' (1837): 'Better fifty years of Europe than a cycle of Cathay'.

If the mockery of China had become harsher by the time of the Great Exhibition this was, surely, on account of wider tensions. The First Opium War had ended in 1842, some nine years earlier. However, the ongoing British attempt to force China open to trade was by no means completed, and the Great Exhibition would be enlisted to the cause.

Charles Dickens was among the writers who contrasted the innovative grandeur of the British empire displayed in Paxton's Crystal Palace with the backwardness of China's 'Celestial Empire'.[29] England and China, he wrote, were the 'two countries that displayed the greatest degree of progress and the least...England, maintaining commercial intercourse with the whole world; China, shutting itself up, as far as possible, within itself'.[30] He suggested that 'the True Tory spirit would have made a China of England, if it could', adding that the likely result could be examined in a little 'Chinese exhibition' that coincided with the Great one.[31] Among the objects to be inspected at the 'Chinese Gallery' in Hyde Park Place was an authentic Chinese Lady. Exhibited as 'a lady of quality' from Canton, she sat there displaying her bound feet and singing for the entertainment of visitors. *Punch* judged the result 'as perfect as Chinese singing can be'.[32]

Together with his co-writer R. H. Horne, Dickens contrasted Britain's massive steam locomotives and industrial machines with the tinkling teacups, medicine roots, rice paper, and joss sticks of the 'flowery Empire'. He extolled the huge and thunderous printing presses that produced *The Times* every morning, contrasting them with the rudimentary and antiquated apparatus displayed at the Chinese Gallery, which boasted of being able to produce two or even three thousand copies a day. He contrasted Britain's vast suspension bridges with the dainty little pagodas and footbridges figured on Chinese porcelain. It was a merciless comparison:

> Consider the materials employed at the great Teacup Works of Kiang-tiht-Chin (or Tight-Chin), the 'bedaubing powder, ready mixed', and the 'bedaubing material:'—pith of stick, to make rice-paper; medicine-roots, hempseed, vegetable paints, varnishes, dyes, raw silk, oils, white and yellow arsenic, saffron, camphor, green tea dyes, &c. Consider the greatness of the English results, and the extraordinary littleness of the Chinese. Go from the silk-weaving and cotton-spinning of us outer barbarians, to the laboriously carved ivory balls of the flowery Empire, ball within ball and circle within circle, which have made no advance and been of no earthly use for thousands of years. Well may the three Chinese divinities of the Past, the Present, and the Future be represented with the same heavy face. Well may the dull immoveable, respectable triad sit so amicably, side by side, in a glory of yellow jaundice, with a strong family likeness among them! As the Past was, so the Present is, and so the Future shall be, saith the Emperor. And all the Mandarins prostrate themselves, and cry Amen.[33]

Three years earlier, Dickens had found another symbol of Chinese backwardness in the *Keying*. This was a Chinese junk, reputedly 160 ft long and made of teakwood, that a band of enterprising Britons had managed to acquire in Hong Kong and then sail around the Cape of Good Hope with a mixed, and increasingly irreconcilable, crew of thirty Chinese and twelve English. Having paused at St Helena, they had set sail for England but were blown off course and ended up visiting New York and Boston first. Since finally arriving in London in 1848, the *Keying* had been moored in the Thames at Blackwall, where it rapidly became established as one of the most popular visitor attractions in London. Like the later Chinese Exhibition, it had provided Dickens with ample illustration of China as a static land devoted, as he now put it, to 'Stoppage' as opposed to 'Progress'.[34]

Compared with the 'stupendous' naval anchors displayed in the outer part of the Great Exhibition, the *Keying* seemed to Dickens a 'ridiculous abortion':[35] more like 'a China pen-tray' than 'a ship of any kind'.[36] It was nothing but a 'floating toyshop',[37] the risible invention of a stagnant country where 'the best that seamanship can do for a ship is to paint two immense eyes on her bows, in order that she may see her way...and to hang out bits of red rag in stormy weather to mollify the wrath of the ocean'.[38] Here, as Dickens had concluded in 1848, was 'the doctrine of finality beautifully worked out, and shut up in a corner of a dock near the Whitebait-house at Blackwall, for the edification of men. Thousands of years have passed away, since the first Chinese junk was constructed on this model; and the last Chinese junk that was ever launched was none the better for that waste and desert of time.'[39]

Dickens was soon to be joined in his view of China as a land of 'stoppage' by Victor Hugo, the French novelist and social campaigner. In 1860, Hugo would fiercely condemn the Anglo-French destruction of the Old Summer Palace outside Peking at the end of the Second Opium War. Yet in his novel of 1869, *The Man who Laughs*, he too went on to evoke China as a morbidly static land in which every innovation was killed off shortly after conception. 'The Chinese', he wrote in an assessment that would surely have interested Joseph Needham, 'have been beforehand with us in all our inventions—printing, artillery, aerostation, chloroform.'[40] And yet 'the discovery which in Europe at once takes life and birth, and becomes a prodigy and a wonder, remains a chrysalis in China, and is preserved in a deathlike state'. China, so Hugo declared, is 'a museum of embryos'. He went on to invent a variation of the Chinese practice of foot-binding in which the so-called 'flowery people' of 1851 appear to have been converted entirely into vegetables:

> In China, from time immemorial, they have possessed a certain refinement of industry and art. It is the art of moulding a living man. They take a child, two or three years old, put him in a porcelain vase, more or less grotesque, which is made without top or bottom, to allow egress for the head and feet. During the day the vase is set upright, and at night is laid down to allow the child to sleep. Thus the child thickens without growing taller, filling up with his compressed flesh and distorted bones the relief's in the vase. This development in a bottle continues many years. After a certain time it becomes irreparable. When they consider that this is accomplished, and the monster made, they break the vase. The child comes out—and, behold, there is a man in the shape of a mug!

Professor Pulleyblank's Brilliant Lecture

On 9 October, while still in Moscow, the members of the late-travelling Second Labour Delegation had assembled to hear their young Canadian Sinologist talk about the historical background to the 'New China' they would soon be inspecting.

Aware that his audience required only the broadest outline, Professor Edwin G. Pulleyblank suggested that the story of modern China opened with the First Opium War of 1839–42. 'Manchus past their best', scribbled Barbara Castle, as her guide explained that China's dynastic ruling class was already in decay when the Western powers forced their way into the Celestial Kingdom in the interests of trade. The Boxer Uprising of 1900 was a failed counter-reform movement, and the subsequent growth of discontent and sedition among students had led to the final collapse of the Qing dynasty in 1911. Western supremacy was effectively killed in Chinese eyes by the 1914–18 war, after which the victorious Allies granted Germany's holdings in China to Japan. Progressive underground movements grew and Sun Yat-sen, who formed his new revolutionary nationalist government in Canton in 1921, looked increasingly to Communist Russia for assistance. As for Chiang Kai-shek, who took over the Kuomintang after Sun's death in 1925, 'Pulleyblank said in his view by the time Chiang had been more busy fighting communists than Japs, there was no alternative to Mao'.

Such, according to Barbara Castle's notes, was the historical path to 'New China' as the young professor sketched it for his delegates the day before they were taken back to Moscow airport to continue their eastern flight. Yet Pulleyblank was also well aware of another challenge facing Western visitors seeking to understand China, whether 'New' or old. 'China but not Cathay' had been the call of Hsiao Ch'ien, a lecturer at the University of London's School of Oriental and African Studies who tried to correct the West's distorted view of his homeland during the Second World War.[41] And Pulleyblank, who had gained his Ph.D. from SOAS a decade later, was articulate on the same theme. He knew that for a Westerner to reach China was a matter not just of travelling many thousands of miles but also of forcing a passage through centuries' worth of accumulated legend, romance, and insult—a 'theft of history' as it has more recently been called, which had surrendered China to the vegetable kingdom.[42]

Pulleyblank would address this problem directly in his inaugural lecture as Professor of Chinese Studies at the University of Cambridge, delivered a few months after his delegation's return, on 24 February 1955.[43] He opened this brilliant oration with an assault on the received view of China as a topsy-turvy kingdom inhabited by exotic flowers, cruel torturers, and effeminate morons—and quite unworthy of serious study. Since assuming his chair in 1953, Pulleyblank had 'met this attitude even in enlightened Cambridge circles'.[44] He was pleased to note, however, that 'our Western complacency is no longer quite so sure of itself. We are, I think, becoming gradually conscious that human history—or all that counts of human history—has not flowed in one main stream from Classical Greece and Rome to modern Western Europe. In our contracted twentieth-century world we are forced out of our parochial attitude, to recognize other peoples and cultures from a standpoint of equality which few if any of our immediate ancestors were capable of adopting.'

Unfortunately, however, it was one thing to recognize 'the desirability of widening one's historical horizons' but quite another to 'proceed to the enormous effort of will that is required to accomplish it'. It was, for example, still possible to open new books published as 'histories of the world' to find China granted only a couple of pages under the heading of 'ancient empires', or to turn to histories of, say, banking or political thought by authors convinced that 'such things did not exist east of the Mediterranean lands'.[45] Though partly due to a 'formidable' lack of knowledge, this failing also reflected 'the lack of a means of fitting the vast mass of detail of Chinese history into familiar patterns of Western history'. So far, the 'translation' that was necessary if Chinese history was to be 'made congruent' with Western history had been left to the 'philosophic historians' of the West.

These thinkers had at least tried to integrate China into their idea of world history. Unfortunately, however, they had used China less to enlarge their understanding than to 'provide illusory support for previously held dogmas'. They too, in other words, had fallen under the spell of their own analogies. The result, Pulleyblank suggested, was 'like the old fable of the blind men who went to the zoo. When they came to the elephant, one touched its trunk and said, "The elephant is like a snake". Another touched a leg and said, "The elephant is like a tree". Another touched an ear and said, "The elephant is like a leaf". Finally one touched its side and said, "The elephant is like a wall". Then they fell into a violent altercation as to which was right.'[46]

Pulleyblank was aware of ancient attempts to 'reconcile Chinese chronology with that proposed in the Bible, to identify the legendary Emperor Fhu-His with Noah, or to prove that Chinese was the primitive language'.[47] However, he chose to take up the story in the seventeenth and eighteenth centuries when knowledge of China began to circulate among 'learned Europeans'. It was Voltaire, the French philosopher of Enlightenment, who had come up with 'the first genuine attempt at a world history' in his *Essai sur les Moeurs*. Drawing on the accounts of Jesuit missionaries, Voltaire had praised Confucianism as an ethics based on reason. Though admirable in its break with 'European prejudice', this manoeuvre remained tied to European perspectives, being meaningful only in its Western context. Pulleyblank saw the same limitation in Montesquieu, who preferred to construe China as a place of 'naked despotism' and fear, where every person was an 'abject slave' subject to the 'capricious will of the ruler'.

In the nineteenth century, China had been denigrated as an unchanging place 'irretrievably sunk in stagnant semi-barbarism, as opposed to a dynamic and triumphant West'. This, to be sure, was how China had appeared to Dickens at the time of the Great Exhibition, but Pulleyblank saw greater damage in the idea of Chinese backwardness as it had been developed by Europe's 'philosophic historians'. He pointed out that, while Oswald Spengler had indeed concluded that China possessed a culture, he was also convinced that the said culture had been stone dead for 'nearly two thousand years'.[48] A comparable assumption was made by the Prussian philosopher of 'Spirit', G. W. Hegel. Writing in *The Philosophy of Right* (1820), Hegel proposed the 'Oriental Realm' as a theocratic order in which the individual personality has no existence, where the external world is 'God's ornament', and 'the history of the actual is poetry'. In this largely prehistoric state, wrote Hegel, 'nothing is fixed, and what is stable is fossilized...Its inner calm is merely the calm of non-political life and immersion in feebleness and exhaustion.' Pulleyblank mocked Hegel, and especially his later *Lectures on the Philosophy of History*, for portraying history 'marching majestically across the map of Eurasia with the sun to culminate in nineteenth-century Prussia'.[49] By identifying China with the most primitive stage of his dialectic, Hegel had converted it into 'the childhood of history', a condition characterized by 'duration, stability—Empires belonging to mere space, as it were—unhistorical history'.

This sort of 'claptrap'[50] would scarcely have merited serious attention, so Pulleyblank would assure his audience in Cambridge, were it not for Hegel's continuing influence. His most consequential follower Karl Marx had also imagined China as 'semi-barbarian', a land 'vegetating in the teeth of time', while its people were bound to their sunken condition by 'hereditary stupidity'.[51] Influenced by Hegel's idea of the 'Oriental Realm', Marx imagined China as the site of a primitive 'Asiatic' mode of production—thereby planting considerable obstacles in the way of the Chinese Communist intellectuals who had struggled, from the 1920s onward, to reconcile their national history with this retarded category. Pulleyblank noted the crazy contortions that followed as European, Japanese, and Chinese thinkers tried to apply Western assumptions about the 'stages' of history to China. In the case of 'feudalism', the beginning of this epoch in China had been placed 'on the one hand, as early as 1500 B.C. and, on the other hand, as late as A.D. 1000 with various intermediate points in between also chosen in one system or another'.[52]

For Pulleyblank, these absurdities only proved the validity of Karl Popper's recent assault on 'historicism',[53] in which human history is assumed to have followed a 'common organic pattern of development'. The 'extreme divergency of the interpretations that had been placed on China' in the name of scientific Marxism indicated that something was 'radically wrong with the whole method'. Having dismissed both the idea of 'Progress with a capital P' and the tendency of Western dialecticians to turn history into a predetermined magic-carpet ride, Pulleyblank would return to his opening question. How indeed should China's history be linked to that of the Western world?

A vast job remained to be done. Against overarching theories, Pulleyblank recommended precise empirical and probably also 'piecemeal' comparisons which would 'help us to analyse the factors at work in complex historical situations'.[54] This approach had been pioneered by Max Weber, whose study *The Religion of China*, demonstrated the soundness of trying to 'abstract logically defined elements from social situations, usually in the form of polar opposites'. It meant paying attention to 'the perennial problems that have assailed mankind everywhere—the basic biological urges of hunger and sex, the struggle with a grudging earth for the means of livelihood, the inadequacies of established social patterns to deal with new conditions, the oppression of the weak by the strong'. By pursuing enquiries of this sort we would, Pulleyblank was confident, 'find that Chinese history throws light on our own history in countless ways and that mankind is indeed one'.

Pulleyblank also recommended the investigation of 'actual historical connexions between China and the outside', insisting that 'Europe was never, even in the Darkest Ages, completely cut off from Asia. China was never completely isolated from the outside world.'[55] The Silk Road across Central Asia was opened two centuries before the Christian era. And the Sung dynasty (AD 960–1279), was 'a major focal point of Chinese scientific and technological development': a time in which many inventions were brought to fruition, including the military use of gunpowder: one of the Chinese innovations that would help to precipitate the collapse of the social order in medieval Europe, having spread there during 'the Mongol dominance of Eurasia'.[56]

In drawing these conclusions, and as he freely acknowledged, Pulleyblank would be much indebted to a Cambridge colleague who, only a couple of years previously, had been savagely denounced as a Communist dupe and traitor. Earlier in 1954, Joseph Needham had published the first volume of *Science and Civilisation in China*, a hugely ambitious work, which would indeed go on to transform Western understanding of China along lines similar to those Pulleyblank recommended in his inaugural lecture. Needham's book, which opened with a formidable blast against Western *chinoiserie*, promised to establish that China, which may well have been a 'museum of embryos' (Hugo) in the sense that many of its innovations had remained unexploited, had been scientifically advanced at various periods of its history, and that its discoveries and inventions had been communicated to the West, with transforming consequences, since ancient times. The first volume of this vastly ambitious work was a ground-clearing manifesto, which introduced both the case for Chinese inventiveness and the evidence of its long-standing influence in the West, and which also traced the routes, over both sea and land, that had made that communication possible.

Needham's opening volume may not have been in Pulleyblank's lap as the plane took off from Moscow, but its implications were certainly unfolding in his mind and, almost certainly, spilling out into his conversations too. In a review published in the *Listener* on 21 October, while the Second Labour Delegation was still in China, Pulleyblank had commended Needham for producing a work of 'heroic magnitude' thanks to which 'We shall be compelled to look at Chinese culture with new eyes'.[57]

Dining out in Novosibirsk

If Pulleyblank's party of trades unionists and Labour politicians showed only limited interest in clearing their minds of *chinoiserie*, this may partly have been because its members were quite worn out by the evening of Sunday, 10 October, when they were driven

back to Moscow Airport to embark on the forty-eight-hour flight
to China. As Denis Mathews wrote, 'we had walked and driven
and talked for several days with very little sleep, and most people
were showing signs of fatigue'. Derrick James recorded his sense
of dismay as their flight itinerary was outlined: 'I had a hangover
anyway, from last night's VOKS banquet and the subsequent sortie
into the Embassy night life.'

They made their first landing at Kazan, which James records as
'dark, cold, and raining'. Scheduled for a short stop, they were
escorted to an old bus, which rushed them 'over the most incredibly rutted muddy track' to a new airport building, where a full-
scale dinner was laid on. 'Needless to say we had to abandon it, as
25 minutes isn't very long for a Russian dinner. But it was long
enough for the chaps to get stuck into the brandy and vodka, and
the party was noticeably cheerful on the next leg of the flight.'

Three hours later, they hit the ground at Sverdlovsk. Passing
through a few weeks earlier, Rex Warner had only noted, 'Lunch
in odd hall. Vodka. Mud Everywhere.' The Second Labour Delegation found a more varied feast awaiting them—'vodka, brandy,
wine, smoked salmon, caviar and so on'. Derrick James was by
now finding this 'a bit too much' and asked for a couple of boiled
eggs instead: 'It was surprising how many people joined me in this
Spartan approach to gastronomy.'

On the way to Omsk, where Professor Hawkes had registered a
'very posh airport' and noted 'Brandy cleared head', the parliamentarians turned out the aircraft lights, stuffed cotton wool into
their ears and tried, without much success, to sleep. Barbara
Castle 'saw the dawn come over wild scrubby mountain country
which gave way to sparsely populated but extensively cultivated
lowland. Among belts of trees and patches of scrub and rock were
vast dark patches of ploughed earth of strange geometrical shapes
and all sizes. Every few miles a group of buildings would line the
roadway, each with its patch of cultivation: here and there clusters
of impressive agricultural buildings. It is a mystery how this sparse
population manages to cultivate these huge strips. One can only
imagine it is wheat cultivation done mechanically on the Canadian model on the prairies.'

The same sight impressed Denis Mathews, or so he informed
his mother. Headed 'In the plane beyond Omsk', his letter reveals

that he too had gazed out over 'the vast flat steppes' and struggled to capture its English likeness: 'immense areas of wheat cultivation and black ploughed earth—a vast Ben Nicholson stretching to the horizon'. Mathews also described the reception that had awaited them in Omsk: 'The plane touches down every three or four hours and tremendous meals are served. The breakfast we have just had began with lashings of red caviar and smoked salmon with the choice of roast duck or turkey, followed by cream cakes, tea and coffee and brandy! This seems a typical diet for almost any time of the day or night.'

The Second Labour Delegation descended on Novosibirsk early in the morning of 11 October. As James writes, 'the Parliamentarians had asked to see a factory there, and we were met at the airport by the Mayor and some of the town council'. They were then escorted to a fleet of cars (Zims equipped with electric windows and other de luxe fittings), and driven into the city. They passed through the derelict and dilapidated old town to reach a square of new buildings, including a vast Palace of Culture, with a concert hall as well as 'the usual huge auditorium'. Having entered this huge edifice—actually the State Academic Opera and Ballet Theatre, which had been completed in 1944—James noted that 'the Russians are very good at cloak rooms. I suppose in their winter they have to be. But everywhere you can hand over your coat, or get it back, very quickly.'

That sorted, they were welcomed by the Chief Architect, who told them about the history of Novosibirsk and, with the help of photographs both new and old, introduced them to the thoroughgoing redevelopment he was visiting on the city, and which was scheduled for completion in 1960. In 1891, so Barbara Castle recorded, Novosibirsk had consisted of 'a handful of wooden houses: the original railway was a couple of wooden platforms'. More wooden houses had been built in the following two decades ('new slums', as these miserable efforts were categorized), but the Soviets had taken the place firmly in hand after the revolution. Over a million people were living there by 1939, and the population rose to 3 million during the Second World War as the Soviet engineering industry was shunted east to avoid capture by the Nazis. After describing the past of his city, the Chief Architect unveiled the future settlement that would bulldoze it into oblivion. There was to be a new bridge over the River Ob, new radial roads

Fig 24. Denis Mathews, Edwin Pulleyblank, Barbara Castle, and William Griffiths (near right), outside the opera house, Novosibirsk (photo: Derrick James).

converging on the central square with its already built Palace of Culture, and a wholescale clearance of old buildings so that the population could be rehoused in new blocks of flats.

Having glimpsed what Novosibirsk was to become, the party were folded back into their limousines and driven out towards the factory that had been selected to receive them. James looked out on 'the most dilapidated wooden hovels; along a narrow, inordinately rough cobbled road. One saw the Russian peasant of fable here, with high boots, padded jacket, & fur cap. There were horse drawn carts, peasants leading cows, a man asleep on a bank by the road, and so on. There were wide stretches of rutted ground alongside the road, and then it would wind through unpainted tumbledown wooden shacks. It was interesting to me that no one minded our seeing this. We came to the Ob, and crossed it on a rough wooden pontoon bridge.' According to Castle, Novosibirsk was 'for all the world like a pioneer city in U.S. or Canada save that their shack development is interspersed with brash cinemas, hotels, shops and public houses whereas in Russia the first buildings to go up are factories, opera houses, workers' clubs, bridges, flats, railway stations'.

Fig 25. Limos outside the opera house in Novosibirsk. (photo: Derrick James)

After cruising past more doomed shacks, they crossed a 'ramshackle pontoon bridge' to arrive at a large works devoted to the production of machine tools and hydraulic presses. Castle noted that the trees, unlike their equivalents in Moscow, quite failed to reduce the ugliness of the place. There was a huge red sign over the gateway—'Peace will Conquer War'—but Castle concluded that it could hardly have been put there for the benefit of foreign delegates, since the Second Labour Delegation was the first party of international visitors to be received here. Welcomed by a 'grim-looking director' and his band of engineers, they were told that the factory employed some 3,000 workers and, having been founded in 1941, was the youngest in the USSR. It was also developing its own workers' settlement, complete with flats, schools, and a technical college. James noted that much of the equipment in the assembly shop hailed from the USA, Glasgow, and France. Castle watched a woman driving a huge overhead crane, and was interested to hear that only 25 per cent of the workers were women because the work was so heavy. On more conventional industrial matters, she deferred to George Doughty, General Secretary of the Association of Engineering and Shipbuilding Draughtsmen, who surveyed the factory's large-scale presses, planing machines, and grinders, declaring that he had seen 'nothing like it except in U.S. and that they leave Britain far behind'.

That judgement would not be repeated in the delegation's formal report, which stated that 'the working pace compared with that in corresponding shops in Britain' and that insufficient time had been available for an inspection of the 'factory organization'. Admiration was also expressed for the fact that the machine-tool factory owned twenty-four blocks of good-quality housing, and also its own rest homes, sanataria (in the Caucuses), and 'Centre of Culture'. The workers were permitted to be absent at harvest time in order that they may help the local farms and, moreover, received their normal pay during the period. The roads were bad, and many of them still lined with terrible housing. 'A word of praise, however, for the Soviet-built cars which conveyed us on the tour. They were based on modern American design and were extremely well sprung and soundly made.'

After a brief 45-minute stop at the factory, the delegates were conveyed to the best hotel in town for what Barbara Castle calls 'an astonishing banquet' laid on by the Mayor: 'excellent and lavish food, excited and friendly waitresses and a local orchestra complete with vocalist. Everyone drank an enormous amount and Denis was sick.' Derrick James also records sitting down at a vast table 'groaning' with bottles and food:

> The Mayor made a speech, we had a toast. Someone replied, we had another. Denis & I were sitting together, & his Russian neighbour kept on toasting him, while a chap opposite did the same to me. To do this sort of thing on vodka is a dangerous practice. So I took things easy, and then tossed off a vast glass of brandy. He didn't finish his, & then he left me alone a bit. But Denis, on my left, got horribly pickled. All this went on while we were eating caviar and smoked salmon. We went on with Georgian wine, fish, soup with dumplings containing beef, chicken and so on. Champagne and fruit saw the party well away. Speeches were incoherent.

Songs were sung, the band played, and all hell was let loose. They kept phoning from the airport that our plane was waiting. It had to wait. We left 2 hours late.

Chairman Ellis Smith must have contributed to those 'incoherent' speeches. His surviving notes, however, says nothing about Novosibirsk, except that the city was being 'extended' and that, with or without the overcoat his socialist comrades at Metropolitan Vickers had bought him before he first embarked for Russia in 1927, it was 'the coldest place I had ever been in'.[58] As for their delayed departure, the Britons were granted more slack than the Bulgarian delegation, which, as Bernal records, had also been 'royally received' in Novosibirsk. Thanks to the 'rush to get on', however, their 'sumptuous meal' could only be eaten 'as far as the soup'.

Fig 26. Mabel Ridealgh (with hat), Ellis Smith, Barbara Castle, and William Griffiths outside opera house, Novosibirsk (photo: Derrick James).

13

A Blue Jacket for Abraham Lincoln
(Paul Hogarth)

Paul Hogarth's delegation left Moscow before sunrise. Having watched the day break over 'a great brown prairie',[1] they reached Sverdlovsk by ten in the morning and then took off again, pursuing an eastern horizon that seemed to stretch away to infinity.

Siberia may have looked disconcertingly empty as well as vast. Yet it was also a land without Americans, and that must be counted a definite virtue in Hogarth's mind: 'utterly without compromise', as John Berger had recently declared that fiercely polarized organ to be.[2] As a British Communist, Hogarth had seen quite enough of the American presence in post-war Western Europe. The best collection of his drawings from the early 1950s, *Das Antlitz Europas* (*The Face of Europe*), published in the German Democratic Republic in 1956, includes a section entitled 'Amis Go home'.[3] Here America is represented by a roadside 'Esso' sign with a native European family plainly going nowhere beneath it,[4] by billboards proclaiming 'Transworld Airlines' or 'General Electric' over Constitution Square in Athens, and by lurid Hollywood films— *Fury at Furnace Creek*, *We Attack at Dawn* or *Lust in the Dust*—pulling crowds at cinemas in far too many demoralized cities.

Hogarth used his crayon to skewer a few transatlantic tourists and businessmen, but his most characteristic Americans in Europe are soldiers. He had drawn these imposing brutes as he found them in the course of his travels: swaggering about with ammunition belts slung over their shoulders, standing by a vast nuclear bomber at an airbase in Norfolk, or overwhelming a modest East Anglian dry-cleaning shop with their smart uniforms. He shows them loafing about on a street corner in baseball caps, or smashing undernourished Englishmen in fist fights and then sweeping their girls into lascivious, loose-hipped rumbas. Meanwhile, US military policemen enjoy their almighty dollars at the best tables in Europe's cafés or stand menacingly in the road—armed, helmeted, and often jack-booted too—as powerless demonstrators march by and the walls around them yell 'Yank Go Home'. Far from being peace-bringing representatives of an optimistic and anti-imperialist 'new diplomacy' such as President Woodrow Wilson had brought to the Paris Peace Conference thirty years earlier, Hogarth's Americans were the tooled-up enforcers of a 'U.S. Imperialism' that had already divided the world into blocs and was now forcing a new round of war preparations on its still exhausted allies in Western Europe.

Yet there was more to Paul Hogarth's idea of America than that. European anti-Americanism has recently been described as a 'cultural mindset' which is 'unthinkable without its flip side, philo-Americanism',[5] and hatred was indeed 'joined at the hip' with a different passion in this British artist's thinking about America. In the years since the Second World War, Hogarth had been among the Western Communists who maintained their intransigency with the help of the New York journal *Masses and Mainstream*, then among the leading organs of American Stalinism. Ferociously dogmatic articles in the issues on Hogarth's shelves likened the picture of the USSR created by assorted 'Trotskyists' and anti-Soviet 'experts' to the propaganda of the Nazis. They condemned psychoanalysis for providing a 'pseudo-scientific rationale for every phase of capitalist activity',[6] and they praised Soviet Russian efforts in realist fiction. As he read Sidney Finkelstein's defence of Soviet culture against its Western critics, Hogarth marked a passage decreeing that 'Today the bourgeois world is no longer interested in the public exploration of reality; it lives in the past; it prefers either no art at all or an art of a dream world. It fears change, and tries to contain and prohibit change. It fears any honest analysis of itself, or of its ties to fascism. Only the working class can afford to know, welcome and fight for the full picture of reality in motion.'[7] Hogarth may also be imagined nodding in agreement with Joseph Starobin's assault on America's foreign policy: 'Let's face it', wrote Starobin: 'Our country has today become the password for everything which Europe suspects, fears and hates.'[8] Starobin commended the public outrage provoked in France by the Communist poet Louis Aragon, who had pointed out that the surviving plinth of a statue of Victor Hugo, dismantled by the Nazis in 1941, had recently been used to display a model of a new car, the Ford Vedette.

Such, however, was the clanking dialectic of history in this period, that America was not only to be deplored, even by its own partisan Communists. While loudly condemning the rise of the new 'American Empire', *Masses & Mainstream* also found contrary American heroes to celebrate. These included John Reed, the enthusiastic participant observer of the Russian Revolution and author of *Ten Days that Shook the World*; Paul Robeson (also one of *Masses & Mainstream's* contributing editors), whose invitations to perform in Europe were threatened by a State Department decision not to grant him a passport;[9] and also the late Agnes Smedley—celebrated for her powerful journalism in the cause of China's revolution, in a tribute that poured predictable contempt on General MacArthur's 'Red-baiting' allegation that Smedley had actually been in China as a Soviet spy.[10]

The vision of China that loomed in Hogarth's mind as he sat in the plane, glancing down to see Siberia's 'endless steppe' give way to the 'convoluted foothills of Mongolia',[11] was shaped by a contrary American perspective: embodied not just in the popular novels of Pearl S. Buck, whose sympathetic portrayal of Chinese peasant life, *The Good Earth*, became a huge bestseller across the world after its first publication in 1931,[12] but also in a strongly anti-Imperialist line of journalistic reportage. Like many on the British left, including those members of the Britain–China Friendship Association who had eventually eased the way for the harried Agnes Smedley to leave America and spend the last months of her life in Britain, he was greatly indebted to American reporters for his understanding of the revolutionary convulsions that had been shaking China since 1911. His sources were not the cowed or compliant reporters of the post-war McCarthy era, but the more vigorous correspondents of the 1920s and 1930s, who had been inclined to associate Mao with Abraham Lincoln and, indeed, to liken China's revolutionary struggle to the American war of independence: both, after all, had been fought against a hated British imperialism.

Hallett Abend, a Californian newspaperman who would go on to become the *New York Times'* chief reporter in the country, had found his 'symbol of the white man in China' after sailing up the Pearl River to the southern city of Canton in 1926. It was a time of blazing revolutionary tension. A general strike had been called in reaction to the 'Shanghai Incident' of 30 May 1925, in which British-commanded police from the International Settlement had opened fire on Chinese demonstrators. The strike quickly spread to other cities: Hankow, Nanking, Chinkiang, Peking, and also Canton, where more fatal shootings had taken place when the international concession was besieged by tens of thousands of striking factory workers, many of whom had made their way upriver from British Hong Kong. Abend's boat had come under fire from the shore as it approached the city. Indeed, the 'pleasant Scot' with whom he was drinking in the dining room had raised his whisky and soda only to catch a bullet that came through the window, smashing his glass, and severing the tip of his index finger. Landing on the island of Shameen, Abend found that the coolies, rickshaw pullers, and servants had withdrawn from the concession under the continuing boycott. Entering his hotel, he was 'accosted' by a 'young Britisher'. The fellow was 'suffering from a hangover of too good a time the night before. Coatless and bewildered-looking, he carried in his hand an unopened tin of salmon. "Can you," he pleaded, "tell me where I can get a dingus to open this damned thing? I am hungry, and there's nothing else on hand for breakfast".'[13]

Similar attitudes prevailed in 'diplomatic and socialite Peking', where Abend found 'China's internal struggles' regarded 'with nonchalant indifference'. As he records, Western expatriates had grown accustomed to ignoring the rumbling of cannon fire that could be heard as they 'dined and danced on the roof of the Peking Hotel'[14] or enjoyed al fresco lunches and cocktail parties at the racetrack between Peking and the Western Hills.

Apprehensive or bone-headed foreigners may indeed have passed round copies of a 'thumping white man's burden' tome named *What's Wrong with China?*[15] and tried to reassure newcomers that the Chinese really didn't mind being beheaded since, as a German would tell Agnes Smedley in Tientsin, they were 'used to it'.[16] However, the events of the National Revolution of 1926/7 had also been sympathetically reported in the Kuomintang's English language paper. The *People's Tribune* was run from the revolution's epicentre in Red Hankow, by two anti-imperialist Americans, William and Rayna Prohme.[17] Based in the same building as the Soviet adviser Mikhail Borodin, the Prohmes also ran a news agency through which they influenced wider American coverage of China. Their busy collaboration was described by Anna Louise Strong, herself an American veteran of the Seattle General Strike of 1919, who had moved to Moscow in 1921 and developed a lifelong and admittedly 'mystical'[18] loyalty to the Bolshevik revolution. Strong had first visited China in 1925. Since there was no effective national government at that time, Peking seemed a bizarrely disconnected talking shop. Full of foreign diplomats and representatives, it was, Strong later remembered, 'like the League of Nations—a place where emissaries of actual powers met and maneuvered through talk. Everybody talked in Peking, in all kinds of assemblies.'[19] For effective action she had to wait until she visited revolutionary Canton as a guest of the busy Mikhail Borodin and his wife.

Returning to South China in 1927, Strong had traced the progress of the nationalist advance through the countryside. She visited 'Red Hankow' (Wuhan), and travelled out into nearby districts in which farmers were taking control of the food supply and setting up local administrations: schools, unions, and the tribunals that tried landlords, gangsters,[20] and 'grafters'—all under the name of 'People's Power'.[21] That same year, she saw Chiang Kai-shek driving the Communist leadership in Canton, Shanghai, and Hankow into hiding, and then extending his 'white terror' into the countryside, where the revolution would be defended by the emerging Red Army. Strong returned to Russia, travelling overland through the north-west and Mongolia with Borodin and his hastily withdrawing Russian advisers. Published in Moscow as well as America, her book, *China's Millions* (1928) told the story of the revolution and its now defeated fight for women's rights among other causes, and it did so from an unwaveringly pro-Moscow perspective.[22]

After the onslaught of 1927, the Communists were driven back into inaccessible areas, often in the remote borderlands between provinces. They were further isolated by a barrage of propaganda and an associated policy of 'corking up the facts'[23] maintained by Chiang Kai-shek even after 1937, when he reluctantly entered a united front with the Communists against Japan. Haldore Hanson was among the Americans who broke through to bring back news from the far side of those nationalist accusations of Communist brigandry and murder. In flight from the depression in Minnesota, he had arrived in Peking in 1934, and was soon foraying out as correspondent for Associated Press and the British *North China Daily News*.[24] Having made his way into the remote north-west held by the Communist Eighth Route Army during the Second Sino-Japanese War, Hanson marvelled at the 'young democracy'[25] being created there: 'On a Buddhist holy mountain in Northern Shansi a replica of Plato's Republic has been organized by a strange congregation of Chinese Communists, Christians, Buddhists, lamas, patriotic college students, and illiterate farmers. They are completely surrounded by Japanese troops. The little state has an area equal to Massachusetts and a population of 14,000,000.'[26]

A more influential account, and one that was certainly known to Paul Hogarth, would be produced by Agnes Smedley, who had entered China from Manchuria and the Soviet Union at the beginning of 1929, and who was indeed involved in Soviet propaganda and espionage. Her abiding hostility to imperialism had been well established by the time of the First World War, when she was jailed in New York for assisting Indian revolutionaries in their opposition to the British empire.[27] Living in Berlin in the 1920s, she had joined forces with the Indian revolutionary Virendranath Chattopadhyaya, and also become involved with the Communist International, which, in the early years of that decade, at least, operated with some measure of independence from Moscow. She had worked with Willie Muenzenburg, the Comintern's highly successful builder of publishing houses and journals, front organizations, and campaigns, including various 'Hands Off China' committees that took the side of the national revolution unfolding in China. With Smedley's assistance, he also organized the First International Congress Against Colonial Oppression and Imperialism, held in Brussels in February 1927, at which the League Against Imperialism was launched.[28]

Having previously felt considerable doubts about the course of the revolution in Russia, Smedley would describe being thrown 'completely into the arms of the Bolsheviks'[29] by the events of 1927.

That was when Chiang Kai-shek had moved against his Communist allies in China, but it was also the year in which Britain broke
relations with Soviet Russia after a police raid at the Soviet trade
mission in London turned up evidence of espionage and subver-
sion within the British empire. As international tension escalated,
Smedley became a journalist for the London-based front organization, the Chinese Information Bureau, and its Berlin partner the
Chinese News Agency.[30] She entered China as a journalist but also
a Comintern agent who was protected, in a way that no Russian
could be after Chiang's severance of relations with the Soviet
Union, by her possession of an American passport.

Basing herself in Shanghai, Smedley monitored Western invest-
ments in China, distributed propaganda, channelled funding to
the Communists, participated in a courier service that kept links
with Moscow, and rallied other sympathetic foreigners to the
cause. She also tried to dodge the attention of various intelligence
services, including the British (which had been aware of her anti-
imperialist activities long before her arrival in China), as they
surveyed her and speculated about her relations with other spies,
including the pair known as Hilaire and Gertrude Noulens (actually the Russians Yakov Rudnik and Tatyana Moiseenko), Richard
Sorge, who passed as 'Johnson' and was eventually executed in
Japan, and various other international Communist agents,
including Arthur Ewert and Gerhardt Eisler.

Smedley's first book about the country, *Chinese Destinies: Sketches
of Present-day China*,[31] offers a number of portraits of people whose
lives and decisions reflected the paths available in the years of
struggle. Published in 1934, these vivid 'sketches' are partisan
allegories in which every decision or event bears simple ideological significance. Rebellious sons break with their mortified families in order to join the revolution. Girls unbind their feet and
refuse marriage for the life of a Communist, or submit and then
find themselves desperately aping Western fashion in an attempt
to keep their husband's eye from wandering in the Shanghai bars.
Landless peasants and coolies raise themselves up from centuries
of exploitation to join the People's Army, and young student
Communists remain heroically true to the struggle despite the
barbaric torture and execution that awaits them at the hands of
Chiang Kai-shek's identifiably fascist 'blue shirts'.

Drawing on hearsay rather than direct observation, Smedley also gave her Western readers a 'first glimpse'[32] of the agrarian Communism being developed under Mao Tse-tung, Chou En-lai and others in the remote rural areas of Kiangsi and Fujian, where the Chinese Soviet Republic was formed at a meeting in Ruijin on 7 November 1931. She includes a version of the fall of Shangpo, in South Kiangsi. This walled city had been hated as the power centre of rich landlords who had luxuriated on the misery of hundreds of decaying villages all around.[33] In 1929, the approach of the Red Army had been preceded by reports that all the landlords in a recently fallen town had been 'slaughtered', so the 3,000 members of the eighteen ruling families in Shangpo had tried to ingratiate themselves to their savagely mistreated peasants by reducing rents and sending wine and even pigs to the villages they had for so long starved and brutalized. They also warned of the horrors to come at the hands of the 'bandit army' approaching under its red banners.[34]

In Smedley's story, however, the 'bandit' army turns out to be a miraculous and improving force. It organizes mass meetings as it advances, promising to hand the land over to the peasants, who would be encouraged to form their own Red Guards to defend themselves in future. Such was the climate of fear the landlords had created among the peasants that the mobilization seemed to fail at first. Refusing to attack Shangpo without having established a Red base among the masses, the Red Army withdraws and the landlords go back to their old ways with relief. The city finally fell to the Red Army when it returned two years later: no longer 'a ragged, barefoot partisan army, it was now uniformed, disciplined and well-armed' and the triumphant peasant masses, who had finally rallied to the Red standard with their hoes, knives, and, spears rushed for revenge: 'blind with hatred' they burn and destroy everything possessed by the landlords, stripping them naked, wrecking their temples, destroying their stores of opium. 'Mau Tse-tung' is introduced at the moment they prepare to kill the landlords, an already 'legendary' figure who tries to limit the wave of executions by sparing the women and children. But the peasants' vengeful rage is overwhelming. Every member of those eighteen families is speared to death and then buried in the fields to fertilize the ground—the landlords themselves, of course, but also their women, children, and babies, one of which is torn from its mother's arms and smashed against the earth by a peasant woman maddened when her husband and seven sons were killed by the landlords.[35]

Smedley neither obscures nor condemns the violence of this improving massacre. Justified by the brutalization the peasants have for so long suffered at the hands of the landlords, the slaughter is portrayed as the necessary settlement without which the revolutionary transformation of Shangpo cannot begin. That job done, unions are formed, industries are brought back into production, and a Soviet government is created. Land is redistributed and opium cultivation, imposed by the hated landlords, is banned: 'In such a way did the Red Army reach into the hearts of the masses and start the long work of creating that which the peasants seemed to have always longed for.'[36] The book could hardly be more firmly on the side of the Red Army, yet it was not published in Russia, where its portrayal of Chiang Kai-shek as a loathsome imperialist killer clashed with an emerging Russian policy of encouraging the Chinese Communist Party (CCP) to form another united front with the Kuomintang to resist China's Japanese invaders.

Smedley followed *Chinese Destinies* with *China's Red Army Marches* (1936), another series of 'stories based on actual events' concerned with the Red Army and its development of the Chinese Soviet Republic from 1928 to 1931. Having helped to introduce Western readers to the revolution as it was carried out by the Red Army in Kiangsi, Smedley hoped to be the writer who would give the world its first insider account of 'the Long March' of 1934–5, a fighting retreat that took the First Red Army an alleged (and still disputed) 8,000 miles, from Kiangsi, where it had been defeated, to the north-west, where it met up with the remnants of the Fourth Red Army, which had withdrawn from Henan, and the Second Red Army from Hubei.

As it happened, however, the Chinese Communists chose a different American journalist to penetrate the 'news blockade as effective as a stone fortress'[37]—or, in Anna Louisa Strong's phrase, 'the steadily narrowing iron ring'[38]—that had isolated their areas for nearly ten years, and to tell their story to a world that had yet to appreciate that they were not simply the murderous 'brigands' of nationalist accusation nor, for that matter, mere puppets of Moscow.

A Missourian like Smedley, Edgar Snow had arrived in Shanghai in 1928, becoming a journalist at the *China Weekly Review* before going on to teach at Yenching University near Peking. He had met Smedley shortly after her own arrival in Shanghai,[39] and later cooperated with her in Peking, where he became involved in her front organization, the League of Civil Rights in China. Unlike Smedley, however, Snow was not known as a Communist sympathizer and, as a journalist who wrote for the *New York Sun*, the *Daily Herald* in London and the *Saturday Evening Post*, his access to the Western media was frankly superior.[40] So, during a lull in the civil war in 1936, and with his passage eased by an introduction from Sun Yat-sen's widow and a letter to Mao Tse-tung, written in invisible ink by a Red commander in Peking,[41] Snow had taken the train from Peking to Sianfu in Shensi. From there he went by truck, over rough roads and through fields of opium poppies, forced on the peasants by 'greedy warlords',[42] to Yenan and Pao An, then the Communist capital, where he stayed to conduct long interviews with Mao Tse-tung, Chou En-lai, and other Communist leaders. The following year, he continued these conversations, before returning to Peking to write his admittedly 'partisan'[43] account of their struggles.

Snow's findings, many of which were written down as dictated by the Communist leaders, were presented in his hugely influential book *Red Star over China*, first published in Britain by Victor Gollancz's 'Left Book Club' in 1937. It was, as Snow pointed out on behalf of his own book, 'one of the amazing facts of our age' that 'not a single "outside" foreign observer had entered Red territory'[44]—either when the Red army was in the south (Smedley was a friend of Snow's, but he apparently viewed her imaginative 'sketches' of the Communist regime in Kiangsi as belonging to merely 'secondary material'), or after the Long March that took the retreating Red Army to the north-west. As the first close-up account of the Communists and their struggle against both Chiang Kai-shek and the Japanese, the widely translated book had a sensational impact, becoming one of the sacred books of the Western left. It would continue to shape perceptions throughout the Second World War, assisted by the fact that the Red Army's liberated areas remained inaccessible for years—isolated by the Japanese occupation and blockaded from the rear by Chiang Kai-shek.

Snow introduced Chou En-lai as he first encountered him in the flood-wrecked town of An Tsai: not the gruesome bandit of nationalist legend, but 'a slender young officer', wearing 'a black beard unusually heavy for a Chinese' and speaking in English in 'a soft, cultured voice: "Hello," he said, "are you looking for somebody?"' Chou's headquarters in a nearby village turned out to be 'a bomb proof hut' that was actually 'half cave' and, as Snow insisted, no grander than the caves lived in by farmers all around.[45] It was barely furnished, with only a couple of dispatch boxes, a wooden table, and a mosquito net suspended over the clay k'ang. A single guard protected the life of the man for whom Chaing Kai-shek had offered a reward of $80,000, and who now welcomed Snow, commending him as a truthful reporter although not actually a Communist, and helped him draw up an itinerary for the ninety-two-day trip that would introduce him to the Communist areas.[46] Like many Red leaders, Chou was 'as much a legend as a man', and Snow wrote nothing that would not enhance the status of this 'Red bandit' who smiled back at him with those 'large, warm, deep-set eyes'.[47]

He met Mao Tse-tung at the Red Army headquarters at Pau An: 'a gaunt, rather Lincolnesque figure, above average height for a Chinese, somewhat stooped, with a head of thick black hair grown very long, and with large, searching eyes, a high-bridged nose and prominent cheekbones'.[48] The Communist leader impressed Snow as having 'an intellectual face of great shrewdness', and he walked about hatless and unguarded, 'despite the $250,000 which Nanking had hung over his head'. After interviewing Mao many times, Snow concluded that 'There would never be any one "savior" of China, yet undeniably one felt a certain force of destiny in Mao. It was nothing quick or flashy, but a kind of solid elemental vitality.'[49] Rejecting the 'strange legends' that had grown up around Mao outside the Communist areas, he was also careful not to place him at the centre of a Stalin-like personality cult: 'while everyone knew and respected him, there was—as yet, at least—no ritual of hero worship built up around him. I never met a Chinese Red who drooled "our-great-leader" phrases, I did not hear Mao's name used as a synonym for the Chinese people, but still I never met one who did not like "the Chairman"—as everyone called him—and admire him. The role of his personality in the movement was clearly immense.'[50] Like Chou En-lai, Mao enjoyed the use of a mosquito net. He also indulged a Hunanese appetite for pepper. These 'luxuries' aside, he ate the same food as the rank and file, and his living quarters were modest.[51] He was well read, knowledgeable about world politics, and convinced that President Roosevelt was at heart an anti-Fascist with whom he could cooperate. He was dignified but 'quite free from symptoms of megalomania'.[52] A soldier told Snow he had seen Mao give his coat to a wounded man at the front, and it was also said that he 'refused to wear shoes when the Red warriors had none'.[53] Snow himself saw Mao's eyes fill with tears as he spoke of dead comrades or remembered how, in famine-struck Yunan during his youth, he had seen starving peasants beheaded 'for demanding food from the yamen'. Mao was a humanist with 'nothing in him that might be called religious feeling',[54] and yet he emerged from Snow's revelatory pages as a positively Christ-like figure.

Yet these were only introductory sketches. In a series of lengthy interviews, the transcripts of which Mao himself corrected for accuracy, the Chinese leader told the story of his life in personal as well as political detail. He reviewed the rise of the Communists from the earliest stirring, and the development of their army, which, though it may have started out as a handful of barely trained men with even fewer rifles, was now rightly legendary for the mobile guerrilla warfare with which it was prevailing against far larger and better equipped enemy forces. He spoke of the Communists' remarkable progress in education and literacy both in Kiangsi and now in the north-west—work that had been led by thousands of young volunteers. He repeatedly affirmed that the Communists were sincere in having suspended their drive towards social revolution, in order to unite with the nationalists in the war against Japan. He also explained why the Communists had not been able to suspend their land redistribution programme, as demanded by their delinquent nationalist partners in the war against Japan: to do so, Mao explained, would be to remove the main factor motivating the peasants in their heroic and self-sacrificing war against the Japanese. Glancing West, the Communist leader, who would later strike Agnes Smedley as a man of off-puttingly feminine demeanour, insisted that the Communists were more than willing to cooperate with America and other Western powers in the battle against fascism.

Not content with offering these sensational portraits of the CCP's leaders, Snow also presented the Communists' own account of key moments in the struggle for China. He provided a new version of the 'Sian Incident', of 11 December 1936, a 'coup de théâtre'[55] in which Marshall Chang Hsüeh-liang and General Yang Hu-ch'eng had kidnapped Chiang Kai-shek, and demanded the formation of a National Resistance Government. Chou En-lai travelled from Yenan to negotiate with Chiang, and the Communists then made the sensational decision to let him go, seasoned killer of Communists that he was. The nationalists agreed to form a common front against the Japanese not long afterwards. There was nothing here of the mysterious background to this still only partly understood incident—of the allegedly Communist allegiances of at least one of the warlords who had captured Chiang, or the communications that passed between Stalin and the Chinese Communists as they decided to restrain their impulse to order Chiang Kai-shek's execution.

It was, however, the Long March that stood at the centre of Snow's account: a legendary trek—actually a fighting retreat—that emerged from the pages of *Red Star Over China* even more fabled than it had been before. The Long March had taken the Red Army from an assembly point in southern Kiangsi over a course of 6,000 miles to Shensi in the north-west, where Snow now found them. The soldiers started by breaking through the nationalist troops isolating them, and then marched through Hunan, battling their way through enemy positions as they went. Snow related it as a story of valour, cunning, and all but impossible endurance, with encounters that, in their own way, are as arresting as those evoked by Marco Polo and other European travellers of the medieval age. The young men of the Red Army climbed barefoot over sky-high mountains, and then descend to plough their way through 'waist-deep mud'. In Szechuan, they made their way through 'Independent Lololand', winning over the 'warlike aborigines' by explaining their policy of granting autonomy for China's national minorities. When they came to the Bridge Fixed by Liu, they found that the wooden planks forming the crossing had been removed, and that nothing remained but the iron chains that had supported them. Undeterred by enemy machine-gun fire, and with great self-sacrifice, they climbed across and then fought their way through the apparently impregnable enemy positions beyond.

Reaching the border of Tibet, they marched through jungles and forests held by the implacably hostile Mantzu tribesmen who lurked invisibly all around them. Soldiers left the road to search for food, and never returned. Well-aimed boulders thundered down on them as they thinned out to file through narrow passes. Then came the Great Grasslands, which turned out to be a swamp, with endless rain and no human habitation at all: a 'weird sea of wet grass' in which animals and soldiers who lost the narrow path simply dropped out of sight, never to be seen again. In a year of marching, they crossed eighteen mountain ranges and twenty-four rivers, breaking through the armies of ten different warlords as well as the government troops that had tried to contain and destroy them.

The survivors of this fatal undertaking arrived at northern Shensi in October 1935, where they were reunited with the remnants of other Red Armies, which had taken different routes. Whatever 'one may feel about the Reds,' wrote Snow, 'it was impossible to deny recognition of their Long March' as 'one of the great exploits of military history'.[56]

Published in 1937, Snow's account of the Chinese revolution was embraced by a wider spectrum of Western opinion than might ordinarily be drawn to a work of what Snow himself would later describe as 'history seem from a partisan point of view'.[57] It was a terrific story, a great documentary fiction, skilfully rather than just dogmatically told, and it did more than any other account to establish the Chinese Communists as heroic freedom fighters in the minds of the Western left. Convinced that the crises and injustices of capitalism faced them with a stark alternative between Fascism and Communism, thousands read the first editions of Snow's book and embraced the leaders of the Chinese Communist Party as the virtuous opposite of Chiang Kai-shek and his sidekicks: scheming and self-interested crooks who were indeed busily diverting Western aid, murdering peasants and idealistic students, proscribing even liberal organizations, promoting gangsterism, and trying to conserve the most despicable aspects of Chinese life. *Red Star Over China* developed new attractions during the Second World War, appealing to the self-interest of the Western powers, who were, so Snow later remarked, 'hoping for a miracle' in China that would keep the Japanese so 'bogged down' that they would never be able to turn upon their 'true objectives' in the Western colonies.[58] If *Red Star Over China* was the sensational first report from the inaccessible Communist republic, it was also destined to be the last for many long years. Thanks to Chiang Kai-shek's breach of the united front, which had been renewed in 1937, *Red Star Over China* would remain the unrivalled account of the Communist leadership through most of the Second World War. Already isolated by the Japanese occupation, the red bases in the north-west were rendered entirely inaccessible to journalists from 1940, when the Nationalists set about blockading them from the rear.

Snow's portrayal of the Chinese Communists still dominated the perceptions of the Western left in 1943, when Agnes Smedley published her *Battle Hymn of China*. She had followed the Fourth Route Army for three whole years, but could do little more than add her own pictures to those in Snow's already established gallery. She covers the Long March and also the Sian incident of December 1936, which she herself had witnessed and, as she would claim rather possessively, first reported. She includes her own close-ups of Mao in his cave at Yenan ('Calling on him at midnight, I pushed back a padded cotton drape across a door in a mountain cave, and stepped into a dark cavern'),[59] of the leader of the Eighth Route Army, Chu Teh, being shaved on the terrace, of Chou En-lai, looking, once again, handsome, highly cultured, and as impressive as Jawaharlal Nehru in his combination of 'education, vision, and statesmanship'.[60] Her own statement of commitment was unhedged: 'I am deeply, irrevocably convinced that the principles embodied in the heart of the Eighth Route Army are the principles that will guide and save China, that will give the greatest of impulses to the liberation of all subjected Asiatic nations, and bring to life a new human society. This conviction in my own mind and heart gives me the greatest peace that I have ever known.'[61]

Paul Hogarth was with Smedley on every word of that. For him, as for many other Western sympathizers, the case had been sealed by events of 1939 when the second Sino-Japanese War, which had already been under way for two years, was subsumed into the wider Second World War. The new alliance brought other Westerners to China, including many who formed a highly positive impression of the Communists in contrast with the nationalists who had reneged on the agreement of 1937. These included Norman Bethune, the Canadian surgeon from Montreal, who ran hospitals for the guerrilla forces under the auspices of the American Committee for Medical Aid to China, and who died as a result of a Japanese gas attack in November 1939. Medical assistance also came from the Indian National Congress, which sent an X-ray unit among other resources, and also from Father Lebbe, a Belgian priest who took his Service Corps into the occupied area in Hopei. American aid included various Red Cross schemes and an anti-malaria mission, funded under the Lend-Lease programme, which worked along the Yunan–Burma railway. The British sent medical missions under the Red Cross and also the Friends Ambulance Unit.

The Cambridge biochemist and Christian socialist, Joseph Needham, had been carried into 'Free China' on that same optimistic wave. Arriving in 1942 to run the British Council's Sino-British Science Cooperation Office, his job, which Needham and his wife Dorothy would remember in *Science Outpost*, was to help break the 'intellectual and technical blockade'[62] imposed by Japan. He travelled widely through west China, visiting scientists in areas under Communist as well as nationalist control, and organizing the provision of equipment, publications, and other supplies. An unnamed Chinese student reporter who heard Needham lecture at West China Union University in Hua Ta, described him as 'a stout man who is very active in his behaviour' who used his 'echoing and quick voice' to urge that science should be considered 'the forecast of the world of tomorrow'.[63] He also records Needham's insistence that, despite the Nazi denial of any idea of common humanity, 'the social development of mankind is approaching the inauguration of one whole collective society...If we make further efforts in this direction, the age of "All within the four seas are one family" will not be far distant.' In the Needhams' minds, at least, the British Council's 'Science Cooperation' project was linked to the wider vision of science as a new 'International', which Joseph Needham would later take with him to UNESCO, when he started work as the agency's first Director of the Section of Natural Sciences in 1946.

While some foreign sympathizers ventured into the Communist north-west from their British Council teaching jobs, as Ralph Lapwood and Michael Lindsay had done from Yenching University, others joined the work of the Industrial Cooperatives, also known as Indusco, set up by the New Zealand Communist Rewi Alley to produce goods for the war effort under the motto 'Gung-ho' or 'Work Together'. Peter Townsend, who had arrived in China in 1941, was soon seconded to the Industrial Cooperatives from the Friends Ambulance Service. Another idealistic young Englishman, George A. Hogg, had reached Shanghai in 1938, a year or so after leaving Oxford, and worked for a while as a reporter for United Press. Having himself attended what Alley describes as 'a "crank" international school in Switzerland',[64] he joined the Industrial Cooperatives as headmaster of a technical school for boys, where he contrived a progressive curriculum in which group singing, daily swimming in the nearby river, and diverse exercises in self-managed activity were obligatory.[65] Hogg contracted tetanus at the school in Shandan, Gansu province, and died in 1945. Full of hope even during his last days, he asked Alley to read him extracts from *Red Star over China* and also *The Communist Manifesto*.[66] Like John Cornford, the young Cambridge-educated Communist and poet who died in the Spanish Civil War in December 1936, Hogg became a heroic figure of sacrifice in the pantheon of the British left.

To the later outrage of Senator McCarthy and his anti-Red crusaders, a number of influential figures in the American military had also formed a very positive view of the Communists during the Second World War. Known as 'Vinegar Joe', General Joseph Warren Stilwell became Chief of Staff to Chiang Kai-shek and commander of the China Burma India Theater. He ran the provision of Lend-Lease to the Chinese government, until recalled from China on the demand of Chiang Kai-shek. Stilwell despised the nationalist government for its incompetence and corruption, its indifference to the welfare of its own starving conscripts, its reluctance actively to take the fight to the enemy, and its manipulation of American aid in an attempt to sabotage the Communist armies with which it was meant to be aligned. He also admired the PLA for its conduct of guerrilla warfare, even if he was less voluble in his praise than Evans Carlson, an American marine officer who would rival both Snow and Smedley (whom Carlson had met and befriended in Yenan), in his praise of the Communist leaders. Carlson commended Mao as 'the most selfless man I ever met, a social dreamer, a genius living fifty years ahead of his time' while also hailing Chu Teh, commander of the Eighth Route Army, as 'the prince of Generals, a man with the humility of Lincoln, the tenacity of Grant, and the kindness of Robert E. Lee'.[67] Described by Smedley as a man whose principles 'were deeply rooted in early American Jeffersonain democracy',[68] he would also remember the 'gung ho' spirit of the Chinese revolution after returning to the United States. Placed in command of the Second Marine Raider Battalion in 1941, he remodelled his force after the example of the Chinese Eighth Route Army. Known as 'the Gung Ho Raiders', his men proved highly effective against the Japanese in the South Pacific.

Paul Hogarth may not have known much about Stilwell and Carlson or their respect for the Chinese Communists. And yet, as he walked back to the runway from the restaurant at Novosibirsk airport, following a company of leather-coated trade union officials from Warsaw and Prague through gardens in which the white plaster figures of Lenin and Stalin loomed 'like ghosts from the dense shrubbery',[69] he surely understood how quickly the moment of Stillwell and Carlson had passed after the close of the Second World War. By the beginning of 1947, the Americans had abandoned their post-war mission, led by General George C. Marshall, to break through the 'overwhelming suspicion'[70] of both the Nationalists and the Communists and establish a lasting truce so that President Truman's dream of a 'united and democratic China'[71] might be realized. Leaving the two sides to resume their civil war, General Marshall flew home to take up his new position as Secretary of State. The fate of his Executive Headquarters in Peking, based in the Rockefeller-funded Peiping Union Medical College, would be decided by the Chinese, already accustomed to mocking this foreign bastion as 'The Palace of Ten Thousand Sleeping Colonels'.[72]

14

How China Came to Cookham

(Stanley Spencer)

Stanley Spencer shuddered 'when the engine went "fit! Fit! Fit!"' At one of these moments, so he would later explain to his brother, 'I looked down into a forest and said to myself "There are bears in there"'.[1] In general, however, the English artist found even 'the plane part' of the flight over Siberia 'a wonderful experience'.[2] He would later claim to have been thrilled by every glimpse, even if he had struggled to spell out the various stops along the route from Moscow. At 'Caygan' (Kazan) he made a pencil sketch which he labelled 'little boy asleep in arms of mother'.[3] He enjoyed 'a good late lunch' at 'Uhlmst' (Omsk), where they had landed on grass and walked along wooden planks to the restaurant, which Spencer found 'very festive…much beaming and smiling. Oh I so love these Siberian places.'[4]

Spencer sometimes identified himself as a socialist, but his socialism was of an idiosyncratically adjusted Christian variety, much closer to the vision of John Ruskin than to the Communism of Paul Hogarth or, for that matter, the fierce 'agrarian reform' pioneered under the name of 'New Democracy' by Mao Tse-tung and his comrades. Spencer liked to paint 'resurrections' not violent revolutions: oddly ecstatic moments in which dead people rise up in their cemeteries and churchyards, pushing aside heavy clods of earth as they step out of their graves and, in some versions, sprouting angelic wings as well as floral dresses and cosy woollen jumpers painted, so Spencer's brother Gilbert remembered, from magazine knitwear and fashion advertisements.[5] No slogan-spouting militants seeking to demolish their way into the future, Spencer's blinking and often lumpish figures are content to bring native flowers into bloom as they emerge in a rapture of amazed fulfilment. So it was with China. News of that remote land had long since found its way into Spencer's mind, but the version of Cathay installed there was hardly a new experiment in Communist power.

Though he may not have shared Richard Carline's interest in politics, 'mild' or otherwise, Spencer had learned from his brother-in-law's knowledge of the peoples of Africa and Asia. The collection of black folk beamed into the churchyard in *The Resurrection, Cookham* (1924–6) together with the cracked and solidified pool of African mud in which they are so firmly stuck is said to have been lifted from photographs that Carline had collected from issues of *National Geographic*. Similar sources informed the painting *Love Among the Nations* (1935), in which a clothed Asian lady stands beneath a vast straw hat among a sprawling carnival of more or less naked people of all races and hues. Here was the separation of peoples overthrown in a curious erotic embrace that Spencer would attribute not to any desire to inject passion into the flagging League of Nations, but to 'my feelings for the east generally'.[6]

For Spencer, the thought of Asia was jumbled up with the power of love to 'break down barriers'.[7] It was also shaped by a long-standing interest in ancient Eastern religions. It is said that, while staying at the Carlines' house in Hampstead in the 1920s, Spencer had read Sir Edward Arnold's poem about Buddha, 'The Light of Asia'.[8] He also became fascinated by Indian friezes, and by the ancient erotic carvings on the Khajuraho temples in Madhya Pradesh, finding in these ingeniously entwined figures inspiration for his *Love Among the Nations*.[9] He is said also to have read the Tao Te Ching, attributed to Lao Tzu, and, in 1932, to have made a drawing of his life modelled on the ninth-century reliefs showing the life of Buddha at Borobudur, in central Java.[10] As Carline himself would remember, Spencer had become 'intensely interested in Asiatic cultures, especially those of Islam, India and China'.[11] The point is confirmed by John Chinnery, who observes that Spencer knew quite a lot about China, even though his understanding owed nothing to the enraptured portraits provided by Edgar Snow and Agnes Smedley, which had so moved Carline, Hogarth, and many others in the circle of the Britain–China Friendship Association.

As an artist who coincided with the modernist movements of the early twentieth century, Spencer may have been aware of Ezra Pound's 'Cathay' (1915)—a brilliant 'invention of China'[12] in which the late Ernest Fenellosa's versions of ancient Chinese texts were used to bring about an 'imagist' renewal of poetic language in free verse. The resulting texts had scandalized more conventional translators, but their admirers included the sculptor Henri Gaudier Brzeska, who carried a copy of *Cathay* with him to the western front, delighted by Pound's confident advance through Li Po's 'valley of the thousand bright flowers'.[13]

Spencer's idea of China may also have been touched by the lower visions brewed up around the tiny Chinese settlement near the docks at Limehouse in London's East End. Here were a few hundred people, mostly men, whose modest lives supported a vast superstructure of onlooking fantasy: the opium dens described or imagined by Dickens, Conan Doyle, and others; the hugely popular fictions of Sax Rohmer's Chinese 'devil doctor' Fu Manchu, with his marmoset, his silk, and his aromatic converted warehouse in Wapping; or the more sympathetically intended evocations of Thomas Burke, whose story 'The Chink and the Child', published in *Limehouse Nights* in 1916, was twice filmed as *Broken Blossoms.*

While it remains impossible to gauge how much early twentieth-century *chinoiserie* had found its way into the back of Spencer's mind, there can be no doubt that he knew quite a lot about the traditional forms of painting and calligraphy practised in the 'flowery kingdom'. He is likely to have seen the collections in the British Museum's Department of Oriental Prints and Manuscripts, run by the scholar and poet Laurence Binyon, and also by Arthur Waley, appointed Binyon's assistant keeper in 1913. He may also have visited the hugely influential International Exhibition of Chinese Art, which opened at the Royal Academy of Arts in November 1935: a prodigious display assembled under the direction of the wealthy collector Sir Percival David, and with the collaboration of many museums and collections around the world, and of Chiang Kai-shek's Chinese government too.

Yet Spencer's knowledge of Chinese art was not based only on ancient relics. A different migration had already been under way by the time of that International Exhibition, and it would soon enough bring twentieth-century Chinese paintings to Spencer's door in Cookham—modern works that were, nevertheless, still informed by the traditional qualities that two British enthusiasts, including the young Alan Watts, had called 'the Spirit of the Brush'.[14]

The Silent Traveller

A significant landing was made on 15 June 1933, when a man about 30 years old arrived in London from France, having just sailed from China in fear of his life.[15] Chiang Yee had grown up in Kiukiang, a district in the province of Kiangsi. Like many Chinese of his generation, he had been inspired by the nationalist student movement, which, in May 1919, opposed the Treaty of Versailles for granting Germany's holdings in Shandong to Japan. After studying chemistry at university in Nanking, Chiang went on to teach and then served with Chiang Kai-shek's northern expeditionary force, which marched from Canton province with the aim of subduing the warlords and unifying China under nationalist rule.

Untouched by Chiang Kai-shek's bloody purge of Communists in 1927, Chiang was appointed to various administrative offices, eventually becoming governor of his own district of Kiukiang. In this role, he had tried genuinely to address the needs of the people in the county. As a consequence, he had fallen foul of Western interests—notably the oil company Texaco, which was involved in corrupt land deals[16]—and also made an enemy of a powerful and increasingly threatening warlord. As the pressure built, he had resigned his job and then been urged to leave China by relatives who feared for his life. He sailed from Shanghai, leaving behind his wife and four young children.

Once in London, Chiang Yee found teaching work at the School of Oriental Studies at London University. He also began to be known for his skills as a painter in the Chinese style. He was approached by Dr Richard St Barbe Baker, a forester and founder of the campaign known as the Men of the Trees, who was planning an exhibition of paintings of the world's trees, and had heard of this accomplished Chinese exile's abilities with brush, ink, and semi-absorbent paper. Chiang Yee contributed a painting of a spray of bamboo, and was surprised, when Baker's exhibition opened, to find his work reproduced in the *Evening Standard*. Encouraged, he applied his skills to other London subjects, and soon placed a painting of ducks in St James's park in the *Illustrated London News*.[17] Before long he was being approached by well-known collectors of Chinese porcelain and paintings, and further opportunities presented themselves with the approach of the International Exhibition of Chinese Art at the Royal Academy of Arts. Chiang was commissioned to write a book about Chinese painting, published as *A Chinese Eye*, just before the exhibition opened in November 1935. With the encouragement of publishers, he went on to produce *A Chinese Childhood*, an autobiographical account of his early years, growing up in Kiukiang, not far from his beloved Lu mountain, and a study of *Chinese Calligraphy* too.

And there Chiang Yee's English adventure might have ended. He was intending to return to China in 1936 or thereabouts, but the Japanese invasion of his tormented homeland wrecked his plans. Staying in England, and feeling both guilty and anxious about the fate of his wife, children, and brother, who had quickly been displaced by the Japanese occupation of Kiukiang, he was soon reaching around for activities that would take his mind off their plight.

Reading various English books about China, Chiang was irritated by the imperialist clichés that seemed to fill them. Opium smokers, beggars, and coolies were indeed part of the Chinese scene, but he knew that these were more or less 'picturesque' details of a history that demanded much deeper understanding, and that the writers and publishers who harped on about them were 'pandering to an unhealthy curiosity in their readers'.[18] As he reflected on these miserable portraits of his country, he conceived the idea of writing about England as it appeared to him, and of doing so with the purpose of seeking out the 'similarities among all kinds of people not their differences or their oddities'.

So it was that *The Silent Traveller* was born. The name was actually derived from the pen-name that Chiang Yee had adopted while still in China. He gave the literal translation of the name as 'Dumb-walking-man', a choice inspired by the fact that, during his years as district governor, he had discovered the truth of Confucius's warning that 'talking too much leads to trouble'.[19]

At first Chiang Yee found British publishers reluctant to join him in the project. They informed him that there would be little interest in his combined commentary and paintings of the British scene, and warned that his proposed title *The Silent Traveller* sounded 'sinister' and might even 'induce inquiries from Scotland

Yard: Why does a Chinaman want to walk silently?' they would wonder. 'Many English people at the time had not forgotten about Dr Fu Man Chu'.[20]

Yet Chiang got a commission all the same. In the first book, the Silent Traveller spent a fortnight in the Lake District. Stepping out in his new persona having taken the train from Euston, he saw unexpected resemblances in the mountains ('I seemed to be back in my own country'[21]). At Derwent Water, he found the rain falling in steady lines 'as if a Chinese screen made of bamboo were hanging in front of my eyes',[22] while the swans and shouting boatmen reminded him 'instantly of the Chinese Westlake in Hangchow'.[23] To illustrate his book, he made brush and ink paintings of lakes, mountains, and fluffy clouds, including one that rolled down purple scree towards him like 'a dragon coming down from the Heavens'.[24] The trees also transported him back to China: especially the weeping willows that he knew as one of the most prominent fixtures in the Chinese landscape. In his text, he reflected on his peregrinations and encounters. He also keeps breaking into verse, quoting from Wordsworth and Shelley, as well as from Li Po or, indeed, from Chiang Yee himself: the latter examples not always being hugely superior to the vegetable lyrics that the British chronicler of East London, Thomas Burke, had a decade earlier planted in the mouth of Quong Lee, his invented poet of Chinese Limehouse.

The Silent Traveller tolerated the attention of more indigenous tourists, who photographed him as an exotic and laughed at his way of 'Boating under the moon' (an operation that involved rowing a dingy facing the bow rather than the stern).[25] Silently aware of the horrors that were unfolding in China, he winced at every reminder of war, whether it be the paper that brought news from the Spanish Civil War, the vexatious announcements of taxi drivers, or even the condition of the town of Keswick, which he found crowded with summer visitors: 'I really felt oppressed with the problem of over-population, a problem which some politicians make an excuse for war.'[26] A previous owner of my copy has scribbled 'nonsense' next to that remark, and 'more nonsense' on the following page, where Wast Water is likened to 'a beautiful woman bathing without much clothing on her body'.

Chiang Yee had met and talked with Laurence Binyon and various other British Sinologists and collectors. And yet as a curious form of reverse *chinoiserie*, the Silent Traveller did not necessarily please the scholars, for whom Chiang Yee's paintings of England may well have appeared just as unreliable and freakish as Ezra Pound's imagist revisions of Li Po. With the general public, however, Chiang Yee had come up with a successful formula. Published by *Country Life* in 1937, the first illustrated book in the series was soon being reprinted and sequels were encouraged. In successive volumes, Chiang Yee led 'The Silent Traveller' out into the Yorkshire Dales, through London, and the generalized partly spiritual condition he named 'War Time'. Bombed out of his Hampstead quarters in the Second World War, he moved to Oxford, where he gathered that Trinity was the only college that still refused to admit Orientals. He took his revenge by standing outside and making his own assessment of a passing group of undergraduates who wore 'brightly coloured woollen scarves wound round their necks so many times that they looked like human giraffes'.[27] They also reminded him of 'a certain type of young Burmese girl who lengthens her neck with copper rings as a means of beautifying herself'. Chiang dreamed of getting hold of a few of these 'long-necked undergraduates for a display in China after the war'.

If there is a certain wistfulness to Chiang Yee's Silent Traveller books, this may be because the concept imposed its own silence on Chiang's own experience of exile. He was, after all, a man who had taken his place in the Chinese struggle. He had loathed the warlords, who rose and, in many cases, also flourished under Chiang Kai-shek, and who had proved every bit as bad as the Manchu emperors in their brutalization of the Chinese people. He was also distinctly sympathetic to the Communists in their struggle against both the Japanese invaders and Chiang Kai-shek's nationalists. In his first years in London he had shared a flat with an exiled Chinese revolutionary, the editor and writer Wang Li-his (Lixi), who, before returning to China (where he would die fighting the Japanese in 1938), became known to the British left as the poet 'Shelley Wang'. Chiang had no doubt that the main reason why the Chinese Communist forces kept triumphing was because they had taken the side of the peasants and set about educating and improving conditions for them. These, however, were hardly causes that could be pressed on English readers under his picturesque persona as 'the Silent Traveller', for whom all talk of politics was corrupting.

By the end of the Second World War, the Silent Traveller books were selling in America too. Chiang Yee was invited to produce new volumes about cities over there. So, in 1946, he boarded the *Queen Mary*, and sailed for New York, together with a legion of British war brides going to join their GI husbands, with no less than 700 babies clutched in their arms.[28] He returned to Oxford after that first visit, only moving permanently to New York when friends found him some teaching at Columbia University in 1955. And here Chiang Yee found it even more sensible to maintain his mask of silent inscrutability—well aware of what Senator Joseph McCarthy and his like might think of a Chinese émigré who expressed any interest in his homeland.

Mr and Mrs Fei

It is impossible to establish what Spencer might have made of the Silent Traveller, but he did get to know some of Chiang Yee's successors. In 1946, the year of Chiang's first departure for America, four Chinese artists arrived in London intending to study at the city's art colleges. Assisted by the British Council, the scheme was inspired by the celebrated Chinese artist Xu Beihong (Hsu Pei-hung) (1895–1953), who had himself studied in Paris in 1919, and who remained convinced that Chinese artists had much to learn from their Western counterparts, particularly their representational techniques and their methods of working from observation.[29] Despite having himself adopted an academic style of history painting that was actually 'moribund' in France at the time he embraced it,[30] Xu hoped that a new synthesis might be possible, and that, after exploring this during their stay in Britain, his former students would bring the fusion back to China, where teaching jobs would be kept open in anticipation of their return two years later. The four visitors had been students of Xu's at the College of Fine Art at the National Central University in Nanking. Two of them, Zhang Anzhi and Chen Xiaonan, appear not to have come into significant contact with Stanley Spencer. The others became good friends with the English artist. Chang Chien-ying, who had worked with Xu Beihong at the China Institute of Fine Arts in Chungking, was unusual as a woman artist who had been on the executive committee of the All China Artists Association: Fei Cheng-wu was a professor at the Suzhou Academy of Fine Art, and had also taught at the Central University in Nanking.

In London, Fei was at first attached to both Camberwell College of Arts and the Courtauld Institute, while Chang was at Chelsea. Held in 1947, their first joint exhibition brought offers of places from Professor Randolph Schwabe, Director of the Slade School of Art, where they would remain until 1950. Settled in Britain, they painted flowers, bamboo leaves, and birds in the Chinese style. In one of Fei's works a squirrel is caught springing along a narrow bough; another shows a sparrow on the point of landing on a sprig of bamboo. They produced peony and orchid designs for printed silks, and landscape murals for ships too.[31] In May 1952, Chang Chien-ying was quoted as saying that her contribution to that year's Royal Academy summer exhibition appeared to be 'the first Academy picture exhibited in the Chinese style of painting'.[32]

Following in the tracks of Chiang Yee, with whom they corresponded (and some of whose contacts they shared), they visited Scotland and the Lake District, painting trees and waterfalls, clouds and mist. Fei's *Waters Meet, Lynmouth, North Devon* (Plate 2) was exhibited at a Royal Academy touring exhibition in 1954. In 1950, *Picture Post* had printed his rendering of a pastoral landscape near Westerham, Kent, in which pines and willows seem like oriental transplants, and an electricity pylon stands bereft of all cables, like a crude Western imitation of a Chinese pagoda. Chang was included in the same feature, entitled *An English Summer Through Chinese Eyes.*[33] A photograph showed her sitting in a flowery English meadow, preparing to 'Write a Picture'. The accompanying text, by L. S. Leguin, explained that calligraphy and painting had long been 'twin arts' in China. Like Fei's, Chang's reproduced brush and ink paintings, *The Sparrows of Middlesex* and *Misty Morning at Bournemouth*, indicated that Chinese artists had long since developed a unique way of striving for reality: 'They do not want to copy nature; but, aiming at perfection, they tried to reproduce the "essence" of the thing painted, recreating, in an imaginative way, the "spirit," without losing the "resemblance".' Strong on clouds, waterfalls and trees, they followed Chiang Yee in finding an affinity between English mistiness and the behaviour of ink on absorbent Chinese paper.

Exhibited and sold by the Leicester Galleries in London, their works appealed to British collectors including William Wilberforce Winkworth, who would eventually become decidedly prim about Chang's tendency to use more colour in her treatment of English themes than he considered appropriate to traditional Chinese technique.[34] When I met her in March 2001, Chang remembered Mrs Attlee as being among her purchasers and Mrs Stafford Cripps too. The pair travelled the country, demonstrating the exotic arts of calligraphy and brush painting on rice paper, and enchanting audiences as they conjured up trees, rocks, fishes, and waterfalls with a few swift strokes of cane-handled brushes made, as enquiring local reporters were duly informed, of the hairs of rabbits, goats, and wolves. One of their champions was Professor John Wheatley, the Director of the Graves Art Gallery in Sheffield, who had previously brought Chiang Yee to Sheffield to illustrate the Chinese techniques he employed as 'the Silent Traveller'. After their demonstration at the Graves Art Gallery in September 1947, others were requested at Durham and at Stoke-on-Trent, where the curator of the city museum and art gallery wrote to say 'the idea of having artists to demonstrate the Chinese method of painting naturally appeals to us in view of our concern with pottery decoration'.[35] It was noted that 'little Miss Chang Chien-Ying' was one of the Kensington artists whose work had been selected by the Royal Academy that year.

There may have been considerable interest in the exotic 'method of wrinkles'[36] that Fei would describe as characteristic of the traditional Chinese depiction of rocks and mountains. Yet Chang and Fei were also studying the techniques of English masters, including Constable and Turner. Indeed, Chang told one reporter 'I want to paint Chinese scenery in the Turner style'.[37] Chang and Fei were no Communists, and their art, whether of traditional Chinese subjects or English scenery, was definitely not polemically driven like the strip-like series of cartoons Jack Chen had produced to make the case for the Industrial Cooperatives in Free China, or the galvanizing revolutionary woodcuts of the Yenan school. This was not the Chinese art the Feis and their collectors had in mind at all. As Lord Methuen would write: 'As you must know by now, we appreciate and love the art of your country and are delighted to know that the great tradition is "still" kept alive and that we have such good representatives in our country, albeit brought here, no doubt, under duress, to continue its practice.'[38]

It was during this period that Chang and Fei's paths crossed with that of Stanley Spencer. The exact circumstances of their first meeting remain unclear, although they might have met at one of the first British shows of the Chinese artists' work, perhaps at the Leicester Galleries, in London, where Spencer himself had exhibited. Whatever the circumstances, the Chinese artists accepted Spencer's invitation to visit him at Cookham in Berkshire. In 1947, Spencer wrote to thank them for sending photographs of their visit, noting that 'we all look very glad to be in Cookham', and also that 'the people in Cookham are saying when are you coming again'.[39] He also talks of making a drawing, either in Cookham or in London, which he was then visiting one or two days a week in order to see Hilda Carline ('my wife and mother of my children'), who was, as he wrote, 'recovering from a serious operation'. The proposed drawings did indeed get made. Spencer had recommended that they meet for this purpose in London, since on their next visit to Cookham, they would probably wish 'to wander about the village' rather than sit drawing in 'my cottage rooms'. In the event, Fei drew Spencer on 28 August 1947. Spencer added his own signature to the image to indicate his approval of the result. He also made three drawings of Chang.

The idea that the four Chinese artists would go home to take up their reserved positions after a couple of years was complicated by the Communist victory of 1949. Zhang Anzhi and Chen Xiaonan returned to China shortly after the 'Liberation'. Chang and Fei had doubts as to the wisdom of such a step. They had no Maoist inclinations, and they feared the suspicion that seemed likely to fall on any Chinese who had willingly engaged with the West. Nevertheless, they booked a passage and wrote to Spencer to say farewell. They were due to sail on 10 February 1950 and, on the evening of the 9th, Spencer turned up unannounced at their house in Edgware hoping to say goodbye. In a letter he intended

Fig 27. Photograph of Spencer, Miss Li, and Fei Cheng-wu in Cookham.

to put through the door if they were out, he apologized for having failed to answer their earlier communications, and regretted that they had never got round to meeting again in Cookham. As it happened, however, Chang and Fei were at home. It was raining, as Chang remembered in 2001, and she had opened the door to find Spencer standing there, 'so small and wet'.

As Spencer discovered, Fei had fallen acutely ill. Chang would later insist that his affliction was entirely genuine, and certainly not an excuse concocted to ease any political embarrassments that might follow from their failure to return to China as planned. Fei was simply too stricken to move so they missed their boat. Stranded by the rain, Spencer stayed overnight. Though he had come with no sign of an overnight bag, it turned out, as Chang remembered vividly, that he was already wearing his pyjamas under his suit. Three years later, he served as best man at Chang and Fei's wedding, held at Kensington Register Office on 27 March 1953.

Katy Talati's Album

By this time, Spencer's friendship with Fei and Chang had opened another contact through which Spencer would deepen his interest in Chinese painting. Katy Talati was of Parsee origin, but had

Fig 28. Photograph of Spencer at Fei and Chang's wedding. The potter, Eleanor Whittall is second from left.

grown up in China.[40] Her uncle had moved to Peking from Bombay in the early 1900s. He began his business in China by bartering trainloads of tallow for Siberian furs and, having made his fortune, married the daughter of a Siberian chieftain. Katy Talati's father joined him in China, and Katy was born in this milieu: prosperous but also mixed since the family had many Chinese friends, which was very unusual at that time. Having developed an interest in Chinese painting, she was introduced to its techniques by the Belgian Catholic Priest, Father Edmund van Genechten, who had learned to paint in the Chinese style in order to proselytize among the Chinese. She went on to win a scholarship, which would have taken her to Chicago, had it not been for the attack on Pearl Harbor on 7 December 1941, and Japan's declaration of war on Britain and America the following day. After a period of enforced residence in the British Legation, she ended up imprisoned by the Japanese in an internment camp at Weihsien in Shantung province, some two hundred miles from Peking.[41]

By 1948, Katy Talati had moved to London, a city she remembers finding 'very drab' on her arrival. The subsequent fate of her uncle, who for a time had been the only non-white foreigner to own property in Peking's Legation Quarter, would do nothing to make her more sympathetic towards the Chinese Communists. He had opened the Talati House Hotel in Tientsin in 1929. During the war against Japan, this luxurious establishment had been taken over as HQ for the Communist Eighth Route Army, but worse was to follow the 'Liberation' of 1949. The hotel had no guests at this time, but the Communist authorities had insisted that Talati must continue to pay his hundred-strong staff. The hotel had quite recently been valued at £7 million, but the revolutionary authorities preferred to take it over 'in lieu of tax'. Talati understood that her defeated uncle had actually dropped dead while trying to deal with this situation in the tax office. She herself had arrived in Britain with a remarkable portfolio of Chinese art. Before leaving, she had assembled an album of what she judged to be the very best Chinese artists. There were no political woodcuts of the Maoist Yenan school in Talati's collection, but she did have works by Pu Quan, a cousin of the last emperor, Pu Yi, and also by the venerated master Ch'i Pai-shih, who she remembers visiting in Peking along with his housekeeper, one of the last surviving eunuchs from the Manchu court, who was later alleged to have faked much of the work that elderly Ch'i Pai Shih was still accustomed to pricing by the yard.

Once in London, Talati kept her distance from the Carlines and their circle, which she recalled as being decidedly 'pink' in complexion. She did, however, get in contact with the Chinese artists she remembered as 'the British Council four'. At the opening of one of their London exhibitions, she saw people clustering around a 'little urchin tramp' who turned out to be Stanley Spencer. Not long afterwards, she too was on her way to Cookham, where she would show Spencer some of her collection of Chinese paintings. The two became friends. Talati accompanied Spencer as his guest at the Royal Academy when Winston Churchill was appointed Honorary Academician Extraordinary (1948).

She also remembers how he would arrive at her home in Ealing without luggage, wearing a paint-spattered blue overcoat and carrying a tatty old string bag—perhaps the very one he is said to have taken to Buckingham Palace when he received his CBE in 1950: 'a small very self-assured man in pebble glasses', as one astonished eyewitness remembers, who turned up wearing 'a grubby beige mac' that made him look like 'a man going to the Windmill' in Soho, and carrying a 'net shopping bag sprouting rhubarb and celery'.[42]

In 1949, or thereabouts, Talati visited Spencer in Cookham, where she found her new friend living in apparent poverty— unlike Patricia Preece who appeared to have done very well out of her spurned and reduced husband: acquiring his house, a number of valuable pictures, and also the expensive jewellery Spencer had bought for her from Cartiers and other such establishments. What Talati remembered most vividly, however, was Spencer's uncontained enthusiasm for her Chinese paintings. When she took them to him at Cliveden View, his modest little house in Cookham Rise, he cleared and, indeed, swept the floor of the upstairs bedroom he used as his studio so that she could unfurl a long silk scroll painted by Pu Quan, whose great-grandfather, the Daoguang Emperor, had ruled China between 1821 and 1850. So there it was on a bedroom floor in Berkshire: a work of ink on silk, of strong lines and evocative wash, unrolled to reveal a landscape of rocks, mists, pines, and water, with little human details: villages, clustered houses, people fishing from the end of a little jetty, or gathered stick-like in a distant field. Made in 1946, and entitled *Rich and wonderful streams and mountains*, the work included a colophon explaining that the scroll had been painted in the style of the artists of the Song dynasty.[43] Spencer was enthralled. In his excitement, so Talati remembers, he kept running downstairs to the lectern holding the family Bible in which he searched out the lines that particular details in the scroll brought to mind. Protestant missionaries had long been accustomed to comparing China with the Israel of the Old Testament,[44] but Spencer wasn't seeking to convert anyone out of their primitive, diseased, and idolatrous ways. For him, as for other travellers, China was a remote land of shimmering otherness. Yet here it was also as a series of inspiring recognitions, unfurled at the centre of his own English experience.

The Dangers of Travel—an Informal Anglo-Chinese Agreement

Spencer's initial hesitation about Dr D. M. Ross's letter inviting him to join the cultural delegation to China reflected the high level of Cold War anxieties at the time. However, it was also connected to Spencer's mistrust of the idea of travel, as he would explain years after returning from China, on 5 June 1957, when he made his way to the neighbouring village of Bourne End to address the local Parents Association on the subject of his travels. In his notes for the talk he would detect a 'puritannical fallacy' in the widespread insistence that travel 'broadens the mind', and state his strong disagreement with those who saw travelling as 'a sort of symbol of getting away from self: "Don't be a stick in the mud."'[45] His own travels had, so he noted, been 'at almost all times forced upon me' and did not arise 'for the fulfillment of any of my own needs'.

As an example of the dangers posed even by walking short distances, he recalled how, in 1906, he had been asked, in his very first commission, to illustrate a fairy tale for a certain Miss White of Bourne End. To deliver his drawing, which survives as *The Fairy on the Waterlily Leaf,* he had been obliged to walk to Bourne End from Cookham and neither he nor Miss White had been happy with the experience. 'Girl too fat' as Spencer noted Miss White's objection, adding 'Well of course it was fat' since the solid daughter of the Cookham butcher had kindly consented to pose as his model. A few years later, and far more alarmingly, he had been persuaded to spend a month in Somerset while he was still a student at the Slade. He remembered feeling he had 'lost caste' when he returned to Cookham. Indeed, 'My work was never the same'.

The mud-caked Africans in *The Resurrection, Cookham,* may come to mind here, but Spencer's habit of clinging to his native ground like a 'stick-in-the-mud', should also be understood in its English context. Nineteenth-century precedents could be found in the writings of Ruskin and William Cobbett, but Spencer's Cookham is particularly close to the idea of 'little England' advocated by another former student at the Slade, namely the writer G. K. Chesterton, with whom Spencer was personally acquainted. Chesterton elaborated his idea of England in an essay entitled 'On Rudyard Kipling and making the world small', included in his book *Heretics* (1905).[46]

Here he took issue with the epigram in which Kipling asked 'what can they know of England who only England know?' It was, contended Chesterton, 'a far deeper and sharper question to ask, "What can they know of England who know only the world?"' With his imperial cosmopolitanism, Kipling might certainly 'know the world; he is a man of the world, with all the narrowness that belongs to those imprisoned in that planet. He knows England as an intelligent English gentleman knows Venice.' The globe-trotting Kipling did not belong to England or, indeed 'to any place; and the proof of it is this, that he thinks of England as a place. The moment we are rooted in a place, the place vanishes. We live like a tree with the whole strength of the universe.'

Spencer would surely have joined Chesterton in taking the side of the untravelled but also unabstracted 'man in the cabbage field' against Kipling's footloose imperialism. Yet, as we imagine Cookham's peculiar genius flying so enthusiastically towards China, sketching the mountains after Lake Baikal in oranges, purples, and reds, or sharing John Chinnery's interest in a freakish-looking grasshopper found by Dr Horn's children on the grass landing strip at Ulan Bator, we might also wonder to what extent going to China really put this extraordinary English artist in breach of his own mistrust of travel. The journey was laborious, but Spencer would surely not have been surprised to find his suspicions confirmed by the wisdom of the sage Chuang Tzu, a Taoist philosopher who lived during the Era of the Warring States, in what the West would measure as the fourth century BC.

In *Three Ways of Thought in Ancient China*, published in 1939, Arthur Waley, the British translator and Sinologist who was also among the signatories of the Statement of Friendship carried by the cultural delegation, quotes Chuang Tzu's discussion of Lieh Tzu, who had been very fond of travelling until he met an adept named Hu-ch'ien Tzu. The wise man warned Lieh Tzu that 'Those who take infinite trouble about external travels, have no idea how to set about the sight-seeing that can be done within. The traveller abroad is dependent upon outside things; he whose sight-seeing is inward, can in himself find all he needs. Such is the highest form of travelling; while it is a poor sort of journey that is dependent upon outside things.'[47] From the moment of that real-ization, Lieh Tzu 'never went anywhere at all, aware that till now he had not known what travelling means'. Like China's Commu-nist rulers, Paul Hogarth is likely to have taken a dim view of such reactionary solipsism. But this was, nevertheless, a Chinese 'way' with which Stanley Spencer could have felt very much at home. China may well have been 'wholly other', in Joseph Needham's phrase, but for Spencer, as for Needham, it would also turn out to be strangely, and sometimes also achingly, familiar.

Rex Warner, meanwhile, really was in Mongolia: 'We came down at the small airfield of Ulan-Bator where we had another and larger breakfast to the accompaniment from the radio of what must have been national, but sounded to me very like Hebri-dean songs. There was time to observe that all Mongolians in sight were wearing wide-brimmed trilby hats.'[48]

15

The Flight of a Brown Phoenix
(Cedric Dover)

As the plane carrying the Second Labour Delegation landed at Ulan Bator, Barbara Castle was delighted to see the Mongolian capital 'encircled with snow peaks, dromedaries and Mongols wandering about in the hot sun'. Britain did not recognize the People's Republic of Mongolia at this time, and none of the outward travelling delegations was in any position to leave the airfield. It remained to the home-bound Labour MP for Pembrokeshire, Desmond Donnelly, to discover that the Chief Lama and his Ministers knew little of Britain, beyond what they had been told by the Dean of Canterbury, who had visited a couple of years earlier and was remembered as the very holy 'lama Johnson', and, indeed, considered Mongolia's 'main contact' with Britain.[1]

The aerodrome consisted of no more than a grass strip attended by a modest control building and '3 beautiful Mongol tents in white canvas lined with felt'. Passing through in September, Rex Warner had mistaken these evocative structures for large huts. Castle, however, got a closer view: 'they were round and decorated with a lower run of yellow wooden slats. They waved us away when we tried to look inside'. Derrick James noticed a stove pipe chimney poking through each of the three 'flattened tops', and that the wooden doors and internal beams were richly ornamented too. The fact that the interiors of these barely modernized yurts were adorned with fine silks and carpets was noted by J. D. Bernal, who had been ushered in together with the Bulgarian delegation to be greeted by a deputation of the Mongolian government. He records that the 'Mongolian entertainment' came with plenty to drink and a great many toasts too. The eating, however, was 'rather disappointing—all out of tins'.[2]

No member of the Second Labour Delegation was more predisposed than Cedric Dover to feel an inspiring history in these nomadic presences. As a 'Man of the Trees', his mind would fill with images of arid and treeless 'badlands' when he recalled the flight over 'deserts, steppes, parched lands, bare mountains, clouds of dust'.[3] Yet those glimpses of the windswept grasslands of Northern Mongolia also reminded him of the legendary Genghis Khan, who built the Mongol empire in the early thirteenth century, and was reputed once to have declaimed 'My archers and warriors are dark like a great forest of trees'.[4]

Dover had long been captivated by the thought of the roving Mongol hordes—an uncontainable horizontal force mixing and interbreeding as they thundered across a world in which no wall, border, or natural barrier could halt their advance. Indeed, nearly two decades previously, he had invited members of India's recently formed Congress Socialist Party to consider the achievements of Genghis Khan, who had started out as an 'obscure Mongol Nomad' from a land 'without a history, without a national existence', and gone on to forge a great empire reaching from the Black Sea to the Pacific Ocean. In 1954, Dover would inform his fellow delegates that the Mongol hordes had even crossed the Behring Straits to enter America ('Hence the American Indians', scribbled Derrick James appreciatively). Back in 1936, however, the thought of the great nomad's conquests had been evoked by the influence that Stalin's Soviet Union then exercised over vast tracts of Asia, including Mongolia, which had come adrift from imperial China after the collapse of the Qing dynasty in 1911, and where, a few years after the Red Army extinguished the brief rule of a vile White Russian 'khan', Baron Ungern-Sternberg,[5] a Soviet-assisted 'Mongolian People's Republic' had been proclaimed in 1924. 'The cycle goes on', so Dover had concluded: 'The story ends and a new story begins.'

Who exactly was Cedric Dover and what, beside an interest in trees and a definite inclination towards Stalin's Russia, was the perspective this 50-year-old Eurasian would bring to bear on New China? Any other airborne delegate puzzling over that question might have begun by conceding, however reluctantly, that Dover probably knew more about twentieth-century Asia than anybody else on the plane. During the Second World War, he had published a survey of the Far East entitled *Hell in the Sunshine*. He opened this polemically driven tract with the observation that three quarters of the world's people were neither white nor European by origin: 'They are the browns, blacks, yellows and middlings who make another world within the world—an oppressed world of poverty, pestilence and misery surging with the impulse to burst its chains.'[6] It was one of Dover's most repeated claims that 'the coloured world'[7] (a phrase that represents his own variation on the 'dark world' championed by his friend and hero W. E. B. Du Bois) held the promise of an emancipated future. It included the great majority of humankind, and its people, though denigrated as well as exploited, were the authentic outcome of a history in which mixture, movement, and interbreeding had actually been the norm since time immemorial. The white man, with his fantasies of racial purity and elevation, belonged to a jumped-up minority, raised to dominance by imperialist power coupled with the technological innovations that had done so much to drive the industrial revolution.

Fig 29. Cedric Dover on the Yellow River, China.

Dover's main purpose, as expressed in *Hell in the Sunshine*, was to assert the conditions under which the coloured majority might actively join the Allied war effort. Reluctant as they may be, the British, French, and American authorities had no alternative but to learn the lesson then being provided by the Chinese Communists as they confronted the far better equipped forces of Japan: namely, that people could hardly be expected to fight with any commitment if victory only offered more of the same old exploitation and misery. In order to enlist the active participation of the Asian peoples in the war against fascism, the Western governments would have to dump their imperialist attitudes and accept that the Second World War actually marked 'the beginning of a world revolution'.[8] The fact that this lesson remained to be learned had been proved by the words uttered by Winston Churchill in a broadcast of 15 February 1942. Speaking directly after the fall of Singapore, Britain's 'chief patriarch' had identified the setback as 'one of those moments when the British race can show its quality and its genius'. For Dover, who naturally aligned himself with those who grasped 'the wickedness of racial thinking', this speech only went to show that, while the British people were certainly 'in the midst of a great company' in the fight against fascism, 'they are in it without being of it. They are not marching shoulder to shoulder with the rest of that company as brothers, as comrades fighting today for a universally better world tomorrow.'[9]

Dover's anti-imperialist analysis of British policy in Asia was not embraced by the British authorities as a useful contribution to the war effort. He had, however, been more willingly accepted as the inventor of 'Dover's Cream': a mosquito repellent which was officially adopted for Allied troops fighting in the Far East and also used, as one witness recalls,[10] to ease the suffering of burns victims during the London blitz.

Some of the more conservative trade unionists on the Second Labour Delegation may have wondered about Dover's qualifications as a scientist, an anthropologist, or, indeed, anything else. There can be no doubt, however, that he had gathered some impressive personal references during the course of his nomadic and largely freelance career. The curriculum vitae he would send to the Library of Howard University in Washington, DC, in January 1956 included glowing testimonials gathered from across three continents.[11] Writing in 1948, the President of the New School for Social Research, in New York, is quoted as having declared Dover a man of 'unique' and valuable experience in the field of 'race and race problems'. This assessment was strongly supported by the Director of the Department of Scientific Research at the American Jewish Committee; by the Chief Counsel of the US Office of Indian Affairs in Washington, DC; and by Dr Charles S. Johnson, the African American President of Fisk University, in Nashville, Tennessee. In 1941, Sir John Megaw, Director General of the Indian Medical Service, had commended Dover for his scientific research and described him as 'a gentleman of high character and agreeable personality'. His view was foreshadowed by the assessment of Sir Martin Forster, Director of the Indian Institute of Science in Bangalore, who, in 1934, had declared Dover 'a highly competent entomologist' and a man of impressive 'earnestness, vision and professional competence'.

An altogether less favourable assessment would not emerge until 2003, when the *Guardian* published the recently discovered list of 'crypto-communists' and 'fellow travellers' drawn up by the mortally ill George Orwell on 2 May 1949 and sent to a friend, Celia Kirwan, who was then working for the Foreign Office. Charlie Chaplin, J. B. Priestley, the novelist Naomi Mitchison, and the actor Michael Redgrave were among those Orwell reckoned should not to be trusted to serve the cause of anti-Communist propaganda in the new Cold War. Cedric Dover was included on the list in the most damning terms of all. Orwell identified him as 'Writer (*Half-caste* etc.) and journalist. Trained as zoologist'. Under 'Remarks', he added: 'Is Eurasian. Main emphasis anti-white (especially anti-USA), but reliably pro-Russian on all major issues. Very dishonest, venal person.'[12]

As Orwell knew, having worked with Dover at the BBC World Service, 'Eurasian' was Cedric Dover's preferred term for his own mixed race origins. Born in April 1904, he had grown up in Calcutta in West Bengal, a member of what others preferred to name the 'Anglo-Indian' population. In the early days of colonization the children of mixed unions between European men and Indian women were welcomed by the Europeans, but their status had changed in the late eighteenth century—an adjustment that Dover attributed to fear of mixed-race uprisings such as had occurred in Haiti, and to rising competition for patronage in the East India Company.[13] Excluded from the military and civil services, and yet still strongly set off against the Indian majority, they developed their own more or less self-reproducing cultural and biological unit. Though the European ancestry of India's Eurasian population (estimated at some 120,000 in a census of 1931)[14] was actually more mixed, thanks not least to the historical contributions of the Portuguese, their members tended to identify with the British colonial power. They lived by deference and preferment in the larger cities of India, typically working as literate employees in the colonial administration or the railways.

By the beginning of the twentieth century, the Anglo-Indian population was in a 'depressed'[15] condition. Its members' habitual identification with Britain was becoming dysfunctional, their customary privileges having been eroded as the British responded to pressure from the Indian nationalist movement. They also faced rising hostility from the Indian population: restless for self-rule and unimpressed, to say the least, by a minority that had so loyally served the imperial authorities.

Dover was born into this increasingly straitened world in 1904, the son of a civil servant who had died when he was 12. He was educated at Jesuit schools in Calcutta, including St Joseph's College, founded in 1890 by the Irish Christian Brothers as their first establishment in India intended to cater for the poor and disadvantaged. Reading about the comparative history of religions, he began to question the absolute distinction drawn by his teachers between true Christianity and 'heathen' error. He went on to discover that Darwin and Huxley were 'not "vile atheists"', as he had been taught, but 'lovers of Truth who had led the most exemplary lives'.[16] Dover became a natural scientist in reaction against a Christian education in which no aspect of reality was allowed to connect with any other for fear of bringing dogmatic theology into question.

This new interest led him to seek out Dr Nelson Annandale, the Scottish Superintendent of the Indian Museum, in Calcutta, and also founder and Director of the Zoological Survey of India. Dover started to work at the Indian Museum while still in his teens, encouraged by Annandale, who also helped him win the scholarship that took him from there to Edinburgh University. This might have been the opening of an orderly scientific career, but something went wrong. In a diary written during the Second World War, Dover would remember the 'prim wraith of Professor Ashworth' and how 'I wilted again under his verdict on my career: "I'm afraid our golden swan has turned out to be a goose after all"'.[17]

Having returned to Calcutta at the beginning of the 1920s, Dover was employed once again by Annandale, as Temporary Assistant in Entomology, Zoological Survey of India, initiating a period in which he combined scientific work with other jobs, including serving as Secretary of the Asiatic Society of Bengal. While still in his late teens, Dover became something of a specialist on Indo-Malayan wasps and bees. He followed Annandale, in surveying the freshwater and estuarine fauna and flora of Malaya, including the water insects of which he built up an extensive collection that would be used by later researchers in future studies. He investigated the transmission of spike disease in sandal wood (claiming that his conclusions were based on 'the first survey and analysis in Asia of the fauna of a single forest tree'[18]), and helped devise ways of preserving wood against termites. Together with Mercia Heynes-Wood, with whom he would go on to have three children, he contributed a volume on the *Cicindelidae* to the Indian government's Catalogue of Indian Insects.

Perhaps his own sensitivities as a Eurasian in British India had some bearing on his various studies of organisms that had success-fully adapted to hostile environments: creatures which might nowadays be described as 'extremophiles'. Surveying the dark Batu Caves, north of Kuala Lumpa (where he was briefly employed in the Malaria Bureau and also by the Federated Malay States Museums), he discovered a primitive ancestral crustacean, *Parabathynella Malaya*, which led to the creation of a new subdivision of the Crustacea. He researched the peculiarly adapted fauna to be found living in the digestive liquor of carnivorous pitcher-plants, and also the thermophilious organisms living in Malayan hot springs, finding the latter, as he would later recall, 'in a way, even more remarkable than the exceptionally resistant eggs of the brine shrimp *Artemia*'.[19]

It was in the course of this fieldwork that Dover contrived the mosquito repellant that would secure his reputation as the inventor of 'Dover's Cream'. Citronella oil was the active ingredient, but Dover found it too volatile to be used unmixed in the tropics. He tried various other bases including liquid Vaseline, which proved too heavy. So he eventually mixed it with cedar wood oil, white petroleum jelly, and spirit of camphor. Dover reported that he had used this mixture very successfully for two years in Burma and Malaya. One application lasted an entire night, and, in addition to its mosquito-repelling qualities, it was 'soothing, antiseptic and beneficial to the skin'.[20]

Between 1921 and 1934, the year in which he reached the age of 30, Dover wrote many articles for scientific journals, both in India and abroad. He also applied his scientific vision to wider questions in a series of polemical essays, ten of which were collected as *The Kingdom of Earth* in 1931. The 'Young Man's Credo' at the heart of this precocious tract was a plea for intelligence, erotic love, and scientific dynamism against cultural ossification. The main enemy was 'dogmatic religion', which enthroned 'blind superstition', deformed the 'powers of the human mind', and repressed understanding of the fact that 'life has within itself unlimited potentiality'.[21] Dover's message was that it was possible to abandon dogmatic religion and the idea of a Personal God or an 'independent creator' without surrendering Hope, Wonder, the basis for personal morality, or even immortality, since 'I am but a living bud' of the wider experience of the World.

Dover espoused materialism and the theory of evolution, but the primary weapon in his struggle against tradition in these years was the science of eugenics. In 1925, when he was still only 21 years old, he wrote a passionate critique of G. K. Chesterton, repudiating the author of *Eugenics and Other Evils* as 'a charming teller of tales'.[22] The Englishman's book impressed Dover as an example of the 'useless verbiage' that is likely to result 'when a man of religious outlook turns his mind to a science of which he admits to know nothing'.

Joining forces with his fellow researcher, Mercia Heynes-Wood, Dover set out to demonstrate how the new science of eugenics might be applied to India, linking it both to child welfare and to birth-control techniques.[23] The challenge of eugenics was also for the Eurasian community to consider. In a lecture delivered at the YMCA in Calcutta on 24 March 1925, young Dover announced that 'As a race we Anglo-Indians are unprogressive, we do not realize the full significance of the relation of biology to human society; we oppose any theory likely to effect a radical change in our mode of living, or what is still worse, we take no notice of it'.[24] It was time, he insisted, for the Anglo-Indians to wake up to the fact that 'small, well-fed, well-educated, well-regulated families are infinitely superior to large ill-fed, badly educated and badly regulated families, even though the latter may provide more souls for heaven (or what is more likely: the other place), or more soldiers for the British army'.

That same year, Dover and Heynes-Wood had launched 'the first Eurasian magazine of any consequence in a hundred years'.[25] The introductory issue of *New Outlook* proclaimed their intention of 'striking a new note in Anglo-Indian journalism'.[26] Its purpose was no less serious for being printed between advertisements for Sanatogen, Pelmanism, and ice-making machines, and alongside articles on the trouble with the Calcutta bus companies, the best recipe for gooseberry cheese, and the virtues of noise in the modern city ('Noise is our birth right. Noise denotes life').[27]

Dover would later claim to have been 'the first Eurasian to ally himself wholly with the struggle for Indian independence'.[28] Certainly, he and Heynes-Wood encouraged Calcutta's Eurasians to stop making their own 'bogey of Swarajism'—and to 'unite' and join 'the great work of reconstruction that is before us'.[29] Rather than sending deferential deputations to beg the favour of British ministers who hardly knew of their existence, they should embrace the new anti-imperialist vision of India as 'a spiritual community to be evolved out of the co-operation of seemingly heterogenous elements of race or creed'. *New Outlook* commended the Eurasian man who had swallowed his pride sufficiently to open a tea-stall at the railway station in Calcutta, thereby breaking with the attitudes that had discouraged other 'Anglo-Indians' from developing their own commercial enterprises in India. This initiative was 'a small event in a large city, but a larger event in a small and myopic community whose members had always relied on government employment. It shows that one Anglo-Indian at least has realized the dignity of honest labour, of straight-forward competition on an equal basis with the people of the country, of the folly of perpetual petty job-hunting.'[30]

In 1934, the year in which the Congress Socialist Party was formed as a caucus inside the Indian National Congress, Dover moved to London, leaving Mercia Heynes-Wood and their three children in Calcutta, and launching himself into a concentrated study of the literature on 'race' and 'race mixture'.

We know something of Dover's life in London in the mid-1930s, thanks to the late Tania Alexander, a woman of high Russian-Estonian extraction and pronounced left-wing sympathies, who herself came to London in 1935 and found work as an editorial assistant to the publisher Fred Warburg. She worked with Dover on his books *Half-Caste* (1937), *Know This of Race* (1939), and *Hell in the Sunshine* (1943), and she would later help at least one of his abandoned dependants with financial assistance. Speaking in 2002, she remembered Dover as 'always penniless'.[31] He lived 'very poorly' and was 'completely irresponsible in many ways': he had left a young family in India but kept forming liaisons and fathering and then abandoning more children in England. Though 'very good-looking', Dover also seemed uncomfortable. Alexander had the impression that 'it worried him to be half-caste'.

By November 1935, Dover had transferred his skirmishing about 'The future of the Anglo-Indian' to the pages of the *Spectator*. Arguing against the suggestion that 'Indianisation' now posed a serious threat to the Anglo-Indian community,[32] he countered that 'thinking Eurasians' saw a very different future than the 'devoted Anglophily' preferred by such as the eminent Anglo-Indian eye surgeon Colonel Sir Henry Gidney: 'I wish my community to be rationally rather than nationally minded...I want it to be unashamed of being Indian, but the dangers of national prejudices prevent me from wanting to be proud of the geographic accident of birth. That is why I suggested cultural alliance with its ethnic kinsfolk outside India.'[33]

Dover found friends in the circle of Britain's Eugenics Society, including Sheila Grant Duff, and, for a while at least, he continued to write about the application of eugenic ideas to India. Though he had previously condemned 'biological twaddle' of the kind that condemned the half-caste as 'an individual who possesses the bad qualities of both races',[34] his youthful interest in the 'science' of eugenics was more seriously challenged during three visits to Germany, where he gathered information about the treatment of Jews and 'the coloured "hybrids" of the Rhine'[35]—the so-called 'black bastards' born to German mothers and North African soldiers (not all of them black, as Dover would insist) employed after the Great War in France's occupation of the Rhine. He also studied the progress of the 'biological outlook' as expressed in a number of innovative exhibitions. He was impressed by the 'incomparable activities'[36] of the German Hygiene Museum in Dresden (founded in 1911), and also by a show entitled 'Frau und Volk' at the Museum of Sociology and Economics in Dusseldorf. In Berlin, he attended the opening of an exhibition entitled 'The Wonder of Life', organized by the Dresden museum. The '*pièce de résistance*'[37] of this hugely popular show was 'The Transparent Man', 'a full-sized, automatically controlled model in which the systems of the body are illuminated and explained in orderly sequence'.

Writing two years after Hitler's accession to power, Dover was still prepared to commend 'the remarkable progress in public appreciation of the biological outlook in Germany',[38] attributing it largely to the long-standing commitment of the museum movement to public education, 'which has survived political changes and economic misfortunes'. He also noted that the exhibitions were displaying 'a somewhat Hitlerised concept of the biological outlook'.[39] Indeed, he had been dismayed by the emphasis placed on racial purity, and also by the anti-Semitic cartoons that had been included in the technically innovative displays: 'The organizers of the Exhibition would have done better if they had refrained from degrading an otherwise excellent scientific exhibition with such propaganda.'[40] Despite the Nazi contamination of the cause, Dover nevertheless remained reluctant to allow the thought that this unwelcome development reflected any fundamental flaw in the biological approach itself. He preferred to use the German museums to grind a more familiar axe of his own. Alarming as he found their concessions to Nazi race ideology, the technical brilliance of these exhibitions and their successful appeal to a wide and popular audience provided an 'instructive contrast' to the 'conservative traditions and administrative inefficiency' that 'impeded the proper development of the museum movement in the British Empire, where museums largely remain storehouses of national treasure'.

Looking back over his life in the 1950s, Dover would attribute his final abandonment of eugenics to the influence of Julian Huxley, who had sent him an early proof of his book *We Europeans* (1935), in which 'racial biology' was condemned as a 'vast pseudo-science', which 'serves to justify political ambitions, economic ends, social grudges, class prejudices'.[41] The book, which must have arrived very shortly after Dover's visits to those exhibitions in Germany, was 'the turning point' at which he resolved to 'discard many of the unproductive and untenable theses and antitheses (including some of my own) of the past'.[42] Reviewing Huxley's work in *Nature* that November, Dover welcomed it as 'an opportune prophylactic against the spreading virus of racialism', agreeing that to grant even 'limited acceptance' to the notion of 'race' would 'help to relegate the Negro, already regarded by numerous morons as "subhuman", to the category of the gorilla in the Western mind'.[43] One of the first British 'morons' he targeted was A. M. Ludovici, a fascist advocate of inbreeding who invoked 'science' to justify his pet hates ('race mixture', Jews, high intelligence in women, etc.) and also his cranky 'preference for skirts, since trousers lead to "constantly artificially warmed scrota", which "may be suspected of causing varying degrees of decline in sexual vigour"'.[44]

Dover's repudiation of eugenics stands at the centre of his first British-published book, *Half-Caste*, issued by Secker & Warburg in 1937. This tract blasts off with a thunderous declamation: 'The "half-caste" appears in a prodigal literature. It presents him, to be frank, mostly as an undersized, scheming and entirely degenerate bastard. His father is a blackguard, his mother a whore. His sister and daughter, dressed by Coward and Cochran in a "shimmering gown", follow the maternal vocation.'[45]

Having thus introduced his insulted and down-trodden hero, Dover starts slashing his way through the pseudo-scientific theories of race with which white opinion has oppressed the world's mixed communities. He finds these in the utterances of Kipling, Goebbels, and the editor of the *Eugenics Review*, and also floating about in a more dispersed state in the 'syndicated xenophobia'[46] of the mass press. He attributes their success partly to the fact that 'the bourgeois libido' is plainly excited by 'experts who deposit coloured horrors on the very doorsteps of Balham— licentious buck niggers and sinister celestials menacing Tooting hymens and the security of roast pork and apple-sauce'. Noting that considerable tracts of Western literature have been devoted to 'smelling strangeness'[47] in people like himself, he quotes a novel by H. Bruce in which the 'Yewrasian' is condemned as 'not a proper human being'—a degenerate, treacherous and 'enfee-bled'[48] specimen who may safely be presumed to have inherited the worst traits of both parental races. Dover scorns the 'yellow Malayan hybrids' of Somerset Maugham and the 'ludicrous mongrels' and 'half-caste harlots' of Linklater and others, and then moves on to condemn the more 'subtle' negative 'propa-ganda of apparently sympathetic writers' including Eugene O'Neill, Carl Van Vechten, Laurens van der Post, and Paul Morand. He acknowledges the attempts at positive representa-tion to be found in the works of the British novelists David Garnett and William Plomer, and pays tribute to Nancy Cunard, the radi-cally inclined shipping heiress who had been viciously assaulted by the Hearst press as well as by the Ku Klux Klan during the years she spent assembling her now famous collection of black writing, *Negro: An Anthology* (1934), to which Dover himself had contributed.[49]

The lesson of history, so Dover proclaims, is that, contrary to the thoroughbred fantasies of the world's ruling classes, humanity has actually 'been in the melting-pot for unknown millenia'.[50] He projects the 'half-caste' back into the Bible, quoting chapter and verse to show that 'mixture and illegitimacy' form the unmistak-able 'heritage of Christ'.[51] He declares that few, if any, civilizations have emerged out of 'uniracial effort', and none has been origi-nated by 'the Nordics alone'. He finds 'ethnic interchange' built into the foundations of the USA too, noting that interbreeding between British settlers and native Americans began with the original Jamestown Colony. Thanks to marriages such as the one entered by John Rolfe and Pocahontas in 1613, the Amerindian 'hybrids of those early days' had gone on to become 'the old aris-tocracy of America'.[52] The African Americans, meanwhile, were not just mixed but superior to the whites 'in many physical and mental respects'. Few peoples, after all, had endured a more 'eugenic' history than was provided by slavery, with its 'rigorous weeding out of the unfit...The Afroamericans have in them the pick of the Negro genes.'[53] Reviewing the contribution of the artists of the Harlem Renaissance, and writers such as Langston Hughes and James Weldon Johnson as well as the tradition of the spirituals, he declares himself in no doubt that the American Negro 'has developed out of the American milieu a form of expression, a mood, a literary genre, a folk-tradition, that are distinctly and undeniably American. This is more than the white man has done.'[54]

Having found racial mixture, or 'miscegenation' a home near the source of all civilizations, Dover goes on to survey 'the world's mixed communities', and to identify the factors genuinely responsible for their problems.[55] The 'Anglo-Indians' among whom he had grown up in Calcutta formed the oldest and largest of these groups, dating back to the Portuguese settlements of the early sixteenth century. But he also surveys smaller communities in Burma, Ceylon, British Malaya, Hong Kong, and Shanghai. He considers the Maori hybrids of Australia and New Zealand, and takes his readers to Norfolk and Pitcairn Islands, where the mutineers of the Bounty mingled advantageously with Polynesians, and then on to Tahiti and Mauritius in the Indian Ocean.[56] These mixed populations, each one born of exposure to 'the winds of trade and evangelism', are treated as islands of subtle variation and adaptation, where the colonizing European stocks have been variously improved by mixture with more native and aboriginal traits, and where the promise of a new humanity can be found. They are praised in ways calculated to offend British racists such as A. M. Ludovici or the Nazi-sympathizing Dorset aristocrat and eugenist, Captain George Fox-Lane Pitt Rivers. As Dover writes of a brown fellow encountered on Cape Barren Island, off the coast of Tasmania, he was 'a superb type of intelligent and vigorous old manhood, such as one sometimes sees among the Sussex farmers'.[57]

Dover has vast numbers of yellow, brown, black, olive, and honey-coloured people arrayed behind him by the time he had pursued his survey across the South Atlantic and through the Americas both North and South. He concludes that the problems facing these populations are the product of political and economic pressures and certainly not of any alleged 'eugenic' degeneration. He also enjoys comparing these often vibrant mixed communities with places where allegedly thoroughbred Europeans had tried and failed to build a new world. He mentions the descendants of Cornish fishermen who failed miserably to sustain their tiny island of Tangier off the coast of Maryland, or the dismal regime that Scottish migrants had established in Newfoundland, which was found to be so corrupt and incompetent that, in 1933, the British legislature had to suspend its constitution.[58] His appreciative survey of African-American art and literature is sharpened by contrast with the illiterate, blood-feuding 'Mountain People' of Appalachia. Dover commended the barbaric and diseased condition into which these claimed descendants of Ulster Scots had since lapsed to the attention of the 'racial writers' who routinely cited Haiti and Liberia as proof of Negro backwardness.

Dover made a considerable impact with *Half-Caste*. It was hailed as 'the Bible of the persecuted' by the *Burma Review*. The African American sociologist Alain Locke commended Dover for his 'eagle-like penetration of vision', while the Indian novelist Mulk Raj Anand, writing in *Life and Letters*, hailed Dover as 'one of the most courageous prophets of a new scientific humanism'.[59] Over the fifteen years since its publication, Dover had continued to insist on how much the world's scattered mixed-race populations had in common. 'There is', as he wrote in 1952, 'a deep underlying unity of kind and sentiment; of comparable geography and economic development, making for a feeling of shared landscape; of cultural similarities brought about by these factors as well as by dispersion; of common symbolic values and ways of symbolisation; and above all of a certain identity of purpose, which facilitates intimacy between brown, yellow and black men'.[60] The consequence of these 'binding mutualities' was that a coloured person could 'feel at home almost anywhere in the vast similitude of the underprivileged world. I have lived in Negro ghettos with an overpowering feeling of intimacy, and they have taken me into their homes as a relative rather than a stranger. I have felt the same kinship on American Indian reservations, and even the dour

Apaches have welcomed me inside their *tipis*. And I have forgiven the Southern States much for reviving the scenes of my youth and the cooking of my people.'

Dover's desire to draw these scattered populations into a more active expression of their 'binding mutuality'[61] led him to place great emphasis on the value of cultural interaction to the coloured world. He considered books to be 'ambassadors'[62] that cut through ignorance and hostile stereotypes to encourage common understanding. It was in the same spirit that he had planned a collaboration with the Jamaica-born former Communist writer Claude Mckay: a co-written volume of autobiographical reflections about growing up in Calcutta and Jamaica entitled *East Indian, West Indian* was announced several times but only fragments appear to have been written by the time McKay died in May 1948.[63]

Dover also wrote a manifesto for 'coloured writers and readers'. Published in 1947 and dedicated to W. E. B. Du Bois, with whom Dover had stayed in Atlanta in 1938, *Feathers in the Arrow* opened with the statement that 'Life within the impositions of an alien culture is the restricting factor in creative achievement amongst coloured minorities and exploited majorities. The resolution of this difficulty, and its intricate persuasions, is a major problem in coloured writing today.'[64] Dover suggested that 'the cultural misfortune' shared by Eurasians, Indians, African Americans, and other 'marginal' peoples, was that they had no mother tongue of their own: 'This I believe is a common experience amongst coloured writers. They are tormented by attempts to clothe the feelings and impressions and ideas aroused by their world in the words, rhythms and ways of expression belonging to another. They, like myself, are not part of the scene which produced the language, and the language is not part of the scene in which they have their being. That is partly why the problems of coloured peoples have been stated more in political, sociological and survey writing than in poetry and fiction.'[65] Having surveyed works by writers such as Sterling Brown (*Southern Road*), Richard Wright, and Mulk Raj Anand, Dover would support the prophecy of the African American critic Alain Locke, who had recently anticipated that the 'race novel' would soon produce 'a new conjunction of art and sociology'. Indeed, he anticipated that 'the great creative works of the next few decades will come mainly from the coloured peoples'.[66]

Dover's view of the coloured world was various and culturally rich—its character expressed less by the abstract strictures of Stalin than by Walt Whitman's big-hearted and welcoming line about 'the vast similitude' that embraces all humanity. What, then, is to be made of George Orwell's sour assertion that Dover was 'Reliably Pro-Russian on all major issues'?

Dover was quite capable of changing his mind, as can be judged from his abandonment of eugenics. By the end of the 1930s, he was warning students at the University of Cambridge that the biological cause he had once espoused with such enthusiasm had degenerated into a pseudo-science that had taken over the role of 'defending imperialism and the ruling class' from the 'social Darwinists' who had earlier stalked the British empire with cranial callipers in order to distinguish 'energetic longheads' from the 'indolent roundheads' born to serve them.[67] As he awoke to this fact, Dover made his apologies to G. K. Chesterton, admitting that the man he had once mocked as a literary ignoramus should be congratulated for 'detecting in the use of science an enormous potentiality for misuse'.[68]

As he became more convinced of the baleful inadequacy of the concept of 'race', Dover admitted the failure of another of his own favourite polemical flourishes. He had once liked to think that 'hybridised groups' were 'superior, by reason of greater adaptability and wider culture, to the more specialised types with which they compete'[69]—an application of evolutionary theory that had enabled him to acclaim the 'half-caste' as 'tomorrow's man' in a poem entitled 'Brown Phoenix'.[70] However, he now recognized it as nonsensical to suggest that 'mixed races are superior because they are mixed, or that some kinds of mixture are better than others'. Any special potential possessed by people of mixed race 'had nothing to do with race or hybridity. It is due to greater cultural adaptability arising from marginal status.'[71] By 1939, his goal was to pull 'race' down from its elevated position, not simply to carry out a 'childish' rearrangement in its pantheon. Dover would hold that position for the rest of his life. As he would eventually put it in a letter to Joseph Needham, 'I have long suspected that the temptation to use the word "race" lies in the fact that it is a strong word of high symbolic and image-forming content rather than a defining one.'[72]

When it came to the Soviet Union, however, Dover appears to have remained entirely rigid. Writing in *Congress Socialist* at the beginning of 1937 he remarked how, since 1929, he had been emphasizing the 'importance and feasibility of closer contact between people of mixed origin', and urging that the framework for this contact be provided by international Communism: 'we must organize our forces if we are to free ourselves from the domination of the white bourgeoisie'.[73] Or again, 'we need to stand together and not 'divorce ourselves from Left Wing ideologies and the international proletariat in so doing'. Some members of India's Congress Socialist Party may have preferred a decentralized, cooperative and, indeed, guild-like idea of socialism, but Dover had insisted on International Communism as the vehicle of 'the movement towards coloured unity'.[74] Stalin's powerful creed would realize the hopes that W. E. B. Du Bois had been expounding against the colour line since the beginning of the twentieth century, and also those of the Eastern Federation, proposed by another figure with whom Dover would become personally acquainted, the anti-imperialist, socialist, and future first Prime Minister of independent India, Jawaharlal Nehru.

There were moments when Dover hesitated about the hot air he imagined might lift his 'brown phoenix' into flight. In *Know This of Race*, he had spoken out against 'unconsidered Left propaganda appealing to racist sentiments', insisting that 'The urgency of supporting Republican Spain does not excuse pictures and paragraphs about the deluded and victimised Moors as the savage, brown, white-raping hordes of Franco'.[75] He also conceded, all too hypothetically, that 'if anti-Semitism, or any similar antagonism, should reappear in the Soviet Union, we should know that socialism had failed there. And anti-Stalinism would be justified.'[76]

After the Second World War, he questioned the unconscious imperial assumptions displayed by the British Marxists who presumed to advise the coloured world, conceiving themselves as 'self-appointed teachers and guides, fitted by pigmentocracy and a supposedly scientific attitude, to teach us about ourselves'.[77] He had been particularly irritated when such imperialist comrades assumed the right to stand in judgement over Asian, African, or Caribbean literature: 'Only too often they are men with a sense of guilt, arising from their own bourgeois origins and advantages, which they compensate by proletarian enthusiasms and parrot cries of "reactionary". We must demand that the use of such words be always supported by a full historical analysis to which the "reactionary" can reply.' But though he would venture such remarks, he would also accompany them with a defensive insistence on 'the enormous value of communist effort in advancing the struggle of the coloured working classes and in breaking down racial prejudice'.

Yet Dover had taken the side of Stalin's Communist International—preferring the 'socialistic concept of a better world' to the confused 'Christian ideals' and fraudulent race theories shaping other versions of internationalism.[78] And that is where he stayed. If he was among those who brought potentially invigorating new questions into the reach of Marxist thinking, he did not use them to transform the framework he found there or, indeed, to question the increasingly evident brutality of Stalinist power. Unlike the great dissidents of the left, people like Friedrich Adler, Emma Goldman, Panait Istrati, and Victor Serge, who aimed their criticism at the conduct of the Communist system itself, Dover appears to have turned a blind eye to its failings. Soviet Communism persists in his books as the clockwork dialectics through which the coloured world would break free from imperialism and history must 'inevitably end in the victory of socialism'.[79]

It was during the economic and political crisis of the 1930s that Dover had squeezed his vision of the coloured world's 'vast similitude' into the shuttered spaces of an adopted Stalinism. As he decreed in *Half-Caste*: 'In Soviet Russia, for all the ethnic and cultural divergences of its component parts, race-building and race mixture are not contemporary issues.'[80] He joined those who admired Stalin's Soviet Union as a place where the radiant future had already arrived: a glorious federation of republics in which people of different cultures and races mixed amicably to their own mutual advantage. In *Know This of Race*, he announced that the tsarist idea of 'a peculiar Russian soul, which could neither be comprehended nor mingled with' had been swept away by the Bolshevik revolution. If Stalin could visit happiness on his people simply by decreeing that it existed, Dover could insist that the ferocious anti-Semitism that had attended this idea of a pure Russian identity was also a thing of the past: 'Today the incomprehensible Russians are as plain as daylight' and 'The innate racial characteristics of the affected Jews disappeared with equal abruptness'.[81]

Having pronounced this fairy tale true, Dover went on to cite Stalin's show trials as proof that 'in Soviet Russia the anti-Semitic serpent has failed even to wriggle its tail. In the recent trials many of the principal defendants were Jews, yet there was not the slightest whisper within the country of a Jewish plot'.[82] The other minorities of tsarist Russia—Georgians, Armenians, Turks, and Tartars—had also been 'repugnant to the Russian soul' and known for their own 'racial hatreds'. But that too had changed: 'Today the Soviet minorities are the only minorities without racialism and minority grievances. Stalin can claim with truth that the October Revolution dealt the legend of racial inequality a mortal blow.'[83] It was with faith rather than reason that Dover contrasted Stalin's sunshine with the darkening fascist and imperialist regimes of its European neighbours: 'You will agree, then, that in one country the abolition of capitalism has resulted in the disappearance of its supposedly inherent racialism, while in the western countries the conflicts of capitalism have rejuvenated this filthy pestilence.'[84] It was this fanciful vision of the various peoples of the USSR happily united under the smiling figure of Stalin that the China-bound Dover had found reprised in the trees planted around Moscow's new university buildings.

Such, then, is the mix of Dover's writing in the 1930s: an admirable critique of 'race' and eugenics; an expansive enquiry into the condition and culture of the coloured world; and an apparently unquestioned faith in Stalinism as the adopted motor of 'the movement towards coloured unity'.[85] Soviet Communism was neither Dover's main interest nor, perhaps, his primary commitment and yet he remained locked in, like his admired companions in struggle, Paul Robeson and W. E. B. Du Bois. His opposition to imperialism and his loyalty to the 'coloured world' were such that he could not abandon the cause of Soviet internationalism with the comparative ease with which Rex Warner, say, had evacuated the revolutionary ardours of his pre-war youth as so much stale vapour.

Having coated his 'brown phoenix' in this leaden stuff during the early 1930s, Dover carried it with him through the years to come. He continued to write and publish in Britain and India. He also went to the United States of America, where he would attempt to link the cause of the Asian peoples with that of the African American population, whose difficulties had been greatly increased by the depression.

In Boston in 1938, Dover had been introduced to the 'far-flung effort at co-operative research and writing' being produced through the Federal Writers' Project of the Works Progress Administration.[86] During the same visit, he had stayed with W. E. B. Du Bois, and also got to know Aaron Douglas, the Harlem Renaissance artist, who showed him something of Alabama. Dover renewed these contacts after the Second World War. In 1947/8, the African American sociologist and educator Charles Johnson invited him to spend a year lecturing in Anthropology at Fisk University in Nashville, Tennessee, where he also served as editor of Fisk's journal, *Race Relations*. He shared a house with Aaron Douglas, who was then director of the Art Department at Fisk, and working closely with Johnson, who was President of the university. By this time, Dover was not just the author of *Half-Caste*, but an informal representative of the newly triumphant independence movement in India. Jawahardal Nehru had become India's first Prime Minister on 15 August 1947—a moment he himself described as India's 'tryst with destiny'. Making some display of his connections, Dover encouraged Johnson to consider taking steps to foster a new relationship between 'Indian and Negro educational institutions' in the USA, pointing out that the recent expansion of higher education in India created new possibilities, and that India was interested in establishing exchanges with Negro colleges in America rather than merely continuing its traditional reliance on British universities.

In October 1947, Dover approached Johnson with the strong support of Yusuf Meherally, one of the heroes of the Indian struggle for independence, an ethical and cultural socialist who had been among the founders of the Congress Socialist Party and who had been elected Mayor of Bombay while incarcerated in Lahore jail in 1942.[87] Dover asked Johnson to initiate an exchange by answering a letter in which Meherally had emphasized how much centres like Fisk and Howard might contribute to bringing about greater understanding between the Indian and African American worlds. He followed this up by offering him the text of a telegram he had been sent by Nehru to read out before W. E. B. Du Bois at his eightieth birthday celebrations ('India will always remember his sympathy during her struggle for freedom', so Nehru had written).[88] Charles Johnson was predisposed to accept Dover's requests: in a contribution to Dover's *United Asia* symposium, he welcomed 'Asian fraternity' and the part it had already played in helping America's 'Negro minority' find 'its place in the larger brotherhood of man'.[89]

After his spell at Fisk Dover went on to lecture in 'Intergroup Relations' as a Visiting Member of the Graduate Faculty at the New School for Social Research in New York and, also in 1949, joined the faculty convened to run a Summer School for teachers of native Americans, held in Nevada by the US Bureau of Indian Affairs. He chaired a twenty-session seminar on 'The Rediscovery of the Classics' sponsored by the New York Public Library, explaining in a related article that he proposed starting not with 'a sonorous and suspiciously dramatic recital of the Declaration of Independence', but with a manual on 'clear thinking' to prepare the way for discussions in which familiar classics would be 'rediscovered' as works of 'social criticism and philosophy'.[90] As an advocate of 'intergroup relations', he made a strong case for books as 'essential sources' of 'mutual learning' between America, India, and Europe, suggesting that space for their consideration needed to be won back from the clichés and international misunderstandings spread by films, radio, pulp magazines, and even supposedly 'high-powered journalism'.[91]

According to his widow, Maureen Alexander-Sinclair, Cedric's return to Britain was partly driven by the fact that he lacked the appropriate work permits, and post-war America was increasingly uncomfortable for a man of known left-wing affiliations whose papers were not in order. So Dover came back to London. He remained a contributing editor of *Phylon*, a quarterly review of race and culture edited by W. E. B. Du Bois and published by Atlanta University, and also of *United Asia*, a bimonthly 'International Magazine of Asian Affairs' published from Bombay since 1948. In the latter role, he edited a special issue on 'The American Negro'.[92] He was impressed by the Labour victory of 1945, thanks to which Britain had, as he had told American librarians, 'never been more vital and wholesome than it is now'.

As for China, here too Dover's views had not changed much since 1936, when he had commended the Chinese Communists' struggle as 'an epic fight for freedom which those in the vanguard of the Indian struggle cannot fail to appreciate'. His knowledge of that struggle was like Hogarth's in being largely drawn from the writings of Anna Louise Strong, Edgar Snow, Agnes Smedley and others working in what he had called 'the best traditions of American journalism'. These reporters had shaped Dover's understanding of such legendary fixtures as the Long March, 'an epic story of endurance',[93] and the Sian Incident, a 'fantastic kidnapping', which had impressed Dover as marking 'the beginning of a new unity in China'.[94]

In his book *Hell in the Sunshine*, Dover had added to this picture with his own accusing sketch of Britain's perfidious reaction to China's struggle for an independent existence, governed as it had been by a cynical policy of self-interest and imperialist exploitation. He noted British refusal to join America in taking action against Japan after it bombed the Chinese city of Chapei in 1932, and he was also aware of British attempts to come to terms with the Japanese puppet regime in Manchukuo, heavily praised in the report of the Federation of British Industries' goodwill mission under Lord Barnby in 1934.[95] He pointed to the financial finagling perpetrated by Sir Victor Sassoon in an attempt to prop up the Chinese currency, and by the British government's Chief Economic Adviser, Sir Frederick Leith-Ross, who, in 1935–6, had also made friendly approaches towards Japan: a disreputable policy with which the British had persisted right up into the Second World War.

In Britain, Neville Chamberlain's policy of 'appeasement' is thought to have applied to Germany alone, but Dover saw it at work in Britain's 'sordid'[96] and unprincipled policy towards China. He cites the events of 1938, when Chamberlain's government had conceded terms with Japan ('He got "peace in our time" and the Japanese got Canton and Hankow').[97] Concerned to protect British interests and perhaps also to keep Japan available for war with Communist Russia, Chamberlain later ordered his ambassador in Japan to draw up the 'Craigie–Arita Agreement' of July 1939, in which it was agreed that 'the Japanese force in China have special requirements for the purpose of safeguarding their own security and maintaining public order in regimes under their control, and that they have to suppress or remove any such acts or causes as will obstruct them or benefit their enemy'.[98] The signing of the Nazi–Soviet pact in Moscow, only a month later, had dismayed some British Communists, including the young Derrick James who had given up on the party shortly afterwards. But not Dover. He defended the USSR's startling new alliance, treating it as Stalin's desperate response to the discovery that Britain had just sold China down the river.[99]

Thanks to his international connections, Dover would be writing about 'New China', not just for The Men of the Trees but as a contributing editor of the bimonthly journal *United Asia*, which had been founded in 1948, in the wake of India's achievement of independence and, more particularly, the associated Inter-Asian Relations Conference of the previous year. Published with the purpose of bringing about 'a greater awareness of Asia's new vital role in the affairs of men', *United Asia* had promised not to view the world through the 'European spectacles' that had produced the atom bomb, and to affirm not just Nehru's idea of unalignment and 'complete freedom' for the Asian nations, but also Gandhi's more challenging declaration that 'it is up to you to deliver the whole world and not merely Asia from wickedness and sin'.[100]

By 1954, Dover was aware of additional reasons for optimism. Burma had been granted independence in 1948, a year or so after India, and the Malayan Emergency was under way, with Commonwealth forces pitched against Communist insurgents. In India, meanwhile, Prime Minister Jawaharlal Nehru, whom Dover looked forward to meeting again in Peking, continued to advocate an 'Eastern Federation' of Asian States, including China and India, a Pan-Asian vision that had earlier been swamped by Japanese imperialism but which Nehru had relaunched at the Inter-Asian

Relations Conference in April 1947. Dover will also have been gratified that India and China appeared to have come to terms over Tibet, reaching an agreement that had been signed in April 1954, suggesting a link between the two countries of the kind anticipated, so Dover may have been predisposed to hope, in Nehru's policy of 'resurgent Asia'.

Such was the optimism that filled Dover's mind as the Second Labour Delegation took off from Ulan Bator and headed out over the 'flat, brown, wildness' (Derrick James) of the Gobi Desert. According to Ben Parkin, Labour MP for Paddington North, the plane followed the line of the 'single camel track' that could still be seen below. 'Then came the jagged mountains and the Great Wall of China rising and falling along the rocky ridges as far as the eye could see. And then, almost too quickly, we were above the north-western edge of the crowded cultivated plain of Hopei, excitedly watching the bright October sunshine winking its welcome from the coloured roofs of Peking. We had reached our long journey's end only to begin another and longer journey into human experience.'[101]

PART IV

Listening to the Oriole
(China)

A delegation of MPs came from England to visit China and they went to a famous Chinese beauty spot just outside Peking. One MP nudged one of the Foreign Ministry officials and said: 'I bet this is a favourite spot for courting couples on a moonlight night,' only to be met with the cold reply: 'We do not do such things in China.' The MP, undaunted, replied: 'Go on, you don't get six hundred million people by immaculate conception!'

Esther Cheo Ying
(*Black Country Girl in Red China,* 1980)

16

Clement Attlee's Break

We were regaled with tea and a lot of statistics
Clement Attlee[1]

Clement Attlee lies stretched out in a bamboo armchair. A ciga-rette smoulders in his right hand and a walking stick rests between his loosely crossed legs. There is an ancient and ornately framed scroll of calligraphy on the wall behind him and a 'Chinese inter-preter', wearing a bright floral dress, looks out from the same terrace with an engaging smile. 'It was a beautiful place',[2] says the General Secretary of the Labour Party, Morgan Phillips, of the government guest house in which the eight members of his National Executive Committee now found themselves.

Britain's very tired former Prime Minister is slumbering in Hang-chow, a city in the Yangtze Delta known for its pagodas and temples. Though the famous West Lake was being energetically dredged of silt by the new authorities, the waters still abounded with lotus flowers and enormous goldfish like those that the American President Richard Nixon and his wife Pat would be shown feeding for the benefit of the world's press ('I never saw goldfish that big') during their altogether more carefully staged visit of 1972.[3]

Claude Roy, a French writer who passed through two years before the Labour leadership, had been puzzled by the various temples of Hangchow, finding them filled with an apparently indistinguishable apparatus of joss sticks, bronze vases, and gongs. He had deemed it impossible to 'unravel the threads' of the ancient Chinese religions that had long since become 'stunted and adulterated into confused cults, monotonous rituals and the like'.[4] Attlee, Bevan, and the other NEC members were also guided round this place of Taoist, Confucian, and Buddhist residues, the latter represented by the Lingyin temple, a large and very ancient Buddhist establishment, which, as they discovered, retained a small community of monks. They were left in no doubt that the temple was undergoing extensive restoration and that the repairs were being done 'at immense cost'[5] too. Evidently, as Attlee would inform his sceptical readers in America, 'the government is careful of its historical monuments'.[6] They were intrigued to hear that the temple's 76-year-old 'Senior Buddhist' monk was about to start serving as 'a representative under the new constitution'.[7] Though informed that this devout elder had attended the 'Communist-inspired' Vienna Peace Conference in 1952, they doubted he was sufficiently 'worldly' really to understand his responsibilities as a member of the government.

Hangchow was laid on as a tranquil interlude in an otherwise busy itinerary. Having travelled there by train from Shanghai, the British politicians were content to boat on the lake, wander in the hills, and, as Morgan Phillips would later attest, inspect the 'Poets' Corner too'.[8] When informed, as was every foreign visitor, of the old Chinese saying: 'Above is Heaven, below is Hangchow', he and his colleagues could only agree that this was indeed 'a place where one can go to rest and thoroughly enjoy the beauties that abound'.

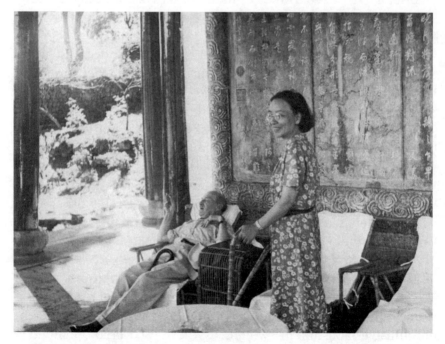

Fig 30. Clement Attlee sleeping at Hangchow (photo: Michael Lindsay).

Attlee's moment of repose in this place of 'peace and beauty'[9] was photographed by Michael Lindsay, erstwhile leader of Britain's China Campaign Committee.[10] Having recently inherited his late father's peerage, Lindsay was now Lord Lindsay of Birker and also, as it happens, a recent emigrant to Australia. He had taken an academic position in Canberra, where he had continued his feud with the Communist advocates of 'friendship' with New China. In 1952, he and two colleagues at the Australian National University had written a critical statement, which was taken to China that October by the Australian delegation to the Preliminary Conference of the Peking Peace Conference. In this he had insisted that while a 'very large' body of opinion in Australia might indeed be prepared to cooperate with any 'genuine attempt to work for peace', no such undertaking would be possible until the Chinese regime stopped exploiting 'Peace' merely as propaganda in the service of its own now fully aligned Stalinist policies. The statement had drawn a predictable volley from one of New China's resident Western admirers. The expatriate New Zealander Rewi Alley had accused Lindsay of 'subjectively making mountains out of molehills',[11] thereby, so Lindsay fired back, proving the truth of George Orwell's idea of 'crimestop' ('the faculty of stopping short, as though by instinct, at the threshold of any dangerous thought').

Having known many of the leaders of the Chinese Communist Party before the Liberation of 1949, Lindsay had returned to China at the beginning of August 1954 to help 'prepare the ground'[12] for the British Labour Party leadership's visit. He was now accompanying the delegation on a mission that was motivated, so Attlee had informed the *New York Times* before leaving London, by the desire to establish whether the Chinese government were seriously bent on 'establishing an "imperial hegemony" in South-East Asia'.[13] The Labour leadership was worried about many of the Chinese Communist Party's policies and yet, as Morgan Phillips would repeatedly insist, their visit was also driven by a desire to 'lift the Iron Curtain'[14] dividing the peoples of China and the West.

Lindsay's photograph shows Britain's former Prime Minister pausing in the midst of that arduous endeavour. Here was Clement Attlee, gathering his resources before moving on to inspect a vast new bridge in the teeming industrial city of Canton, and also taking a break from strife: not just his ongoing dispute with Aneurin Bevan over Labour Party policy towards the soon to be established South-East Asia Treaty Organization and the equally pressing question of German rearmament, but also the wider clamour of warring accusations and propaganda slogans put about by partisans on both sides of the Bamboo Curtain. It was a racket that threatened to obliterate his quietly optimistic faith that 'the Chinese people have more in common with the rest of the world than would be gathered from the highly-coloured stories one sometimes reads, and that the more we of the West have close and friendly relations with the Chinese people, the better for the peace of the world'.[15]

Just like Bedford

Attlee, Bevan, and the six other members of the Labour Party's National Executive Committee had landed at the airfield outside Peking on Saturday, 14 August. Stepping down from their plane, they were handed bouquets of flowers and welcomed by more than fifty smiling representatives of the Chinese government, the People's Institute of Foreign Affairs, and the local Peking Soviet. Lord Lindsay and his wife were also there to greet them, together with the British chargé d'affaires, Humphrey Trevelyan. Even the weather was encouraging. As they flew in from Mongolia, Phillips had been pleased to see the sun shining brilliantly for the first time since they had left England.[16] The countryside was surprisingly green—the *Daily Herald's* attendant reporter, Deryk Winterton, detected a positively 'English-like greenness'[17]—and their limousines (a car was provided for each of the eight visitors) had stirred up huge clouds of dust as they approached the city along a road lined with poplars and acacias. They passed caravans of mule carts 'led by mahogany-brown Chinese, wearing shorts and soup-plate hats'. They saw people labouring in the fields, and were impressed by the efficiency with which 'every inch of available land'[18] seemed to be growing sorghum, maize, and other vegetables: even the roadside verges were being used to raise fruit. Catching sight of these foreign visitors, who, judging by Phillips's example, were already deducing that 'the Chinese landworker is a very good farmer', the peasants in question stared back, leaving the visiting Britons to wonder 'whether their attitude was one of indifference, curiosity or hostility'.

Entering the city, they passed through narrow streets surrounded by single-storey buildings, and crossed the newly constructed 'Red Square' in front of Tiananmen Gate. Though Peking had only a small numbers of motor cars, the air of this traditional 'city of contemplation' seemed filled with incessant hooting: 'All motor cars are driven on the horn',[19] noted Attlee, with some concern for his sleep over the coming nights. In the first 'Peking broadcast' he sent back to Britain, Morgan Phillips offered a more homely first impression: 'As I saw the great mass of cycles on the road I was reminded of a day in Bedford during the last war. I had just started to drive. I was passing through the town at the time when the workers were leaving the factories for the lunch hour break. All at once I seemed to be submerged in cycles. Peking is just like that.[20]

According to the *Daily Herald*, the first of countless toasts were drunk in 'a fiery, evil-smelling vodka-like drink' known as mao-tai: a smiling Chou En-lai is said to have clinked glasses with each member of the delegation, and then welcomed them to China with the words 'Bottoms up'. At another banquet the following day, he toasted the Queen, announcing before 1,300 guests gathered in the Hall of Magnanimity that China was 'ready to strive with the British people to safeguard the peace of Asia and the world'. As had been agreed in preliminary negotiations, Attlee responded by toasting Mao: here, as the *Daily Herald* also informed its readers, was the 'typical leader of Britain's bloodless revolution, now exchanging pledges with the men who, in blood and sacrifice, had carved a new nation out of the decay of the old'.

After musing that 'both, in their different ways, represent the same aspects of the old patterns of life', Mr Winterton cast an apprehensive eye over the menu. For any rationed and stodge-fed Englishman of the time, it was frankly staggering. He counted up 'lice soup' (the *New York Times* replaced this unlikely dish with 'soybean soup'[21]) shark's fins ('Socialists dine on shark's fins', was the *Daily Mail's* headline[22]), mushrooms, winter bamboo shoots, chicken legs with stalks of artificial flowers as handles, and 'melons cooked in the shape of the head of one of Buddha's disciples'.

Having made their way through this prodigious lunch with the assistance of thoughtfully provided knives and forks rather than chopsticks, the delegates were taken to the Pavilion of Purple Light, a lakeside building in the Zhongnanhai, an exclusive Imperial Palace compound (if not yet the new Forbidden City it had become by the time of President Nixon's visit in 1972),[23] which, since 1949, had served as the residence and headquarters of the Chinese Communist Party. Here they talked for five hours with Chou En-lai,[24] who impressed Bevan as 'outflowing, versatile, superlatively knowledgeable'.[25] As for the Chinese leader's view of Bevan, we are left with Michael Foot's suggestion that 'not since Marco Polo probably had a phenomenon so strange alighted on those shores'.[26]

The receptions, lunches, and dinners would continue throughout the Labour leadership's eighteen-day visit. A modest entertainment was provided by the Trevelyans in their house in the British embassy ('a lovely compound of great size,' noted Attlee, 'only smaller than formerly'), where they were also intrigued to meet 'old-timers' who had seen the rule of the empress, the warlords, the Japanese, and Chiang Kai-shek as well as the Communists.[27] Other, more sumptuous, occasions coincided with various 'National Days', the first of which was held in honour of Pakistan—a reception and dinner at which Attlee remembered 'how strong are the ties which bind together the members of the Commonwealth'.[28]

There would be many more speeches too, in which feathery expressions of friendship were released into the air. 'We are resolved that wars must cease',[29] so Attlee informed a dinner given by the People's Consultative Assembly in a brand new concert hall with red tasselled lanterns hanging from the ceiling: 'We sympathise with the Chinese people in their struggle against the forces of reaction in China and we wish well to new China.' His stated belief, which enabled him to be friendly without explicitly sanctioning the policies of the Chinese Communist Party, was that 'we would seek to think always of the things which unite us and not of the things that separate us'. In conformity with this judiciously hedged aspiration, he sought common ground in the fact that, while China was indeed considerably older than Britain, both countries had been obliged to 'make great changes in accordance with modern needs'. It was true that the Labour Party had been able to carry out its reforms 'by peaceful and constitutional means'. Yet 'we had to bear not only with internal problems but with the external, in particular with the historical position of Britain as a world power'. After that reference to his post-war government's management of the rapidly disintegrating British empire (the phrase 'Empire into Commonwealth'[30] with which Attlee would later recall that bloody transition gives little indication of the difficulties he had encountered in Burma, India, Malaya, Iran, and Palestine), he shifted to another common experience. 'We know how much China has suffered in war', he said, before reminding his audience that Britain too had come through agonies in 'two great world wars. The flower or our youth died. We endured many days and nights of bombing in which men, women, and children died.'

Attlee took this idea of shared victimhood and rolled it out like a carpet over the mountainous embarrassments of modern history. For a moment, at least, he may successfully have suppressed the memory of the vehement anti-Communism that he as Prime Minister had shared with his Foreign Secretary Ernest Bevin; of the British excesses so fiercely documented by Agnes Smedley and other American anti-imperialists in the 1930s; and also, for that matter, of the propaganda stories that the British government had circulated through China during the First World War: an arsenal of lies that included the notorious 'falsehood', calculated to be especially repulsive to Buddhists, Muslims, and Hindus, alleging that the Germans were bundling up the corpses of their own fallen soldiers and shipping them to a factory near Coblenz where they were boiled up in vast cauldrons to produce fat, glycerine, and, in some versions of this disgusting legend, pig food too.[31]

Turning to the future, Attlee extended a promise of international exchange, speaking of the renewal of trade as well as his desire to see Western 'scientific knowledge and technical skill' made available to all peoples united by 'the desire for peace'. Like a man posting Christmas cards to the far side of the world, he appealed to the common ground of 'simple family life. As we see here in China the fathers and mothers and children, we think of our own families at home.' Indeed he suggested that the job of 'those in positions of responsibility' was to enable 'those families' to enjoy happy lives, free from fear of war and hunger, and, as he added pointedly, 'free to think and act as they please while being conscious of the rights of others'.

Such were the former Prime Minister's concessions to the Soviet creed of 'peaceful coexistence'. He would not go so far as Nye Bevan, who later told an audience at the Hong Kong Reform Club that the Communists were 'at least "as sincere as ourselves" in their expressed desires for peaceful contact with the West'.[32] Many of his utterances took refuge in a more abstract idea of shared humanity. As fluffy as Pablo Picasso's white doves, perhaps, they were only slightly less vaporous than they would have seemed had Attlee sought common ground in the fact that people everywhere breathed air and that the great majority of them, even after the admitted disasters of the previous decade, possessed a full set of arms and legs too.

Attlee would not be the last Labour Prime Minister to pursue wars, hot or cold, while in office, and then to express a humanitarian concern with peace as he walked away from the responsibilities of Downing Street. Together with his Foreign Secretary Ernest Bevin, Attlee had robustly taken the Western side over the previous decade. In January 1949, indeed, he had approved a Foreign Office Memorandum sent to British posts overseas, urging that 'Iron Curtain' should be used alongside other 'carefully selected graphic phrases' such as 'Kremlin Imperialism' and 'Satellite states' in reference to the USSR.[33] Delivered in the warm light of Geneva, his Peking orations were no longer devoted to bloc-building, and their approach to the Iron Curtain had changed too. Indeed, they were more consistent with the use made of that particular 'graphic phrase' in 1920, when Christian socialist members of the first British Labour delegation to visit Bolshevik Russia had employed it to condemn the blockade with which Britain and other Allied governments had tried to starve Bolshevism in its cradle.[34] Then, as in Attlee's Peking speeches, the aim was to lift the curtain itself, and not just to line up with the partisan adherents on one side or the other.

Keeping ahead of the Press

Together with the opulent receptions, with their toasts and friendly speeches, the Chinese authorities staged encouraging performances for the benefit of their British visitors. These events were a

gift to the seven visiting members of the British press, the first to
have come to China since 1949, who are said to have chased the
Labour leadership's cars around Peking in 'a convoy of pedicabs'.[35]
The *Daily Mail* found its own malicious pleasure in a 'brilliant three-
hour dancing display' arranged by the Indonesian ambassador to
celebrate Indonesian Independence Day (17 August). Attlee had
tactfully withdrawn to his bed after the preliminary banquet and
'before the dancing began'.[36] Aneurin Bevan, however, proved an
'enthusiastic spectator'—as did the *Daily Mail's* nameless reporter
and also Chou En-lai, said to have 'watched attentively as girl
dancers swung and gyrated with exquisite hand movements and
twinkling feet to the music of xylophone, gongs, bells and drums'.

The Times 'Special Correspondent' preferred a choral concert,
held in the poorer north-west quarter of Peking, in which attempts
were made to render the creed of 'peaceful coexistence' in music
and song. According to this mocking observer, the brand new
theatre was 'Odeonesque without the frills' and the British delegates were ushered into their seats by girls dressed in 'demure,
blue, governessy dresses with white collars': an outfit that looked
'sleek and chic' by contrast with 'the prevailing proletarian
uniform'. When the time came, the choir burst into a rendition of
'Our Beautiful Motherland', prompting the reporter to smirk at
the programme notes: '"Wheat ripples in her fields fair," says the
brave attempt at an English translation, "And gold and coal mines
are everywhere."'

An allegedly 'British' folk song turned out to be 'Londonderry
Air'. 'Mr. Bevan delightedly joins in. At the end Mr. Wilfrid Burke
leaps to his feet with applause.' The 'young invited' audience
(said to be workers, but they looked 'more like university students'
to the man from *The Times*) note his gesture and applaud in
return. A contemporary choral work, which evoked the Red
Army's heroic crossing of the Tatu River during the Long March
of 1935, was followed by an ancient duet in praise of plum blossom,
performed by whispy-bearded elders on flute and a 'strange, evocative, stringed instrument the Chinese call the *cheng* which lies
flat on the table and is plucked'. A lotus dance that seemed to
'owe something to the early Agnes de Mille tradition' was itself
followed by a folk song from Sinkiang, adjusted to arrive at an
ideologically sound ending:

> Now all nationalities are united together,
> All sing the praise of our Chairman Mao Tse-tung!

Russian folk songs were thrown in, presumably as 'a tribute to the absent yet ever-present friends', as were extracts from *The Marriage of Hsiao Erh Hei*, a modern Chinese opera in which two young people 'struggle against the forces of feudalism and win free love—though not quite in the English sense as the interpreters of Peking might note'. In the view of *The Times*' superior British reporter, however, the concert was at its most successful in its rendition of 'the colourful and vital songs and dances from China's minorities:

> The minorities have been a triumph for the stage managers in Peking. Whatever may or may not be the policy pursued towards them in the new administration, as a stage turn they are the *dernier cri*. Seeing the group with long black gowns with bright blue sashes and red turbans being introduced to Mr. Bevan at the reception—the photographers are busy—one wonders: are they students at the academy for national minorities? Are they recruits to the central administration? Or are they—as they sometimes look—just a troupe coming on from the wings when required and after their six months stint in the capital, do they go back to their wild hills and their potent liquors to be relieved by another troupe?

Unlike devoted adherents such as the Red Dean of Canterbury, the NEC delegates were by no means so credulous or ignorant of recent developments in China as the smirking newspaper coverage may suggest. They knew a lot about the international manoeuvres of Communism, both Russian and Chinese, and the documents that survive among Morgan Phillips's papers in the Labour Party archives attest to considerable preparation for their mission. Together with highly critical statements by recently returned businessmen, these include a detailed analysis of internal developments in China since the Liberation of 1949, provided by the Royal Institute of International Affairs (Chatham House). Communist China was here described as 'a land of slogans, of campaigns and of movements which though they are ostensibly popular in origin are in fact turned on and off by the Communist Party to suit its purposes as one would a tap'.[37] By February 1951, so this informative document reminded its readers, the Communist leadership had decided to resolve its party's position by a show of force and 'to associate the mass of the people with this process'. The resulting movement, in which 'land reform' was coupled with an ongoing war against 'bandits' and 'reactionaries', took the form of a campaign of public accusation meetings followed by public executions, the 'pogrom' spirit having been whipped up by what Chou En-lai had called 'the stimulated revolutionary initiative of the masses'. Precise numbers were not available, but the Chatham House researchers estimated that the public executions demanded by this centrally 'stimulated' movement in the first half of 1951 must be tallied in the hundred thousands.

Attlee and the other members of the National Executive Committee were informed that this extraordinarily brutal

Fig 31. Attlee in Summer Palace, 19 August 1954.

programme of 'land reform' had coincided with a 'Resist America and Aid Korea' campaign, intended to foment nationalist feeling and, as the seasoned Marxist writer Kuo Mo-jo (now President of the Chinese Academy of Sciences) had claimed in a report on cultural work, to produce 'a fundamental change in the ideology of the Chinese people'. Determined to rid China of imperialist influences, the leaders of this campaign had damned Western support for Chinese universities, now coded 'cultural aggression', and attacked Western churches and foreign missionaries, who were, in some much publicized cases, accused of murdering babies and children in their care.

The Labour Party's International Department had also provided the leadership with a 'Memorandum on Repression and the Forced Labour System in China'.[38] This gave details of the Maoist system of re-education, in which those condemned to death were spared for two years and consigned to forced labour. Since their sentences were only 'suspended' rather than commuted, their survival beyond that was dependent on the decision of their jailers, who might be merciful if convinced that the prisoner in question fully accepted his or her own guilt. It also stated that the Communist-led government had created a considerable chain of concentration camps, run by the Ministry of Public Security and distributed throughout China. Indeed, the authors of this Memorandum provided Phillips with a list giving the whereabouts of many such establishments.

Further information had been supplied by twenty-one émigré 'cultural workers and writers'—publishers, scholars, editors, literary critics, and 'ex-legislators'—who petitioned the Labour Party's National Executive Committee from Hong Kong. Their 'open letter' announced that China was in 'unprecedented distress; pinned, as it were, breathless in between two dark forces in the garbs of the Communist totalitarianism and of Nationalist autocracy in Taiwan (Formosa)'.[39] It also warned the Attlee delegation against trusting in appearances. They should understand that their servants and drivers were likely to be of higher rank in the Communist Party than the returned students who served as their interpreters. They could expect to be reassured that there were no beggars to be seen on China's streets, without also being informed that all such unfortunates had been rounded up and dumped in forced labour camps. They would be shown many new buildings but not the 'concentration camp' labourers who had toiled under frightful conditions to construct them. They would find themselves surrounded by happy children, but they would not be told that of the 4 million emerging from primary school each year, the vast majority would find no place in middle school, or, for that matter, that no schools of any sort would accept the children of 'capitalists or merchants'.

These warnings were largely justified. As various more or less credulous Western 'pilgrims' had already proved by 1954, the Chinese had learned a lot from Moscow about the art of seducing foreign visitors. To be a delegate was to be flattered and indulged as well as sometimes wilfully blinkered and led by the nose. That, at least, was how New China's way of receiving delegations seemed to dissenters such as Dr Chow Ching-wen, who had participated in the People's Consultative Conference as a leader of the China Democratic League. By August 1954 he had already seen his party turned into 'a tool of the Communists' and he would soon retreat to Hong Kong to write *Ten Years of Storm*, the book in which he points out the priority placed by the Chinese Communists on 'hospitality' and stage-managed foreign 'visits'. After hearing Chou En-lai talk about this at the time of Dag Hammarskjöld's visit in January 1955 (the UN Secretary-General would go to Peking to negotiate the release of eleven imprisoned American airmen) he would declare that, for the Communist leaders, the reception of international 'visitors' was 'sometimes more important than normal diplomatic relations'.[40] Inviting delegations enabled them to 'create controversies and oppose the governments' of countries that themselves remained opposed to recognition of the People's Republic. It was because he understood this that the British journalist James Cameron, the *News Chronicle*'s determinedly independent reporter, prided himself on his ability to stray far beyond any delegation's tightly managed itinerary, and to see through the official presentations too. 'I grew out of the practice of believing my eyes some time ago',[41] so Cameron would write of his own tour of China, which began when he lugged his bag across the railway bridge from Hong Kong at the end of September 1954.

The Labour leadership too had been well aware that their delegation might be exposed to 'rigging' of the kind that had been used to make fools of the Webbs, George Bernard Shaw, and other British visitors to Stalin's Russia in the 1930s. Before leaving London, Attlee had tried to reassure the *New York Times* that 'there would be neither rose-coloured spectacles nor blinders in his baggage'.[42] Agreeing that 'on tours such as this "you are often shown only what your host wants you to see"', he explained that he had been 'exposed to lots of eyewash' in his time: 'I know it when I see it'. In the event, he and the other members of the delegation would insist that they were neither manipulated nor, for that matter, censored—although, as Morgan Phillips concedes, they did go along with the request not to take photographs 'at railways, on rivers and at airports'.[43] Indeed, their hosts proved willing to adjust their programme on arrival, shortening it after their longer than expected stay in Moscow, and also ensuring that it contained 'some free days to wander at will'.[44] On these occasions, they visited indoor and open-air markets, where they found 'all the traditional colour of China', and shops of the private, co-operative, and state-run varieties.[45] Phillips himself found 'real old world charm and courtesy' in a street devoted to silk and embroidery work. In an open market area they came across a number of 'entertainment tents' in which workers could buy tea and listen to Chinese opera during their breaks. In tribute to these international visitors, the gramophone in one of these was soon grinding out a version of 'Roll out the Barrel'—a performance, indeed, but hardly one that had been scripted in advance.

Morgan Phillips noticed that 'some people were very reluctant to have their pictures taken'[46] and, indeed, fled at the mere sight of his camera. Yet this was, perhaps, only a minor inconvenience. Labour Party funding being what it was, he had good reasons to point his camera in other directions. Before leaving Britain, he had made arrangements to broadcast statements back home from China, and also, if wanted, to supply 'Topical Talks' to interested takers, including the BBC, which never transmitted his 'Impressions of Moscow' but did broadcast a talk from Peking on the Light Programme on 28 September.[47] While Attlee would produce no less than seven articles for the *New York Times*, Phillips had arranged for his own written despatches to appear in the Labour and co-operative Sunday paper *Reynolds News*. Indeed, the appearance of his 'exclusive' despatches on the front page of that paper prompted the *Daily Telegraph* to cancel its more lucrative agreement to take three articles from Phillips.[48] He had, however, found a market for his photographs. *Life* magazine promised £200 for North American rights, and the picture editor of the *Daily Mirror* offered £100 for first option to use the same pictures in Britain: 'The sort of pictures we want are personalities—the Labour delegates with Chinese leaders, Attlee and Bevan in a rickshaw, and so on'.[49]

While in Peking, Phillips managed to snap the bulky figure of Nye Bevan in a pedicab (an unimproved rickshaw may have seemed more picturesque to the *Mirror*'s picture editor but in 'New China' such conveyances stood condemned as degrading relics of the imperial past). He took various photos of Attlee and the other delegates standing by famous ancient monuments or next to tiny old ladies with bound feet, as Edith Summerskill is shown doing at the Temple of Heaven, or surrounded by a horde of smiling, clean, and apparently well-nourished Chinese children. Phillips snapped various banquets too but, when it came to assembling the slim book—'a pictorial history'—he had also contracted to produce of the visit, he was obliged to rely on agencies for some of the most important shots, including the symbolic 'first handshake' between Attlee and Chou En-lai and the picture of Mao clutching a cigarette and a fork as he had tea with Attlee, seated directly opposite.

Rather like Tilbury

The delegation made various attempts to look behind the prepared scenery during the course of their tour. Two members were shown round a prison in Peking—identified by the *Daily Herald* as 'the Spartan Ching Ho prison' (perhaps the 'farm camp' of Ts'ing Ho', said to have been established in 1950 by the Peking Bureau of Public Security on the list provided by the Chinese oppositionists in Hong Kong). Here, as in the show prisons seen by visitors to Russia during the early years of the Bolshevik revolution,[50] attempts were made to reassure the visitors that the emphasis was placed on 'education' rather than punishment.

As for the new government's widely reported campaign against foreign churches and ministers, they visited various broadly reassuring religious leaders, and happened also to run into a Catholic

Fig 32. Aneurin Bevan and Mr Sam Watson visit a mine at Tangshan, 1954.

priest in the street: the fellow was 'surrounded by women and children' and, when questioned, 'said that he had held three masses
that morning, at which one hundred people attended'.[51] A Meth-
odist preacher claimed an attendance of seventy at his service,
giving them further grounds to conclude that 'though there has
been a campaign against superstition in all its forms, religion is
still being practised in Communist China'.[52] The church leaders,
however, appeared to be spokesmen of the new regime, as they
found after a revealing encounter with a party of boys in a courtyard within the Forbidden City. Some were reading picture books
which, as the interpreter explained, showed 'American "imperialists" torturing North Korean prisoners'.[53] Raising his concern
about such material with religious leaders, Sam Watson found that
they approved of the use of such books. This too, he was informed,
was a matter of education not 'indoctrination': 'Imperialism is, by
Christian standards a sin. Children must be taught not to sin.'

From Peking, the Attlee delegation were flown north-east to
Mukden (Shenyang) for a tour of industrial Manchuria, which

they knew to be at the centre of China's attempts to deliver on its first five-year plan,[54] and which reminded Attlee 'of the grimness of the industrial towns in the north of England'.[55] They inspected vast new housing projects, the quality of which was, as the Labour leader admitted, 'not high by our standards...but one must consider them in relation to the miserable mud hovels in which so many do live'. At a recently collectivised co-operative farm they were 'regaled with tea and a lot of statistics' to support their already positive impressions. The new nursery school was encouraging though obviously also a 'show place': Attlee himself had been 'seized by the hand' by two charming little girls who guided him through the village and towards the conclusion that 'the lot of the peasants has been improved'. They were taken around the steel works at the new city of Anshan, where they also watched another vast housing estate being built by a large force equipped only with 'primitive' equipment. It was here that Nye Bevan cast a critical look at the library and asked why the works of Kropotkin were not available. Detecting a policy of censorship, the delegates got nowhere when they accused their hosts of behaving like 'reactionary rulers and high priests throughout the ages'. As Attlee concluded from this episode, 'These hundreds of millions of illiterates will be given just enough education to enable them to become effective instruments of the slogan: "Increase production." Otherwise, they will hear only with the ears and see only with the eyes of their masters.' They also visited the coal mines at Kailan, where they were led in their assessment by Aneurin Bevan, a former miner, and Sam Watson, leader of the Durham miners, who found the place 'well-timbered and reasonably safe. There was no sign of gas. Output was much lower per man than in this country.'[56] The trip to Manchuria left Morgan Phillips in no doubt that 'the developments there are being tackled with vigour and energy'.[57]

They pursued an independent line of enquiry whilst in Shanghai, where an orchestra and choir played them Chopin and Beethoven, and the views from the Bund over the Yangtze River, now largely idle thanks to the 'Formosan business', impressed Attlee as 'rather like the Thames at Tilbury'.[58] After attending an official function laid on by the Mayor, they joined members of the much reduced British business community in that city. They were

taken around two still working British-owned factories, the China
Printing and Finishing Company and the textile works of Paton
and Baldwin. They visited British residents in their homes and
met others at a cocktail party hosted by the British consulate.[59]
Here they learned more about the British businessmen who had
effectively been treated as 'hostages' by the Communist regime:
refused exit visas until the 'levies' retrospectively imposed on
their immobilized companies had been paid. They later raised
this matter with Chou En-lai, who accepted that there had been
'defects' in government policy on this matter. *The Times* correspondent hoped that 'any outstanding problems of British traders
here will disappear as Chinese–British trade develops along new
patterns'. In the same spirit of conciliation, Morgan Phillips would
note that some British businessmen had made their own decision
to stay in China. Despite the problems faced by many firms, representatives of this optimistic group insisted that pilfering had effectively stopped under the new government, and that the streets
were now much safer for foreign women.[60]

In Canton, a southern city with tall houses and arcaded streets,
the NEC delegates were told about the 60,000 people who lived
on the river in an 'infinite variety' of boats some of which reminded
Attlee of 'very old and battered Oxford College barges',[61] and
who were no longer banned from coming ashore as they had been
before 1949: indeed, they were assured that special schools had
already been built for the children of this floating population. It
was here, as he watched infants running about on the banks of
the river, that Morgan Phillips worried about China's rapidly
increasing population, said to be rising by 12 million a year[62]—a
pressing problem that could easily seem to confirm Western fears
of the alarmingly fecund 'yellow peril' that threatened to overwhelm the world by sheer numbers. As far as Phillips could establish, 'no serious thought was given to family planning', and the
rapid increase in numbers threatened to overwhelm New China's
proudly displayed attempts to build new housing'.[63] It was an issue
that Nye Bevan raised repeatedly during the trip, breaking
through the layers of political jargon—'a terminology of weari-
some repetitiveness',[64] as he called it—to insist that the Communist leaders really should address themselves to the booming
population and its implications for China's food supply. He got

into the habit of asking guests at official receptions and dinners how many children they themselves had, and then wondering pointedly how they proposed to teach family planning to the far more productive peasants. He was unimpressed by the 'evasive' stock answers—that the peasants could never be taught, or that industrialization and 'Marxist economic planning would ensure plenty for all'.[65]

Landlords, Flies, and the Marriage Law

Throughout their tour the Labour leadership tried to take stock of the Communist regime—including Bevan, whose insistence on arguing with his hosts is said to have astonished those of the NEC members 'who at home might fat-headedly sneer at him as a Communist fellow traveller'.[66] Though dismayed by the regime's dogmatism, the smothering jargon, and its leaders' apparent incuriosity about the outside world, the delegates concluded that New China's close relationship with the USSR—a curious outcome of a long struggle for independence from interfering outsiders— would increasingly be strained by a rising sense of national and also wider regional identity. 'It is', wrote Phillips, 'not only a Communist revolution—it is a Nationalist and an Asian revolution. It is the culmination of the process of activity that has taken place since the Russo-Japanese war of 1905, when there have been growing movements against Western imperialist exploitation'.[67]

Despite their declared reservations about Communist methods of government, however, they could hardly remain unimpressed by many of the new regime's works, which loomed up as monumental accomplishments by comparison with their own now outvoted efforts to rebuild post-war Britain. Unchecked population growth may have threatened everything, but the visitors had seen undeniable evidence of vast industrial reconstruction and prodigious schemes of irrigation and flood control. They had seen new schools, hospitals, universities, and public housing schemes far larger than those they themselves had been able to get off the ground in bankrupt Britain—the latter even equipped with 'a very efficient central heating system', as Attlee would remind Phillips to mention in his account of an example in Mukden, Manchuria.[68]

Their cautious attitude towards the claims made on behalf of New China's 'expansion of agriculture' was certainly influenced by knowledge of the violence with which land reform had been carried out. It may also have been lent an extra poignancy by the memory of how one of their own modest attempts in this direction had exploded into the Crichel Down Affair, a protracted dispute over the British state's retention of some 725 acres of chalk downland in Dorset, which had initially been taken over, with due compensation paid to the owner, in order to create a practice bombing range during the Second World War.[69] After the war, this patch of ground had been transferred to the Ministry of Agriculture, so that it could be improved and used to demonstrate new industrial farming techniques. This modest exercise in English land reform had provoked a fierce resistance movement, led by a band of floridly reactionary Dorset landowners whose battle against the usurping state wouldn't have stood a chance in New China. The men from the ministry had been pilloried as if they were Soviet functionaries, and the long drawn-out row had culminated, only a few weeks previously (on 20 July 1954) in the resignation of Sir Thomas Dugdale, Minister of Agriculture in the Conservative government that had, by that time, replaced Attlee's administration in office.

New China's bloody land reforms remained alarming, but the British visitors could readily concede that a 'great deal' had been done in 'the field of public health' and especially in matters of 'simple hygiene'. Huge strides had been made in this area, and not just through vaccination campaigns, street cleaning, and exemplary schemes such as the draining of a formidable open sewer known as the Dragon Beard Ditch behind the Temple of Heaven in Peking.

The public health programmes pursued by the Chinese government in the years following the Liberation are comparable to those implemented in Bolshevik Russia in the chaotic years after the revolution of 1917. There, the people had been bent to the purposes of the Bolshevik state with the help of campaigns driven by slogans such as 'Lice are the enemy of socialism'.[70] And so it had been in China. Far from relying on medical specialists or even speedily trained 'cadres' alone, the Ministry of Health had set out to enlist the people in the war against disease-bearing pests and the results were remarkable.

Indeed, by the summer of 1954, many international visitors were lining up behind the official propaganda statements to agree that there were precious few flies on Mao. The anti-fly campaign had been observed a few years earlier by Basil Davidson, who asserted that, 'by the autumn of 1952, there were practically no flies in Peking'.[71] He describes three medical men in one party of visitors counting up the flies in markets in villages or on Peking streets and, after watching the swatters mobilize against the very few specimens that did dare to appear in these no longer infested places, marvelling at what could be done if public health was turned into 'a public adventure'.

And that was indeed the official claim. As the returned missionaries Ralph and Nancy Lapwood had explained for the benefit of British readers, New China's Ministry of Health had launched a movement against the 'Five Poisonous Things' in 1952. In so doing, they had 'enlisted the popular will behind a nation-wide campaign for positive health'.[72] Dogs had been annihilated, in an unpopular move that sceptics suspected may actually have been motivated by the secret police's desire to get rid of troublesome guard dogs.[73] War had also been waged against rats, disease-bearing snails, malarial mosquitoes, fleas, lice, and house flies. Holes in trees had been cemented up as potential breeding grounds. Canvas bags had been hung behind mules to catch the droppings. Quotas had been set for individuals to meet. Rewi Alley reports that 'thirty a day' was the number of dead flies expected of the workers attending the kitchens and lavatories in the Summer Palace, and that 'criticism' awaited anyone who turned up at the morning meeting having failed to slay and collect that number.[74] By the summer of 1953, the anti-fly campaign had even been joined by American prisoners of war in North Korea. At Camp Four, near Wiwon, inmates noticed guards swatting flies and carefully collecting their corpses in paper bags and envelopes. Having enquired into this new development, they requested permission to join in, and began improvising their own flytraps with socks and toothpaste tubes. Since 200 squashed flies could be exchanged for one factory-made cigarette, the prized corpses were soon being used as currency in poker games too.[75]

The fly campaign had impressed the rarely less than thrilled Hewlett Johnson, who accidentally indicated how it provided a domestic context for the Chinese government's allegation that American planes had been dropping plague-bearing insects on China and North Korea. During his visit of 1952, the Red Dean had not just joined his fellow Christian socialist, Joseph Needham, in supporting the Chinese government's charges accusing America of waging bacteriological warfare. He also insisted, with his usual polarized faith, that the other disease-bearing menaces in China— including the flies, mosquitoes, and rats—were the responsibility of Chiang Kai-shek, whose Kuomintang had reduced China to 'a land of filth and superstition',[76] where war, exploitation, and an absence of proper public health measures had left the people hostage to ancient customs such as 'painting white circles on the walls to "keep the wolves away"'.[77]

Great improvements were achieved through New China's public health campaigns, as was appreciated by Attlee, Summerskill, and also Aneurin Bevan, who had been responsible, in 1948, for facing down Britain's doctors in order to set up the National Health Service. They recognized this despite the expatriate Chinese intellectuals in Hong Kong who had written to warn the Labour Party NEC that the campaigns against flies and rats actually served the regime as another way of forcing its will on the Chinese people: it was alleged that those who did not show their loyalty by filling their daily quotas of slaughtered pests could expect to end up in 're-education' camps. Be that as it may, Attlee and the other delegates can hardly be faulted for not anticipating how the phobic imagery that had been stirred up to drive the anti-pest campaigns would live on—right up to 1999, when the president of the state-run China Human Rights Society, Zhu Muzhi, would inform an audience at the Foreign Correspondents Club in Beijing that the government had no need to reassess the Tiananmen Square massacre of June 1989, since the crushing of the pro-democracy protestors had been no worse than 'cracking down on flies'.[78]

Attlee himself declared of Shanghai that 'Flies seem to have been successfully exterminated in the city'.[79] He went on to note that campaigns had successfully been pursued against 'other long-standing evils': opium smoking had been taken firmly in hand by the 'almost puritanical' regime, as had prostitution, burglary, bribery, corruption, and pilfering too. Overcrowding remained terrible, but the people seemed clean and the streets were free of

1. Chiang Yee, *Sleeping in a Gas-mask*, a scene encountered under a chestnut tree in St James's Park, London which appeared in *The Silent Traveller in Wartime* (London: *Country Life*, 1939).

2. Fei Cheng-wu, *Waters Meet, Lynmouth, North Devon*, c.1947.

3. Chang Chien-ying, *Winter Landscape*, 1953

4. Chang Chien-ying, *Landscape with Distant River*, 1954

5. Paul Hogarth, *Shansi Peasant* or *The Village Chairman*, 1954, conté with colour wash.

6. Paul Hogarth, *Shansi Village*, 1954, conté with colour wash.

7. Paul Hogarth, *The Coal Hill, Peking*, 1954, conté and ink.

8. Paul Hogarth, *Building a New Hotel, Peking*, 1954, Hardtmuth charcoal lead.

9. Paul Hogarth, *Yangtse Boatmen*, 1954, conté with colour wash.

10 . Denis Mathews, *Waterfront, Chungking*, 1954–5, oil on canvas.

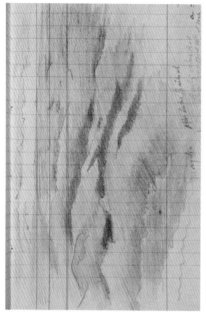

12. Stanley Spencer, *Mongolian Landscape* ('After Lake Baikal'), 1954.

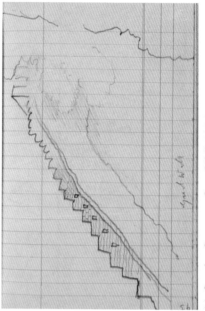

14. Stanley Spencer, *Great Wall*, 1954.

11. Stanley Spencer, '*Plane's Wing*' (*drawn from an aeroplane*), 'Prague–Moscow, September 15th 1954'.

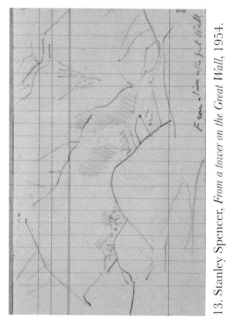

13. Stanley Spencer, *From a tower on the Great Wall*, 1954.

15. Stanley Spencer, *Ming Tombs, Peking*, 1954, oil on canvas.

16. Stanley Spencer, *The Ministers, Ming Tombs, Peking*, 1954, oil on canvas.

17. Stanley Spencer, *Tree and Chicken Coops, Wangford*, 1925, oil on canvas.

litter too. In one of its reports, the NEC delegation would attribute these improvements to the fact that 'It is a police state with a large armed police force'.[80] Attlee, however, preferred to think of them as a triumph not so much of the Communist state as of 'the voluntary action of the individual citizens who regard these old evils as being unworthy of the new China'.[81]

The British politicians found various other achievements to compare with their own reformist endeavours. In Peking as in Hangchow, they were impressed with the zeal with which selected relics of imperial China were being preserved and used to project an idea of the Communist Party as a rapidly modernizing force that was, nevertheless, fully worthy of the dynastic national past it now commanded. In its own way, Attlee's post-war Labour government had also yielded quite a lot of ground to the cause of historic conservation: it had backed the establishment of national parks, set up a new Ministry of Town and Country Planning, taken steps to ensure that comparatively expensive local building materials could be used to create council housing in sensitive historical environments, and also enabled the National Trust to assume ownership of large country houses on behalf of the nation. Yet Morgan Phillips, for one, did not really see the necessity, symbolic or otherwise, of such considerations. Indeed, he declared himself surprised to find a Communist government prepared to expend so much energy on the restoration of monuments such as the Lingyin temple at Hangchow: 'I doubt whether any State, with such a great need for housing and factories would have devoted as high a proportion of manpower and equipment in that town to the rebuilding of that vast edifice of the Buddhist temple.'

They worried about the fact that the decisions of the law courts could be overruled by the government (a Chinese rather than distinctly Communist measure, as Attlee thought likely), but they welcomed the new marriage laws, which had been 'revolutionised' to bring about fundamental changes in the position of women. Arranged marriages and child marriages had been banned. Widows, who had once been regarded as social outcasts, were now permitted to remarry while divorce had been made available by common consent.

Edith Summerskill would reflect on the industriousness of new China, and the amazingly productive energy unleashed by the

Liberation. In a letter of advice to her daughter Shirley, then a student at Oxford, she would regret that some people appeared to be both 'congenitally lazy' and 'totally devoid of ambition'.[82] She reckoned that Britain's temperate and changeable weather was an advantage here: far less enervating than the climates of hot countries in which 'unpunctuality becomes the rule, time is of little consequence and a casual, happy-go-lucky attitude often marks the behaviour of the people'. Old China, she went on to say, had been just like that, and its philosophers, poets, and scholars had 'established in their society the superiority of the loafer'. Discussing this aspect of China's tradition with Chou En-lai, she had been glad to learn that 'modern China rejects these teachings, and the bustle and enthusiasm for work there today are their practical answer to the over-fat and lazy sages of the past'.[83]

Writing from Japan, where she had inspected a brothel only a few days after leaving China, Britain's former Minister for National Insurance again commended the absence of prostitution from New China's streets: 'I am not sure how this has been done, but apparently it is made quite clear to those who might be tempted to enter the ranks of prostitutes that this method of securing a livelihood does not accord with Communist practice.'[84] She also ventured that the reform of the marriage laws had opened the way for the emergence of a superior form of 'conjugal affection'. In old China, as in other 'Eastern countries which can boast an ancient civilisation the attitude of husbands towards wives was primitive in its stark brutality...It was considered "good form" in old China for a man to beat his wife, and if a peasant spared her it was only to ensure that her capacity for agricultural labour was not impaired. The crippled old women I saw in China hobbling along on tiny deformed feet... tell a tale of the cruelties which were inflicted on women. Child marriage was commonplace, and I was told that these girl-wives were subjected to such abominable treatment that the only way of ensuring that they would not run away from a brutal husband was to bind their feet.' Not so, in present-day China, where 'it is a delight to see the young, tall grand-daughter, with feet size seven, strolling beside her diminutive toilworn grandmother'.[85]

Tea with Chairman Mao

In various public statements, the NEC delegates declared themselves impressed to meet a Communist regime whose leaders
asked, with apparent sincerity, for criticisms and advice. Though
'rigidly doctrinaire' over principles, as Morgan Phillips noted, the
Chinese leaders appeared unlike other Communist regimes in
being 'ready to experiment' in their application.[86] In a confidential report for the National Executive Committee, the delegation
commended this sign of flexibility as indicative of an interest in
'empirical' reality: 'Other Communist countries usually claim
their achievements to be the best in the world. Chinese leaders,
however, are ready to admit defects in their policy.'[87]

And yet their discussion with Mao Tse-tung, which took place
on 24 August, did not go quite like that. Having been driven, as
Attlee would remember, through 'a great red wall' into the
Forbidden City and then around a lake, they were received by the
Chinese leader and his 'chief colleagues' at Mao's official residence in the 'palace of the old empress'.[88] It was, in its way, an
historic encounter: 'the first time', as the *Daily Mail* would concede,
that Mao 'had received western statesmen since he came to full
power'.[89] Ushered into a panelled reception hall, the Britons sat
facing Mao, Chou En-lai, Liu Shao-chi, and other members of the
Chinese government across a long and narrow table. In the works
of the *Daily Herald*, 'They drank the fragrant tea of China, smoked
cigarettes, and ate pastries'.[90] During the course of the three-hour
discussion, which Attlee describes as 'vigorous but quite friendly',
Mao informed his visitors that 'the United States of America had
replaced Japan as the chief enemy of the Chinese people'.[91] He
declared that 'American foreign policy was determined on the
basis of a crusade against Communism'—evident in the emerging
South-East Asia Treaty Organization (SEATO) in which Britain,
France, New Zealand, Australia, and the USA were about to enter
a defence agreement with Pakistan, the Philippines, Thailand,
and Bangladesh. While condemning the Chinese people for
getting rid of Chiang Kai-shek—'a great crime' in American
eyes—the US had used its belief that 'New China is but the catspaw
of the Soviet Union', to justify their own imperialist designs. 'They
desire to occupy every area between the United States, China and

Russia. They were re-arming Japan and were taking the lead in securing the re-armament of Germany.'

Attlee would later admit to finding a characteristically British way of smiling at the 'violent hostility to America' his party encountered in China: 'it had its humorous side', he would inform readers of the *New York Times*, 'when one considers the diatribes against British imperialism which used to come from across the Atlantic'.[92] This particular diatribe, however, was far too rigidly expressed and, after listening for a while, Attlee 'intervened to ask whether Mao really thought that the U.S. wanted satellite states like the Soviet Union'.[93] Mao yielded no ground, while admitting that the two sides were 'of a different nature'. Russia's armed forces had 'liberated Eastern Europe. The people there recognised that their interests were identical with those of the Soviet Union. There was therefore a natural unanimity of views.' Attlee let that pass before pointing out that 'it was rather frightening to other nations who often had disagreements among themselves, to see a group of countries acting as a single monolithic bloc'. He added that this sort of behaviour 'actually gave the whole of the case to those elements in the United States who argued that the world was divided into two blocs. After all, why should we support revolutions if they merely added additional nations to the monolithic bloc?'

Mao, who was himself becoming something of a monolith, was not to be shifted. He replied that the Western nations had long 'conspired' against the USSR, before moving on to insist that the Chinese Communist Party had no wish 'to fight either Socialism or Toryism'. They were quite prepared to live 'side by side' with social democracy. He 'did not believe that social democracy could ever replace capitalism' and yet cooperation was vital, especially considering that China's main resources consisted of her people and natural resources. 'Peace' would certainly help. Indeed, Mao suggested that the Labour Party's greatest contribution might be to 'persuade the United States to change her policy; refuse to participate in the Southeast Asia Pact; persuade America not to re-arm Japan and oppose German rearmament'. It was an impossible demand, and one with which only Bevan among the British delegates may have felt inclined to agree. It also prompted Attlee to point out that 'a two-way traffic was needed, and that they might propose to their Russian friends the giving of complete freedom to all the satellite states to choose their own governments, the reduction of armaments in the most heavily armed state in the world, Russia, and the cessation of Russian-inspired activities in other countries'.[94]

The Britons stood back from Mao over many things, from American policy in Asia, to the nature of democracy, or Mao's dogmatic insistence that the standard of living was only higher in Europe because of exploitation of the colonies (What about Sweden, Denmark, and Norway? asked Attlee). Bevan would place 'a serious question mark'[95] against Mao's judgement, citing the reliance on 'old-fashioned Marxist theology' in his suggestion that the planned and centralized economy promised such prosperity that 'birth control' remained unnecessary. In general, however, they were respectful of the Communist leader: 'an impressive character with a quiet strength', as Attlee would inform readers of the *New York Times*. Sam Watson had been dismayed by 'the enslavement of the trade unions by the state',[96] and to hear the Communist leaders talking about 'the worker and the labourer as just a piece of raw material—"the masses"— another brick, another paving stone, something to fit into the pattern'. Neither was he remotely convinced by Mao's suggestion that it had been 'a serious failure' of Britain's post-war Labour government 'not to have eliminated the bourgeoisie'. Yet he also wrote that 'no single man has impressed me so deeply as Mao Tse-tung. He and the men around him seem powerful, dedicated and dignified.'[97]

If they were unable to come to terms with Mao, the British politicians could at least bring home the facts and statistics dumped into their reports by their hosts. Their second report to the National Executive Committee recites pages of figures about agriculture, industry, employment, and the rapidly proceeding construction of buildings in Peking and other cities.[98] It also reproduces the answers received to the questions they had put to Chinese leaders and officials. Some of these concerned 'industrial' issues close to the heart of the trade union leaders on the delegation. They enquired about the comparative wages of bricklayers, firemen, train drivers, and shop workers, and they had many questions about China's trade unions. Were they under direct government control, and what was the precise mechanism by which they might participate in drawing up the National Economic Plan? After visiting Cotton Mill No. I in Peking, they wondered exactly how the trade union committee at such plants was elected. They also wanted to know exactly how labour was recruited for 'great public works such as water conservancy and railroad building', and about the conditions in which the peasant 'volunteers' laboured. In the case of water conservancy projects, they were reassured that workers' travel expenses were picked up by the government and that hygienic temporary housing was provided at the sites, along with hospital facilities, coal to cook with, and sufficient food (including 'meat dishes several times a month'). In the absence of motorized equipment, work was indeed done by manual means, but a rich 'cultural life' was laid on too, consisting of clubs, reading rooms, literacy classes, and also artistic performances and film shows. The delegates may have refrained from enquiring into the extent to which this programme was devoted entirely to propaganda. However, they did ask detailed questions about the various forms of intimidation employed at the 'People's Courts' in cases concerned with '"economic sabotage" and other alleged crimes against the state': indeed, they asked if they might watch such a 'political' case in action, and received a hedged reassurance ('You will be invited to such a trial, when it occurs').

Many of the NEC's questions were designed to clarify the possible terms of trade between China and Britain. What goods was China not already able to acquire through the USSR and its East European states? Would any future exchange be conducted in sterling, and was China prepared to resume its disrupted export of tea to Britain? They asked questions about the treatment of British businessmen in China: why were their 'domestic and business' personnel 'constantly questioned by the police', and why did Chinese friends 'no longer dare visit foreign businessmen' legally resident in the country? They also asked after Robert Ford, a British subject, who had been arrested as 'wireless operator to the Tibet government' when China occupied Tibet in 1950, and who remained imprisoned though never charged. Informed that Ford had pleaded guilty to various crimes, including 'instigating Tibetan separatism' and 'inciting former local officials of Changtu to poison the living Buddha Geda, our negotiating-delegate to Tibet', they still wanted to know why the British Chargé d'Affaires' official enquiries about Ford's welfare had not even been answered—an allegation that Chinese officials denied.

These enquiries may well have been useful to the British diplomatic mission in Peking, although Douglas Hurd plainly resented the way Aneurin Bevan in particular walked into the embassy compound and proceeded to lecture the staff there 'about the state of China as though we were the visitors'.[99] He acknowledges that the Labour NEC delegation generally 'acquitted itself well' in China. Its members had refused to toast Mao unless Chou En-lai agreed to toast the Queen. The Durham miners' leader, Sam Watson, cut short a long spiel about religious freedom in New China by asking the offending 'bloody bishop, "Where's your loyalty lie, man, to Jesus or this lot here?"'[100] Morgan Phillips had responded to a tour of a new housing estate by declaring that he would never have expected to see Gorbals tenements 'built with a sense of pride'. Even Bevan had determinedly informed his hosts that socialism could be achieved by parliamentary democracy. Yet Hurd's would be a grudging tribute: 'Any disappointment the Chinese may have felt while the Labour circus were here has, I am sure, been removed by the fatuity of nearly all their statements since they left.'

Coming Home: the Cold War Resumed

Just before leaving Canton at the end of their eighteen-day visit, Attlee and his colleagues held a press conference for British and Chinese journalists. In their statement, they expressed 'warm enthusiasm' for the hospitality shown to them, and also for the time accorded to them by both Mao Tse-tung and Chou En-lai, with whom they had had several meetings. They commended the regime's ongoing attempt to 'build the nation on modern lines' in the face of China's 'primitive industrial inheritance and the many centuries of social stagnation', and suggested that 'sympathy and understanding should be shown by the rest of the world in immediate and practical form'. They condemned the 'lack of communication' that had led to so much misunderstanding on both sides of the Bamboo Curtain, and reciprocated 'most heartily' the 'earnest desire' they had seen in various 'spokesmen of revolutionary China to end this isolation'.

In short, they reaffirmed the creed of 'peaceful coexistence', insisting that the 'great ideological differences' existing between New China and the Western democracies should not be allowed to stand in the way of 'cooperation in the field of common interests'. In response to a question asked by a Chinese journalist, Morgan Phillips repeated his conviction that the easing of international tension demanded an end to isolation and a strengthening of Chinese–British relations. It was on this basis that the Labour government had recognized the Communist government of China in 1950, and he looked forward to trade and cultural exchanges, and to the eventual establishment of full diplomatic relations after the now rapidly approaching arrival of a Chinese chargé d'affaires in London.

Having dispatched that thank you letter, Attlee and his fellows embarked for Hong Kong. As a concession to the spirit of 'peaceful coexistence', their train was allowed to cross the frontier to arrive at Lo Wu station in Hong Kong. It was the first time such a passage had been permitted since the Liberation—a nice gesture that broke with the precedent according to which people entering or leaving China had been obliged to walk across a bridge to continue their journey on the other side. It would not, however, command reality. The bulk of the delegation went on to visit labour leaders in Japan, where Aneurin Bevan would refuse to give a press conference ('No, no', he is reputed to have said at the suggestion before adding a Welsh expletive), and provoke further controversy by reminding assembled Japanese trade unionists that, while he felt 'almost ashamed' of aspects of Britain's imperialist past, they too had a history to think about.

Attlee, meanwhile, stayed for three days in Hong Kong—he had those seven articles to write for the *New York Times*—and then went on to Singapore where he was joined by his wife, before proceeding to Australia and New Zealand. By the time they arrived in Canberra, where Attlee was welcomed as a guest of the Australian government, the Iron Curtain that he and his delegation had struggled briefly to lift was descending all over again.

The British Labour leader had tried to resist the usual polarized views when asked, at a press conference in Hong Kong, whether he had experienced any 'Communist eyewash'[101] in China. He commended the 'frankness' of the Chinese officials he had met, and insisted that the delegation had been 'allowed to go where they wished and see what they wished'. He also volunteered that, while his party had indeed found China 'being run by Communists, with whose principles we do not agree', they had also been 'impressed' by 'certain definite reforms which constituted new departures in China', by the 'incorruptibility' of the government, and by the great energy with which it was 'applying the general principles in which it believed'. As an example of the latter, he cited the zeal applied to 'the extinction of flies'.

There were, of course, problems too, but Attlee was diplomatically moderate about them, noting his delegation's concern about China's rapidly increasing population, which placed 'enormous pressure' on the country's natural resources, yet appeared to be considered 'a benefit' by the government. On international matters, Attlee had indicated, in reply to Mao's suggestion that he try to influence American policy over Formosa and the UN, that there were 'certain things'[102] the Chinese leader might pass on to the USSR. It would be 'a good thing', he had observed, if the USSR reduced its armaments and freed the 'satellite countries' in Eastern Europe. He recommended that Formosa be 'neutralised' for a short period in which that island's 'final status' might be sorted out.

A few days earlier, Morgan Phillips had informed readers of *Reynolds News* of the delegation's view, formed in defiance of the Iron Curtain, that it must be possible for Britain to have both China and the USA as friends, and that the Communist government of China should be granted China's 'rightful place' in the United Nations. It was true, as claimed by those who condemned such a measure, that this would add another nation to 'a group that acts and votes as a single communist monolithic bloc while the western nations differ among themselves'.[103] The 'bloc' already existed, however, and the danger surely had to be faced.

Though offered in a spirit of conciliation, these remarks were quickly attacked in Moscow. An editorial in *Pravda* condemned Attlee as 'a tool of reactionary circles in the United States and Britain': the British leader had 'slandered' both the Soviet Union and China 'immediately after enjoying their hospitality' and he had done so 'in order to curry American favour'.[104] As for his alleged attempt to get Mao Tse-tung to persuade the Soviet Union to reduce its arsenal, this was dismissed as particularly 'ill starred'.

Pravda's condemnation was entirely predictable. Within days, however, Attlee's efforts were being assailed on equally familiar grounds by cold warriors in the West too. Writing in *Tribune* while the Labour leaders were still in China, Michael Foot had alleged that the British Foreign Office's publicists had been 'playing down' the mission in response to American pressure, even putting it about that Attlee had only joined the delegation for 'Party' reasons to keep the left-wing Aneurin Bevan from stealing the initiative.[105] These hostilities were now renewed. Asked by Australian reporters if his mission represented a form of 'appeasement', as some American observers had suggested, Attlee reminded them that 'Appeasement comes from governments, and not from members of the opposition like myself. We were individuals seeking to find out for ourselves'.[106] He also repudiated American suggestions that he had been 'played for a sucker' by the Communist leaders: 'I have had a longer experience of the Communists than has had the United States, and I ought to know whether I was being played for a sucker or not.'

The American response had indeed been hostile. Speaking at the national convention of the American Legion, George Meany, the fiercely anti-Communist President of the American Federation of Labour, had condemned the drift to 'peaceful coexistence' as so much 'defeatism'.[107] Without explicitly naming Attlee's delegation, he had deplored such missions to Moscow and the city America still knew as 'Peiping', as 'wining and dining with Communist murderers'. And Meany was by no means the only critic of 'British gullibility', as the *Daily Mail* wanted its readers to know. The Socialist MP for Nottingham Northwest, Mr Tom O'Brien, had suggested that Attlee should visit Washington on his way home to calm the worries his visit had caused to the Americans he had described as 'Senators, bartenders, drug-store attendants'.[108] Churchill's Cabinet was also said to have been affronted by the fact that Mao and Chou were 'seizing a unique opportunity for world publicity', and that the smiling 'receptions and talks involving the socialist visitors are taking place in an atmosphere which the outside world assumes to be extremely threatening'.[109]

By the time he got back to London, Attlee was embattled on both sides, and being accused of inconsistency for his efforts. In one of his *New York Times* articles, he had written that China's illiterate masses would only be 'educated' sufficiently to make them 'effective instruments of the slogan: "Increase production".'[110] But how, as Attlee's own former Minister of Civil Aviation (and, later, Governor of Cyprus), Lord Winster wondered on the letters page of *The Times,* did he reconcile that observation with his suggestion, made while in Canberra, that a commendable 'idealism' was among the forces driving the Chinese government? William Empson wrote from Hampstead to defend Attlee ('It is a usual difficulty of the returned traveller that people find the truth patently self-contradictory unless it is specially pre-digested for them'[111]), but Attlee chose to leave the question unanswered. After a brief thaw, the Cold War appeared to be refreezing around him, and he could release no statement, whether dove-like or more hawkish, that would not be blasted—probably from both sides at once.

Attlee would return to the argument at the annual Labour Party conference, which opened in Scarborough on 27 September. In his speech he recognized that Chinese and Soviet Communism were not the same thing at all. Indeed, his recent visit had left him convinced that 'the Chinese, with their great traditions, would not fall for the cruder forms of Communism',[112] and that they should indeed be admitted to the United Nations. As for Chiang Kai-shek and his followers, they 'should be retired to some safe place to live out their lives in peace'.

These rhetorical concessions may have pleased the left of the Labour Party but they were made in the service of a larger battle. The Confederation of Peace Committees of West Yorkshire had laid on a demonstration fronted by two men wearing SS uniforms and followed by others carrying black crosses bearing the names of concentration camps.[113] Yet no such antics would prevent Attlee and his National Executive Committee defeating the Bevanites and committing the party both to the rearmament of West Germany and to the recently established South-East Asia Treaty Organization.

Lord Lindsay's Last Word

It fell to Lord Lindsay to communicate the mission's more critical objections to the Chinese authorities. He was no longer convinced that the Communist leaders with whom he had worked during the Second World War were, as he had once declared, infinitely more reasonable than the British Stalinists he had earlier encountered in the industrial areas of South Wales. He had also revised his judgement of the 'new form of educational practice' he had seen being developed by the Chinese Communists guerrillas in their base areas in the north-west. Writing in the earlier 1940s, he had concluded that this reflected an 'unresolved contradiction between education and indoctrination'.[114] The University of Yenan had been explicitly committed to the objective of 'cultivating the ability of independent and critical thought'. Yet other Communist educational institutions, especially in Manchuria, had emphasized 'the subordination of individual thinking to the mind of the group and the unquestioning acceptance of the authority of the Party'. Since then, he now believed, the cause of propaganda and thought control had won.

On 23 August 1954, Lindsay, who remained in Peking for a while after the Attlee delegation had left, wrote to Chi Ch'ao-ting, a Columbia-educated former spy who was now a Communist diplomat, objecting to the absurdly misinformed view of the West presented in New China's press. The British delegates had 'been led to believe that Chinese opinion is grossly ignorant of conditions and opinion in Britain, and in the rest of the outside world' and, moreover, that the government appeared 'quite uninterested in reducing this ignorance'.[115] He suggested that the Labour leadership had become more pessimistic about the possibility of avoiding another war, 'not because they think that the Chinese government wants war, but because they feel that its ignorance of the outside world may lead it to blunder into a war without intending to produce one'.

Attlee and the other NEC members may have been 'too polite to complain', but Lindsay was not so restrained: 'when I see my old friends acting in a way which seems to me to increase the danger of a new war which would involve all of us in disaster, I feel it is my duty to warn them.' In this spirit, he went on to explain what Attlee had meant when, at a press conference in Hong Kong on 2 September, he had talked about the 'many delusions about the west' he had come across in China. The slanted stories peddled by the New China Press Agency implied that 'the Australian Communist Party has the support of most Australians' and that the British masses were largely Communist, but held down through 'violent persecution by the ruling class'. In his view, the 'record of Communist action', and not just against democratic socialist parties, wholly justified the suspicions held by 'large sections of the British people' about the 'good faith of Communist claims to co-operate with people of differing political views'.

These widespread fears were a major hindrance to 'peaceful coexistence' as it might be embraced in the West. Lindsay warned his former friend that, by drawing a veil over their existence, the Chinese Communists were systematically depriving their own people of the opportunity to understand and reduce these powerful obstacles. In an argument that would be repeated in Morgan Phillips's 'pictorial story' of the delegation, he added that they were also increasing the likelihood of a new war breaking out over Formosa, which China was more likely to attack if it came to believe its own lies about the strength of anti-Communism in America. By the time Lindsay wrote these words, however, the difficult business of awakening the Chinese people and their regime to the truth about Western opinion was left to the motley group of scientists, artists, politicians, and writers who followed in the wake of Clement Attlee's departed delegation.

17

Popeyed among the Tibetans: The Undiplomatic Rapture of the Cultural Delegation

'There it sits...four square, ruled and patterned, bang in the middle of a sepia landscape.'[1] It was 'the colour of milk chocolate' and seemed 'as self-assured and inexplicable as a dog biscuit on a beach'. Seeing no river ford, harbour, or mountain pass that might explain Peking's position on the North China plain, the airborne Hugh Casson portrays himself wondering 'Why is it there and not somewhere else?' In truth, he already knew the answer from the Danish architect Steen Eiler Rasmussen, whose study *Towns and Buildings* (1949) opens by evoking Peking as a temple city that owed its position to necromancy and ritual rather than to 'common-sense' or the demands of trade.[2]

By the time the plane landed outside this fabulous settlement where 'the ideal city became reality',[3] every member of the cultural delegation surely understood why Stanley Spencer had likened them, as they braced themselves to walk out into the streets of 'grey despairing Prague', to death-watch beetles trapped in their boreholes and condemned only to go forward. It was Friday, 24 September and the six exhausted men peered out of the fuselage to see a guard of honour waiting with a dais and even a brass band. Their leader, Professor Leonard Hawkes, muttered in disbelief and, so Casson also claims, 'vanity and alarm' shuffled for supremacy as the rumpled cultural luminaries straightened their ties and prepared to step out into the blinding light. A. J. Ayer would turn the moment of disembarkation into a mock-heroic joke centred on himself. Claiming to have been first to emerge, he was 'astonished to hear a band playing and to see what I thought I recognized as the leaders of the Chinese Government waiting to greet us'.[4] As he began to step down, however, 'the band stopped playing, the dignitaries retreated, and our aeroplane was hastily shunted to a remote corner of the aerodrome where five men in horn-rimmed spectacles stood waving small union jacks'. Two planes, it seemed, had arrived in the wrong order: 'We had usurped the place of the Rumanian Government's delegation.'

It's an amusing story, which would surely go down well over lunch at Bertorelli's in Charlotte Street after Ayer returned to London. It also disregards the facts as recorded by other observers. 'Brilliant Sunshine', wrote Rex Warner, whose diary records that a band and troops were indeed on hand to welcome the 'Rumanian Parliamentary delegation' and also that the British cultural delegation were in fact met on board their plane by members of a committee who treated them with 'the greatest courtesy'. After descending into their own more modest 'battery of cameras'[5] they sipped politely offered lemonade in a newly decorated reception room and were then driven into Peking, their cars raising the same dust as the Attlee delegation's had done a month or so earlier. No doubt they also passed the 'endless rows of donkey carts' that the Birkbeck physicist J. D. Bernal, who had landed in Peking only one day earlier, found 'very reminiscent of Ireland'.[6]

Casson looked out to see blindfolded donkeys circling endlessly around wells, and cabbage fields that 'surged' right up to the 'new factories and office blocks crystallising behind their bamboo scaffolding'. No tower cranes or bulldozers here, he noted, but a new Peking was still rising at incredible speed outside the 40-ft high grey walls surrounding the historical city. Passing through those ancient ramparts, they joined the blue-clad masses in crowded streets, where bicycles shoaled like 'silver herrings' (more even than in Cambridge, as Bernal had noticed), and the trams had been made both festive and correct with flags and other decorations.

Warner registered 'one-storey buildings of great charm', the additional red or 'pink-washed' wall surrounding the Forbidden City, and also the huge stands outside the Gate of Heavenly Peace, already prepared for the fifth anniversary celebrations to be held on 1 October. He noticed fragile-looking rickshaws, girls wearing trousers, and vast wicker baskets full of earth being hauled about by horse and donkey. 'Good-looking people' he scribbles, shortly after entering his party's brand new hotel in the old Legation

Quarter. 'At last a room to oneself', he sighs with an abundant
sense of relief, which turns into positive satisfaction as he discovers
that the 'very comfortable' room in question is generously
equipped with cigarettes, matches, sweets, ink, books on Peking
and modern China, and also copies of a daily news sheet printed
in English. He could tolerate the crudely purposeful art on the
hotel landings, even if it did consist of 'strapping sculptured girls'
and 'keen male workers'[7] far too reminiscent of the Metro stations
in Moscow.

The 'Sin Chiao' Hotel seemed 'a pleasant, orderly looking
building' to Hugh Casson's architectural eye: 'Western in style
but with agreeably Chinese details at roof level and round the
entrance doors'. One of three 'huge, barracks-like hotels'[8] built
in Peking for the exclusive use of the new government's international guests, its 'modern amenities' included lifts, hairdressers,
and 'dancing on Saturdays'. The dining room offered round
tables for guests who favoured Chinese food, and square ones for
those who preferred Sheffield cutlery and European-style cuisine.
The place was packed with delegates from various parts of the
world. Casson counts his way through parties 'from Pakistan and
Indonesia, from France and Central Europe, from Italy, Germany
and Japan', plus a few 'jokers like ourselves'. Among the more
individual travellers, he remembers a cancer surgeon from Chile,
a few 'professional and paunchy' delegates who appeared to live
entirely for World Youth Conferences, a Swedish novelist (probably Artur Lundkvist), a Dutch photographer, and a 'British
artist' who was almost certainly Paul Hogarth. It was James
Cameron who would track down a single paying guest in one of
these monstrous hostelries: an unusually principled reporter
named G. K. Reddy of the *Times of India*.[9] Though themselves
'Guests' of the Communist regime, the cultural delegation also
felt 'prim and purse-lipped' in the company of these altogether
more partisan visitors. None of them would feel obliged to repay
their hosts with enraptured promises such as 'I'm betting everything I've got on China' (an example recorded by Rex Warner at
one of the many banquets laid on for international visitors). Yet,
as Casson confirms, they would soon find their own ways of
'falling to the spell of China and its people' if not exactly of its
new regime.

In the Steps of Kublai Khan

Having bathed and otherwise refreshed themselves, the newcomers joined their hosts and interpreters for what Casson described as a 'difficult' lunch. 'They gave us Toast of Welcome and Toast of Pleasant Stay', scribbled Leonard Hawkes, '& I gave Toast of Thanks and Pleasant Anticipation'. Yet it was also here that the Britons became aware of the itinerary dawn up for their visit and started to plead that they be spared 'factories and clinics, mines and blast-furnaces'. Afterwards, if the sequence of events presented in Casson's *Red Lacquer Days* is accurate, they climbed the wall of the Tartar City and gazed north over the magical settlement they would begin to explore properly the next morning. Still informed as much by his reading of Rasmussen as by the actual city that now stretched out before him, Casson describes the view as follows:

> a city of low grey houses, seamed by tiny alleys, and geometrically dissected by great boulevards laid out by Kubla Khan. The hous-es—Rasmussen calls them 'Petrified tents'—are built round mini-ature courtyards each of which contains a tree, so that in summer the eye commands a giant walled garden five miles across.[10] Above this green and leafy sea ride the palaces and temples of the Impe-rial and Forbidden Cities—'the greatest palace that ever was' wrote Marco Polo—golden roofed, emerald-eaved, scarlet walled, their royal height unchallenged by the homes of citizens. Above these again, but still within the Imperial City, rise two artificial mounds, one decked with pavilions, the other crowned with a white whisky-bottle shaped pagoda. A haze of charcoal smoke hangs over the scene and through it drifts the city's noise—clamorous and bewil-dering—bells, gongs, horns, drums, shouts, rattles, and snatches of music.

Peering around the edges of his first impressions, the British architect acknowledges various signs of new development: a 'thin black scribble of wire' reaching out over the roofs of the city, the trams and Cadillacs, the 'Croydon-esque' silhouettes of the new public buildings, even the odd 'flash of scarlet' given off by a flag or scarf. In fact, Peking was already caught in a storm of recon-struction. It would be said that the Chinese delegates who went from Peking to Geneva earlier in the year had returned to find that four new hospitals, six factories, and eleven Ministerial blocks had been laid out, built, and occupied during their absence of only a few weeks.[11] To Casson's eye, however, the modern interruptions were not on a scale that could 'destroy this feeling of being in a place unchanged'. Peking remained, so Ayer also concluded, 'in the main a medieval town'.[12]

After returning to their hotel for a short rest, Hawkes and his band were met by their Chinese hosts and a group of welcoming intellectuals who toasted them with what Warner found to be 'a kind of cherry wine', and took them off to dinner. The food, which was served in Western style, was excellent, Warner notes, as was the Chinese wine named 'Young Bamboo Shoot'. Casson was still worried about the guided tour awaiting them. 'Clearly we shall not be left alone,' he scribbled: 'Bed at 10.30 ready for heavy day.'

Over the next week, a great deal of their time would be 'spent simply in sight-seeing',[13] as Ayer later informed listeners to the Third Programme. Their introductory bus tour of the city commenced at 10 a.m. on Saturday, 25 September, the morning after their arrival. Warner was impressed by the many shops, most of them still small private enterprises, which seemed to be selling everything—flowers, fruit, sewing machines, bicycles, great woolly coats. They saw a quarter devoted entirely to the sale of old tyres, much used on the city's innumerable carts, and there were children everywhere. 'During the whole of our stay', writes Casson, 'we never saw a child in tears, nor a child barefooted'. Warner watched office workers performing their morning exercises (Paul Hogarth would record that these thrice daily public PT exercises—or 'Physical Interludes',[14] as they were described by James Cameron—were often carried out to 'the strains of revolutionary songs'),[15] Warner also noted 'Police numerous'—although these figures may only have been directing the traffic, dressed in white uniforms and using red megaphones to bark such improving instructions as 'The lady comrade with the basket is asking to be run down if she continues to ignore the crossing'.[16]

Later that day they were taken south into the outer Chinese City to visit the Temple of Heaven—actually, as Warner noted, 'two groups of buildings separated by a long avenue with cypresses at each side'. If the teeming city had seemed 'a fantastic cauldron of life', this impressed Casson as a place of 'miraculous serenity'.

Warner was especially taken by 'the temple where emperors prayed for harvest'—presumably the 'Temple of the Happy Year', which one early twentieth-century guidebook describes as 'the noblest example of religious architecture in the whole of China'.[17] In fact, this marvellous edifice had been rebuilt after being destroyed by a lightning strike in 1889—allegedly, so the same guidebook explains, after the wrath of Heaven was provoked by a trespassing centipede. 'Wonderful building', wrote Warner, 'with extraordinary perspective & feeling of space to enter'. Casson notes that these once neglected buildings had now been so carefully restored and redecorated that they 'glittered' on their 'blindingly' white marble terraces 'like freshly unwrapped toys'. Spencer, meanwhile, felt as if he had walked into Heaven itself—and the Heaven he found here was not, as he would later insist, some otherworldly domain. Like his English 'resurrections', which could break out in a churchyard, or overwhelm a person as he read a newspaper or love letter, it was actually present in 'the great open spaces, the miles long "pastures" and the little shallow carved marble bridges that are so lovely to come to'.[18]

Lunch was a struggle for Warner, who could handle a glass anywhere but admitted to being utterly incompetent with chopsticks. After a rest, they were led out of their hotel for a second excursion. This time the tour bus conveyed them to the Forbidden City, and the walled enclosure known as the Pei Hai (Beihai) or Northern Sea Park, where they looked out over a 'wonderful lake with willows', saw goldfish exhibited in great tubs ('bred for strangeness'[19] was Ayer's assessment of these extravagant and rarely just golden creatures), and climbed one of the Imperial City's two artificial hills to visit the 'White Dagoba'. Built in the Tibetan style by the Emperor Shun Chih on the occasion of the first confirmed Dalai Lama's visit to Peking in AD 1652, this famous stupa impressed Warner as being 'shaped like a bottle of VAT 69'. Having stood beside it and surveyed the various palaces below, they descended through a tunnel and then found themselves being punted across the 'North Sea' in a 'delightful' boat propelled by a man at each side. Bats were fluttering about in the dusk by the time they arrived at the Emperor's fishing pavilions. Warner loved the 'feeling of calm, space, pleasure' conveyed by this astonishing artificial landscape. He was pleased to see 'lots of young people enjoying themselves, Girls in boat with Chinese fiddle'. And 'all this under the care of v. beautiful girl'. That same '*sweet* fifteen year old' also appears in Casson's notebook, where she is said to have been quite overthrown by Stanley Spencer ('S.S. gives guide hysteria').

And that is how things were to be for the cultural delegation as they were guided through the 'legendary world' (Casson) of Peking. They spent their first week in 'a stupor of visual delight', sampling the wonders 'of temples and gardens, of palaces and lakes, of secret courtyards and absurd pavilions with delicious elegant names: "The Palace of Pleasant Sounds," "The Studio of Pure Fragrance", "The Hall of Vast Virtue", "The Pavilion for Watching the Spring"'.

Coping with the Crowds

Having arrived in a holiday period, they found these amazing places teeming with visitors—'soldiers strolling with linked fingers, old ladies tottering on misshapen feet…parties of school children in scarlet scarves'. The cultural delegates were noticeably less emphatic in their admiration for these crowds than was Paul Hogarth, one of whose most widely reproduced Peking drawings seems to congratulate the citizens shown wandering through the Summer Palace for having reclaimed their no longer forbidden inheritance (Fig 50).[20] According to Casson, such busy crowds might well have seemed 'unwelcome' to Western visitors, who would quickly discover that the quiet in which they preferred to contemplate such ancient places was only available at dusk or early dawn. Yet he also turned this popular Chinese interest in the no longer reserved luxuries of imperial Peking into a stick with which to beat the Marxist levellers at home: 'How wrong surely are those who, in the interests of equality, would remove from public gaze all evidence of another's wealth.'

In Britain, the rise of popular tourism had seemed alarming not just to landowners, but to upper-class 'socialists' such as C. E. M. Joad, who had agonized over the 'untutored townsman's' invasion of the countryside.[21] Yet none of the cultural delegates felt inclined to transfer that class-bound sense of alarm to the peasants, soldiers, and workers to be found enjoying

Fig 33. Stanley Spencer, Leonard Hawkes, Rex Warner, Hugh Casson, and A. J. Ayer, Summer Palace, Peking (photo: John Chinnery).

the imperial palaces and gardens of Peking. Writing for the *Sunday Times*, Warner describes the new visitors as 'remarkably orderly'.[22] On his first visit to the Summer Palace he found 'every path and building was packed with people of all ages, happy, smiling, unhurrying and unhurried'. With the help of John Chinnery, he also ascertained that the Public Authorities treated these sightseers with remarkable courtesy: 'Instead of what with us would have been the notice "No Entry", written outside a building reserved for official entertainments, the Chinese inscription, so I was told by an English Sinologist, read "Meandering people cease their steps". Nor did there appear to be any real need for the moral injunction stating that "Those who deface the people's property should inwardly reprimand themselves".' In defiance of such familiar Western clichés as the 'yellow peril' or the emerging denigration of the newly clothed Chinese people as 'blue ants', Warner wrote that the Chinese mass now seemed to him 'less like a many-headed monster than like many scenes of crowded streets and buildings'. Though normally 'averse to crowds', these ones were 'surprisingly human beings with smiling faces'. Perhaps it was this observation that encouraged the *Sunday Times* to entitle Warner's article, 'Peking, the City of Smiling Discipline'.

The six men composing the cultural delegation were not invited to follow Clement Attlee and Aneurin Bevan in taking tea with Mao Tse-tung. They were, however, guided through Sun Yat Sen Park, where Warner saw 'great rocks like Henry Moore everywhere, sometimes arranged in small mountains'. Ayer was similarly impressed by those erratically shaped boulders—'agonised rocks' was Casson's description—which were in fact naturally formed and gathered in from all over China. Like the goldfish and the trees that had been 'groomed' to resemble trees in ancient paintings, they convinced him that the Chinese had 'a great passion for what one might describe as natural deformities'.[23]

They picnicked among the still unrestored ruins of the Summer Palace, where they were shown the hulk of the rusting iron steam yacht presented to the empress dowager by the emperor of Japan. Warner was perhaps more impressed to see an exhibition of slogans and pictures carved on single grains of rice, by the 50-year-old Mr Ching Chin-yi: one of this strange prodigy's works, so Casson was assured, bore the text of the Stockholm Peace Appeal. Before leaving, they visited the Hall of Listening to the Oriole, where they enjoyed a lunch that included Shark's lips, duck's liver, crab's stomach (which turned out to mean roe), washed down, as Warner notes, with 'lots of yellow warm wine'. The Oriole, as he noted of this very busy place, appeared to have 'migrated'.

At the Lama temple (also known as the Yonghe temple) in the north-east of the city, Warner surveyed the statues and paintings and concluded that 'All Buddhas have long ear-lobes'. He was also impressed by a chapel that seemed to be positively crawling with 'frightful' images of 'protective spirits'. One of these demons was 'riding with a dead man for saddle'. Another had 100 arms, and was 'apparently copulating'.

On another day, they were equipped with masks against the dust and driven to the Great Wall of China, some 50 miles north of Peking. On the way they passed innumerable carts and 'odd' ruins. They watched Bactrian camels drinking from a stream and surveyed the mountains beyond: 'like N. Wales' as Warner concluded, before moving on to admire the 'stupendous sight' of the Great Wall, which 'unrolled like toothpaste', and seemed 'strong, solid & well-made, like everything here'. After enjoying sandwiches and lemonade, and concluding that the Wall was 'a wonder of the world alright' (Warner), they were driven on to the valley of the Ming Tombs, which Ayer would describe as 'perhaps in their setting the most beautiful works of architecture I saw in China'.[24] Situated in a natural amphitheatre surrounded by low hills and a mountain that reminded Warner of Mount Hymettus near Athens, the tombs were approached by a long avenue—a 'spirit way'—guarded by vast silent stone animals: elephants, horses, dragons, and camels. As Casson wrote, 'Here restoration work is only just beginning and the atmosphere is pleasantly melancholy. The late afternoon sun fills the deserted courts as though with golden syrup, and grey long-tailed birds call and flutter in the cypresses.' Warner was particularly enchanted by the Changling tomb, which had grass growing on its roofs, and vast pines, cypresses and oaks in the courtyards: though 'more like a ruin' than some of the other tombs he found it a place of 'immense, haunting serenity'.

The Price of Conservation

If they were dazzled and amazed by these ancient Chinese places, this wasn't only, so Casson mused, because of the inherent magnificence of the temples, palaces, and parks they were shown: 'Today, once behind the Iron Curtain, every building, however well-known, every monument—even such prosaic objects as trolley-buses or chocolate cake—are invested with a new mystery, an atmosphere of the other side of the looking glass which gives a keener edge to everything observed. When this is added—as in China—to the fantasy of other cultures which have for thousands of years regarded all customs of the West as barbarous and contemptible, then the resulting visual experience is so disturbing in its impact as to be almost physical in effect.'

The members of the cultural delegation spent days reeling with this politically enhanced sense of astonishment, and reaching for words as the tide of unfamiliar impressions started to test the anchors of habitual Western assumption. They also began to acquiesce to New China: not abstractly to the politics of Mao and Chou En-lai, but to the smiles of the children and the charm of the people with their memories of corruption and oppression under Chiang Kai-shek and their brave hopes for the future; to the cleanliness of the streets and the absence of flies, which impressed Rex Warner just as it had earlier done Clement Attlee; and also to the care and attention that the forward-looking new government seemed to be lavishing on the monuments of old China. Ayer accepted that much in China would have to be changed in the years to come. The rickshawmen, most of whom actually drove old pedicabs, would be allowed to 'continue their trade so long as they keep their rickshaws in repair',[25] but no new rickshaws were to be built and these petty capitalists would have to learn new ways as time went on. He knew there would be more trams, buses, and cars, and that 'many of the old houses will have to be pulled down' to make way for them. Having toured the historical sites of the city, however, he was encouraged by the fact that 'those who are now in power show themselves to be extremely conscious of at least the aesthetic values of the past. Monuments and temples which, so we were constantly informed, were allowed to fall into disrepair during the Kuomintang regime, are now being faithfully restored.'

Warner, who had been much concerned with the meaning of history and, indeed, of the idea of 'heritage' in Britain, will surely also have been provoked to thought by this discovery. Writing at the close of the Second World War, he had worried about the loss of 'living tradition'[26] in Europe—the recent history of which had amply confirmed the prophetic truth of W. B. Yeats's warning about the fate of an age in which 'the centre cannot hold'. The death of God had left a void at the heart of Western liberal societies that the slouching 'rough beast' of fascism and other versions of 'the Cult of Power' had soon enough tried to fill. While 'Science' and 'efficiency' had become new superstitions, the idea of national history appeared to have declined into a disconnected if sometimes also spectacular totem. Severed from its connection to 'living tradition' and no longer able to promise a convincing future, so Warner suggests, history only persisted in the present in the form of monuments, 'ghosts', and more or less reliable 'portraits of the past'.

The members of the cultural delegation surely knew that China was a land in which culture had, in Ayer's phrase been 'made subservient'[27] to politics. And yet, as they were guided around the monuments of old Peking, they do not appear to have been much troubled by the thought that by restoring these ancient sites the new regime might also be transforming them into decor with which to impress their own people as well as international visitors. No suggestion of cynical manipulation was implicit in Casson's remark that the buildings of the restored Temple of Heaven looked like freshly unwrapped 'toys'. Even James Cameron, the foreign correspondent who prided himself on his ability to see through the show that powerful interests might choose to place before his eyes, recited the list of 'protected places' to be preserved within the walls of Peking without a hint of irony. The exotic-sounding names of these sites—the 'Pavilion of Melodious Sounds', the 'Palace of the Passing Time', the 'Wells of the Precious Concubine', etc.—were allowed to accumulate through a paragraph in Cameron's book *Mandarin Red*, and no great sense of alarm was provoked by the fact that the rest of the country was, as Cameron understood, increasingly dedicated to an utterly contrary process described by the *People's Daily* as 'Forsaking the feudal roots of an unconstructive past'.[28]

Talking Back and Getting the Dalai Lama's Autograph

So the cultural delegation's 'red lacquer days' floated by in a kaleidoscopic storm of delight, luxury, and surprise. When they weren't feasting or admiring ancient buildings, they were shown documentary films about the revolution in Peking, or about a farm that had been converted into an agricultural co-operative (the latter example struck Warner as 'naïve, but rather charming'). They visited art galleries and were taken to the Peking opera for an 'absolutely fascinating' performance in which a wicked landlord was justly murdered by a fisherman and his wife. Their tour included visits to appropriate institutions, including the Historical Museum, then being set on a new footing in the Forbidden City, where they heard about the rudimentary training being given to 'barefoot' cadre archaeologists, and examined some of the tens of thousands of items recovered in the course of reconstruction work over the last few years.

Over tea, the director, Mr Han, gave them the new regime's interpretation of the missing remnants of 'Peking Man', the story of which had been running for a couple of years as a palaeontological accompaniment to the Chinese government's germ warfare allegations. 'Stolen by Americans', was Mr Han's brisk judgement of the fate of the fossilized skulls and cranial fragments which had been recovered to great international interest at Zhoukoudian, 30 or so miles south-west of Peking, during the Rockefeller-funded excavations of 1927–37, and then gone missing while being conveyed to the USA for safe-keeping in 1941. As Dr Pei Wen-Chun explained in a then current issue of *China Reconstructs*, the claim, which was brought into sharp relief by the long history of Western looting of China's historical sites, had been supported by the British paleontologist, D. M. S. Watson, Professor of Zoology at University College London, who was alleged to have told scientific colleagues in the spring of 1951 that he had seen the missing fossils, sensationally associated with the idea of the 'missing link', in the American Museum of Natural History.[29] Though repudiated by American museum officials,[30] the misunderstanding persisted and, like other foreign visitors, the British delegates were challenged to take sides.

While in Peking, they also undertook a number of individual activities. Leonard Hawkes talked with experts in geology and natural resources and was also taken off by archaeologists to further 'probe the mystery of the Peking Man'. Rex Warner had his own engagements too. After one discussion with Chinese literary figures, he noted, 'Very nice. We talked about children, wine and Badminton.' Talking shop, for him, also meant comparing notes with a well-known Chinese author who explained that his publisher would normally issue editions of between 10,000 and 20,000 copies of a new book: a figure that will have contrasted starkly with Warner's recent publication of *Escapade*, his more or less instantly forgotten novel in which Stalin and Hitler were found hiding in the little English village of Average.

Hugh Casson stepped up to 'add my quota of warning to the local architects and students against the danger of adopting current

Soviet architectural styles'. By way of alternative, he apparently recommended that New China's architects and planners might derive more fruitful lessons from the example of Britain's still rising New Towns. He warned against despoliation by 'wirescape' too.

A. J. Ayer gave a lecture on Logical Positivism at the University of Peking, where he also claims to have dissected and revealed the true significance of Mao's theory of Contradiction. The latter, as Ayer summarized, argued in favour of the 'particularity' of contradiction, suggesting that, while all natural processes are 'dialectical', each is 'dialectical' in its own way. This really meant, so Ayer informed an audience that may not have felt entirely at ease in its polite applause, that 'you cannot deduce from any general law of dialectics what will happen in any given type of circumstances: you have to study the facts'. This seemed to Ayer a sensible, indeed a potentially momentous modification in Marxist thought. The author of *Language, Truth and Logic* tried and, in his own estimate, 'failed' to convince his audience that Mao's theory really amounted to 'the purest empiricism' and an abandonment of the dialectic. 'Marxism becomes, when treated in this fashion, a linguistic framework into which you try to fit your empirical observations, and not a theory about the character of the events you may expect to observe.' Ayer ventured to suggest that such an interpretation 'should suit the Chinese, who have hitherto shown themselves to be a people of a predominantly practical turn of mind'. Back at the hotel, as Warner records, the lecture was followed by dinner, a 'very good' show by acrobats and jugglers, and, of course, a lot more of the Chinese wine known as 'Fragrant Snow'.

Though their visit was unofficial and without any formal diplomatic purpose, the members of the cultural delegation were 'hospitably entertained' over lunch in the British embassy compound, where they also 'discover old friendships'—Casson's way of referring to the fact that one member of the embassy staff, John Addis, had once been taught by A. J. Ayer. Casson's notebook reveals that Humphrey Trevelyan warned them not to be taken in by the official presentations, or to forget the importance of 'what you don't see and what can never be seen or known at any time'. In the latter category the diplomat included the fate of the lost relics of Peking Man, which may, he suggested, have fallen

victim to Japanese rather than American looting as Chinese
officials had suggested. Silent on this matter, Rex Warner, who
had previously recorded Mr Han's accusation, only notes that
'H. Trevelyan's house' in the embassy compound reminded him
of 'Wimbledon Common'. He did, however, enjoy the 'very nice
lunch', and was happy to go along when Mrs Trevelyan offered to
take the visitors on an afternoon shopping trip in which they
could spend the Chinese dollars handed to them by their hosts.

The meal provided by the British embassy was a modest affair
compared with the banquets laid on by the Chinese authorities.
That very evening, the six members of the cultural delegation
joined a thousand other foreign guests at a perfectly organized
event that Warner describes as 'Chou En-lai's party'—'surprisingly
wonderful', as he found it, with representatives of every nation
imaginable, and 'terrific cheers for Chairman Mao' going up at
the end. The speeches were 'interminable', especially those of
the Russians, but Warner escaped into the garden and talked with
some 'v. nice Indians'.

It was at this event that Hugh Casson caught sight of 'a grave
spectacled young man in a golden-yellow topée' who turned out
to be the 19-year-old Dalai Lama. His attendance in Peking
together with the already 'completely sinacized'[31] tenth Panchen
Lama, had been proclaimed as a sign of 'unprecedented friendship, unity and co-operation of all nationalities in China'.[32] Their
presence was a triumph for the Chinese government, which had
earlier worked hard to soften up the two spiritual leaders of Tibet
by presenting them with gifts: peacocks had been sent for the
private zoo of the animal-loving Panchen Lama, and cars for each
lama were bought in Calcutta and then dismantled and carried
through 'snowbound passes' into Tibet.[33] The two lamas had
made the two-month journey to Peking to attend the annual
National Peoples Congress, at which Mao, Chu Teh, and others
were elected to the leadership. The Dalai Lama himself was
incorporated as a vice-president of the Congress's standing
committee, in which real power was alleged to reside.[34] Perhaps
the appearance of Tibet's spiritual leader prompted Casson to
wonder about the exact nature of Communist China's 'Liberation'
of Tibet, formalized in a Seventeen-Point Agreement signed by a
Tibetan delegation in Peking on 23 May 1951, at a time when a

large force of Chinese troops was arrayed at the Tibetan border. His diary, however, only records that he managed to extract an autograph—written with a fountain pen filled with green ink—from this exotic and supposedly immortal child, whose people were already worrying that their leader might not be allowed to return to Tibet.[35] Casson admits to having been undeterred in his advance by 'the half-horrified, half-envious glances of my friends', or, for that matter, by the 'top-booted Bulgarian girl folk-dancer' he had to elbow aside to clear a passage. Warner's diary entry for this event closes with the phrase 'Rather tight'.

The Greatest Parade in the History of the World?

As they feasted on Peking duck, sea slugs, abalone, fishes' lips, and other barely imaginable delicacies, the cultural delegates did begin to wonder, as Humphrey Trevelyan had urged them to do, what lay behind the brilliant scenes unfolding before them. 'We see what we see,' repeated Casson in *Red Lacquer Days*, helpfully rephrasing Trevelyan's words of warning as his own: 'Is what we do not see, or even what nobody can see more significant?' They conclude that the government is both popular and in full control, and they ask themselves, without much apparent result, whether there is any opposition. Casson is troubled by the realization that 'as every traveller to Orwell-land soon finds out, he cannot remain a referee. He must play on one side or the other. You can respect the vigour and strength of a new system that has brought stability and dreams of untold industrial prosperity to a nation that is no doubt accustomed to tyranny, but to yield such respect means that you must also accept the basic premises of the system—the distortion of truth, the insistence upon official infallibility, the mutual suspicion and informing, the closed frontiers, the need for the accused man to prove his innocence and not the accusers his guilt.' None of this was really acceptable to Casson, who anticipated that the massive National Day celebrations of 1 October would be particularly testing for 'an effete Liberal from the West'.

This was not the first openly political function the members of the cultural delegation attended during their visit. They had been to receptions held for the Russian delegation, and for other Communist countries too. On 27 September, they had also sat at the back of the Chamber of Deputies, decked out in scarlet and silver as if for 'a children's matinee at the Odeon' (Casson notebook), and watched as the young Dalai Lama and some 1,210 other voting delegates lined up for the 'election' of the Chairman, President and other leaders of the National People's Congress. Here, the more official foreign delegates were 'at last at ease', being entirely familiar with the 'familiar setting of rostrum and agenda, of voting papers and points of order'. For the cultural delegation, however, time dragged as the 'interminable' (Warner) proceedings droned on, unassisted by Mr Khruschev who took a full hour to deliver his formal tribute. Mao, Chu Teh, and the other Communist leaders got their preordained positions unopposed, and none of the British delegates noted the absence of Kao Kang (Gao Gang), the purged former Communist leader in Manchuria, who had, in the words of *The Times*, 'not been heard of for months'.[36]

Back in the hotel, Casson endured an 'intolerable' dinner, in which Chilean, Glaswegian, and other international Communists toasted Mao and the other 'elected' leaders in a spirit of 'embarrassingly competitive fervour' ('Now we know what it must be like to be a Swiss when the British celebrate Christmas in some winter-sports hotel'). A. J. Ayer 'retired to bed in despair', but Casson joined Warner, Spencer, and others in a trip to the Peking Opera, which he described as 'formal, noisy, squeaky'. Warner and Spencer found their appreciation of the performers' remarkably communicative gestures complicated by their misgivings over the 'foregone conclusion' of the 'election' they had seen earlier. Indeed, Warner records the unquestioning enthusiasm shown by a man he took to be Indian, and probably a trade unionist, condemning it as 'v. unEnglish'. Like the memory of the events that provoked them, however, these anxieties would, for most of the delegates at least, be quite overshadowed by the 'National Day' celebrations of 1 October, the climax beside which all other ceremonies and banquets paled.

This event took the form of a vast parade through Tiananmen Square, and formed the main attraction for no less than forty-seven delegations visiting from twenty-six countries.[37] Such was the depressing realization that dawned on James Cameron of the *News Chronicle*. His request for a visa had long been ignored, but on 24 September he had received a call from Chinese officials in

Berne granting him permission but only on condition that he crossed the border into China by the 29th.[38] It was not until after he reached Peking that this proudly independent correspondent realized he had been obliged to endure a 'lunatic scramble across the earth' in order that he could join 2,000 other international spectators at a tightly managed 'military fiesta' of the sort he had already witnessed, and thoroughly loathed, in too many countries across the divided world.

The celebrations of 1 October were, as Ayer would later inform listeners to Britain's Third Programme, 'perfectly organized' in every aspect. The great parade, which the left-wing Swedish novelist Artur Lundkvist also hailed as a 'masterwork' of 'Chinese mass-organization',[39] opened punctually at 10 a.m. Ayer recalled it as an 'exhausting spectacle, since one had to stand to watch it, but impressive in its way'. Stanley Spencer had ducked out ('Some Mongolians or something came in, and I went upstairs',[40] as he would later tell his brother Gilbert), but the other members of the cultural delegation were there to see the proceedings open with a formidable hour-long military display—'troops, marching & mechanised', as Warner put it, and there were gun salvoes and plenty of tanks, jets, and rocket-launchers too. The military display was followed by 'a great liberation of pigeons & balloons by children', and then the civil parade began, with countless masses marching by carrying huge 'pictures of the saints' (Stalin, Lenin, Gorky, and various moustache-bearing Balkan leaders too), and 'model locomotives, model Ketchup bottles, missiles, aircraft, everything'. Paper flowers seemed to fill the entire square. Great floats rolled by, symbolizing particular factories and industries. Balloons carried slogans aloft and enormous Picasso doves also 'wafted' through the air.[41]

Picasso's peace doves had flown through a whole series of congresses before turning up in China. Destined to become a hugely prominent fixture of Cold War iconography, the first version of Picasso's dove had appeared on posters advertising the first Congrès Mondial des Partisans de la Paix, in Paris, April 1949. The man responsible for that poster was the Communist writer Louis Aragon, who had found its image of a standing dove when looking through some of Picasso's recent lithographs.[42] Launched there, the 'Peace dove' quickly spread its wings. The first version that

Fig 34. Paul Hogarth, National Day, Tiananmen Square, 1954, conté.

Picasso designed specifically for the use of the Peace Movement was produced in 1950, for the Second Congrès Mondial des Partisans de la Paix, eventually held in Warsaw after the British authorities barred entrance to many international delegates who tried to attend it in Sheffield. It was this particular airborne specimen that was to make the journey to China. It passed through Warsaw, where it was displayed in the Theater Polski, on 22 November 1950: an enlarged version had loomed up behind Pablo Neruda as he accepted the Stalin Peace Prize on Picasso's behalf. A huge reproduction of the same image had stood between rows of national flags behind the praesidium at the Asian and Pacific Peace Conference in Peking, in 1952. By 1954, Picasso's thoroughly propagandized dove had coupled with the famous pigeons of old Peking, known for their fluting whistles and allegedly once used as 'Food distributors' by owners who are said to have trained them to fly into the imperial granaries, fill themselves with rice and then return to their lofts where they would be forced to disgorge their prize.[43] According to James Cameron, the descendants of Picasso's dove now adorned Tien An Men, the Gate of Heavenly Peace. Indeed, they were 'everywhere, completely replacing the Dragon'.[44]

As he looked on, James Cameron counted 'workers at this and that, unions and federations, trades and associations'. He was amazed to see 'a section of Roman Catholic nuns, with a banner saying: "Christians for Democracy!" and—to stretch credulity until it creaks—a group among the "minorities" labelled the "New Chinese Capitalists' Association"', whose banner cried, or perhaps pleaded, 'Long Live Private Enterprise in the Glorious Revolution'. As they filed past the Praesidium, marchers shouted 'slogans of fidelity' (Ayer) to their leaders. They also rallied to the Minister of Defence's opening call for the liberation of Taiwan, expressing fierce 'hostility to their enemies—including, I am afraid, the United States'.[45] The watching crowds, meanwhile, cheered wildly. Their cry 'Down with American Imperialism' also battered at the ear of Professor Hawkes, who gazed on as children released 'thousands of toy aeroplanes' to compete with the slogans already born aloft by massed balloons. Paul Hogarth saw these elastically propelled devices gliding about 'like ceremonial wasps'.[46] Cameron watched as they eventually 'stalled among the banners'.[47] Even the Communist celebrities in the 'mammoth tribunal' (Cameron mentions Khrushchev, Bulganin, Shvernik, Bierut of Poland, and Kim Il Sung from North Korea) looked 'somehow subdued and muted' by the unprecedented scale of the display of adoration unfolding before their eyes.

As they 'watched the military ironwork clattering by' (Casson), the members of the cultural delegation found their attention wandering—despite the 'miracle of organization' that Leonard Hawkes too had detected in the proceedings. Looking around

Fig 35. Hugh Casson, National Day, Tiananmen Square, 1954, ink drawing.

the stand, Warner's eye settled on 'Lamas in yellow basin hats & robes' while Casson surveyed the other Western delegates. Some of the latter were inclined to take a heroic view of their own presence, convinced that they were 'punching' the Iron and Bamboo Curtains full of holes.[48] But it was with a feeling of dismay that Casson appraised the motley company of adherents, dreamers, and human doves in which he found himself. He noted 'the mild faces of the Fighters for Peace, faces that we have seen above a hundred platforms. Gold-rimmed spectacles misted with emotion, cheeks creased with years of well-meant service in this cause or that, shirts defiantly open at the neck, badges in lapels, and there in the middle—could it have been?—an M.C.C. tie.'

That unexpected item also found a place in Warner's diary, where it is said to have been sported alongside more predictable 'Soviet' insignia. It belonged to Ivor Montagu, the pamphleteering British Communist and fiercely anti-American son of a Jewish banking family. Montagu was a film critic and director, the friend and translator of Sergei Eisenstein and Vsevolod Pudovkin, and a considerable table tennis champion as well as a cricket lover. A seasoned curtain-crosser for the National Peace Council, and an early advocate of sports exchanges between the blocs, he admired the people of New China for seeking 'betterment' in coordinated 'physical jerks' and sports such as basketball and table tennis, and also for flexing their sinews against the indolent old world in which 'rich men regarded walking as something you paid those less fortunate to do on your behalf'.[49] He was there with his wife, having previously visited the All-Union Agricultural Exhibition in Moscow as a guest of the Soviet Writers' Union, and then enjoyed a 'holiday' in the Mongolian People's Republic where he had identified the yurt as 'the perfect prefab',[50] and disparaged the Buddhist lamas for robbing the Mongols of their traditional bravery, as well as for spreading venereal disease. There was rapture in Montagu's eyes as he found his image of the promise of New China in the form of 'two stalwart, striding girls, matchless in face and beauty of limb, heading the athletics section of the parade'.

Montagu's decision to sport an MCC tie alongside Communist regalia made for an incongruous juxtaposition, to be sure, if one that was no less of a period piece than the hammer and sickle with which the pre-war socialist aristocrat Charles Philips Trevelyan is said to have adorned the entrance to Wallington Hall, his country seat in Northumberland. Casson found his own way of wondering about this oddly decked Marxist sportsman, who admired the urge for 'physical, mental and moral betterment'[51] being promoted by the All-China Athletic Federation, but would conclude that New China's table tennis players lost by being just a little too relentless in the attack. So too would the Chinese interpreters and minders when the athletic Montagu insisted, despite a ban—which he considered quite unnecessary if not positively misguided—on taking 'a short off-season dip'[52] in the shallow lake of the Summer Palace.

Casson's appraisal of his fellow freeloaders will have radiated out from Ivor Montagu to include other foreign observers of New China's triumph. It will have encompassed the rapture of institutionalized old Communists such as Rewi Alley. It will have taken in Dr Joshua Horn who was also standing there, almost certainly with the wife whose dogmatic certainty had impressed Casson as 'beyond all bearing' in Moscow. Casson had surely felt relieved to say farewell to this 'humourless devotee' at the airfield outside Peking, abandoning him and his family to the smiling 'pig-tailed girl with rosy cheeks' who, as Horn later described, 'caught a praying mantis for my six year old daughter, and tied a length of plastic thread from one of her braids round the insect's leg so that the little girl could play with it and feel at home'.[53] But here was the Birmingham injury surgeon smiling up at him once again: 'I had never before experienced such a mass demonstration of unity, joy and confidence,' he would write, remembering how he had watched the fifth National Day celebrations as delightful proof that the Chinese people had finally liberated themselves from the diseased and depraved past he had seen when visiting Shanghai as a young ship's doctor in 1937.

There too was Birkbeck College's Marxist physicist, J. D. Bernal. He had arrived in Peking the day before the cultural delegation and endured a similarly unspectacular reception at the airfield. Thanks to the priority accorded to the Bulgarian delegation with whom he had travelled, he was obliged to stay on the landed plane until 'the ceremonies of reception and the playing of the Bulgarian and Chinese national anthems, the reviewing of the Guard of

Honour, the speeches on both sides'. Only when these were completed was he permitted to step down into the 'very discreet' and, indeed, hardly noticeable reception laid on for him by members of the Chinese Academy of Sciences. Bernal lacked an MCC tie but he was sporting the Stalin Peace Prize medal he had just picked up in Moscow: 'the only time I have ever worn it', he records, 'and I believe that in this case I pinned it on the wrong side'.[54]

Placed in the 'Minorities Section' among Mongolians and Tibetans 'who looked very rakish and liberated and smelt most terribly of garlic', James Cameron was by no means the only Western observer who speculated that he might be watching 'the biggest crowd of humans ever assembled anywhere on the earth'. He confessed to having 'no love of multitudes', and also to a 'personal, and probably psychologically revealing, distaste of men walking in parallel lines'. As he watched, he also suffered 'a sudden, rather terrifying mental flashback to the old childhood analogy: if all the living Chinese should march past a given spot, they would *never* stop, so endless is their number'. And yet, long before the procession came to an end at precisely 3 o'clock as planned, Cameron was captivated. He described the 'phenomenal' proceedings as a 'superb extravagance'[55] and 'the greatest show on earth'—while also noting that the Chinese presenters remained modest and, indeed, 'carefully refrained' from calling it any such thing.

The cultural delegates may not have stood quite so 'popeyed among the Tibetans'[56] as James Cameron claims to have done. They must, however, have noticed what he identified as 'the twin emphases on the great contemporary paradox', namely 'the demonstration of military might beside the call of peace'. That conjunction was, Cameron thought, 'the *pons asinorum* of the time, the contemporary rationalization so blandly shared by both contending sides'. 'There were, therefore, the big battalions and the dancing-girls with fans: the rumbling heavy tanks and the endless ranks of workers waving olive-branches: the four-engined bombers and the screaming MiGs high above the vast fluttering multitude of doves, suddenly and symbolically released above the soldiers, trailing silk banners with the double message: "No More War!" and "Taiwan!"'[57]

As the temperature rose and the marchers continued to troop by at the rate of 100 or 200 per second, Warner relieved the tedium by sporadically quitting the viewing stand, making his way down to the 'rest room' below, also heavily populated by yellow robed lamas, where it was possible 'to smoke and drink quantities of tea'. Though hugely enthusiastic about the proceedings, J. D. Bernal made the same descent: 'I went down just once…and found myself seated at a small table next to the Dalai Lama, who was occupied, as I was, in sucking orange juice through a straw.' Casson had gone down much earlier. Unlike Bernal, he was uninterested in the procession of war machines, depressed by the sight of the troops 'packed like jerking toys in lorries', and frankly appalled by 'the fatuity' of the other international delegates' beaming smiles. So, 'as soon as the minimum time for courtesy has been expended', he and Ayer headed below for tea, over which they discussed 'the prim futility of their gesture, the self-justifying gymnastics in which every traveller behind the Iron Curtain is constantly and inevitably engaged'.

Casson tried, perhaps idly, to interest Ayer in his theory that military demonstrations should only be allowed to take place in the countries of potential enemies, where they really might exercise a deterrent effect and contribute to the maintenance of peace. Their interpreter encouraged them to go back up to be photographed, but the two men refused to return until the students, workers, and children had taken over from the soldiers. Ayer would later admit of the jubilant masses that 'the enthusiasm displayed was genuine, that the loyalty of the people, at least of the people of Peking, has been largely captured by the present Government'.[58] Yet, as he added, this fact did not in itself prove that government to be good. Indeed, he was troubled by the sight of the Communist leaders smiling and greeting the people from the grandstand in front of the Gate of Heavenly Peace. Bernal would declare himself greatly moved by 'the simple affection that Mao creates.' Ayer, however, was troubled by the 'analogy' of the Nuremberg rallies: 'the old Liberal in me felt that this was not the way in which people ought to react to the presence of their rulers.' A similar sense of alarm was felt by at least one onlooking British diplomat. Describing the parade as a 'fantastic sight' in a letter to his mother, Douglas Hurd declared that 'the most terrifying thing was the great multitude of children, brightly and charmingly dressed, almost hysterical with excitement as they shouted their way past Mao's balcony'.[59]

Rex Warner liked the closing scenes best. Great columns of dancers were driven forward with clashing cymbals and drums, mixing with athletes, wearing white with coloured jumpers, as they passed in front of Mao, Chou En-lai, Chu Teh, and other leaders arrayed behind the marble balustrade on top of the Gate of Heavenly Peace. Hundreds of thousands had been involved. Indeed, Warner concluded that it must have been 'the biggest and most colourful parade ever seen'.

J. D. Bernal was more systematic in his praises. In his detailed description of the proceedings he fought his own war against the anti-Communist stereotypes that construed the Chinese people as a faceless mass, pressed into a mould of inhuman orthodoxy by the grinning Communist emperor who now stood there accepting their tribute. He had found himself 'very impressed by the way in which two small school girls, one with a green and one with a red ribbon, started the whole thing off, stepping out even before the soldiers and the airmen'. Insisting that the military parade was both 'extremely brief and only symbolic', he suggested that the 'heaviest thing that anyone had to carry' in the procession was probably the pneumatic picks carried by proud miners in the trade union section. He emphasized the 'holiday atmosphere', the 'ease and gaiety' of the proceedings, declaring that 'there was nothing monotonous about it at all' since each of the processing groups 'brought in some new idea'. In contrast to those who saw only coerced uniformity in the Chinese masses, Bernal emphasized the kindness of the individuals who stepped out of the crowd to rescue the pigeons which got tangled in their ribbons and 'fell down into the Little River', and the variety of the citizens groups who came after the peasants had marched by with their harvest trophies. These included 'the different religious communities, i.e. Mohammedans in their little white caps, the Buddhists in their yellow robes, each carrying a peace dove on a stick, the Catholics, the Christians much better dressed and very respectable people hardly to be distinguished from those that followed them—the patriotic businessmen'. He derived the same message from the procession of China's varied national minorities, dressed in their distinctive 'national dresses' and demonstrating their own traditional dances. Far from being exhausted by the proceedings, Bernal was with those who felt 'sorry and disappointed when it was all over. We felt, although we were standing all the time, that we wanted to go on seeing this kind of thing forever.' Ayer may have worried about the reverence shown to Mao, but Bernal saw the smiles and greetings passing between him and the people as 'the most intimate linking of the people with the leader...He does not even need to say very much, he just smiles and the people know what he has done and what he is doing.' Dr Joshua Horn saw the event through a similar ideological lens. He emphasized that while the military units carried 'excellent' weapons, they wore 'simple cotton uniforms, devoid of badges of rank, epaulettes or decorations'. And he was touched to see that some of the peasants in the parade were 'a little undisciplined. They had come a long way to see their beloved Chairman and they wanted more than a fleeting glimpse of him. So when they saw him, they stopped, waved and shouted and the Chairman waved back.'

Paul Hogarth may have exchanged polite smiles with Casson, but he was fiercely untroubled by misgivings of the kind experienced by the more liberal Britons. He made a drawing of the parade (Fig 34), an act for which he had to secure special permission (even though he left out all Casson's 'military hardware'), and he too loved the embarrassment brought to certain class enemies by the vast popularity of the event. Delighted by the convivial internationalism of the foreign delegates' stand, where 'Yellow-robed lamas with English-style sun helmets drank lemonade with Birmingham trade unionists' and 'Indonesians stood with Italians', he was also pleased to see 'the entourage of the British chargé d'affaires' making its way from the separate stand of the diplomatic corps 'with the aplomb of a party who had lost everything at Ascot'.[60] We can be sure that the scowl was returned, at least by Geoffrey Hurd, who disapproved of the fellow-travellers and their deference to the grotesquely superior Chinese leaders. As he would write of the great parades and receptions of 1954 and afterwards, 'it was painful to watch our progressive thinkers such as D. N. Pritt and Kingsley Martin crouching before this performance, just as their predecessors had crouched before Stalin'.[61]

After struggling for a time to find their bus, the five members of the cultural delegation were driven back to their hotel through streets crowded with jubilant people. 'Their intelligent smiling faces & waving & clapping made a moving experience,'[62] noted Hawkes. 'No more spontaneous demonstration could be imagined,' he concluded with the help of an interpreter who reassured him that the Chinese people, despite their amply displayed enthusiasm for fierce anti-American slogans, were always delighted to meet 'good' foreigners. It was all too much for the trade union delegate who sat next to Casson on the bus with 'tears running down his face'. The same emotional fellow features in Warner's diary, where the 'obvious' belligerence of the slogans shouted during the parade is contrasted with the great generosity of the people ('Cheers, handshakes & smiles everywhere'), who seemed 'wonderfully friendly, happy and powerful'. It had, as Casson conceded, been an 'at times most moving' spectacle.

Lunch was served at about 3.25. Warner consumed 'a lot of mao tai', and then fell into a deep sleep until 7, when there was a banquet for all the external delegations, served with 'grape wine' that turned out, sadly, to be 'v. unpalatable'. The 'tremendous' two-hour firework display that followed was further proof, to Casson at least, that China did these things better than any other nation in the world. Not so the propaganda that Warner found himself leafing through over a beer after making his way back to the hotel through streets filled with drumming and dancing: 'Everyone in the office chipped in to criticise & help'; 'The round-faced representative consented with a nod'; 'She is a good wife because she has read & understood the marriage law'.

Shanghai and Hangchow: Fragrant Snow and more Mao-tai

The cultural delegation's last appointment, before they left Peking for a tour of Shanghai and Hangchow, took place at the Institute for Cultural Relations at 9 a.m. on Sunday, 3 October. In a ceremony that had been shunted down their itinerary due to more pressing business, they presented both the 'statement of friendship' and the book of supporting signatures they had brought from London. Speaking in a hall 'filled with the elite of Chinese

Arts and Sciences', Professor Hawkes explained that the 672 signatories spoke for 'many thousands of others anxious for a real effort to increase the interchange of ideas'.[63] Flanked by his vice-president, the geologist J. S. Lee (Jonquei su-Kwang Lee), the President of the Academy of Sciences, Kuo Mo-jo, replied by praising 'the great gifts' of British science and literature, which were surely the 'cultural heritage not only of the British but also of the Chinese people and all the world'. He added that the Chinese considered cultural isolation to be 'unfortunate' and hoped that the British gesture of friendship would 'enhance the exchange of ideas'. Rex Warner judged it a 'moving' occasion, and the President's speech both 'v. good' and 'excellently trans-lated'. Over tea, this time served with apples and grapes, he talked to the Hunan-born writer Ting Ling (Ding Ling), and to a colleague of hers, identified as 'Ko Ching Ping', who repeated the Maoist nostrum that 'The people are like water & the poet is the fish', leaving Warner to add a puzzled question mark of his own.

The Chinese authorities appear to have been happy enough with the presentation. A few months later Kuo Mo-jo would recall that the presented statement of friendship had 'kindled a warm response all over the land'.[64] Indeed, sixty-five prominent Chinese scientists, writers, and artists had sent a joint reply 'expressing thanks to our British friends and our wish to join hands with them to promote the progress of culture and achieve lasting peace for mankind'.

After the presentation, the visiting cultural luminaries embarked on a five-hour flight to Shanghai. Casson was tempted to another imagistic flight of fancy as they passed over the direly flooded plain of the Yellow River, dotted as it was with 'village islets'. If Peking had resembled a dog biscuit on a beach when he first saw it from the air, these marooned settlements reminded him of a handful of 'raisins floating in coffee custard'.

Arriving at Shanghai on the afternoon of Sunday, 3 October, the delegates were met, as they both expected and dreaded, by a large reception committee and driven through the city to a skyscraper hotel. Warner and Ayer forayed out in a vain attempt to find the fabled 'Largest Bar in the World'.[65] They returned in time to be picked up by their attentive 'Chinese friends', who took them to the banquet at which Casson found himself 'happily seated next to a charming young actress trained at the Old Vic'. That was followed by a tour of the illuminated city, still brilliantly decorated for the recent National Day, and the visitors were then delivered into a private cinema where they dutifully watched a film that Warner remembered only as 'White Butterfly', and Casson as 'New China's first full-length, full-colour, fully talking film'. Neither records any judgement of its content. 'Three vain attempts to get whisky', notes Warner: 'bed about 12.45'.

Like Clement Attlee before him, Warner 'hoped for a bit of peace and quiet' in Hangchow. He had managed to acquire some alleged 'whisky' by the time his party boarded the evening train, but was vexed to discover that it tasted 'too peculiar to drink'. Casson notes that the delegation travelled in a 'special wagon-lit' attached to the regular express. They were provided with every form of comfort—a compartment each, slippers, beer, bananas, and other refreshments, and excessively 'perfect service' too. The latter included an attendant who came every fifteen minutes to top up the flask of hot water, to the disappointment of Ayer and Warner, who were hoping it would cool sufficiently to be mixed with their unpalatable 'whisky'.

Disembarking in Hangchow after midnight, they found to their 'flattered dismay' that, here as in Shanghai, the promised 'literary circles' awaited them at the station, along with 'black limousines' in which they were soon whisked off to their 'charming faded old hotel'. The air was 'soft as milk' (Casson); they also reported a 'terrific smell of perfumed flowers & sound of crickets & cicadas' (Warner). 'Once a dilapidated health hazard', as the guidebook put it, watery Hangchow was 'now a National Park of rest' where they would see the same sights as the Attlee delegation and be paddled from islet to islet on the lakes in a blue and white cano-pied gondola with a central table set for tea. As Casson remem-bered, 'Butterflies dance, fish jump, water lilies yawn in the sun'. Warner, whose own early poems had produced various odes to British birds as well as to class war and the coming revolution, adds 'one dab-chick' and 'a kite' to the list. Spencer used the rare moment of stillness to make 'an hour-long study of a willow leaf', but the cultural delegation was otherwise quite motionless, drifting along with its collective 'fingers trailing in the pewter-coloured water of the lake'.

They came to life for the 'most excellent lunch' that followed, served with 'pale yellow' wine. This version was named 'Fragrance of Snow', and Warner judged it 'Very good & really fragrant'. They then proceeded to the Art Institute, where Warner noticed a 'traditional picture with red flag figures' but 'not much evidence of Stalinist art'. Enlarging on this perception for the *Sunday Times*, he would explain that the picture in question was 'a typically classical Chinese landscape, with its tufted rocks, cascades and pines'. It had been 'rendered "modern" by the insertion of some tiny figures of men, dwarfed further by a waterfall, yet seen to be carrying, if very closely examined, minute red flags'.[66] Gratified by the fact that the work had nothing in common with the 'dim, unintoxicating, dispirited art' he had seen in Moscow, Warner ventured the hope that 'the Russian fashion' may not 'extend eastward without undergoing considerable modification'. His diary reveals that the 'cultural dinner' was 'very good' too: 'mandarin fish, lots of good wine'.

They had returned to Shanghai by the time Stanley Spencer drew an exclamation mark from the normally undemonstrative Professor Hawkes. He did this by revealing how much money he needed to maintain himself and, as may be presumed, the expensive ruins of his marital life. As Hawkes scribbled in his notebook: '<u>Spencer.</u> Outgoings £45 a week!'

By 8 October, they were back in Peking, where Hawkes proceeded to follow up D. M. Ross's list of scientists with British connections and to lecture students at the Geology Building of Peking University. He noted that 20 per cent of the 3,700 students in the various departments were women—a development that may have interested him particularly, since Bedford College, where he was Head of the Geology Department, was a women's college. The previous year, he had looked forward to the day when Bedford College would 'grow up and admit men undergraduates'—a view that was said, by a disapproving student reporter on the college paper, to put him openly 'in opposition to the progressive spirit of the founders'.[67]

Warner's turn came on Sunday, 10 October, when he went to the Writers Club to make a speech about translation and other literary matters. After a 'delightful' lunch with a group of leading writers, they went back to the courtyard home of Gladys Yang, a literary translator who, having been born to a missionary family in Peking, had gone on to become the first person to graduate in Chinese from Oxford University, where she had also met her future husband Yang Xianyi.[68] The couple had returned to China in 1940 and—repelled by the brutality of the nationalist government—developed links with the Communist underground. In the early 1950s, they had moved to Peking, where they were now employed by the Foreign Languages Press to make English versions of Chinese literature. As Chinnery recalls, Warner won a considerable drinking contest with Yang Xianyi, which may cast some light on his diary, wherein Yang is described as 'drunk; but very nice'.

That really should have been the end of it, but when Ayer, Warner, Casson, and Hawkes got up, early on 11 October, expecting to begin their arduous journey back to London, they discovered that they lacked the visas required to re-enter the USSR. During the delay of twenty-four hours, they visited the Institute of National Minorities where they examined various national costumes and sampled Tibetan food. They also heard the director, Professor Fei, explain that the institute had been founded in 1951 with the aim of training 'cadres' who would work to integrate their minorities into 'New China'. Though 'constantly interrupted by Stanley Spencer', as Warner records, Fei maintained his '100 candlepower smile' (Casson) and held forth, as he was evidently very used to doing, about the work of his institute. The political project, he explained, involved educating elected representatives from China's various nationalities. The wider policy, however, was to develop the language and culture of each minority group. There was great need for interpreters, so students were taught Han Chinese. Literacy varied greatly between the different minorities. In the 'primitive tribes', which had no experience of written language, the policy was to record and transcribe the native language into Latin script and then 'analyse the results grammatically' in order to devise a written version that could be taken back and taught to the people in question.

Like the new marriage law, the Communist regime's policy towards the national minorities was a matter about which some members of the cultural delegation were prepared to be openly impressed. Praising this evident 'desire to preserve continuity in the midst of radical changes',[69] A. J. Ayer likened the government's approach to its commitment to archaeology and the restoration of palaces and temples. Given that the 600 million people in China were divided into forty-five nationalities, he thought it would be understandable if the new government's policy might be to have done with the complexity and establish the Han language as the 'single official language' of all China. Considering that there were some 25 million people in China who spoke languages without any written script at all, he also ventured that 'one might expect that steps would be taken to make these languages obsolete'. Listening to Professor Fei, however, he was persuaded that the regime was actually moving in an altogether more admirable direction. Here as with museums and religious monuments, he concluded approvingly, revolutionary transformation was accompanied by a policy of preserving and fostering 'distinctive social customs'.

That night the cultural delegates were informed that they really would be taking off first thing on Wednesday, 13 October. Their final unexpected encounter occurred on their last evening, when they returned to the hotel after a second visit to the Temple of Heaven and found the newly arrived Second Labour Delegation sitting in the dining room. Derrick James records that Casson and Hawkes, 'poor devils', were prevailed upon to speak about what they had seen in China. Though they were 'good about it, and witty', James decided that Hawkes must have 'picked up the early Watson story about Peking Man from the [British] Charge d'Affaires here'. Casson, meanwhile, found the newcomers a 'not very impressive bunch'—although he did make exceptions of Barbara Castle and Edwin Pulleyblank. He also admitted to a sense of 'irrational irritation' when he noticed that his own delegation's interpreters were already 'busy accustoming themselves to a new set of Western idiosyncracies'.

It was only a brief encounter for Hawkes, Warner, and Casson, although not for Spencer who that evening had gone to the theatre with Ayer. Frustrated by the impossibility of combining drawing and painting with the continuous moving about of sightseeing,[70] the idiosyncratic artist from Cookham had decided to stay in China for an extra ten days in order to work. He would be accompanied by John Chinnery, who may also have recognized that the homebound journey would be rather less of an ordeal for everyone if the delegation split up.

For Warner, however, none of this mattered very much. 'We all made speeches & I talked to Lewis, member for West Ham—Bed by 11.00.' According to James, the allegorically minded classicist used his speech to inform the weary newcomers that mao-tai was 'the best sort of booze' to be had in China. He was less cautious on this matter than J. D. Bernal, who would remember mao-tai as 'a strange drink which smells rather of decaying cheese, and is about the most powerful drink that I have ever come across in my life'.

18

Cadillacs, Coal Mines, and Co-operatives: The Second Labour Delegation Grapples with the Facts

There was even Doctor Globo—an engaging, mad Brazilian who wandered around in an agonized way, seeking everything and finding nothing.

James Cameron[1]

The mule-carts were to be expected. But what was the National Secretary of the Women's Cooperative Guilds of Great Britain to make of the gleaming American cars that could also be seen gliding, where imperial elephants may once have paraded, along the wide boulevards of Peking?

Mrs Mabel Ridealgh would carry that question with her when she, together with other members of the Second Labour Delegation, trooped into the offices of China's Committee for Promotion of International Trade. The meeting took place on the afternoon of Saturday, 16 October and the officials gathered to receive them included the Deputy Manager of the China Import Export Association. As members of a late-travelling and down-graded delegation, this particular band of Britons would meet a lot of deputies and Vice-Presidents during the course of their visit. On this occasion, however, they were also received by a senior official from the 3rd department of the Ministry of Foreign Trade: an authoritative cold warrior who proved a fierce wielder of statistics.

As Barbara Castle describes in her diary, Mr Chang informed them that China's foreign trade had risen by 81 per cent between 1951 and 1953, and that during the previous year 75 per cent of it had been with the Soviet Union. Of course, the government had always wanted to trade with the West too, and the rising standard of living in China provided a 'sound basis' for hoping that this would indeed be possible now that the Geneva Conference had improved relations so much. Mr Chang ventured that a good beginning had been made the previous June, when a Chinese trade mission visited England, and that his ministry was now preparing to 'welcome another U.K. mission next month to work out details' of the general agreement reached.

Chang had strong views about the US-led trade embargo against China, explaining that everything depended on the definition of 'strategic materials' and 'purposes connected with war', phrases which had plainly meant very different things on either side of the alleged Bamboo Curtain. He was adamant that New China only wanted imports 'for peaceful purposes', but the embargo's enforcers had refused to accommodate that fact: 'unless you limit it to armaments, anything can be included—even bread'. Asserting that the proscription had been more damaging to other Western countries than to China, he suggested that 'U.S. monopolists' had actually been manipulating the phrase 'purposes connected to war' in order 'to monopolize trade with the west'. At Barbara Castle's request, he went on to provide a detailed list of what China hoped to import from Britain, and also the goods, mostly raw materials and food stuffs, that China was ready to export immediately in exchange.

Fig 36. The Second Labour Delegation under the wing of a plane, China, (photographer unknown).

Fig 37. The Second Labour Delegation standing by a plane.

And what, Mrs Ridealgh wanted to know, of the gleaming American cars that she had noticed cruising among the shoals of silver bicycles? Had these conspicuously new-looking vehicles—the 'Cadillacs' that feature in Hugh Casson's diary and the 'glossy Buicks'[2] noted by James Cameron—come to China via Japan? And was the UK, which had suffered economically from abiding by the export embargo, actually 'being had' all along by its most powerful ally?

Chang's answer was that, while the 'U.S. monopolists' insisted on the embargo, American business and economic interests actually wanted to trade with China: 'in recent years we have received constantly letters and offers from American firms'. Under these circumstances, it was surely not surprising to see new American cars in Peking. 'They are being imported direct. Through the "open door", not the "back door": we have no embargo here.' This reply prompted George Doughty, the General Secretary of Britain's Association of Engineering and Shipbuilding Draughtsmen, to mutter that the offending vehicles were probably transported in British ships to Hong Kong. Chang, however, only pressed his point deeper by adding: 'We also think British cars are good and want to import them.'

One Smoke-Stack after Another

The Second Labour Delegation had landed at the aerodrome outside Peking on the evening of 12 October. Derrick James was pleased to find 'a nice lad called Jim' there to witness their arrival. James Cameron had turned up bearing a bottle of vodka, with which he obligingly 'strengthened' the lemonade laid on, together with cigarettes ('rather superior to Players'), by the official reception committee. James also noticed how 'courteous and kind' the welcoming Chinese were: 'They speak quietly, simply, and humorously. They smile charmingly and readily, and don't make restless or unnecessary movements. I was tremendously impressed.' The bleary-eyed company in which he had disembarked did not benefit by comparison. Watching the Chinese, 'I became uncomfortably aware of how uncouth a party we were'.

This particular batch of dishevelled stragglers had not reached Peking until nearly two weeks after the main anniversary celebrations. Their lateness, however, did not deter the smiling guides and interpreters, who opened their tour with the usual historical attractions before proceeding to a string of 'industrial' sites of the kind the cultural delegation had been so anxious to avoid. Like their predecessors, the newcomers spent their first morning at the Temple of Heaven, and were then wafted into the Pei Hai Park, formerly part of the Winter Palace. Here they saw the lake known as the North Sea—famous, as Osbert Sitwell had remarked in the 1930s, 'for its lotuses, and the extensive wooded park which surrounded it'.[3] They were also invited to admire one of Peking's 300 new nursery schools. Castle records that the selected example, which also impressed James as 'the most enchanting' he had ever seen, was situated in a garden where the empress had once reared silkworms. James, who happened to have left London only a few days before his wife was due to give birth, appears to have been touched by every infant he saw during the trip, but the Chinese children were especially fetching. He found them 'quite exquisite with their black hair and brown slanting eyes, and here were dozens & dozens of them'. They were friendly and uninhibited too: 'they rushed at us and within a few moments we were all carrying at least two.'

Fig 38. New school by old palace wall, Peking (photo: Denis Mathews).

While James rode on the playground slide and entertained those delightful infants with the magic of his exposure meter, Barbara Castle practised the Fabian art of getting the facts straight. Notebook in hand, she recorded the number of children, the fees paid by their parents, the dietary and health provisions, and the additional fact that, while housing conditions remained so bad, it was considered necessary to provide residential accommodation for the children over five nights of the week. Having transcribed the claim that the children also spent two and a half months of each year at lakeside resorts, Castle spared a moment for the clambering infants, leading them, as James recalls, into a version of '"ring a ring a roses", and so on'. It fell to James to make a brief

Fig 39. Derrick James with children on slide, Peking (photo: Denis Mathews).

speech on behalf of the delegation. 'I said I liked children all over the world, but had lost my heart to Chinese children. This went down very well.'

The next day's attraction was, perhaps, a little less captivating. 'No 1 Textile mill', in the eastern suburbs of Peking, had opened only a month earlier. It turned out to be a considerable establishment equipped with 50,000 'mostly East German' spindles and over 11,000 looms. The delegation met the head of the trade union and also the man in charge of 'rationalization proposals'. Castle appraised the impressive machinery, the central heating and air cooling systems, the 'special flooring' that had been introduced to 'ease workers' feet', and also the associated canteens, barbers' shops, and bath houses. The factory had an 'excellent modern layout' and the tour also revealed a day nursery for workers' children, a library, no less that four canteens, a clinic capable of dealing with minor injuries and a workers club—the later being still under construction. The regular Saturday night dance was said to be joined by half the 2,500 workers, and there was a Workers' Congress too, which elected representatives each year to keep an eye on health conditions and sort out family problems.

Castle noted that the many women working at the mill enjoyed conditions of equal pay, and that the workers' quarters were quite acceptable, even if the furniture was 'solid but uninspiring' and the kitchen 'rather primitive'. She was also informed that two more such textile mills were soon to be built in Peking alone. It all seemed highly impressive and, at the close of their visit, the delegates were pleased to receive a 'tremendous send off' from the workers, who gathered round their bus to hear Ellis Smith's farewell speech. According to Castle, there was 'enthusiastic applause' as dove-like invocations of 'peace and goodwill' slowly struggled out of the mouth of the English Chairman and took to the air.

There would be many more such visits before Tuesday, 9 November, when the Second Labour Delegation were guided back to their departing aeroplane. On the evening of 16 October

Fig 40. Rewi Alley with children (photo: Derrick James).

they were put into a sleeping car and trained north, together with
a Polish delegation, to the site of the Kwantung reservoir scheme,
being made by damming the Yung-ting River, 90 or so miles from
Peking. As Barbara Castle recorded, they stepped off their train
early in the morning and peered through thick mist to see 'tiny
blue-clothed figures swarming everywhere'. Taken to the administrative director's office, they found a well-rehearsed presentation
waiting for them: 'A model showed us the dam, the proposed
lake, the water discharge tunnel and the spillway. The dam is
complete, so is the valve tower and most of the basin of the lake.
A hydro-electric plant is being built to the side of the lake. They
are immensely proud of the whole thing: the first water conservation scheme they have built since liberation. Pointing to the
model, the director told us that the capacity of the reservoir will
be 22,000 million cubic metres (500,000 million gallons?) though
the dam is only about 300 yards wide.'

Castle was informed that the flood-prone river had originally
been known as 'Wu-ding—"The river which has never been
tamed"—and that the Chinese people had at last tamed it. 'The
proposal is (1) to plant more trees round upper reaches to hold
soil and sand and to reduce silt coming down and (2) to build 3
reservoirs of which this is the middle, and biggest one. Its construction enables 97% of the basin to be controlled. The water will also
be used to supply electricity to Peking and agricultural areas and
for irrigation. The lake is to be stocked with fish, trees planted on
banks and railway built to make a lakeside holiday resort.'

Perhaps this vast dam impressed some delegates as New China's
riposte not just to the floods menacing vast areas of China, but also
to the North Sea Lake in Peking's Imperial City, where they had
inspected a small metal grating installed to prevent the emperor's
stocks of fish escaping into the river.[4] For Castle, however,

> the most astonishing sight was to see this modern scheme being
> built with almost entirely manual labour: men were digging tunnels
> with shovels and carrying the stone away in baskets slung on poles
> and carried on the shoulders of two men. There seemed more
> baskets than trucks and little donkeys plodded by weighed down
> with loads of brushwood. The experts on our delegation said the
> scheme needed heavy drilling and firing equipment, bulldozers,
> excavators and loads more trucks: every kind of large-scale earth-

moving equipment. The director said they had some equipment of this kind left over from pre-liberation days, but not enough. The Soviet Union had let them have a little but its help had taken the form chiefly of lending technicians and helping them with expert advice as their own engineers had little or no experience of such large schemes. Over the 4 years of construction they had gradually built up a skilled labour force. As we walked round in the hot sunshine, loudspeakers filled the valley with 'music while you work'...The most significant lesson of this visit is that all the machinery needed for this project is on the embargo list. China is getting by because she has masses of man power (40,000 men work on this project at peak periods) but the West is refusing to lighten her labours as she struggles to fight floods and irrigate land.

As General Secretary of the National Union of Mineworkers in the Midlands Area, Mr J. H. Southall is likely to have felt more in his element when visiting a large coal-mining complex in Fushun, during the delegation's instructive visit to the Manchurian power-house of New China's breakneck industrialization. Here too, the delegates started by meeting the Directors and Trade Union officials who supplied them with 'a large amount of data'[5] about the operation, which included both open-cast and deep-shaft mining, and had now fully recovered from a standstill following the 'departure' of the Japanese from the area. They were told about production figures, the apparently vast sum of money set aside for safety improvements, the recently introduced rule that now barred those under 18 from working underground. After being informed about the various recreational and welfare facilities laid on for the workers, including the schools and the nine 'Clubs, with their 106 shops' and 117 'Amateur Troupes', they were divided into groups and taken around various parts of the plant.

The Open Cast Mine interested the inspecting Britons, not least because it seemed remarkably well supplied with steam locomotives, electric haulage motors, and cranes. They noticed large amounts of electric cabling and also that water hoses lay ready to deal with outbreaks of spontaneous combustion. They were assured that the latter problem had been brought under control for the first time, and that smoke from such heatings had routinely 'filled the air' in the dark days when the hated Japanese ran the mine.

It was considered noteworthy that the subgroup who, after lunch, made the descent into 'the Dragon and Phoenix Mine', included two women, Mrs M. Ridealgh and a lady interpreter. In preparation they were provided with garments similar to those worn by Aneurin Bevan and other members of the Labour leadership on their visit to the once Anglo-Belgian Kailan coal mines elsewhere in Manchuria: 'overalls, gum-boots, a very curious but nevertheless effective pit-helmet, white gloves and a small towel to act as a sweat cloth'. As they prepared their helmet lights, they were impressed to find that a special canister had been provided to reduce the risk of battery acid corroding the clothing.

They discovered another 'very curious feature' as they prepared to make their descent. They were lowered into the shaft in a small box-like cage situated at the side of the shaft so as not to interfere with winding operations. Thanks to this apparently alarming arrangement, people were routinely lowered into the shaft at the same time as coal-winding operations were under way—a procedure that would never have been tolerated in a British mine. Generally the underground roadways were well lit and safely constructed, with the 'walking' road well fenced off from the passing mine cars. The investigators waded through areas of water, and along steeply sloping stretches where bamboo matting was used to secure footholds. They watched the coal face being worked by shot-firing, and noticed that it was 'very wet', with 'water seeping from the whole length of the face, and into the gob'. Despite its unexpected characteristics, they were persuaded that this was generally a well-run mine. Having been informed about the miners' wages and also inspected some of the admittedly overcrowded new housing, they left the site convinced that 'China is very conscious of the value of its miners and consequently is moving rapidly towards a betterment of their working and social conditions just as fast as the economic position will allow this to be done'.

Just like the Co-op?

Many large industrial plants hove into view as the delegation was led through China: a steel-rolling mill in Anshan, Manchuria; a Railway Engine Repair Works in Chengdu; machine-tool and textile machinery factories in Shanghai...Yet some members, including Mrs Ridealgh and Barbara Castle, were also interested in taking stock of the cooperatives that seemed to promise a different approach to socialism than the collectivization—or 'Democratic Centralism'—that Stalin had imposed on the USSR. Though central to the officially promulgated idea of post-Liberation China as a 'new democracy', these organizations acquired a particular glint for those who viewed them through a British lens.

Six years after producing his report on *Social Insurance and Allied Services* (December 1942), which would soon be acclaimed as the founding charter of Britain's post-war welfare state, the elderly Liberal peer William Beveridge had extolled the virtues of 'voluntary action', in a book of that name written in association with the National Council of Social Service. Far from being cast into history as a primitive anachronism, Beveridge suggested that this form of 'social advance' was the necessary accompaniment to state action if the latter was not to become oppressive and overwhelming.[6] Conceived as 'charity', the idea of voluntary action was viewed with considerable suspicion by some British socialists, for whom it smacked of interfering social patronage and the Conservative Primrose League, and who believed that, however much Beveridge might worry about the 'totalitarian' model, all such responsibilities should be transferred to the new agencies of the welfare state.

Cooperation, however, was a different story. This form of self-managed activity could claim an honourable place in the pantheon of British radicalism and a long lineage going back to the nineteenth-century inspiration of Robert Owen and William Morris among others. Moreover, and as Mabel Ridealgh knew, British cooperators had been among the international constituency that had supported and provided funds for Rewi Alley, George Hogg, and others as they set out to create a network of Industrial Cooperatives in Free China during the war against Japan.

Mrs Ridealgh had hoped to visit the Guild Hospital built in Sandan in the north-west with funds donated by members of the Women's Co-operative Guild in Britain. Sadly, this 'little mud hospital' had been destroyed by an earthquake earlier that year,[7] but she would have liked to discover more about its restoration.

In the event, Sandan proved too far away for a visit and, like other visitors before her, she had to settle for the reassuring word of Rewi Alley, who had been 'largely responsible' for promoting the hospital to its overseas funders, and who happened, as he said, to have been at the site only six weeks previously. He was able to inform Ridealgh that the building had been reconstructed, using its original timbers. He also told her that the doctors who had been trained at Sandan were now running hospitals all over China and that the teaching work once carried out there had been 'transferred to a very large new modern hospital in Lanchou where they look forward to passing out more and more qualified doctors on an ever increasing scale'.

Sandan proved beyond reach, but the delegation did enquire at some length into the place of cooperatives in New China, and also the extent of State ownership of the economy. During a visit to the All-China Federation of Supply and Marketing Coopera-tives, they were informed that, though the State had indeed 'nationalised the larger concerns', it had 'no intention, at this stage, of making any sweeping extensions of public ownership either in production or distribution'. There were, consequently, three coexisting systems of distribution: the State shop, the private shop, and the co-operative store, and the proportion of each varied considerably between town and country.

Since 1949, the enquirers were told, China had set out to build two types of co-operative organizations: retail co-operatives and consumer co-operatives in the towns; and supply and marketing co-ops in the country. There were also credit co-ops and others organized around particular handicrafts or among fishermen, but it was these two types that formed the bulk of the rapidly growing movement. Membership of consumer co-operatives had grown from 3 million to 10 million since the liberation. Growth had been even faster in the villages, where there were now 30,000 Supply and Marketing Co-ops, with a membership of 149 million. These organizations now handled 50 per cent of the retail trade in the countryside, and 'their turnover has multiplied 18 times since 1950'. Special schools had been set up to train co-operative workers and over 11,000 productive enterprises had been formed to supply these stores with co-operatively produced goods: the phrase 'Something like the Co-operative Wholesale Society' appears in the delegation's report.[8] It was, the visitors concluded, a most impressive record of achievement, and all the more persuasive for the fact that the Vice-Chairman of the All-China Federation admitted that both the service the co-operatives provided and the choice of goods they made available needed improvement.

Having heard that 'the extension of co-operatives' formed the principal way in which the government had so far sought to 'socialize' production and distribution, the delegation were invited to inspect selected examples during their travels. They visited a larger embroidery and lace co-operative organized as part of the Handicrafts Producers Co-operative in Peking. This producers' organization had nearly 4,000 members and, while it had started as a factory, most of its output was now made by women working at home as a 'supplement to their domestic duties'. The delegates were generally impressed, even though their report also concludes that 'the workshop is too small and the tools for production are not modern. The flat iron is used and washing boards in preparing goods for sale. The range of 147 patterns is not sufficient to meet popular demands.'

At His Pu Hsiang, Chengdu, they were welcomed in the 'ex-landlord's house' and shown round the Second Workers' Co-operative Farm: introduced as one of thirty such co-ops formed in the area since February, and one that also claimed greatly increased production (43.3 per cent). The Vice-Chairman explained that she had owned nothing before the liberation, having been exploited by landlords and condemned to the most abject poverty. The recent land reform had lifted the yoke, however, enabling her to restore her previously starved and scattered family. The visitors were also told that the government had assisted the 152 families in the new co-operative by providing loans and chemical fertilizers, and by training some members in relevant skills including tractor driving and sanitation.

The Shanghai Consumer's Co-operative claimed a membership of 880,000, scattered over thirty-one administrative districts. Its stores seemed to be 'well stocked with a good variety of consumer goods', and the supply of 'soft furnishings and hardware' was also judged fairly impressive. At a tea co-operative outside Hangchow, they were informed that members retained their own piece of

Fig 41. Man with pedicab, Shanghai (photo: Derrick James).

ground for growing vegetables and perhaps keeping chickens and a pig, while also greatly benefiting from collective action—not least in the creation of irrigation schemes and the destruction of pests. Here as elsewhere, the improvement was narrated as a story of Before the liberation, when the people had worn rags and suffered, and After, when they had been raised up by the Communist Party and started to thrive.

And so the delegation marched on, passing through a co-operative hosiery factory in Shanghai, where workers were allowed fifty-six days maternity leave on half pay while the day nursery provided milk powder and porridge or biscuits every three hours as part of the service, and a Co-operative village community near Fushun, Manchuria, where they saw scores of new buildings and a great expansion in the village school. It was an impressive story, and not one that was to be dragged down by insinuations of the violence of the land reforms from which so much of it had emerged. Mrs Ridealgh was left in no doubt, as she would eventually report back to her membership, that 'Co-operation was raising the standard of life and bringing happiness to the families of an ever growing membership that had then reached 160 millions'.[9]

Before and After: Facts Become 'Bricks'

According to Barbara Castle, the entertainments laid on for the Second Labour Delegation in Peking included a display of 'brilliant acrobatics with the best and most amusing illusionist any of us had ever seen'. In their attempt to take stock of Chinese realities, the Britons might reasonably have wondered whether they were also being offered a different kind of illusionism. James Cameron, for whom the word 'delegate' suggested a new kind of eunuch, distinguished himself from such observers as a practised foreign correspondent.[10] Not so easy, he implied, for closely chaperoned drones such as the members of the Second Labour Delegation, who were indeed highly reliant on their hosts and interpreters, and who lacked any means of testing the figures they dutifully wrote down at their many meetings with Chinese officials, or of telling true facts from the optimistic propaganda in which they were so carefully wrapped.

Their report informs its readers that the All-China Federation of Trade Unions boasted 11 million entirely voluntary members, 90 sanatoria and 42 rest-homes in 'health resorts'. Repeating official claims about the newly introduced system of social insurance and the ongoing campaign to raise literacy among workers, it also accepts the estimate that wages had further to rise notwithstanding recent increases. Officials from the Ministry of Education provided the British trade unionists and politicians with a 'general picture' of the school system, and assured them that New China's students of English really did study Mark Twain among other modern authors. At the Institute of Economics, the more collectivist Britons worried that the continued existence of private enterprise might be 'a contradiction in a socialist state'. They were briskly informed that 'socialism could only be built on the basis of production', and that, according to the officially adopted theory of three stages, it was envisaged that private capitalism would be replaced first by state capitalism with co-operatives, and only after that by true socialism.

The tables were turned at the People's Institute of Foreign Relations, where the Vice-President confronted the British visitors with, not just a barrowful of prepared facts and statistics, but a series of pointed questions about British policy towards the rearmament of West Germany and American-led plans to form an anti-Communist South-East Asia Treaty Organization (SEATO). In reply, Ellis Smith skirted the official Cold War policies pursued by his party's National Executive Committee and accepted at the annual party conference the previous month. He preferred to insist that the idea of 'peaceful coexistence' had actually found 'mass support' within the rank and file of the Labour Party. Ben Parkin gave a 'detailed account of events leading up to the Labour Party's recent decision to back German Rearmament', explaining the range of opinions held, including the opposition voiced by Aneurin Bevan, Barbara Castle, Harold Wilson, and others in the Tribune pamphlet *It Need Not Happen*.[11] He emphasized that many Labour supporters had 'opposed American pressure', as had French public opinion over the proposal for a 'European Defence Community'.

Barbara Castle also joined the discussion, asserting that the British Labour Party's position on SEATO was not actually the same as that of the USA, 'bedevilled' as the latter country was by its support for Chiang Kai-shek. On the contrary, she insisted, public opinion in Britain actually 'supported China's claim for a seat in the United Nations'. At the end of the meeting, so Castle records, the President of the Institute for Foreign Affairs suggested that the solution to the problem of Taiwan would be for America to withdraw the 7th fleet from the area: 'Then we would have no difficulty in liberating Taiwan as we liberated the mainland from the traitorous regime of Chiang Kai-shek.' When Ernest Thornton recommended an exchange of ambassadors, the same man affirmed that China's chargé d'affaires would be leaving for Britain shortly.

It would not be for another twenty years that the Parisian semiologist Roland Barthes would visit China with a group of leftist intellectuals, and find himself oppressed by both the guided tour and the boundless enthusiasm shown by some of his fellow visitors.

It was outside Nanking, at the tomb of the first Ming emperor, Zhuy Yuanzhang (1328–98), that Barthes finally refused to get out of the car, fed up with an itinerary of entirely pre-scripted sites and a guide who was grimly determined to limit any encounter offering the possibility of 'surprise'.[12] He could take no more of the unceasing commentary of revolutionary slogans and stereotypes: an 'avalanche of bricks',[13] as he called it, designed to obliterate all possibility of independent reflection.

Although the situation was far looser in 1954, the guided tours were well under way and facts as well as dreams and illusions were already being packaged as 'bricks'. Castle, Ridealgh, and other members of the Second Labour Delegation encountered a primary example in the making, when they visited the offices of the Women's Democratic Federation, to enquire after the genuinely improved status of women in New China and particularly the new marriage law, said to give women equal rights to property and divorce. Everything mentioned was presented as a contrast between Then and Now, and all the more plausibly since so much progress had been made. Before the liberation, women had been

Fig 42. Roadside encounter (photo: Cedric Dover).

little better than domestic animals. Confined to domestic chores and deprived of education, they had been beaten, abused, and deprived of all agency. Their oppression had been justified by primitive superstition, which had claimed that if women were allowed to work the land the crops would fail. In some rural areas, so the delegation was informed, poor families had been in the habit of drowning their baby girls. 'One found the boiler-suited women a little de-sexed',[14] Barbara Castle would later admit, but the improvements on this front were hugely promising.

They submitted to more ideologically wrapped statements of fact in a long session about the Constitution of New China, in which their questions were answered by the Vice-President of the Chinese Institute of Law and Political Science, whose words were scribbled down by Barbara Castle. There were indeed, this authority confirmed, many parties in New China, and there was 'nothing to stop' any group of persons setting up another new party either. The Association of National Democratic Construction represented capitalist interests ('i.e. factory owners and bankers'). The Party of 3 September represented intellectuals ('e.g. professors'). There was even a party made up of former members of the Kuomintang who had stayed in China...As for the visitors' worry that the Standing Committee of the People's Congress had the power to 'interpret laws' in particular cases, they were assured that this body never interfered with the outcome of trials. The people's courts did indeed report to Congress at different levels, but this was only to 'allow Congress to decide what changes are necessary in law or judicial administration'. With the British Habeas Corpus Act in mind, the delegates wanted to know whether there was an obligation on the prosecution to produce the accused in court within a given time, and whether the accused had effective rights of defence. In reply they were battered with more facts: presidents of courts must be qualified lawyers, and there were already more than 2,000 women judges.

There is ample indication that the politicians and trade unionists forming the core of the Second Labour Delegation were convinced by the atmosphere of industrious improvement they found in China. They favoured the establishment of trade and other forms of exchange between China and Western countries, believing that such a development would demonstrate that China's path need not pass through Moscow alone. Determined to make this case against

American-led anti-Communist opinion in the West, they were not inclined to wonder, in their public reports at least, whether the remarkable things they had seen were already being manipulated by a Communist Party that was, as its critics claimed, using the optimism and mass mobilization of the Chinese peoples to create the

Fig 43. Foreigners welcomed to school of National Minorities (photo: Derrick James).

conditions for an increasingly autocratic seizure of power over everything. Like the British Labour Party's first delegation to Bolshevik Russia in 1920, they were inclined to blame the problems they saw on Western policy and to reserve much of their irritation for their own country's official representatives.

On 18 October, a party was laid on for the Second Labour Delegation by the British chargé d'affaires. Derrick James describes how they entered the British legation compound to find themselves in 'a warm English sofa-and-armchair-and-whisky sort of scene' that might indeed have seemed more at home in Wimbledon, as Rex Warner had also earlier suggested. James judged the people there to be 'quite nice chaps', and was pleased to be shown 'some lovely porcelain' that John Addis had collected in Peking: 'it was nice to be able to feel the smooth polish of the stuff, rather than peer at it from behind glass.'

James would express different views a day or two later. After another dinner in the embassy, this time in a smaller group including Denis Mathews and Barbara Castle, he wrote 'These chaps are so nice and polite, but they really are shockers, running down the Chinese and doing it within the hearing of the servants. I didn't like them much, but we had an English dinner in English surroundings of incredible beauty. They live awfully well, and even gave us a bottle of red.' There had been 'great alarm' when James broached the subject of Chinese visits to British universities. 'Didn't I think the Chinese would spread Communism?' asked the staff, adding that the government was 'very worried' about this: 'They don't have much confidence in us, perhaps correctly.'

Generally, the members of the Second Labour Delegation accepted the portrayal of China as a place of dramatic contrasts in which the Liberation of 1949 served as the moral as well as political pivot between opposed worlds. 'Before' had indeed been a place of abject demoralization, exploitation, disease, flood, war, and want. 'After' was the present: already improved and filled with the promise of far greater things to come. Though an officially nurtured impression, this was not just a stage-managed illusion conjured out of nothing. Remarkable reforms had taken place in many different spheres of life, and if war could be avoided, the future seemed wide open. Their conclusion was remarkably similar to that of Alan Winnington, the British Communist journalist who stayed in Peking after Anthony Eden had refused to renew his passport. He would later recall how many of his Chinese friends had come to refer to the first half of the 1950s as 'the golden years'. 'The Communists rode on a wave of success: currency stabilised; famine ended, railways restored; industry booming; coal, steel and power leap-frogging. We found workers everywhere at lathes while building workers were finishing the factories. Everyone was better off—very little better off but in China that could make the difference between life and death.'[15]

Second Thoughts in Chungking

Though its more diligent members kept writing down the figures and statistics offered as proof of this inspiring narrative, the Second Labour Delegation was hardly unanimous on all matters, and neither were its members happy to swallow every 'brick' served up by New

Fig 44. Pioneers welcoming visitors (photo: Cedric Dover).

China's presenters. One of their more heated internal disputes took place at the end of a long day on 22 October in Chungking, formerly Chiang Kai-shek's much bombed provisional capital in the south-western province of Szechuan. They had left Peking early in the morning, flying in two more or less demilitarized Dakotas. James found himself in a converted American model, which proved greatly superior to the noisy and vibrating Russian versions that had brought the visitors to Peking from Moscow. They made their first fuelling stop at a military aerodrome where they looked out at rows of jets—'Maybe the fabulous MIGS', speculated James. They disembarked for a 'vast European lunch' at Sian, after which they sat in the sunshine, with their jackets off and their sleeves rolled up. 'It was wonderful', James noted, just 'like a hot English summer day'.

That evening in Chungking, however, the delegates had 'a great argument' about the vast new State Building in which they were staying. Though it had been built in 1951, Barbara Castle felt that this provocative edifice 'looked for all the world like a larger edition of the Imperial Palaces in the Forbidden City. It dominates the town from its hill, standing out in its red and green tiled magnificence and its traditional ornamented pagoda style. You climb hundreds of steps to its entrance which leads to the largest auditorium and stage we have yet seen, capacity 5,300 with electrically operated curtain.' The bedrooms arrayed around this vast auditorium were spacious and each was equipped with its own private bath—an 'enormous swimming pool affair'. Noting that the sense of luxury was only a little diminished by the fact that the 'vividly coloured distemper was already peeling off the walls', Derrick James thought the place both 'gigantic' and 'rather atrocious'. The new State building was also 'an eye-opener'[16] for Ernest Thornton, MP for Farnworth, and former Secretary of the United Textile Factory Workers Association of Great Britain. Having earlier visited Chungking in 1946, when it was still the much-bombed 'wartime capital city' of nationalist China, he remembered it as 'the most dilapidated, neglected, ramshackle city I have ever seen'. Though the crowding remained terrible, he could not but appreciate the new buildings and the ongoing road construction that could now be seen everywhere. Nevertheless, he too had his doubts about the 'modern "Temple of Heaven"' that was the Chungking's new State Building.

The British visitors were duly entertained by the city dignitaries but, for James at least, the 'cavernous' halls of this gaudy 'monument to the post-liberation period' were hardly lightened by the speeches made by the 'chaps' on the delegation, or, even by the songs they began to exchange. James writes that John Horner, a charismatic firebrand well known to the British press as the 'Communist General Secretary of the Fire Brigades Union',[17] contributed an 'idiomatic ditty about the fire service', and 'things, as they say, warmed up'.

The Chinese watched these increasingly lubricated proceedings with expressions of 'blank politeness' on their faces, and then took their guests up onto the hotel roof and enlisted the sight of the city below into another recitation of the epic story of China Before and After. Where once there had only been lanterns and candles, there was now electric street lighting. James granted their point, even though he had heard many such claims by now. 'It was rather wonderful', he wrote, 'and one must remember that this was a thing they had created...It was an impressive moment, I thought, because they were so proud of it.'

Despite the hospitality, this brazen new palace on a hill remained more than some members of the delegation could bear. In a heated discussion, some protested that it should never have been built—certainly not before something had been done about the 'hovels' the delegation had passed when driven into the city along the Yangtze River from the airfield. Ernest Thornton himself understood why 'some of us expressed criticism of such a profligate use of labour and materials on so obvious a show-place, whilst living conditions were so wretched for scores of thousands'.[18] 'Even John Horner was worried', as Castle notes in her diary. She, herself, disagreed with the objectors, as did Ellis Smith, who pointed out that Chungking was 'the admin centre' for a number of south-western provinces, and that people travelled for hundreds of miles to attend meetings here. This defence was acknowledged by Thornton, who reveals that this was also the 'emphatic' defence mounted by the Chinese officials, and who went on to insist that 'there could be no doubt but that the people of Chungking liked and were proud of this great incongruous edifice'.

Castle's defence was different, and connected to her belief that socialism must be inspiring and not just about equal rations of

austerity all round. She argued that 'in every society there must be
some luxury to satisfy the craving of the most high-minded of us'.
'In Labour Britain, we had never attacked the capitalist ideology,
we had provided the security of the welfare state but left people
with the desire, and the opportunity, to contract out of it (capital
gains, football pools, legacies, etc.)'. In these backward areas, she
thought, 'the Gov. must concentrate all its energies on getting
people to contract in; luxury must therefore not be private but
communal'. The 'hovels' they had seen on the road from the
airport had indeed looked dismal, but Castle and Smith would be
reassured, when driving out of Chungking to visit a steelworks the
following day, to see many buildings, either just built or still under
construction, that would be of direct value to ordinary workers:
'flats, sports stadium, gymnasium, hospital, trolley bus station, road
widening'. With these in mind, Castle concluded that 'So long as
bureaucracy does not corner the luxury, a few palaces won't hurt'.

She found the outlying steelworks impressive too. Driving past
'blocks of new workers' flats and through a garden', their interpreters drew their attention to a poster at the gate reading 'We
will make our factory a garden'. They were informed that the
Kuomintang had done its best to wreck the plant on the eve of
Liberation, destroying the blast furnace, the power plant, and
also the open hearth. The factory had since been nationalized
and restored with the help of Soviet experts. The delegates, some
of whom will have had their doubts about 'joint consultation'
schemes of the toothless variety then being offered by industrial
managers in Britain, were informed that '4,000 rationalisation
proposals' had been received from the workers in 1953 alone.
Wages were said to have trebled since the liberation, and prices
had been 'stabilized' too. Workers had once lived in air-raid shel-
ters, but there were now 480 blocks of flats in which 10,000 were
housed: 'the people were keen to show them to us'. Vast canteens
dispensed nutritious diets and there were cultural programmes,
as well as a cooperative store, for each group of flats. The visitors
saw, or were told of, a cinema, library, even a skating rink.

All this was registered by the trade union leaders, who will have
known, even if they had never before seen a skating rink, that
many people in Britain were still living in temporary prefabs, to
say nothing of those who were sleeping rough or, as the novelist

Jack Lindsay had emphasized in a recent assault on 'the British way', obliged to improvise homes out of old anti-aircraft gun pits and abandoned Nissen huts on bombed-out waste land around the London docks.[19] Perhaps they were reassured to identify certain imperfections in the steelworks' equipment. The open-hearth furnace did employ modern methods, including both an electric charger and oxygen, which helped to speed up proceedings. The plant was not a continuous mill, however, and its 'hot mill strip' was a considerable distance from the furnaces. The pre-war rolling machinery was 'rather old and slow', and material was conveyed in baskets rather than electrically operated trucks. Indeed, Arnold Hardy, Council member of the Amalgamated Union of Foundry Workers, noticed that the blast furnace was distinctly antiquated: in the absence of water coolers he feared that there was even some 'danger of explosion'.

It was not the steelworks that restored Ernest Thornton, who had concluded of the new State Building that 'an overseas visitor could not fail to wonder whether they had got their priorities right in this case'.[20] His optimism was renewed by the new railway connecting Chungking and Chengdu. This, as he knew, had been 'talked about' for forty years. Plans had been drawn up, taxis levied, tunnels blasted, and stations built too. The railway, however, had remained 'an expensive and illusory dream' until 'the new regime' came along and 'tackled the job' triumphantly in two years. And now here he was, looking out of the window at steamers and junks on the Yangtze River, and smiling back at the crowds gathered by the railway to watch as the trains crawled by: slowly, as Thornton admitted, but impressively punctual too. 'Here, simply, lies the story of the strength and success of the Communist regime. It not only promises, but fulfils its promises—at least in respect of big spectacular projects which the populace can see. To the Chinese masses this impresses more than the ideological propaganda which is passed out in good measure. But it lends credence to the propaganda at the same time.'

Mrs Ridealgh's Nocturnal Ordeal

One evening in Peking, James had found Castle in 'a great panic'. She explained that, before leaving London, she had arranged to be an 'accredited correspondent' for the *Daily Herald*, and that, in this capacity, she had managed to make a breakfast appointment with India's Prime Minister, whom the party had earlier met at the Summer Palace. If Nehru agreed to publication of their discussion, it would, Castle estimated, represent a considerable 'scoop'. Yet she was also worried that the other delegates, who were 'all trying the same stunt', would 'hate her for life' if they were not invited too. 'It all seems childish', wrote James, 'but this, believe me, is as childish world.'

That fear of missing or hogging a 'scoop' was by no means the only cause of aggravation between the British politicians who visited China that year. J. D. Bernal reveals that, for all their espousal of 'peaceful coexistence', the members of the Second Labour Delegation were far from friendly to one parliamentary colleague. On 27 October, the British physicist came across Desmond Donnelly, Labour MP for Pembrokeshire, who was in Peking to pursue his interest in developing trade links in China. Donnelly informed Bernal that he was on 'very bad terms' with the Labour delegation, having recently fallen out with Aneurin Bevan 'because of his attitude, which I had not known, of voting for German rearmament'. Donnelly was actually making his second visit to China, having previously visited as a reviled dissenting member of the Britain–China Friendship Association's largely Communist delegation of 1952, and once again he had argued with the regime's presenters. He questioned the greatly increased Soviet influence he now detected, and suggested that the apparently miraculous eradication of flies noted by so many sympathetic tourists had at least as much to do with the copious use of DDT as with the people's heroic swatting programmes. He visited show institutions, such as were used to impress the Second Labour Delegation, and challenged them directly. At one of Peking's much admired crèches, he told the director that the inculcated 'group spirit', thanks to which children were said to 'get to love the staff here more than their parents', was really an attempt to break up the family and 'an affront to the dignity of the common man'.[21] After seeing through that 'fantasy from "1984"', he took on a textile mill, interrupting the director as he spouted patently false production statistics, and challenging him until he admitted that he had formerly been a journalist with the People's Liberation Army, and understood little about the business he was apparently now running. "'You see,'" he pleaded, "'the 'delegations' that come here do not ask such questions. They accept what I tell them".'[22]

Donnelly may have conducted himself as a principled outsider, but the civil war between right and left in the Labour Party was capable of fracturing the delegation internally too, since some of its members, including Vice-Chairman George Lindgren, were well to the right of the party, and being in China exacerbated the mistrust that lay between them and their Bevanite colleagues. Speaking in 2002, Barbara Castle recalled that right-wing eyebrows would be raised even over apparently trivial matters, such as a person's choice of tables in the dining room of Peking's 'Sin Chiao' Hotel.[23] It was fine to sit at a square table, at which European-style food would be served. But to opt for Chinese food at a round table was to be suspected of an unhealthy softness for Communism, while 'to pick up a pair of chopsticks', even if only to reveal Western incompetence in their manipulation, was perceived by some as an act of flagrant treachery.

The British MPs may have looked a haggard as well as uncouth rabble when they landed at Peking but this didn't prevent them from squabbling absurdly, at the end of their first day in China, about whether they had been 'slighted' by Chou En-lai, and indeed, by Mao himself, who had also failed to turn out to greet these stragglers at the airfield. Yet, as James goes on to note, this particular manifestation of 'childishness' was nothing compared to the drunken carousing. James had his own ideas about the delegation's susceptibility on this front: 'I think people are nervous about flying, so when they land they are very uninhibited. After a day's flying the release of tension usually leads to something of an orgy.' That this habit could get out of hand became painfully apparent on the train that brought the delegates back to Chungking after their excursion to Chengdu, where they had visited the Agrarian Exhibition and inspected a new Railway Engine Repair Works. The delegates started by singing 'Auld Lang Syne' on the platform, to which their Chinese hosts replied—'I hope in kind', as James wrote. They then took to the restaurant car, where they 'had a party'. Ben Parkin ('He's a rude bastard at first sight, but witty and very intelligent') sat down to play poker with James and Charles Royle. The 'other boys', meanwhile, were 'whooping it up in a maudlin sing song way. So we sang lewd songs for a while and went to bed late.' In this case, 'late' meant about 1.30 a.m.

They woke early to find that 'a great fuss' had broken out over Will Griffiths' nocturnal manoeuvres. This particular MP may have helped the 1945 Labour government over its plans for British dentistry and also served as an effective Parliamentary private secretary to Aneurin Bevan, with whom he remained a close friend.[24] As James explains, however, he was also 'quite hopeless when he gets drunk. He becomes obstreperous and an annoyance.' His weakness had been revealed in Moscow, where they had been obliged to abandon him at an embassy party because he refused to leave with the rest of the delegation. He had 'got plastered' in Peking, 'going so far as to hit Ben, and eventually coming into our room, trying to sit on a chair, falling over and splitting his ear on a glass topped table. I had to staunch the blood, which was considerable. And send him off to get stitched up.' On the train to Chungking, a different idea had entered the mind of this intoxicated Labour fact-finder and, at some point in the night he had tried to climb into Mrs Mabel Ridealgh's bunk. 'She is a pleasant, middle aged woman, but naturally she doesn't enjoy that sort of thing. There's been a great row about it.'

19

'Nuts about Pavlov'? Resuming the Scientific Dialogue

By the end of their second full day in China the four 'professional' members of the Second Labour Delegation were united in horror of the 'tour itinerary' organized for them. As Derrick James wrote in his diary, this included many industrial sites associated with the delivery of China's first five-year plan, 'but that's not quite what some of us came here to see'. In order to overcome the assumption that the entire delegation must be guided through a single set of visits and receptions, James, Dover, Pulleyblank, and Mathews had to negotiate their way through a love of 'tidy arrangements' exhibited not just by their welcoming hosts, the Chinese People's Association for Cultural Relations with Foreign Countries, but also, and perhaps no less formidably, by the Secretary of their own delegation, Mr George Doughty.

As General Secretary of Britain's Association of Engineering and Ship-Building Draughtsmen, this baron of the block vote had decided views about internal discipline, and these can only have been intensified by political antagonisms within the group. The theory, as James notes, was 'more or less that if one wanted to have a haircut one should submit an application in writing to George, admittedly not in triplicate, but that is not the sort of arrangement that suits me'. At an early meeting James therefore spoke up about his desire to see 'university people', explaining that 'it was a waste of my time to see textile mills and so on'. This prompted a certain amount of 'acrimony' from the trade unionists, who did not warm to the incipiently bourgeois idea of 'individuals making private arrangements'. It was eventually agreed, however, that the professionals should have a word with Mr Chou, their head contact in China, and see what might be done.

Chou proved to be 'a nice chap', if 'a trifle effusive in his handshaking', and obliging too. As for the British delegates, it quickly emerged that the professionals were not the only ones interested in loosening George Doughty's grip. Indeed, James found that most of the MPs were also 'getting a little restive' under his 'attempted autocracy'. So the itinerary was diversified considerably. Some receptions, meetings, and visits would still be shared by all, but for others the delegation was divided into more specialized sub-groups. The 'professionals' would visit the same cities and be put up in the same hotels, but they were enabled to pursue their own specialized interests during the day. For Derrick James that meant finding out as much as he could about New China's pursuit of the biological sciences in the rapidly expanding universities.

Dr Derrick James Investigates

By October 1954, China's universities were just emerging from what the delegation's final report would describe as a 'tremendous reorganization'. The Liberation of 1949 had brought an end to the Western support that had previously sustained various privately run colleges, which had subsequently become reliant on State funding. Since 1952, a rationalization had been under way, based, as so much in New China, 'on the Russian pattern'. It was learned that fourteen 'combined universities' had been established in the larger centres, and specialized institutions had also been created to teach medicine, engineering, agriculture, and other technical subjects. The students, whose numbers had been greatly increased, were, so it would be claimed in one of the more bucolic sections of the Second Labour Delegation's report, 'happy, healthy, well-cared for, and noticeably free from the psychological problems common in Western universities. They study with so much concentration that many professors and lecturers said that one of the problems of student welfare was to ensure that work did not intrude excessively into holidays and other periods of rest. We imagine that many teachers in the West would welcome the opportunity to handle such a problem.'

Perhaps that outsider's flourish was the work of Cedric Dover, who also took an interest in New China's universities. Certainly, it is not how Derrick James described the situation in his diary. He began his enquiries on 15 October, when he visited the rapidly expanding University of Peking, formerly Yenching University, to the west of the city. Passing the Student Health Centre, a 'rather shabby' building with peeling walls that reminded him of a medium-sized country house, he walked in, despite the protestations of his young interpreter, a 'sweet little girl with ribbons in her hair', who was worried that 'arrangements' for such a visit should have been made beforehand. It turned out that the Medical Officer in Charge, Dr Sun Tsoong La, was able to speak English, so the two men launched into a discussion about the incidence of psychosomatic disorders among their students.

James was interested to hear that some 10 per cent of students exhibited such symptoms, which he recognized as the same figure given by an earlier investigator. He was informed that the main incidence of illness fell in the final year of study, when students were expected not just to complete their own course but also to lecture non-scientists for some six hours a day. Dr Sun, who used the old-fashioned term 'neurasthenia' as James noted with some apprehension, declared himself convinced that the problems arose from 'overfatique'. However, he also insisted that the fault lay with the students, who were failing to 'face up to their own difficulties'. Dr Sun was accustomed to treating mild cases with 'Pavlov's mixture', which consisted of 0.2 per cent caffeine and 5 per cent bromide, but he also divided his patients into 'symptom groups' so that they could receive 'explanation' of their condition from the medical staff.

While bracing 'explanation' formed one of the two main 'bases' of treatment, the other took the form of 'Exercise'. James had already noticed that exercise was 'a big thing in China'. All sedentary workers were meant to exercise to music for two half-hour periods each day and, like every visitor, he had seen workers doing gymnastics in groups all over the city. He noted that 'this sort of thing goes on in the university too, much to my distress, and the student health doctor said he was sure that exercise was immensely beneficial to the health of the students'.

As proof of his claim, Dr Sun cited the fact that the number of patients seeking his assistance had failed to increase in proportion to the recent increase in student numbers. James was intrigued to hear this but also, after a moment's reflection, unconvinced by Dr Sun's explanation. He asked whether conditions had not improved recently in the rapidly expanding university. Wasn't the food better, and wasn't there now less overcrowding? Hadn't the financial situation of students become easier too? Dr Sun confirmed that conditions were indeed less challenging, yet he seemed 'nonplussed' when James went on to suggest that 'factors other than physical exercise' may be playing their part in improved student health. James proposed a 'controlled experiment' to establish the truth of this situation, but quickly realized that it was unlikely to succeed since exercise was more or less compulsory under government policy. He concluded that Dr Sun 'seemed to deny environmental factors in psychosomatic disease, and insist on some personal "weakness", to be overcome by determination'. This, as James hardly needed to note down, was not the way things were done at University College London.

Having started his investigations in the Student Health Building at the University of Peking, James moved on to the Zoology Department, another new building in which he examined the second-year students' blackboard, filled as it was with bracing slogans ('Don't Waste Time', 'Work Harder' etc.), and spoke to Professor Chang Lung-Hsiang, whose experimental apparatus seemed more limited than those James had earlier seen at research institutes in Moscow. The Professor asked to be sent catalogues of books and scientific instruments, and admitted that, like his colleagues both here and in other universities, he had been so busy coping with vastly expanded student numbers, that it was only now becoming possible to concentrate on research in accordance with the programme recently adopted by Academia Sinica.

The same point was made at the Peking Medical College, which James visited together with William Griffiths, the dentist and MP for Manchester Exchange. Here the visitors were met by various professors, who explained that they too had greatly expanded their student numbers, shifting from 400 students before the Liberation to the present 2,800. Courses had been shortened to hasten the qualification of much-needed doctors, and there was not yet a state registration scheme for nurses, also in short supply. Buildings appeared generally good, although the anatomy school seemed pressed for space: students were dissecting twelve to a cadaver, on tables that were very close together. It turned out that the Dean, Professor Wu Chuan Kuai, spoke very good English, a discovery that prompted James to wonder about the point of using an interpreter to translate his opening statements. Teaching methods were designed to promote 'mutual assistance' rather than competition. Examinations were oral, and no student had yet exercised his or her right to complain about the awarded grade.

James continued his 'professional' enquiries the next day. After visiting the Historical Museum in the Forbidden City, where he joined the rest of the delegation as it traipsed through the apartments of the dowager empress (he records 'exquisite pottery and hideous European clocks of brazen and disastrous complexity'), James broke off again to visit the Academy of Public Health, an eight-department research institute where he met the assembled heads of department, and was, once again, 'impressed by their courtesy and air of competence'. He learned that many public health workers had been trained and dispatched to public health stations around the country. Indeed, every ten families now had a 'public health representative' drawn from among themselves, whose job it was to 'keep abreast of recommendations'.

As for research, the director explained that China 'must presently concentrate on preventative medicine', and that research was being concentrated on the solution of 'immediate practical problems'. The institute's scientists were therefore beginning to investigate the challenges faced by workers labouring under especially humid and hot conditions, and researching the disposal of factory effluents containing phenol. Their nutritionists were examining traditional Chinese cooking methods in order to establish the extent to which they preserved or destroyed vitamin C. They were also researching the soya bean and its possible uses as a source of protein and developing substitutes for maternal milk. Their virus section, which James judged 'most extensive and well equipped', was beginning to work on polio, while other scientists were advising the municipality of Peking on the design of new water and sewage systems.

There were, as yet, no reliable public health statistics for China, but typhoid and dysentery seemed under control in Peking and a large part of the rest of the country. Steps were also being taken against malaria in the south, where DDT was being manufactured and employed against mosquitoes, along with spraying and draining and 'a great campaign against stagnant water'.

While James strongly approved of this policy of harnessing science to the social needs of the time, he was by no means blinded by an adherent's faith in Soviet methodology. His notes of his conversation with J. H. Cort, held in the Palace Hotel as he passed through Prague, suggest that he might have envied the simplicity at least of centralized state funding for scientific research as it appeared to work in the Soviet bloc. At the same time, however, they reveal his pronounced scepticism about Soviet ideas of 'proletarian science', elsewhere increasingly discredited but still, apparently, being extended into New China. In the physiology department, he was shown 'a luxurious Pavlovian set-up', consisting of a vast soundproof room with a control room alongside it. There was 'a viewing panel and a battery of switches and coloured lights like the control panel of a power station'. Work had yet to begin, but James found the director 'uneasy' when he tried to 'pin him down about Pavlov'. Asked about the practical projects he planned, the man explained that 'they proposed to work on the conditioned reflexes that lead people to be conservative about their diet, and in fact controlled their dietary prejudices'.

A few days later, he met up with an elderly Professor whose name he records as 'Mawen Chao': described as 'a dear old boy' who works on wounds. The Soviet influence here was not represented by Pavlov, this time, but by Olga. B. Lepeshinskaya, the elderly Bolshevik researcher who had won Stalin's admiration for the experiments with which she claimed to have vanquished the bourgeois theory that new cells can only be produced by the division of other cells. James was by no means an admirer of Lepeshinskaya, whose star, following the death of Stalin, was also falling in Moscow, where scientists who had been humiliated and bullied into promoting her preposterous theories about 'the vital substance' had started to protest about the imposition of such pseudo-science. In Prague, he had heard that the scientists in the Czechoslovak Academy of Sciences were anything but convinced by Lepeshinskaya's claim to have proved a hunch expressed by Engels in *The Dialectic of Nature*. The same disbelief had prevailed in London. Indeed, on hearing of Lepeshinskaya's alleged discoveries, news of which had emerged from the Soviet bloc at the beginning of the decade, James's scientific colleagues at University College had joked that, to get her supposedly revolutionary results, the primitively equipped old Bolshevik must have strained the egg yolks used in her experiments through a very dirty sock.[1]

That news, however, had apparently yet to penetrate New China, whence Lepeshinskaya claimed to have received 'numerous letters' written by interested researchers.[2] 'Mawen Chao' told James he had anticipated Lepeshinskaya's 'discoveries' by his own researches in 1930. Studying repair in lymph nodes, he had established, to his own satisfaction at least, that the cells were 'formed anew' from acellular granules identified as 'living protoplasm'. James remained polite but doubtful when this researcher showed him sections of rabbit's ears he had treated 'with crude leather rubbed into the skin'. 'It seems that this increases the epithelial connective tissue and cartilage in the treated ear, which becomes much thicker.' James conceded that this thickening was 'certainly demonstrated' in the sections he had been shown, although he also noted that there had been 'no quantitative measurement data'.

The professor also expounded his experimental work on wounds, which again involved the ears of unfortunate rabbits. After snipping the tips off his chosen examples, he claimed to have observed epithelial thickening that was too early to be accounted for by mitosis, and too extensive to be accounted for by cell migration, since the remaining epithelium remained of normal thickness. Describing these claims as 'interesting', James noted that, here again, the scientist had 'no quantitative measurements at all, and this is such a quantitative sort of thesis'. His enquiries were cut short when the interpreter told him it was time to return to the hotel to meet a professor Li, who had worked with J. B. S. Haldane in London.

As with the new Academy of Sciences in Prague, the reorganization of science in New China was based on the Soviet model, and attended by predictable remarks about the mechanistic and reactionary nature of science in the imperialist West. And yet a considerable number of the scientists met by James had studied and in some cases also worked in Britain or America before the Liberation, and there were many connections to renew. Some remembered working directly with Joseph Needham's Science Cooperation Office during the war, and others asked him to pass on greetings to various scientists in Britain, including Lionel Penrose, the Professor of Genetics at University College London. James met the Deputy Minister of Health, Dr Ho, in the company of an American-trained paediatrician. They talked about dentistry, the training at four new colleges, and the difference between dentists and dental 'technicians' who could be trained for 'routine stuff like fillings'. They also 'bandied questions' about the two different systems. He found them 'very interested in the mode of operation' of Britain's National Health Service, and noted that, when it came to the separation of mothers from their sick young children, they were 'very interested in Freddie Brimblecombe's home care scheme'.[3]

James extended his enquiries in Chungking. While the rest of his delegation were visiting an outlying steelworks, he went to the university, which was now 'more like a polytechnic' having been shorn of its Arts faculties and, as the smiling director explained, closely harnessed to the industrial and technological 'requirements of the State'. At Chengdu, where 'the chaps' went off to see a new Railway Engine Repair Works being built without the benefit of mobile cranes or lifting and handling equipment, James and Dover were taken round the Medical College. The director, who appears in James's diary as Professor Liein, impressed James as an immensely likeable man who had been at Oxford, London, and Brussels before returning to China in 1936. His medical school, meanwhile, was utterly huge. The department of anatomy was housed in a 'bare but fabulously clean' building. There was another 'vast Pavlov set-up', with lots of dogs in a brand new animal house, and the two visitors were also shown a vast collection of skulls, retrieved from graves so that they could be measured.

Concerned that this looked like 'pure research with a vengeance', James asked 'What for?' The researcher's answer was 'elusive', leaving James to conclude politely that here, as elsewhere, resources had been concentrated on teaching and research was 'only just starting up'. Liein left no doubt about the progress that had already been made since 1949. Over tea, he explained that he had been 'afraid to open his mouth in the past, ill-paid and unable to publish'. And now here he was building this vast organization, with every help and encouragement from the State. The students were friendly, keen, and enthusiastic. He was having a wonderful time, so James was to understand, and his experience made nonsense of the idea that the government was 'divorced from the interests of the people'.

A year or so earlier, the Red Dean of Canterbury, Hewlett Johnson, had fervently approved of the fact that 'Though many of China's leading doctors and surgeons are western-trained, there is a revolt in Chinese medical circles against implicit faith in America's medical science'.[4] Nothing James saw in China convinced him that, either here or in Russia, a new form of science was being developed. And yet there was one synthesis that did interest him. This lay not between 'proletarian' and 'bourgeois' science or in Lepeshinskaya's 'struggle of the old and moribund against the new',[5] but between Western and traditional Chinese forms of medicine.

In Shanghai, where he found the best-equipped anatomy department he would see in China, James also visited the 11th People's Hospital, a new institution founded only two months previously in August 1954 and staffed entirely with practitioners of Chinese Medicine. Here he learned that the new Chinese government's policy was not to establish 'a system in opposition to Western medicine', but rather, as he later informed readers of the Lancet, to initiate a 'systematic investigation'[6] of the remedies and methods of traditional Chinese medicine, and to re-establish them on a modern scientific basis. It was, as Dr Wu Chih-chung, Dean of the Medical Institute at Shenyang (Mukden), further explained, a matter of extracting and 'remoulding' what was valuable from a practice that consisted of a 'previously neglected mixture of experience and superstition'. This enquiry had been under way before the Liberation—as was suggested by the fact that the drug ephedrine had long since been isolated from a herb named ma huang, employed in traditional Chinese prescriptions. However, the investigation was now being carried out on a much larger scale. Indeed, James was informed that over 300 prescriptions had been analysed on the advice of workers studying the old literature. Public-health scientists had already isolated a drug that promised to be effective against both amoebic and bacillary forms of dysentery, and it seemed likely that research into ancient methods of sewer construction might also yield materials and methods that could be 'rediscovered' without burdening the limited manufacturing resources presently available.

It was, however, the revival of Chen Chiu therapy (acupuncture combined with cauterization or burning) that seemed most 'striking' to James. This was now being reviewed in accordance with the methods of the Pavlovian school, the latter being taken to offer a scientific grounding that would remove this branch of traditional medicine from 'the domain of empiricism'. As he wrote, the Chen Chiu Institute, set up in 1951, was forging ahead with this synthesis and claiming 'remarkable success' in the treatment of rheumatism, malaria, hypertension, tuberculosis, and other conditions. In its publications, the institute claimed its treatments had been successful in 90 per cent of 5,115 cases of malaria in army units, and 80 per cent of 263 cases of hypertension. It claimed also to have trained 1,400 practitioners posted to army and local government organizations. James would use an exclamation mark, carefully placed between brackets, to distance himself from some of the claims relayed in his *Lancet* article...Yet he also came home convinced that considerable advances were being made and that a renewal of the interrupted exchange between British and Chinese scientists would only help both sides.

Cedric Dover's Freelance Eye

Dr James shared some of his visits with other interested delegates, including Mr Cedric Dover, who would claim to have visited six universities and three medical colleges, and who joined James in applauding the fact that New China's scientific research was planned and responsive to social need, and by no means 'haphazard'. His own investigations, however, followed a more erratic path.

Dover's perspective was less that of a practising scientist than of an anti-imperialist partisan, who embraced New China as the promising inspiration of a wider resurgence that might, he hoped, inspire liberation movements throughout Asia. His fellow delegates may have been impressed by the fact that Dover was greeted personally by Jawaharlal Nehru. The Indian Prime Minister's arrival in Peking on 19 October had been witnessed by J. D. Bernal, who happened to be in the road as he was driven into Peking from the airfield: Bernal saw Nehru 'standing up in his car looking very pleased with himself' as he was hailed by the crowds lining the route all the way from the aerodrome. Dover had been acquainted with Nehru during the struggle for independence, and he would return from China to tell his English wife that the Indian leader had urged him to understand that running a government was 'very different' from maintaining principled positions while in opposition.

Derrick James, meanwhile, would go back to London with some doubts about Cedric Dover's standing as a scientist.[7] His fellow investigator may have researched and published as something closer to a 'natural historian' in his younger days, but he remained unqualified and the fact that his name had become attached to a simple citronella-based insect repellent hardly indicated a competent analytical scientist of the kind Dr James respected. Dover's concept of 'science' was at once popularizing and loose, and by no means confined to the disciplined model espoused by James, Needham, Bernal, and others inclined to see science harnessed to state planning as the rational basis for a new International. In an article published earlier in 1954, Dover had hailed his former mentors in Calcutta, both Nelson Annandale and his colleague Sunder La Hora, as practitioners of a characteristically Asian approach to evolutionary biology. He would claim their study of adaptation to be founded on the 'old Indian basis' of 'observing living things in their natural milieux'—an ecologically attuned perspective that set out to investigate life 'as process, as interrelatedness, as a totality of subtle harmonies rather than a Darwinian war on many fronts'.[8]

Dover's anti-imperialism also lent elasticity to his account of New China's indebtedness to Soviet science. Having met Dr Tchou-Su at the Institute of Experimental Biology, Dover passed no judgement when reporting that Tchou-Su was researching the formation of cells from 'pro-cells', a programme inspired, as he noted without any trace of Derrick James's scepticism, by 'Academician Lepeshinskaya'.[9] He did admit to some more practical doubts over the same institute's 'revolutionising' of silk production. Tchou-Su was proud to have produced a hybrid of the Indian and Chinese silkworms, which could be induced to spin on thin plywood boards rather than in the customary cocoons. This innovation promised an 'obvious economic advantage': it would be possible to 'transport silk in package boards instead of cocoons containing only 13 to 17 per cent silk' and also to utilize the

eliminated cocoons for oil production and animal food. Unfortunately, as Dover also recorded, 'some old-fashioned sericultural-
ists'—presumably those who continued to operate on a private
basis—had objected that the boarded silk was 'practically useless
for weaving'. One, indeed, had muttered contemptuously that
the supposedly miraculous new material was 'an excellent substi-
tute for leather'.

While James focused his efforts on investigating the true state
of Chinese science and the possibility of a renewed exchange with
British institutions, Dover's interests seemed to spread out all over
the place as he prepared the articles he would later scatter through
the pages of *United Asia, Trees,* and other publications in which he
had a hand. He commended China's heroic achievements in
locust control, and repeated the story as it was told to him: many
breeding grounds had been destroyed in 1951, when 12 million
peasants had been mobilized in a 'campaign of extermination' to
destroy locust nymphs across sixteen provinces.

He was intrigued by the work of a 'Laboratory of Vertebrate
Paleontology'. This small institute was struggling to keep pace
with the finds made possible by the huge construction projects
under way in China. Since the Liberation, it had recovered more
materials than had previously been produced by fifty years of
sponsored digging. Its finds ranged from the skeleton of a duck-
billed dinosaur, unearthed in East Shantung, to a 'Diplodoccus-
type' creature, exposed by construction work in the upper Yangtze
region of Szechuan. It was also responsible for the site at Chouk-
outien, south-west of Peking, where 'Peking Man' had been
unearthed by Davidson Black in 1927—although, as Dover
explained, quoting from Dr Pei Wen-chung's article in *China
Reconstructs,* 'most of the major discoveries' were made by Chinese
scientists, who had suffered 'the common colonial experience of
being regarded "simply as collectors, not as colleagues"'.[10] Given
the 'cultural awakening' of the Chinese masses, Dover reckoned
the work of the laboratory had already achieved 'a unique place
in the public regard'.

Dover had long emphasized the importance of literature in
articulating the experience and common interest of the world's
divided and oppressed coloured, if not always 'half-caste', populations, and he now set out to apply this interest to New China too.

Assisted by the veteran dramatist Chen Pai-chen (Baichen), the Shenyang novelist Ma Chia, and other members of the Writers Union, he surveyed the literature of New China with the same enthusiasm he had earlier applied to Indian writing or to the work of Langston Hughes and other artists of the Harlem Renaissance. He opened the story with the Sun Yat-sen revolution of 1911, asserting that the decadence of the Manchu dynasty had by that time reduced literature to 'little more than an indulgence for aesthetes'[11] Since then, things had changed remarkably. Following the Communist interpretation of modern Chinese literature, he celebrated the stories of Lu Hsun, the Shanghai writer who had developed 'a realistic colloquial literature of protest, satire and reform, coupled with revaluation of the classical humanist works'. In the 1920s and 1930s the movement initiated by Lu and extended by others, including the president of the Academy of Sciences, Kuo Mo-jo, had been 'encumbered by necessary caution', but its achievements had been 'as remarkable as its failures had been understandable'.

As it became a 'dynamic force' in China, the Communist Party had strengthened the movement for an engaged new literature, assisted by Mao Tse-tung who, at a conference of artists and writers held at Yenan in May 1942, had famously urged writers to 'penetrate and express the lives of the people',[12] and insisted that an art sourced in the life of the people would 'put fabricated literature and art to shame'. This was the struggle that Dover wanted to hear more about. He was convinced that Mao had unleashed 'a great movement which will lead Asian literature for many years to come'.

Yet he also acknowledged that the movement faced considerable problems. Not surprisingly, it had encouraged a kind of fiction that was really a form of 'creative reportage', and there were other difficulties too. Given the extreme violence of China's recent experience—in Korea as in the civil war and the struggle against the Japanese before that—it was obvious why so many Chinese novels seemed 'too black and white', or only concerned with war. This impression may have been partly due to the English translations, which were admittedly poor (a problem to which Yang Xianyi and his wife Gladys had already turned their attention). Yet Chinese writers also admitted that the 'tempo of change' going on around them left them little time for the meditation and 'sheer hard work' needed to 'mould understanding works of art'. Thus it happens, as a young Chinese writer told Dover, that '"correct writings may not appeal, while appealing writings may not be correct. We find this contradiction very disturbing, but we must resolve it."'

Too respectful to accuse any of New China's writers of mistaking slogans for literature, Dover was nevertheless alarmed by the zeal with which some younger authors had been rounding on their elders. Specifically, he regretted the treatment of Professor Yu Ping-po of Peking University. Yu had spent thirty years researching *The Dream of the Red Chamber*, the vast and classic Chinese novel written during the Qing dynasty by Tsa Hseu-chen (Cao Xueqin), but was now coming under attack for having devoted 'years of research to obscure and unimportant details of the author's life'. Dover accepted that Professor Yu may have reduced literary history to 'fascinating detective work', pursuing 'clues' rather than searching for 'social understanding'. But the debate initiated by Li His-fan and Lan Ling in the autumn of 1954 also worried him as being tinged with the attitude of 'youth versus age'. Knowing better than to couch his criticism in Western bourgeois terms, Dover suggested that Yu's critics may have forgotten Mao's insistence that there were 'different kinds of satire' to be employed for dealing with enemies, friends, and 'people in our own camp'. By this definition Lu was surely a 'friend', and Dover scolded those who had derided him so savagely, suggesting they were not being so 'Marxist' in their ardour as they believed.[13]

As the 'anthropologist' of the Second Labour delegation, Cedric Dover also took great interest in the regime's policy towards the National Minorities. He and James visited the National Minorities institutes in both Peking and Chengdu. They saw the costumes and were shown the folkloric displays, and they heard the presentation about the raising of cadres, and the conversion of previously unlettered languages into written form. Like A. J. Ayer and other members of the cultural delegation, they were impressed by what they were told: a picturesque imagery of concord and difference within an overall framework of New China. It took someone else to raise doubts about the regime's policies in this area. Rewi Alley was a tireless defender of the

Chinese revolution, who now spent his time collecting maps of China to send to his old friend Joseph Needham and talking foreign visitors out of their hesitations about the course of the Liberation. Yet he was plainly still his own man on the national minorities question. As J. D. Bernal describes, he was 'very critical of the tendency towards centralisation' in education, and convinced that you really could not 'show respect' to the national minorities 'by bringing people to Peking'. Instead, it would have been better to 'do it in relation to the practical means of the cultures, whether the Mongolians in the north, or the Tibetans, or the Forest people in the southwest'.

While Cedric Dover surveyed China in the knowledge that he would soon be assembling a special issue of *United Asia* devoted to 'the Chinese scene', he also continued his investigations as a member of Richard St Barbe Baker's Men of the Trees. He opens his report to this international and ecologically minded constituency by establishing that China's interest in silvestral matters stretched far back into antiquity. Waterways and roads had been planted with elms and willows during the Sui dynasty (581–618), and mature trees were moved from distant forests 'to grace the palaces'. Kublai Khan himself had been a man of trees, who believed, if Marco Polo is correct, that 'those who plant trees are rewarded with long life'.[14] Despite the vandalism unleashed against it by the French and British in 1860, the 'fabulous' Summer Palace in Peking 'still affords superb examples of the architectural use of trees'. Not for Dover, then, the idea that the Summer Palace, created after 1737, according to a plan commissioned from the Italian painter Fra Castiglione, had actually been a fanciful Chinese treatment of European themes, or, indeed, an exercise in reverse *chinoiserie* all along.[15]

Trees were decorative and inspiring, and Dover was by no means the first foreign observer to sense, in China's traditional appreciation of them, a distinctive way of being in harmony with nature, rather than just setting out to conquer it, as had occurred in many parts of Asia and Africa under Western imperialism. Yet beauty and ornamentation were not the only considerations governing New China's employment of trees. Recalling how badly the forests had suffered 'from war, neglect and sheer cupidity' in the decades before the Liberation, Dover was pleased to report that a thoroughgoing greening of the nation was now under way. New forestry laws had made indiscriminate felling 'impossible', and the new Ministry of Forestry was launching 'vast protective, regenerative and replanting schemes' that promised to raise the nation's tree cover by 25 per cent over the following decade. There were new trees along the country's new roads and railways and smoke-tolerant trees (such as Ailanthus), were being planted in industrial towns.

Dover pursued this theme throughout his tour of China, identifying a great variety of species as he went. He praised Hangchow as 'a city of trees and waters', and finally naming Sun Yat Sen University in Canton as the place where he and his increasingly tree-minded interpreter, Lee Cheng Ling, had been at their happiest. The botanical garden here included a remarkable collection of ancient trees, some of which Dover recognized 'as colourful species I had known in India'.

Many of those trees, of course, were older than the Chinese Communist Party, and yet the greening of New China dwarfed anything Dover would later see in India, where the Chinese authorities generously enabled him to spend a few weeks on his way home from Canton, and where forestry seemed to proceed at 'a snail's pace' thanks to 'the present stage of Indian nationhood'. China had imported timber before the Liberation, but it now had timber and forest products such as tung oil available for export— a development that had been achieved by large-scale regeneration of existing forests as well as by new planting. It was also using forestry for protective, ecological reasons, creating windbreaks or, in the case of the 600-mile-long shelter-bed in the north-east, using trees to halt and even to reverse the advance of the Gobi Desert. Made possible by 'mass support and organization', and also by the extensive training and research schemes introduced by the new government, large-scale planting schemes were being used to protect crops, reclaim land, and control rivers all over China. 'In a few years', Dover prophesied optimistically, 'floods and silt-laden waters will exist only in literature and memory'. Standing with Barbara Castle on the Great Wall of China and surveying 'the brown parched treeless earth' that stretched out below, he had no hesitation in announcing, as Castle's diary records, that 'Geographically, Communism came just in time to save China'. It was too early, perhaps, to anticipate the negative ecological consequences that might follow in the wake of the new regime's vast water regulation schemes, or, for that matter, of the unprecedented industrial revolution spreading through China from its heartland in Manchuria.

J. D. Bernal's Marathon

If James knew better than to mistake Cedric Dover for a qualified analytical scientist of his own kind, he harboured no such concerns about another British visitor who was then making similar rounds to himself in China. J. D. Bernal, who was both a well-known Marxist and a distinguished Professor of Physics at Birkbeck College, London, spent two months in the country lecturing and visiting scientific research institutes as a guest of the Academy of Sciences. By the time he left for Hong Kong, he had visited some sixty institutions in all, given thirty scientific lectures and conversed with hundreds of scientists, administrators, and engineers. His general impression of New China, so he would write in an article reprinted in Dover's special issue of *United Asia*, 'was that the transformation of civilisation, the grafting of the new scientific culture on the old stock of literary tradition, had been achieved smoothly and in an incredibly short time'.[16] He also suggested that 'the greatest revolution' in China had been the 'moral' one, which had made the people both 'happy and hopeful'. Their energy had been released, and their future lay in the application of 'scientific planning' and the heroic industrialization with which they had set out to transform their 'semi-feudal, semi-colonial economy' within the span of 'less than a generation'. The planned harnessing of science on a massive scale was an important part of the story, but the revolutionary transformation of China was also based on 'the rapid bringing out of the latent ability and knowledge of the whole people and no longer merely of a traditional elite'. Bernal was convinced, as he would later tell readers of *United Asia*, that what China had already achieved represented 'a major example to the other Asian countries'.

Bernal saw more of New China's science than did Derrick James, and he surveyed its scientific endeavours from a more privileged position too. He was no mere member of a 'delegation' as he would explain when trying, unsuccessfully, to convince an editor at Penguin to commission an already drafted book on his findings.[17] Instead, he was a senior and internationally well-known scientist, who had been welcomed in China as in the Soviet Union for his sympathy with the Communist states, and who remained a controversial figure in Britain for the same reason.

Birkbeck College's Professor of Physics had hardly assisted the cause of the Western scientists who shared his opposition to the Cold War by granting his seal of approval to the 'proletarian science' given exclusive sanction by Stalin in 1948. In the early years of the Cold War he had defended Trofim Lysenko, with his bogus claims about the inheritance of acquired characteristics, against Julian Huxley, who had condemned 'Soviet genetics' with the charge that 'a great scientific nation has repudiated the universal supranational character of science'.[18] In a defence entitled 'Science in the Soviet Union', produced for the East–West Relations Committee of the National Peace Council, in May 1950, Bernal had approved the assertions of Soviet Professor N. I. Nushdin, who had glorified in the fact that Soviet science was 'partisan science' and unlimited by the 'reactionary fetters that capitalism forces upon science' in the West. Like Needham's defence of China's allegations of US bacteriological warfare (and also the more fatuous speculations of the Red Dean), Bernal's assertion had been intended as a rejection of the polarizations of the Cold War. However, it was also based on the partisan delusion that the Soviet Union was 'consciously founded on science, which appears as a central, integrating mode in economic, political and cultural life'. He suggested that the paradox for Western observers was that, while science was being developed and applied on an unprecedented scale in the USSR, it was also developing 'features that seem to make it different and largely unrecognisable from what we have known as science in the past'.

In 1950, Bernal's contention had been that dialectical materialism did not conceive science to be 'an eternal category of abstract truth' as Western scientists were trained to do: 'an objective body of knowledge, impartially collected according to methods independent of all considerations of class or nationality, and approximating ever more closely to one absolute truth'. Insisting that Western science was actually 'no more universal or eternal than capitalism itself', he had described it instead as 'a series of efforts, not made by men in general, but by those dominant or rising classes in society, to achieve even greater control of [the] environment for their benefit'. In justification of his argument, he pointed out that the twin founders of modern science as the West understood it had based their ideas partly on fields that were actually far from natural science. Newton had drawn on Platonic and Arian world views, while Darwin had drawn on Malthus's 'reactionary' picture of social struggle while formulating his idea of 'the survival of the fittest'.

In the Soviet Union, meanwhile, scientists understood their responsibility to 'improve, on both a short and long term basis, the conditions of the people'. Theirs was a 'far wider, more relative and dynamic conception of science as once facet of social activity, determined in its findings and its methods'. Bernal had praised Soviet science for its 'enormous range of effort and deep seriousness'. He quoted Soviet Academician Alexander Oparin's endless optimism about atomic energy, the coming harnessing of photosynthesis to man's needs, and to agricultural transformation: 'In the place where one ear of grain was growing in the past', so Oparin had argued, 'not two ears of which Swift's Gulliver dreamed, but scores are growing at present'. Protesting that the 'genetics controversy' associated with Lysenko had been used to 'blacken Soviet science', he backed the right of Soviet scientists to differ and repudiated the 'alleged suppression and ruin' of Russian science 'at the hands of Lysenko'. As he had once written, 'In the creation of a new world it would be idle to look for the quietly pursued excellence and sound and acute scholarship that characterize our old-established and stable society'.[19]

Bernal was wrong in these arguments, as many knew at the time. His own growing awareness of this fact may be further indicated by the fact that, during his visit to China in 1954, he does not appear to have sought out any signs of the extension of Soviet 'proletarian science' to this younger land. Just as it reveals absolutely no interest in probing the allegations of bacteriological warfare, which had recoiled so strongly against his friend Joseph Needham, Bernal's unpublished chronicle of the trip betrays no sign of any enquiry into the Chinese adoption, such as it may have been, of Pavlov, Lysenko, or, for that matter, Bernal's fellow Stalin Prize Winner, Olga B. Lepeshinskaya. Indeed, when he had lunch with Dr Joshua S. Horn, the British injuries surgeon who had moved with his family from Birmingham to take up residence in Peking, Bernal advised against his intention, expressed with a newly arrived pilgrim's zeal, to give up on 'the techniques of encephalography' he had previously worked with, and which now seemed altogether 'too mechanistic', in order to adopt a fully Pavlovian approach.[20] Bernal counselled that it might be more valuable to 'try and combine the advantages he had with technical measurements of nerve responses with the Pavlovian approach', rather than simply abandoning his British work and trying to 'break into an entirely new field'.

Like James, he would claim that many of the scientists he met in China had 'only recently returned' not from Moscow but 'from Britain and America'. As he travelled through China, meeting scientists in Peking, Shanghai, Tientsin, Hangchow, or Changchun in Manchuria, Bernal set out to renew these contacts and derive transferrable lessons not so much from Soviet examples, which he admitted might also be valuable, but from recent British attempts to harness science to the planned economy under the Labour government of 1945.

One of the many lectures he gave before finally leaving China from Canton was entitled 'Application of Science to Building Construction'. It is not recorded at which institution in China this was delivered, but the surviving text reveals it to have been a detailed examination of the endeavours of the Attlee government to apply science to the nation's acute housing shortage. Bernal was specifically concerned with the Building Research Station in Watford, which had made a considerable effort since 1945 'to see how science could be applied to building problems of all kinds, but particularly those of houses and many storied apartments'.[21] As Chairman of the Ministry of Works' Scientific Committee, Bernal had helped to establish and oversee this institute, which had started out with 660 trained scientists in its employment but since been much 'diminished' thanks to 'the economies imposed by rearmament at the time of the Korean War' and also 'the general atmosphere of non-interference with private industrial interests'.

Despite this recent falling off, which he saw as all too characteristic of Clement Attlee's post-war government, Bernal reckoned the experiment worth reviewing in some detail for the benefit of his Chinese audience. The scientists of the Building Research Station had set about creating 'minimum standards' for various materials, and improving fitments for heating, ventilation, and water supply. They had built experimental houses and studied the behaviour of their occupants in order to establish that far too much coal was used in heating, and that temperature was regulated 'only in the very wasteful way of opening and shutting windows'. They had sought to minimize the use of 'traditional materials that required coal in their manufacture', preferring materials such as plywood, resin-bonded chips, and even sawdust. Bernal himself had been most concerned with the improved use of concrete and cement. Research in Bernal's own Crystallography department at Birkbeck College had been stopped before its full consequences could be exploited, but it had established that Portland cement was a crystalline product rather than a gel as previously thought, thus making it possible to calculate stresses far more accurately. It had also suggested other ways of reducing waste: avoiding the use of concrete in places where small loads met, for example, or exploiting new forms of lime mortar to save scarce materials.

Before their work was curtailed, the scientists of the Building Research Station had demonstrated that 'great economies' could be made in the construction of houses and blocks of flats, where unnecessarily 'large factors of safety' were being allowed in the absence of precise and reliable calculation. They could also claim 'great success' in their investigations into prefabrication, although progress in this area had been hampered by 'an individual, uncollective approach to the problem'. Indeed, Bernal told his audience that the Building Research Centre's initiative had turned into one long battle against 'tradition and vested interests' and that 'mechanization is entering British building at a pitifully slow rate'.

Here, as in Bernal's earlier discussion of 'bourgeois' as opposed to 'proletarian' science, we encounter the polarized logic of the Iron Curtain, in which initiatives considered to have failed in one bloc are relocated and placed entirely to the credit of the other. It had been left to the Soviet Union to 'show the way' by bringing 'the effects of the industrial revolution into building'. While

Bernal hoped to see China gaining much from that source, he argued that the lesson to be learned from the recent British experience was essentially about 'economy of material'. He advised his audience that 'the vast assembly of scaffolding which decorates the Chinese building site must be wasteful if not of timber at least in the transport to bring it to the site...and certainly your brick buildings have walls much too thick for their height and some form of hollow or sandwich construction would save much bricks and cartage'. He was adamant that China 'cannot afford the waste of material and effort which is implied in the reliance on old tradition'. On another occasion, and for similar reasons, he would be concerned when he heard that bricks were not included in the central production plan, and that it was left to local councils to supply them. This was 'a definite weakness'[22] since bricks could certainly be produced more cheaply under a centralized plan.

Such was the spirit in which Bernal travelled through China, lecturing, conversing, and inspecting works and facilities as he went. He advised the heads of the new Academy of Sciences to devote more attention to 'the principles of scientific organization and planning', since it was all too easy to lose sight of longer-term objectives in 'a period of very rapid growth'. And he was impressed when the Academy's scientists emphasized the importance of learning not just from the Soviet Union, but from other countries too: 'I think that the Chinese science will be in a position almost at once to make use of a great deal of experience from England for example.' In the same spirit, he advocated a future exchange between the scientists of the two countries and handed over journals and publications given to him for that purpose by the Royal Society in London. Though mistrusted by many in the West for his strongly pro-Soviet views, Bernal was certainly not simply banging the drum for Moscow. Throughout his trip, indeed, he actually sought to establish exchanges that would contribute to broadening the international reach of New China's scientists and engineers, in effect pulling them away from exclusive reliance on Soviet sources.

Bernal had not been immeasurably impressed by the new Iron and Steel Institute in Peking, but that was largely because 'I found for the first time signs of slackening on the sanitary front in the presence of quite a few flies, which I duly complained about'. For the most part, however, he was full of praise for the work of Chinese scientists. In the 'boom frontier town' of Changchun in Manchuria, the bacteriologists at the Institute of Applied Chemistry and Technical Engineering were doing 'excellent' work to improve agriculture by devising new ways of fixing nitrogen in the soil, or of releasing phosphorous from organic phosphates in the acid soils of the north-east. At a still privately owned chemical factory in Nanking, he found scientists trying to work out how to crystallize ammonium sulphate into larger and heavier crystals that would not get blown away when spread on China's windswept fields. The scientists at Shanghai's Institute of Physiology and Biochemistry in Shanghai were engaged in 'extremely promising' work testing cerebral rhythms and investigating neural control of various biochemical mechanisms.

As for the ongoing attempt to teach science to members of the national minorities, Bernal shared Rewi Alley's view of the methods most likely to achieve results. Having talked to a science teacher at the Nationalities College in Peking, Bernal emphasized the need to approach the subject 'from the practical side'. He formed the impression that difficulties were arising from the fact that the college was pursuing 'rather the opposite attempt of producing a rather stylized and dogmatic scientific world picture'. 'Many of the northern people simply refused to believe that the sun and moon eclipses could be due to such simple processes as one block of matter turning round another, and considered that their demoniacal explanations were more satisfying'. They were also reported to find evolution a 'rather difficult doctrine' to embrace. The teacher informed Bernal that science was 'more easily grasped by agricultural people including the primitive ones of the south-west, than by nomads and animal breeders of the north and west'. Counting could also be a challenge, with some minorities finding the number 10 too large really to grasp. As for Geometry, Bernal reckoned it might be 'better taught through the nationalities' experience of art'. Overall, he reckoned that teachers would get further if they 'left the theory out and stuck to the practice'.

It was at Hankow that Bernal found his most dramatic example of what modern expertise could do when combined with a fierce mobilization of the masses. He was given the story by Mr Fang, the engineer who, a few weeks previously, had been responsible for the city's defences during that summer's terrifying flood of the Yangtze and Han rivers. His struggle against nature had been concentrated on the Tchang-Kung Dike, which surrounded the three cities of Wuhan and extended over a length of some 136 kilometres. In the floods of 1931, in which approximately 100,000 people were said to have died (other estimates would be much larger), the water had reached 28.8 metres above sea level and the three cities were submerged for three months. That height had been exceeded in July 1954, and the water reached an unprecedented height of 29.73 metres in August. Indeed, the aerodrome here was normally at a safe distance from floods, but when the Attlee delegation passed through, the waters were said to be 'lapping at the end of the runway'.[23] In 1931, and as Rewi Alley would explain in due course, the nationalist authorities had utterly failed in their responsibilities to lead the flood-defence work rather than just using it as another opportunity to line their own pockets.[24] That, however, was Before the Liberation, and everything went differently under the Communist-led government. Bernal was told how the people had been organized into 'flood fighting campaign units', while Engineer Fang and his comrades oversaw a vast programme of works designed to strengthen and heighten the dike. Bernal heard that the defences had been raised to a height of 31 metres above sea level in four stages of construction. This had involved shifting nearly 3 million cubic metres of earth, vast quantities of sacking and mats, and great rafts of timber, much of which was coming down the river anyway.

The embargo-hating members of the Second Labour Delegation would come away from their inspection of Hankow's defences convinced that the work must have been 'considerably hampered due to the absence of earth moving machinery, motor trucks and similar equipment', but this was not how the Chinese relayed the story to Bernal. Indeed, Engineer Fang informed the British professor that 32 locomotives had been involved, together with 2,419 tractors, 141 lorries, 21,790 junks, and 640 ordinary boats. Power pumps had been brought in from all over the country to dispose of surface water seeping into the barricaded city. From within the population 90,000 people had been mobilized to carry out this flood protection work, and 170,000 were always on duty to deal with accidental breaks. In all 2,733 partial breaches had occurred, nearly all in moments of terrible rain and gale-force winds that caused great waves to beat in against the dykes. Many heroes had emerged during those moments of crisis, and the skill of the peoples' engineers had been proven too. The three cities of Wuhan had been saved from an inundation that Rewi Alley would describe as the greatest in the history of the Yangtze River's history,[25] and the waters were successfully diverted into newly constructed flood detention areas and over the countryside. The latter step required the evacuation of millions of peasants and caused considerable loss of property and cattle but not of human life. Bernal wrote down the same figures that were given to the Second Labour Delegation. So the story sits in both reports as another shining and statistically arrayed example of what is possible when modern scientific technique is harnessed to the power of a resurgent people directed by what Ernest Thornton MP recognized to be a 'ruthless Central Government'.[26] Perhaps Thornton had the comparatively very modest but still out-voted works of Britain's post-war Labour government in mind when he added that 'It would be folly to think that because the masses in Britain or America would refuse to take such a cruel route, the Chinese, with their different background and experience, will revolt during their arduous journey'.

PART V

The Artist's Reckoning
(China)

20

Revolution Comes to the Art Schools and Museums

Though repeatedly confronted with a revolutionary breach between China as it was 'Before' the Liberation and 'After', the British visitors nevertheless found various ways of praising the Communist-led authorities for their attention to tradition. For Derrick James, it was the determination to renew, rather than just sweep aside, the inheritance of Chinese medicine. The sports-minded Ivor Montagu was more interested in the traditional movements being incorporated into New China's bracing athletic routines. He appreciated the fact that some of these manoeuvres were drawn from 'duck boxing' perhaps, or originally derived for acrobatic purposes from close observation of animals,[1] and he did not share Douglas Hurd's retrospective concern that the regime's more or less compulsory exercise sessions reflected an oppressive new 'uniformity being fastened on the Chinese people'.[2]

The Second Labour Delegation's final report found the same respect for tradition in the regime's still emerging approach to 'The Visual Arts'. Indeed, New China's rulers are here commended for encouraging the arts on more fronts than the high-minded gentlemen running Britain's still fledgling Arts Council would ever have dreamed of. They are praised for conserving and restoring 'the treasures of old China' after many years of neglect: 'This applies to a Pagoda still occupied by Buddhist monks near Hang-chow, as much as to the Imperial Palace, Ming tombs, or new work on archaeological sites of importance'. They are commended for supporting traditional opera and theatre, for introducing a basic wage for painters and 'art craftsmen', and for their reorganization of the art schools, which had been expanded and redirected in order to make the artist's approach 'one that will be appreciated by the great mass of the people'. In the case of new works, the report approved of the fact that 'High authorities recognise that pictures should be creative works not illustrations, that they should be realist not naturalist'. Its authors were also pleased to note that 'the traditional art of China, which has never copied nature but has recreated it, still lives in the works of such respected old masters as Chi Pai Shek [*sic*] and the late Hso Peon [Xu Beihong]; and many younger painters are applying this tradition to contemporary themes'.

The man most likely to have written this enthusiastic, if inaccurately typed, assessment was no slack-minded dupe or conformist zealot. The artist and critic Denis Mathews had been among the keenest of the 'professionals' when it came to breaking out of George Doughty's collectivist regime. Born in 1913 as the son of the Edwardian artist R. G. Mathews and a dancer and former Tiller Girl, Lily Nanton, Mathews would sometimes attribute his rebellious outlook to an attack of acute illness that struck him after he failed out of University College, London, where he had gone to study maths at a precociously young age.[3] Diagnosed with pleurisy, this derailed prodigy had spent a year in a London temperance hospital, where the protocol of the civil defence ward left him with a horror of tight regimes of any kind. An instinctive libertarian as well as the 'strong left-wing socialist'[4] remembered by Michael Foot, Mathews later spent six months studying at the Slade under the sponsorship of Professor Schwabe. Primarily, however, he was a self-taught artist and photographer (his paintings were much admired by Foot's wife, the film-maker Jill Craigie), and a man of wide-ranging interests: 'he could talk about anything under the sun.' He was, as Foot also volunteers, popular with women. Both during and after the trip to China, he got on particularly well with Barbara Castle ('whether they had an affair I don't know', adds Foot, 'but I think it quite likely').

Foot reckons that Denis Mathews, like the other delegates, was 'out to be friendly with China'. He may not have believed everything claimed in *China Reconstructs*, the garishly upbeat bi-monthly propaganda magazine that could be picked up at Collets or Central Books in London, but he was well aware of the many trials suffered by the Chinese people over recent decades, and strongly in favour of getting New China into membership of the United Nations. He was also keen to foster a wider appreciation of the difference between China and the USSR, to counter the Cold War idea of the Communist world as a singular monolithic bloc, and to see Britain differentiate itself from the intransigent Cold War policies of the USA. Mathews's letters from Peking confirm Foot's recollection, just as they leave no doubt that the visual arts, both ancient and modern, formed the main arena in which he pursued this goal.

Mathews made his first autonomous forays in Peking. His widow, Margaret, remembers him talking of stepping out to wander through the city at night, and the pleasure he took in the alleys, shops, and street markets, where he spent hours watching people making noodles or spinning fantastic animal figures out of melted

Fig 45. Muslim slaughter house, Peking (photo: Denis Mathews).

sugar. It was, she remembers him saying, 'like wandering in a medieval world'. His photographs of Peking attest to this. A few are fully aligned with the perspectives of the guided tour. He was prepared to photograph radiant children smiling out from a newly built kindergarten pressed up against a palace wall in Peking, and yet he had no eye for the official parades or the sight of red flags flying over voluntary work brigades of the kind that, in 1952, had inspired the Red Dean of Canterbury to turn himself into a grinning propaganda machine ('silk is a lovely material for banners, floating and waving in soft and graceful curves').[5]

Many of Mathews's chosen subjects were found on the street: children clad in Pierrot-like fabrics or selling little birds on sticks, or a man staring back unyieldingly as he reclines on his battered old pedicab. He made a remarkable series of photographs documenting the treatment of cows as they passed through a Muslim slaughterhouse in Peking. There are also many pictures of temples, palaces, and other historical monuments—including the Lama Temple, and the ancient Buddhist caves at Daton in Shansi province, north-west of Peking. Indeed, very many of Mathews's photographs are not really of 'New China' at all…

As the delegation flew to Chungking, in Szechuan province, a thousand miles to the south-west, Mathews gazed down to see flooded terraced fields resembling 'an ornate antique mirror, studded with small pieces of glass which reflect the landscape and sky'.[6] Writing to his parents in England, he informed them that 'there is a lifetime's painting material in this wonderful scenery unlike any other that I have ever seen'. There were many signs of 'appalling' poverty in the city of Chungking, 'but even here is the amazing struggle which the people are making to bring their country into a modern nation. Roads, hospitals, factories and flats are being built with every load of earth and rock by hand… Their enthusiasm is infectious and no one who has been here can doubt the success of the whole experiment.' Indeed, 'a backward nation is lifting itself up by superhuman effort: while the living conditions are still most primitive but everyone is made to feel that the success is their own'. Having stayed with the Second Labour Delegation in the new State building at Chungking, Mathews noted that the authorities were also building conference centres, theatres, and concert halls. Remembering how the delegation had worried and argued about the flashy palace in which they were accommodated, he accepted that such initiatives might appear 'extravagant' to Western eyes unable to grasp that New China's luxury was actually shared and communal: 'they feel it belongs to them all'.

Deeply impressed by these heroic strivings, Mathews once again extracted himself from the delegation, which after only a day in Chungking was taking the train for Chengdu, where its industrially inclined members would inspect farms undergoing agrarian reform and also various new factories and a railway repair shop. Mathews stayed behind to spend four days on his own in Chungking. 'It's a millionaire's life,' he joked to his parents. He had the benefit of an interpreter and two cars as well. He only had to mention his interest in the river, and a launch with a crew of six would immediately be provided. So it would be too with rice fields or hot springs some fifty miles away. The slightest suggestion of interest prompted the offer of a chaperoned drive.

He used this opportunity to make drawings and photographs. He produced images of men working flooded rice terraces with buffaloes, and of others building roads, winding bobbins for the

Fig 46. Men carrying load down steps, Chungking (photo: Denis Mathews).

looms in little open sheds in village streets, or making shoes by the roadside. He spent much of his time down on the wharves on the River Yangtze, where he watched the 'heavy labour' of teams of perhaps fifty people, as they carried vast loads—including massive electrical transformers—up from the river whilst singing the 'urgent, monotonous chant which keeps them in step'. He made many photographs here: of labouring men and of women doing embroidery by the quay, of a curious tea-house or 'pub' perched on stilts to prevent it being washed away by floods, of a new ship being displayed as the first 'small liner' ever built in a Chinese shipyard. The latter carried 950 passengers and was equipped with bunks of three different classes. The queue of 'happy faces proud to see their own ship' was some three quarters of a mile long. Mathews would later use some of the photographs he made here as the basis for paintings produced after his return to England (Plate 10).

As Organizing Secretary of Britain's Contemporary Art Society, Mathews was determined to discover more about Chinese art as it

Fig 47. Raised tea-house and steps, Chungking (photo: Denis Mathews).

was being developed under the new regime. He had arrived in China with a letter for Chou En-lai, written by Isobel Cripps, who had visited both nationalist and Communist-held areas of China in 1946.[7] As a result of this recommendation, or so he suggested in a letter to his parents, he had been assigned to the Secretary of the Artists' Association, Mr Hua Chun Wu, (Hua Junwu) a well-known cartoonist who had placed his talents in the service of the revolutionary struggle after making his way from Shanghai to Yenan in the 1930s, and who now accompanied Mathew on his travels through China. The two men got on 'tremendously well', and Mathews was all the more impressed when his fervent companion announced, when speaking of Clement Attlee's delegation, 'We refused to sing the Red Flag with the British socialists'.

Mathews was determined to explore the activities of Chinese artists as they tried to follow Mao's decree that they should dedicate their art to the cause of revolutionary mobilization. Though his interest was broadly sympathetic, he was also seeking a critical dialogue. Like the other British artists connected to the ongoing attempt to develop a new practice of 'social' rather than formulaically 'socialist' realism,[8] he was worried about the Chinese emulation of official Soviet aesthetics. Derrick James records a discussion he and Mathews had, shortly after arriving in Peking, with a 'cartoonist' who was also, as James remembers, vice-chairman of the Academy of Arts. (This was surely Hua Junwu, although Margaret Mathews remembers her husband also speaking of his meetings with the revolutionary cartoonist Mi Gu.) The men were toasting and drinking after dinner, and Mathews renewed his attempt to 'trap' the cartoonist into saying whether or not he really liked the Soviet art being promoted as a model for New China's artists. James records that Mathews had first raised this question while his newly arrived delegation was still at Peking airport, but it had been sidestepped and 'left over for further discussion'. When he broached it again, he did so with the question, 'What better time than now could there be for this discussion?' But the smiling cartoonist fended off the question once again, replying 'Is there anything you want to see in Peking? We want to help you all we can.' And that, as James noted, was that.

Mathews kept his questions primed as he proceeded through art academies in the various Chinese cities he visited with the

Fig 48. Child with two Chinese artists. Hua Junwu is standing second from right (photo: Denis Mathews).

Second Labour Delegation. In Chungking, he pursued his enquiries with Mr Ling, a well-known Szechuan artist. Having joined the delegation in inspecting a new iron bridge and the immense new dykes heaped up under Engineer Fang to prevent flooding at Hankow, he was taken by Mr Hua to see the still only partly built art school. He was shown the life rooms, studios, and dormitories, and introduced to the work of various artists, who turned out to be 'painters in the traditional school who were choosing contemporary subjects for their motifs'. For Rex Warner, visiting the Art Institute in Hangchow a little earlier in the year, this might only have meant insinuating a few tiny figures waving almost invisible red flags into a corner of an otherwise unchanged traditional painting. But Mathews saw something altogether more worrying. James, who was with him, notes that a course of 'literature' had been introduced into the curriculum. He and Mathews had wanted to know what books were included in this, but could get no answer except for 'a long diatribe about the place of art in society, and so on'. He also records that, after examining a lot of student work in a classroom, 'Denis was dismayed at its similarity, as if the teaching were markedly dominant'.

Throughout these encounters Mathews continued his argument about art and its ongoing reformation. All the evidence suggests that he was seeking a genuine dialogue between different traditions and perspectives, and also that he allowed for the possibility that his concern about the directions taken by Chinese artists may only have reflected his own presuppositions: 'I have had long talks with the artists here and my disagreement with certain aspects, such as their predominant interest in subject matter, may well be my wish to see them achieve a similar culture to our own.'

Mathews expressed the hope that 'their own methods may in time produce something quite different and more exciting than our own introspective expression'. Having taken that swipe at Western bourgeois aesthetics, however, he found himself disagreeing strongly with 'certain aspects' of the Chinese artists' thinking. He had no trouble with their determination to engage popular culture. And yet this could hardly be achieved satisfactorily by painting heroic scenes from the Long March, or portraits of muscular peasants and workers, standing there with hammer, mattock, or sickle held aloft—one painted 'brick' after another, to anticipate Roland Barthes's expression. He feared an over-zealous abandonment of Chinese tradition and also a confusion of realism with a dim form of Stalinist naturalism.

This concern did not belong to Mathews alone. Paul Hogarth would argue in very similar terms. And so too would J. D. Bernal, who was familiar with Pablo Picasso, whose work Hogarth, Mathews, and others hoped would provide the inspiration for a new style of figuration in realist art. The Birkbeck scientist had met the Spanish artist when he passed through London on the way to the Soviet-backed British Peace Committee's officially aborted Sheffield peace conference in November 1950. Indeed, Picasso had created an already famous mural on Bernal's wall in Torrington Square, London. So it was not in ignorance that Bernal went into a poster shop in Peking and then walked out again, declaring himself disappointed by 'this new style of heroic, optimistic poster, which is an imitation of the Russian...I do not like it so much as those large brightly coloured posters that used to come from China a year or two ago. In fact, I was altogether rather disappointed at the trend of art here.' Visiting the Soviet Exhibition in Peking, he regretted both the primitivism with which mineral specimens were exhibited (as if one lump of socialist coal could be differentiated from another merely by identifying its place of origin with a label), and also the supposedly exemplary works of socialist realist art on display, which were surely dull enough to account for the fact that the galleries were also largely deserted.

It was neither the socialism of New China's art that worried these British observers, nor the idea that the artist should be prepared to serve a wider cause. They objected instead to the particular mode of naturalism, which was dull, academic, and, as Hogarth also declared repeatedly, stuck in the most mediocre conventions of nineteenth-century Russian painting...This was not at all the kind of realist art he or Mathews wanted to see. It was both detached from Chinese methods and traditions, and ignorant of the fertile new ground opened by Western artists—Picasso, to be sure, but also Renato Guttuso, the Italian Communist artist whose work was then becoming known to a wider British public (thanks partly to his illustrations in Elizabeth David's *Italian Food*, published in 1954), and who—if Hogarth remembered correctly—would also have visited China in 1954 had it not been for the prohibition of his wife, who knew him to be an incorrigible womanizer.

Mathews would return to London convinced that the dialogue between Chinese and British artists should continue. His views are implicit in the Second Labour Delegation's report which declares, in its section on 'The Visual Arts', that 'the many artists we met expressed the hope that British painting should be seen in China. The urgent desirability of such loan exhibitions cannot be too highly stressed. They would promote cultural ties which would lead to better understanding between the two countries and they would help to show the Chinese a Western alternative to the influence of naturalism'.

It was from Shanghai that Mathews eventually embarked on his most ambitious excursion into China's ancient past. Travelling with the Second Labour Delegation, he had encountered astonishing displays of hospitality even in the slums of this city: 'everywhere', he told his parents, 'it is like a triumphal tour with people smiling and clapping, shaking hands and inviting us into their poor homes'. It happened after a meeting with British businessmen at a 'magnificent buffet lunch' at the British Consulate-General on Sunday 31 October. The Consul-General was there with his wife and staff and the Indian Consul-General too. The expatriates represented engineering companies, Shell oil company, and various trading firms including Jardine Matheson, and Butterfield and Swire. Yet the group was dominated by representatives of various Western banks.

Derrick James, who has left the most detailed account of this meeting, arrived half an hour late to find the event 'in full swing' and the conversation lubricated with 'lots of drink'. He also found the British businessmen 'quite contradictory' in outlook. The bankers, especially, seemed to hate the Chinese. One, who had been in the country for thirty-seven years, hadn't even bothered to learn the language, justifying his negligence by saying that his 'clerks spoke English'—and this from a brute who was also quite prepared to fend off questions with the superior injunction that 'you have to live in a country to know it'.

Another expatriate, who introduced himself as the representative of an American company, was unable to leave because he was arguing with the Chinese authorities about taxes said to be due. His lament only convinced James of the truth acknowledged by a factory manager, who described the Chinese as 'helpful and cooperative', and also reckoned that the Chinese treated British businesses just like other foreign enterprises: 'no better, no worse'. Most of the party, meanwhile, got horribly drunk and, when the time came to leave, proved reluctant to 'break it up'. Before he left them to it, James saw Will Griffiths lapse into his cups once more. 'Boozed again', the MP for Manchester Exchange began to make 'a speech about "we know what we think of the Shanghai business men, and we know what they think of us". Luckily he fell off his chair at this point.'

Later that day, they had dinner and the Second Labour Delegation then divided for the last time. The main body of politicians and trade unionists set off for Tientsin, where they would plod around the 'Jen Lee Piecegoods Factory', before moving on to visit diverse industrial attractions in Manchuria. James, Castle, Pulleyblank, and Mathews, saw them off 'with a sigh of relief'. The next day they visited a 'wonderful' antique shop, full of enticing 'nooks, crannies & recesses', where a Tang horse could be bought for about £3—a price reflecting the fact that it was now normally impossible to take such things out of the country. They then embarked on journeys of their own.

James, Charles Royle, and Barbara Castle would travel by train to Canton—a journey of 1,800 miles during which, as Castle informed readers of the *New Statesman*, they would live, sleep, and eat with the 'new democracy',[9] becoming intimately acquainted with the suggestion book, the fly-swatting conductor, and the loudspeaker with its bracing music and encouraging injunctions. After inspecting some medical schools and the activities of a women's trade union in Canton, the three left China, going back through the 'Bamboo Curtain' to re-enter 'private enterprise society' in Hong Kong, where they looked about themselves in horror as 'values' became 'monetary' again, sex postured at them from the advertising hoardings, and 'the Chinese women, in their tight slit skirts, looked provocatively different'.

Mathews, meanwhile, joined Edwin Pulleyblank on the first of a series of trains that would take them back to the city of Sian, far away in Shensi province in the north-west, where they would spend two astonishing days before boarding the night train back to Peking. Seeing them off on 1 November, Derrick James notes that they faced a total of 72 hours in trains, and that the first 25 hours of this gruelling ordeal would be spent without the convenience of a sleeping car. As it was, the train journey to Sian took more like 48 hours. Reaching the Yangtze River by the first evening, they were then ferried over from Nanking, where Mathews sampled the delights of Nanking Duck: salted and steamed and served together with 'fungus, bamboo shoots and sea slugs' from trolleys on the platform. They had the use of a sleeper compartment as far as Hsu Chou, where they changed trains, climbing into a carriage 'filled with friendly, smiling faces' for a journey that Mathews described in vivid detail:

We rumbled on our way to a raucous loudspeaker accompaniment. Chinese music is vigorous, strange and above all loud. The percussion is ear splitting. The eccentric modulations of the singer, the violent tattoos of the drummer were interspersed with cautions not to lean out the window, one person not to take the place of two, or two the space of three. There was the news, recent history of Formosa, and then there was that drummer!

The Chinese girl feeding her child next to me was unmoved by him. Her other girl of two tottered across and shook hands solemnly. Chinese children greet you everywhere with unsurpassed charm. By the age of four they project themselves at you—waist level. In a matter of moments one is festooned with little laughing faces like the fruits of persimmons on a tree. The hours and the flat countryside rolled by. The rice harvest was being beaten into tubs in the fields. The peanuts were being uprooted. The cotton collected in large baskets. A short violet dusk slipped down from the hills. We were beginning to climb.

People bundled themselves into the strange contortions of uncomfortable sleep. A group murmuring at a game of cards; a baby's cry; someone blundering to the lavatory broke the uneasy rest. The half erect figures twisted themselves into a different form. Outside, the sandy cliffs rising in terraces from little wheat sown valleys were punctured by caves cut into the vertical cleavage of the earth—the homes of the peasants who are richer now than they'd ever been before.[10]

This fascinating and also laborious journey was not motivated by Mathews's interest in contemporary art or in gauging the Chinese response to Soviet socialist realism. It was, as Edwin Pulleyblank would later explain, 'principally to gratify my antiquarian interest'[11] that he had persuaded the delegation's Chinese hosts to organize an excursion which was to prove, so Mathew noted as their train entered the T'ung Kuan valley, a 'journey back in time'. It hauled them back through the recently annulled past of corruption and 'squeeze', disease, famine, and war over which the hated Chiang Kai-shek had presided with the help of his Western allies, and into a far deeper past in which great dynasties had risen and fallen, leaving their relics buried in the ground on which 'New China' was now staking its claim.

Two thousand years ago, so Mathews learned from his admired and more learned Canadian companion, Shenshi province had been more prosperous than anywhere else in China. Sian stood in the place of the much larger city of Chang-an, which had, as Pulleyblank would also explain, been 'the capital of all China' in the former Han and Tang dynasties, which was to say 'the periods of its greatest imperial splendour'.[12] That city, however, had been sacked at the end of the Tang dynasty, and the present walled city of 'Sian', a name which means 'Western Peace', dated only from the Ming dynasty. It was a mere sixth of the size of its predecessor, which may have had 1 million inhabitants and, thanks to its place at the end of the Silk Road, had drawn 'merchants and ambassadors from all over Asia from Japan to Baghdad'.

According to Mathews they found Sian 'lying in rather drab rectangular sections on a large flat plain'. Visiting the North Western Historical Museum, which had, they were informed, only really been established in the last two years, he commended the archaeological research carried out since the liberation: 'A priority of first importance in these difficult times, under these hard conditions, has been to guard the heritage of the past.' Here in the domain of archaeology as also in science and engineering, they might have found ancient objects pressed into the 'brick'-like shape of official showmanship. The exhibits, however, proved truly astonishing. Mathews describes Edwin Pulleyblank 'genuflecting reverently before the massive carved stones of the Pei Lin 'Forest of Tablets', great steles carved with ancient poems and classical texts in the ninth century AD, many of them, as Mathews noted, mounted on the back of a giant tortoise. They saw 'well known treasures such as horses in high relief from the tomb of the Tang emperor T'ai-tsung', and many sculptures and pottery figurines unearthed in excavations connected to the ongoing building programme that would, so Pulleyblank was assured, eventually bring the city back to the size of ancient Ch'ang-an. Looking over these often recently recovered treasures, they saw great dynasties rise and fall, starting perhaps with the Ch'in empire, whose first emperor, Shih Huang-ti, introduced road systems and a unified currency, scripts, and weights and measures, and who also ordered the destruction of earlier records of Confucianism in order to project himself into posterity as the first emperor.

Standing in amazement before ancient 'stone carvings of great delicacy and grace', Mathews sensed 'a similar approach that we see perhaps in the archaic Greek just before the classical period'. The two men studied the casts of carvings that had been brought from Buddhist caves far away to the west. They also discussed the archaeological finds of the last few years, aware that 'scholars all over the world' were anxious to hear about them. Working in candlelight, Pulleyblank took the opportunity of that exceptional moment to search the steles for 'evidence of musical notation in the Tang period'.[13] Looming above the city, they saw the Drum Tower and Bell Tower, 'great wooden structures, gaily painted, dating from the Ming period', which had fallen into neglect but been 'magnificently restored'[14] since the Liberation: 'traditional carvings added, decoration carved out in meticulous detail'.

Mathews too was delighted to find the remote past being reinstated in this way. 'I arrived in Sian', he wrote, 'and history threw a glow onto the plain and the provincial town'. And yet he would not lose sight of the more recently degraded past from which 'New China' was struggling so heroically to emerge. He and Pulleyblank were put up in a brand new guest house, but the ordinary houses and shops of Sian 'told the same tale of neglect which you see all over China', as did the 'hard, back-breaking work' that surrounded the visitors both in the city and as they ventured out through the southern suburbs. They saw people driving pedicabs over wet and sticky mud roads, and toiling at treadles as they turned raw cotton into thread. They saw others sharing the condition of mules as they walked 'in closed circles to pump water into the fields', heaved immense loads past 'cave dwellings carved in the vertical sand cliffs' or ground corn in 'a hollow of the cliff face'.

The same combination of ancient and modern persisted beyond the walls of Sian. The two visitors were taken through the southern suburbs to visit the Great Falcon Pagoda, where, as Pulleyblank explained, 'the most famous of Chinese Buddhist pilgrims to India, Hsuan-tsang', had retired in AD 645, in order to translate the many sutras he had collected during the course of a recent journey. They were also driven out to the famous Huaqing Pool, a hot spring at Li-shan that had once been the resort of Tang emperors, and also Emperor Xuanzong's legendary courtesan Yang Guifec and where, as both Mathews and Pulleyblank repeated in their written accounts of the visit, Chang Hsüeh-liang had kidnapped Chiang Kai-shek, in the famous 'Sian Incident' of 1936.

While revering the relics of the ancient past alongside Pulley-blank, Mathews professed himself to be in no doubt that the developments of the last five years had already established the Liberation as 'a nodal point in Chinese history'. He saw new homes and gardens, new schools and universities, intended both for technical and cultural development, and, outside the town, a vast new textile factory built in accordance with China's first five-year plan, in which he gathered that 3,000 people worked to turn out 100,000 miles of cotton every year. In all, as Mathews wrote, it was a revelatory journey, in which the new and old combined to promise a brighter future: 'The journey to Sian gives me great hope', he wrote. The judgement would be repeated, and its lesson bluntly spelt out, in the Second Labour Delegation's report, 'It is a matter of great interest that in spite of their intense concentration on new development and construction, Chinese leaders and the people are also most actively concerned with preserving her past... This type of restoration has been in evidence everywhere we have gone in China. One may cite as further examples the Lama Temple in Peking, the Summer Palace and Buddhist temples in Hankow.'

They had, of course, come to see New China, but most of the visiting Britons, whether artistic or scientific, zealots or doubters, could not help but be touched by the relics of China's dynastic past—now, apparently, being brought under vigorous new management. The first B–CFA delegation, a collection of Communist sympathizers who visited China in 1951, had appreciated 'the many beautiful things left by the emperors'.[15] Led by the geologist Leonard Hawkes, the members of the cultural delegation of 1954 had also approved the resumption of archaeology in New China, and not just in those brick-shaped arguments about imperialist looting and the lost fossilized fragments of Peking Man ('Now stolen by the Americans', as J. D. Bernal repeated).

The report of the Second Labour Delegation went further in this direction, expressing 'great interest' in the regime's pursuit of archaeology and conservation, and welcoming the fact that, even in the rush to redevelop China, archaeological surveys were carried out on sites as they were cleared for new development. Such was the 'immense scale' of the ongoing construction work that China's twenty to thirty fully trained archaeologists 'had a hard time keeping up' with the pace of development. The 'quality and thoroughness' of their work had inevitably suffered, but a new course had been started at Peking University, which would help to train archaeologists for the future. Some areas, meanwhile, were more fully protected—including, as Professor Pulleyblank had been informed, parts of the Tang city of Ch'ang-an to the north of Sian, which was to be spared immediate redevelopment so that the rich archaeological finds anticipated could be reserved for 'more leisurely exploration'.[16]

There were two perspectives governing the presentation of the past as the foreign delegates saw it in New China, and they were not always easily reconciled. One defined the past as an evil to be swept away by traditional muscular methods if bulldozers, cranes, and scientific techniques were unavailable thanks to the American embargo. The other conceived it as an ancient inheritance to be secured in the present. Some of the more ardent foreign supporters of the Communist-led regime tended to be wary of conceding too much value to 'old' China. Cedric Dover, for example, would include a selection of Denis Mathews's photographs of ancient monuments into his special 'China' edition of *United Asia*, but not without making it quite clear in a cautionary caption that he himself believed 'the human achievements of the new China are so much more impressive'.[17]

For Rewi Alley, the resident New Zealander whose mind was every bit as polarized as that of the Red Dean of Canterbury, the quandary could only be dispatched by taking the side of the new. Standing in his room in a Peking hotel one day in March 1953, Alley had looked out, over a street that was busy with industrious people and rubber-wheeled carts, bicycles, and trucks, towards the wooded Coal Hill and 'the long sweep of gold-tiled roofs of the imperial palaces that stretch out from it'.[18] That, of course, would be preserved, but what about the block of old housing near the hotel, which was then being demolished to make way for a new building?

Though wary of anti-revolutionary sentimentality, Alley appears to have been saddened by the sight, for he allegorized his description in order to place the demolition on the side of history. The old beams of the wrecked building 'looked solid enough', as he put it, 'but as I watch one drops to the ground and simply disintegrates, its core being completely rotten'. If that revealing collapse was not enough to justify the tearing down of the old, Alley then looks on as an old lady, who is walking by on the arm of 'a tall young worker', sways on her bound feet as she views the destruction. 'She evidently has memories of former times', writes Alley, before concluding briskly: 'But the ancient building has had its day... In a few months' time a useful, brand-new modern building will stand where the old one stood. The local people will become completely accustomed to it, as they are accustomed to the new ones opposite our hotel built only last year, and the old will slip out of their memories.' Demolition, in other words, may be painful for those who remember, but it is also emblematic of the revolutionary change that is necessary if China is to emerge from 'the agony of the past century'.

This was one way of dismissing conservation as an indulgence of over-sensitive Westerners who cared more for old buildings than for the pressing needs of the people. Yet that crude choice was not accepted by some of the other travellers, including the angular Marxist physicist J. D. Bernal, who saw a lot of Alley during his stay in China and shared his view of many things.

Bernal understood that the renewal of China would entail many breaches with tradition. In his own field of expertise, he fully embraced the rhetoric of Before and After, believing that science should be harnessed as an engine of the planned future. Whether the subject was floods, pestilential diseases, or cement, the idea of the conquest of nature caused the Birkbeck professor no anxieties at all. And yet Bernal was concerned about how the reconstruction of China would effect the historical built environment.

He was, it is true, far from captivated by the imperial palaces—particularly the Summer Palace which he described as 'just a mounting set of horrors of bad taste'. He had been inclined to blame this on the empress dowager, until Rewi Alley explained that it was actually not entirely her fault. In Kuomintang days, officials had crammed the place with 'every bit of Chinese and foreign rubbish they could find, and the new regime had chosen not to alter it. So here it was to delight the visitors: the clocks disguised as battleships or light houses, the lampshades in various hideous coloured glass and all the other rubbish which even the multiple looters of Peking had not thought worthwhile to take away. One horror was piled on another.' The emperor's garden, meanwhile, was filled with 'any amount of nonsense, much of which had been brought from western countries, including some ridiculous miniature lamp-posts of the London type'.

Bernal had tired of the guided tours that led him and every other visitor through such absurd places but, like Mathews and others, he loved exploring the popular quarters of old Peking. In the evening of 1 October, after watching the great parade and then chewing his way through a solitary meal at his hotel, he ventured out into the hutongs, which he greatly appreciated as narrow and twisting alleys 'with one-storeyed grey-walled houses on each side, never any windows...All you see are doors, usually with a little stone ornament on each side of it, a door vermilion or black with a brass lion-headed knocker.' Stepping through one of these entrances, the visitor would be ushered into a series of courtyards with one-storey pavilions opening onto them. There may have been some shrubs and flowers in pots, but grass was 'discouraged because it is supposed to produce mosquitoes'. It was in one such courtyard house that he met up with Alan Winnington, Mike Shapiro, and other Communist expatriates. A celebration was under way, although not yet the one at which, so Winnington would later claim, the ginger beer was laced with vodka and 'Professor J. D. Bernal' learned to jive.[19]

The Titanic crystallographer also enjoyed some of Peking's privately operated traditional restaurants...Winnington declares that it was the done thing to take foreigners to eat Peking Duck at a famous restaurant called the Quan Ju De (Meeting of All Virtues).[20] Other possibilities included grilled mutton at the Kao Jou Chi,[21] and The Clay Saucepan which 'served only pork from the tip of the tail to the grunt'.[22] It remains unclear which of these establishments was also known as 'The Dump', mentioned in Bernal's drafted memoir. However, he does describe joining various fellow-travelling expatriates for 'a strange and rather nostalgic kind of evening' at an ancient establishment said once to have been frequented by moonlighting emperors, where the resident foreigners recreated their English background by singing English songs, and exchanged stories about the heroic old days of the Communist underground in pre-war Shanghai. Like the hutongs, these restaurants were an essential part of 'old Peking' and Bernal valued them greatly, along with many buildings that, as he also recognized, 'with the best will in the world it will be impossible to preserve, but should be recorded'.

This expert on Portland cement and prefabrication was troubled by the already gathering destruction of Peking, which Winnington too would come to see as an unnecessary disaster (after relocating to East Germany, the latter would later lament the demolition as if it were the consequence of China's abandonment of the correct path of loyalty to the USSR). On the way to the recently built Iron and Steel College, to the north of the city just past the Liang old town, Bernal saw an ancient wall, 'far the oldest in Peking', and regretted that it was 'being rapidly broken down and its material being used'.

He felt a larger pang of regret when he visited the Municipal Offices on 29 October. He had gone there to meet the gifted city architect, Liang Ssucheng, and to hear about the Peking plan. Fascinated as he had been by the hutongs, he accepted that the city could not possibly 'be allowed to go on as a collection of one-roomed shed and courts'. 'What they are proposing to do, and do gradually, is to weed it out, so to speak, leaving every historic temple and so forth, as well as all good and interesting houses, and setting them out in little parks by themselves. For the rest they are going to try and build buildings which are not skyscrapers, but will have to be more than the one storey insisted on by the Emperors.'

This sounded reasonable enough to Bernal, as did Liang's assurance that the future plan did not rely heavily on building 'inside the old city boundary'. He was pleased to hear that the railways, which were 'completely crazy, and designed mostly for security troop movement to protect the legations', would be wholly 'altered and taken out of the city altogether'. There would be a new residential area to the south-west, and industrial expansion to the east—a direction that suited the fact that the prevailing wind came from the west. Attended with the promise of new provision for culture and recreation, this left Bernal feeling pretty positive about the planned future of Peking.

There was, however, one consideration that kept nagging at the back of Bernal's mind. He was unable to establish whether the vast old city walls were to be retained. 'I was very much in favour of retaining them, but perhaps only for sentimental reasons. In fact I would rather like to restore them to their former glory by adding the little pavilions over each of the bastions. It must have made them one of the gayest and most exciting sights in the ancient world.' Hindsight suggests that Liang may silently have agreed with this assessment, but Bernal feared that New China's 'traffic designers are only too anxious to pull them down'.

It was the same in Hangchow, where Bernal was shown the West Lake. He was, of course, happy for this artificial sea to be dredged of the silt that, 'having been there for several hundred years, should provide an extremely rich source of nitrates and phosphates'. But it was the fate awaiting the trees that brought him up to the limit of his enthusiasm for New China. Informed that the authorities were planning to fell and replace the aged willows alongside the causeway, 'I said I would like to raise my voice against that'.

No consideration here for the emerging counter-claim—not just that traffic mattered, but that many of Europe's cities had once been walled too, or that the walls surrounding China's cities, towns, and villages were symbolic of an age of chaotic warfare that New China must overcome. As the pro-Communist artist and political journalist Jack Chen would write in his appreciative account of the revolutionary attempt to make a new 'garden city' out of the wrecked and pillaged town of Hsinteng in Chekiang province: 'The battlements of the old confining town walls have been pulled down so that the town seems to stand on a terrace. Their stones are used to build new houses.'[23]

21

Paul Hogarth's Sky Full of Diamonds

The line is English, the eyes, the restraint, the draftsmanship, the determined duty to his subject.

James Aldridge [1]

A man stands bolt upright, wearing a broadbrimmed straw hat and a tightly fastened jacket of indigo cotton. Identified only as a 'Shansi peasant', he stares back with an expression that could hardly be mistaken for a meek or even particularly friendly smile. His left arm is extended to grip a large six-pronged wooden hayfork—a primitive implement that may or may not be intended to defy America's export embargoes as it looms up beside his head.

The drawing (Plate 5), which avoids portraying its subject as exotically other, anthropologically quaint, or charitably abject, was made somewhere not far from the rapidly expanding city of Sian in the autumn of 1954. Created during an 'idyllic afternoon' spent wandering through villages 'built like medieval walled towns with gate towers and ramparts',[2] it is the work of Paul Hogarth, who used his charcoal crayon and a later application of colour wash to confirm that 'the Chinese people have now stood up'. Mao had proclaimed that momentous fact on 21 September 1949 in his opening address at the First Plenary Session of the Chinese People's Political Consultative Conference. The phrase 'China Stands Up' was taken as the title of the Common Programme adopted a few days later. It found echoes in 'The March of the Volunteers', the song chosen as the national anthem of New China, the chorus of which, 'Arise, Arise, Arise', was speedily adopted by many of the regime's international admirers too—although not by Hugh Casson, A. J. Ayer, or, for that matter, by Rex Warner who, so John Chinnery recalls, jokingly converted the frequently heard but, to him, incomprehensible Chinese refrain into a drinking song, 'Gin, gin, gin'.

The British Communist Arthur Clegg, who had visited China with a B–CFA delegation in the early summer of 1951, concluded a fiercely anti-American hymn of praise to the new regime by affirming that 'The people of China have most definitely stood up, and are continually awakening to life'.[3] The phrase became an instant chapter title in the books of New China's foreign admirers. Indeed, it served as the name of an entire enraptured book by R. K. Karanjia, an Indian journalist and editor who visited China as Deputy Leader of the first Indian Goodwill Mission in September/October 1951 and, having returned to Bombay, announced that the contrast between Old and New China had 'struck us like an apocalypse, something of a revelation'.[4] Mao's declaration impressed the partisans among New China's foreign residents too. Looking out of his room in the Peking Hotel in June 1952, Rewi Alley had watched a gang of labourers shifting bricks on a construction site opposite. To a less committed observer these toiling men may have looked more or less exactly as labourers had done before the Liberation, but Alley was in no doubt of the 'change in their very bearing. Waiting to cross the street tramway lines they stand erect and the leader, a magnificent bronzed figure of a man, stands in unconsciously heroic pose. I think that is the answer. They stand up.'[5]

Paul Hogarth also approved of this transformation, and by no means thanks only to the 'giant bearded Sikh' he befriended on the train to Hangchow, a highly knowledgeable man who for thirty years had lived in China as a guard at the Indian Consulate in Shanghai, and would only say of the Liberation that 'the Chinese could now lift up their heads'.[6] Admiration for the same revolutionary levitation is implicit in the proudly erect posture of his industrious Shansi peasant—a nameless fellow who, as Hogarth's later caption would reveal, had also risen to the position of 'village chairman'.[7] We know nothing else about this man, but we can be sure that he is not grovelling, or kow-towing, before anyone.

Comrade Winstanley and the Eunuchs of Bloomsbury

The viewer of Hogarth's *Shansi peasant* may well feel inclined to wonder about the reality 'behind' this flatly presented figure. In many of his Chinese portraits, Hogarth situates his subjects in their fields, factories, or building sites, granting the figure a place in an

attentively depicted wider reality. Although Hogarth also made a
drawing entitled *Shansi Village* (Plate 6), his more frequently reproduced *Shansi Peasant* has no more background than a shadow
puppet. His world is not shown and the graphic manoeuvres with
which Hogarth brings him forward as a representative of 'New
China' leave him standing in a field full of unanswered questions.
Who is this standing fellow with his by no means conventionally
'inscrutable' expression? And what course had he followed through
the land reform, recently declared completed, in which countless
hated landlords had been dragged into 'accusation meetings',
'struggled with', and, in many cases, killed—all in the cause that
one fiercely unapologetic propaganda book of the time named
'Extracting the Poisonous Shaft'.[8]

If Hogarth's drawing seems to confirm the official presentation
of 'New China' as a land of emphatically upright people who had
at last seized control of their own destiny, it may also be suspected
of drawing its subject into a different kind of illusion projected
from Hogarth's side of the image. The British habit of visiting
China only to encounter things that seemed oddly familiar was by
no means born of the 'Liberation' of 1949. Earlier travellers had
also made a sport of contriving far-fetched analogies to strike
sparks of contrast as well as unexpected likeness between English
and Chinese realities. A characteristically exotic example is to be
found in Osbert Sitwell's description of the months he spent in
Peking in 1934.

One afternoon, Sitwell and a friend who spoke some Chinese
had driven out into the dusty plain surrounding Peking. Their
destination was the Kang T'ieh Temple and Refuge of the Palace
Eunuchs, where they hoped to meet some of the doubly emascu-
lated creatures who had survived the abolition of their traditional
world by the new Republic of China (1911), and who lived on in
this isolated and rarely visited refuge. Having driven as far as the
roads allowed, they had parked their car and set off on foot,
walking over 'small, dry, rounded hills'[9] and through winds full of
stinging dust. The first building that loomed up in the 'thick
golden haze' turned out to be the Pa Pao Shan Golf Club, where
they were briskly assured by gin-drinking expatriates in plus fours
that that their universally respected member, General Cruikle-
bury, was nobody's Eunuch General.

After walking on, they came upon a group of low buildings among tall cedars and pines. Crossing a courtyard, they knocked at a door behind which they heard chatter and a clinking of tea-bowls. They were received by some fifteen elderly eunuchs gathered in a 'long, low hall'.[10] Raised in an unimaginably opulent world, these men were now reduced and poor. Dressed in stained gowns and forced to live by subsistence farming, they were unvisited and deprived even of the gossip that had once sustained them. Sitwell alleges that some of them were still groaning with pain from the terrible wounds that had launched them into service many decades previously. Their home, however, still reminded him of 'a Women's Club or Institute, in which only constant cups of "nice hot tea" could keep up the spirits of the members'. Eager to make the most of their unusual visitors, these 'last, lost refugees of a dead past',[11] enquired after the world outside. 'Did they drink tea in England?' they wondered. 'And were there still eunuchs in the Palace?' An Englishman who had visited these human ruins two years previously had informed them that the eunuchs of Buckingham Palace had recently been abolished, but that they still survived 'in...a difficult word for them...Bloomsbury. It was, he said, a refuge for eunuchs, like their own...How they longed to visit it, and see for themselves English ways of life.'

A less decadent clutch of scenic English analogies had crowded the mind of Joseph Needham in February 1943, when he first went to China to set up the Sino-British Science Cooperation Bureau. His friend the anthropologist Margaret Mead had asked him to record the impressions of his initial thirty-six hours, and he obligingly did so in a letter. Driving into Kunming from the airport, he notes the colour of the ground there: 'very nice yellow, warm like Cotswold stone'.[12] Entering the town, he saw paved roads with mostly earthen pavements, and two-storey houses: 'All faintly reminiscent of an English village street',[13] he suggested. Lodged at the consulate, he remarks: 'Weather almost exactly like Cambridge in Spring or autumn, and with innumerable rooks cawing, one might think oneself at Duxford vicarage if one closed one's eyes.'[14] He continues: 'Everything seems so strangely familiar (having thought so much about China for so long) yet like a dream...The Consulate and most of the houses I've seen are all slightly hick, reminding me of Ringstead Mill [a windmill near Hunstanton in Norfolk], as if one should have to live permanently in the depths of the country.'

The more or less stylish exploitation of such 'glimpses of familiarity' continued after the Liberation. Some of the English analogies applied to post-Liberation China were like many of their predecessors: trivial flourishes that enfolded otherness and similitude for the sake of a momentary effect. Others, however, now took on the heavier job of cutting through the bamboo curtain, rejecting polarization and insisting, convincingly or otherwise, that the 'New China' emerging on the far side was neither so completely 'other' nor so fully identified with the USSR as cold warriors in the West loudly assumed. 'It's the same in Marylebone High Street', wrote the veteran actor and dramatist Miles Malleson, of New China's admirably well-funded theatre and its admitted hunger for plays with a contemporary message.[15] A similarly unlikely analogy came to the mind of Basil Davidson, who was introduced to a Chinese group leader in her alley in the southern city of Canton, and insisted that the good lady was 'as much a spy on her fifty families as the chairman of my parish council, in rural Essex, is a spy on me'.[16]

In the commentary he eventually wrote to accompany his drawings of New China, Paul Hogarth himself played this game with some flair. He likened Hangchow to 'a South Coast English seaside resort whose better days lay at the beginning of the century'[17] and declared arriving in Shanghai to be 'like pulling into Manchester from Sheffield'. In Shenyang (Mukden) in Manchuria he found the industrial skyline 'reminiscent of the Midlands', while the hotel, which was actually packed with a raucous troupe of Bulgarians, recalled the gloomy 'Peabody buildings' to be found in British cities. The affable Rex Warner had reserved 'Wimbledon' for the British embassy compound in Peking, but Hogarth, who as a Communist could hardly be expected to enter that particular bastion of imperialism, was transported back to the same dreaded suburban milieu by the former British Concession in Canton, strategically placed on the offshore isle of Shameen, but now 'Alas' turned into 'a sort of park'.[18] Its hotels and clubs had become 'the haunts of exhausted delegations and foreign visitors' but they still had English water-closets bearing anachronistic 'coats of arms and Edwardian trade names'. Their English taps still creaked and dribbled, but it was the chimes of their clocks that finally picked up a horrified Paul Hogarth, already reduced to feeling as if he had somehow been trapped in the pages of 'old volumes of the *Illustrated London News*', and dumped him down in Wimbledon.

For many Britons in China during the first years of the revolution, this habit of striking more or less plausible comparisons between the two countries extended to political considerations too. Encountering the self-confident but not overbearing Miss Wang Mei, a head teacher in Canton, Basil Davidson thought that she had 'a great deal in common with our suffragettes of not so long ago'.[19] George Hardy, the British-born operative of Stalin's Communist International who returned to China with the first B–CFA delegation in 1952, gazed out over fiercely reformed fields and saw 'co-operative farmers learning in practice the principles of Britain's Robert Owen and the Rochdale Pioneers'.[20]

Hogarth's drawing of the Shansi peasant surely participates in a related Englishing of 'New China'. Avoiding all reference to Stalin's murderous collectivization of agriculture in the USSR, it evokes an earlier analogy that linked the agrarian reforms introduced under the Chinese revolution less to Owenite cooperators than to the demands made by the Diggers and Levellers of England's seventeenth-century civil war. The Diggers had long had an honoured place in the minds of English radicals. As an enemy of the 'Hireling Clergy' as well as of the enclosure of common land, Gerard Winstanley was among the past promoters of 'social reconstruction' commended in *The Ploughshare*, an anti-war magazine run by Quakers during the Great War.[21] The Communist historian A. L. Morton fêted him and his fellow Diggers in *The People's History of England* (1938) and again in *The English Utopia* of 1952. Hats, and perhaps also a few cloth caps, were doffed to Winstanley in *Music and the People*, a vast historical pageant written by the English Communists Randall Swingler (a writer who would later become something of a father figure to Paul Hogarth) and Alan Bush (composer), and first performed at the Royal Albert Hall on 1 April 1939. Twelve composers were involved, including Ralph Vaughan Williams, Elizabeth Lutyens, and Norman Demuth; and the vast cast included Paul Robeson, twenty-three London cooperative choirs, the Rhondda Unity Male Voice Choir, and a contingent of children from the Woodcraft Folk who performed a 'Stag Dance' in the interval before assorted 'Diggers' marched on stage singing Winstanley's *Stand Up Now.*[22]

Winstanley's inspiring example had also been remembered by Joseph Needham, who, in 1939, had interrupted his work as reader in Biochemistry at Cambridge to produce, for the Left Book Club, a short and pseudonymously published book entitled *The Levellers and the English Revolution*. Writing as Henry Holorenshaw, he celebrated the Diggers and Levellers as 'true-born Englishmen every one',[23] and commended them for standing well to the left of Cromwell's Parliamentary cause and demanding 'a much greater measure of economic equality, so that England could be a Commonwealth in reality as well as in name'.

Recovering this past struggle at the close of a decade torn between fascism and Communism, Needham praise the Diggers for proving that 'the ideals of Socialism and Communism are not, as so many people, think, something of foreign origin, French or Muscovite, alien to the genius of the English people'. He described how the Levellers had turned up with their spades at Cobham in Surrey, and started to 'dig up the common land near or on St. George's Hill with the intention of growing corn, roots, beans and other produce'. In their 'Large Declaration', issued under the signatures of Winstanley and Everard, they railed against the Norman Conquest, which had extinguished the liberties of the English people, and claimed God as their supporter in their determination to take land that was 'common and untilled' and 'to make it fruitful for the use of man'. They were radical English democrats, throwing off the yoke of feudalism and stepping up to the plate of history at a moment of transformation. Fired by the belief that the English revolution should not only grant freedom to the gentry and clergy, they had started digging at Cobham in order to create 'what we should now call a "collective farm"'.[24]

A Christian Socialist himself, Needham noted that, far from denouncing religion as the opium of the people, Winstanley had claimed Jesus Christ as 'the Head Leveller'.[25] He had also written about nature in a manner that reminded Needham of the great scientific movement of the seventeenth century, a connection that combined with an understanding of the class struggle and its driving role in history to give Winstanley's arguments 'an extremely modern ring'.[26] Needham invited English socialists to wake up to their own tradition, not least because they would then find it easier to outfox the anti-Communist propaganda imagery used against their cause: 'the Bolshevik with beard and bomb is a figure of straw invented and manipulated with much skill by the forces of reaction and privilege to terrify the simple-minded.' The pamphlet closed with an airy prophecy. 'And the day will come, when England is a Commonwealth again, when Thriplow Heath, Corkbush Fields, Burford Churchyard, and St. George's Hill at Cobham will see the sea-green ensigns once again afloat upon the wind.'[27]

A decade later, Needham would be convinced he had seen that violently suppressed English future winning through at last. The ensigns, however, were of scarlet silk and he was a world and at least two curtains away from Thriplow Heath. It was during the Korean War in 1952, the year of the germ warfare allegations, that Needham revealed his transported vision in a Foreword to his friend Rewi Alley's emphatically entitled book *Yo Banfa!* (*We Have a Way!*): 'The Resurgence of Asia. China's real Renaissance. The upsurge which has made the 500,000,000 black-haired people stand up and speak out. To democratic English ears the phrase, embodied in the national song of new China, echoes the song of the 17th century Levellers, "Ye Diggers all, Stand up now, Stand up now."'[28]

Needham's analogy had been reaffirmed a year later by Basil Davidson: 'I do not think that any Englishman', so he wrote, 'could look at the People's Liberation Army, as the army of New China is called, without groping in his mind towards Cromwell and the Roundheads. You cannot easily find your russet-coated captain in the People's Liberation Army, because this army has no badges of rank of any kind, but you can hardly prevent a strong sense of conviction that these soldiers know what they are fighting for, and love what they know.'[29] And now here was Paul Hogarth, standing in village or field in Shansi province, perhaps with the usual crowd of interested children, pedlars, muleteers, and barking dogs gathered around to observe and comment on his progress, using his crayon to confirm that China's long-suffering peasants knew what they were doing too.

Peking and the New Landscape

Hogarth's first impressions of Peking were mixed with a feeling of sheer relief at finally being able to unload his delegation of shop stewards and councillors into the care of their waiting interpreters and guides. The parting, however, was by no means as final as he would have liked. At the banquet provided to welcome them to New China, the nameless delegates got so 'pissed'—the word is Hogarth's own—that none was able to muster even a few words in reply to the welcoming speeches of their hosts, so Hogarth found himself having to perform that task for them too. Once that was done, however, he left them to their insularity, their ignorant jokes, and their timorous insistence on Western food, and stepped out to explore what post-war 'Reconstruction' might look like in this most legendary of Communist lands. As he wrote in his illustrated journal of the visit, it was immediately apparent to him that 'whatever Red China is or is not, it is a country which is undertaking an immense task of bringing benefit to the millions of its people; and doing it at the expense of the very few'. As he added of his determined attempt to look New China in the eye, 'I tried to capture something of it as I journeyed round.'[30]

Hogarth started by meeting his hosts at the Chinese Artists Union. Here, like Denis Mathews, he was introduced to Hua Junwu, 'a distinguished caricaturist and Yenan veteran'[31] with whom he discussed the excursions he would make into various parts of China over the following three months. The smiling Hua promised that he would be allowed to draw 'everything but military secrets'. He also provided an interpreter named Tu and, since New China hoped to learn from Western artists, also a 23-year-old 'apprentice' named Ho-i-min, a graduate of the Central Art Academy who would accompany him on his travels.

Hogarth spent his first days 'padding round the streets'[32] of the exuberant city that Peking turned out to be. He wandered through jostling bazaars and 'markets where flies no longer dared to live'. He reeled at the noise of the place and found himself recovering 'half-forgotten sensations of childhood' as he gazed into 'great bowls full of goldfish, fur hats and ear-cleaning outfits'. Like Denis Mathews and J. D. Bernal too, he was amazed by the street life and the popular energy it conveyed, and he soon set his crayon to work, capturing selected 'string-makers, potters and scribes' as they went about their work, and interspersing these portraits with sketches of the vast, teeming, and flag-dressed construction sites that reminded him of sets from 'some Cecil B. de Mille historical epic'. As was his way, he drew in the open, often surrounded by a crowd of 'three or four hundred children' who 'relentlessly' followed his every move.

Hogarth may have brought his own conté and graphite crayons, a lifetime's supply of which had been presented to him the previous year at the newly nationalized Hardtmuth pencil factory in Czechoslovakia.[33] Paper, however, was another matter, as he discovered when Ho took him to the Lui Li Chang, a street devoted to the sale of antiques and artists' materials. Here he quickly decided to replace the cartridge paper he had brought from England with large sheets of fine bamboo paper, much of it 'exquisitely coloured with vegetable dyes'. When I met him nearly half a century later, he could still produce the ragged remains of the large portfolio a Peking craftsman had made for him out of confiscated American canvas, and which had also accompanied him on his travels around China.

Tu and Ho guided their resolute English guest on his excursions into different regions of China. They went to Shenyang (Mukden) in Manchuria, where Hogarth drew the rampant industrialization that people would never have associated with China in the past. Like Attlee and Bevan before him, he found a land of smoke and booming construction sites adorned with red silk banners, of literate and skilled workers who had been 'raw young peasants' only a few years ago, and who now stood at the heart of a 'fundamental transformation of China's economy'.[34] Visiting the pulsating 'beehive' that was the Number One Machine Building Factory, he singled out a 19-year-old woman turner named Kuang So-yen, who explained, while he drew her, how women now received the same opportunities and also the same rights and pay as men. She had learned to read and write at the factory's cultural club, and she was a member of the dance ensemble too. At the School of Art, he watched as students gathered under red flags to form a volunteer work brigade and spend their Saturday afternoon levelling a stretch of waste land to make a park.

At Anshan, he went to work in the Soviet-built iron and steel works, portraying various scenes in the Automatic Rolling Mill, the Rail Shop, and at the blast furnaces. In the commentary he wrote at the time, he gave no anticipation of his later confession that his drawing of an 'Anshan Steelworker' showed a stock hero who had been lined up for him by vigilant minders. He did, however, admit that to draw in such busy factories and industrial plants was 'an exacting task', in which the artist had to abandon any idea he may have had of playing 'the detached observer'.[35] To draw from life in such situations was, he explained, like being 'a film producer': it entailed seeing past the 'eager official' who was trying to 'tell you all', selecting your subjects, and then taking steps to extract them from their work routines and put them at ease so that their 'true qualities can be observed in the little time there inevitably is'. The background, meanwhile, was constantly changing, making it quite impossible to be 'literal even if this was desirable; the artist has to interpret by extracting the relevant and the significant in the scene which he is a part of for so short a time'.

After Anshan, Hogarth was conveyed to Fushun where he drew 'the world's largest open-cast coal-mine'[36] and, no doubt like many other Western visitors, heard the story of its transformation from an old miner who remembered how dreadful life had been when the mine was under Japanese rule. Counting up the new schools, literacy classes, and hospitals, this fellow dutifully declared that the liberation was 'like the day is to the night'. In 2001, Hogarth would remember what he had see of industrial Manchuria as proof that China was already embarked on the wrong route.[37] At the time, however, he described that industrialization as 'not debauching in its effects', and approved the government's declared aim of hauling China 'out of the Middle Ages in as short a time as possible'. Had he seen the slogan, 'Throw off nature's insolent yoke', said to have been among those displayed at the time of the Liberation, the young Hogarth would surely have nodded in approval.

Not long after returning to Peking from Manchuria, Hogarth packed his crayons again for a short train excursion in which he followed the delegates' well-beaten track to both the Kwantung Dam and the Great Wall. Shortly afterwards, he boarded a train for a longer visit to the north-west, in the course of which he too would find Sian to be a city of astonishing contrasts, where vast new factories loomed up under 'great webs of scaffolding', and barbers 'plied their shears' in the shadow of mud-baked city walls, while a new university quarter mushroomed on the other side.[38]

Travelling out, they came to the walled villages near which the 'Shansi peasant' was discovered, together with itinerant pedlars who carried great bundles on shoulder poles as they walked from one village to the next. Outside the mountain spa of Hua Ching Chi, they pulled up at an ancient Buddhist monastery, where 'gargantuan' monks 'lived as though it was the seventh century, and only the slogan "Long Live Peace" whitewashed on the walls outside gave the whole thing away'.[39]

From Sian, Hogarth travelled south. At Chungking he examined the ongoing reconstruction but found himself, like Denis Mathews, gravitating to 'the sublime spectacle of the waterfront',[40] where he saw 'the age-long backwardness that Asia is only just beginning to throw off'. At Hangchow, he visited a model tea-growing co-opera-tive, and also the enormous Buddhist temple of Lingyin. In Shanghai, where he stayed high up in the King Kong Hotel, formally the famous Cathay Hotel, he approved of the new life that thronged around 'the silent tomb-like foreign-built banks and commercial buildings'.[41] For Hogarth as for other delegates, Hankow was largely about the heroically constructed dikes with which the people, earlier that summer, had saved the three cities of Wuhan from floods. Near Canton, on the Pearl River, he and his attendants tasted 'extraordinary' citrus fruits while brushing off 'enormous wasps that hovered about like helicopters in the Garden of the Hesperides',[42] and strolled through 'great groves of bananas and pineapples feeling like Lilliputians in some tropical paradise'.

In the 'Author's Preface' to *Looking at China*, Hogarth introduces the drawings he made in the course of these excursions by suggesting that he had all the time been working in 'an English tradition' of travelling and recording: one that is at heart 'a tradi-tion of regard and warmth for the common man'.[43] His pursuit of this goal in 'New China' sometimes demanded manoeuvres of a kind that were hardly available to his claimed Victorian precur-sors. Edward Lear may have carried a pocketful of stones with which to repel dogs during his sketching tour of Macedonia in 1848,[44] but Hogarth was more likely to be troubled by swarming representatives of the 'common man' himself. On one occasion, when he had resolved to draw an ancient and ornately decorated tea-house in the southern city of Canton, Hogarth 'took up a position behind the front window of a book shop' opposite, but his view was soon obscured by smiling faces pressed up against the window. Interpreter Tu tried to disperse them, but his attempts only swelled the crowd of interested observers, who soon advanced into the shop, forcing Hogarth's retreat to an upstairs window (Fig 4). By this time the whole street was alive with clamouring spectators, and people were also leaning out of the tea-house windows to stare back at the artist. His view interrupted, Hogarth had little choice but to withdraw for a lunch of baked carp and doves' eggs.[45] He managed to complete the drawing in the afternoon, but only after arrangements were made to hide him, not in a car of the kind in which a visiting Soviet artist—Stalin's long-favoured Alexander Gerasimov—had quickly been detected, but in a covered truck borrowed from 'a local military unit'.

Some of Hogarth's drawings present the official story of New China's ascent and ongoing reconstruction, including his sketch of the vast parade of 1 October as seen from the viewing stand by Tiananmen Gate (he later recalled not just that he had to get special permission to make this work (Fig 34), but also that he could only get out his paper and crayon after the military display was over and the square was dominated by the people's parade, with the banners and flags he duly portrayed).[46] In many of his drawings he serves as the respectful 'artist-reporter' recording the heroism of the people as they struggle to lift their reforming country out of the chaos of its recent past. Just as he had earlier done in the post-war European states, Hogarth drew what he was shown: the vast building sites, new bridges and dams like the one at Kwantung north of Peking, great industrial sites, and cooperative farms too. Whether or not these drawings achieve the new sense of figuration sought by the 'social realists' championed by John Berger at home, they are often skilfully realized works which successfully avoid naturalistic scene-building of the kind associated with Russian Socialist Realism. One of his most dramatically achieved drawings uses a few strokes to conjure a solitary Chinese

Fig 49. Paul Hogarth, Voluntary Work Brigade.

Fig 50. Paul Hogarth, In the Summer Palace.

Fig 51. Paul Hogarth, 'Culture for the People', opera audience at the Chungking People's Palace of Culture.

Fig 52. Paul Hogarth, Landlord.

Fig 53. Paul Hogarth, Peking clerk.

Fig 54. Paul Hogarth, Woman director of lace-making co-operative.

Fig 55. Paul Hogarth, Rice Fields in Szechwan.

Fig 56. Paul Hogarth, Banana workers.

Fig 57. Paul Hogarth, The Great Wall.

peasant driving off into the future with a red flag waving from his cart (Frontispiece). Others show people combined in densely knotted collective configurations as they come together in their labours—clustering around a rope as they heave a junk across fierce currents where the Yangtze and Kialang rivers meet (Plate 9), or building emblematic works such as the all important dykes that, earlier in the year, had saved Hankow from terrible floods and the new steel bridge over the Han river in the same city. These drawings are indeed celebratory, and all the more effective because their line is both curious and assertive, by no means confined to cartooning in the service of what Attlee had described as 'hardshell'[47] Communist dogma.

As in his previous travels, Hogarth also made many portraits of representative individuals. Two years earlier, he had singled out famous figures such as Madam Sun Yat-sen as she appeared along-side Jean Paul Sartre and others at the Soviet-backed Vienna Peace Congress of 1952, but in China as in Poland he chose to portray examples of 'the common man' and sometimes also woman. In this respect, Hogarth passed the test failed by the British sculptress Clare Sheridan when, to the embarrassment of her uncle Winston Churchill, she visited Soviet Russia in 1920 with the intention of making busts of the leading Bolsheviks. She had been roundly told off by Angelica Balabanova, the increasingly disillusioned former secretary of the Communist International, who informed this idiotic visitor that, rather than helping to make cult figures of the leadership, she would do better making sculptures of representative workers, and especially the long-suffering women, without whom the revolution meant nothing.[48]

It is also to Hogarth's credit that the portraits gathered in *Looking at China* try not to leave their subjects merely as abstract stereotypes, or the human 'bricks' of an abjectly celebrated governing regime. Although they may indeed have been selected as stock types, they are portrayed in their individuality and not always confined to their places of work either. Besides the later disowned Anshan Steelworker, his subjects included the elderly Fushun Miner who recalled the brutality of the Japanese, and 'the old revolutionary', Huang Yeng, a veteran of the Canton Commune (which had been violently suppressed under Chaing Kai-shek in 1927), who had also served as a seamen in British Army transports during the Great War, and who suddenly broke the silence by asking, in remembered sailor's English, 'Ow are yew today?'[49] There is also a thoughtful-looking Peking office worker (Fig 53), a 'gargantuan' Buddhist monk in Shensi, a worker in a banana plantation in the south (Fig 56), a stonemason in Szechuan, a schoolgirl in Canton. No minder would have objected to Hogarth's drawing of 'Miss Wang-yang', a former leader of an underground women's organization, who was now director of a lace-making cooperative in Peking (Fig 54). In Shansi province, and despite the misgivings of interpreter Tu, Hogarth drew a former landlord, a still proud-looking man who now survived as a working farmer whose estate had been reduced to the allotted one third of an acre for each member of his family (Fig 52). In many cases, he spoke to his subjects through his interpreter as he drew them. Indeed, in his journal he would sometimes tell their stories, to the extent that he had been able to glean them through his interpreter, emphasizing their struggles and suffering, their heroic determination to climb out of the slough of despond that was China's recent past.

When, in 2001, I asked Hogarth what China had meant to him as an artist, he remarked 'I found it a country that was completely different to any of the socialist countries I had visited. It was a complete breakthrough stylistically.' When asked how this breakthrough was manifest in his drawings, he did not refer to his portraits or his pictorial 'reportage' of New China's industrious works of reconstruction. 'It gave me a subject matter I thought I'd never see in those days ... It released in me the landscape painter.' Hogarth's Chinese landscapes do indeed feel wider and freer than his drawings of building sites, mills, and smoking factories. A remote Honan village crouches, as pictured villages tend to do all over the world, among trees and hills. The Great Wall reaches out and upwards from behind the slogans draped over its first few yards. A wooded park rises to a many-staged Pagoda in Hankow, and further closely observed trees line a remote country road near Sian, revealed to be the habitat of apparently un-Communist chickens as well as a thoroughfare for mules and carts. Hogarth also used his crayon to conjure up vast stretches of water with a few brilliantly spaced strokes. One of his more maritime drawings casts a wide prospect over the Yangtze and Kialang rivers as they meet at Chungking, while another, perhaps seen from his hotel room, sweeps over the once imperialist river front of Shanghai before spreading out to capture a great expanse of water crowded with junks and sampans. At Hankow the view from the shore belongs to the cormorant fishermen, shown with their birds roosting 'like chickens' on the bows of their tiny boats.

Sometimes Hogarth would plant his Chinese landscape with industrious citizens, sewing rice in a paddyfield or kneeling in slowly advancing rows to weed spinach in a wide cooperative field. In some drawings he seems even to bring this newly discovered sense of space indoors, finding landscapes in the interiors of various houses, or even in the ferocious sword-brandishing southern Heavenly King looming over no longer frightened visitors in the Hall of the Heavenly Kings in the Buddhist Lingyin temple at Hangchow.

Some of these landscapes may certainly be counted among Hogarth's finest drawings of China, yet we should not necessarily assume that these skilfully rendered views show the artist escaping his political harness. His apparently neutral drawings of landscapes and historical buildings in Greece and Poland had been exhibited as indicating the national strength and legitimacy of the Communist movement in both countries. And before judging Hogarth's Chinese landscapes innocent of partisan Cold War politics, we should remember the arguments of the French anti-Stalinist leftist Boris Souvarine. Writing in 1929, he fiercely condemned the Western fellow-travellers who went to the USSR and came back hymning the natural beauties of Georgia, or ancient historical buildings such as the Kremlin itself, as if these, like the Moscow ballet and the sun that sometimes shone over the Volga, were to be placed to the credit of Stalin's emerging regime.[50]

On Temples and Popular Culture

Speaking in November 2001, Paul Hogarth recalled that the achievements of New China had seemed impressive even allowing for the fact that the foreigners who went in 1954 had all been invited in the expectation that they would write 'a favourable report'. 'As far as anyone could see, it was going very well. It was in its pure phase. There had been a big change and they hadn't yet blotted their record. The past was still there. That was what impressed Spencer and me and Denis.'

Hogarth was engrossed by old China as well as new, and yet the 'diary' printed alongside his drawings betrays no trace of preservationist anxiety of the kind shown by Casson and also J. D. Bernal. Just as, in his book of drawings in Greece, he had shown the familiar tourists' view from the Parthenon in order then to go 'behind' it and reveal the true Greece of the American-backed military dictatorship, he opens the Chinese chapters of *Looking at China* with a drawing of the Coal Hill (Plate 7). This wooded and temple-clad artificial mound had been a legendary feature of imperial Peking since the days of Marco Polo, but Hogarth's drawing makes no attempt to escape into the dynastic past. It shows the Coal Hill as seen from a considerable distance, hemmed in by vast construction sites, its pagodas dwarfed by towering cranes adorned with red flags, and further challenged by telegraph wires and their supporting poles. The untidy 'wirescape' that troubled Casson as an unwelcome imposition is, in Hogarth's drawing, simply part of the transforming scene. As for the Summer Palace, one of the most widely reproduced of Hogarth's Peking drawings (Fig 50) shows a group of 'citizens' enjoying that popular amenity, which had, as his caption explained, been 'open to the public since 1949'.[51] He himself, however, dismissed 'the Hampton Court of Peking' as a site that 'looked too Chinese to be real...It was all like some extraordinary Butlin Camp to which you had been invited on opening day.'[52]

The Chinese traditions that most interested Hogarth had little to do with the newly accessible imperial palaces and gardens, but were instead embodied by the vibrant popular culture to be found in the markets and streets. Like the other visitors, Hogarth was guided around the Temple of Heaven, but it was the nearby fair that really excited him. It was, he wrote, like 'some vast Breughel come to life. Amongst the workshops of tinkers, gilders, wood-carvers, cobblers and blacksmiths and the wheel-carts stuffed with sweetmeats and vegetables, lay one of the most fascinating sights I have seen.'[53] He had entered the Tien Shiao, which he described as 'three square miles of popular life such as one saw on early English broadsheets'. Hogarth surveyed it with amazement.

'Past the tables of scribes and the stoves of chestnut-sellers were crowded tents in which audiences solemnly watched swords and fire swallowed like hors d'oeuvres; ancient ballads were recounted to the accompaniment of two-stringed fiddles and clashing cymbals. There were jugglers, conjurors, comedians and mountebanks. All the intensely colourful popular culture of China, unchanged for centuries and fascinating to Westerners for the very reason that it still existed in the twentieth century.' Hogarth was doubly impressed when informed that the continued existence of Tien Shiao was down to a new accommodation reached between the city authorities and the acrobats, story-tellers, players, and musicians themselves. Having long been 'vagrants', condemned to travelling around China from one end of the year to the next, they had 'at last stood their ground and organized themselves'. Whilst maintaining their pitches here, they now also performed at 'factory cultural clubs and theatres'. Hogarth was informed that 'an entire State ensemble' had been raised from among these no longer strolling players, and that several of them had won the award of 'Honoured People's Artist'.[54]

Hogarth was fascinated by the ongoing popularity of China's traditional art forms. In Sian he found theatres that 'pulsated with Chinese opera' and, in their vitality, reminded him of 'the Globe at Southwark'. It was here, in Shensi province, that he saw his first 'enchanting' shadow-play. The music and movement seemed 'similar to the classical Chinese Opera', and the dialogue was delivered by 'a male singer who renders all the various roles with not a little ventriloquy'.[55] The artfully manipulated figures were 'fashioned from translucent fish-bones, exquisitely coloured and jointed with wires'. The play was apparently 'a rather complicated court drama', but Hogarth was far too fascinated by the technique to keep up with the plot. It was followed by a puppet play in which the legendary Monkey King 'wanted to "borrow" a magic fan' from a princess in order to extinguish a volcano threatening the province. This too impressed Hogarth as a work of great pace, with 'elaborate fighting-scenes and vigorous musical accompaniment'.

Meanwhile, traditional story-tellers could be found performing at fairs and in villages and market-places throughout China's interior. These raconteurs dramatized their tales and 'ancient legends' with the help of clap-sticks and often also a child who, as the story unfolded, would 'turn over the heavy pages of a volume of coloured prints mounted on an easel'. Hogarth was inspired to discover that China's popular art forms had themselves become 'mass media' and 'were more than [holding] their own with the cinema as a means of information and entertainment'.[56]

One Sunday morning in Chungking, he visited a 'quiet court-yard' that turned out to be a busy cultural centre: 'for sixpence you could take in the latest antics of the Monkey King whilst sipping tea and chewing melon seeds. Workers with their families strolled about, looking at a small exhibition of woodcuts under a bamboo veranda. Around the courtyard, although you would not have realised it, were small theatres which played Peking and Szechuan opera, music-hall and shadow plays.'[57] In one of these, a local opera was being performed for 'an appreciative audience of dockers and steelworkers'. Surveying the crowd, Hogarth recognized many of the faces he had earlier seen while making drawings on the waterfront.[58]

In Shanghai, he was pleased to discover that the race track had been turned into a park, and also that 'huge popular cultural centres' had been established in former department stores. He counted 'seven such Palaces of Culture, each as big as Selfridges', and they contained libraries, exhibition halls, theatres, and reading rooms too. They were managed by a trade union committee, which also oversaw a total of 500 cultural clubs attached to the city's facto-ries. In one of these halls, he looked around an amateur art exhi-bition. Many of the woodcuts and cartoons had been produced by factory workers, originally for 'wall-newspapers' in their work-places. They were 'crude', as Hogarth admitted, but they also 'did a job a professional artist could not do'.[59]

Watching an artist taking a party of 'keenly interested' indus-trial workers around an exhibition of his work, Hogarth concluded that New China's artists really could claim to be 'working for the people'. It compared rather painfully to the situation in Britain and the failure to sustain the spirit of common purpose that had attended the wartime activity of the Council for the Encourage-ment of Music and the Arts: 'It was the sort of interest that one remembered had existed in Britain during and immediately after the war, when the CEMA art-shows were shown in libraries, elec-tricity showrooms and factory canteens. The creation of a popular audience, hungry for a share of the enjoyment of a living accessible culture, brought about a breakdown of the old barriers—the barriers between people and artist, spectator and performer. For a few years art was integrated into the life of the nation as a whole. We have lost that integration in Britain through no fault of the artist, and I found it inspiring to see it again in China.'[60]

New China's artists did not seek autonomous expression or art for its own sake. Nor did they pursue liberal ideas of aesthetic distinction of the kind espoused by Britain's BBC, with its top-down mission to inform, educate, and entertain, or by the Arts Council with its habit of beaming already-made Henry Moore sculptures into public spaces used by people who refused in such large numbers to visit public art galleries. As Hogarth saw it, the best of New China's artists worked with this vibrant popular culture, and sought to articulate and assist its progress. Their model had been provided by the Communist Eighth Route Army, which, long before the Liberation of 1949, had enlisted traditional story-telling to their cause. They had added musical accompaniment and coloured film-strips, which soon rivalled the traditional album in popularity. They had encouraged writers to produce new scripts, including 'new or revised versions of traditional stories of rebellions against feudal tyrants',[61] telling the story of Marx, Mao, or Lenin and the life stories of brave patriots who outwitted the Japanese or the Kuomintang. Many of the performances, which now also took place in more formal settings such as village halls and schools, dealt with officially current topics such as land reform, popular science, and hygiene. The performances were watched in 'breathless silence' although emotion might be expressed during 'news' items. Hogarth was pleased to see this happening during the course of 'an alter-nating display in which Chou En-lai argues with Dulles; the relevant dialogue is spoken by a commentator and both characters render stereotyped facial expressions of anger, strength and frustration. The cartoons are brightly coloured; the commentary is punctuated with shrill passages from the *erh-hu*, a two-stringed fiddle.'

English Realism?

New China's visual artists had embarked on a comparable march, driven forward by Mao's injunction that they should be trying not 'to raise the people to the old cultural level of the feudal classes but rather to elevate them in the direction in which they were already travelling'.[62] Hogarth had started to investigate the art of New China during his first days in Peking. Yu Feng of the Union of Artists, had taken him to the National Exhibition of Graphic Art in the Imperial Palace, where most of the artists represented seemed to be working in 'a Western idiom blended with the decorative forms of Chinese paper-cuts and folk-art'. The subjects were drawn from everyday life, and they reminded Hogarth of nineteenth-century English images of the industrial revolution. Though many of the works on display seemed 'vigorous and useful', Hogarth noted that they 'retained little of the urgent realism of the revolutionary woodcuts of the 1930s'.[63] When he expressed surprise that 'very few of the original Yenan wood-engravers were represented', he was informed that, since 1949, most of these veterans 'had been engaged on administrative tasks related to the establishment of art publishing houses, new museums and art schools', and that they were only now returning to their creative art.

That evening Hogarth continued the discussion with the draughtsman and illustrator Shao Yu, director of the People's Art Publishing House, and also Yuan Han, 'one of the most outstanding of the Yenan wood-engravers'.[64] Yuan showed Hogarth a selection of his prints from the 1930s to the present day. Recognizing some of the prints that 'had conveyed the very substance of an incredible revolutionary moment to the Western world', Hogarth politely observed that he found the prints from after 1948 less interesting. Yuan replied that the present task of 'peace and reconstruction' demanded a different approach than had the war pursued by the Communist armies in the north-west.

The modern Chinese woodcut had emerged as part of a 'militant, partisan art' in a revolutionary situation, and the artists responsible for its development had been 'intimately in touch with the life of the Border Regions'. It was 'by no means so easy' for artists now to keep in touch with 'the widening range of the country's new life'. New subject matters generated greater aesthetic interest than could easily be satisfied by China's trained artists who, like the scientists encountered by J. D. Bernal, found themselves in very short supply and faced with a 'greatly increased demand' for their work. Huan explained that young artists were increasingly portraying realities of which they themselves had no direct experience, and that many were exhibiting and publishing work while they were still art students. If the modern woodcut techniques and imagery pioneered in Yenan were losing their currency, Hogarth suspected this was also because 'the initiative had passed into the hands of those artists who had received a traditionally Chinese training because their art of large scroll-paintings fitted into the monumental demands of the numerous new buildings that were going up throughout the country'.[65]

Pleased to discover that some Chinese artists were still working in the traditional style associated with the venerable Ch'i Pai-shih (Qi Baishi), Hogarth was less impressed by the main source of international inspiration reflected in much of the work he saw. Among the exhibitions in Peking, as he remembered, was a show of art from the Soviet Union, which he remembered as 'not so good'. He was concerned because a nucleus of Chinese artists, including Ho's wife, were undergoing, or had recently completed, training in Soviet techniques of socialist realism in Moscow and Stalingrad. For Hogarth, who was committed to developing a very different practice of 'social realism', the Soviet example being thrust on New China's artists could only bog them down by detouring them into the fusty styles of nineteenth-century naturalism.

It was a problem that Hogarth, like Denis Mathews, would attack with some vigour during the course of his travels. Talking about the advantages of East–West exchange during their three-day-long train journey from Peking to Sian, Hogarth told Ho that, while he was happy with the socialist country's 'ambitious plans to re-establish the Fine Arts as an integral part of human society and on a monumental scale', he did not believe 'a Western-style Chinese art' could satisfactorily develop under the influence of Soviet Russian examples alone. For Hogarth, the key point was that the Soviet model of Socialist Realism, with its roots in nineteenth-century academic tradition, should emphatically not be adopted as the only, or even the primary model by artists in New China: 'I had said that a Western-style Chinese art could not satisfactorily develop on the foundations of Russian and Soviet art *alone*.' Recognizing that China's artists and historians had not, for various reasons, 'been able to freely commune with Western Europe as a means of studying the infinitely richer traditions of Western European art', Hogarth argued for a much wider cross-fertilization, but accepted that 'this was difficult in a divided world'. The desirability, even the necessity, of that exchange was 'readily admitted', but 'what western countries were well-disposed enough to make this possible? Ho had me there.'[66]

Hogarth would continue this conversation with other artists as he met them in various cities. In Canton (also visited by a touring show of Soviet art), he pursued it with Huang Sin-pu and Huang Pot-wei. And when he returned to Peking, he would share his concerns with the Chilean painter José Venturelli, a friend and illustrator of Pablo Neruda's, who was living in Peking as a political exile, and who introduced Hogarth to a Chinese printer in whose tiny workshop he went on to make some lithographs.

It was, however, in Shanghai that Hogarth made the discovery that seemed to clinch his case for a wider international exchange between China and the West on artistic matters. It also suggested that the kinship between China and England need not just be a matter of straining to detect an echo of the Diggers and Levellers in the anthems of the newly upright 'tillers' of New China's soil. Among the sights offered to culturally minded foreign visitors in this city was the house of the writer Lu Hsun, off the Shanyin Road. A well-known author and co-founder of the League of Left-Wing Writers, Lu Hsun was by 1954 installed in New China's memory as one of the great heroes of the revolutionary movement of the 1920s and 1930s. The museum that had recently been made of his house would not impress all British visitors that year. Hugh Casson, who himself considered it no more faked up than Ann Hathaway's cottage in Stratford, records that A. J. Ayer was dismayed by 'this piece of hagiography where not only the books and furnishings but the yellowing cigarette holder, the balding hair brush, the stomach pills and the plaster death mask of the writer (sprouting "genuine moustache hairs") are preserved with solemn care'.[67]

Paul Hogarth was not to be distracted by such purely personal relics either. He knew about Lu Hsun, perhaps partly through the account of Agnes Smedley, who had befriended the Chinese writer in the 1930s, and gone on to describe how many of his students had been harassed and murdered by nationalist 'blue

Lu Hsun's Bedroom –
Shanghai.

Fig 58. Hugh Casson, Lu Hsun's living room, Shanghai 1954.

shirts' who hadn't dared to finish off the famous writer himself (Lu Hsun died of natural causes in 1936).[68] What really fascinated Hogarth about Lu Hsun, however, was less to do with his writing than with the fact that he had also turned his house into 'a laboratory of an art which expressed the values and ideals of the Chinese revolutionary movement'.[69]

More specifically, Hogarth was interested to know more about the sources of the simple woodcut technique that Lu Hsun had famously introduced to China in the late 1920s, seeing it as particularly appropriate to the Chinese struggle. Now commemorated as the earliest organization of graphic artists in China, Lu's Chinese Woodcut Association had, after no more than a week, been forced to disband as a 'subversive centre', but various of Lu

Hsun's followers had taken their knowledge of the new technique to Yenan in the north-west, and used it to produce a new kind of propagandistic art capable of rallying the illiterate masses to the growing Communist cause in the wars against both Chiang Kai-shek's Kuomintang and the Japanese. It was this art—engaged, reproducible, and directly connected to the experience of its intended audience—that Hogarth, like Mathews, Bernal, and others, had liked so much more than recent Soviet-inspired versions of socialist realism, and he was interested to learn more of its origin.

Some, including Hogarth's friend Jack Chen, would assume that, in creating this 'vigorous school of modern graphic art', Lu Hsun had drawn wholly on 'the traditional art of the people'.[70] Hogarth, however, learned from the new museum that the Shanghai writer had been a man of altogether more cosmopolitan interests, who had collected works by the Belgian Frans Masereel, the Soviet artist Kravchenko, and, a favourite of Hogarth's own, Käthe Kollwitz from Germany. Indeed, as he looked through the folios and anthologies preserved in the Lu Hsun

Fig 59. Jack Chen and Paul Hogarth, China 1954 (photo: Cedric Dover).

museum, he was intrigued to find works by various English artists too: Robert Gibbings, Stephen Bone, Edward Bawden, David Low, Eric Dalglish, and Gwen Raverat among them.[71]

In their subjects, the woodcuts made by Lu Hsun's followers in Yenan have little if anything in common with the pastoral outlook of Bawden, Gibbings, and Raverat, who could never be accused of having produced 'a dramatic record of the savage nature of the political struggles' in Shanghai or, for that matter, in Cambridge or north Essex, where both Bawden and Hogarth himself were then living. And yet surviving members of Lu Hsun's Woodcut Study Association had taken the techniques they had learned partly from the example of these European artists when they escaped to join the Communist forces in Yenan in the north-west. In 1938, they had founded a Lu Hsun Academy of Art at Yenan, and also a Woodcut Artists' Group whose members 'joined guerrilla units in the Japanese rear'.[72] These innovators had gone on to develop their own bluntly revolutionary and nationalist themes. They had also studied the Chinese graphic tradition as they set out to make their prints more appropriate to their intended audience. Hogarth, however, delighted in the thought that the new revolutionary art of China shared its technique with Gwen Raverat's leafy glimpses of the river Cam. Though nothing to do with anybody's idea of 'social' or 'socialist' realism, this unexpected line of descent nevertheless proved Hogarth's point as he carried on arguing for 'the increased vitality that can be given to art through judicious cross-fertilisation'.[73]

22

Stanley Spencer's English Takeaway

> When I contemplate what the time of one whole day may
> reveal to me, I am filled with the romance of adventure.
> I am Treasure Island...the most unexpected thing I ever
> came across was myself.[1]

To call Stanley Spencer a solipsist would be greatly to underestimate his self-absorption, which embraced so much of the world that he stepped into China like a vagrant prophet astonished to find himself suddenly at home.

In a note written some twenty years before his visit, Spencer had recorded his desire to write the story of his life as if it were a wandering existence, both physical and mental, like 'a journey from here to China' in which everything was examined 'externally and internally at the same time'.[2] And now here he was, peering about with a sense of startled recognition: 'As I drove along the roads from the airports to the towns it was almost comic to see these dreams of mine coming true on either side of the road.'[3]

A. J. Ayer and the other members of the cultural delegation may well have felt relieved to 'leave him behind'[4] in Peking, as the *Manchester Guardian* would imply when reporting their return to London. With or without the copy of William Blake's *Songs of Innocence* that Paul Hogarth would remember him clutching,[5] Spencer could indeed be a tiresome presence. He kept interrupting guides and interpreters with apparently hare-brained observations, and there seems to have been nothing in all of China that he couldn't match with a reference to the little English world of Cookham.

Britain's chargé d'affaires in Peking found the English painter peculiarly infuriating. Humphrey Trevelyan had seemed polite

enough when he welcomed the visiting delegation of 'cultural
giants' to lunch at the embassy and he raised no objections when
his wife led some of them out on shopping trips. Later, however,
he would look back on their mission as a ridiculous initiative—all
the more despicable for the fact that the 'giants' in question had
'accepted the pocket money offered to them by their hosts'.[6] Trevelyan declared himself especially dismayed by the 'fatuous
performance' with which they presented their 'message of peace'
to New China's Minister of Culture, Kuo Mo-jo, whose purpose, as
Trevelyan knew, was to 'exploit the word "peace" for political
ends'. Britain's official representative had shuddered as Spencer
'guilelessly expatiated to their hosts on the delights of Formosa',
without apparently getting round to explaining that the 'Formosa'
he was talking about had precious little to do with the American-
buoyed nationalist bastion that the Communist slogans fiercely
insisted was really New China's Taiwan. Spencer's 'Formosa' was a
little offshore island—an 'ait' in traditional English usage—in the
River Thames at Cookham. Named through some local quirk of
imperial *chinoiserie*, it included a creek, a field in which the local
boy scouts were accustomed to assembling, and an eighteenth-
century house of decidedly picturesque appearance.

Buddha and the Resurrection

Whatever it may have done for his dreams, China was by no means
an easy place for Spencer. During the tours, receptions, and sight-
seeing he shared with the cultural delegation, he felt increasingly
frustrated in his desire to paint and draw: 'I would either have to
sight-see or work; it was not possible to do both. The sight-seeing
meant continual movement & very few short pauses.'[7] He had
fallen ill on the second day, withdrawing from the planned itinerary on account of a cold and sore throat. He couldn't cope with
Chinese food either. Where Bernal and others enjoyed exploring
barely imaginable delicacies such as lotus porridge and abalone,
Spencer was definitely a square-table man, who coaxed the waiters
into 'bringing me only what I could fancy, like toast and eggs and
tea and suchlike'.[8] 'Suchlike' could be demanding. Paul Hogarth
remembered Denis Mathews coming up to him in the Peking
hotel and saying, 'You will never believe it, but Stanley has just

asked for fish and chips'.[9] Shortly after returning to Cookham, Spencer would himself claim to have lost one and a half stone in weight, and been considerably weakened by 'not being able to eat in China'.[10]

Spencer disliked the triumphalist style of the banquets and parades, and he recoiled from the Chinese masses too—partly, so Chinnery recalls, because he couldn't bear the smell of garlic. This reaction should perhaps be considered together with Osbert Sitwell's assertion, made after visiting Peking in 1934, that this sensation was quite 'unprecedented' and 'an unforgettable experience of the senses...to compare Chinese garlic to European would be like comparing a gasometer to a violet'.[11]

Though he shrank from the crowds, Spencer found the Chinese people highly sympathetic as individuals, and was delighted to use his pencil to single them out. In all, he made 'about a dozen drawings', many of them produced in the studio provided for him at the Central Academy of Fine Arts after the rest of the cultural delegation had gone home. Most are individual portraits in which a 'blue ant' is picked out of the ideologically moulded mass and revealed, quite unmistakably, to be a unique human being. Paul Hogarth would later recall these now dispersed drawings as a series of 'Holbeinesque pencil portraits of Chinese officials',[12] yet 'officials' were by no means dominant either in Spencer's own scribbled list of his Chinese drawings, or in the eleven examples he would offer for sale at Agnew's gallery in October 1957,

Fig 60. Stanley Spencer, *Hangchow Girl, Hangchow farmer,* and *Peking Child,* (drawings, 1954), *Sunday Times,* 31 October, 1951.

Fig 61. Stanley Spencer, *Hangchow Girl*, drawing.

alongside drawings and watercolours of China by Richard Carline, Sir Hugh Casson, Paul Hogarth, and Denis Mathews.[13] These included his drawing of *Professor Leonard Hawkes, the Geologist*, made in Peking, and two others, entitled *Shu Chang, 1954. The Interpreter at Peking* and *Mr. Wu, 17th October, 1954. One of the Masters of the Peking School of Art*. But the list is dominated by drawings of children. There was *Peking boy*, drawn on 17 October, and also his cousin, drawn on the 13th, and described only as *Peking girl. Peking*

Child was left undated, as was *A Girl of Hangchow.* Retrievable examples show beautifully simple sketches of faces caught somewhere on the spectrum between apprehension and curiosity. Unlike the drawings in which Paul Hogarth set out to establish the humanity of New China's representative types (peasant, steel worker, textile worker, stonemason, etc.), Spencer's are not even loosely framed by ideology. All he tells us of one of the young girls who came to his studio at the Academy is that she arrived for the sitting with 'about 6 other grown up girls for "safety"'. Having finished with the child and moved on to make a drawing of one of the older guardians, he added 'My God they have such charm, & humour & with such repose & ease. I said because all girls have hair done in two plaits: "Must hair always be in plaits?" & the girl smiled & in a desultory way began to undo one but I shouted at the interpreter "no, no, don't bother, it's alright".'

During his final ten days in Peking, Spencer also set out to explain himself and his work to an audience at the Central Academy of

Fig 62. Spencer talking with the artists Huang Miaozi (third from left) and Yu Feng (centre) at the Central Academy of Fine Arts, Peking.

Fine Arts. Edwin Pulleyblank, who attended the English artist's lecture, remembers his feeling of admiration and sympathy for John Chinnery, who was charged with producing a Chinese translation on the spot. He remembers Spencer's oration as 'a very personal and idiosyncratic lecture and I doubt whether many of the audience got anything at all out of it'.[14]

Spencer, of course, had his own memory of the event. Thinking of the pencil portraits he had been drawing in his studio at the Academy, he had informed his audience that 'it is well I am a Head Hunter & not a Clothes Hunter because all their clothes are the same'.[15] He devoted more time, however, to his main topic: 'I felt it necessary to make it as clear as possible that with all due respect to delegations & Attlee that I was possibly the most marvelous visitor to China they had ever had [-] something on a par with the coming of Buddha. Apart from my wish to be seen as who I am I found it as I say urgent & necessary because in England if people <u>don't</u> know who I am I am at once called upon to carry heavy suitcases.'[16]

In order to introduce his work to the Chinese, who would surely never have mistaken their visitor either for Buddha or a porter, Spencer had brought copies of various books with reproductions of his work. On arrival, however, he had found that this 'cut no ice' (hardly an expression, as he conceded, that could rightly be used with reference to 'the warmhearted Chinese people') because 'out there in China almost any artist of the least note has his work published at once by the Government in de luxe editions. So my books were just lost among the welter of beautifully reproduced books of modern Chinese artists with which all hotel bedrooms were furnished.'[17]

It is impossible to establish whether or not Spencer introduced his audience to any of his large 'Shipbuilding on the Clyde' paintings, which might have suggested what an idiosyncratically Christian socialist version of industrial realism looked like. He does appear to have shown examples from his ongoing series, 'Christ in the Wilderness', which Barbara Castle remembers him likening to 'with Kitchener in Khartoum', and also from another recent group of paintings on the theme of 'Christ Preaching at Cookham Regatta'. In the latter he had shown Christ seated in Cookham's old horse ferry barge, and speaking out among the crowded and cushion-filled punts, spitting fiery words at the gaudily clad diners, the barmaids, and the avaricious proprietors of the Ferry Hotel, and causing one listening woman in a punt to faint away as he converts Cookham's annual summer festival into its final Day of Judgement.

We can't be sure whether Spencer showed his Peking audience a recent addition entitled *Girls Listening*, which John Berger had described as 'superb'[18] in the *New Statesman* when it was first exhibited in London in February 1954. But the regatta series is mentioned by Barbara Castle. Having spent the day touring food markets and visiting the offices of the Women's Democratic Federation to hear about the improving situation of women in New China, she met up with Spencer at the hotel as he returned from delivering his lecture. She remembered the artist, whom she described as 'great fun', explaining that his aim in these paintings was to show Christ 'out-regattaing the regatta'. He also informed her that he had told his audience at the Academy of Art that 'they didn't want to hear about art methods from him: they were only likely to have one chance of meeting him and he'd better talk about himself. Heaven knows what they made of him!' As Castle wrote in her diary, 'he is sweepingly unconcerned with methods of mechanics of art. All I'm interested in is my soul. If my soul feels it, the painting's all right.'

Denis Mathews, who attended the lecture, noted that it was actually highly impressive, and that it moved the Chinese, who came to regard Spencer as an old master: an English equivalent, indeed, of Ch'i Pai-shih. This perception was confirmed by Yu Feng who was among the Chinese artists who welcomed Spencer to the Central Academy and attended his lecture. Speaking on the phone from Beijing nearly fifty years later, she looked back through the memory of her later years in jail to remember Spencer as 'a very good artist' and to remark more generally of 1954 that 'the time was good'.[19] The comparison with Ch'i Pai-shih would have pleased the English artist. Together with Pulleyblank, Chinnery, Mathews, and Cedric Dover, he had visited the Chinese master, then a great eminence though all but overwhelmed, and within a few months of his death. Chinnery remembers him as very old, reliant on his assistant, and fumbling with an apparently endless collection of keys as he retrieved and showed his work.

There was also, Chinnery recalled, some suspicion that the old man was hardly in any condition to have painted the work still being produced under his name.

Spencer greatly admired the venerated Chinese artist. Indeed, where the other delegates went out shopping for silk, porcelain, or other souvenirs such as the Tang horse brought back by Barbara Castle, Spencer left the Chinese money he had been given to his hosts so that they could buy three paintings by Ch'i Pai-shih, and send them to him at Cookham. He also worried about his ignorance of Chinese art and the difficulty he had in really appreciating it. Ruminating on this matter, he would note that the artists who, like Ch'i Pai-shih, worked 'in the traditional way' seem 'excellent to me', but also that he lacked the ability to differentiate adequately between their work. 'When I think of some English artist', he observed, 'I don't think of English art & when I think of a French artist I don't think of French art.'[20] But with Chinese art in the traditional style, everything seemed more or

Fig 63. Mathews, Dover, Spencer, and Pulleyblank with Ch'i Pai-shih.

less identically 'Chinese'. He hoped he could see the distinction of Ch'i's work, but much of what he saw left him feeling like the chauffeur in Shanghai, who had informed the interpreter that he couldn't tell the six British cultural delegates apart.[21]

Spencer showed absolutely no interest in the statistics dutifully noted down by the visiting trade unionists and Labour MPs, and which also turned James Cameron quite grey. He disliked the ideological clamour and the bricklike slogans, and was more than happy to ignore China's rapidly proceeding industrialization. Twelve years earlier, he had felt unexpectedly at home in the 'communal atmosphere' created by shipworkers at Lithgow's various shipyards in Port Glasgow, where he went as an official war artist to produce his great series of paintings of welders, burners, caulkers, riggers, plumbers, and furnace men at work. In China, however, Spencer was happy to leave the factories, mines, and hydro-electric schemes to Paul Hogarth, who had yet to join him in fearing that 'the coming of Communism and industrialization is completely destroying China'.[22]

Yet there can be no doubt that Spencer delighted in many aspects of the Chinese scene. At Hangchow, John Chinnery remembers the British artist bending down in fascination at the sight of a worm emerging from the body of a dead praying mantis. The same encounter, which happened near the Lingyin temple, was also recorded in both Casson's and Rex Warner's diaries. Some children had killed the insect and the worm emerging from its corpse was large and black. It seems safe to presume that Spencer had also shared Warner's fascination over breakfast that morning, when their guide told them about the Chinese habit of cricket fighting, explaining that it was necessary to goad the insects into action by prodding them with a brush made of whiskers from a live rat, and that champion crickets were often buried as heroes in tiny coffins of ivory.

The freakish prodigies of Chinese nature were one thing, but Spencer was also enraptured by the visible legacies of old China. Chinnery remembers being with him as they drove out of Peking, heading north in order to visit the Ming Tombs. The road took them past a field of ancient-looking brick kilns, odd-shaped conical structures surrounded by ladders and improvised walkways and scaffolding with people carrying things up to them. Spencer

Fig 64. Smelting iron (photo: Denis Mathews).

was greatly excited by the sight. Within seconds, indeed, he was exploding with quotations from the Old Testament.

One of the letters Spencer wrote to his niece Daphne Robinson gives an enraptured account of a performance of traditional opera he had just seen at Hankow. He praised the simple scenery, the ceremonial robes and gestures, the miming, and the 'exactness' of the movements through which the actors evoked a whole world of mountains and streams without ever leaving the flat stage. Taken backstage and introduced to the performers after the show, he wrote 'It seemed so strange to be shaking hands with these...remote beings'. As he wrote to his niece, the performance 'gave me such a sense of utter loveliness that I wished you could have been here'.[23]

The music at that performance impressed Spencer as both 'enchanting' and 'haunting'. Like so much in China it seemed 'strangely familiar', to repeat Joseph Needham's phrase, and its melodies 'not unlike in mood to Irish ones'. Spencer felt a comparable sense of recognition in many of China's ancient buildings. He never completed the oil painting he began at the Summer Palace: 'just by a tree-bordered stream like one of the back streams at Cookham',[24] as he later explained to his brother. Yet he marvelled at China's traditional temples and 'religiously concerned' buildings, emphasizing their 'spacing' and their areas of paved ground standing open to the sky.[25] The marvellous series of carved marble bridges at the Temple of Heaven in Peking were carefully spaced, not for reasons of traffic management or 'avoidance of bottlenecks', but according to ideas of 'belonging and harmony with people's wishes, and architecturally of course heavenly: that is the word. Especially as you approach and as you see people here & there on them. I so wanted to draw a group of these bridges & get the effect.'

Spencer celebrated the remaining traces of Buddhism and other Eastern religions wherever he found them, placing his own emphasis on their engagement with this world rather than any abstract idea of the next. In China, as he would suggest in the same note written in March 1959, mountains were not merely 'a symbol of holiness' but 'a factor in degree of holiness'. He ventured that 'the geographical shape of China with its mountains, rivers & valleys is the shape of the Chinese people's soul', and that China was a land where spiritual beauty was uniquely 'concrete'. People in the West might look at the Alps and see and comment on their beauty, but it was 'all done in a secular way'. The Chinese might feel the same about their mountains, and yet there was surely also something far from secular in their contemplation, which had inspired 'some of the profoundest religious joy' and also the 'great creative wonder'. Hence, he suggested, the temples that adorned so many Chinese mountains, and became more and more marvellous the higher you go. Europeans might feel driven to climb and conquer mountains—as in Edmund Hillary and Sherpa Tenzing's first ascent of Mount Everest in 1953 or the Italian expedition to K2 at the end of July in 1954. Spencer, however, was singularly unimpressed by such feats: 'Nothing whatever of wonder has been added to Everest in that it has been climbed, except perhaps [that] Sherpa Tensing had some religious urge giving the meaning that I love. But the presence, the all-pervading presence of the Tibetans & their lamaseries: that makes it alright for me.'

The sense of sacred geography Spencer associated with both China and Tibet confirmed his idiosyncratic idea of 'resurrection', as most famously expressed in his large canvas *The Resurrection, Cookham*, painted in Richard Carline's studio in the Vale Hotel in Hampstead, and completed in 1926. 'With me happenings & place are inseparable. They constitute the religious fulfillment of creative beings. No wonder I do the Hampstead picture, no wonder I make a "temple" of that small hill between the Priors and the Vale Hotel.' In other paintings he had associated that same sense of suddenly embodied revelation with reading newspapers, love letters, and other unexpected phenomena: 'No wonder I make a heaven of "Mails" & "Mirrors" & letters & people's happenings.'

If this was how the Chinese saw mountains, it was a similar story with their art. Spencer formed the view that in China, the religious sensibility found its 'first & chief outlet and expression in art'. Undeterred by any poster artist from Yenan, he also came home convinced that, in the prevailing Western sense of the word, 'there is no such thing as art as such (with us art has now a secular connotation) in China'.

The Great Wall of Cookham

Haunting melodies, primitive and scaffolded kilns, and temple-dressed mountains were among the Chinese presences that Spencer loved. Yet if we are to understand how China kept thrusting this very particular delegate back into his own English preoccupations, we need only consider one of the most celebrated features of Peking, which remained the ancient city of 'walls within walls'[26] that had so impressed the American writer Caroline Singer, when she had arrived there with the artist Cyrus Leroy Baldridge in 1925. Within the great grey walls that surrounded the entire city, there were the walls of the so-called Chinese city, and the taller ones of the Tartar City. There were the walls of the Forbidden City too. 'Box within box', as James Cameron wrote, 'of curling coloured fantasy'.[27] Lesser walls lined the hutongs said to be situated according to a pattern descended from the days when the Mongols pitched their tents where courtyard houses were later built, and when the routes that later became walled alleys were paths providing access to water. As J. D. Bernal also appreciated, these residential gateways in the hutong walls often opened onto screening 'spirit walls',[28] built to prevent the entry of evil powers.

Walls had long been of singular significance to Stanley Spencer. His grandfather had been a master builder, but the many walls that appear in his English paintings suggest more than a practical understanding of brick, flint, and lime mortar. Cookham was full of high garden walls and Spencer, even as a child, was unusually short. The village's walls lent a sense of mystery to his childhood experience, and they had also brought a characteristic sense of the other side, palpably present and yet also unknowable, into his paintings and drawings. One such metaphysical wall appears in Spencer's famous painting *The Last Supper* (1920), set in a Cookham malthouse. Here, Christ sits at the head of the table, and the low brick wall behind him stands forward sufficiently to indicate hidden space behind—the end of a room, but also a suggestion of the world beyond. Spencer often uses walls to define the metaphysical composition of his paintings: the brilliant brick and flint wall of *The Betrayal* (1922–3), for example, or the curved white example shaping the visual narrative of *Zacharius and Elizabeth* (1913–14). In *The Resurrection, Cookham* (1924–6), now in the Tate collection, Cookham church itself seems to have been flattened into a wall—as if to suggest that indicating the presence of the beyond is the primary thing that a church must do. The curious proceedings of *Love on the Moor*, commenced in 1937 but not completed until 1955, are set in front of a high brick wall, which wanders along in an erratically serpentine way, filling the background and creating the compositional field of this exceptionally wide painting.

Just as in Cookham, the walls of Peking appear to have lifted Spencer's gaze up to the heavens. After visiting the Forbidden City, he wrote to his niece, 'very lively wandering about in these great paved courtyards with the red walls & gold tiles & blue sky above the walls except where some Palace Hall rises out of them. Birds floating overhead: the Chinese said they were eagles but I think they must have meant kites.'[29] He also found himself oddly at home on the Great Wall of China, duly laid on as an attraction for Spencer, as for the other members of the cultural delegation, who were taken out of Peking to see it on 28 September. Rex Warner describes being driven along a cart-filled 'metalled rd. with dusty margins' and 'huge sunflowers' beside it, which then gave way to a 'dusty track' heading out towards mountains that resembled North Wales. This monument drew similes from several of the visitors. Rex Warner likened it to a squirt of toothpaste, whereas James Cameron thought of a bootlace laid out over the mountains.[30] Spencer, however, appears to have walked along it with a more closely remembered comparison in mind.

'Yesterday we visited the Great Wall. Sun blazing & grasshoppers very noisy. The young interpreters are very charming & are taking great care of me'—so he wrote on 2 October, before going on to deliberate about the Chinese name for sunflower and how it appeared to be 'one of those words that "means what it does"'.[31] He would reveal more about his encounter with the Great Wall of China three years later, when he made his way from Cookham to the neighbouring village of Bourne End in order to address the local parents' association on the subject of his travels. Characteristically, his notes for the talk pass through various detours and then break off before he has ever really reached China. They do, however, suggest how the Great Wall came to figure in his imagination. As he approaches his encounter with the Badaling section of China's relic, Spencer breaks off into another crazily local digression, this one accompanied by an imagined audience objection to his wandering manner:

> But I must get back to Cookham for a breather and to our own childhood garden wall along which I used to walk (Say! When's this guy going to get to China?). I walked from the coal cellar along it until it gets to the branches & blossoms of the cherry tree & many changes occur; here it is clear there it is nearly impassable because of the lid of the dustbin that leans back over it then it becomes covered in ivy & I scramble through & then I find the great trays of yew tree branches sweeping over it & I am not sure if I am still on the wall or in the fir tree. Little thought I that one day I would be walking along the great wall of China; well some of it. And how similar the feeling, that wall passed through Peking and through jungle, it is a symbol of life with all its vicissitudes but still persisting.[32]

This is likely to appear chaotic stuff to anyone sympathetically disposed towards Edwin Pulleyblank's reasonable suggestion, made in his inaugural lecture in Cambridge in 1955, that only disciplined expertise will enable a researcher to escape the theatre of misrecognitions that has so long governed the relations between China and the West. For Spencer, however, the English analogy was not just a visual cliché about rooks and yellow stone, or a fancifully imagined connection between Mao's agrarian reforms and the defence of the commons mounted by English Diggers and Levellers in the seventeenth century. It was instead a vivid experience that ran through his whole personality, and never more so than when he found the Chinese monuments he really wanted to paint.

The Valley of the Ming Tombs, Suffolk

Together with the other cultural delegates, Spencer had visited the valley of the Ming Tombs on the same day as they were taken to see the Great Wall. No doubt he had registered what Casson called the 'secret silence' of these monuments, which lay 'deserted in the shaggy little valleys outside Peking'. After Casson, Warner, Ayer, and Hawkes had set off for London, he and Chinnery made two further visits, in one of which they were also accompanied by Denis Mathews. It was during his return to this strangely evocative and apparently abandoned place that Spencer finally 'did a little oil painting'.

Built between 1409 and 1644, the walled Mausoleums of thirteen Ming emperors were laid out in accordance with the principles of feng shui, in a natural amphitheatre encircled by high hills. Created by and dedicated to the emperors of the last Chinese dynasty before the coming of Manchu rule, this ancient 'place of the dead'[33] had changed relatively little since 1898, when it was visited by Sarah Pike Conger, wife of the Minister in charge of the American Legation in Peking. She had noted that this amphitheatre was crossed by a rocky river-bed featuring the arched ruins of ancient granite bridges. Monumental places of teak and stone, the walled tombs were approached by means of a 'wonderful avenue of marble men and beasts'.

This 'Spirit Way' was guarded by the Dragon Hill and Tiger Hill, artificially created mounds on either side, and the large statues placed at regular intervals along its edges had seemed strangely imposing. 'First in line on each side were four priests, six or eight times natural size, cut out of solid blocks of granite and, like the tombs themselves, carved in exquisite detail. They faced the centre of the avenue. After the priests were eight warriors on either side, making twenty-four statues in all. Then followed twelve pairs of animals, one of each pair standing, and the other lying down. There were four horses, four unicorns, four camels, four elephants, four lions, four tigers, in all twenty-four.'[34]

Having survived centuries in their bare and dusty landscape, the entire site seemed to defy time. For Mrs Conger, the ancient 'thought-force' incarnated in the place seemed to give 'inherent power' even to the arches of the ruined bridges, which combined with the temples, the gateways with their towering columns, and other monolithic presences, to offer a 'thrilling dream-picture'.[35] Standing there, Mrs Conger had felt confirmed in her impression that 'Our life in China is a dream from beginning to end'.[36]

Though perhaps less mystically attuned than Mrs Conger, the Marxist physicist J. D. Bernal had found things much the same when he visited the Ming Tombs on Sunday, 3 October 1954, counting it 'the most perfect day that I have yet spent in China'. He was driven out of Peking on the 'quite good road' he took to be 'an artificial construction, I imagine built for tourists under the Kuomintang'. Arriving in the circular valley, he noted that the ancient Imperial Road was broken in places—some of it had been reclaimed by the fields and a bridge had been swept away. Passing through a couple of gates, he came to 'the celebrated parade of animals and officials—all in correct hieratic order—some kneeling, some standing, with the military definitely lower than the civilians'. 'Only in China', he concluded of the entire site, 'could a dynasty plan so accurately for its collective tombs. Only in China could successive emperors stick to the arrangement laid down for them by a distant ancestor'. As for the present condition of the tombs, he noted that one temple courtyard floor was being used as a threshing floor while another more remote tomb had been converted into a stable and was filled with brushwood and straw. He was confirmed in his anti-imperialism by the discovery that 'the tablet chamber of one of the most important tombs' had been 'scratched over with the names of the various invading troops that had at one time or another been quartered there. It was curious to see cheek-by-jowl the Irish of the Inskillings and the Yugoslavs of the Trieste regiments of the Austrian army of fifty years ago, and even some Russians.' Restoration of these neglected and more or less vandalized monuments was yet to come, but Bernal placed the fact that he was able to visit the site at all to the credit of New China: 'it amused me to think of Osbert Sitwell, not being able to get as far as the tombs in his time, only twenty years ago, because of the bandits.'[37]

Cedric Dover also saw what he wanted at the Ming Tombs. For him, the fact that they occupied a wooded area enclosed by bare hills only went to show that trees had been 'felled on a spectacular scale' in imperial China and often for reasons of 'despotic egotism'. Writing in their journal *Trees*, he left his fellow Men of the Trees in no doubt that the Ming Tombs, like other historical monuments in China, had been created at 'an incalculable cost' in human life and also in 'the ruthless destruction of the finest trees'.[38] Evidence was provided by the 'Dragon Tree', an ancient bole that survived in the courtyard of the central Ming Tomb ('it should be stabilised by tree surgery'), and also by the fact that the main Ming Tomb was 'supported by 32 giant cedar pillars, each measuring 16 hands around'. More generally, Dover would declare himself surprised that the new government had not yet really turned their attention to this ancient site. The new 'motorway', which he thought had actually opened in 1953, would make the cost of restoration more manageable and the tombs, together with their 'fabulous approach of monumental statuary', could 'appropriately be used as a special museum in full conformity with the ideology of the state'.[39]

Fig 65. The Ming Tombs, camels (photo: Denis Mathews).

Denis Mathews, who accompanied Spencer on one of his visits, photographed the tombs and some of the monolithic statues lining the spirit way. His pictures show signs of the recent planting, with which the authorities had already begun to re-establish the Ming Tombs as curated attractions in New China, and which would eventually grow up to place the statues in an avenue of rich foliage. In 1954, however, and as Douglas Hurd found on his picnicking days out from the embassy compound in Peking, the tombs stood 'derelict' with 'trees growing out of walls' and 'carved sacrificial vessels' lying in the grass of a bare valley now devoted to maize and glowing red persimmons.[40] Hurd judged the site even more impressive than the tombs of the Pharaohs near Luxor. As they appear in Mathews's photographs, the statues forming the Avenue of Beasts may also recall the Ancient Greek ruins encountered by nineteenth-century travellers in north Africa—relics of a vanished civilization surviving in a discontinuous world that hardly knew what to make of them.

By that time Spencer too had returned to the site on a working visit. While John Chinnery talked with a peasant, who listened to his Chinese and then declared himself pleased to discover how similar were the English and Chinese languages, Spencer set to work on two oil paintings of the 'Sacred Way' with its statuary. One, showing the stone camels, is called *Ming Tombs, Peking* (Plate 15). The other, of officials, is entitled *The Ministers, Peking.* (Plate 16).

Typically, Spencer found his own way of engaging with these abandoned presences and their dusty amphitheatre. After his first visit, which took place on the same day his delegation visited the Great Wall, he wrote to friends declaring, 'But the great thing of yesterday was the Ming Tombs, & becoming personally acquainted with that lovely double row of animals. Oh they are wonderful.' He found the two 'wall-eyed' horses 'particularly beautiful & moving'.[41] Three weeks later, he described the scene for his niece Daphne: 'Imagine a great plain with a road wandering across the center of the plain. On either side of this road & rising unceremoniously out of the fields at the side of the road large figures of annimals [*sic*]. These line the road either side & recur at about telegraph pole distance, after the animals come generals looking very ferocious & then ministers looking very saintly. All these (annimals & all) are meant to be mourning for the Emperor. I begin my journey home on Friday morning (22nd Oct) early.'[42]

Fig 66. The Ming Tombs, warrior (photo: Denis Mathews).

By the time he arrived at the Ming Tombs, Spencer had surveyed much of Russia and China in a strange spirit of recognition. And the two paintings he made here were no exception. He registers the otherness of those enigmatic statues, relics of a long gone world in a wide, bare landscape that was itself suspended between marginal agriculture and an erosion that, in *Ming Tombs, Peking* especially, has produced a parched and yellowed appearance that might have seemed more appropriate to the Gobi Desert. They stand there, holding out against time and the dust of their flat plain, and oblivious to the row of recently planted trees or shrubs sprouting just behind them. Each one is upright and isolate: a stone echo, perhaps, of the robed and menhir-like figures standing in the flat fields of Spencer's youthful painting *John Donne Arriving in Heaven* (1911).

Of the various works he made while in China, Spencer's paintings of the Ming Tombs were not greatly favoured by the 'cultural' members of the Second Labour Delegation. Barbara Castle quite liked one of them, but Derrick James had written that 'the oils

Fig 67. The Ming Tombs, councillor (photo: Denis Mathews).

seemed to miss, to me', unlike Spencer's 'drawings of Chinese types', which impressed him as 'superb', and which Barbara Castle also thought 'very good'. Posterity has so far gone along with this evaluation of the two paintings—registering them only as misfired eccentricities, which sit strangely alongside Spencer's better known, and far more highly valued, English works. Yet, as much as any of Spencer's Cookham paintings, the two Chinese oils are deeply felt works.

It was not until after returning to Cookham from China that Spencer provided an indication of the sense of 'personal acquaint-ance' he had discovered in the valley of the Ming Tombs. In November 1954, when he may still have been finishing off the two oil paintings, he wrote a 'letter' to his first wife, Hilda Carline, who had divorced him in 1937, when he took up his disastrous relationship with Patricia Preece. In this he expressed the wish that she had been with him on the recent journey. Transposed to the Mongolian steppe, she would have found herself surrounded by 'hundreds of miles of nowhere', in a world where 'the only happening is yourself'.[43] Spencer also reminded Hilda of a comparison he had made many years before his trip to China. Writing to her in 1948, he had recalled the day on 23 February 1925 when they were married in the village of Wangford, a few miles inland from the coastal town of Southwold in Suffolk, where Hilda had worked as a land girl during the Great War. In particular, he recalled 'the time when, at last, we were alone'.[44] The guests had just left the vicarage in a taxi. 'I can feel the gravel & tarmac under my feet now...We did not hurry but listened to ourselves loving. We stood singly about like things set adrift. How lovely it was. In our apparently aimless standing about we loved & mentally hugged each other. I could have sat on the low garden wall of Hill St. for ever...The one thing we both had so longed for, & which we had been suspended from being, was now possible. We could each be our self. We were both one: each a new part of the other's self. We freely, and without scruple, invaded our new selves.'

The '"us" birth', so Spencer remembered, had occurred 'on the road' as they walked out from the house at Hill Street. They went to the bottom of the garden and then turned right along a lane, where they had paused before continuing on their way:

> It was like in my (Tate) Resurrection; no one was in any hurry to go anywhere, everywhere was this new place of our love, it was air round our face. When we decided to walk along that road for a bit, it was just for the sake of deciding & and not that there was or needed to be any purpose in the decision; we loved the right turn because it gave us something to decide upon. Everything had a new meaning; its right meaning, we tumbled from our marriage shells & eyed each other. In this birth of married life, like the chick & its scratching, our first essay was to mooch along, you dawdling a little behind me, & stopping here & there to look at something. Everything was as if we had never seen it before, we were walking about in our marriage looking at this marriage substance, the straw & the grit of it.

After this great moment, they had walked on, wanting 'to get to where there was, on the right, a great plain. Our longing to marry seemed like a longing to see that place & our approach now was as if we were on the way to be married.' Soon enough, they came to a place where 'there was an opening to the right, at a corner of a road crossing our lane, & there we could see it going away to left & ahead & to right; in some part of it maize was growing'. In one sense, this was obviously an entirely English view, and yet for Spencer, 'It was the vast Gobi desert of you that I longed to wander into & about in & to put here & there the me of things.'

As Spencer remembered surveying it with Hilda, that north Suffolk 'plain' was the landscape of their married life to come, and 'in distant or mid distance we could see shapes & forms all of which were the various parts of it'.[45] It had seemed then like the 'vast Gobi desert of you': the prospect of their future together-ness, its distant 'shapes and forms' suggesting 'various parts' of the life they would share. It was all wrapped up in a feeling that 'The performance of our love was upon us. We loved the rehearsals we had already had on a previous visit to Wangford, but now the great plank of our life: our marriage had begun.'[46]

Writing a few weeks after returning from China, Spencer now informed Hilda that the 'plain' they had discovered at Wangford had not just been the Gobi Desert. It was also their 'place of the Ming tombs'.[47] 'We had seen photos of the place & we felt our together selves was like the remoteness of these animals. And now I have visited our marriage mecca & am back home again.'[48]

Though found at the other side of the world, Spencer's paint-ings of the Ming Tombs are, as these scribbled letters to Hilda suggest, peculiarly autobiographical images. Like Hilda as Spencer had earlier imagined her in the Gobi Desert of Wangford, the monuments on either side of the spirit way rose out of bare earth as the 'only happening' in their plain. Spencer's two oil paintings show them as the enigmatic and perhaps now barely legible remnants of a lost age and its future promises. They stand cracked and, like Spencer's broken marriage, forsaken in an empty and, in *Ming Tombs, Peking* particularly, parched and desertified land-scape. Both paintings are resistant and regretful images of 'shapes and forms' that might have lived had the course of events not gone off in other directions. They reminded Spencer of the 'somethingness'[49] with which Hilda might have constellated his world had mental illness, cancer, and his own impossibly selfish behaviour not laid waste to its promise; had he resisted his own disastrous impulse to recapture his 'early lost vision' with Patricia

Preece; had he never opted for 'the-thief-getting-over-the-wall dodge of divorce',[50] with which he had turned their marriage into stone.

It is characteristic of Spencer that he could journey to the far side of the world and still find himself painfully at home. Hilda Carline would never receive her former husband's explanation of his Chinese paintings, nor any of the letters that he continued to write her ('Dear ducky...'). She had died in 1950. The sense of despair and regret that assailed Spencer in China was perhaps not much diluted by the knowledge that he had cared for her quite attentively during her last weeks in the Royal Free Hospital in north London: sometimes sleeping out on Hampstead Heath in the intervals between his visits to her bedside, and occasionally also turning up in the morning at the Abbey Road house of Michael Foot and Jill Craigie, who would cook him breakfast and listen kindly as he asked preposterous questions, such as 'Why do you think it is that I am so attractive to women?'[51]

At Home with Chou En-lai

It was late Autumn in Peking by the time of Stanley Spencer's most notorious interaction with China. The nights were growing cold, fallen leaves were gusting about in the streets, and the citizens were already resorting to padded suits and 'fantastic fur hats'.[52] Carpets had been taken up in the Sin Chiao Hotel, and the rooms vacated by the departed foreign delegations had been occupied by an opera and ballet company from Moscow, shortly to open with a performance of Reinhold Glière's *Esmerelda* in a theatre that, as Paul Hogarth remembered, had been only half built when he drew it not so many weeks previously.

It was 21 October and Hogarth was having lunch at the hotel with Spencer and also Denis Mathews, who was enthusing about the fabulous reliefs and frescoes he had just returned from seeing at the ancient Buddhist sites at Tatung, in Shansi province in the north-west. Suddenly, a 'breathless courier' arrived to say that they had been invited to join an audience with Chou En-lai, organized for the politicians and trade unionists of the Second Labour Delegation, who were about to embark on a two-week tour of China. To the alarm of the courier, Spencer declined, as was his habit with all such events, explaining that he had to 'take a nap and afterwards finish an important drawing'.[53] He added that he was convinced that Mr Chou, to whom he had already been presented as a member of the cultural delegation, would quite understand. At this, the courier is said to have looked 'very unsure', and Spencer eventually changed his mind, although not before 'several appalled M.P.'s had remonstrated with this mani-festation of the dreaded artistic temperament'. '"I agree to go," said the not so rude genius of Cookham, "on one condition: that politics are not mentioned".'

As Hogarth recalled, this typically impossible remark prompted 'ribald hilarity from the British parliamentarians, which made us feel like naughty children'. True to his promise to Spencer's friend and former brother-in-law, Richard Carline, Hogarth tried to shelter the wayward Englishman from the joking and 'merri-ment' that continued as they boarded the coach. However, it was not just those grimly unimaginative MPs and trade unionists who found Spencer's protestations exasperating. As Denis Mathews wrote a few days later in a letter to his mother and father, 'Stanley Spencer, who carries his individualism to a rather potty extent, was puffing and blowing in the bus saying he "wouldn't stay there to be involved in politics...Very experienced!"

"Of course the Premier is," I replied.
"No, I am," he rapped back. "I don't know about him."'[54]

Soon enough, the bus pulled up outside the red-lacquered gates of Chou En-lai's residence, where the party were led into a courtyard by a pavilion adjoining the Imperial Palace. Hogarth, whose eyes had been considerably widened since he wondered about the pot plants adorning the arrival halls of Moscow airport, recalls filing through 'the exotic magnificence of a garden ablaze with yellow and plum-coloured blooms onto a terrace where shrubs flourished luxuriantly in great green urns'.[55] Having been greeted by 'the familiar faces of the Committee for Cultural Rela-tions', the British visitors passed into the green-tiled pavilion, which was adorned with red-tasselled lanterns, scroll-paintings, and classical calligraphy. Here they found themselves 'ranged informally' in front of the welcoming Premier, who had the usual 'knot of athletic-looking interpreters and stenographers gathered about him'.

Chou opened by 'formally welcoming our visit to China'. The wizard of Geneva then launched into a highly impressive talk—speaking in Chinese, as Barbara Castle noted, even though he was fluent in English and, indeed, kept stepping in to correct the interpreters. Derrick James describes a man of 'tremendous charm & personality', who sat there, 'loose and relaxed', emphasizing his points with 'graceful, expressive hands'.

As Barbara Castle recalls, Chou looked forward to a future of cooperation, in which the two world systems might advance in communication rather than continued ideological warfare. In the course of his presentation, which was delivered with great charisma and panache, Chou En-lai also talked flatteringly about the advantages of travel. Denis Mathews noted that Chou would have experienced these 'above the Chinese who have mostly not left their country', and the Chinese leader apparently informed his British audience that they had the same advantage over the Chinese. As Hogarth wrote in his journal, the Chinese leader concluded his presentation with an encouraging suggestion: 'We are new friends, but new friends can be old friends.'

To Castle, Chou En-lai's speech seemed 'a real breakthrough. We were so full of delight at the breakthrough.'[56] It fell, however, to Mr Ellis Smith, the MP for Stoke-on-Trent South, to reply on behalf of the British delegation. It was a dangerous moment, as Derrick James recognized, having already heard many of Chairman Smith's orations. After a show at a theatre in Chengdu, in the south-western province of Szechuan, he had mounted the stage and addressed the invited audience in 'a splendid fighting speech', ending with the declamation 'Peace to the world & long live Mao, Chou En-lai and the Chinese people'. This particular example had been 'a damned good speech' that 'brought the house down'. Yet Smith had also continued to prove capable of horrors such as the 'most appalling speech' he had delivered in Shanghai. The company that time had included various 'witty and sophisticated' Chinese hosts, but Smith blundered his way through a 'condescending and most embarrassing' oration in which he commended the new bridge to which the delegation had been introduced earlier that day as a 'bridge over the Yangtse', when it actually crossed the River Han.

As if that was not embarrassment enough, he had then trotted out the excruciating line that 'the Chinese treat you right if you treat China right'. 'It was horrible', wrote James as he remembered Chairman Smith 'dropping great bricks all over the place'.

On this occasion, as Paul Hogarth remembered, the Lancastrian Labour Party stalwart kicked off with a dismal cliché, venturing that it had been 'a slow boat to China'. He then looked up, as if remembering that his delegation had actually travelled by plane, and added, ponderously, that the slow boats were actually 'fast ones now'. Smith's tongue liked to wander and his mind was stuffed with memories associated with China, any of which, as his cringing fellow delegates had good reason to fear, he might have offered up to Chou En-lai. He might have gone all the way back to the comradeship of the British Tank Corps with which he had served in the First World War, and his encounters with the Chinese auxiliary units that had serviced this new force in northern France. He might have lingered, as he had in Moscow, over his experiences in Soviet Russia in 1927: the sight of Trotsky being chased out of Red Square, the 'Homeric banquets'[57] that the Bolsheviks had laid on for the international guests who gathered to celebrate the tenth anniversary of their revolution, or the British Workers Delegation's 'extremely interesting'[58] meeting with a Chinese youth delegation in Moscow.

That particular encounter, as Smith could easily have elaborated for the benefit of Chou En-lai, had taken place in a large hall 'filled with an excited, jolly crowd of Chinese students. There were many girls among the students, looking extremely attractive with their black hair and beaming countenances; the audience was the most enthusiastic we have ever experienced, and the whole meeting went with a swing.' A Chinese delegate had also left them in no doubt that the recent 'temporary defeat'—actually a bloody slaughter as Chou En-lai knew well—of the Communist movement in China had been chiefly due, not to Stalin's misguided policies towards Chiang Kai-shek, but 'to the protection given by foreign imperialist troops to the reactionary elements'. It had been a poignant encounter, as Chairman Smith will have remembered, and all the more so given that the majority of the Chinese youth delegation are said to have been 'captured and beheaded' by Chiang Kai-shek's forces on their way back into China.[59]

Smith might have taken the opportunity of the moment to tell the Chinese Premier a thing or two about his experience as a pattern-maker at Metropolitan Vickers in the late 1920s. He had been joined in his labours by college apprentices from around the world, including China and Japan. Many of these had visited him at his house, 'which was an open door to them'.[60] They had, as Ellis wrote in the same autobiographical note, learned 'a great deal from one another'. Indeed, one of these students had sent him a copy of the still unpublished Tanaka Memorandum, in which Japan's imperialist ambitions towards China were revealed. Smith had tried to interest 'a well known and respected newspaper' (almost certainly the *Manchester Guardian*) in this document, but they 'doubted its authenticity'. So, in March 1932, he had broken the news in *The Plebs,* journal of the National Labour Colleges, denouncing the still little-known Memorandum which revealed Japan's imperialist ambition to capture Mongolia and Manchuria, and to rule them, and perhaps later China ('the one great area left open for capitalist penetration'[61]) with a policy of 'Blood and Iron'.[62] He might also have reminded the Chinese Premier of the stand he had taken in 1937 when, as a new MP, he had spoken at a meeting in Manchester, condemning the Japanese invasion of China and tabling resolutions calling on the British government to express its 'profound abhorrence aroused by the barbaric slaughter of non-combatants with which Japan has sought to destroy the moral of the Chinese people'.

Whatever Smith drew from the capacious lumber room occupying the back, and perhaps also much of the front, of his mind, Chou En-lai heard him out with a smile and then invited a broader discussion, asking the delegates about their impressions of China and about how a new Anglo-Chinese cultural exchange might be made into a reality. The immediate result of this offer was, so Hogarth recalled, 'a tongue-tied silence' into which some witnesses would still be thrusting accusing explanations many years later. Perhaps some of the British delegates were simply stunned by the cumbersome thoughts of Chairman Smith or, indeed, awestruck by the superior presentation of Chou En-lai. Perhaps, as even the ex-Communist Paul Hogarth was still inclined to believe in 2001, they were just scared of appearing too conciliatory or 'pro-Communist' in the articles they knew each other to be hoping to sell to newspapers back home.

There are various versions of what Stanley Spencer said, when he eventually stepped in to break the deafening silence. According to his brother Gilbert, Spencer responded warmly to Chou En-lai's declaration that the Chinese were a 'home-loving people': 'So am I,' said the English stick-in-the-mud, adding that 'it took China to get me away from Cookham'.[63] In John Rothenstein's account, it was Chou's remarks about 'New China' that triggered the painter: 'Yes...we ought to know the New China better. And the New China ought to know Cookham better. I feel at home in China because I feel that Cookham is somewhere near.'[64] Another variation would soon be circulating in Bertorelli's restaurant, in London's Charlotte Street—although by the time word of Spencer's encounter had followed A. J. Ayer back to Bloomsbury, Chou En-lai had apparently been converted into Mao. After hearing this mockingly inflated version at a Wednesday Club lunch, Peter Vansittart wrote, 'after Freddie's return, I imagined new maps of Great Britain being issued to Chinese schools, marking Edinburgh, London, Heathrow and Cookham'.[65]

According to Denis Mathews, who was present at the meeting and later made a drawing of the encounter,[66] Spencer responded to Chou En-lai's remarks about the advantages of travel, declaring 'well, I have just come from my village of Cookham! Spent all my life there! I don't travel in France or Italy but China is a different matter. I left Cookham for that!'[67] In other accounts, he also confirmed that the two worlds were indeed not that far apart and, indeed, that China was on the edge of Cookham, a point that may partly have been derived from the coincidence of 'Formosa' being the name of Cookham's island on the Thames. Though he had declared himself quite uninterested in international politics and Cold War manoeuvring, Spencer's point, as Hogarth later described it, was that 'it was important for nations to rub along together'.[68]

At the time Hogarth recorded the event a little differently, describing how that 'tongue-tied silence' was suddenly broken by Stanley Spencer's voice saying that, 'international tensions aside, people are what really mattered. He lived in a typical English village, a real world, where people were at one with each other and that this spirit should prevail everywhere in the world today.'[69] The point, as Hogarth later added, was that people 'loved one another' in

Cookham. Love could be found in China too, and it 'should and could prevail everywhere in our world'.[70] The sentiments expressed by Spencer may have seemed 'inconclusive' to some of the delegates, but 'Chou En-Lai responded warmly'.[71] Spencer had 'broken the ice' with a simple and guileless message, that nevertheless moved Chou En-lai and, as Barbara Castle also recalled, opened the way for a lengthy discussion that seemed full of promise.

Derrick James noted some of the content of that exchange in his diary. Castle asked whether Chou was really prepared to encourage visits, reporters, and student exchanges. The Chinese leader replied that such things would be more and more welcome, once resources became available. Outlining the kinds of cultural exchange that might be developed, Chou suggested an encounter between the two traditions of dance and opera, venturing that Chinese audiences might appreciate a visit by Sadlers Wells with Margot Fonteyn. Deploying the winning smile that had proved so powerful in Geneva, he asked the question that he would soon trot out again at the Bandung Conference: 'Was there an iron or bamboo curtain as far as we could see?' When Mabel Ridealgh asked 'some involved hopelessly phrased question about religion', Chou cited the presence of the Dalai and Panchen Lamas in Peking and also the regime's provision for its other national minorities as proof that freedom of worship was, of course, accepted in the New China, and there were other measures for the national minorities. In answer to a question about the causes of world tension, Chou defended the achievements of the Geneva Conference against the intransigent policy of the US, determined as it was 'to divide the world into two blocs'. China wanted collective security, as did Nehru, whose visit had proved so encouraging. He commended the British Foreign Secretary, Anthony Eden, for proposing that 'collective security' might be built along the lines of a 'Locarno Pact for Asia', and expressed his regret that this initiative had been defeated by America's determination to press ahead with the creation of the South-East Asia Treaty Organization. There was loud laughter, when Ellis Smith entered a discussion of student exchanges in which Chou and Pulleyblank had considered the choice between Oxford and Cambridge, insisting that Manchester was obviously the best British university to host such a programme.

And so the conversation continued. Chou insisted that the world must demand peace from the USA and not China, and he had little to offer Ernest Thornton when he asked if China would allow independence to the people of Taiwan if the island was returned to China. The meeting lasted for a couple of hours in all, and Barbara Castle's enraptured account appeared in the *Daily Herald* a few days later. Published under the heading 'China Does not Want War',[72] her article quotes Chou as promising emphatically that China 'had no intention of going to war with the United States'. She was by no means alone in her admiration. After the discussion, indeed, James was 'horrified' to see the MP for Salford West, Charles Royle, and a handful of no longer tongue-tied delegates rushing up to Chou En-lai to clamour for his autograph: 'It seemed to be a bit thick, as he is a busy man, and I was glad to find that others felt as I did.'

In the bus on the way back to the hotel, the awe-struck trade unionists and MPs returned to their joking with the English painter who had felt nothing but contempt for their timorousness and their petty political calculations. They asked Spencer why he had not left as soon as politics was discussed. 'He fixed them with a piercing eye and said that he did not hear the word mentioned, but he had heard the words of a man concerned with the future of mankind and not its destruction.'[73]

Afterword

Holy China?

Personally I think the amount one can learn from these trips is extremely limited.

David Hawkes
(*New Statesman*, 6 November 1954)[1]

One of the first reports of the cultural delegation's return to England appeared in the *Manchester Guardian* on 20 October. Headed 'Culture but No Politics', it conveyed some of the impressions brought back by Sir Hugh Casson, Professor Leonard Hawkes, and A. J. Ayer—identified, only a little mockingly, as 'three cultured men just back from taking the greeting of 600 cultured men to China'. The unnamed reporter also noted that Rex Warner had excused himself as being 'unable to come up from Oxfordshire', and that Stanley Spencer had apparently been 'left behind' in China.[2]

'They do some research', said Hawkes of New China's university science departments, before adding that the need for short-term practical training programmes remained overwhelming. 'I do not think logical positivism is taught', said Ayer, 'but the professors had heard of Wittgenstein' and their Marxism was 'still pretty elastic', despite the danger that it might soon be turned into 'an orthodoxy'. 'They are very conscious of Russian architecture', added Sir Hugh Casson, who may already have been thinking about the scenery he was designing for the approaching premier of Sir William Walton's first opera, *Troilus and Cressida*, at the Royal Opera House in Covent Garden:[3] 'the Russian permanent exhibition building dominates Peking in a rather bossy sort of way'. The article closed on the three men's claim not to have been asked a single political question during the course of their visit: 'Was not that a bit odd? Well, they were hosts, we were guests.

"No, we did not ask a single political question either—perhaps that was a little odd too".'

Ayer went on to present a lecture announced as 'A Visit to Pekin and Moscow' at University College on Tuesday, 2 November 1954.[4] A few days later, on Wednesday the 10th, he joined Casson, Warner, and the now returned Stanley Spencer for a discussion entitled 'News from Abroad: China'.[5] This event was held at the Institute of Contemporary Arts, a new agency of the avant-garde, which had recently brought the American composer John Cage to London to introduce a performance of music for prepared piano. The discussion was chaired by William Empson, whose wife, Hetta, was that very same evening speaking on the theme of 'Women in China' at Friends House in Euston Road. Ten days later at Caxton Hall it was the turn of three political members of the Second Labour Delegation, John Baird, George Doughty, and Ben Parkin, to speak on the subject of 'Our Visit to China' at a fortieth anniversary meeting of the Union of Democratic Control, where they were introduced by Basil Davidson.[6] H. W. Franklin, also of the Second Labour Delegation, spoke on the subject of 'China and the USA' for the National Peace Council, on 13 November.[7]

Along with public meetings such as these, often organized by campaigns or more local organizations closely associated with the Britain–China Friendship Association, there were radio broadcasts to the wider public and newspaper articles too. Clement Attlee's reflections had been stretched over no less than seven articles in successive issues of the *New York Times*, and the similarly sceptical thoughts of Aneurin Bevan, who had been dismissed as an untrustworthy left-winger by the *New York Times*, now appeared in *Tribune* on four consecutive days in October. Warner's three articles for the *Sunday Telegraph* and Casson's for the *Observer* followed soon afterwards. Other papers preferred news of the Arsenal team, which had been so badly trounced in Moscow.

These reports and discussions joined a stream of potentially encouraging indications that the 'spirit of Geneva' might have some practical results in Britain. China's new chargé d'affaires, Mr Huan Hsiang, arrived in London on 27 October: still appointed on an 'ad interim' basis, but a great improvement on nothing.[8] There were to be more trade missions too, of an altogether more official kind than the reviled 'Icebreaker' mission of June 1953.[9]

As for the distribution of encouraging books and propaganda, at the end of October, Collets, the Soviet- affiliated London bookshop, opened a dedicated Chinese outlet.[10]

The cause of rapprochement also gathered support beyond the reaches of the more or less partisan 'friendship' organizations. The Bevanite left had never been in much doubt as to the rapprochement they hoped Britain would reach with New China, but the altogether more cautious Clement Attlee remained moderately encouraging too. At the end of November, while speaking at a reception held by the British Council to mark United Nations Day, he affirmed that 'there was a little melting of the ice in international relations',[11] and that 'personal contacts' were what was needed if 'friendship' was to become real. A British Parliamentary Mission to Moscow had also returned to London, with its leader, Lord Coleraine, declaring that they had seen no evidence of discontent with the new government nor of any desire for war.[12] Winston Churchill responded to the thaw too, suggesting, or at least not exactly denying, that he might be prepared to meet Mr Malenkov after all.[13] Perhaps he felt encouraged in this direction by the *New York Times*, which had credited him with first calling for face-to- face meetings with leaders on the far side of the Iron Curtain, while also suggesting that Attlee had stolen his thunder by going to China and shaking hands with Mao.[14]

For a tiny company of those who might, in Attlee's phrase, be called 'hardshell'[15] Communists, the demand for a new settlement with China may have been driven by loyalty to the big brother in Moscow. But this was not the impulse that kept a wider range of liberal, democratic socialist, and Christian opinion hoping for a rapprochement through those years of acute nuclear tension. As the Geneva-born cult of Chou En-lai had revealed so clearly, the cause of 'friendship' was shaped by an imaginative reflex that was particularly tempting to Western liberals and leftists in the time of the Iron Curtain. Finding the dominant powers on their side of the division—in this case Eisenhower and Dulles—both intransigent and beyond influence, they may well have been tempted to project their wishful aspirations over, or under, the curtain, and use them to convert the leaders on the far side into more benign and reasonable figures.

For many Britons, the cause of peace and international cooperation was also sustained by a strong sense of affronted patriotism.
It was possible, after all, to have welcomed the end of empire, and
yet to remain firmly—if not quite imperiously—convinced that
Britain, despite its near bankruptcy, still had a leading and independent role to play in the wider world.

The country's abject reliance on dollar loans was only part of the
problem. A more diffuse 'Americanization' accompanied the hard-
ening 'Natopolitan' mould opposed by those who favoured an
independent British foreign policy. The year 1954 was marked by
the Geneva Conference, but it also saw the first Wimpy Bar opening
at the Lyons Corner House in London. It would, perhaps, have
taken a defeatist to see the coming triumph of the industrialized
hamburger in that modest 'fast-food' counter, named as it was after
a figure in the 'Popeye' cartoons. But Churchill's government was
already being lobbied to take action against American comics,
accused of filling the minds of British youth with what one Labour
MP called 'rather beastly material'.[16] Objections were also being
raised against the corrupting influence of American advertising
techniques and Hollywood cinema. As for America's slickly
produced popular music, this would be famously damned as a
pernicious kind of 'spiritual dry-rot' in Richard Hoggart's study of
'English Mass Culture', *The Uses of Literacy* (1957).[17]

Far from only being a matter of the 'American slouch'[18] adopted
by feckless British teenagers as they plugged coins into jukeboxes
in milk bars around the country, this loss of independent British
character was also detected in the government's capitulation to
American demands at home. There had been considerable protest
in July 1954, when Churchill's cabinet had buckled to pressure
from Washington and expelled the alleged US draft evader
Dr Joseph Cort, who only escaped his American prosecutors by
crossing the Iron Curtain and taking up 'political asylum' in
Prague. And now came the news that British authorities had been
assisting American prosecutors in their persecution of the Johns
Hopkins sinologist Owen Lattimore: 'scraping together'[19] information from publishers and other British sources that had been
used to support charges against the traveller, writer, and scholar
who had been fingered by Senator Joseph McCarthy as the top
Communist spy in America. Having grown up in China and trav-

elled widely through central Asia in the 1920s, Lattimore had met and approved the Communist leadership in the early 1930s, but his present troubles stemmed from his later years of service as an adviser to Chiang Kai-shek during the Second World War. He had affronted members of what one Guardian letter-writer described as the 'evil and nefarious'[20] China lobby in the USA (funded by Chiang Kai-shek, using recycled American money as the same resolute American correspondent explained) by recoiling from the corruption of the Kuomintang and suggesting that America should at least establish contact with the Communist forces in China. Another correspondent deplored the hounding of Lattimore, who would eventually leave America to take up a teaching position at the University of Leeds, as an 'utterly unBritish business'.[21]

If these were among the considerations driving those Britons who wanted a more conciliatory and Geneva-like British foreign policy, they would be severely challenged as Mao and his fellow Communists proceeded to convert China into a nuclear-armed, fully industrialized, and totalitarian superpower. Remembering his own flight out of China with the NEC Delegation, Sam Watson of the National Union of Mineworkers had likened 'New China' to 'a great plane in the period of take-off. It rises higher and higher, faster and faster, generating more and more power, and if it stops doing so for a second, it crashes to the ground'.[22] The 'price of power' during the course of the Great Pilot's flight would prove steep and then catastrophic, and, as Watson also anticipated, it would largely be paid for by the forcibly collectivized peasants and the workers whose trade unions had already been 'enslaved' by the state. The private traders who, on 1 October 1954, had marched through Tiananmen Square behind banners professing their loyalty to the revolution, were soon swept aside as the economy was nationalized. Time also ran out quickly for the British banks and other companies that had held out through the first five years of the revolution. The Communist government may have been welcoming of the idea of resuming trade with the West, but it was still, as the Foreign Office minister Lord Reading pointed out, pursuing a 'deliberate policy' of making it 'impossible for most British and foreign firms to remain in China, and to force them to surrender their assets'.[23] The regime's presentation of its apparently benign and enlightened approach to China's national minorities would soon be thrown further into question—most obviously by China's behaviour in and around Tibet, whence the Dalai Lama, who had composed one of the more picturesque attractions of Peking for foreign visitors in 1954, would flee in 1959. Western intellectuals might have liked the sound of Mao's 'Hundred flowers' campaign of 1956–7, which encouraged educated people to express their criticisms of the regime. However, it was soon followed—as may have been intended from the start—by the 'Anti-Rightist' campaign, in which the figures who had been encouraged to reveal themselves were rounded up to be denounced, dispatched into forced labour, executed, or driven to suicide.

In the summer of 1954 Mao had informed Aneurin Bevan that, while the collectivization of land was indeed the 'ultimate aim' of his government, 'It will be many years, perhaps scores of years, before we can bring it about'.[24] In the event, collectivization was being forced on the countryside within months: a 'slave-driving'[25] initiative that would remove all autonomy from the co-operatives that had so impressed the smiling national secretary of the Women's Co-operative Guild and even prompted the more cautious Clement Attlee to apply Lord Beveridge's liberal English phrase 'voluntary action' to the examples he inspected.[26] The creation of vast 'People's Communes' commenced in 1958,[27] which was also the year of the Great Leap Forward, intended to industrialize all China in a few years. The result was ecological disaster as forests were felled to fuel notoriously incompetent 'backyard steel furnaces', many of which turned out pig-iron of such poor quality that it could never be used,[28] and a barely imaginable famine in which as many as 38 million are said to have died. Liberal-minded 'friends' of China would find no comfort in these developments, including the measure that had the modest virtue of vindicating one of Attlee's and Bevan's prophecies: a breach with the USSR which became total in December 1962. It appears to have been the latter event that finally prompted the passportless Briton Alan Winnington to quit the by now bitterly divided circle of foreign Communists in Peking. Assisted by Harry Pollitt, General Secretary of the Communist Party of Great Britain (and 'the greatest Englishman I have known'[29]), he moved to East Germany, leaving behind Rewi Alley and the American Anna Louise Strong, who would struggle on as Maoist mouthpieces.

During the years that saw these events unfold, many of the delegates would reconsider their attitude to China. Professor Leonard Hawkes had agreed to become a Vice-President of the Britain–China Friendship Association in April 1955,[30] but there is no indication that he allowed this symbolic position to compete with his more engaging commitments as a senior geologist. The MPs returned to their constituencies and the House of Commons, where the Labour Party would remain in opposition for the rest of the decade. A number of the Bevanites, who can hardly have expected to thrive in the Labour Party under Attlee or his successor Hugh Gaitskell, took their struggle against the 'Natopolitan' mould into other arenas. Ben Parkin, the MP for Paddington North, was among those who re-emerged as members of the Campaign for Nuclear Disarmament, founded at the end of 1957. He also devoted considerable energy to campaigning against rent-racketeering by Peter Rachman and other slum landlords in his Notting Hill constituency.

Cedric Dover was among the most industriously optimistic of the returned delegates. Having made his way back to Britain via India, he compiled his special issue of *Trees*, and started gathering up articles from the other delegates for his special 'China' edition of *United Asia*. He also wrote a series of articles about aspects of New China's activities for more specialist journals—In 'Biology and China', printed in the journal *Science and Culture*, he claimed to have detected a feeling among China's teachers, that, while the Western science of 'genetics' was indeed to be criticized and rejected in accordance with Soviet practise, 'it would be an advantage' at least 'to teach it in an introductory way'.[31] Despite this concession to Western reason, he once again praised the work of Dr Tchou-Su, the silkworm specialist he had found pursuing the Soviet Academician Lepeshinskaya's path at the Institute of Experimental Biology, repeating that it was reminiscent not just of the distinctively 'Asian' approach to evolutionary biology pursued by Nelson Annandale and his colleagues in Calcutta but also of the theories about the cell surface advanced by the African American scientist Ernest Everett Just (1883–1941). In 'Museums in China', published in the *Museums Journal*, he praised the fifty new museums claimed by the Chinese Ministry of Culture, and associated this praiseworthy growth with both an awakened interest in education and culture, and a determination—assisted, he ventured, by 'the eagerness of the people to donate their hidden treasures'—to repair the damage done by 'wanton pilfering' and 'the depredations of Western collectors for more than a century'.[32] A small measure of criticism was implied by his observation that the people responsible for this remarkable development had yet to realize that 'natural history is also history of a socially and culturally indispensable' kind.

With those reports written, Dover threw himself back into his primary causes. He continued to contest the idea of 'race' as a spurious construct, integral to imperialism but undeserving of any place in the true science of man.[33] An advocate of the very different approach he, like the various researchers who had passed through his seminar at the New School for Social Research in New York, preferred to name 'intergroup relations', Dover would continue to oppose the rising industry of 'race relations',[34] whether it appeared in UNESCO's well-intentioned programmes and publications or in the tendency of journalists and politicians to transform 'outbreaks of hooliganism at Notting Hill and other microcosms of heterogeneity into "race riots"'.[35] He continued to speak at meetings such as the International Congress of Black Writers and Artists, held at the Sorbonne in September 1956. He also resumed his use of the Reading Room in the British Museum, the quarry in which he had long been excavating the works of historical figures who should be remembered by 'the rising coloured world'[36]—an alternative pantheon presented through a series of essays in *Phylon*, the 'Atlanta University Review of Race and Culture', edited by W. E. B. Du Bois. Having already produced studies of the fourteenth-century Tunisian scholar Ibn Khaldun, the twelfth-century Spanish Jewish poet and physician Jehuda Halevi, and Antar, the sixth-century 'Negro warrior-poet' of North Africa, he now welcomed the eighteenth-century French botanist Jean Baptiste Christophe Fusée Aublet into his brown pantheon as 'the first secular abolitionist'.[37]

Dover also returned to the engagement with African American culture he had first developed with the help of W. E. B. Du Bois, Alain Locke, Charles Johnson, Paul Robeson, and others. Published in the year before his sudden death, on 9 December

1961, his last book, *American Negro Art*, is an illustrated survey dedicated to Aaron Douglas, the great artist of the Harlem Rennaissance: 'An epoch ago, at Tuskagee, you and William Dawson took me into the sick heartlands of Alabama to visit an ex-slave, Mr. Baker, whom you were painting. I still see him hurrying across his proudly cultivated farm with outstretched hands, "Now I can see," he said, as you introduced your friend from a faraway corner of the coloured world, "us niggers is getting together at last"'.[38]

As for the British artists who visited China in 1954, their work was eventually brought together for a group exhibition at Thomas Agnew & Sons' gallery in Albermarle Street, London W1. Entitled 'The Contemporary Chinese Scene', this was a group exhibition of paintings and drawings by Casson, Hogarth, Mathews, Spencer, and also Richard Carline, who had visited China in 1955.[39] They retained their political and aesthetic differences but there wasn't a zealot among them by the time the show opened on 23 October 1957.

Several people remember Stanley Spencer's irritation at Casson's claim, published in the *Observer*, that he had turned up at Heathrow with a pyjama cord hanging out of his suitcase: the English artist is alleged to have insisted, more or less indignantly, that this could not be true since he was actually wearing his pyjamas under his suit at the time. Neither man, however, would have apologetic adjustments to make on the more important matter of China and its political governance. While in Peking, Spencer may indeed have described Chou En-lai as a man of peace but he was no admirer of the new government or its programmes. As he informed members of the Bourne End Parents' Association in June 1957, the China of his dreams was an old China of temples, holy mountains, and ancient religious ways, and it was being destroyed by Communism and its frantic indus-trialization. His China was closer to that of Alan Watts, the US-based British author of *The Way of Zen* (1957), than to the fren-zied course of Chairman Mao, and there is no indication that he changed his view before his death in 1959.

For a time Paul Hogarth seemed to remain loyal to the revolu-tion as well as to the vast Chinese landscapes that had transformed his pictorial perspective in a manner that would, eventually, allow him to leave his increasingly awkward political views behind. He was still in Peking on 24 November 1954, when an exhibition featuring ninety of his Chinese drawings went on show at the Central Academy of Fine Arts, accompanied by a press statement in which he praised the Chinese people for their 'insatiable interest and appetite for culture'.[40] He also declared that 'only good could result from closer relations between the British and Chinese people', and hoped that his drawings would go on to 'assist the British people to acquire a fuller understanding of the historic transformation of society which is now taking place in China'. By that time the drawings were already going into circulation in Britain and Europe. The *News Chronicle* used some to illustrate James Cameron's articles about China, and the Bevanite paper *Tribune*, edited by Michael Foot, published a sequence of Hogarth's portraits, each one accompanied by the artist's written appreciation of its heroic subject. Thanks to Hogarth's international contacts drawings were reproduced in various left-wing papers in Europe too: the Danish Communist Party's daily *Land Og Folk*, the French Communist Party's *Lettres francaises*, and *Horizons: La Revue de la paix*, to mention only three.

Through the initiative of Sir Hugh Casson, Hogarth was also invited to prepare a selection of his Chinese drawings for the very respectable *Architectural Review*. They appeared alongside a critical appreciation by the art critic Robert Melville, known for his advocacy of Picasso and Francis Bacon, who now likened Hogarth's Chinese drawings to those made by Henry Moore and Graham Sutherland in London during the blitz. Melville was pleased to report that, with one or two flag-draped exceptions, the ongoing reconstruction of China had enabled Hogarth to 'use his sensitive topographical draughtsmanship purposefully, but without symbolic and propagandistic gesticulations'.[41] He praised Hogarth's river landscapes above all, pointing out that these pictorially impressive 'studies in uncentred composition' actually failed to gratify the artist-reporter's earnest desire to produce emblematic images of 'man's constructive energies'. If in future Hogarth found a way of harmonizing his strong sense of moral and political purpose with his evidently expanded pictorial sense, he would, so Melville estimated, be capable of giving 'topographical drawing a new raison d'être'.

Whilst grateful for the respect of that far from Communist publication, Hogarth had also been busy giving readers of the *Marxist Quarterly* another dose of the bracing stuff they expected. The issue for January 1955 carried his assault on the post-war resurgence of 'the reactionary doctrine of art for art's sake',[42] condemning the especially 'revolting' abstractions of Francis Bacon and the praise bestowed on them by American critics and also by the influential Museum of Modern Art in New York, which Hogarth accused of no longer being prepared to display its collection of American realist art from the 1930s. He discharged a secondary cannonade in the direction of London's Institute of Contemporary Arts: guilty of a recent exhibition on the Human Head in which 'drawings by lunatics flanked Renaissance portraiture' and, more generally, of attracting younger artists in search of meaning and then turning them away from 'the cultural heritage and the tangible problems of reality'.

At about the same time Hogarth had also joined John Berger, Randall Swingler, and John Willett, the writer and translator of Brecht, in founding the Geneva Club, a formally non-aligned left-wing dining club and discussion group named after the conference of that year, which held the first of its irregular meetings in Bertorelli's restaurant in Charlotte Street before moving to the Duke of Argyll in Soho. Hogarth would remember the initiative as an attempt on Berger's part 'to build bridges to an earlier generation of pacifists, which included a lot of the conscientious objectors from the First World War, like A. E. Coppard and Miles Malleson'.[43] J. D. Bernal attended some of its meetings, as did J. B. S. Haldane, Eric Hobsbawm, and Doris Lessing. Besides Paul Hogarth, the meetings were attended by a number of artists variously associated with *Realism*, a short-lived publication of the Communist Party artist's group, and the so-called kitchen sink school: Derrick Greaves, Edward Middleditch, George Fullard, and Peter de Francia too.[44]

Some of Hogarth's drawings of China had been augmented with colour by the end of 1955, when they went on show at the Leicester Galleries. The exhibition was opened by Aneurin Bevan on 30 November, and the invitation cards bore a reproduction of the fork-bearing 'Village Chairman': the Chinese Winstanley who had already put in an appearance in *Architectural*

Review and was now captioned 'Peasant with Pitchfork'. The man from the *Manchester Guardian* noted that Nye Bevan seemed 'sober in dress and speech'—an unusually 'inconspicuous' figure among 'so many flamboyantly dressed artists'. The figure-head of the Labour left 'wedged himself reticently into a corner between a charcoal sketch of a haggard Manchurian miner and a watercolour of rice fields in Szechwan, and spoke in a quiet voice. "I think one's dominant feeling, coming away from China, is one of sadness," he said: "One is sad that human beings should have to pit themselves against such a great mass of poverty and backwardness. Perhaps Mr. Hogarth's drawings will help to stir an attitude of sympathetic pity and enable people here to appreciate better what is happening in China today."'

Sympathetic critics had indeed liked what they saw. Hogarth's 'delicate, realistic water-colours' reminded Tom Driberg of the work of Edward Lear. This former Communist and now Labour MP for Maldon, in Essex, reckoned that readers of *Reynolds News* would like 'even those with such stark titles as "Weeding spinach on a Co-operative farm"'.[45] Writing in the *Manchester Guardian*, Stephen Bone commended Hogarth's drawings as 'remarkably sensitive to the spirit of a place', noting that China had demanded 'considerable enlargement of his technique and his pictorial ideas'.[46] For John Berger too, the drawings gave 'a real sense of the scale of China. A harbour scene implies the control of a whole coast line: a street scene the activity of thousands. A magnificent portrait of a steel worker redeems from all propaganda and restores to their full meaning the words "a people's hero." The explanation of this is obviously Hogarth's own excitement at what he saw; one of the incidental results is that his drawing has altogether ceased to be static: his line no longer just records, it embraces.'[47]

That exhibition went well enough, but other things were happening in Hogarth's life. Having already lost his teaching job at the Central School of Arts and Crafts in London, where his departure for China had apparently been the last straw for an envious director, he set his hand to various commissions, including some none too badly paid jobs from state publishers in Czecho-slovakia for whom he prepared illustrated editions of Charlotte Brontë's *Jane Eyre*, Dicken's *The Pickwick Papers*, and a translation of a pointedly northern working-class autobiography by Jane Walsh entitled *Not Like This*.[48] For a year or two, he also persisted with his travels in the Soviet bloc. He went to Moscow in December 1954, taking up an invitation that had been extended to him by the Soviet Society for Cultural Relations while he was in Peking. Here he met the famous writer and journalist Ilya Ehrenburg, who was horrified to read Hogarth's attack on Abstract Impressionism, published in *Soviet Culture* during the British artist's visit. Ehrenburg informed Hogarth that in the USSR abstraction, far from being a poisonous American plot, was a vital resource for independent-minded artists who refused to become the mere illustrators of state ideology. After riding to Leningrad (he was given a first-class berth on the Red Arrow express), Hogarth also met up with Nazim Hikmet, the Turkish Communist poet, who had found refuge in Russia after eighteen years of imprisonment in his homeland. He too warned his visitor that the USSR was not a paradise, urging him not to 'believe all you have been told!'[49]

The autumn of 1955 found Hogarth lodged in another 'plushy' hotel, this time in Bucharest, Romania. Travelling in a delegation alongside an expert in folk art from the Horniman Museum and Montague Slater, journalist, novelist, and librettist for Benjamin Britten's *Peter Grimes*, he enjoyed excursions into a still medieval countryside featuring walled villages, herdsmen in striking astrakhan hats, and gypsies riding by in 'gaily decorated' caravans. That, however, was only a picturesque interlude when compared with the journey of March 1956, which took him to Rhodesia and then South Africa, travelling with the then still more or less Communist author Doris Lessing, who made this return to Africa in order to write her book *Going Home*. Having seen some of his drawings of New China, she had approached Hogarth at John Berger's suggestion, and asked if he would accompany her to make some drawings for a book intended as an 'exposé of colonialism and apartheid'.[50] They scraped together the funds from various sources—Hogarth suggests that Lessing raised a contribution from the Soviet press agency TASS—and then flew to Salisbury.

The collaboration went well enough in Rhodesia but Lessing, already well known for her opposition to the pass laws and other apartheid policies of Johannes Gerhardus Strijdom's governing

National Party, was refused entry to South Africa. Hogarth got through, having sat separately on the plane into Johannesburg with this possibility in mind. Assisted by Ruth First, then married to the ANC leader Joe Slovo, he took his paper and crayons out into the townships, facing down the scowls and glaring suspicion of his whiteness to make a series of drawings that derive their considerable power from their opposition to the dictatorial government and its apartheid policies.

Hogarth would have made portraits of the leaders of the ANC but was disconcerted to find that they 'had the expressions of Communist Party apparatchiks'. Not so, however, the future Nobel prize-winner Albert Lutuli, to whom First introduced Hogarth in a village west of Durban, where he was running a small shop. Lutuli was then known as 'Ex-chief Luthuli', having been deposed from his position as elected Chief of the Zulus by the apartheid government when he refused to resign from the presidency of the African National Congress. Hogarth's drawing shows this dignified former teacher wearing a broad-brimmed hat against the sunlight and looking back at his visitor with the open spaces of South Africa behind him and an expression of quietly defiant strength that seeks nobody's pity. It is an exceptional portrait, which insists on the possibility of solidarity even in this police state where the Iron Curtain that Winston Churchill had seen descending between Communism and the Western democracies in March 1946 had quickly been embraced by the recently elected National Party and reconstituted as the colour line.[51] When, in 1958, Hogarth published a book of his African drawings under the title *People Like Us*, they were introduced as a 'lovely and inspiring collection'[52] by Father Trevor Huddleston, himself a great enemy of apartheid who had spent many years working for the Community of the Resurrection in Johannesburg. By that time, the drawings—and especially the portrait of Lutuli—had achieved a new sense of moral and political urgency thanks to the ongoing 'treason trial', a prosecution that commenced in December 1956 with the arrest of Lutuli, Nelson Mandela, Oliver Tambo, and more than 150 others associated with the ANC and the wider 'Congress Alliance'. The drawings had not fared so well in Britain before that. A few had been used in Lessing's book: though accepted with enthusiasm by

Michael Joseph, they were only printed as chapter headings, 'not much bigger than postage stamps'[53] as Hogarth later complained. They had also been turned down by the Leicester Galleries, his normal outlet in London, which shrank from exhibiting such 'challenging' work.

It is possible that this encounter with apartheid served briefly to buttress the cause of Communism in Hogarth's mind. Within eighteen months, however, events in Eastern Europe had brought that teetering edifice crashing down. Hogarth is likely to have been discomforted by Khrushchev's condemnation of Stalin's crimes, made in a secret speech at the Twentieth Party Congress on 25 February 1956, but a more dramatic shock came six months later. In October 1956 he was in Sofia, Bulgaria. After attending a retrospective exhibition of his prints and drawings, he boarded a train that would take him through Hungary to Warsaw for a reunion of men who had fought in the Spanish Civil War as members of the International Brigades. He reached Budapest in the opening stages of the uprising that began on 23 October, when a great mass of protesting citizens took to the streets and soon drew fire from the State Security Police. Barred from leaving the train, Hogarth and his fellow passengers were shunted on to Poland, where they would quickly discover what they had passed through in Budapest.

Arriving in Warsaw on 25 October, Hogarth left the railway station to find the city full of clamorous demonstrations, partly mounted in defence of Hungary and its reinstated reformist leader, Imre Nagy. Some 150,000 demonstrators had gathered outside Stalin's towering Palace of Culture and Science. It was said, so Hogarth later recalled, that the city was surrounded by Russian tanks and that Khrushchev was threatening military intervention. The crowds, however, refused to disperse until the moderate Communist leader Wladyslaw Gomulka, whom Khrushchev had agreed should be released from jail in order to form a new government, had appeared before them. Those who lingered to demand 'complete democratization', faced 'a series of savage and brutal attacks' from squads of riot police.[54] As Hogarth also recalled, the protest spilled over into the Congress on the international brigades, where Soviet observers were challenged to produce the Polish and Hungarian heroes of the brigades, including some who, it was rumoured, had long since been shot on Stalin's orders.

He met up once again with the graphic artist Jerzy Zaruba, who declaimed 'Our revolution is beginning!' He also heard Basil Davidson, who was there for the *Daily Herald*, say of the ferocity with which the military police assaulted the crowd, that 'it was difficult to imagine this happening in England'. Realizing that he had 'nurtured too many illusions' in his years as a Communist artist-reporter, Hogarth resolved that it was time to 'speak out'. The result of his now 'total disbelief' in Soviet Communism was an article that appeared under his name on the front page of the *Sunday Times* on 28 October. Hogarth later recalled feeling 'like Judas'[55] as he dictated this to the newsdesk from Warsaw. He reported that Gomulka had already removed the first secretaries of various party committees and sacked the entire Warsaw provincial committee for their attempts at 'curbing popular support' for the 'progressive forces' of the moment.[56] Yet his article was not merely a reluctant reformist's acceptance of the newly empowered moderate leader who might be expected to save Communism from the wrath of the people by making a few visible adjustments here and there. Hogarth went on to praise Poland's new 'revolution' altogether more thoroughly, placing himself on the side of the students who, 'wholeheartedly supported by factory workers', had demanded the truth from the 'frightened party officials sent to placate' stormy mass meetings. Having observed that 'Intellectuals appear jubilant at the break with all that is imitative of the Soviet in the arts', he closed by declaring: 'I have visited Warsaw many times since the war but never have I seen it so alive. In the words of a student "an oppressive fog has lifted from our eyes".'

In hindsight, Hogarth would be more inclined to describe these events as the moment of revelation in which he finally joined those who had lost their faith in the God that Failed. In actuality, his abandonment of Communism appears to have been a more gradual process. He did not resign from the British Communist Party immediately after the Soviet invasion of Hungary in November 1956[57] and, for a couple of years at least, his drawings would continue to circulate on both sides of the Iron Curtain. It may, for example, be assumed that Hogarth's reservations remained unknown to the still forcibly befogged readers of the

East German edition of his drawings, published with a long introduction by the orthodox British Communist Derek Kartun in 1956. And yet Hogarth would find straddling the Iron Curtain increasingly uncomfortable as the year of Hungary and Suez rolled on.

In December, he received an embarrassing call from a *Daily Mail* journalist who was pleased to have tracked 'prosperous Mr. Hogarth' down to his lovely 'rural retreat' at the Red House, Little Maplestead, Essex. He wanted to know what his target made of being welcomed as 'an artist of the proletariat' in the Union of Bulgarian Writers' paper, *Literature Front.*[58] Written by a certain G. Chajkorgki, the incriminating article in question alleged that Hogarth 'lives and works in one of those gloomy, dismal areas of Manchester plunged in desperate misery so vividly and touchingly described in the novels and poems of English writers'. In truth, as the man from the *Mail* found out, it had been '17 years since Mr. Hogarth lived in Gatley', which was actually 'a white-collar suburb in Manchester's green belt'. Hogarth could find few words with which to defend himself except 'Oh dear!' and 'Nonsense!' as the journalist read him further extracts claiming that unemployed workers in Manchester were dying of hunger and, indeed, that all Lancashire was ready to explode with 'tumultuous communal strife' such as it had known in the time of the Chartists. 'That', muttered the embarrassed artist-reporter in reply, 'is what they want people to think England is like...'.

By that time, the partisan in Hogarth was reeling if not yet stone dead. It was in a gentler spirit of 'détente'[59] that he revisited Russia in 1957, perhaps with Ilya Ehrenburg's condemnation ('You have done a great deal of harm') still ringing in his ears. He travelled with a group exhibition he had assembled under the title 'Looking at People'. Modelled on the exhibitions organized by the Artists International Alliance during the Second World War, this show had appeared in earlier versions at the Whitworth Gallery in Manchester, where it is said to have drawn unprecedented crowds in August 1955, and later at the South London Gallery (April 1957). By the time it reached the USSR, 'Looking at People' had been much expanded. With a catalogue introduced by John Berger, it included works by Carel Weight, the sculptor Betty Rea, George Fullard, Ruskin Spear, Edward Ardizzone, Alistair Grant, and Derrick Greaves, the latter representing realism of the 'Kitchen Sink School' also associated with John Bratby.

A seasoned opponent of Soviet socialist realism and its associated aesthetics, Hogarth is unlikely to have been worried by the comments scrawled by 'enraged visitors' in the visitors' book: 'Looking at People—all right...but why distort them?', or 'These pictures...have made me sick and I regret the time I spent here'.[60] Hogarth was by now no longer a Communist, a near teetotaller, nor, indeed, a Puritan of any sort. His big break came in 1958, when he met Brendan Behan. The notoriously uproarious and hard-drinking Irish writer, who was in London to promote his hugely successful autobiography *Borstal Boy*, had seen a copy of Hogarth's African collection, *People Like Us*, and one thing led to another when Randall Swingler introduced the two men to one another in a Soho pub (the York Minster). They agreed to collaborate on a book about Ireland, *Brendan Behan's Island* (1962), which went on became a best-seller on both sides of the Atlantic. Hogarth may have discovered his interest in landscape in Communist China, but the success of this book brought him prestigious and also lucrative commissions from *Fortune* magazine, which began by inviting him to visit the American south to draw the ongoing construction of a new 2,600-mile-long oil pipeline. 'In China,' as Hogarth would later say of the contrast, 'industrial construction had been characterised by the use of manpower on a massive scale. Here, state-of-the-art machinery had replaced muscle and brawn.'[61]

One literary collaboration led to another too. *Brendan Behan's Island* was followed by *Brendan Behan's New York*. Then came Majorca with Robert Graves, swinging London with Malcolm Muggeridge, Haiti, Cuba, and West Africa with Graham Greene, the Mediterranean with Lawrence Durrell, and eventually also Provence with Peter Mayle, the author of *Wicked Willie's Guide to Women* and other educational works... Hogarth became an influential teacher, working at the Cambridge School of Art before moving to the Royal College of Art in London, where his colleagues would include Sir Hugh Casson, who eventually also welcomed him into the membership of the Royal Academy. In 1952, Hogarth had knocked on Picasso's door and asked the great man to contribute a painting to an 'Artists for Peace' exhibition at the

London Royal Hotel. By the early 1980s, it would fall to him to approach the no longer despised figure of Francis Bacon at Wheelers restaurant, in Soho's Old Compton Street. He asked the triumphant artist, who had by now inherited the mantle of Picasso as well as many other prizes, to join him as a member of the Royal Academy—an invitation that Bacon rejected with a contemptuous hiss, promising that he never joined '*anything*, not even a dinner party'.[62]

The fact that the artistic exchange with China continued after 1954 was due not to Paul Hogarth but to Denis Mathews and Richard Carline, who joined forces to organize a series of three exhibitions that would be taken to China through the agency of the Chinese government. The first of these was an exhibition of British graphic art 1450–1956, including works by Phiz, Gilray, Beardsley, Baines, William Hogarth, and Samuel Palmer. Richard Carline accompanied it to China in 1955, and his widow Nancy remembered that he found the visit a 'greatly enjoyable' experience. That was hardly to be the case in 1960, when Mathews made his return to China, accompanying an exhibition of twentieth-century British oil painting. Entitled 'Sixty Years of British Painting in Oils', this included paintings by Duncan Grant, John Singer Sargent, L. S. Lowry, and Victor Pasmore among others. There was an industrial scene by Julian Trevelyan, a work by Mathews himself, and Josef Herman's painting of a helmeted and head-lamp-wearing Welsh miner—one of the many works that the Polish-born Jewish artist had produced since moving, in 1944, to the small mining village of Ystradgynlais in South Wales.

By this time the difficulty of taking these shows around China had increased greatly—as is revealed by the typescript of an unpublished book about the journey written by Anna Mathews, who accompanied her husband and, like him, embarked in a mood of excited optimism. Tensions persisted between these unofficial 'friends' of China and the British consular officials who, while unimpressed by their upstart initiative, nevertheless felt obliged to put in an appearance at the exhibition's openings in Peking and Shanghai. Yet Mathews was serious about seeking to establish a critical dialogue between Chinese and Western artists, and certainly not just queuing up to praise the regime and its politically orientated artists. He treated the visit as an opportunity to resume the exchange about realism, Soviet influence, and traditional Chinese aesthetics that he had initiated within minutes of stepping down from the plane outside Peking in 1954.

Anna Mathews records some of the comments left by visitors to the exhibition in Shanghai. One of these supposedly 'ordinary citizens' declared that there was too much work that displayed 'formalist' tendencies, a decadence that seemed especially to afflict more recent work such as Paul Feiler's modernist Cornish seascape, *Morvah, White* (1958), which was said only to demonstrate 'the decline of painting'.[63] 'Bourgeois formalist—no ideological content', as another had written of most of the exhibited work, going on to excoriate the British exhibition as an example of 'Art for Art's sake'. Josef Herman's lanterned figure *The Miner*, was plainly commendable for its proletarian subject—obviously 'an expression of the working people'—but not for its treatment. The objection was not so much that the figure was resting, as so many of Herman's miners are (not for him the Stakhanovite hero struggling at the coalface): 'It isn't bad, but what a pity the image has been smeared and made ugly.' These judgements prompted Anna Mathews to the observation that 'Chinese attitudes to painting are a complete reversal of our own. In England, painting as a profession is considered useless, expensive and (unless it is atrophied academic) rather neurotic; it bears, in the popular mind, little relation to life and not at all to such life-moulds as politics. In China, art is useful, costs little, propagates ideology, and is as healthy as a run around the hockey-field.' The Chinese artist had to accept that 'Chi-chi is out' and that he is 'a worker who holds a brush or a pen instead of a shovel'. And yet he is also a 'privileged and cosseted figure in a still-struggling society': respected, comparatively well paid, and, she thought, secure.

Anna Mathews saw nothing wrong with the 'excellent theory' of the artist as a committed servant of the people who would 'help the masses push history forward'—at least as this theory had been presented by Mao at the Yenan Forum of 1947. Yet, she would come home from China in no doubt that Mao's doctrine had since 'degenerated into a sort of mystic incantation of fair meaninglessness'.

She cites a discussion she and Denis had with some unnamed artists and officials in Nanking. They had gathered in the private room of a restaurant, the walls of which were covered with reproductions of scrolls by that most famous of China's traditional painters, Ch'i Pai-shih. One of the hosts asked Mathews if he liked Chi's work. When Mathews answered that he did, the host went on to indicate one particular scroll and ask his visitor if he agreed that it was 'the best of the ones here'. Mathews replied, 'Frankly no, I imagine it is a late one'. The host replied 'Yes, it is. Therefore it is better than the others.' This prompted Mathews to point out that, while Ch'i Pai-shih was indeed 'a great painter', he had also been 'ninety, frail, and almost blind when he died, five years after the revolution'. It was therefore hardly surprising that his later scrolls really 'do not compare' with his earlier work. The suggestion was quite unacceptable to his host, who insisted that the master had painted in 'a freer and more lively way after the Liberation, rejoicing at the workers' victory. Painting with a free spirit, he painted better pictures.' Horrified by this dogmatic statement, and well aware that most Peking critics also considered the late work 'highly inferior', Mathews restrained himself from remarking that Ch'i Pai-shih had been 'almost too ill to hold a brush' when he and Stanley Spencer had met him in 1954, and 'only his will-power kept him going'. Instead, he wondered what would have happened if Ch'i Pai-shih had died five years before the revolution, rather than after it. He would surely have been 'a good artist' all the same? The answer came in the form of a brick: 'a reactionary society never produces good artists'.

Further dismay was to follow when the Mathews returned from Nanking to Shanghai, to participate in an artists' forum on 20 June 1960. The event was convened to discuss the exhibition 'Sixty Years of British oil painting', at the Shanghai Exhibition Hall, in Nanking Street. The assembled artists and academics talked a lot about flowers, and whether this favourite subject matter of traditional Chinese art was actually 'without socialist content', as Mathews appears to have suggested. He was told that, since the Liberation, this too had changed. Like those working in the recently imported medium of oils, Chinese artists working in the traditional style now felt a 'strong urge' to reflect the spirit of the present time.

This prompted Denis Mathews to wonder: 'what is the difference between a socialist and a reactionary peony?' Informed only
that 'Some are healthy, some are unhealthy', he pushed back,
asking, 'How do you decide what is healthy and unhealthy in
flower painting?' In answer, a professor named Yang Ke Yang indicated one of the British works, a painting of green peppers by the
New Zealand-born modernist Frances Hodgkins, which was not at
all 'like real life'. 'Art permits exaggeration,' granted Yang, 'but
those peppers are not lovable'. His suggestion was that these
painted fruits 'seem rotten, therefore unhealthy', so Anna
Mathews recorded. Yang also indicated a painting by Rodrico
Moynihan, formerly Professor of Painting at the Royal College of
Art and closely associated with the realist Euston Road School,
suggesting that the fishes and ham it portrayed were unmistakably better than Hodgkins's peppers.

Mathews replied that, while he did not personally agree with
Yang's judgement, this might indeed be a 'fruitful theme' to
pursue. Rather than basing his criticism on the work's subject
matter, as Mr Yang had done, he suggested that the problem was
actually connected to a 'way of drawing' that may not 'convey
enough' about the fruit. Hodgkins's pepper was adequately
painted, but if it was beautifully painted, it would not matter if the
fruit was rotten or fresh. He then went on to wonder how Professor
Yang might go about choosing between two hypothetical paintings. The first was a work of unmistakably modest ability illus-
trating an epic achievement of recent history, such as a celebrated
incident in the Long March. Though painted in an 'ordinary &
unimaginative way', it might still be judged 'adequate' as an illustration. It would be considered to have 'fulfilled' the purpose of
the artist in socialist society, even though it was a work of weak
vision. The second painting showed 'a superb & beautiful peony
growing from a rock'. It was, he repeated, a 'superb & beautiful'
painting but it had 'no socialist content'. Having outlined these
alternatives, Mathews asked 'which is healthier?'

Yang refused to answer this question, preferring to counter
with one of his own. He recalled something that had happened to
Ch'i Pai-shih during the war against the Japanese. The Chinese
master had come to Shanghai, where the Kuomintang head of
the garrison headquarters asked him to paint. Ch'i refused at

first, but gave in when pressed. What he painted, however, was a picture of a crab. When the reactionary leader saw this, he became 'very excited', recognizing that the crab conveys 'man riding roughshod over the people'.

Mathews thought Yang's story 'very nice', but it also proved his earlier point. He suggested that the crab only conveyed this hostile comment because of a 'mutual background of knowledge'. It was not the painting itself that upset the nationalist leader, but the meaning of the crab, which was to say an 'intellectual not visual concept'. The story merely indicated that the two men were criticizing pictures from a different standpoint.

At this juncture another artist, whose name is only recorded as Mr Sheng, returned to the discussion, repeating that the important thing was whether or not the painter had 'a healthy mind'. If a painter had an unhealthy mind, he would not paint pictures that had a positive influence on people in industry. Traditional flower paintings, meanwhile, were 'much appreciated' by the workers because they showed the flower 'blooming to its full'. In doing so, they reflected the fact that working people hope for 'a more colourful and better life' and wished to struggle to pursue this noble aim.

Anna Mathews appears to have been increasingly horrified as the discussion dragged on for nearly four hours. Her note of the meeting gathers asterisks as it goes, each one attached to a scribbled marginal comment. 'What makes him think conformity is colourful?' she asks as the chairman decrees that 'socialist life is more colourful than any other'. 'In other words, ram it down their throats', she scrawls furiously as the same functionary explains that the quality of an art work is decided by a 'combination of audience and experts': a process he described as 'elevation on base of popularisation'. In her later account of the episode she would admit to stifling exasperated 'literary screams' as the debate dragged on—'what price Dostoievsky' and 'What's the difference between this and advertising?' Her final judgement was severe:

> Conclusion I am forced to: it is good to paint shrimp. It is better to paint the Long March. It is best to paint Chairman Mao. But if I paint a sick shrimp I am politically unreliable. If I paint 2 sick shrimps I am an aggressive imperialist reactionary.

Though guests of the government, the Mathews had encountered many such frustrations. Their request to have the same guides and interpreters as Denis had met six years earlier in 1954 was ignored. The authorities in Peking curtailed plans to tour their exhibition to other cities beside Peking and Shanghai, and Mathews was not invited to lecture or hold study groups, even though that was ostensibly the reason why he had made the journey. They soon found that all conversation was based on ideological concerns: Anna Mathews records that they encountered absolutely no interest in aesthetic considerations or even questions of technique or method. One young acquaintance told them, quite seriously, that 'a worker's criticism is as good as an art-expert's criticism, because there is nothing to stop the worker being an artist'. The new cry, as Anna Mathews wrote, was 'anyone can do anything'. A typical encounter occurred in Nanking, where they met artists who claimed to prefer making 'collective paintings' to working on their own. They were also approached by a laughing interpreter who came brandishing a newspaper article about a Dutchwoman, 'an artist who put paint on the canvas by kissing it. In order to furnish an exhibition, she had kissed the canvasses millions of times.' 'Listen', said the interpreter, 'did you ever hear anything so funny', quoting the paper that cited this as 'a ridiculous extravagance of capitalist art'. 'Ridiculous', it may well have been but, as Denis went on, it was 'also exceptional. You Chinese have finger-painting. What's the difference?'

It was not long after this depressing episode that Denis reminded his wife about an interaction that had taken place earlier in London. He had been visited by an attaché from the Chinese embassy who hoped that he might be able to provide some printed reproductions to be sent back to China to indicate the work present-day British artists were producing. The desired list included paintings produced by a chimpanzee at London Zoo. As Mathews admitted, this surprisingly gifted chimpanzee actually existed. Named 'Congo' it had become something of a star on the television programme *Zootime*, presented by a young zoologist named Desmond Morris. Mathews, however, was fully aware of how those images were likely to be used in a China that was predisposed to mock such 'decadent' Western trends as abstract expressionism. He refused to include any simian endeavours objecting that they were in no sense representative of British art.

There would be further meetings and receptions to attend at the Chinese embassy in London. Indeed, in the spring of 1964 the Britain–China Friendship Association hosted an exhibition entitled 'Arts From China', which brought some of Ch'i Pai-shih's marvellous crabs, prawns, and dragonflies to London's Royal Festival Hall and was accompanied by a programme in which an anonymous commentator expressed the hope that 'The Chinese hold the view that they should preserve all that is good and best in the past; to break away from tradition does not necessarily mean to deny tradition but to develop it; new flowers bloom forth from the soil which has been enriched by the ashes of the old'.[64] By this time, however, the intellectual exchange that Mathews had been trying to sustain with Chinese artists was effectively dead. It was Richard Carline, rather than Mathews, who had returned to China with an exhibition of English watercolours in 1963. His widow Nancy remembered him finding it 'not nearly so enjoyable' as his earlier visit of 1956. Some of the artists and critics he had befriended then were under house arrest, and he himself felt hectored and harangued: 'He said he never wanted to go again.'

That only left the London-based Polish-Jewish artist Feliks Topolski. During the Second World War, this muralist and pictorial 'chronicler' of the twentieth century had proclaimed, so Paul Hogarth wrote in *Looking at China*, that 'our generation was not bred for war; we were expecting revolutions'.[65] Having tried hard but failed to secure an invitation in 1954, he finally made it to the land of his dreams in the early stages of the cultural revolution, launched by Mao in May 1966. 'One goes to China as if on the last remaining Voyage on the otherwise tourist-industry bound globe',[66] so he would declaim in the large book of revolutionary *chinoiserie*, filled with ferociously engaged drawings and paintings, which he would publish under the title *Holy China*. Mocking the 'smirks' of more cautious 'Western "travellers"', Comrade Topolski came home to heap inordinate praise on China's violently renewed revolution and to pronounce, in solidarity with the Red Guards who were already persecuting many of the artists and writers who had engaged in dialogue with the British visitors of 1954, that the future belonged to the young.

They, after all, were already protesting under 'pop-portraits of Mao' across 'the entire West', and they would surely soon sweep away their 'mindless, possession-bound civilization' and replace it, as their Chinese comrades were doing, with 'the selfless "society of continuous change"'. Better the Royal Academy than that, as Paul Hogarth had by then decided.

APPENDIX

Membership of Three Delegations

Delegation of the Labour Party National Executive Committee (August–September 1954)

The Rt. Hon. C. R. Attlee, OM, CH, MP (Leader)

The Rt. Hon. Aneurin Bevan, MP

Wilfrid Burke, MP (Chairman of the Labour Party 1953–4)

Harry Earnshaw, OBE (United Textile Factory Workers' Association)

Henry Franklin (National Union of Railwaymen)

Morgan Phillips (Secretary of the Labour Party)

The Rt. Hon. Edith Summerskill, MP (Chairman of the Labour Party 1954–5)

Sam Watson, CBE (National Union of Mineworkers)

The Cultural Delegation (September–October 1954)

Professor Leonard Hawkes

Hugh Casson, RDI, FRIBA, Hon. ARCA

Professor A. J. Ayer

Rex Warner

Stanley Spencer

John Chinnery

The Second Labour Delegation (October–November 1954)

Capt. J. Baird, MP for Wolverhampton North

Mrs B. Castle, MP for Blackburn East

Capt. W. D. Griffiths, MP for Manchester Exchange

Mr A. W. J. Lewis, MP for West Ham North

Mr G. S. Lindgren, MP for Wellingborough

Mr B. Parkin, MP for Paddington North

Mr C. Royle, MP for Salford West

Mr E. Smith, MP for Stoke-on-Trent

Mr E. Thornton, MP for Farnworth

Mr C. Dover, Anthropologist, Author, Biologist and Lecturer

Dr D. W. James, Lecturer in Anatomy, University College, London

Mr D. Mathews, Art Critic and Secretary, Contemporary Art Society of the Tate Gallery

Professor E. G. Pulleyblank, Professor of Chinese Studies, Cambridge University

Mr C. Cooper, General Secretary, Society of Technical Civil Servants

Mr G. Doughty, General Secretary, Association of Engineering and Shipbuilding Draughtsmen

Mr A. Hardy, Council Member, Amalgamated Union of Foundry Workers

Mr J. Horner, General Secretary, Fire Brigades Union

Mrs M. Ridealgh, National Secretary, Women's Co-operative Guilds of Great Britain

Mr B. Roberts, General Secretary, National Union of Public Employees

Mr J. H. Southall, General Secretary, National Union of Mineworkers, Midlands Area

Notes

Preface

1. Curated by Timothy Hyman and myself, this exhibition was held at Tate Britain from 22 March to 24 June 2001. My article about Spencer's trip to China appeared as 'Berkshire to Beijing' in the *Guardian*'s Saturday Review, 17 March 2001.
2. Marc J. Selverstone, *Constructing the Monolith: The United States, Great Britain, and International Communism, 1945–1950* (Cambridge, Mass., and London: Harvard University Press, 2009).
3. E. P. Thompson, 'Outside the Whale', an essay first published in Thompson (ed.), *Out of Apathy* (1960), and republished in full in Thompson's *The Poverty of Theory and Other Essays* (London: Merlin, 1978), 1–33.
4. Ibid. 1.
5. Patrick Wright, *Iron Curtain: From Stage to Cold War* (Oxford: Oxford University Press, 2007).
6. James Cameron, *Mandarin Red: A Journey Behind the 'Bamboo Curtain'* (London: Michael Joseph, 1955), 13.
7. Jack Goody, *The Eurasian Miracle* (Cambridge: Polity Press, 2010), 1.
8. *Manchester Guardian*, 20 October 1954.

1. Embarkation

1. This introductory description is largely drawn from Hugh Casson, *Red Lacquer Days: An Illustrated Journal Describing a Recent Visit to Peking* (London: Lion and Unicorn Press, 1955). The text of this unpaginated book reproduces three newspaper articles printed in the *Observer* ('Journey to Peking', 31 October 1954, 'Journey to Peking—2', 3 October 1954, 'Journey to Peking—3', 14 November 1954) and derived from Casson's notebooks, written at the time. It is worth noting that in his notebook, Casson quotes the desk clerk as asking 'Is this the p. delegation?' The 'p' probably stood for 'political', in which case Casson's decision to opt for 'cultural' instead may itself reflect the undoubtedly political anxieties of the time.
2. See John Falmer, 'Is Britain Tilting into the Sea?', *Portsmouth Evening News*, 29 January 1954. Cuttings of this and the following articles survive in Leonard Hawkes's staff file at Royal Holloway, University of London, Archives, BC AR/150/56/D645.
3. Frank Lambe 'Part of Britain is disappearing into the Sea', *Glasgow Evening News*, 27 April 1953.

4. Thucydides, *The Pelepponesian War*, trans. Rex Warner (Harmonds-worth: Penguin, 1954). See also Stephen E. Tabachnick, *Fiercer than Tigers: The Life and Works of Rex Warner* (East Lansing: Michigan State University Press, 2002), 292–5.
5. Rex Warner, *Poems* (London: Boriswood, 1937).
6. *The Wild Goose Chase* (London: Boriswood, 1937), *The Professor* (London: Boriswood, 1938), *The Aerodrome* (London: John Lane The Bodley Head, 1941), *Why Was I Killed? A Dramatic Dialogue* (London: John Lane The Bodley Head, 1943). For a wider discussion of Warner's life and work see Stephen E. Tabachnick, *Fiercer than Tigers*.
7. Rex Warner 'May 1945' in *The Cult of Power* (London: John Lane The Bodley Head, 1946), 135–45.
8. Tabachnick, *Fiercer than Tigers*, 281.
9. Rex Warner, *Ashes to Ashes: A Post-Mortem on the 1950–51 Tests* (London: MacGibbon & Kee, 1951). For a discussion of this book, conceived while Warner drank hot champagne with Lyle Blair at Lords Cricket ground, see Tabachnick, *Fiercer than Tigers*, 276. Peter Vansittart remembered how Ayer shared Warner's interest in cricket, and was also amused by Warner's willingness to publish detailed descriptions of games he had never seen (telephone conversation with the author, 5 April 2002).
10. Rex Warner, *Escapade: A Tale of Average* (London: The Bodley Head, 1953).
11. John Chinnery, interview with the author, 2 March 2001.
12. Conversation with Olive Cook, Saffron Walden, Essex, 2002.
13. Kenneth Pople, *Stanley Spencer: A Biography* (London: Collins, 1991), 12.
14. Peter Vansittart, telephone conversation, 5 April 2002 and interview with the author, Kersey, Suffolk, 8 June 2002.
15. José Manser, *Hugh Casson: A Biography* (London: Viking, 2000), 138.
16. In his obituary of Leonard Hawkes, Professor A. J. Smith records that he showed his 'contempt for administration' by keeping all the records for his department in two ledgers. He also recalls that in committee meetings Hawkes was inclined to overstate his case—a habit he claimed to have developed because Bedford College was a women's college, and this was 'the only way to make women argue back'. *Bedford College Old Students Association Journal*, 64 (1981/2), 17–18. Royal Holloway, University of London, Archives, BC AS 903/1/3.
17. Stanley Spencer, letter to his niece Daphne Robinson, 30 August, 1954. Transcribed by Dr. Jeremy Hardy. Copies of this and other letters to Daphne and her mother Marjorie Spencer are lodged with the Stanley Spencer Gallery in Cookham and also the Tate Gallery Archive.
18. Stanley Spencer in his notes for a 'Talk to Bourne End Parents Association', presented on 5 June 1957, Tate Archive, 733.10.191.

19. Margaret MacMillan, *Seize the Hour: When Nixon Met Mao* (London: Murray, 2006), 7.

20. Ibid. 6.

21. For Winston Lord's account of the closely 'choreographed' nature of the Nixon/Mao handshake see the transcript of 'Transforming the Cold War', a conference sponsored by the US State Department, and held in Washington DC, on 25–7 September, 2006. Available at www.state.gov/s/pa/ho/88112.htm (accessed 14 August 2007).

22. Humphrey Trevelyan, *Worlds Apart: China 1953–6, Soviet Union 1962–5* (London: Macmillan, 1971), 80.

23. Yafeng Xia, *Negotiating with the Enemy: U.S.–China Talks during the Cold War, 1949–1972* (Bloomington and Indianapolis: Indiana University Press, 2006), 79.

24. Barbara Tuchman, *Stillwell and the American Experience in China 1911–1945* (London: Phoenix Press, 2001), 487.

25. Mao Tse-Tung, 'On People's Democratic Dictatorship; written to commemorate the Twenty-eighth Anniversary of the Communist Party of China (1 July, 1949)', in Otto B. van der Sprenkel, *New China: Three Views* (London: Turnstile Press, 1950), 186.

26. R. H. S. Crossman et al., *Keep Left* (London: New Statesman and Nation, 1947), 31.

27. 'Communism in the Public Services', *The Times*, 30 March 1954, 4. See also Dianne Kirkby, '"Ecclesiastical McCarthyism": Cold War Repression in the Church of England', *Contemporary British History*, 19/2 (June 2005), 187–203.

28. 'The Far East', *The Times*, 2 January 1950, 7.

29. John Haffenden, *William Empson: Against the Christians* (Oxford: Oxford University Press, 2006), 187.

30. Ibid. 189.

31. Tuchman, *Stillwell and the American Experience in China 1911–1945*, 526.

32. Ibid.

33. Evan Luard, *Britain and China* (London: Chatto & Windus, 1962), 83.

34. Trevelyan, *Worlds Apart*, 17.

35. *A Chronicle of Principal Events Relating to the Korean Question 1945–54* (Peking: Shihchieh Chihshih, 1954), 28.

36. Alan Winnington, *I Saw the Truth in Korea* (London: People's Printing Press Society, 1950).

37. Monica Felton, *What I Saw in Korea* (London: self-published, 1951). For the parliamentary debate in which Hugh Dalton, Labour Minister for Local Government and Planning, justified his immediate dismissal of Felton from her £1,500 a year post as Chairman of the Stevenage Development Corporation, see *Hansard*, House of Commons, 13 June 1951, 488:2306–13.

38. Quoted from the 'Editorial note' introducing *Bacterial Warfare*, a special number of the Chinese *Medical Journal*, 70/9–12 (September–December 1952), 335.

39. 'Report on the Crime of American Imperialists in Spreading Bacteria in Korea'. Quoted from an unattributed English-language edition of a report by the Chinese People's Commission for Investigating the Germ Warfare Crime of American Imperialists, first made public on 24 April 1952.

40. An English version of the 'Report of the International Scientific Commission for the Investigation of the Facts concerning Bacterial Warfare in Korea and China' was published in a 'Special Number' of the *Chinese Medical Journal*, 70/9–12 (September–December 1952).

41. Martin Buxton, letter to Professor P. A. Buxton, 24 October 1952.

42. See *Out of Their Own Mouths: Revelations and Confessions Written by American Soldiers of Torture, Rape, Arson, Looting and Cold-Blooded Murder of Defenceless Civilians and Prisoners of War in Korea* (Peking: Red Cross Society of China, 1952).

43. For a Chinese version see Mne Andrew M. Condron, Ex-Royal Marines, Sgt. Richard G. Corden, Ex-U.S. Army, and Sgt Larance V. Sullivan Ex-U.S. Army, *Thinking Soldiers by Men who Fought in Korea* (Peking: New World Press, 1955). For a Western account of the psychologically 'subjugated' prisoners-of-war—one Scot and twenty-one Americans—who in January 1954, decided not to come home from Korea in an agreed exchange of prisoners but to move to Communist China instead, see Virginia Pasley, *22 Stayed* (London: W. H. Allen, 1955).

44. Pasley, *22 Stayed*, 159.

45. Alan Winnington, *Breakfast with Mao* (London: Lawrence & Wishart, 1986), 171.

46. Ibid. 162.

47. Ibid. 164.

48. James Cameron, *Mandarin Red: A Journey behind the 'Bamboo Curtain'* (London: Michael Joseph, 1955), 272.

49. Edward Hunter, *Brain-Washing in Red China: The Calculated Destruction of Men's Minds* (New York: Vanguard, 1951, new and enlarged edition, 1971). Hunter first wrote of Red China's 'brainwashing' in an article for the *Miami Daily News*, in September 1950. In a statement to House of Representatives UnAmerican Activities Committee on 13 March 1958, he went on to apply his idea to the battle for opinion in the West, announcing that '"Peace", in the Communist vocabulary, is the period when all have accepted, in a so-called voluntary manner, the inevitability of a Communist world' (www.crossroad.to/Quotes/globalism/Congress.htm). For a contemporary review of Hunter's book, in which the idea of 'brainwashing' is welcomed as an early 'peep through the bamboo curtain', see Fred R. Riggs, *Far Eastern Survey*, 21/15 (29 October, 1952), 159.

50. Claude Roy, *Into China* (1953) (London: Sidgwick & Jackson with MacGibbon & Kee, 1955), 267, 277.

51. Peter Townsend, *China Phoenix: The Revolution in China* (London: Cape, 1955), 338–9.

52. William G. Sewell, *I Stayed in China* (London: Allen & Unwin, 1966), 101.

53. A. J. Ayer, *More of My Life* (London: Collins, 1984), 99.

54. Stanley Spencer, 'Talk to Bourne End Parents Association', 5 June 1957, Tate Archive, 733.10.191.

55. Entry for 14 September in Rex Warner's diary of 'China Trip', in the possession of Mrs Frances Warner.

56. Hugh Casson, *Red Lacquer Days: An Illustrated Journal Describing a Recent Visit to Peking* (London: Lion and Unicorn Press, 1956), unpaginated.

57. Ayer, *More of My Life*, 102. Georgy Malenkov was Premier of the USSR between 1953 and 1955, briefly sharing power with Nikita Khrushchev, then General Secretary of the Soviet Communist Party.

58. Rex Warner, diary, 15 September, 1954.

59. John Chinnery, interview with the author, 2 March 2001.

2. Holding Out in the Legation Quarter

1. Denton Welch, *Maiden Voyage* [1943] (Harmondsworth: Penguin, 1986), 229–31.

2. See John Gittings's obituary of Derek Bryan, *Guardian*, 3 October 2003.

3. Humphrey Trevelyan, *Worlds Apart: China 1953–6, Soviet Union 1962–5* (London: Macmillan, 1971), 61.

4. Trevelyan replaced Sir Lionel Lamb, who had been posted to Peking in March 1951, and who had himself succeeded J. C. Hutchinson, appointed as chargé d'affaires *ad interim* when Britain recognized the People's Republic of China in 1950. He was the first to find himself in the position to drop the *ad interim* from his title. See 'Chargé D'Affaires in Peking', *The Times*, 21 May 1953, 8.

5. Trevelyan, *Worlds Apart*, 21.

6. Juliet Bredon, *Peking: A Historical and Intimate Description of its Chief Places of Interest* (Shanghai: Kelley & Walsh, 1922), 14.

7. Hedda Morrison, *A Photographer in Old Peking* (Hong Kong: Oxford University Press, 1985), 15.

8. Hetta Empson, 'Notes from Peiping on Aspects of North China (1948 and 1950)', *Contemporary Chinese Woodcuts* (London: Fore & Collet's, 1950), unpaginated.

9. Ida Pruitt, *Old Madam Yin; A Memoir of Peking Life 1926–1938* (Stanford, Calif.: Stanford University Press, 1979), 16.

10. Caroline Singer and C. Le Roy Baldridge, *Turn to the East* (New York: Minton, Balch & Company, 1926), 32.

11. For one contemporary description of these pigeons see Claude Roy, *Into China* [1953] (London: Sidgwick & Jackson, 1955), 41.

12. Arnold Toynbee, *A Journey to China or Things Which are Seen* (London: Constable, 1931), 213–14.

13. John and Alice Chipman Dewey, *Letters from China and Japan* (New York: Dutton, 1920), 215 and 7.

14. Basil Davidson, *Daybreak in China* (London: Cape, 1953), 28.

15. Toynbee, *A Journey to China*, 213.

16. Douglas Hurd, *The Arrow War: An Anglo-Chinese Confusion 1856–1860* (London: Collins, 1967), 239.

17. For an account of the 'Guest Ritual' governing the Qianlong emperor's reception of Lord Macartney, see James L. Hevia, *Cherishing Men from Afar: Qing Guest Ritual and the Macartney Embassy of 1793* (Durham, NC, and London: Duke University Press, 1995). Hevia points out that the emperor's letter, which was been much quoted in twentieth-century accounts of Sino-Western relations, only became widely known after 1896, when it was first translated. His account of the ritual governing the reception of the Macartney embassy confirms Bertrand Russell's suggestion that 'no one understands China until this document has ceased to seem absurd'. See Hevia, *Cherishing Men from Afar*, 238.

18. Juliet Bredon, *Peking*, 39.

19. Karl Marx, 'Revolution in China and in Europe', *New York Daily Tribune*, 14 June 1853.

20 Juliet Bredon, *Peking*, 43.

21 Sarah Pike Conger, *Letters from China: With Particular Reference to the Empress Dowager and the Women of China* (London: Hodder & Stoughton, 1910), 140.

22. Amaury de Riencourt, *The Soul of China* (London: Cape, 1959), 187–8.

23. Arthur H. Smith, *China in Convulsion* (Edinburgh and London: Oliphant, Anderson & Ferrier, 1901), i. 240, 270.

24. Grant Hayter-Menzies, *Imperial Masquerade: The Legend of Princess Der Ling* (Hong Kong: Hong Kong University Press, 2008), 93.

25. Hugh Trevor-Roper, *Hermit of Peking: The Hidden Life of Sir Edmund Backhouse* (New York: Knopf, 1977), 35.

26. Conger, *Letters from China*, 170.

27. Bredon, *Peking*, 44.

28. Anonymous letter, written in the British Legation quarter and dated 13 September 1900. See 'The Peking Legations', *The Times*, 4 December 1900, 3.

29. 'Details of the Capture', *The Times*, 1 September, 1900, 3.

30. See B. L. Putnam Weale, *Indiscrete Letters from Peking: being the notes of an eye-witness, which set forth in some detail, the real story of the siege and sack of a distressed capital in 1900——the year of great tribulation...* (London:

Hurst & Blackett, 1907), 258–9. Weale was the pen name of Bertram Simpson, as is revealed by Cyrus Baldridge, who also explains that Simpson, thanks to the 'indiscretion' of his book, would remain forever a '*persona non grata* with the British in Peking'. When Baldridge visited the city in 1924, 'the best eyebrows of the Peking Club' were still being raised 'at one seen too often in his company'. See Cyrus LeRoy Baldridge, *Time and Chance* (New York: John Day, 1947), 216–17.

31. Peter Fleming, *The Siege at Peking* (London: Hart-Davis, 1959), 243.
32. Sarah Pike Conger, *Letters from China*, 188–9.
33. Ibid. 176.
34. I owe this information to Grant Hayter-Menzies, whose book on the friendship between Mrs Conger and the Empress Dowager Cixi is forthcoming from Hong Kong University Press (email exchange, 27 February 2010).
35. Hsiao Ch'ien, *China but not Cathay* (London: The Pilot Press, 1942), 8.
36. Denton Welch, *Maiden Voyage* [1943] (Harmondsworth: Penguin, 1986), 232–3.
37. Trevor-Roper, *Hermit of Peking*, 25.
38. Somerset Maugham, *On a Chinese Screen* [1922] (Hong Kong and Oxford: Oxford University Press, 1986), 29.
39. Caroline Singer and C. Le Roy Baldridge, *Turn to the East* (New York: Minton, Balch & Company, 1926), 56.
40. Baldridge, *Time and Chance*, 215–16.
41. Ibid. 219.
42. The American journalist Nathaniel Peffer speaks of both the 'over-enthusiasm' and the 'maladjustment' of Peking's foreign residents in the course of differentiating Singer and Baldridge's book from the usual 'impressions of the Orient'. See his 'Foreword' to Singer and Baldridge, *Turn to the East*, 1.
43. Singer and Baldridge, *Turn to the East*, 53.
44. Cyrus LeRoy Baldridge, *Time and Chance*, 228.
45. Trevor-Roper, *Hermit of Peking*, 1977.
46. Stacey Pierson, *Percival David Foundation of Chinese Art: A Guide to the Collection* (University of London: School of Oriental and African Studies), 11–12.
47. Baldridge, *Time and Chance*, 229.
48. Haldore Hanson, *'Humane Endeavour': The Story of the China War* (New York: Farrar & Rinehart, 1939), 22.
49. Peter Fleming, *News From Tartary* (London: Cape, 1936), 69.
50. Ibid. 21.
51. Peter Fleming, 'Hidden Asia. To India From Peking. 1.—A Flank Attack', *The Times*, 18 November 1935, 15.

52. Ella K. Maillart, *Forbidden Journey: from Peking to Kashmir* (London: Heinemann, 1937), 6.
53. Somerset Maugham, *On a Chinese Screen*, 28.
54. Ibid. 12.
55. Sir Harold Acton, *Peonies and Ponies* [1941] (Hong Kong: Oxford University Press, 1983), 92.
56. Derk Bodde, *Peking Diary: A Year of Revolution* (London: Cape, 1951), 18.
57. Trevelyan, *Worlds Apart*, 22.
58. Telephone conversation with Michael and Julian Morgan, who followed Martin Buxton in the British embassy after his second posting there in 1957, 26 September 2007.
59. Trevelyan, *Worlds Apart*, 27.
60. Douglas Hurd, *Memoirs* (London: Little Brown, 2003), 105.
61. Rewi Alley, *At 90: Memoirs of My China Years* (Beijing: New World Press, 1986), 241.
62. Ralph and Nancy Lapwood, *Through the Chinese Revolution* (Letchworth: People's Book Co-operative Society, 1954), 5.
63. John Haffenden, *William Empson: Against the Christians*, 233–5.
64. Ibid. 233–5.
65. For the Buxtons' infant daughters, the embassy compound in Peking really would be the centre of the world. Born in Peking in 1950 and 7 years old when her father's second posting ended, Eleanor Kovar remembers the vast entrance, with its vast studded doors, one of them penetrated by a small wicket gate, and the Western-style houses inside. She recalls a stable, with horses—her father used to ride a pony to work—and also a herd of goats, kept because fresh cow's milk was quite unobtainable. Most of all, her memory is defined by the vast high wall surrounding the compound. Though forbidden, she and other children used a well-placed tree to climb up onto it in order to gaze out at the parades on national days. She remembers the Chinese marching past in ranks of at least ten deep, dressed in blue or grey Mao costumes, each group bearing their flag and chanting patriotic songs in perfect unison.

She and her younger sister Rachel were objects of fascination to Chinese children, who had never before seen anyone with red or even curly hair. But if curious stares were part of the city's human architecture for a British child, there were occasional political irruptions too. One day her *amah*, a Christian like the other Chinese staff, came to work bearing nasty bruises, which she would only later recognize as evidence of Communist hostility towards Christianity. On another occasion she remembers being driven back from school at the 'Convent of the Sacred Heart', the only international school in the city, and the car being halted by a crowd chanting and staging a protest against some or other British perfidy outside the gates of the embassy: a disconcerting encounter that quickly gave way to smiles and informal displays of friendliness once the driver explained that he was bringing the children home from school. Eleanor Kovar, telephone conversation with the author, 2007.

66. William Empson, letter to John Hayward. Quoted in Haffenden, *William Empson*, vol. ii: *Against the Christians*, 105.
67. 'The Fate of Peking: Faded Glories of the Former Imperial Capital,' *The Times*, 16 December 1948, 5.
68. Bodde, *Peking Diary*, 78.
69. Ibid. 139, 74, 80.
70. Ibid. 68.
71. 'The War in China', *The Times*, 20 January 1949, 5.
72. Bodde, *Peking Diary*, 97, 85.
73. Ibid. 64.
74. Alan Winnington, *Breakfast with Mao: Memoirs of a Foreign Correspondent* (London: Lawrence & Wishart, 1986), 103.
75. Bodde, *Peking Diary*, 105.
76. Ibid. 109–10.
77. Ibid. 99.
78. Sybille van der Sprenkel, telephone conversation, 18 September 2007.
79. Bodde, quoted in Haffenden, *William Empson: Against the Christians*, 152.
80. Haffendfen, *William Empson: Against the Christians*, 171.
81. Ibid. 153.
82. Bodde, *Peking Diary*, 224.
83. Ibid. 181.
84. Ralph and Nancy Lapwood, *Through the Chinese Revolution*, 45.
85. Alun Falconer, *'I Saw New China'* (London: Britain–China Friendship Association, 1950?).
86. Otto B. van der Sprenkel, in Otto B. Van der Sprenkel (ed.), *New China: Three Views* (London: Turnstile Press, 1950), 2.
87. Ibid. 5.
88. Mrs Sybille van der Sprenkel, 'Mr. Martin Buxton', Obituaries, *The Times*, 26 October 1966, 12.
89. John Haffenden, *William Empson: Against the Christians*, 144–5.
90. Douglas Hurd, *Memoirs* (London: Little Brown, 2003), 97, 101.
91. Ibid. 105.
92. Douglas Hurd, letter to Walter Hamilton. Ibid. 106.
93. Ibid. 111.

3. Paul Hogarth's Marxist Shudder

1. Obituary of Paul Hogarth, *Independent*, 7 January 2002.
2. Ronald Searle quoted in Richard Ingrams's 'Introduction' to Paul Hogarth, *Drawing on Life: The Autobiography of Paul Hogarth* (Newton Abbot: David & Charles, 1997), 6.

3. Paul Hogarth, interview with the author, Cirencester, 1 November 2001.
4. John Berger, 'Portrait of the Artist No. 101: Paul Hogarth', *Art News and Review*, 4/23 (13 December 1952), 1.
5. Hogarth, *Drawing on Life*, 14–15.
6. John Berger, 'Paul Hogarth' [1952/3], in *Paul Hogarth: Cold War Reports* (Norwich: Norwich Institute of Art and Design, 1989), 5.
7. Stanley Evans, *East of Stettin-Trieste* (London: Fore Publications, 1951). In Budapest, Evans attended and thoroughly approved the trial of the violently mistreated Hungarian Cardinal Mindszenty (35–43).
8. Paul Hogarth, 'Afterword', Andy Croft (ed.), *A Weapon in the Struggle: The Cultural History of the Communist Party in Britain* (London: Pluto Press, 1998), 209.
9. Paul Hollander, *Political Pilgrims: Travels of Western Intellectuals to the Soviet Union, China and Cuba* (New York: Harper Colophon, 1983), 347–399.
10. For an account of Iron Curtain Potemkinism and its emergence in the wake of the Bolshevik revolution of October 1917 see my *Iron Curtain: From Stage to Cold War* (Oxford: Oxford University Press, 2007), 140–9, 191–7.
11. Paul Hogarth, handwritten annotation to typescript of interview with Andy Croft, 19 November 1993.
12. Hogarth, *Drawing on Life*, 20.
13. Ibid, 24–5.
14. Paul Hogarth, *A Vienne Au Congrès des Peuples Pour La Paix: Trente Dessins pris sur le vif de Paul Hogarth* (Paris: Editions Défence de la Paix, 1953).
15. At the time of the Ambateilos trial in Athens, Betty Ambatielos was identified by *The Times* as a Communist and former Athens correspondent for the *Daily Worker*. See '10 Greeks Sentenced to Death', *The Times*, 5 November 1948, 4.
16. Paul Hogarth, *Defiant People: Drawings of Greece Today* (London: Lawrence & Wishart, 1953), 22.
17. Hogarth, *Drawing on Life*, 25.
18. Ibid. 23.
19. James Aldridge, 'Introduction' to Hogarth, *Defiant People*, 1.
20. Jack Lindsay, 'Introduction' in *Catalogue of an Exhibition of Drawings and Prints of Poland by Paul Hogarth* (London: Christopher Foss, 1954), 3–4.
21. Hogarth, *Drawing on Life*, 29.
22. Katarzyna Murawska-Muthesius, 'The Cold War Travellers Gaze: Jan Lenica's 1954 Sketchbook of London', in Wendy Bracewell and Alex Drace-Francis, *Under Eastern Eyes: A Comparative Introduction to East*

European Travel Writing on Europe (Budapest and New York: Central European University Press, 2008), 342–5.

23. Paul Hogarth, *Das Antlitz Europas* (Dresden: VEB Verlag Der Kunst, 1956), 179.

24. For the 'Panzaic principle' as it has been applied to the novel, see Wayne Burns, *A Panzaic Theory of the Novel* (Seattle: Howe Street Press, 2009).

25. Hogarth, *Drawing on Life*, 30.

26. Paul Hogarth, *Zeichnungen Aus Polen* (Wydawnictwo Artystyczno-Graficzne R.S.W. 'Prasa').

27. Murawska-Muthesius, 'The Cold War Traveller's Gaze...', 341.

28. According to Murawska-Muthenius, a selection of drawings appeared as 'American Occupation of Great Britain: Correspondence from London' in *Świat*, 1/8 (1951). See 'The Cold War Traveller's Gaze...', 343.

29. 'Poor District of London' appeared in *Świat*, 4/20 (1954). See Murawska-Muthenius, 'The Cold War Traveller's Gaze', 344. Murawska-Muthenius leaves no doubt that Hogarth, together with British Communist friends such as the *Daily Worker* journalist Derek Kartun, participated in the Stalinist framing applied to his drawings as they appeared in Polish publications such as *Szpilki, Świat*, and *Przeglad Artystyczny*. At the same time, it is possible that, even in these tightly corralled settings, the drawings were less than reliable bearers of the interpretations placed on them. Murawska-Muthenius describes how one of *Świat*'s selections of his drawings was 'crowned' by a portrait of a certain Lennie Baxter, described as both a 'trade union activist' and a 'fishmonger'. She has Baxter standing there boldly with his arms crossed, 'looking straight into the viewer's Eye ("I") as if answering the call of the Communist Manifesto: "Proletarians of the whole world unite!"' By the time this portrait was republished in *Das Antlitz Europas*, an East German collection of Hogarth's drawings, Lennie Baxter was being described as a 'fish porter' in the market at Billingsgate, which was not in the East End at all (Hogarth, *Das Antlitz Europas*, 49). As he stands there, gazing back at Hogarth with a sceptical eye, we may be sure that his gaze was never exactly intended to convey 'a message of solidarity from the East End workers to their Brothers in Eastern Europe' (Murawska-Muthenius, 'The Cold War Traveller's Gaze', 344).

30. Hogarth, *Drawing on Life*, 30.

31. Ibid. 33.

32. Ibid. 32.

33. Randall Swingler, 'Bohemia to the Tatras', *The Countryman*, 49/1 (Spring 1954), 58.

34. Croft, *Open Heart*, 220.

35. Ibid. 220–1.
36. This is how José Ortega y Gasset conceived 'realism' in his 'The Nature of the Novel', trans. Evelyn Rugg and Diego Marin, *Hudson Review*, 10 (1957), 40.
37. Transcript of Andy Croft's interview with Paul Hogarth, November 1993.
38. Paul Hogarth, 'Humanism versus Despair in British Art Today', *Marxist Quarterly*, 2/1 (January 1955), 37–47.
39. In its wider presentation, the British dispute between realism and abstraction would be organized into two opposed camps arrayed around the art critics David Sylvester and John Berger, both of which would lay claim to the inheritance of Picasso. If Bacon was to become central to Sylvester's vision, Hogarth played a comparable role for Berger who, in December 1952, had commended Hogarth for a political consciousness that, having never been 'merely a romantic, intellectual theory', was supported by 'action and experience and commitment to the progressive working class movement' (John Berger, 'Portrait of the Artist No. 101: Paul Hogarth', *Art News and Review*, 4/23 (13 December 1952), 1). Hogarth identified with other realist artists, hoping that the work shown in Berger's exhibition 'Looking Forward', at the Whitechapel Art Gallery in 1952, would form 'a bloc which represents a challenging alternative to the despair and decadence of abstract and non-representational art'. As he saw it, the project was continuous with the pre-war Euston Road School as represented by William Coldstream, Lawrence Gowing, and, before his turn to abstraction, Victor Pasmore. It also found inspiration in the work of Diego Rivera and other Mexican realists, exhibited at the Tate Gallery in 1953. Mistrustful of the conventional art gallery, it would find its venues with the help of 'enlightened trade union patronage' of the kind that had already sustained a travelling exhibition of Hogarth's drawings and lithographs in Britain, as well as commissioning Cliff Rowe's murals of the general strike of 1926 at the Electrical Trades Union College in Esher. For a survey of this argument, see James Hyman, *The Battle For Realism: Figurative Art in Britain During the Cold War 1945–1960* (New York and London: Yale University Press, 2001).
40. Paul Hogarth, *Drawing on Life*, 54.

4. The Battle of British 'Friendship'

1. George Trevelyan, *Worlds Apart; China 1953–5, Soviet Union 1962–5* (London: Macmillan, 1971), 30.
2. Alan Winnington, *Breakfast with Mao: Memoirs of a Foreign Correspondent* (London: Lawrence & Wishart, 1986), 168.

3. Anne-Marie Brady, *Friend of China—the Myth of Rewi Alley* (London and New York: Routledge Curzon, 2003).

4. Rewi Alley, *At 90: Memoirs of My China Years* (Beijing: New World Press, 1986), 43–9.

5. Anne-Marie Brady, *Friend of China*, 52–3.

6. 'Lines Written at the House of a Swedish Friend' (August 1952), in Rewi Alley, *Fragments of Living Peking* (Christchurch: New Zealand Peace Council, 1955), 115.

7. Rewi Alley, 'Peking' (5 February 1951), ibid. 95.

8. Marian Ramelson, *British Woman in New China* (London: British Committee, Women's International Democratic Federation, 1949(?)), 16.

9. R. K. Karanjia, *China Stands Up and Wolves of the Wild West* (Bombay: People's Publishing House, 1952), 249.

10. Rewi Alley, *At 90*, 240.

11. Arthur Clegg, *Aid China 1937–1949, A Memoir of a Forgotten Campaign* (Beijing: New World Press, 1989), 11.

12. Shijie Guan, 'Chartism and the First Opium War', *History Workshop Journal*, 24 (1987), 17–31.

13. Bertrand Russell, *The Problem of China* (London: Allen & Unwin, 1922), 82.

14. Ibid. 250.

15. John and Alice Chipman Dewey, *Letters from China and Japan* (New York: Dutton, 1920), 228.

16. Ibid. 161.

17. Ibid. 194.

18. Cyrus LeRoy Baldridge, *Time and Chance* (New York: John Day, 1947), 214–15.

19. Hallet Abend, *My Years in China 1926–1941* (London: John Lane, 1944), 52. See also 'Slow Strangulation', *Time*, 9 May 1927.

20. Philip Short, *Mao: A Life* (London: Hodder and Stoughton, 1999), 178.

21. 'Statement Issued in Protest against the Violation of Sun Yat-sen's Revolutionary Principles and Policies' (14 July 1927) in Soong Ching Ling (Mme Sun Yat-sen), *The Struggle for New China* (Peking: Foreign Languages Press, 1952), 6. For an account of this farewell statement's publication in the *Hankow People's Tribune*, see Baruch Hirson and Arthur J. Knodel (eds), *Reporting the Chinese Revolution: The Letters of Rayna Prohme* (London and Ann Arbor: Pluto Press, 2007), 82.

22. 'Hands Off China!' appeal quoted from a leaflet published by the Communist Party of Great Britain, London. The Communist signatories included Harry Pollitt, Tom Mann, Shapurji Saklatavala, Ben Tillett, and Will Lawther. The appeal was also signed by the radical Liberal journalist H. N. Brailsford, the Countess of Warwick, Liam O'Flaherty, and Sean O'Casey.

23. Clegg, *Aid China*, 17.
24. Quoted from 'Stop the War on China!: League Against Imperialism Calls to British Workers', a single-page leaflet published in London by the League against Imperialism, n.d.
25. Clegg, *Aid China*, 22.
26. George Hardy, *Those Stormy Years; Memories of the Fight for Freedom on Five Continents* (London: Lawrence & Wishart, 1956).
27. Quoted from *China: The World's Oldest Civilisation Fighting Against Japanese Aggression*, an illustrated brochure published by the China Campaign Committee (London) in 1937.
28. Clegg, *Aid China*, 38–9.
29. Ibid. 114.
30. Ibid. 32.
31. Ibid. 19.
32. Shelley Wang's article 'China's struggle on four fronts' appeared together with his poem 'The Eagle' in a special Chinese supplement to *Left Review*, 3/12 (January 1938), 717–24. See also his 'Poem' included in the 'China Symposium' in Stefan Schimanski and Henry Treece (eds), *Transformation* (London: Gollancz, 1943), 174. Wang was killed in 1939, having returned to China to join the fight against Japan.
33. Yuan-tsung Chen, *Return to the Middle Kingdom: One Family, Three Revolutionaries, and the Birth of Modern China* (New York and London: Union Square Press, 2008), 303–6.
34. Jack Chen (Introduction), *Five Thousand Years Young: Modern Chinese Drawings and Woodcuts* (London: Lawrence & Wishart, 1937). See also *Progress of China's Industrial Cooperatives: A Series of Twenty Drawings* by Jack Chen (New York: American Committee in Aid of Chinese Industrial Cooperatives, n.d.).
35. Clegg, *Aid China*, 29–30. For a memory of General Yang's last interview before leaving London (given in a dingy hotel in Southampton Row), and his insistence that the Communist contribution to the war against Japan would be greater than many had yet understood, see Richard Goodman, 'The New Napoleons', *Left Review*, 3/13, February, 1938, 773–8.
36 Clegg, *Aid China*, 110.
37. Ibid. 83.
38. Ibid. 114.
39. Ibid. 26.
40. Ibid. 34.
41. Clement Attlee was himself chairing this Committee from May 1947. See David Kynaston, *Austerity Britain 1945–51* (London: Bloomsbury, 2007), 224.

42. Michael Lindsay, *The Unknown War: North China 1937–1945* (London: Bergström & Boyle, 1975), unpaginated.

43. Hsiao Li Lindsay, *Bold Plum: With the Guerillas in China's War against Japan*, (Morrisville, NC: Lulu Press, 2007), 99–101.

44. This is how they were described when they were republished by the China Campaign Committee. See Lord Listowel's Preface to Michael Lindsay, *North China Front* (London: China Campaign Committee, 1944), 1.

45. 'China at War. Political Obstacles to Military Unity. The Chinese Communist View', *The Times*, 18 December 1944, 5.

46. Lindsay, *North China Front*, 22.

47. Hsiao Li Lindsay, *Bold Plum*, 325–6.

48. Lindsay, *The Unknown War: North China 1937–1945*.

49. Hsiao Li Lindsay, *Bold Plum*, 339.

50. Ibid. 339–40.

51. Clegg, *Aid China*, 156.

52. Lindsay, *China and the Cold War*, 9.

53. Ibid. 4.

54. Ibid. 20.

55. Ibid. 4.

56. Clegg, *Aid China*, 175–6.

57 Arthur Clegg, *New China, New World* (London: Birch Books, 1949), 4.

58. Clegg, *Aid China*, 173.

59. George Orwell, letter to Humphry House, 11 April 1940, in Peter Davidson (ed.), *The Complete Works of George Orwell*, xii: *A Patriot After All, 1940–41* (London: Secker & Warburg, 1998), 140.

60. See his letter against the suggestion, made in the previous day's paper by a retired naval captain named M. H. Scott, that Franco's Spain should be allowed into the new Western European Union 'because it is anti-Communist'. This was, he suggested, to play into Soviet propaganda claims that 'the spokesmen of western democracy are hypocritical when they talk of maintaining freedom; that they really have no objections to a police State provided only that it is a police State which protects the rights of property'. *The Times*, 13 May 1948, 5.

61. Michael Lindsay in Otto B. Van Der Sprenkel, Robert Guillian, and Michael Lindsay, *New China: Three Views* (London: Turnstile Press, 1951), 147.

62. Ibid. 149.

63. Ibid. 147.

64. Ibid. 145.

65. Ibid. 147.

66. Ibid. 132.

67. Ibid. 131.

68. Michael Lindsay, *Notes on Educational Problems in Communist China 1941–7. With Supplements on 1948 and 1949* (1950) (Westport, Conn.: Greenwood Press, 1977, p. i.

69. Ibid. 44.

70. Michael Lindsay, *China and the Cold War: A Study in International Politics* (Victoria: Melbourne University Press, 1954), 240.

71. Michael Lindsay in Van Der Sprenkel, Guillian and Lindsay, *New China: Three Views*, 149.

72. Russell, *The Problem of China*, 250.

5. The Charms of Anti-Americanism

1. Ruth Fischer claims that her brother Gerhardt had been 'sent to China at the end of 1929 to liquidate the opposition to the Russian politburo'. See her *Stalin and German Communism: A Study in the Origins of the State Party* (London: G. Cumberlege, 1948), 618.

2. Quoted from Wolf Biermann's account of Eisler's return to Europe. See J. K. Miller, 'Interview with Wolf Biermann', http://eislermusic. com/biermann.htm (accessed 15 August 2007). See also the account of the captain of the *Batory*, Jan Cwiklinski, *The Captain Leaves his Ship: The Story of the Captain of the S.S. Batory by Jan Cwiklinski, Formerly Master of the Polish Motorship Batory, as Told to Hawthorne Daniel* (London: Robert Hale, 1955), 205.

3. Quoted from Wolf Biermann's account of Eisler's return to Europe. See J. K. Miller, 'Interview with Wolf Biermann', http://eislermusic. com/biermann.htm (accessed 15 August 2007).

4. Kingsley Martin, MP, 'The international scene as I see it, No. 30. (The case of Gerhardt Eisler)', script of radio talk for the BBC's USSR section, transmitted 7 June 1949, Kingsley Martin archive, Special Collections, University of Sussex library.

5. *The Journey to Berlin: Report of a Commission of Inquiry into certain events at Brussels, the Channel Ports, Innsbruck and Saalfelden in August 1951* (National Council for Civil Liberties, 1952).

6. These are the words of Harry Backer, Secretary of Birmingham Trades Council. For a fuller account of the Corts, the campaign to keep them in Britain, and their subsequent plight see my *Iron Curtain: From Stage to Cold War* (Oxford: Oxford University Press, 2007), 9–15, 358–74.

7. Stanley Evans, *East of Stettin-Trieste* (London: Fore Publications, 1951), 84.

8. MG 2/1/51. Michael Lindsay, 'Anglo-Chinese Relations; the Story of a Delegation', *Manchester Guardian*, 2 January 1951. Lindsay would write more about the Liu Ning-I delegation in *China and the Cold War: A Study in International Politics* (Victoria: Melbourne University Press, 1954), 12–16.

9. Lindsay, *China and the Cold War*, 15. For Lindsay's latter account of this 'friendship delegation's visit, 12–18.

10. Liu Ning-I, Introduction' to Arthur Clegg, *New China New World* (London: Birch Books, 1949), p. viii.

11. *Tribune*, 3 November 1950.

12. Betty England, Introduction in *Britons in China: Report of the First British Delegation to Visit New China* (London: Britain–China Friendship Association, 1951), 6.

13. George Hardy, *Those Stormy Years: Memories of the Fight for Freedom on Five Continents* (London: Lawrence & Wishart, 1956), 210. (CUL NF6 624:5.c.95.461.)

14. Ibid. 245–6.

15. Ibid. 252–3.

16. Michael Lindsay, *New China: Three Views* (London: Turnstile Press, 1951), 147.

17. Ibid. 253.

18. Hardy, *Those Stormy Years*, 254.

19. Ibid. 255.

20. Ibid. 256.

21. W. J. Ellerby, 'Foreword', Geoffrey Bing QC, MP, *M.P. in New China* (London: Britain–China Friendship Association, 1952/3), unpaginated.

22. Geoffrey Bing, *M.P. in New China* (London: Britain–China Friendship Association, 1952), unpaginated.

23. Desmond Donnelly, *The March Wind: Explorations behind the Iron Curtain* (London: Collins, 1959), 39.

24. Ibid. 53, 52.

25. Hewlett Johnson, *Searching for Light* (London: Michael Joseph, 1968), 307.

26. Ibid. 307.

27. Hewlett Johnson, *China's New Creative Age* (London: Lawrence & Wishart, 1953), 29.

28. The phrase is quoted from the Conclusion of the report of Joseph Needham's 'International Scientific Commission for Investigation of the Facts concerning Bacterial Warfare in Korea and China', in *Exhibition on Bacteriological War Crimes Committed by the Government of the United States of America* (Peking: The Chinese People's Committee for World Peace, 1952), 15.

29. Report of the International Scientific Commission for the Investigation of the Facts concerning Bacterial Warfare in Korea and China, *Chinese Medical Journal*, 70/9–12 (September–December 1952), 459.

30. Tom Buchanan, 'The Courage of Galileo: Joseph Needham and the "Germ Warfare" Allegations in the Korean War', *History*, 86/284 (October 2001), 504.

31. Simon Winchester, *The Man Who Loved China: The Fantastic Story of the Eccentric Scientist who Unlocked the Mysteries of the Middle Kingdom* (New York: Harper Collins, 2008), 201.

32. *Exhibition on Bacteriological War Crimes Committed by the Government of the United States of America* (Peking: The Chinese People's Committee for World Peace, 1952), 17.

33. Ibid. 3.

34. Anne-Marie Brady, *Friend of China: The Myth of Rewi Alley* (London and New York: RoutledgeCurzon, 2003), 61–6, 81.

35. Harold W. Rigney, *Four Years in a Red Hell: The Story of Father Rigney* (Chicago: Regnery, 1956), 145.

36. 'Dean of Canterbury on Germ Warfare', *The Times*, 9 July 1952, 3.

37. 'Primate and the Dean of Canterbury, *The Times*, 16 July 1952, 4.

38. Hewlett Johnson, Dean of Canterbury, *I Appeal* (London: Britain–China Friendship Association, 1952).

39. Johnson, *Searching for Light*, 328.

40. Report of the International Scientific Commission for the Investigation of the Facts concerning Bacterial Warfare in Korea and China, *Chinese Medical Journal*, 70/9–12, (September–December 1952), 399.

41. Tom Buchanan, 'The Courage of Galileo: Joseph Needham and the "Germ Warfare" Allegations in the Korean War', *History*, 86/281 (January 2001), 513.

42. Winchester, *The Man Who Loved China*, 207.

43. Buchanan, 'The Courage of Galileo', 509.

44. Winchester, *The Man Who Loved China*, 208.

45. Kingsley Martin, quoted in Buchanan, 'The Courage of Galileo', 513.

46. Letter to *The Times*, 8 October 1952, 7.

47. L. O. Lyne, letter to *The Times*, 10 October 1952, 7.

48. Desmond Donnelly, *March Wind: Explorations behind the Iron Curtain* (London: Collins, 1959), 223.

49. Buchanan, 'The Courage of Galileo', 521.

50. Winchester, *The Man Who Loved China*, 210–11.

51. Percy Timberlake, *The 48 Group: The Story of the Icebreakers in China* (London: The 48 Group Club, 1994), 1.

52. Ibid. 3.

53. 'British Shipowner's "Crime"', *The Times*, 5 May 1953, 5.

54. 'Trade with China', *The Times*, 6 May 1953, 9.

55. Timberlake, *The 48 Group*.

56. Ibid. 5.

57. Ibid. 9.

58. Ibid. 20.

59. Ibid. 13.

60. 'Franco-Chinese Trade Agreement', *The Times*, 8 June 1953, 7.

61. 'Moscow Trade Talks', *The Times*, 7 November 1957.

62. Joan Robinson, *Letters from a Visitor to China* (Cambridge: Students' Bookshops Ltd, 1954), 30.

63. Ibid. 27.

64. Ibid. 18.

65. Ibid. 12.

66 Evan Luard, *Britain and China* (London: Chatto & Windus, 1962), 145.

6. Barbara Castle's Bevanite Sigh

1. Barbara Castle, Conversation with the author, 23 February, 2001.

2. Edwin Pulleyblank, email to the author, 26 April 2002.

3. Derrick James, diary. Unless otherwise specified, all quotations from James are from this unpublished source.

4 Denis Mathews, unpublished note headed 'Tuesday October 5th 1954'.

5. See Olga B. Lepeshinskaya, *The Development of Living Processes in the Pre-cellular Period...* (London: Society for Cultural Relations with the USSR, 1951), and *The Origin of Cells from Living Substance* (Moscow: Foreign Languages Publishing House, 1954). For an account of Lepeshinskaya's baleful career in Stalin's Russia, see Yakov Rapoport, 'Olga Lepeshinskaya: The Vital Substance and its Inglorious Demise', in Rapoport, *The Doctors' Plot* (London: Fourth Estate, 1991), 254–72.

6. Barbara Castle, diary of China trip 1954, typed version as received 11 February 2002.

7. The Kem Amendment, named after the Republican Senator James Kem from Missouri, was introduced in May 1951 and had indeed been more draconian than the later Battle Act, introduced in October, which allowed the President some flexibility over the imposition of penalties on allies in receipt of American aid.

8. Richard. T. Cupitt, *Reluctant Champions: US Presidential Policy and Strategic Export* (New York and London: Routledge, 2000), 77.

9. *Economist*, 25 August 1951, 431–3.

7. Chou En-lai's Winning Smile

1. Robert Guillain, *Blue Ants: 600 Million Chinese Under the Red Flag* (London: Secker & Warburg, 1956), 32.

2. Yafeng Xia, *Negotiating with the Enemy: U.S.–China Talks during the Cold War, 1949–1972* (Bloomington and Indianapolis: Indiana University Press, 2006), 26.

3. Alec Nove and Desmond Donnelly, *Trade with Communist Countries* (London: Hutchinson, 1960), 120.

4. Lindsay was scathing about Madame Sun Yat-sen's 1951 article 'On Peaceful Co-existence': 'On the one hand she argues that peaceful co-existence is possible and that the great majority of the American and British people want peace. On the other hand, she denounces both Truman and Attlee as the willing tools of minority groups who want war, though even when the article was written it was clear that the only alternative governments which the British or American people were likely to choose would be still further to the right politically. That is, while talking of peaceful co-existence she uses arguments which imply that war is inevitable.' (Michael Lindsay, *China and the Cold War* (Victoria: Melbourne University Press, 1954), 9.)

5. Robert F. Randle, *Geneva 1954: The Settlement of the Indochinese War* (Princeton University Press, 1989), 143.

6. James Cable, *The Geneva Conference of 1954 on Indochina* (London: MacMillan, 1986), 18.

7. Ibid. 29.

8. Ibid. 35.

9. 'Seeking Five-Power Conference', *The Times*, 11 January 1954.

10. Randle, *Geneva 1954*, 26.

11. Cable, *The Geneva Conference*, 52.

12. Ibid. 53.

13. Ibid. 57.

14. Ibid. 58.

15. Philippe Devillers and Jean Lacouture, *End of a War: Indochina 1954* (London: Pall Mall Press, 1969), 122.

16. 'More Delegates Arrive in Geneva. Sunshine and Eastern Colour', *The Times*, 24 April 1954, 5.

17. Devillers and Lacouture, *End of a War*, 124.

18. As the *Manchester Guardian* reported of Krasin, 'A being...erect upon two legs and bearing the outward form and semblance of a man was seen to approach 10, Downing Street, yesterday, to ring at the door and gain admission...Mr. Lloyd George has seen him and lives.' *Manchester Guardian*, 1 June 1920. Quoted in W. P and Zelda K. Coates, *A History of Anglo-Soviet Relations*, (London: Lawrence and Wishart, 1944), 26.

19. Yafeng Xia, *Negotiating with the Enemy: U.S –China Talks during the Cold War, 1949–1972* (Bloomington and Indianapolis: Indiana University Press, 2006), 78.

20. Hewlett Johnson, *China's New Creative Age* (London: Lawrence & Wishart, 1953), 146.

21. James Cameron, *Mandarin Red: A Journey behind the 'Bamboo Curtain'* (London: Michael Joseph, 1955), 285.

22. George Trevelyan, *Worlds Apart; China 1953–5, Soviet Union 1962–5* (London: Macmillan, 1971), 77.

23. Ibid. 79.

24. Douglas Hurd, *Memoirs*, (London: Little Brown, 2003), 107.

25. Ibid. 69.

26. Robert F. Randle, *Geneva 1954: The Settlement of the Indochinese War* (Princeton University Press, 1969), 341.

27. Ibid. 351.

28. Ibid. 353.

29. Ibid. 350.

30. Cable, *The Geneva Conference of 1954*, 127.

31. Randle, *Geneva 1954*, 357.

32. Cable, *The Geneva Conference of 1954*, 89.

33. See, for example, Nicholas Read-Collins, *Report on the War in IndoChina* (London: Union of Democratic Control, 1953).

34. Francois Joyaux, *Chine et le règlement du premier conflit d'Indochine: Genève 1954* (Paris: Publications de la Sorbonne, 1979).

35. Drew Middleton, *New York Times*, 27 June 1954. Quoted in Randle, *Geneva 1954*, 301.

36. See the text of Liu Shao-ch'I, from 1949, quoted in Joyaux, *Chine*, 366.

37. Randle, *Geneva 1954*, 281.

38. Ibid. 305.

39. Ibid. 285.

40. Ibid. 188.

41. Ibid. 310.

42. Hurd, *Memoirs*, 111.

43. Joyaux, *Chine*, 306.

44. Ibid. 360.

45. Hurd, *Memoirs*, 111.

46. Morgan Phillips, *East Meets West: A Pictorial Story of the Labour Delegation to the Soviet Union and China* (London: Lincolns-Prager, 1954), 12.

47. Michael Foot, interview with the author, 4 June 2002.

48. A. J. Ayer, *More of My Life* (London: Collins, 19874), 99.

49. 'British Art Show on Red China', *Glasgow Herald*, 24 October 1957.

50. This assertion surfaced at the time Tate Britain's exhibition of Stanley Spencer's paintings and drawing, curated by Timothy Hyman and myself, in 2001. It was made, courtesy of a letter from Mrs Angela Hodson, in a diary article in the *Sunday Telegraph* on 3 February 2001.

51. John Chinnery, interview 12 March 2001.

52. Ross's letter is quoted in Spencer's letter to his niece Daphne Robinson, 30 August 1954. Spencer's letter to Daphne and her mother Marjorie Spencer, which remain in the Robinson family's possession, have been transcribed by Dr. Jeremy Harvey. Copies are held in the Tate Archive and also in the Stanley Spencer Museum, Cookham.

53. Stanley Spencer, letter to Daphne Robinson, 1 November 1954.

54. Stanley Spencer, letter to Daphne Robinson, 30 August 1954.
55. Stanley Spencer, letter to Marjorie Spencer, 1 December, 1954.
56. See James Hyman, *The Battle for Realism: Figurative Art in Britain During the Cold War 1945–1960* (New Haven and London: Yale University Press, 2001), 71.
57. Nancy Carline, telephone interview, 8 March 2001.
58. Paul Hogarth, *Drawing on Life: The Autobiography of Paul Hogarth* (Newton Abbot: David & Charles, 1997), 42.
59. Paul Hogarth, interview with the author, 1 November 2001.

Part II. One Good Elk and Dinner with the Politburo

1. Michael Davie, 'With Arsenal in Russia', *Observer*, 10 October 1954.

8. Flowers for Edith Summerskill

1. Paul Hogarth, *Looking at China: With the Journal of the Artist* (London: Lawrence & Wishart, 1956), 1.
2. The phrase 'techniques of hospitality' is quoted from Paul Hollander, *Political Pilgrims: Travels of Western Intellectuals to the Soviet Union, China, and Cuba* (New York: Harper Colophon, 1983), 347–399.
3. Morgan Phillips, *East Meets West: A Pictorial Story of the Labour Party Delegation to the Soviet Union and China* (London: Lincolns-Prager, 1954), 18.
4. Sir William Hayter, KCMG, *The Kremlin and the Embassy* (London: Hodder & Stoughton, 1966), 32.
5. Paul Hogarth, *Looking at China*, 1.
6. Ibid. 2.
7. John Chinnery, interview with the author, London, 2 March 2001.
8. Hewlett Johnson, *Searching for Light* (London: Michael Joseph, 1968), 334.
9. Stanley Spencer, note in Tate Archive, 733.10.162.
10. Hogarth, *Looking at China*, 2.
11. A. J. Ayer, *More of my Life* (London: Collins, 1982).
12. Eric Hobsbawm, *Interesting Times: A Twentieth-Century Life* (London: Allen Lane, 2002), 198.
13. A. J. Ayer, *More of My Life*, 103.
14. Clement Attlee, 'Attlee Reports on Trip to Moscow', *New York Times*, 7 September 1954, 1.
15. Hogarth, *Looking at China*, 2.
16. Ernst Bloch, quoted from Jack Zipes, 'Christa Wolf: Moralist as Marxist', in Christa Wolf, *Divided Heaven* (New York: Adler's Books, 1979), p. viii.
17. Denis Mathews, letter to his mother, written 'in the plane beyond Omsk', 11 October 1954.

18. *The Times*, 7 August 1954, 2. Surviving papers suggest that the invitation had actually come much earlier, but political sensitivity encouraged a different explanation.

19. Michael Foot, *Aneurin Bevan: A Biography*, ii: *1945–1970* (London: Davis-Poynter, 1973), 446.

20. Sir William Hayter, *The Kremlin and the Embassy* (London: Hodder & Stoughton, 1966), 37.

21. Ibid. 40.

22. Andrew Rothstein, *Peaceful Coexistence* (Harmondsworth: Penguin, 1955).

23. Quoted from Chou En-Lai, Report on Foreign Affairs at the 33rd Session of the Central People's Government Council, Supplement to *People's China*, 1 September 1954, p. 9.

24. Chou also spoke in English '("Excuse my poor English," he said, and then spoke in excellent, fluent English, not one word of which was comprehensible to his Russian hearers')'; Hayter, *The Kremlin and the Embassy*, 36.

25. Morgan Phillips, 'Labour Party Delegation to China—Report No. 1', report to the National Executive Committee, October 1954. Morgan Phillips General Secretary's papers, Labour Party Archive, Museum of Labour History, Manchester.

26. Hayter, *The Kremlin and the Embassy*, 37.

27. Ibid. 38.

28. Phillips, *East Meets West*, 20.

29. Foot, *Aneurin Bevan: A Biography*, ii: *1945–60* 444.

30. Phillips, 'Labour Party Delegation to China—Report No.1'.

31. *The Times*, 12 August 1954, 6.

32. Hayter, *The Kremlin and the Embassy*, 39.

33. Clement Attlee, 'Attlee Reports on Trip to Moscow', *New York Times*, 7 September 1954, 9.

34. Sam Watson, 'China's Attitude to the West', *Observer*, 26 September 1954, 6.

35. Foot, *Aneurin Bevan: A Biography*, ii: *1945–1970*, 445.

36. Aneurin Bevan, 'Kremlin Personalities', *Tribune*, 1 October 1954, 1–2.

37. Hayter, *The Kremlin and the Embassy*, 39.

38. Morgan Phillips, *East Meets West*, 20.

39. Morgan Phillips, 'Our Moscow Talks', *Reynolds News*, 15 August 1954.

40. Morgan Phillips, pencil text of article sent from Moscow (clipped to a typescript, significantly different but of the same article), entitled 'Moscow Revisited', General Secretary's Papers, Labour History Museum, Manchester.

41. Morgan Phillips, undated draft of article for the *Daily Telegraph*. General Secretary's Papers, Labour History Museum, Manchester.

42. *Daily Sketch*, 14 August 1954. *Reynolds News* responded the following day with an article entitled 'Give it the fool's cap and bells', attacking the *Sketch* for its 'barmy logic'.
43. Theodore Rothstein, *Peaceful Coexistence* (Harmondsworth: Penguin, 1955), 62.
44. Ibid. 63.
45. Ibid. 70.
46. Ibid. 135.
47. Edith Summerskill, statement broadcast on 11 December 1954, quoted in Rothstein, *Peaceful Coexistence*, 167.

9. Just Like Manchester a Hundred Years Ago

1. A. J. Ayer, *More of My Life* (London: Collins, 1982) 104.
2. Michael Davie, 'Heard and Seen in Moscow', *Observer*, 10 October 1954, 7.
3. Stanley Spencer, undated letter to Dickory Frank from Moscow, transcription in Tate Archive, 733.1.546.
4. Ibid. 104.
5. Denis Mathews, letter to his mother, written 'in the plane beyond Omsk', 11 October 1954.
6. Hayter, *The Kremlin and the Embassy*, 47.
7. Stanley Spencer, letter to Dickory Frank, Tate Archives, 733.1.546.
8. A. J. Ayer, *More of My Life*, 104.
9. Martin Thompson, 'Back to the Future', *Cambridge Alumni Magazine*, 37 (Michaelmas Term 2002), 27.
10. Ellis Smith, 'Two Views of Russia', *Labour's Voice* (January 1962) (copy among the Ellis Smith papers at Salford Local History Library).
11. Clement Attlee, 'Attlee Reports on Trip to Moscow', *New York Times*, 7 September 1954, 9.
12. A. J. Ayer, *More of My Life*, 105. Ayer gave a different description in a radio talk delivered on the BBC's Third Programme shortly after his return: 'we were struck by the closeness of the analogies with Victorian England. There is the same expanding economy, the harsh conditions of labour, the belief in a Utopia to be attained through material progress, the jingoism, a certain sanctimoniousness and moral earnestness, and almost exactly the same artistic tastes' ('Impressions of Communist China', *The Listener*, 2 December 1954, 941).
13. Rex Warner, *The Aerodrome* (London: Bodley Head, 1941), 49–60.
14. On 10 August 1954, *The Times* reported that a delegation of British agriculturalists had been invited to visit the Moscow Agricultural Exhibition. The group included a number of men who were leading figures in the state-led modernization of British agriculture: Professor Sir

James Scott Watson, chief scientific and agricultural adviser with the Ministry of Agriculture and Fisheries; G. D. H. Bell of the Plant Breeding Institute in Cambridge; and Sir William Ogg, Director of Rothamsted Experimental Station.

15. Clement Attlee, 'Attlee Reports on Trip to Moscow', 9.
16. Morgan Phillips, 'Moscow Revisited' (typescript for *Reynolds News*), General Secretary's Papers, Labour History Museum, Manchester.
17. Stanley Spencer, undated note written 'about 11 o'clock Saturday night' in Moscow, Tate Archives, 7333.10.162.

10. The Tragic Thoughts of Chairman Smith

1. Ellis Smith papers, in Salford Local History Archive, U294 Z38946.
2. Denis Mathews, letter to his mother, headed 'In the plane beyond Omsk. Monday Morning, October 11, 1954'.
3. 'Our London Correspondence', *Manchester Guardian*, 14 November 1941, 4.
4. Ben Pimlott (ed.), *The Second World War Diary of Hugh Dalton* (1986), 773, 866. See also David E. Martin and John B.Smethurst's entry on Ellis Smith in Joyce M. Bellamy and John Saville (eds), *Dictionary of Labour Biography*, vol. ix (London: Macmillan, 1993), 265–70.
5. P. M. Williams (ed.), *The Diary of Hugh Gaitskell 1945–1956* (1983), 9.
6. 'We still Need 1,000,000 People's Commandos', *Reynolds News*, 15 May 1949, 4.
7. Paul Robeson, 'Why a Singer must Fight', *Reynolds News*, 15 May 1949, 4.
8. Gerald Brown, 'Ellis Smith, Champion of the North, Dies', *Manchester Evening News*, 8 November 1969.
9. Ellis Smith, 'A New Ginger Group', *Reynolds News*, 22 May 1949, 4.
10. Ellis Smith, 'A Letter to an Engineer', U294/27, Salford Local History Library.
11. John Dummelow, *1899–1949* (Manchester: Metropolitan-Vickers Electrical Company Ltd, 1949), 91–2.
12. The course attended by Smith was taught by Fred Casey, an advocate of 'Independence in Working-Class Organization', whose book, *Thinking: An Introduction to its History and Science*, had been published by the Labour Publishing Company in 1922. Raphael Samuel has argued that the movement for 'independent working-class education', as represented by the Plebs League and also the network of labour colleges, was much concerned with teaching workers 'How to Think' at this period, in contrast with the Communist Party of Great Britain, which broke away from the Plebs League in 1922, and concentrated on teaching a self-contained, Marxist and 'Party-minded' version of 'What to Think'. See Raphael Samuel, 'Staying Power: The Lost World

of British Communism, Part Two', *New Left Review,* 156 (March/April 1986), 74–6.

13. Barbara Castle, *Fighting All the Way* (London: Macmillan, 1993), 61.
14. Ibid. 142.
15. Johny Smethurst, telephone conversation with the author, 2002.
16. Ellis Smith, MP, House of Commons, 20 May 1938, *Hansard,* 336 cc799–804.
17. Quoted from John Parker, who entered the Commons as a Labour MP after the same election (Joyce Bellamy and John Saville (eds), *Dictionary of Labour Biography* (*DLB*) (London: Macmillan 1993), ix. 267).
18. See David E. Martin and John B. Smethurst, entry on Ellis Smith in *DLB* ix. 269.
19. The Second Report to the NEC is indeed full of statistics, which may be incomprehensible, since Morgan Philips, who assembled it, elsewhere admits that it was impossible even to establish what the exchange rate was in Moscow.
20. 'Reflections 16' in Salford Local History Library U294/27.
21. *Soviet Russia Today: Report of the British Workers' Delegation, 1927* (London: Labour Research Department, 1927), 17–18.
22. Ruth Fischer, *Stalin and German Communism: A Study in the Origins of the State Party* (London: Oxford University Press, 1948), 575.
23. Ibid. 595.
24. Ellis Smith, handwritten and untitled notes describing his 1954 trip to China, Ellis Smith papers, Salford Local History Library, I294/Z95.
25. Tom Fraser, quoted, David E. Martin's entry on George Lindgren, Joyce M. Bellamy, and John Saville (eds.) *Dictionary of Labour Biography,* Vol. II (London: Macmillan, 1974), 236.

11. Stanley Spencer's Pyjama Cord and the Socialist Tree

1. Vernon Lee, 'On Modern Travelling', in *Limbo and Other Essays* (London: Grant Edwards, 1897), 67.
2. Peter Vansittart, telephone conversation with author, 5 April 2002.
3. A. J. Ayer, *More of My Life* (London: Collins, 1984), 101.
4. Peter Vansittart, conversation with the author, Kersey, 8 June 2002.
5. Peter Vansittart, *In the Fifties* (London: Murray, 1995), 140.
6. José Manser, *Hugh Casson: A Biography* (London: Viking, 2000), 173.
7. Cedric Dover, 'Keep it Dark', *Reynolds News,* 8 October 1939, 10.
8. Cedric Dover, 'Biology; the Study of Living Things', in William Freeman et al., *The Complete Self Educator* (London: Odhams Press, 1947), 160.
9. Cedric Dover, 'Asian Journey', *Trees,* 18 (April 1955), 243–56.
10. Cedric Dover, *Know This of Race* (London: Chatto & Windus, 1939), 50.

11. Ellis Smith, 'Two Views on Russia', *Labour's Voice* (January 1962).
12. See Smith's book of often unidentified press cuttings, Salford Local History Archive.
13. *News Chronicle*, 14 January 1949.

Part III. Anticipating China

1. Vernon Lee, 'On Modern Travelling', in *Limbo and other Essays* (London: Grant Richards, 1897), 63.
2. Aneurin Bevan, 'The China Tour Part Three: Marx Versus Birth Control', *Tribune*, 8 October 1954, 1.

12. Ghosts over Siberia

1. Hugh Casson, *Red Lacquer Days: An Illustrated Journal Describing a Recent Visit to Peking* (London: Lion and Unicorn Press, 1955), unpaginated.
2. Dinah Casson, personal communication, 13 July 2009.
3. A. J. Ayer, *More of My Life* (London: Collins, 1984), 106.
4. Ivor Montagu, *Land of Blue Sky: A Portrait of Modern Mongolia* (London: Dennis Dobson, 1956), 13.
5. Casson, *Red Lacquer Days*.
6. In his notebook, Casson recorded Spencer's words as 'How terrible to see an army and not feel protected by it'.
7. Ayer, *More of My Life*, 106.
8. Joseph Needham, *Science and Society in Ancient China; delivered at Conway Hall, Red Lion Square, W.C.1, on May 12, 1947* (London: Watts, 1947), 19.
9. Andrew L. March, *The Idea of China: Myth and Theory in Geographic Thought* (Newton Abbot, London and Vancouver: David & Charles, 1974), 36.
10. John De' Marignolli, 'Recollections of Travel in the East', in Henry Yule, *Cathay and Way Thither; being a collection of Medieval Notices of China*, vol. ii (London: Haykluyt Society, 1866), 339, 346.
11. 'Travels of Friar Odoric', in Yule, *Cathay and the Way Hither*, ii. 182.
12. Ibid. 186.
13. Ibid. 240.
14. Ibid. 222.
15. Ibid. 219.
16. Jean-Denis Attiret, *A Particular Account of the Emperor of China's Gardens near Pekin*, trans. Sir Harry Beaumont (London: Dodsley, 1752), 34–6.
17. Ibid. 6.
18. Ibid. 44.
19. Ibid. 34–6.
20. See Hugh Honour, *Chinoiserie: The Vision of Cathay* (London: John Murray, 1961).

21. Dawn Jacobson, *Chinoiserie* (London and New York: Phaidon, 1993), 60.

22. From 'Three Old German Palaces', in Vernon Lee, *The Tower of Mirrors* (London: John Lane, 1914), 125.

23. Honour, *Chinoiserie*, 225.

24. 'Punch's Own Report of the Opening of the Great Exhibition', *Punch*, 20 (1851), 190.

25. Prince Albert's Royal Commission appears to have encountered some difficulty in its attempt to establish a Chinese presence at the Great Exhibition. The Chinese emperor would not participate, and the merchants and traders invited to help the British consuls in assembling 'a tolerable representation of Chinese industry' also proved unenthusiastic—even if their reluctance was not directly connected to their attempt to convince the British government of their need for access not just to treaty ports such as Canton and Shanghai but to the interior of China too. In the event, the Great Exhibition's Chinese displays appear to have been assembled in by a certain Mr William Hewitt, hired by Prince Albert's Royal Commission to acquire exhibits that were already in England. Hewitt is reported to have spent £1,000 gathering objects in London and Liverpool, and also to have recruited 'a Chinese attendant at the cost of £50'. See Frances Wood, *No Dogs and not many Chinese: Treaty Port Life in China 1843–1943* (London: John Murray, 1998), 57.

26. See James L. Hevia, *Cherishing Men from Afar: Qing Guest Ritual and the Macartney Embassy of 1793* (Durham, NC, and London: Duke University Press, 1995).

27. See Eric Reinders, *Borrowed Gods and Foreign Bodies: Christian Missionaries Imagine Chinese Religion* (Berkeley: University of California Press, 2004), 212.

28. 'A Dissertation on Roast Pig', in Charles Lamb, *Essays of Elia*, 1st Series (New York: Appleton, 1890), 193–201.

29. Charles Dickens, 'The Chinese Junk', first printed in *The Examiner*, 24 June 1848, and collected in Michael Slater (ed.), *Dickens's Journalism*, ii: *The Amusements of the People and other Papers: Reports, Essays and Reviews 1834–51* (London: Dent, 1996), 100.

30. Charles Dickens (with R. H. Horne), 'The Great Exhibition and the Little One', first published in *Household Words*, 5 July 1851, and collected in Harry Stone (ed.), *The Uncollected Writings of Charles Dickens: Household Words 1850–1859*, i (London: John Lane, 1969), 320.

31. Ibid. 320.

32. 'A Chinese Puzzle', *Punch*, 21 (1851), 19.

33. Dickens and Horne, 'The Great Exhibition and the Little One', 320.

34. Ibid. 329.
35. Ibid. 322.
36. Charles Dickens, 'The Chinese Junk', *The Examiner*, 24 June 1848, collected in Slater (ed.), *Dickens's Journalism*, ii: *The Amusements of the People and other Papers: Reports, Essays and Reviews 1834–51*, 100.
37. Ibid. 101.
38. Dickens and Horne, 'The Great Exhibition and the Little One', 323.
39. Dickens, 'The Chinese Junk', 101.
40. Victor Hugo, *The Man Who Laughed* (1869), Salt Lake City: Project Gutenberg e-text no. 12587 (prepared by Steve desJardins), quoted from section IV of 'Another Preliminary Chapter'.
41. Hsiao Ch'ien, *China, but not Cathay* (London: Pilot Press, 1942).
42. Jack Goody, *The Theft of History* (Cambridge: Cambridge University Press, 1996).
43. Pulleyblank would later explain that his inaugural lecture 'attracted a good deal of interest at the time' and that, in 1956, Tom Harrisson, ethnologist and founder of Mass Observation, had published an abbreviated version in the *Sarawak Museum Journal*, of which he was then editor. See the preface to Edwin G. Pulleyblank, *Essays on Tang and pre-Tang China* (Aldershot and Burlington, Vt.: Ashgate Variorum, 2001), p. vii.
44. E. G. Pulleyblank, *Chinese History and World History: An Inaugural Lecture* (Cambridge University Press, 1955), 5.
45. Ibid. 7.
46. Ibid. 26.
47. Ibid. 8.
48. Ibid. 15.
49. Ibid. 12.
50. Ibid. 13.
51. Ibid. 17.
52. Ibid. 23.
53. Ibid. 24.
54. Ibid. 26.
55. Ibid. 29.
56. Ibid. 32.
57. Edwin G. Pulleyblank, review of Joseph Needham, *Science and Civilisation in China*, vol. i, *The Listener*, 21 October 1954, 683–4. This review, which was published without attribution, is included on the list of Pulleyblank's publications in Marjorie K. M. Chan and Hana Kang (eds), *Proceedings of the 20th North American Conference on Chinese Linguistics, 2008*, vol. ii (Columbus, Oh.: The Ohio State University, 2008), 1061–75. Pulleyblank writes that the first volume of *Science and Civilisation in China* had destroyed any remaining excuse for the

popular habit of opposing the 'spiritual east' with the 'materialistic west'. It had demonstrated that 'China has never been so completely cut off from the outside world as is sometimes supposed, and in certain periods, notably the time of the Mongol domination over most of Asia, intercourse between east and west has been very active'. Then as now, an outsider who produces such an ambitious and ground-breaking work risked stirring resentment in the heart of a professional Sinologist. But though Pulleyblank had indeed spotted a few errors ('inevitably [Needham] has occasionally trusted an unreliable source or made blunders'), he was also among the first to admit that these were only minor slips 'which a pedant might cavil at'.

58. Quoted from Ellis Smith's expanded notes of the delegation's visit to China, in the Ellis Smith papers at Salford Local History Library.

13. A Blue Jacket for Abraham Lincoln

1. Paul Hogarth, *Looking at China: with the Journal of the Artist* (London: Lawrence & Wishart, 1956), 4.

2. John Berger, 'Portrait of the Artist: Paul Hogarth', *Art News & Review*, 12 December 1952, 1.

3. Paul Hogarth, *Das Antlitz Europas* (Dresden: Verlag der Kunst, 1956), 161–76.

4. It may be noted that Hogarth had no such reservations about the British oil company Shell International. Indeed the artist James Boswell, whom Hogarth had met in the Artists International Association, had become art director at Shell International, and employed Hogarth as his assistant from 1946 to 1949 (Paul Hogarth, *Drawing on Life: The Autobiography of Paul Hogarth* (Newton Abbot: David & Charles, 1997), 19). In that capacity, he illustrated and designed various books issued to commemorate Shell's contribution to the war effort. One such, in which his illustrations stand alongside those of his friend, Ronald Searle, is W. E. Hope Stanton, *Tanker Fleet: The War Story of the Shell Tankers and the Men who Manned Them* (London: Anglo Saxon Petroleum Company, 1948).

5. Jessica C. E. Gienow-Hecht, 'AHR Forum: Always Blame the Americans: Anti-Americanism in Europe in the Twentieth Century', *American Historical Review* (October 2006). www.historycooperative.org/journals/ahr/111.4/gienowhecht.html> (30 Dec. 2008).

6. Lloyd L. Brown, 'Psychoanalysis vs The Negro People', *Masses & Mainstream*, 4/10 (October 1951), 16.

7. Sidney Finkelstein, 'Soviet Culture: A Reply to Slander', *Masses & Mainstream*, 3/1 (January 1950), 61.

8. Joseph Starobin, 'Europe Judges the Smith Act', *Masses & Mainstream*, 4/10 (October 1951), 1.

9. Elizabeth Moon, 'Free Paul Robeson!', *Masses & Mainstream*, 4/10 (October 1951), 8–10.

10. Ting Ling, 'Agnes Smedley', *Masses & Mainstream*, 4/8 (August 1951), 81–6.

11. Hogarth, *Looking at China*, 4.

12. See Hilary Spurling, *Burying the Bones: Pearl Buck in China* (London: Profile, 2010).

13. Hallet Abend, *My Years in China 1926–1941* (London: John Lane, 1944), 10.

14. Ibid. 48.

15. Rodney Gilbert's *What's Wrong with China?* (London: John Murray, 1926) was described as a widely discussed 'lifesaver to the foreign community' by Rayna Prohme, in a letter written from Peking on 8 September 1926. See Gregor Benton et al. (eds), *Reporting the Revolution: The Letters of Rayna Prohme* (London and Ann Arbor: Pluto Press, 2007), 36. For Benton's description of the book, see p. 180 n. 22.

16. Agnes Smedley, *Battle Hymn of China* (London: Gollancz, 1944), 40.

17. Benton et al., *Reporting the Chinese Revolution*.

18. Anna Louise Strong, *I Changed Worlds: The Remaking of an American* (New York: Garden City, 1937), 226.

19. Ibid. 229.

20. Ibid. 258.

21. Anna Louise Strong, *China Fights For Freedom* (London: Lindsay Drummond, 1939), 59.

22. See Anna Louise Strong, *China's Millions: A Vivid Personal Narrative of an American Woman's Recent Adventures in China*, books I and II (New York: Coward-McCann, 1928). See also Strong's *China Fights for Freedom* (London: Lindsay Drummond, 1939).

23. Edgar Snow, *Red Star over China* (London: Gollancz, 1968), 384.

24. Haldore Hanson, *'Humane Endeavour': The Story of the China War* (New York: Farrar & Rinehart, 1939).

25. Ibid. 244.

26. Ibid. 241.

27. Ruth Price, *The Lives of Agnes Smedley* (Oxford: Oxford University Press, 2005), 77–9.

28. Ibid. 154, 153.

29. Ibid. 155.

30. Ibid. 156.

31. Agnes Smedley, *Chinese Destinies: Sketches of Present-Day China* (London: Hirst & Blackett, 1934).

32. Price, *The Lives of Agnes Smedley*, 251.

33. Smedley, *Chinese Destinies*, 267.
34. Ibid. 268.
35. Ibid. 279.
36. Ibid. 280.
37. Snow, *Red Star*, 35.
38. Anna Louise Strong, *China Fights For Freedom* (London: Lindsay Drummond, 1939), 80.
39. Price, *The Lives of Agnes Smedley*, 186.
40. Ibid. 275.
41. Snow, *Red Star*, rev. edn (London: Gollancz, 1968), 46.
42. Ibid. 55.
43. Ibid. 16.
44. Ibid. 185.
45. Ibid. 70.
46. Ibid. 71.
47. Ibid. 70–1.
48. Ibid. 90.
49 Ibid. 91.
50. Ibid. 92.
51. Ibid. 93.
52. Ibid. 94.
53. Ibid. 95.
54. Ibid. 95.
55. Ibid. 380.
56. Ibid. 205.
57. Snow, 'Preface to the 1968 Edition', ibid. 16.
58. Ibid.
59. Smedley, *Battle Hymn of China*, 121.
60. Ibid. 121–2.
61. Agnes Smedley, *China Fights Back: An American Woman with the Eighth Route Army* (London: Gollancz, 1938), 116.
62. Joseph Needham and Dorothy Needham (eds), *Science Outpost: Papers of the Sino-British Science Co-operation Office (British Council Scientific Office in China)* (London: Pilot Press, 1948), 13.
63. 'Science and Society: Dr. Needham's lecture in Hua Ta (West China Union University) Yesterday', in Joseph and Dorothy Needham, *Science Outpost*, 121.
64. Rewi Alley, 'Introduction', in George A. Hogg, *I See a New China* (London: Gollancz, 1945), 5.
65. Hogg, *I See a New China*, 140–1.
66. Rewi Alley, *At 90: Memoirs of my China Years* (Beijing: New World Press, 1986), 194.
67. Quoted in Hanson, '*Humane Endeavour*', 243.
68. Smedley, *Battle Hymn of China*, 143.

69. Hogarth, *Looking at China*, 4.
70. 'General Marshall's Recall and Final Statement', in *United States Relations with China: With Special Reference to the Period 1944–1949*, Washington: Department of State Publications 3573, Far Eastern Series 30 (1949), 217.
71. 'President Truman's Statement of December 18, 1946', *in United States Relations with China: With Special Reference to the Period 1944–1949*, 218.
72. Jack Belden, *China Shakes the World* (London: Gollancz, 1952), 13.

14. How China Came to Cookham

1. Gilbert Spencer, *Stanley Spencer: By his Brother Gilbert* (Bristol: Redcliffe Press, 1991), 189.
2. Stanley Spencer, letter to Marjorie Spencer, 1 December 1954.
3. This drawing and caption is in an accounting style notebook, held in the Tate Archive, London, No. 733.3.77.
4. Ibid. 7–8.
5. Quoted in Keith Bell, *Stanley Spencer: A Complete Catalogue of the Paintings* (London: Phaidon, 1992), 194.
6. Bell, *Stanley Spencer: A Complete Catalogue*, 114.
7. Ibid. 114.
8. Keith Bell attributes this information to his conversations with Richard Carline. Ibid. 114.
9. Ibid. 117.
10. Ibid. 114, 117.
11. Richard Carline, *Stanley Spencer at War* (London: Faber, 1978), 68.
12. For an account of Cathay and its English critics see Hugh Kenner, *The Pound Era* (Berkeley and Los Angeles, University of California Press, 1971), 192–222.
13. Quoted from 'Lament of the Frontier Guard', originally published in *Cathay* and collected in Ezra Pound, *Collected Shorter Poems* (London: Faber & Faber, 1952), 144.
14. Launcelot Cranmer-Byng and Alan W. Watts (eds), *The Spirit of the Brush: Being the Outlook of Chinese Painters on Nature, from Eastern China to Five Dynasties AD 317–960* (London: John Murray 1939).
15. Chiang Yee, *China Revisited: After Forty-two Years* (New York: Norton, 1977), 34.
16. Ibid. 31.
17. Ibid. 35–6.
18. Ibid. 39.
19. Chaing Yee, *The Silent Traveller in Edinburgh* (London: Methuen, 1948), 1–2.
20. Yee, *China Revisited*, 39–40.

21. Chiang Yee, *The Silent Traveller: A Chinese Artist in Lakeland* (London: Country Life, 1937), 10.
22. Ibid. 38.
23. Ibid.
24. Ibid. 19.
25. Ibid. 43.
26. Ibid. 26.
27. Chiang Yee, *The Silent Traveller in Oxford* (London: Methuen, 1944), 17.
28. Chiang Yee, *China Revisited: After Forty-two Years* (New York: Norton, 1977), 48.
29. David Priestley, 'Two Chinese Artists in London', *Asian Art in London Journal* (Winter 2000), 30–3.
30. Craig Clunas, *Art in China* (Oxford University Press, 2009), 115–16.
31. Mary Sorrell, 'Chien-Ying Chang and Cheng-Wu Fei', *The Studio* (November 1952), 144–7.
32. Quoted from *Kensington News and West London Times*, 11 May 1951.
33. L. S. Leguin, 'An English Summer through Chinese Eyes', *Picture Post*, 12 August 1950, 22–25, 40.
34. In 1959, Winkworth would tell Fei to advise his wife that, when she attempts a new theme, ' it is very important to use the most typically Chinese technique—such as, when painting a primrose for instance, not to use natural colours, to paint it in ink, only faintly indicating the colour of the flowers and painting the leaves only in ink with a slightly blue or green shader, and not in green, which makes it all too light. If this is not done, the primrose looks like an ordinary English watercolour and does not harmonise with the peaches, plums and orchids which Chien-ying usually does in pure Chinese style.' William Wilberforce Winkworth, letter to Fei, 20 June 1959, in the possession of Nong Priestley.
35. Geoffrey Bemrose, letter to Chang and Fei, 25 November 1947, in possession of Nong Priestley.
36. Fei Cheng-wu, *Brush drawing in the Chinese Manner* (London and New York: Studio Publications, 1957), 72.
37. 'Star Man's Diary, *The Star*, 31 March 1947. Cutting in the possession of Nong Priestley.
38. Lord Methuen, letter to the Feis, 6 November 1954.
39. Stanley Spencer, letter to Miss Chang and Mr Fei, dated 6th of an ungiven month, 1947. In the possession of Nong Priestley.
40. Katy Talati, interview with the author, Oxford, 2002.
41. See also Frances Wood, *No Dogs and not many Chinese: Treaty Port Life in China 1843–1943* (London: John Murray, 1998), 285–6.

42. Mrs Judith B. Kelly, telephone conversation 24 April 2001. Mrs Kelly had written from her home in Bedfordshire after hearing me on BBC Radio Four's *Start the Week* at the time of the opening of Tate Britain's Stanley Spencer exhibition in March 2001. She remembered attending the honours ceremony with her father, Reuben Kelf-Cohen, Under-Secretary at the Ministry of Fuel and Power, who was there to be made a Companion of the Order of the Bath. Mrs Kelly had been impressed by the highly formal nature of the occasion. The footmen were in livery, and George VI, who was very ill at the time, was almost certainly wearing make-up. All the men had followed protocol and donned formal coats and black striped trousers—except Stanley Spencer, who was also the only one to arrive alone and not accompanied by members of his family. Mrs Kelly could not be sure whether Spencer was wearing sandals or a pair of boy's shoes, but he was certainly sporting a coloured shirt and a patterned tie too. Despite the evident dismay of the footmen, he showed no signs of nervousness and seemed impressively sure of his 'absolute right to be there'. After the ceremony, the footman who helped Spencer on with his raincoat looked greatly relieved to be wearing gloves. As for England's honoured artist, he 'popped his CBE in with the veg and walked off across the courtyard'. It is also said that Spencer had taken a painting to the palace in the hope of presenting it to the Queen Mother, and been disappointed when told that presents were never accepted, so he had a painting of flowers in his bag too.
43. This and other works from Talati's collection are reproduced in Shelagh Vainker and James C. Lin, *Pu Quan and his Generation: Imperial Painters of Twentieth-Century China* (Oxford: Ashmolean Museum, 2005).
44. Hilary Spurling, *Burying the Bones: Pearl Buck in China* (London: Profile, 2010), 53.
45. 'Talk to Bourne End Parents Association', note headed Cliveden View, Afternoon of June 5, 1957, Tate Archives, 733.10.191.
46. G. K. Chesterton, *Heretics* (London: John Lane, 1905), 46–53.
47. Arthur Waley, *Three Ways of Thought in Ancient China* (London: Allen & Unwin, 1939), 60–1.
48. Rex Warner, 'In Communist China—1. Peking the City of Smiling Discipline', *Daily Telegraph*, 31 October 1954, 7.

15. The Flight of a Brown Phoenix

1. Desmond Donnelly, *The March Wind; Explorations behind the Iron Curtain* (London: Collins, 1959), 222–3.

2. J.D. Bernal, drafts for projected book about China, Bernal papers, Cambridge University Library, B.472.

3. Cedric Dover, 'Asian Journey', *Trees*, 18 (April 1955), 256.

4. Cedric Dover, 'So the cycle goes on', *Congress Socialist*, 26 September 1936, 13–14.

5. James Palmer, *The Bloody White Baron: the Extraordinary Story of the Russian Nobleman who became the Last Khan of Mongolia* (New York: Basic Books), 2009.

6. Cedric Dover, *Hell in the Sunshine* (London: Secker and Warburg, 1943), 11.

7. Dover wrote frequently of 'the coloured world' – as in his essay, 'Inter-group Relations and the Coloured World, *Asia* (Saigon), 6, (September 1952), 193–197.

8. Cedric Dover, *Hell in the Sunshine*, 89.

9. Ibid. 86.

10. Tania Alexander, telephone conversation with the author, June 2002.

11. Cedric Dover, 'Annotated Bibliography 1920–1950', copy marked in Dover's hand 'The Library, Howard University, 20 January 1957'. A second typescript, entitled 'Biographical Notes', includes 'Extracts from Testimonies' and 'Some Opinions on Books'. I have used these two documents, copies of which were received from Michael Banton, to guide and inform my reconstruction of Dover's project.

12. 'Orwell's List', *The Guardian Review*, 21 June, 2003, 7. See also Timothy Garton Ash's associated article, 'Love, death and treachery', 4–7.

13. Dover, *Cimmerii? Or Eurasions and their Future* (Calcutta: Modern Art Press, 1929), 10.

14. Cedric Dover, *Half-Caste* (London: Secker and Warburg, 1937), 117.

15. Ibid. 117.

16. Ibid. ii.

17. Cedric Dover, 'Moods of yesterday', *United Asia*, Vol. 8, No. 3, June 1956, 198.

18. Cedric Dover, Biographical Notes, p. 2.

19. Cedric Dover, 'Annotated Bibliography 1920–1950', p. 2.

20. Cedric Dover, 'An Improved Citronella Mosquito Deterrent', *Indian Journal of Medical Research*, 17 (1930), 961.

21. Cedric Dover, *The Kingdom of Earth (Ten Essays)* (Allahabad: Allahabad Law Journal Press, 1931), 21.

22. Ibid. 131.

23. See Cedric Dover & Mercia Heynes Wood, *Eugenics and Birth Control* (Lahore: Times Publishing Co.), 1931. Also Cedric Dover and Mercia Heynes Wood, *Eugenic Problems and Research in India* (New York: Third International Congress of Eugenics, 1932).

24. Cedric Dover, 'An Ideal of Anglo-Indian Education and its Relation to Eugenics', *New Outlook*, 1/1 (April 1925), 226–28.

25. Cedric Dover describes it thus in his 'Biographical Notes', 2.

26. 'Editorial Musings, *The New Outlook*, Introductory No. (March 1925), 1.

27. D. D. Bedi, 'A Plea for Noise', *New Outlook*, Introductory No., March 1925, 22.

28. Cedric Dover,' Annotated Bibliography, 1920–1950', p. 10.

29. 'Editorial musings', *New Outlook*, 1/1 (April 1925), 2.

30. 'Editorial musings', *New Outlook*, 1/2 (May 1925), 33.

31. Tania Alexander, telephone conversation with the author, June 2002.

32. J. R. Glorney Bolton, 'The Future of the Anglo Indian', *Spectator*, 22 November 1935, 850–1.

33. Cedric Dover, letter to the editor, *Spectator*, 27 December 1935, 1071–2.

34. These are the words of Dr. H. N. Ridley FRS, a Malayan botanist quoted by Dover in *Cimmerii?*, 16.

35. Quoted from Dover's 'Biographical Notes'.

36. Cedric Dover, 'Welfare Museum's in Germany', *Museums Journal*, 35: 9, December 1935, 328.

37. Ibid. 327.

38. Ibid. 325–9.

39. Cedric Dover, 'Biological Education in Germany', *Biology: A Journal for Schools and Teachers*, 1/2 (1935), 74–5.

40. Cedric Dover, 'Biology and the Nation in Germany', *Nature*, 135: 3416, 20 April 1935, 629.

41. Julian S. Huxley & A. C. Haddon, *We Europeans: A Survey of 'Racial' Problems* (London: Cape, 1935), 7.

42. Dover, 'Annotated Bibliography', 10.

43. Cedric Dover, 'The Racial Myth', *Nature*, 136, 9 November 1935, 736.

44. Cedric Dover, review of Anthony M. Ludovici's *The Choice of a Mate*, in *Marriage Hygiene* (Bombay), 2, 3 February 1936, 342–3.

45. Cedric Dover, *Half-Caste*, 13. The 'Cochran' in this opening blast is presumably Noel Coward's London producer, Charles B. Cochran.

46. Ibid. 14.

47. Ibid. 16.

48. Ibid. 163–4.

49. Ibid. 69.

50. Ibid. 19.

51. Ibid. 79.

52. Ibid. 204.

53. Ibid. 213.

54. Ibid. 227.

55. Ibid. 17.

56. Ibid. 181–2.
57. Ibid. 184–5.
58. Ibid. 255–6.
59. Dover, 'Biographical notes', 20.
60. Cedric Dover, 'Intergroup Relations and the Coloured World', *Asia* (Saigon), No 6. September 1952, 193.
61. Ibid. 193.
62. Cedric Dover, 'Books as Ambassadors', *The Crisis* (NAACP), (December 1947), 368–9.
63. See Claude McKay, 'Boyhood in Jamaica', *Phylon: The Atlanta University Review of Race and Culture*, Second Quarter (1953), 134–145.
64. Cedric Dover, *Feathers in the Arrow: An Approach for Coloured Writers and Readers* (Bombay: Padma Publications, 1947), 7.
65. Ibid. 9.
66. Cedric Dover, 'Intergroup Relations and the Coloured World', 196.
67. Cedric Dover, *Know This of Race* (London: Chatto and Windus, 1939), 65.
68. Ibid. 109.
69. Dover, *Half Caste*, 277.
70. Cedric Dover, *Brown Phoenix* (London: The College Press, 1950), 11.
71. Dover, *Know this of Race*, 40.
72. Cedric Dover, Letter to Joseph Needham, 25 July 1955, Joseph Needham, Papers ca 1901–1984, Cambridge University Library, M170.
73. Cedric Dover, 'Towards Coloured Unity', *Congress Socialist*, 23 January 1937, 14.
74. Dover, *Feathers in the Arrow*, 12.
75. Dover, *Know This of Race*, 81.
76. Ibid. 51.
77. Dover, *Feathers in the Arrow*, 22.
78. Dover, *Half Caste*, 278.
79. Ibid. 276.
80. Ibid. 71.
81. Dover, *Know This of Race*, 47.
82. Ibid. 49.
83. Ibid. 50.
84. Ibid. 50–1.
85. Cedric Dover, *Feathers in the Arrow*, 12.
86. Cedric Dover, 'Literary Opportunity in America', *Left Review*, 3/16 May 1938, 982–3.
87. Cedric Dover, 'Closer Relations Between Negro and Indian Universities', Memorandum to Dr. Charles S. Johnson, Fisk University,

29 October 1947, in the Johnson papers at Fisk University Archives, Box 128f.1.

88. Cedric Dover, 'The Encouragement of Asiatic Students at Fisk', Memorandum to Dr. Charles S. Johnson, 9 March 1948, in Johnson papers at Fisk University Archives, Box 128f.1. See also 'Cedric Dover introduces this number', *United Asia*, 5/3 (June 1953), 148.

89. Charles Johnson, 'The Negro Today', *United Asia*, 5/3 (June 1953), 147.

90. Cedric Dover, 'Looking Forward from Yesterday', *Wilson Library Bulletin*, Vo. 23, No. 6, February 1949, 439.

91. Ibid., 440.

92. *United Asia: an International Magazine of Asian Affairs*, 5/3 (June 1953).

93. Dover, *Hell in the Sunshine*, 45.

94. Ibid. 49.

95. Ibid. 45–6.

96. Ibid. 55.

97. Ibid. 55.

98. Ibid. 62.

99. Ibid. 63.

100. *United Asia*, First Issue, May–June 1948.

101. Ben Parkin, caption to Denis Mathews' photograph of the Great Wall at the opening of *United Asia*, Cedric Dover's issue of United Asia dedicated to 'The Chinese Scene', 8/2 (1956).

16. Clement Attlee's Break

1. Clement Attlee, 'Attlee Tells of Manchurian Tour; Decries "Curtain of Ignorance"', *New York Times*, 10 September 1954, 3.

2. Morgan Phillips, *East Meets West: a pictorial story of the Labour Party Delegation to the Soviet Union and China* (London: Lincolns-Prager, 1954), 48.

3. Margaret Macmillan, *Seize the Hour: When Nixon Met Mao* (London: John Murray, 2006), 299.

4. Claude Roy, *Into China*, London: Sidgwick and Jackson with MacGibbon and Kee, 1955, 301.

5. Morgan Phillips, *East Meets West*, 48.

6. Clement Attlee, 'Old City in China Impresses Attlee', *New York Times*, 15 September 1954, 3.

7. Morgan Phillips, *East Meets West*, 52.

8. Ibid. 48.

9. Clement Attlee, 'Old City in China Impresses Attlee', 3.

10. The photograph is printed at the end of Michael Lindsay's unpaginated book *The Unknown War: North China 1937–45* (London: Bergström & Boyle, 1975).

11. Michael Lindsay, *China and the Cold War* (Carlton: Melbourn University Press, 1955), xii.

12. 'Don't be misled by these arguments', *Daily Sketch*, 2 August 1954.

13. Drew Middleton, 'Attlee to Study China Carefully', *New York Times*, 29 July 1954, 3.

14. Morgan Phillips, *East Meets West*, 14.

15. Clement Attlee, 'Foreword', in Morgan Phillips, *East Meets West*, 9.

16. Morgan Phillips, 'Peking Broadcast No. 1', typescript copy stamped 'Labour Party Press Dept', in among Morgan Phillips' papers ('the General Secretary's Papers') at the Labour Party Archive, Labour History Museum, Manchester.

17. Deryk Winterton, '"Attlee and Co." get busy at five hour lunch', *Daily Herald*, 16 August 1954, 1.

18. Morgan Phillips, 'Peking Broadcast No. 1'.

19. Clement Attlee, 'Bicycles Impress Attlee in Peking', *New York Times*, 8 September 1954, 6.

20. Morgan Phillips, 'Peking Broadcast No. 1'.

21. 'Chou En-lai fetes Attlee Group; Trade is Major Luncheon Topic', *New York Times*, 16 August 1954, 1.

22. 'Attlee and Chou Talk Five Hours: Socialists Dine on Shark's Fins', *Daily Mail*, 16 August, 1954.

23. Margaret Macmillan, *Seize the Hour*, 71.

24. 'Attlee and Chou Talk Five Hours', *Daily Mail*, 16 August, 1.

25. Michael Foot, *Aneurin Bevan: a Biography. Volume Two: 1945–1960* (London: Davis-Poynter, 1973), 446.

26. Ibid. 447.

27. Clement Attlee, 'Busy Peiping Impresses Attlee; Streets Swarming with Bicycles', *New York Times*, 8 September 1954, 6.

28. Ibid. 6.

29. Deryk Winterton, 'Why we are here – by Attlee', *Daily Herald*, 19 August 1954.

30. This was the title under which Attlee gave the Chichele lectures at Oxford in 1960. See Clement Attlee, *Empire into Commonwealth* (Oxford: Oxford University Press, 1961).

31. Arthur Ponsonby, *Falsehood in Wartime* (London: Allen & Unwin, 1928), 102–113.

32. 'Bevan at Hong Kong Dinner', *New York Times*, 8 September 1954, 6.

33. Marc J. Selverstone, *Constructing the Monolith: the United States, Great Britain, and International Communism, 1945–1950* (Cambridge Mass. & London: Harvard University Press, 2009), 125–6.

34. I have described this mission in *Iron Curtain: From Stage to Cold War* (Oxford: Oxford University Press, 2007), 133–190.

35. 'Chou En-lai fetes Attlee Group; Trade is Major Luncheon Topic', *New York Times*, 16 August 1954, 1.

36. 'Chou and Bevan watch the dancing girls', *Daily Mail*, 18 August 1954.

37. S.O. (Chatham House), 'Communist China 1949–1953: an Outline of Internal Development', typescript held in the Morgan Phillips papers, Labour Party Archive, Labour History Museum, Manchester.

38. A typescript of this 'Memorandum of Repression and the Forced Labour System in China', apparently prepared by Saul Rose, is held among the Morgan Phillips papers in the Labour Party Archive, Labour History Museum, Manchester.

39. Wu Hsien-tse and 20 other 'Cultural Workers & Writers in Hong Kong', 'Petition to the British Labour Party: an Open Letter', copy in the Morgan Phillips papers, Labour Party Archive, Museum of Labour History, Manchester.

40. Chow Ching-wen, *Ten Years of Storm; the True Story of the Communist Regime in China* (New York: Holt, Rinehart and Winston, 1960), 289–91.

41. James Cameron, *Mandarin Red; a journey behind the 'Bamboo Curtain'*, London: Joseph, 1955, 26.

42. Drew Middleton, 'Attlee to Study China Carefully', *New York Times*, 29 July 1954, 3.

43. Morgan Phillips, *East Meets West*, 30.

44. Ibid. 30.

45. Morgan Phillips, 'Peking Broadcast No. 1'.

46. Morgan Phillips, *East Meets West*, 30.

47. Details of Phillips' arrangements with the BBC are contained in a letter dated 22 September, in the Morgan Phillips papers, Labour Party Archive, Museum of Labour History, Manchester.

48. In a letter to Phillips, dated 1 September 1954, Colin R. Coote, General Manager of the *Daily Telegraph*, cancels his paper's agreement to buy three articles for fifty guineas each, citing his repeated articles in *Reynolds News*. Morgan Phillips papers, Labour Party Archive, Museum of Labour History, Manchester.

49. Letter to Phillips from Sydney Jacobsen of the *Daily Mirror*, 2 July 1954. Morgan Phillips papers, Labour Party Archive, Museum of Labour History, Manchester.

50. For a British appreciation of the Bolshevo prison, near Moscow, see G. Allen Hutt, 'In the hands of the O.G.P.U', *British Russian Gazette & Trade Outlook*, 7/8 (May 1931), 186–7.

51. Morgan Phillips, *East Meets West*, 52.

52. 'Labour Party Delegation to China - Report No. 1', N.E.C. 27 October 1954. A copy of this 'Private and Confidential' Laobur Party document

is held in the Morgan Phillips papers at the Museum of Labour History, Manchester.

53. Sam "Watson, 'My Impressions of New China', *Observer*, 19 September 1954, 8.

54. The preparatory documents among the Morgan Phillips papers in the Labour Party Archive include the minutes of a lecture and discussion of 'China's Industrialisation and Trade Prospects', held at the Royal Institute of International Affairs (Chatham House) on 25 May 1954. The meeting was chaired by Sir Frederick Whyte, and the opening address given by Mr. T. J. Lindsay, a businessman who had recently returned after spending 21 years in China, and who described the development of the first five year plan, and how major projects were at that time still largely concentrated in Manchuria.

55. Clement Attlee, 'Attlee Tells of Manchurian Tour; Decries "Curtain of Ignorance", *New York Times*, 10 September 1954, 3.

56. Morgan Phillips, *East Meets West*, 40.

57. Morgan Phillips, 'Peking Telegram No. 1'.

58. Clement Attlee, 'Attlee Finds Port in Shanghai Idle', *New York Times*, 14 September 1954, 3.

59. 'Chinese Attitudes to British Enterprises. Assurances during Visit of Labour Delegation', *The Times*, 28 August, 1954, 5.

60. Morgan Phillips, *East Meets West*, 46.

61. Clement Attlee, 'Old City in China Impresses Attlee', *New York Times*, 15 September 1954, 3.

62. Morgan Phillips, *East Meets West*, 32.

63. Ibid. 50.

64. Aneurin Bevan, 'I put a question mark against his judgement', *Tribune*, 11 October 1954, 4.

65. Quoted from *Tribune* (8 October 1954) in Michael Foot, *Aneurin Bevan: a Biography. Volume Two: 1945–1960* (London: Davis-Poynter, 1973), 446–7.

66. Ibid. 446.

67. Morgan Phillips, *East Meets West*, 42.

68. Ibid., 32. While commenting on the draft text of Phillips' book, Attlee wrote that 'a reference might be made to the central heating of the workers' flats'. Clement Attlee, letter to Phillips, 18 October 1954 in the Morgan Phillips papers, Labour Party Archive, Museum of Labour History, Manchester.

69. See I.F. Nicolson, *The Mystery of Crichel Down* (Oxford: Oxford University Press, 1986).

70. Ben Turner, *About Myself, 1863–1930* (London: H. Toulmin, at the Cayme Press, 1930), 223.

71. Basil Davidson, *Daybreak in China* (London: 1953), 76–7.

72. Ralph and Nancy Lapwood, *Through the Chinese Revolution* (People's Books Co-operative Society, 1954), 71.
73. Ibid. 73.
74. Rewi Alley, *The People Have Strength* (Peking: Rewi Alley, 1954), 152.
75. Akira B. Chikami 38 Ing C., Co., 'Lord of the Chinese Flies'. *http://www.2id.org/warstories.htm#lord.* Accessed June 2003.
76. Hewlett Johnson, *China's New Creative Age* (London: Lawrence & Wishart, 1953), 77.
77. Ralph and Nancy Lapwood, *Through the Chinese Revolution,* 72.
78. *China Reform Monitor,* No. 189, 12 April 1999.
79. Clement Attlee, 'Attlee Finds Port in Shanghai Idle', *New York Times,* 14 September 1954, 3.
80. 'Labour Party Delegation to China—Report No. 1.
81. Attlee, 'Attlee Finds Port in Shanghai Idle', 3.
82. Edith Summerskill, *Letters to My Daughter,* (London: Heinemann, 1957), 114–5.
83. Ibid. 115.
84. Ibid. 195.
85. Ibid. 118–9.
86. Morgan Phillips, 'We CAN Have China and U.S. as friends', *Reynolds News,* 29 August 1954.
87. 'Labour Party Delegation to China - Report No. 1'. Typescript headed 'N.E.C. 27th October 1954', Morgan Phillips papers in the Labour Party Archive, Labour History Museum, Manchester
88. Clement Attlee, 'Attlee Describes Debate with Mao', *New York Times,* 13 September 1954, 8.
89. Quoted from a picture caption, *Daily Mail,* 31 August 1954, 8.
90. Deryk Winterton, 'Mao Talks with Attlee', *Daily Herald,* 25 August 1954.
91. The delegation's meeting with Mao is here reconstructed from 'Labour Party Delegation to China—Report No. 1'.
92. Clement Attlee, 'Attlee Finds Chinese More Candid about Defects than Russians Are', *New York Times,* 9 September 1954, 3.
93. 'Labour Party Delegation to China—Report No. 1'.
94. Attlee, 'Attlee Describes Debate with Mao', 3.
95. Bevan, 'I Put a Question Mark Against his Judgement', 4.
96. Sam Watson, 'China: the Price of Power', *Observer,* 3 October 1954, 2.
97. Sam Watson, 'My Impressions of New China', *Observer,* 19 September 1954, 8.
98. 'Labour Party Delegation to China Report No. 2.', typed document marked' N.E.C. 27th October 1954', Morgan Phillips papers in the Labour Party Archive, Labour History Museum, Manchester.
99. Douglas Hurd, *Memoirs* (London: Little, Brown, 2003), 111.
100. Ibid. 110.

101. 'Mr Attlee on his Peking Visit', *The Times*, 3 September 1954, 6.
102. 'Attlee Bade Mao Ask Russians to Free Peoples, Cut Arms', *New York Times*, 3 September 1954, 1.
103. Morgan Phillips, 'We CAN Have China and U.S. as Friends', *Reynolds News*, 29 August, 1954.
104. '"Pravda" attack on Mr. Attlee', *The Times*, 9 September 1954, 8.
105. Michael Foot, 'Soapy Sam Soaps the Wrong Baby', *Tribune*, 20 August 1954, 4.
106. 'Mr Attlee Leaves Australia', *The Times*, 14 September 1954, 8.
107. 'Laborites Tour Derided to Legion, *New York Times*, 2 September 1954.
108. 'What I told Mao – Attlee', *Daily Mail*, 3 September 1954.
109. 'Concern over Attlee and Chou', *Daily Mail*, 26 August 1954.
110. Quoted in Lord Winster, letter to *The Times*, 15 September, 1954, 9.
111. W. Empson, 'Mr. Attlee's Remarks', *The Times*, 17 September 1954, 9.
112. 'Labour Support for S.E.A.T.O.', *The Times*, 28 September 1954, 8.
113. 'German Arms Issue at Labour conference', *The Times*, 27 September 1954, 6.
114. Michael Lindsay, *Notes on Educational Problems in Communist China 1941–7* (New York: Institute of Pacific Relations, 1950), 1.
115. Michael Lindsay, letter to Chi Ch'ao-ting, written from the Peking Hotel on 23 August 1954. A copy is retained in the General Secretary's Papers (Morgan Phillips), Labour Party Archive, Labour History Museum Manchester.

17. Popeyed among the Tibetans: The Undiplomatic Rapture of the Cultural Delegation

1. Hugh Casson, *Red Lacquer Days: An Illustrated Journal Describing a Recent Visit to Peking* (London: Lion and Unicorn Press, 1956), unpaginated. In this chapter as elsewhere, I am also drawing on Casson's notebooks.
2. Steen Ellis Rasmussen, *Towns and Cities* (1949; 1st English edn 1951; Cambridge, Mass.: MIT Press, 1961), 2.
3. Ibid. 3.
4. A. J. Ayer, *More of My Life* (London: Collins, 1984), 107.
5. This and other citations are from Leonard Hawkes's diary, a red Century notebook held in a folder entitled 'Leonard Hawkes. Cuttings, letters and photographs relating to his visit to China', Geological Society, London, Ref. No. LDGSL 1040.
6. This and other citations are from J. D. Bernal, 'China—projected book. Transcripts of tapes recording his visit day by day'. Box 53, B.470, University Library, Cambridge.
7. Rex Warner, 'In Communist China—2 The New Puritanism in New Dress', *Sunday Times*, 14 November 1954, 7.

8. James Cameron, *Mandarin Red: A Journey behind the 'Bamboo Curtain'* (London: Michael Joseph, 1955), 65.

9. Ibid. 65.

10. Casson is quoting from Rasmussen's *Towns and Buildings*. In fact he has got Rasmussen wrong here—the Danish architect was talking about the upturned eaves of the temples and other buildings in the forbidden city as a 'petrified tent city', not the south-facing courtyard houses in the hutongs, which were contrastingly low, grey and colourless—the opposite of what the West imagined in many versions of *chinoiserie*.

11. Cameron, *Mandarin Red*, 28.

12. A. J. Ayer, 'Impressions of Communist China', *The Listener*, 2 December 1954, 941.

13. Ibid. 941.

14. Cameron, *Mandarin Red*, 25.

15. Paul Hogarth, *Looking at China: With the Journal of the Artist* (London: Lawrence & Wishart, 1956), 5.

16. Cameron, *Mandarin Red*, 29.

17. Juliet Bredon, *Peking: A Historical and Intimate Description of its Chief Places of Interest* (Shanghai: Kelley & Walsh, 1922), 142.

18. Stanley Spencer, note dated 17 March 1959, 7333.10.201, Tate Gallery Archives.

19. A. J. Ayer, 'Impressions of Communist China', 941.

20. Captioned 'In the Summer Palace', the drawing in question appears in Hogarth's *Looking at China*, opposite p. 10. It would also feature on the cover of Cedric Dover's special edition of *United Asia*, devoted to 'The Chinese Scene'.

21. C. E. M. Joad, *The Untutored Townsman's Invasion of the Countryside* (London: Faber, 1946).

22. Rex Warner, 'In Communist China—1. "Peking The City of Smiling Discipline"', *Daily Telegraph*, 31 October 1954, 7.

23. A. J. Ayer, 'Impressions of Communist China', 941.

24. Ibid. 944.

25. Ibid. 942.

26. Rex Warner, 'May 1945', *The Cult of Power* (London: John Lane, 1946), 140.

27. Ayer, 'Impressions of Communist China', 941.

28. Cameron, *Mandarin Red*, 28.

29. Pei Wen-Chun, 'New Light on Peking Man', *China Reconstructs*, July–August 1954, 36.

30. See 'Bones of "Peking Man"', *The Times*, 5 January 1952, 6. It would later be suggested that Watson had made a 'genuine mistake', having actually been shown a fragment of skull from Java man at the American Museum, and then communicated his misunderstanding to a

colleague in East Germany, whence the story of American perfidy passed to China. ('Scientists urged to dig for Spemens of Peking Man', *Science Newsletter*, 75/15, 11 April 1959, 232–3).

31. 'Three Years of Bondage', *The Times*, 29 May 1954, 7.
32. 'Panchen Lama on Way to Peking Congress', *The Times*, 7 July, 1954, 5.
33. 'Peacocks for the Panchen Lama', *The Times*, 24 March, 1954.
34. 'Heir to Mao in Peking', *The Times*, 28 September 1954. For a Communist assumption that the Dalai Lama was henceforth an elected representative of the government, see Ivor Montagu, *Land of Blue Sky: A Portrait of Modern Mongolia* (London: Dobson, 1956), 47.
35. *The Times*, 8 October 1954, 6.
36. 'Heir to Mao in Peking', *The Times*, 28 September 1954, 8.
37. Cameron, *Mandarin Red*, 65.
38. Ibid. 12.
39. Artur Lundkvist, *Den Förvandlade Draken: En resa I Kina* (Stockholm: Tidens Förlag, 1955), 23.
40. Gilbert Spencer, *Stanley Spencer: By his Brother Gilbert* (Bristol: Redcliffe Press, 1991), 188.
41. Hogarth, *Looking at China*, 18.
42. Gertje R. Utley, *Picasso: The Communist Years* (New Haven and London: Yale University Press, 2000), 114–17.
43. Osbert Sitwell, *Escape with Me!: An Oriental Sketch-book* (London: Macmillan, 1939), 190–1.
44. Cameron, *Mandarin Red*, 29.
45. Ayer, 'Impressions of Communist China', 942.
46. Hogarth, *Looking at China*, 18.
47. Cameron, *Mandarin Red*, 35.
48. Montagu, *Land of Blue Sky*, 12.
49. Ivor Montagu, 'Sports and Pastimes in China', *United Asia*, 8/2 (1956), 150.
50. Montagu, *Land of Blue Sky*, 84.
51. Montagu, 'Sports and Pastimes in China', 180.
52. Ibid. 181.
53. Dr.Joshua S. Horn, *Away With All Pests: An English Surgeon in People's China, 1954–1969* (New York and London: Monthly Review Press, 1971), 27.
54. J. D. Bernal, 'China—projected book. Transcripts of tapes recording his visit day by day'. Box 53, B. 470, University Library, Cambridge.
55. Cameron, *Mandarin Red*, 31.
56. Ibid. 36.
57. Ibid. 34.
58. Ayer, 'Impressions of Communist China', 942.
59. Douglas Hurd, *Memoirs* (London: Little, Brown, 2003), 113.

60. Hogarth, *Looking at China*, 18.

61. Hurd, *Memoirs*, 111.

62. Leonard Hawkes, notebook (red Century) in file entitled 'Leonard Hawkes. Cuttings, letters and photographs relating to his visit to China', Ref. no. LDGSL 1040, Geological Society, London.

63. 'Cultural Links with China. British Delegates' Letter', *The Times*, 6 October 1954, 5.

64. Kuo Mo-Jo, 'We Want the Same Things', *China Reconstructs* (January 1955).

65. I take this to be a reference to the 110-foot bar boasted by the Shanghai Club at No. 2. The Bund, which was famous in the 1920s and 1930s, as 'the longest bar in the world'.

66. Rex Warner, 'In Communist China—2. The New Puritanism in New Dress', *Sunday Times*, 14 November 1954, 7.

67. 'Olympians No. 5, *Bedford News*, 7 June, 1953, 1.

68. John Gittings's obituary of Yang Xianyi, *Guardian*, 24 November 2009, 33.

69. Ayer, 'Impressions of Communist China', 942.

70. Stanley Spencer, Tate Archives, 733.10.162.

18. Cadillacs, Coal Mines, and Cooperatives: The Second Labour Delegation Grapples with the Facts

1. James Cameron, *Mandarin Red: A Journey behind the 'Bamboo Curtain'* (London: Michael Joseph, 1955), 62.

2. Ibid.

3. Osbert Sitwell, *Escape with Me! An Oriental Sketch-book* (London: Macmillan, 1939), 178.

4. Ibid. 178.

5. 'COAL MINING: Visit to Open-Cast Mine and Shaft Mine at Fushun', in 'British Visiting Group to China: October–November 1954'. A copy of this duplicated 63-page typescript, which assembles reports written by various members of the Second Labour Delegation survives among Cedric Dover's papers in the possession of Mrs M. Alexander-Sinclair, London.

6. Lord Beveridge, *Voluntary Action: A Report on Methods of Social Advance* (London: Allen & Unwin, 1948).

7. *Women's Co-operative Guild, Seventy-Second Annual Report for the year 1954* (London: Women's Co-operative Guild, 1955), 18.

8. 'British Visiting Group to China: October—November 1954'. A copy of this duplicated 63-page typescript, which gathers in reports written by various members and appears to be the Second Labour Delegation's agreed report, survives among Cedric Dover's papers.

9. Women's Co-operative Guild, *Seventy-Second Annual Report for the Year 1954*, 18.
10. Cameron, *Mandarin Red*, 26.
11. Aneurin Bevan, Barbara Castle, Richard Crossman, Tom Driberg, Ian Mikardo, Harold Wilson, *It Need Not Happen: The Alternative to German Rearmament* (London: Tribune, August 1954).
12. Roland Barthes, *Carnets du Voyage en Chine* (Paris: Bourgeois, 2009), 95–6.
13. Ibid. 141.
14. Barbara Castle, interview with the author, 23 February 2002.
15. Alan Winnington, *Breakfast with Mao; Memoirs of a Foreign Correspondent* (London: Lawrence & Wishart, 1986), 177–8.
16. Ernest Thornton, 'China Re-visited', *United Asia*, 8/1 (October–November 1956), 344.
17. 'Arms Policy Vote at T.U.C.', *The Times*, 7 September 1954, 8.
18. Thornton, 'China Re-visited', 345.
19. See Jack Lindsay's *Rising Tide: A Novel of the British Way* (London: Bodley Head, 1953), 10.
20. Thornton, 'China Re-visited', 345.
21. Donnelly, *The March Wind*, 142.
22. Ibid. 143.
23. Barbara Castle, Interview with the author, 23 February 2002.
24. Michael Foot, *Aneurin Bevan: A Biography*, ii: *1945–1960* (London: Davis-Poynter, 1973), 508.

19. 'Nuts About Pavlov?' Resuming the Scientific Dialogue

1. Dr Elizabeth James, interview with author, 2001.
2. Olga B. Lepeshinskaya, *The Origin of Cells from Living Substance* (Moscow: Foreign Languages Publishing House, 1954), 79.
3. For details of Dr Brimblecombe's scheme see F. S. Brimblecombe et al., 'A London Trial of Home Care for Sick Children', *Lancet*, 272/6963, 9 February 1957.
4. Hewlett Johnson, *China's New Creative Age* (London: Lawrence & Wishart, 1953), 83.
5. Lepeshinskaya, *The Origin of Cells from Living Substance*, 8.
6. D. W. James, 'Chinese Medicine', *Lancet*, 21 May 1955, 1068–9.
7. Elizabeth, interview with the author, 2001.
8. Cedric Dover, 'The Significance of the Cell Surface: the work of E. E. Just', *Journal of the Zoological Society of India*, 6/1 (June 1954), 3–4.
9. Cedric Dover, 'The Uses of Biology in China', *United Asia*, 8/2 (April 1956), 135.

10. Pei Wen-Chung, 'New Light on Peking Man', *China Reconstructs* (July–August 1954), 34. Dover quotes from this in 'The Uses of Biology in China', 135.

11. Cedric Dover, 'New Writing in China', *United Asia*, 8/2, 2 April 1956, 153.

12. Ibid. 154.

13. Ibid. 157.

14. Cedric Dover, 'Asian Journey', *Trees*, 18 April 1955, 246.

15. Sacheverell Sitwell, *Spanish Baroque Art* (Duckworth), ch. 6. Quoted in Osbert Sitwell, *Escape With Me! An Oriental Sketchbook* (London: Macmillan, 1939), 221. In 1737, Emperor Ch'ien Lung united the buildings erected by his two predecessors, and entrusted the painter Fra Castiglione, to produce the general plan.

16. J. D. Bernal, 'Science in China', *United Asia*, 8/2 (1956), 129.

17. J. D. Bernal, draft letter to A. S. B. Glover of Penguin Books, J. D. Bernal papers, University Library, Cambridge, B.472.

18. J. D. Bernal, 'Science in the Soviet Union'. Document produced for the East–West Relations Committee of the National Peace Council, 22 May 1950, Box 53 B. 4.60, J. D. Bernal Papers, University Library, Cambridge.

19. J. D. Bernal, FRS, 'Present-Day Science and Technology in the Soviet Union', in J. Needham (ed.), *Science in Soviet Russia* (London: Watts & Co., 1942), 2.

20. For the chronicle of the book, which consists of edited transcripts of interviews describing the trip, see J. D. Bernal, 'China. Projected book. 256pp. Taken from tapes mostly corrected', Cambridge University Library, MS. Add. 8287: B.4.72.

21. J. D. Bernal, 'Application of Science to Building Construction. Lecture in China', Cambridge University Library, MS. Add. 8287: B.4.71.

22. J. D. Bernal, 'China. Projected book', 86.

23. 'China Revisited. Acceptance of the New Order', *The Times*, 28 August 1954, 5.

24. Rewi Alley had gone to Hankow from Shanghai to inspect the 1931 floods as a representative of Sir John Hope-Simpson of the League of Nations, who was himself leading the rehabilitation work at the invitation of the Kuomintang government. His reflections on this experience, together with his charges of incompetence and corruption against the KMT leaders who failed to rally to the cause, are given in Rewi Alley, *Man Against Flood: A Story of the 1954 Flood on the Yangtse and of the Reconstruction that Followed it* (Peking: New World Press, 1956), 11–17. My copy of this book once belonged to the Political Section of the American Consulate in Hong Kong. It has been conspicuously and

repeatedly stamped with the words 'Chinese Communist Publication', in case any dim reader mistook even one of its claims for the truth.

25. Rewi Alley, *Man Against Flood*, 24–5.
26. Ernest Thornton, 'China Revisited', *United Asia*, 8/5 (October–November 1956), 347.

20. Revolution Comes to the Art Schools and Museums

 1. Ivor Montagu, 'Sports and Pastimes in China', *United Asia*, 8/2 (April 1956), 151.
 2. Douglas Hurd, *Memoirs* (London: Little Brown, 2003), 118.
 3. Margaret Mathews, interview with the author, 2 November 2001.
 4. Michael Foot, interview with the author, 4 June 2002.
 5. Hewlett Johnson, *China's New Creative Age* (London: Lawrence & Wishart, 1953), 81.
 6. Denis Mathews, letter to his mother and father, consisting of sections written in Chungking between 23 and 30 October 1954. Transcript in the possession of Margaret Mathews.
 7. Peter Clarke, *The Cripps Version: The Life of Sir Stafford Cripps 1889–1952* (London: Allen Lane, 2002), 467–8.
 8. For an account of John Berger's arguments in favour of 'social' as opposed to 'socialist' realism during the early 1950s, see James Hyman, *The Battle for Realism: Figurative Art in Britain during the Cold War 1945–1960* (New Haven and London: Yale University Press, 2001), 113–31.
 9. Barbara Castle, 'Sleeper to Canton', *New Statesman*, 11 December 1954, 775–6.
10. Denis Mathews, 'Sian', 1954. The typescript of this article, together with the letter cited in this chapter, is in the possession of Margaret Mathews.
11. E. G. Pulleyblank, 'A Sinologist in Sian', *United Asia*, 'The Chinese Scene: A Symposium', 8/2 (1956), 137.
12. Ibid. 137.
13. Denis Mathews, 'Sian'.
14. Pulleyblank, 'A Sinologist in Sian', 138.
15. Betty England, writing as Secretary of the delegation, in 'Britons in China: Report of the First British Delegation to Visit New China', London: Britain–China Friendship Association, London, 1951.
16. Pulleyblank, 'A Sinologist in Sian', 137.
17. *United Asia*, 8/2 (April 1956), 71.
18. Rewi Alley, *The People Have Strength* (Peking: Rewi Alley, 1954), 274.
19. Alan Winnington, *Breakfast with Mao*, 194. The 'jiving' epsiode is reliably said to have taken place at a party held by the Winningtons during Bernal's later visit in 1959.
20. Ibid. 182.

21. Ibid. 181.

22. Ibid. 182–3.

23. Jack Chen, *New Earth: How the Peasants in One Chinese County Solved the Problem of Poverty* (Peking: New World Press, 1957), 15.

21. Paul Hogarth's Sky Full of Diamonds

1. James Aldridge's 'Introduction' in Paul Hogarth, *Defiant People: Drawings of Greece Today* (London: Lawrence & Wishart, 1953), 3.

2. Paul Hogarth, *Looking at China: with the Journal of the Artist* (London: Lawrence & Wishart, 1955), 40.

3. Arthur Clegg, 'New China as I Saw it', *Labour Monthly: A Magazine of International Labour*, 33/8 (August, 1951), 375.

4. R. K. Karanjia, *China Stands Up* (Bombay: People's Publishing House, 1952), 3.

5. Rewi Alley, *The People Have Strength* (Peking: Rewi Alley, 1954), 61.

6. Hogarth, *Looking at China*, 67.

7. Ibid. 42. Repeated in Paul Hogarth, *Cold War Reports 1947–1967*, Norwich: the Norwich Gallery (Norfolk Institute of Art and Design), 1990), 26.

8. Hsiao Ch'ien, *How the Tillers Win Back Their Land* (Peking: Foreign Languages Press, 1951), 63.

9. Osbert Sitwell, *Escape With Me!: An Oriental Sketchbook* (London: Macmillan, 1939), 310.

10. Ibid. 314.

11. Ibid. 320.

12. Joseph Needham, letter dated 26 February 1943 in Joseph Needham and Dorothy Needham (eds), *Science Outpost: Papers of the Sino-British Science Co-operation Office (British Council Scientific Officer in China)*, (London: Pilot Press, 1948), 27.

13. Ibid. 27–8.

14. Ibid. 28.

15. Miles Malleson, *An Actor Visits China* (London: Britain–China Friendship Association, 1953), 7.

16. Basil Davidson, *Daybreak in China* (London: Cape, 1953), 162.

17. Hogarth, *Looking at China*, 70.

18. Ibid. 61.

19. Davidson, *Daybreak in China*, 115.

20. George Hardy, *Those Stormy Years: Memories of the Fight For Freedom on Five Continents* (London: Lawrence & Wishart, 1956), 255.

21. L. H. Wedmore, 'The Lonely Furrow and Some who have Ploughed it. II—Gerard Winstanley, The Digger', *The Ploughshare*, 1/2 (March 1916), 52–5.

22. Andy Croft, *Comrade Heart: A Life of Randall Swingler* (Manchester and New York: Manchester University Press, 2003), 90–4.

23. Joseph Needham, 'Foreword' in Henry Holorenshaw, *The Levellers and the English Revolution* (London: Left Book Club, 1939), 6.

24. Ibid. 21.

25. Ibid. 24.

26. Ibid. 27.

27. Ibid. 94.

28. Joseph Needham, 'Foreword' in Rewi Alley, *Yo Banfa! (We Have a Way!)* (Shanghai: China Monthly Review, 1952).

29. Basil Davidson, *Daybreak in China*, 125.

30. Hogarth, *Looking at China*, p. vi.

31. Ibid. 6.

32. Ibid. 5.

33. Hogarth, *Drawing on Life*, 33.

34. Hogarth, *Looking at China*, 33.

35. Ibid. 24.

36. Ibid. 31.

37. Paul Hogarth, conversation with the author, 1 November 2001.

38. Ibid. 39.

39. Ibid. 47.

40. Ibid. 55.

41. Ibid. 72.

42. Ibid. 61.

43. Ibid. p. v.

44. Ibid. 66.

45. Ibid. 64.

46. Paul Hogarth, interview with author, November 2001.

47. Clement Attlee, 'Attlee Reports on Trip to Moscow', *New York Times*, 7 September 1954, 9.

48. Angelica Balabanov, *My Life as a Rebel* (London: Hamish Hamilton, 1938), 218.

49. Paul Hogarth, *Looking at China*, 60.

50. Panait Istrati [this volume was actually written by Boris Souvarine], *Russia Unveiled*, trans. R. J. S. Curtis (London: Allen & Unwin, 1931), 23–5. For an account of Souvarine's argument, see my *Iron Curtain: from Stage to Cold War* (Oxford: Oxford University Press, 2007), 273–7.

51. Paul Hogarth captioned this drawing 'In the Summer Palace', and explained it as follows on the reverse of a surviving photograph: 'The Former Imperial Summer Palace (Yi-Ho-Yuan) is the Hampton Court of Peking and is a Favourite Week-End Spot of Citizens. Grounds are full of young People. Palace has been opened to the public since 1949.'

The drawing was later used on the cover of Cedric Dover's Chinese issue of *United Asia* (8/2, April 1956).

52. Hogarth, *Looking at China*, 12.
53. Ibid. 10.
54. Ibid. 12.
55. Ibid. 39.
56. Ibid. 40.
57. Ibid. 56.
58. Ibid. 58.
59. Ibid. 72.
60. Ibid. 76.
61. Ibid. 40.
62. Ibid. 17–18.
63. Ibid. 14.
64. Ibid.16.
65. Ibid. 17.
66. Ibid. 38.
67. Casson, *Red Lacquer Days*.
68. Agnes Smedley, *Battle Hymn of China* (London: Gollancz, 1944), 60–6.
69. Hogarth, *Looking at China*, 73–4.
70. *Five Thousand Years Young: Modern Chinese Drawings & Woodcuts*, with an introduction by Jack Chen (London: Lawrence & Wishart, 1937).
71. Hogarth, *Looking at China*, 74.
72. Ibid. 74.
73. Ibid. 74.

22. Stanley Spencer's English Takeaway

1. Stanley Spencer, extract from a lecture delivered at Oxford in November 1922 and transcribed by Richard Carline. Adrian Glew (ed.), *Stanley Spencer: Letters and Writings* (London: Tate, 2001), 119.
2. Ibid. 170.
3. Notebook entry, composed as a letter to the late Hilda Carline ('Dear ducky'), addressed as from Cliveden View, Spencer's house in Cookham Rise, and dated 3 November 1954. Ibid., 241.
4. 'Culture, but no Politics', *Manchester Guardian*, 20 October 1954, 16.
5. Paul Hogarth, *Drawing on Life; the Autobiography of Paul Hogarth* (Newton Abbot: David & Charles, 1997), 42.
6. Humphrey Trevelyan, *Worlds Apart: China 1953–5, Soviet Union 1962–5* (London: Macmillan, 1971), 120.
7. Stanley Spencer, Tate Archive, 733.10.162.
8. Gilbert Spencer, *Stanley Spencer: by his brother Gilbert*, 189.
9. Paul Hogarth, interview with the author, November 2001.

10. Stanley Spencer, letter to Daphne Robinson, 1 November 1954. He told his brother Gilbert he came home weighing only 6 stone 10. (Gilbert Spencer, *Stanley Spencer: by his brother Gilbert*, 189).

11. Osbert Sitwell, *Escape with Me! An Oriental Sketch-book*, (London: Macmillan, 1939), 171.

12. Paul Hogarth, *Drawing on Life*, 42.

13. Catalogue of 'Exhibition of The Contemporary Chinese Scene, Water-colours and Drawings' (London: Thomas Agnew & Sons, 1957).

14. Edwin Pulleyblank, email to the author, 26 April 2002.

15. Stanley Spencer, letter to Marjorie Robinson, 1 December 1954.

16. Ibid.

17. Ibid.

18. John Berger, quoted in Keith Bell, *Stanley Spencer: A Complete Catalogue of the Paintings*, (London: Phaidon, 1992), 499.

19. Yu Feng, telephone conversation with the author, 9 May 2003.

20. Stanley Spencer, 'Slimline' notebook, 1954, Tate Archive, 733.3.78.

21. Ibid.

22. Spencer, note dated 17 March 1959, Tate Archive, 733.10.201.

23. Stanley Spencer, letter to Daphne Robinson, undated but headed 'Hangchou', 1954.

24. Gilbert Spencer, *Stanley Spencer:: by his brother Gilbert*, 189.

25. Stanley Spencer, note dated 17 March 1959, Tate Archive, 733.10.201.

26. Caroline Singer and C. Le Roy Baldridge, *Turn to the East* (New York: Minton, Balch & Company, 1926), 52.

27. James Cameron, *Mandarin Red*, 25.

28. Hedda Morrison, *A Photographer in old Peking* (Hong Kong: Oxford University Press, 1985), 3.

29. Stanley Spencer, letter to Daphne Robinson, 20 October 1954.

30. James Cameron, *Mandarin Red*, 276.

31. Stanley Spencer, letter to Angela and Peter Hodson, Peking, 29 September 1954, copy in the possession of the Stanley Spencer Museum at Cookham.

32. Stanley Spencer, notes for a talk to Bourne End Parents Association, 5 June 1957. Tate Archive, 733.10.191.

33. Sarah Pike Conger, *Letters from China: with particular reference to the Empress Dowager and the women of China*, (London: Hodder and Stoughton, 1910), 14 & 16.

34. Ibid. 16–17.

35. Ibid. 17.

36. Ibid. 18.

37. Describing his stay in Peking in 1934, Sitwell writes that 'owing to the increasing number of bandits in the nearer countryside, we were only able with safety to penetrate to some twenty or thirty miles along two

broken-down roads; down the rest, it was wiser to turn back toward the walls after a mile or two'. (*Escape with Me!*, 215–6). He also found that every night the gates of Peking were 'locked and barred against bandits', a fact that had prompted one American visitor to remark: '"Well, I can tell you here and now, we wouldn't stand for it in Detroit!"' (Ibid., 223).

38. Cedric Dover, 'Asian Journey', *Trees*, 18, April 1955, 248–9.
39. Cedric Dover, 'Museums in China', *Museums Journal*, 55:2, May 1955, 33.
40. Douglas Hurd, *Memoirs* (London: Little, Brown, 2003), 115.
41. Stanley Spencer, letter to Angela and Peter Hodson, 29 September, 1954.
42. Stanley Spencer, letter to Daphne Charlton, Peking, 20 October 1954.
43. Stanley Spencer, letter to the late Hilda Carline, Notebook, Tate Gallery Archive, 733.3.79. Quoted from Adrian Glew (ed.), *Stanley Spencer, Letters and Writings*, 241–2.
44. Stanley Spencer, Letter to Hilda Carline, August 1948. Tate Gallery Archive, 7331.1663. Quoted from Glew, Adrian (ed.), *Stanley Spencer: Letters and Writings*, 129–131.
45. Ibid. 130.
46. Ibid. 131.
47. Stanley Spencer, letter to the late Hilda Carline, Notebook, Tate Gallery Archive, 733.3.79. Quoted from Adrian Glew (ed.), *Stanley Spencer, Letters and Writings*, 241–2.
48. Ibid. 241.
49. Glew, 242.
50. Ibid. 243.
51. Michael Foot, interview with the author, 4 June 2002. See also Michael Foot, 'My First Home', Property supplement, *Daily Telegraph*, 18 May 2002.
52. Paul Hogarth, *Looking at China: with the journal of the artist* (London: Lawrence & Wishart, 1956), 83.
53. Ibid. 84.
54. Denis Mathews, letter to his mother and father, 30 October 1954.
55. Ibid. 84.
56. Barbara Castle, interview with the author, 23 February 2002.
57. Margaret McCarthy, *Generation in Revolt* (London: Heinemann, 1953), 113.
58. *Soviet Russia To-Day: Report of the British Workers' Delegation, 1927* (London: Labour Research Department, 1927), 83.
59. Margaret McCarthy, *Generation in Revolt*, 137.
60. Ellis Smith, 'Reflections 16', a typescript held among the Ellis Smith papers at Salford Local History Library (U294/Z102).
61. Ellis Smith, 'The Struggle in the Far East: The Economic Background', *The Plebs*, 34/4 (April 1932), 78.

62. Ellis Smith, 'The Gathering World War-Clouds', *The Plebs*, 34/3 (March, 1932), 49–51.
63. Gilbert Spencer, *Stanley Spencer: by his brother Gilbert*, 189.
64. John Rothenstein, *Modern English Painters*, ii: *Lewis to Moore* (London: Eyre & Spottiswoode, 1956), 172.
65. Peter Vansittart, *In the Fifties* (London: Murray, 1995), 140.
66. Denis Mathews' picture *Stanley Spencer meets Chou En-lai* would be offered for 18 guineas at Thomas Agnew and Sons' Exhibition of the Contemporary Chinse Scene: watercolours and drawings, which opened on 23 October 1957. Its present whereabouts is unknown.
67. Denis Mathews, letter to his parents, 23–30 October 1954.
68. Paul Hogarth, Interview with the Author, 1 November 2001.
69. Hogarth, *Looking at China*, 84.
70. Hogarth, Dr*awing on Life*, 42.
71. Hogarth, *Looking at China*, 84.
72. Barbara Castle, 'China does not want war', *Daily Herald*, 25 October 1954, 2.
73. Hogarth, *Looking at China*, 86.

Afterword

1. David Hawkes, 'Two Views of China', *New Statesman*, 6 November 1954, 589.
2. 'Culture but no Politics: A Mission to China', *Manchester Guardian*, 20 October 1954, 16.
3. 'Sir William Walton's First Opera', *The Times*, 27 October 1954, 9.
4. *New Statesman and Nation*, 30 October 1954, 564.
5. *New Statesman and Nation*, 6 November 1954, 596.
6. Ibid.
7. *New Statesman and Nation*, 13 November 1954, 632.
8. 'Peking's Envoy to London', *Manchester Guardian*, 27 October 1954, 7.
9. Percy Timberlake, *The Story of the Icebreakers in China* (London: The 48 Group, 1994), 15–22.
10. An advert announcing the opening of Collets' Chinese bookshop in Great Russell Street appeared in *Tribune*, 29 October 1954, 2.
11. 'International Ice Melting', *Manchester Guardian*, 26 November 1954, 1.
12. One of the members of this Parliamentary Mission to Russia, the Labour MP Christopher Mayhew, admitted that he had been forced onto the defensive when one Soviet leader, Mr Gromyko, had insisted that Marxism had proved correct in its prophecies and was spreading all over the world, and then asked him what 'philosophy' Britain might put against it. Mayhew found himself talking about Bertrand Russell and A. J. Ayer, whose work 'seemed to be concerned mainly with the

meaning of words. It did not seem very constructive to me'. (Christopher Mayhew, 'The Kremlin's Code for Co-Existence', *Observer*, 24 October 1954, 4). In his article Mayhew actually went on to explain that this apparent fixation with language at least had the definite advantage of revealing the 'errors' of Marxist claims to truth. That qualification had disappeared by the time Mayhew's objection was quoted in the *Marxist Quarterly*, where Peter Fryer quoted it at the head of a hostile review claiming that the recent books by Russell and 'Professor Ayer' breathed 'the miasma of a society in decay', and that the two bourgeois philosophers should stop worrying about such piffling questions as 'Can I feel somebody else's headache?', and wake up to the fact that 'ordinary men and women engaged in mass struggle' are capable of 'noble, selfless and disinterested action in support of their workmates'. See Peter Fryer, 'Russell, Ayer and Bourgeois Morality', *Marxist Quarterly*, 2/1 (January 1955), 48–9.

13. 'Meeting with Mr. Malenkov', *Manchester Guardian*, 27 October 1954, 2.

14. Drew Middleton, 'Labour's Prestige Rising in Britain', *New York Times*, 14 September 1954, 1.

15. Clement Attlee, 'Attlee Reports on Trip to Moscow', *New York Times*, 7 September 1954, 9.

16. 'Action Against U.SA. Comics', *Manchester Guardian*, 22 October 1954, 2.

17. Richard Hoggart, *The Uses of Literacy: Changing Patterns in English Mass Culture* (1957) (Boston: Beacon Press, 1966), 204.

18. Ibid. 203.

19. 'Our London Correspondence', *Manchester Guardian*, 21 October 1954.

20. Marc T. Greene, letter to the editor, *Manchester Guardian*, 26 November 1954. In an earlier letter to the *New Statesman and Nation*, Greene had identified himself as an American journalist living in London, and declared the 'shameful' persecution of Dr Lattimore as 'the very negation of democracy and the affirmation of totalitarianism' (New Statesman and Nation, 6 November, 1954).

21. P. J. Pitman, 'The Lattimore Case', letter to the editor, *Manchester Guardian*, 25 October 1954.

22. Sam Watson, 'China: The Price of Power', *Observer*, 3 October 1954, 2.

23. 'British Firms in China', *Manchester Guardian*, 21 October 1954, 12.

24. Aneurin Bevan, 'The China Tour Part Three: Marx Versus Birth Control', *Tribune*, 8 October 1954, 3.

25. Jung Chang and Jon Halliday, *Mao: The Unknown Story* (London: Jonathan Cape, 2005), 411.

26. Clement Attlee, 'Attlee Finds Port in Shanghai Idle', *New York Times*, 14 September 1954, 3.

27. Chang and Halliday, *Mao*, 452.
28. Alan Winnington, *Breakfast with Mao: Memoirs of a Foreign Correspondent* (London: Lawrence & Wishart, 1986), 210.
29. Ibid. 251.
30. The invitation was extended by J. Dribbon, the Secretary of the B-CFA in a letter of 7 April 1955. Hawkes notes that he accepted on 11 April. Leonard Hawkes papers, Geological Society, LDGSL 1040.
31. Cedric Dover, 'Biology in China', *Science and Culture*, 20 May 1955, 520.
32. Cedric Dover, 'Museums in China', *Museums Journal*, 55/2, May 1955, 31–5.
33. Cedric Dover, letter to the editor, *Man*, 1951, 95.
34. Dover had expressed his resistance to the post-war formulations of 'race' and 'race relations' in the following articles: 'UNESCO on Race', *Eugenics Review*, 112 (October 1950), 177–9; 'Racial Studies', *Nature*, 168/ 862, 17 November 1951.
35. Cedric Dover, 'What is a Race Riot?', *United Asia*, 11/3 (1959), 234–7.
36. Cedric Dover, 'The Black Knight Part 1', *Phylon*, 15/1 (1954), 41.
37. Cedric Dover, 'Aublet: the First Secular Abolitionist', *Phylon*, 17/3 (1956), 291–5.
38. Cedric Dover, *American Negro Art* (London: Studio, 1960), 7.
39. It is worth mentioning. Keith Bell, Stanley Spencer,
40. *Daily News Release* (Peking), 25 November, 1954, No. 1797.
41. Robert Melville, 'Paul Hogarth', *Architectural Review* (August 1955), 75–9.
42. Paul Hogarth, 'British Art Today, *Marxist Quarterly*, 2/1 (January 1955), 37–47.
43. Paul Hogarth, interview with Andy Croft, November 1993.
44. See James Hyman, *The Battle for Realism: Figurative Art in Britain During the Cold War 1945–1960* (New Haven and London: Yale University Press, 2001), 84–5.
45. Tom Driberg, 'The Beams that Blind Us', *Reynolds News*, 4 December 1955.
46. Stephen Bone, 'Chinese Drawings', *Manchester Guardian*, 1 December 1955.
47. John Berger, 'Greaves and Hogarth', *New Statesman and Nation*, 10 December 1955.
48. An undated note entitled 'Money Expected Between Xmas & Easter' anticipates receiving £60 for *Pickwick Papers* and £100 pounds for Walsh's *Not Like This*. Both translations were published in Prague in 1956. The note is folded into Hogarth's copy of Peter Townsend's *China Phoenix* (1955), or one that appears to have been given to his third wife Pat Douthwaite by his second wife Phyllis Hayes, and which I happened to buy from a second-hand book dealer.

49. Paul Hogarth, *Drawing on Life*, 47–8.

50. Ibid. 68.

51. For Dr Daniel Francois Malan's response to Churchill's Fulton speech see my *Iron Curtain: From Stage to Cold War* (Oxford: Oxford University Press, 2007), 46.

52. Father Trevor Huddleson, 'Preface', in Paul Hogarth, *People Like Us: Drawings of South Africa & Rhodesia* (London: Dennis Dobson, 1958), 6.

53. Paul Hogarth, *Drawing on Life*, 73.

54. Ibid. 45.

55. Ibid. 46.

56. Paul Hogarth, 'Red Army Pulls Back in Poland', *Sunday Times*, 28 October 1956, 1.

57. As Hogarth himself once put it, 'I didn't leave because of the Hungarian business, because nobody, there was no change in the leadership. I think I must have left in '57.' Paul Hogarth, interview with Andy Croft, November 1993.

58. John Hobson, 'The Reds Betray a Guest', *Daily Mail*, 18 December 1956.

59. Paul Hogarth, *Drawing on Life*, 50.

60. Ibid. 52.

61. Ibid. 94.

62. Ibid. 179.

63. Anna Mathews, 'Untitled book on China', unpaginated typescript in folder from the literary agency A. M. Heath & Co. Ltd. I have also drawn on Anna Mathews's notes of an 'artists' forum' held in Shanghai on 20 June 1960. Here Denis Mathews discussed his exhibition of British oil paintings with ten or so Chinese artists, including two recorded as 'Yang Ke Yang' and Mr Sheng. Both documents are in the possession of Mrs Margaret Mathews.

64. *Arts From China at the Royal Festival Hall, from 17th March – 12th April 1964* (London: Britain–China Friendship Association, 1964). An annotated copy of this catalogue survives among Denis Mathews's papers.

65. Paul Hogarth, *Looking at China*, p. vi.

66. Feliks Topolski, *Holy China* (London: Hutchinson, and Boston: Houghton Mifflin, 1968), unpaginated.

Photographic Acknowledgements

Courtesy of Bonhams/© The Estate of Stanley Spencer 2010. All rights reserved, DACS: **fig 61**; private collection/photo © Christie's Images/The Bridgeman Art Library/© The Estate of Stanley Spencer 2010. All rights reserved, DACS: **plate 16**; copyright by Hugh Casson, reproduced by permission of the Estate of Hugh Casson: **figs 10, 11, 12, 13, 14, 22, 23, 35, 58**; reproduced by permission of the Estate of Chang Chien-ying: **plates 3, 4**; reproduced with permission of Chien-fei Chang: **plate 1**; © John Chinnery: **fig 33**; © Bettmann/Corbis: **fig 8**; © Hulton-Deutsch Collection/Corbis: **fig 31**; courtesy of the Cedric Dover Collection: **figs 4, 29, 42, 44, 59, 63**; reproduced by permission of the Estate of Paul Hogarth: **frontispiece, figs 5, 34, 49, 50, 51, 52, 53, 54, 55, 56, 57, plates 5, 6, 7, 8, 9**; reproduced by permission of the Estate of Derrick James: **figs 16, 17, 18, 19, 24, 25, 26, 40, 41, 43**; Derrick James Collection: **figs 15, 21**; © Michael Lindsay, reproduced by permission of James Lindsay: **fig 30**; reproduced by permission of the Estate of Denis Mathews: **figs 38, 39, 45, 46, 47, 48, 64, 65, 66, 67**; © Crown copyright: UK Government Art Collection, reproduced by permission of the Estate of Denis Mathews: **plate 10**; RIA-Novosti: **fig 20**; private collection/photo courtesy of Sotheby's/© The Estate of Stanley Spencer 2010. All rights reserved, DACS: **plate 15**; © The Estate of Stanley Spencer 2010. All rights reserved, DACS: **fig 60**; © Tate, London, 2010: **fig 62**; © Tate, London, 2010/© The Estate of Stanley Spencer 2010. All rights reserved, DACS: **plates; 11, 12, 13, 14, 17**; TopFoto: **figs 1, 2, 3, 9, 32**; courtesy of Hull History Centre: University Archives (DPB): **figs 36, 37**

In a few instances we have been unable to trace the copyright owner prior to publication. If notified, the publisher will be pleased to amend the Acknowledgements in any future edition.

Index